The Italics Are Mine

THE ITALICS ARE MINE

NINA BERBEROVA

Translated from the Russian by
Philippe Radley

ALFRED A. KNOPF   NEW YORK   1992

THIS IS A BORZOI BOOK
PUBLISHED BY ALFRED A. KNOPF, INC.

PUBLISHER'S NOTE: *The Italics Are Mine* was originally
published in the United States in 1969 by Harcourt,
Brace & World, Inc., New York, as translated from the
Russian by Philippe Radley. That translation was also
published in Great Britain by Longmans in the same year.
The original Russian edition, *Kursiv Moi*, was published
in 1972 and revised in 1983. In 1989, Actes Sud,
Arles, published a French edition of the book, *C'est moi
qui souligne*, with revisions by the author. For this
Knopf edition, originally published in Great Britain
in 1991 by Chatto & Windus Ltd., Philippe Radley's
translation was extensively revised, incorporating corrections and new material from the Actes Sud edition.

Library of Congress Cataloging-in-Publication Data
Berberova, Nina Nikolaevna.
[Kursiv moi. English]
The italics are mine/Nina Berberova; translated from
the Russian by Philippe Radley. —1st Knopf ed.
p. cm.
Translation of: Kursiv moi.
Includes index.
ISBN 0-679-41237-9
1. Berberova, Nina Nikolaevna—Biography. 2. Authors,
Russian—20th century—Biography. I. Title.
PG3476.B425Z4713 1992
891.73′42—dc20
[B] 91-58549 CIP

Manufactured in the United States of America
FIRST KNOPF EDITION

If you can look into the seeds of time,
And say which grain will grow and which will not,
Speak then to me.

                                   – *Macbeth*, I:3

CONTENTS

Contents

PART ONE

The Nest and the Anthill

I WOULD LIKE TO WARN THE READER: THIS BOOK is about myself, not about other people; an autobiography, not a set of memoirs, not a collection of portraits of famous (or not so famous) contemporaries, and not a series of vignettes. It is the story of my life, and in it I loosely follow the chronological order of events and uncover my life's meaning. I loved and love life and love the meaning of life almost as much. I will speak more about myself than about other people. My mind lives in the past as memory and in the present as my awareness of myself in time. There may be no future at all, or it may be brief and meaningless. This I have to face.

The tale of my long life has a beginning, a middle, and an end. As it unfolds it will become clear where I see its interest and its value. With no deliberate effort on my part, the meaning of life will unfold, the meaning of *my* life, or, indeed, of every life. This meaning will never be put before life itself to obstruct it; it will creep into the tale and coexist with time and space, and other things which are on the same level for me as the air (of two hemispheres) I breathe. I will speak of things that were essential to me: 'knowledge of oneself', liberation of oneself, revelation of oneself, maturity that grants the right to this revelation, and solitude in an anthill, which has always been for me something more appealing than solitude in a nest.

Of the three possibilities, living for the future life, living for future generations, or living for the present moment, I very early chose the third, the 'most ferocious immanence', in Herzen's words. In some ways I developed prematurely but I learned to think very late. This is my main shortcoming: I was so determined *not to lose time* that I often did the wrong thing. Not losing time has been my permanent concern since I was three years old, when it dawned on me that time is the warp of life, its very fabric, something that you cannot buy, trade, steal, falsify, or obtain by begging. Not to lose time – for what? For coming to know oneself, understand one's human condition, and learning to think about it.

I never could look into anyone as intensely as I could into myself. And I have not met anyone who could look more intensely into me than I myself can. *Know thyself* – this has always been a rule of my life, one that appeared in my consciousness before I can remember. Know not so much men in general, nor people, nor friends, but above all know thyself. I remember very well how I first learned that the earth is round, or that adults were at one time children, or that my father was not a Russian. I cannot, however, remember when I started looking into myself. In childhood and after fifty this was quite intense. Between my twentieth and thirtieth years it slowed down; there was obviously not much time for it. As I look into myself today, I see among other things some events, thoughts, and feelings that I would not really like to bring to light. Let them stay where they are. I am writing an autobiography, not a confession. They are my 'secrets'. Everybody has his secrets. Some carry them through life as a burden, some cherish them. I see my secrets not as dead weight but as forces that give life to my life; I do not drag them behind, I allow them to flower in me in their own way. It looks now as if everything has been profitable to me. And if the payment has sometimes been excessive, it was after all the payment *for life*, and there cannot be and is no excessive payment for life.

I never felt cut off from the world and, indeed, felt a conscious fusion with it twenty-five or thirty years ago, when I did not even suspect that man and rock were one and the same, that there was no organic and inorganic universe, that the nebulae repeat the pattern of newly discovered elements, and that man by his dimensions stands midway between these nebulae and the atom. The charge of electric energy that lives in me, that I feel like a wave of heat passing through me when I say the word 'I', cannot be isolated from all the energy or the sum of energies of the world in a rock, a star, or another man. It is part of the whole and I am a part of the universe. There are moments when I feel this part is *greater than the whole*. I know, when I take into account my longevity, health, self-awareness, and the possibility until now of self-transformation, that at my birth I was given an electrical charge, a colossal charge of tremendous strength. And that the moment this energy comes to an end – it will come to an end.

I said 'self-transformation'. Knowing oneself was only the first task; the second was self-transformation. That is, once you reach an inner equilibrium, once you have unravelled the knots, you must bring the whole 'pattern' down to a few simple lines. The emotional anarchy of youth, all the intellectual toying, the pro-longed *Weltschmerz*, and the fears and tremblings of the quivering creature of the twentieth century must become past. No more fears, hesitations, superstitions, no more keeping up with fads of the day. These monsters, if one does not get rid of them in time, will later become fixed ideas from which there will be no salvation in old age.

All this sounds terribly serious. Perhaps the reader already sees in front of him a severe face, spectacles, whiskers, false teeth, straight grey hair closely cropped at the neck and thinning at the crown, and the dull, fat, 'mighty' pen which is held by an arthritic, blue-veined hand. The picture is inaccurate. Not only have I no whiskers but I have only delicate eyebrows. As a young girl I had a rather pretty face, though it lacked expression; at about forty the face became thin and very sad. Now I cannot judge what it is. Indeed, I don't much remember it as I write. I only know that time has worked with its axe over my features. It has sharpened the chin, outlined the mouth, lifted up the cheekbones, cut out the cheeks. The forehead has become hard, and the whole oval in its shadows now lives much more intensely than in earlier photographs, but my nose is still short! And I am writing with an ordinary pencil.

The 'beyond' scarcely interests me. In my estimation it lies somewhere not far from the 'opium of the people' and is exploited like coal or oil. That does not concern me. However, as soon as it emerges and tries to intervene in my life, I prick up my ears. It bears false truths, easy answers; you must never let it come near. Everything in the Christian religion (one of the elements of civilization which today merges with culture) that is significant exists and existed in other religions, which are and were elements of civilization also. God has been killed, God has been 'eaten' many times. Neither the Acts nor the Apocalypse nor the church dynamited slavery. The New Testament says not one word about animals and the sorrow in their eyes. Nineteen centuries after the

5

Sermon on the Mount people still laughed at hunchbacks, freaks, cripples, impotents, cuckolds, and old maids. Though it uplifted people spiritually, Christianity did not free them socially; and only the democracy of the nineteenth and twentieth centuries taught people not to preen themselves on wealth, not to scorn poverty, and gave everyone the right not to be bought or sold.

One conviction constantly lived and still lives in me, that my century is the only suitable century for me. I know that many judge our time differently. I speak now, however, not about world stability (was there ever such a thing?) or about the joy of living in one's own country (Russians flee theirs a good deal), but of something else. As a woman and as a Russian, where – in what time – could I have been happier? In the nineteenth century, amid Pushkin's Nanettes and Zizis? Or Herzen's Natalias and their wards? Or, later, among the mothers and daughters of the rising bourgeoisie? Or the scholarly advocates of the feminist movement? Or, perhaps in the eighteenth century or still earlier, when all over Russia people slept, ate, and prayed, when young and old prayed, ate, and slept?

I arrived at the right moment. Treasures lie all around me. One need only grab them. I am free to live where I want, as I want, to read what I want, to think about anything I wish, to listen to whomever I please. I am free in the crowded streets of big cities, where no one sees me as I walk in the pouring rain, not knowing where I walk to or from, muttering lines of verse; and in the woods and at the seashore, where in blessed solitude music resounds within me; and in my room, where I can lock the door. I can know all that I wish to know and I can ignore the rest. I ask any question and get an answer to it. I choose my friends. I am happy that all the riddles of my immature years have been solved. I never pretend to be cleverer, more beautiful, younger, kinder than I really am in order to appear other than I am, for I do not need such lies. I live in a fantastic, indescribable luxury of contemporary problems and solutions that are close to me and among which I am free to make a choice. I am in the centre of a thousand possibilities, and a thousand responsibilities, and a thousand unknowns. The horrors and misfortunes of my age have helped me, the Revolution liberated me, exile tempered me, World War Two pushed me into another dimension.

I did not need to liberate myself from the consequences of a 'bourgeois upbringing', a tough task which in France occupied Jean-Paul Sartre and Louis Aragon for fifty years. I grew up in Russia at the time when there was no doubt that the old world would in one way or another be destroyed, where no one seriously clung to old principles – at least not in our milieu. In the Russia of the years 1912–16, we saw everything shake, everything fall apart. Protest was our environment and my first strong feeling. Only very late, at about twenty-five, did I learn that I belonged by birth to the 'bourgeois class'. Though I felt no ties to it, essentially because all my life had been spent among déclassé exiles (a group I belonged to along with all the heroes of my novels and short stories), I must nevertheless say that the bourgeoisie as a class was always more engrossing and exciting to me than, say, the remnants of the feudal-aristocratic class, and at least as engrossing and exciting as the working class, but much less so than the class of the so-called 'intelligentsia', déclassé or not, to which I felt closest.

It is good to feel one's own effort at getting one's daily bread. But for me all toil for a living, however hard, must bear some symbolic meaning. It would be easier for me to put new soles on old shoes or to sew bags than to tally up debts or trade in unnecessary things. But the problem of making a living is only the horizontal dimension of our general existence. What of the vertical? There was a time when few lived in the vertical dimension (the intellect) and those who did suffered from a feeling of guilt among others who lived in the horizontal dimension. Now all who wish to may learn to live vertically with easy consciences. To do this three conditions must be met – one must want to read, want to think, want to know. As Jaspers has said, you don't have to learn how to sneeze and cough, but you must learn how to think. Thinking is not an organic function.

When I recall myself in early childhood (I remember myself first when I was almost three), I see giant people and huge objects, all deformed because I look at them from underneath, as a very small being. High above me I see the branch of an apple tree (actually it comes up to the waist of a grown man). I can't reach it, though I stand on my tiptoes and stretch my hands towards it. I see a huge pink house which was, in fact, one of those noblemen's dwellings about which Chekhov wrote. I see a giant with an entire lilac bush

7

in his hands sitting opposite me on the deck of a boat that is moving down the Neva from Smolny to the Admiralty on a sunny summer day. He smiles and gives me a branch. He is a stranger, but I am not afraid of strangers. I take the bunch of lilac from him and am pleased he likes me. Somewhere beneath the sky I see a window, and a ghostly figure, all white and rather terrifying, nods and beckons to me. The panes are being wiped by a white rag on a mop. Finally, the branch of the apple tree, after being bent down, falls into my outstretched hands. I hang over it and rock, imagining that the tree is simply a huge flower and that I hang on this flower like a small bug. I fall, having broken loose, but am not hurt. I stand up and run to where the greenery is thicker, where there is an odour of dampness, and the grass is silken. At the old wooden parapet there I stop and bend over a well, which seems an abyss to me, until I am grabbed from behind and pulled aside. This is the old well, and each summer I will look into it. It is empty and dry and black, and there has been no water in it for a long time. But every year I will look into it, deeper and deeper, until at about the age of twelve I will feel the desire to go down into it. But there is nothing to climb down on. You can only stand and listen while, at the bottom, long dry, something crackles and rustles. Then it dawns on me that someone could leave me there and forget me, and I would die of thirst. Suddenly I want this to happen as quickly as possible, so I can find a spring, a source to water me at the bottom of the well. I will find it and drink from it, and no one will know I am alive, that I continue to think, to compose verse about the well and the source, and that this source works for me alone.

My maternal grandfather belonged to the most liberal zemstvo of Tver, and looked like a perfect Tatar. His name was Ivan Dmitrievich. Using Dmitry Lvovich, Ivan's father, as a model, Goncharov wrote his *Oblomov*, and once, while visiting his hero, forgot his beaded watch–case, which I played with in my child-hood. The case was worn and terribly soiled, and I was not allowed to put it in my mouth, but I managed nevertheless to nibble at it. Its taste reminded me of a chicken croquette. When Dmitry Lvovich's father, Lev Ivanovich, was living there, the old Empire house burnt down and a new pink one, the one I knew, was built. Only one thing was known about Ivan Semenovich, that he had built the church at the very end of the garden and was buried beneath it.

Nothing was known about Semen Yurevich, but Yury (no patronymic known) was the very man who received almost fourteen thousand acres of muddy marshes, woodlands, meadows, fields, including six villages, from Catherine II. The gallery of ancestors hung in the half-dark hall: Yury (no patronymic), like Derzhavin, all medals and powdered curls: Semen Yurevich and his wife, with slanting eyes; Ivan Semenovich, placid and devout, in a high collar; Lev Ivanovich and his three sisters, all four in profile and drawn in pastels; and finally Dmitry Lvovich, who weighed almost four hundred pounds in old age. Until I was about six I confused my own great-grandfather with Ilya Ilyich Oblomov and his author. It seemed to me that Oblomov was the writer who had visited our home and written a famous novel on the life of Dmitry Lvovich, who had become so fat because he was lazy (a family fable with an appropriate moral).

Kara-Ul came from the Tatar 'black city' during the reign of Ivan the Terrible, or perhaps was brought to Muscovy. He was baptized and did not return to his Tatar realm. What his descendants did to survive those two hundred years until the day Catherine bestowed the estate on Yury, why the estate was bestowed by her, and how Yury obtained his medals and curls is unknown to me. There were only a few antiques in the house, all from the last century, the preceding one having been forgotten. Covered with cobwebs in disorder in the attic, old crinolines were scattered, with velvet albums, a globe, a complete set of the monthly *The Messenger of Europe*, and a lot of waxen orange blossoms, the symbol of innocence which brides wore on their heads on their wedding day. I once made a wreath for an old Saint Bernard dog from them.

My maternal grandfather was short, had a round belly, one black tooth in his mouth, and a curly, greenish-grey beard in which, every now and then, something would stick. I remember him in casual dress, and in formal clothes when he lay dead in a coffin, dressed by an undertaker's employee in his uniform, with his orders and ribbons, and painted a rosy colour (this made the corpse look alive and attractive). The employee locked himself up with my grandfather for about two hours and made him up to look so ruddy, cheerful and smart that the beard was no longer green, but azure. In everyday clothes he was completely different. Often (this was when he was very old) his trousers would be in disarray, and a drop would hang from under his nose (it was said this was because he took iodine). I don't know exactly what he did in Petersburg, where he lived during the winter. All his life was dedicated to the town of Ustyuzhna and the district of Vesyogonsk in the Tver province. The Rybinsk reservoir was built in this area in the thirties to feed the Volga with the waters of the wide and lazy Vologda, Tver, and Yaroslav rivers. In my childhood years these were miserable places. The peasants lived in poverty, the land yielded scantily, the railway was about seventy miles from the estate. As a child I would hear how my grandfather christened peasant children, helped them to obtain scholarships to the district school, got the sick into a hospital in the provincial town, hired a new medical assistant for the volost, kicked a drunkard priest out of a neighbouring parish.

Yes, these were grim, wretched, wild places. In the slumbering and indeed virgin forests you found wolves and bears. The Savanka River, a tributary of the Mologa, was inaccessible owing to the large number of mosquitoes that flew above it in great dark clouds. It was, moreover, easy to sink into the swampy shore. Fields stretched on for a hundred miles. The horizon was straight and hard, and paths, often merely log paths, led off into the limitless distance where only skylarks sang their song.

The Karaulov family was large, and now, as I recollect my childhood, I see that not everything in it was *comme il faut*. My grandmother, my mother's mother, had obviously made something of a misalliance in marrying my grandfather, a man who belonged with all his heart to the time of the Great Reforms, and later to the K.-D. Party along with all his friends, all members of the Duma – Petrunkevich and, of course, Fedor Rodichev, the famous Duma orator. My grandmother came from a family of high rank and did not like 'freethinkers'. Some of her relatives were ministers and other high-ranking persons, and all those hospitals and schools that Grandfather helped build were complete anathema to her, I would say. She died when I was twelve, and I think she differed little from her mother or grandmother, who felt serfdom to have been an evil of only average significance.

Rodichev, who had such a powerful voice that Mademoiselle and I could hear him from the other end of the garden when he arrived, and Korsakov, another K.-D., who was married to the daughter of a former serf, a radical and a well-educated woman, and was the father of 'Vanechka', a classmate of Osip Mandelstam's at the Tenishev School, were all friends of Grandfather's. District leader of the gentry, trustee of the girls' high school, justice of the peace, founder of the vocational school – he was all of these. Zemstvo occupations filled his life. I do not know why he attained high rank and how it was that he died an actual councillor of state. I don't even know why he was portrayed with a red-and-white ribbon across his chest, and an Anna or Stanislav Medal on his neck (which he also wore when he lay in his coffin), in the official portrait of him that hung in a district institution that he had apparently founded. I only saw him once on his way to an official reception. It was some kind of review of the gentry set up by Nicholas II, and Grandfather took off his comfortable frock coat, covered with dandruff, put on a uniform sewn with gold, and even wore a cocked hat (all carefully ventilated in the frosty air of the courtyard) and began to look like the mayor in *The Inspector General*, as played by Davydov in the Aleksandrinsky Theatre. Later he recounted how he had stood to attention at the reception. Nicholas walked slowly, stopped, asked questions. He paused near Grandfather and asked if the railway was far from his lands. Grandfather could not restrain himself and answered, 'Seventy miles, your majesty. It's time, indeed, to build a branch in our area.' 'Russia is very large,' said the tsar, smiling sadly as becomes tsars. 'You can't do everything at once in such a big country.' (What tempo, exactly, did he consider suitable for changes in Russia? He himself was driven out one hundred years too late.)

This was in Petersburg. That year, for the first time, I rode on a tram with Grandfather. They had started a line from the Nikolaevsky Station. Before that there had been only horse-cars. We were off to visit one of his two sisters, both of whom I knew, of course, only as old ladies. I would like to say a few words about them here.

Olga Dmitrievna was always a sort of Anna Karenina for me. She was married to Prince Ukhtomsky, had an affair with another man by whom she had a son (in later years a sculptor, who was shot in 1921 as a member of the Tagantsev plot), separated from her husband, then she returned to him, went abroad, and never got a divorce. The son by her lover bore her husband's name, and although he knew the boy was not his, her husband never gave up the child and tortured him and his mother in every possible way. This grievous story ended when everyone finally died, after suffering, shame, 'scandal', and ruin. Why Grandfather took me to visit her, I do not know. I, of course, knew nothing of her life and saw only an old but still attractive and gentle woman. Grandfather got on and off the tram groaning. All this left a rather melancholy impression on me.

Grandfather's other sister, whose name was Alina, had a completely different fate. From time to time she appeared at the estate, and was, in the full sense of the phrase, the laughing stock of the servants. She cropped her hair, wore male clothes, spoke in a bass voice, and was neither man nor woman, but probably a hermaphrodite. She never married, of course, had her own strong opinions about everything and expressed them sharply, not caring what impression they made on anyone. I always wondered if she shaved. There were ten years of her life which were never discussed. The last time I saw her I was thirteen. She was half paralysed and just managed to get into the carriage and sit next to me. At that time, she wore floor-length calico skirts and smoked a pipe. I took the reins in my hands, and we quietly moved down a dusty rutted path to the fields and rode around leisurely without any definite aim. To entertain her, I read her verse aloud – mine and Blok's, which I pretended was mine. She liked it. Is it necessary to add that Alina and Olga were invited to my grandmother's house only when there were no other guests?

In Grandfather's study, where Goncharov once sat and, as I imagine it, studied his hero, I now sat. In the mornings, peasants, or, as they were called then, muzhiks, came to consult Grandfather. They were of two kinds, and it seemed to me that they were two completely different breeds. Some muzhiks were demure, well bred, important-looking, with greasy hair, fat paunches, and shiny faces. They were dressed in embroidered shirts and caftans of fine cloth. These were the ones who were later called kulaks. They lived on their own farms, liberated themselves from the village com- mune, and felled trees for new homes in the thick woods that only recently had been Grandfather's. They walked in the church with collection trays and placed candles before the Saint-Mary-Appease- My-Grief icon. But what kind of grief could they have? The Peasants' Credit Bank gave them credit. In their houses, which I sometimes visited, there were geraniums on the window sills and the smell of rich buns from the ovens. Their sons grew into energetic and ambitious men, began new lives for themselves, and created a new class in embryo for Russia.

The other muzhiks wore bast sandals, dressed in rags, bowed fawningly, never went further than the doors, and had faces that had lost all human expression. These remained in the commune. They were undersized, and often lay in ditches near the state-owned wine shop. Their children did not grow because they were underfed. Their consumptive wives seemed always to be in the final month of pregnancy, the infants were covered with weeping eczema, and in their homes, which I also visited, broken windows were stopped up with rags, and calves and hens were kept in the corners. There was a sour stench. But in the homes of the fat ones, for some reason, agile, cheerful, industrious sons grew up and married healthy, pretty girls. When grandchildren appeared, they were sent off to a technical school in a regional town. Grandmother, of course, could endure neither one nor the other.

Grandfather, who was against Stolypin's reforms with all his heart and was completely for the commune, was often visibly tormented by all this. The awareness that the three-field system continued all around him, that threshing was still performed with chains in the barns of neighbouring villages, that in some districts there were no schools except parochial ones, that the supporters of McCormick (inventor of the reaping machine) were mainly in America and not in Russia, visibly saddened him at times, and suddenly for no special reason, having paced to and fro in the hall for almost two hours, hands behind his back, he would order the carriage to be harnessed and leave for a week. He would return somehow unnoticed, close himself up in his study (where he slept on a sofa as was customary then), and later appear in the dining room with a slightly guilty expression. He rarely conversed with his wife. Much later I learned he had a second family in the province of Novgorod: a woman he loved who was much younger than he, and three children. I was happy to discover this.

I was ten when I got the idea that it was necessary for me to choose a profession quickly. As I mentally return to this period and burrow into the early events of my childhood, I can now explain, perhaps only partly, this desire to find a 'trade' in life for myself.

About four years before this I quite accidentally, but with irrefutable force, learned that boys have something girls don't have. This made a stunning impression on me, though it in no way bothered me and did not produce envy or a feeling of misfortune. I soon forgot about this discovery and it had no effect, at least explicitly, on my later development, though it probably stuck in my subconscious (or wherever such awareness is supposed to be). I now see my strong desire to have a profession 'for life', to have something that would grow with me like an arm or a leg and be part of me, as a kind of compensation for what I lacked as a girl. I sought not only the profession itself, but the act of choosing it, of conscious decision. But I have come to know that in the course of sixty years not all my decisive and 'irrevocable' actions were the result of *conscious* decision. My departure from Russia in 1922 was not, but my staying in occupied France in 1940 was. In my entire life I have made responsible, existential choices no more than four or five times that bore meaning for the structure of my life and personality (in the 'global' or 'totalitarian' sense); but I must admit that each time these conscious choices gave me an awareness of the force of my existence and freedom, a sharp sense of the 'electric charge', which one can call bliss whether or not the choice led to happiness or an evident despair. And the sense of 'electric happiness' is not diminished by the fact that my choices were partly conditioned by the two great laws – of biology and sociology – for I do not conceive of myself outside of them.

The realization of my first strong desire to choose, to decide, to find, to move myself consciously in a chosen direction gave me all my life, as I now see it, a feeling of victory not over someone else but over myself, not bestowed from on high but personally acquired.

So I wrote a long list of possible professions on a piece of paper, completely disregarding the fact that I was not a boy, which meant that professions such as fireman and postman had properly to be excluded. Between fireman and postman, among forty possibilities, there was poet (I didn't follow alphabetical order). Everything in me boiled up and I thought I had to decide then and there what I would like to be so that I could begin to live accordingly. I looked at my list as at a counter all laid out with wares. The dark corner of the Russian alphabet, where the *yat* and the hard sign and the soft sign play hide-and-seek with the *yu* and *ya*, was not yet very clear. But the world was wide open before me, and I began to climb over its shelves and boxes.

After lengthy reflection completely alone and in secrecy, I came to my decision. Verses gushed from me. I choked with them, I couldn't stop, I wrote them at the rate of two or three a day and read them to myself, to Dasha, to Mademoiselle, to my parents, to their friends, to whoever was there. This rigorous sense of vocation has never left me, though in those years it was rather peculiar; it seems to me. At ten I was an ordinary child, played games, tried to avoid homework, got punished, stood in a corner picking at the wall plaster. In other words, I behaved like everybody else. Yet a constant thought ran parallel to this – I am a poet, I will be a poet. I want to be friends with poets; I want to read poetry; I want to speak about verse. Now as I look back I see that my two strong and enduring childhood friendships were with those who, like me, wrote verse and had chosen a calling for themselves before they had actually entered life. One was shot in the years of Stalin's terror, the other lost two husbands in Stalin's purges.

I well remember that summer and my search for a profession. I had decided to try everything possible and not to lose time, which I already prized highly. The first question that arose was: Should I be an acrobat? For several days I did some gymnastics, but I was very quickly bored. Then I turned to botany and for hours looked for algae in a can filled with pond water. But this, too, seemed uninspiring. When I discovered there were people who studied folklore, I took a notebook and pencil and went to watch cows being milked in the evening. There young peasant girls sang, 'Peas today and peas tomorrow. Milk the cows and come to me.' It wasn't hard to write that down. The song was sung over and over about two hundred times until all the cows were milked; and there were many of them because in those years Grandfather lived principally off the sale of butter and Edam, which were manufactured in a barn we called the 'factory'. But folklore did not satisfy me either; something like a black storm cloud now hung over me. I feared I would be made fun of. And it was clear I could not procrastinate about finding myself a profession. I had loafed for entire days in the house, in the garden, in the yard. I had fallen into nettles, I had been bitten by a goose, had sobbed under the hoop skirts in the attic, but a profession would not come to me.

Yet the village priest's seven daughters, the two youngest of whom were my age, knew from their earliest years that they would become village teachers; I liked this very much. The priest was poor and completely uneducated, but his daughters had scholarships and they lived in the town during the winter. The poverty in their house was horrifying. They were ashamed when I found the older ones barefoot, washing the floors, and the younger ones squelching through manure in the yard, running from a pig to a cow which were all covered with flies. The houses that stood between Grandfather's house and the church were surrounded by dense lilac, jasmine and honeysuckle. The deacon had a deaf-mute wife, and the poverty was such that the sacristan's children walked about naked until the age of ten. The fourth house belonged to two old women, one of whom had no nose. They would rush out to kiss my shoulders, my hands, my dress when I walked by. The housemaid, Dasha, told me once that they were 'former strollers' and that if one strolled a lot, one would end up without a nose. They were sent the remains of our holiday dinners. Who were these women? Why did Grandfather give them a house between the deacon's house and the priest's? They were called dressmakers, and it is possible this was once so. When I knew them they were dishevelled, filthy, terribly thin, and looked like old crows.

I was ashamed that they kissed me, I was ashamed of the bare legs of the priest's daughters, of my own bare legs, even of my bare arms in the summer, not to mention the bathing suit that was put on me even though I did not go in the water or only went in with a howl. As I remember it, until the age of about twelve or thirteen, I was ashamed of my feet, of my own stupidity, of my mother's ball gown in which she showed her beautiful shoulders. Sometimes I was ashamed of the stupidity of others, too, of the mistake of some idol of the moment. (Khodasevich jokingly called shame for another's stupidity 'hypertrophy of the feeling of responsibility.') But, of course, I was ashamed most of all of my bare toes. When I was washed in a wooden tub, I tried to make the soapy foam cover them, dress them. What was most terrifying for me was a pair of light, scraping sandals. 'They won't sink in water or burn in fire,' said the clerk of the shoe store in the Gostiny Dvor, proud of his wit, as he fitted them to me. It goes without saying that I was wearing ribbed black stockings so that I would somehow endure this without yelling. Those non-burning, non-sinking sandals became a symbol of summer horror for several years.

I didn't go to church. At first I was 'taken'. Then, when I grew up and could no longer be forced to go, I tried to stay away from the Saint-Mary-Appease-My-Grief icon, and other things I felt nothing in common with. I remember, when I still had to attend church, that every Sunday in the chapel there was a row of small coffins containing the bodies of newborn infants – six, eight, sometimes even more. The infants were all alike, slightly similar to dolls, or rather like Easter suckling pigs (in the mouths of which you put a leaf of lettuce). Unchristened babies were buried on one side of the cemetery, christened ones on the other. Grandfather would say with nostalgia, 'Yes, my boy,' (he said 'my boy' to me) 'that's how it is. A godforsaken place! This is not Moscow province, or Orel province. Here, my boy, are our roads – seventy miles to the railway, thirty-five miles to the nearest hospital, twenty-five miles to the doctor's assistant. And so on, my boy, and so on. No roads – that's how it is, my boy, lack of roads. Woods, swamps, mud. There you are in the slush,' (he waved his hand) 'when the bridges are carried off, and you can't fetch the doctor or anyone else. You hop, but you can't hop far enough. Filipp Gennadievich left the day before yesterday and has still not returned. So it is, my boy.' ('All in good time,' said the tsar with a sad smile.)

I often sat behind the sofa, in a corner in an old armchair, when the staid muzhiks discussed their mortgages in the Peasants' Credit Bank, saying 'they' to Grandfather and 'we' to themselves in their low-class style of address. One of them, Savva Kuzmich Karaulov (most of them used the name of the nearest landowner to get passports), who had a clever face and clean, strong hands, had recently been made a church elder. His son had set out to open a hardware store in the volost. The conversations, which both Karaulovs found interesting, went on for a long time, for Savva and Grandfather had nowhere to rush to. It started getting dark. Dasha would bring in the freshly filled kerosene lamp, with its frosted lamp shade covered with all kinds of curious designs. A portrait of Uncle Serezha, my mother's brother who had accidentally shot himself while on a hunt at the age of eighteen, sparkled on the wall. The armchair I sat in was upholstered in some kind of ribbed material. I ran my fingers over the ribbing and dreamt I had suddenly become blind and was learning to read with my fingers. You see, I would say to them, I have become blind, but this means nothing. I can read all that I want with my fingers. Then it dawned on me it was time to have supper, that Grandmother would be angry at Grandfather and me, and, astonished, I saw that Savva Kuzmich Karaulov no longer sat in front of Grandfather, but had been replaced by Timofey, who had no surname, wore shabby bast sandals and sat on the edge of his chair, crumpling his cap in his hands. With tear-filled eyes he looked at Grandfather, who said:

'Eh, eh, my boy, I will give you land for a house, but who will build it for you? Anisya? Matrena? You have to marry them to someone first and get sons-in-law. Your older daughter will soon be twenty? Soon she will be a spinster. She has stayed on too long! Nevertheless, my boy, I will think it over. For the moment you take the timber – do you hear, I'm talking to you? – you take the timber. We will arrange some sort of an agreement. But no land. I have to think about it. I can't think that quickly. I am an old man, my boy, a very old Russian man, not some kind of a French fop. And now go to the kitchen. Go, go you will be given what's needed.'

He went out to the dining room and I followed. He said, 'Give me that ointment that Dr Wasserkwelle in Kissingen prescribed for me when I ate too many oysters. Timofey keeps scratching himself under his arms.' To this his wife, a fastidious and humourless society woman, answered, 'He keeps scratching himself because he is full of lice. His foot-cloths have poisoned the whole atmosphere for us. Now we must air the place or we will all be *suffoqué*.'

She had an uncle who was a minister for Alexander III, and a cousin who was a minister for Nicholas II. But it all ended right there: the nephews were good for nothing, and the son had perished on a hunt.

There was a peculiar stillness in the dark Russian night. It lasted and lasted, as if it had had no beginning and would have no end. 'And if you sink in it with your dreams and hopes,' I said to myself, 'it will drag you in, suck you in, swallow you up, this soundless-ness, motionlessness, and lifelessness in the garden, the fields, the woods, right on out to the horizon.' I sat on the window sill and thought I might perhaps take up curing the sick, or become a village schoolteacher like the priest's daughters, or till the fields like Tolstoy, or learn to build those splendid izbas with geraniums on the window sills and carved cockerels on the eaves, where I would later put Timofey and his relatives. I was still choosing a profession for myself, and could not decide yet. There was no one to get advice from, because at that time mankind, for me, was divided into two halves – well-wishers, who in my opinion understood even less than I about these matters, and enemies, who out of sheer meanness would not give good advice.

I knew how to love people and things then, but I also knew how to hate. I chiefly hated everything to do with the 'nest', with family spirit, paternalism, the defence of small ones – that is, me – from something terrible or dangerous or simply risky. To warm myself near someone, settle in some secure place, find a shelter – in a way this seemed to me not only repugnant, but humiliating. I remember how I once, almost roughly, cast my mother's hand from my shoulder. This gesture, a pat on the shoulder, suddenly seemed to me not merely a tender hand movement but the symbol of protection and defence, which I could not endure. I cast the hand away and gave a deep sigh, as if I had pulled a pillow off my face which was about to suffocate me. From what – from what horrors and fears, visions and catastrophes, sicknesses and sadnesses – did they want to protect me? I am ready for them, I expect them, I burst out towards them. I am learning to write with both hands so that if someone cuts off my right one I would outwit him. And if I were condemned to the loss of both legs, I would crawl on the stumps, like that beggar on the church porch. It was not for nothing that for two days I had been learning to crawl on the floor when no one was looking, much to the astonishment of two dogs, a Saint Bernard and a dachshund.

Living in the 'nest', I still, of course, did not understand the full significance of this concept, but as I saw more than a gesture in the hand placed on the shoulder, so I saw a symbol in the nest. Never in the whole of my life have I been able to free myself of this, and even now I think that an anthill is better than a nest, that there those near you *warm* you less (this warming is particularly repulsive to me), that in the anthill among a hundred thousand or a million you are

19

freer than in a nest, where all sit around and look at one another, waiting until scientists finally discover ways to make us mind readers. This does not mean every family is a nest to me. There are exceptions and there will gradually be more of them. But the psychology of the nest is loathsome to me, and I always sympathize with one who flees his nest, even if he flees into an anthill, where it may be crowded but one can find solitude – that most natural, most worthy state of man, that precious and intense state of being conscious of the world and of oneself.

The fundamentally romantic idea that the rock or the stone lives alone, while man lives in a collective, in close unison with his equals, is not only wrong, but in its very essence quite the opposite of the truth. The rock lives in the close unison of its molecules. It is a kind of indivisible unity of billions upon billions of parts that make up one whole. But the further we go from the stone and the closer we get to man, the more clearly the necessary and immutable differences appear. How surprisingly alive false ideas are! They even have their own evolution. At first they are highfalutin' 'truths', then humdrum 'laws', and finally superstitions. The concept of immortality also belongs to superstitions. Who needs immortality? Who, having lost the ability to change himself, wants to prevent others from changing? Indeed, what is immortality? We are told that that which does not die is immortal. But precisely what in nature does not die? Only that which *multiplies by dividing*. The amoeba is immortal because it is halved when it multiplies, and so, in a manner of speaking, it lives eternally. But we, who multiply through sex, die and cannot be immortal, because we do not divide.

Fear, and sometimes horror, of solitude belong to that type of truthless superstitions: it has become a kind of scarecrow. Nevertheless, before knowing anything of this, from my earliest years I strove to be alone. Nothing could have been more terrible for me than a whole day, from morning till night, spent with someone else rather than with my own thoughts – not giving an account to anyone for my actions, carrying on dialogues with myself, reading all that I came upon. At first, these were ads in *Speech* which I was taught to read from – 'We recommend our experienced cook' or 'Flat with firewood up for rent.' Then, 'Here is the cat. Is that a cat? Where is the rat? There is the bat,' from a then modish ABC book (I have forgotten the name of the author); then, *Childhoodandyouth* (I learned much later that this was not one but three words – my eyes raced across them in a hurry to learn 'what was next'); and, finally, *Crime and Punishment*, as I lay on my stomach under a tree, completely immersed, chewing on bits of grass, sometimes swallowing a tasteless spider along with the juices.

I remember one evening: I am lying in bed with fever, the Petersburg winter evening is blue and black outside, while next to me on the night table are a lamp, tea with lemon, and medicine. The clock shows ten minutes to six, a compress squeezes my throat. Mother sits stiffly and severely on a straight chair next to me. Why is she sitting? Why doesn't she go away? I want to be alone, to cover my head with my blanket, so that quietly in the darkness, warmth, and concentration I will overcome my illness; but she is there so that I won't feel lonely. I am trying to imagine what will happen when she finally leaves and the room will become mine. I will hear the bells of trams from Liteiny Avenue. I will imagine the sparks that shoot out in the snow from under the tram cars. I will think about the people walking home in their fur coats and hats, people about whom I would like to know everything knowable that I will never know. I will finally pull my book out of its hiding place under the mattress. But she still does not go away. She offers me tea, a cutlet, and, horror of horrors which turns me to ice, she offers to read aloud. 'What's this? You have feet like ice!' she exclaims, though she doesn't go for the hot-water bottle but calls Dasha instead, who brings me a metal hot-water bottle wrapped in a towel, curved obviously in anticipation of someone's very round stomach, and from which water continually seeps. A thousand years pass and still she sits, until an odour of cabbage pie escapes from the kitchen. The telephone rings. Freedom! Everything is over somehow instantaneously. There I am alone in the large half-dark room, while the reflection of a lantern floats by on the foggy window. A cab driver is conveying someone, for some reason, to some place. I will never, never find out who he was, where he was going, who lives next door, who thinks of me that very minute as I think of him (though we do not know each other). How much of everything there is in me – even more, it would seem, than there is around me. Life is big and beautiful. Life is long and huge, like the universe itself. I won't have time . . . I won't have time . . . to . . . Wait! Wait! Last a little longer, maybe some twenty or thirty years . . . No, that is too short a time. The fortune-teller said sixty. When will this be? It will be in the year 1961. Oh, what joy that this is still so far off, so infinitely far off, as from Kazan to Ryazan, from Ryazan to Erevan, to Lebedyan, to Tmutorokan . . . 'You were delirious and reciting a lesson of geography,' I am told when I open my eyes. It is time to take my temperature.

The Christmas tree belonged to the realm I detested wholeheartedly, its branches hung with crackers, candles, and foil. To me, it was the symbol of the 'nest'. I hated paper angels with stupid pink faces. I was bored by crackers. No dunce cap could fit my head, as later, hats would not. Candles flickered with the false assurance that it was more splendid to live by them than by tungsten lamps. It was impossible to accept this. I considered people who affirmed it were my personal enemies. What was most important was: in the apartment a centre would suddenly appear where I had to be instead of remaining alone and free, instead of sitting on the window sill behind the curtains admiring the frost patterns on the window pane, or at my desk in my room, or under the dinner table, or in the kitchen where the solitaire 'Napoleon's tomb' was being played. But I had to sit and admire the burning candles, look as if I liked angels and expected presents. Yet only unexpected things brought joy. I had to share the adults' affectation that was so displeasing to me, in the same way as when people read bad verse or listened to gypsy songs. On the other hand, what joy I felt when the dead bare fir was finally carried out!

I feared affectation and false melancholy more than fire. It seemed to me that there was too much of it around, that it would somehow reach me and wear me out, and that I would then perish. There was indeed a lot of it around; for before the 1920s, when for the first time man's profound and important inner depths were unlocked and people revealed themselves, his lyric élans blossomed, and because they were universal, they were not only cheap but mediocre. I remember covers of magazines with whiskered men, and the expanded nostrils of Vera Kholodnaya, snake-woman, bird-woman, fairy-woman, lioness-woman, into whom some of my classmates dreamt of transforming themselves but who only threw me into a state of panic. As usual, pushed to extremes either by the instinct of self-preservation or by cold reflection, I came to doubt, along with the affectation of lyricism, lyricism itself, with those awful verses about moonlit nights – and the nights themselves. All the Liebestraums gave me the same aftertaste – of something that is touched with finality, that will not survive the first shock, wherever it may come from, and prevents me from being fully armed for a first encounter with fate. Liebestraums rang out everywhere, bringing astounding delight to our mothers, who, then still quite young, felt that the sources of emotionalism and affectation had opened up to them, about them, for them. They no doubt dreamt that we would follow them into all these romances and nuances as into a worn shoe. As for our children, they would happily settle among them. But we refused to profit from these boons, and instead of semolina kasha, from childhood on we gnawed on the devil knows what, breaking our teeth, and very often hearing a rustling reproach somewhere: ungrateful, coarsened souls, insensitive and dry, they like poetry without metre, music without melody, painting without mood. I must confess that at about twelve I began to doubt the dialogue of Natasha and Sonya at the window, the night Prince Andrey spent at Otradnoe, the charm of Kitty. To me, all this seemed to be a smoke screen, a camouflage for real life; all these lovely girls were in the very centre of their Liebestraums, in the midst of their nest, and further from me than a Polynesian savage.

No smoke screen over life, no emotional overtones of religion (twilight, icon-lamp, candles, chants for the dead). I developed a profound aversion to false comfort and cosiness. I wanted a hundred-watt light shining on a book in which everything was expressed, everything was said, a clear day, a black night, no ambiguous meanings, no sad improvisations that were covered by veils of glances, sighs, and hints. These Fata Morganas seemed to me more terrible than cannon fire. Behind them lay my very own life, which I foresaw with the actual cannon fire that thundered over me three times, my own struggle in which no one dared replace me, where I would not cede my place under fire. Life was gradually becoming a reality from which I had no intention of hiding behind anyone's back.

All dualism is painful for me, all splitting or bisecting contrary to my nature. When Lenin speaks about matter in opposition to energy, when Berdyaev speaks about material principle (reaction) and spiritual principle (revolution), when idealist philosophers speak about spirit and flesh, I am jarred, as by a false note. My commandment was the truth that matter is energy. My whole life has been the reconciliation within myself of the old dichotomy. Now all these diverse and often contrasting traits fuse in me. Long ago I stopped thinking of myself as being composed of two halves. I feel physically, that a *seam*, not a *cut*, passes through me, that I myself am a seam, that with this seam, while I am alive, something has united in me, something has been soldered, that I am one of many examples in nature of soldering, unification, fusion, harmonization, that I am not living in vain, but there is sense in that I am as I am, an example of synthesis in a world of antitheses.

I carry the fact that two origins – Russian (northern) and Armenian (southern) – fuse in me, like a precious gift of destiny. To a great extent this conditioned me from my childhood on. This contrast, like a whole host of other contrasts and even contradictions which I saw and knew in myself, gradually ceased to be a source of conflict. I began to feel them like a union of polarities and consciously rejoiced in being the focus of their unification.

My grandfather on my father's side, Ivan Minaevich Berberov, was a descendant of those nameless Armenians who, by dint of a complicated historical process, found themselves in the middle of the eighteenth century on the southern shore of the Crimea in a very poverty-ridden state. Potemkin informed Catherine of this. She decided to take these people out of the Crimea and give them land on the shores of the Don (where it empties into the Sea of Azov), near Cossack villages and the city of Rostov, so they could settle and begin new lives, in commerce and working at various trades. This, of course, was in line with her Crimean policies. I remember that at the centre of the little city of Nakhichevan (named in honour of the Transcaucasian Nakhichevan, an old Armenian city), in front of the Armenian cathedral (behind it stood a Russian cathedral which faced the market square), was a huge bronze monument to Catherine, bearing the inscription: 'To Catherine the Second – from grateful Armenians.' This monument was removed in 1920 by local authorities and thrown into the rubbish heap, where it lay upside down for a long time. Later it was found and turned into a cannon, perhaps, or a plough. Now, according to rumour, Karl Marx stands there.

Armenian affairs in the new place went enviably well. Grandfather Ivan Minaevich's father, who obviously had the means, sent Grandfather at the end of the 1850s to study medicine in Paris. On a daguerreotype of the time he is shown in a top hat, with long hair, an elegant jacket, a cloak, and a cane. The names of Charcot and Pasteur, even that of Gambetta, were in the air until the end of my grandfather's days (he died at the beginning of 1917). From Paris, Grandfather returned with an M.D., got married, had seven sons and one daughter. He became known in the area as a doctor to whom money meant little, one of the most learned of the people of his generation, that is, of the people of this really *nondescript* town, which was somehow unlike all other southern Russian centres.

My father, Nikolai Ivanovich, was the third of his seven sons. All the boys were sent in time to Moscow to study at the Lazarevsky Institute of Oriental Languages. There they crammed into their memories 'You are a sneak, you are a slave, you are an Armenian'* and 'The timid Georgians run away,'† which they later remembered with humour. After the Lazarevsky Institute, they all went to the university. In my childhood I was always exhilarated by the symmetry with which every two years, so I was told, they took state exams and then went on their way into a host – or rather an assortment – of all kinds of professions: physician, lawyer, mathematician, journalist, banker, etc. They stood shoulder to shoulder in the family group – one in civilian clothes, two others in university outfits, three in Lazarevsky Institute jackets, and one on the knee of my grandmother, wearing a lace collar. All, as if made to order, were tall, straight, handsome, the older ones with black beards and fiery eyes, the younger ones with serious and sombre faces.

Grandfather Ivan Minaevich lived at the other end of Russia and everything about him was in sharp contrast to the son of Oblomov. He was the first European I met. From his European youth only the cane remained at this time, held in his dry, carefully manicured hand. The cane-head was of ivory with a small hole in it, as was then the fashion. I sometimes looked into this hole and saw Paris, the view from the hill of Montmartre – minus, of course, the Eiffel Tower. It was a walking stick that had been purchased at

*Pushkin.
†Lermontov.

25

Charville's in 1861. The sky was blue, without a single cloud. The cupola of the Invalides and the towers of Notre Dame gradually became my close acquaintances. I could have entered that hole like an insect as small as a crumb and remained there. Only in roundabout ways, however, did I finally reach that city, to stay there a quarter of a century.

Standing at Grandfather's desk, which at that time came to just below my chin, I carefully considered medical journals, newspaper clippings, pencils, pens, envelopes with foreign stamps, a hand mirror in a silver mounting. Grandfather liked to have it at hand, like his bottle of subtle perfume with which, not embarrassed by those near him, including me, he would spray his white, straight, silken beard from time to time; to my cheeks his beard was not at all like the grey-green, curly, rigid one of Grandfather Ivan Dmitrievich, where it was sometimes possible to find a crumb from a roll eaten that morning. Both of them, of course, like all grandfathers of that time, had something of the Almighty in them; but while the Russian grandfather was a mixture of Jehovah and a water-goblin, the Armenian grandfather was a combination of Jehovah and Prospero.

In a spick-and-span black frock coat and a white satin tie, scented, combed, he would appear at morning tea and take in the table with a quick, sharp glance (so it remained until his death). The table was overflowing with cream, pancakes, rolls (some crusty, some soft), butter, pressed and fresh caviar in blue tins, smoked and half-smoked grey mullet, vimba with a shiny red back, balyk, all kinds of ham chosen with great care at the grocery, an omelette in the skillet, little pies with cottage cheese, waffles with jam, sausages, Edam cheese, Swiss cheese – some with drops of condensation. He took all this in with a penetrating glance, drank his glass of tea with lemon and ate a biscuit, since at approximately this time he had, as was said in the family, a 'cracked idea', that the less one ate, the better. This was then so new, incomprehensible, and at cross purposes to the preparations in the kitchen, pantries, and cellars, that very soon news that Dr Berberov advised eating six grapes instead of beef Stroganoff, and that his sons (one a doctor) would take him to Switzerland to see a famous psychiatrist, affected the people in the town, and his practice began to suffer. It is true that every morning the sick continued to come from Don villages and the lower city, which lay on the shores of the Don – villagers, cossacks, petit bourgeois, small house-owners, farmers. But all of these people were *Russian*, that is, people who were comparatively poor and simple, whereas the society to which Grandfather had belonged all his life was Armenian.

His wife was pushed around in a wheelchair. As I remember this house and the life in it, I now strongly doubt that Grandmother was, in fact, paralysed. It seems to me that she simply got over-tired during her long life, that everything had come to fatigue her. So she sat in a wheelchair and announced she had had enough. She travelled abroad in that very chair with a faithful servant. Probably she realized that if she stood up – in other words, 'got better' – she would again have to nurse, if not her children, then her grand-children, to carry out all of Grandfather's whims, supervise the cook, the coachman, the housekeeper, the maids, greet guests, feed dinners to forty men at once, order dresses from Paris, toast members of the party of 'Dashnaktsutiun' who had come to visit Grandfather from the Transcaucasus, enter into the family affairs, general and monetary, of her seven sons, and busy herself with relatives who filled the house with their stormy lives (each living here in his own way and insisting that ordinary standards could not be applied to him). Grandmother found the way out. She pretended to be overcome by paralysis and now enjoyed life.

I assessed the difference between the two breeds very early. At about eight I gathered that I came from two different, though not inimical, worlds. On the one side, people who not only did things like everyone else, but who tried to be like everyone else – Olga Dmitrievna, tortured by the 'shame' and 'scandal' of her family life, about which no one spoke, and Alina, hiding ten years of her life from everyone. On the Armenian side, there was a whole world of original characters and lives and fates. This nonconformity, as I later realized, was rooted in the people themselves, in their life-energy, their eagerness, and constant consciousness that nothing comes easily all by itself, that nothing gets done by itself, and every day is a special day. They had hot blood, strong passions. Among them were gamblers who broke the bank of 100,000 roubles in the Merchants' Club, and progressive people who had fought for ideas dear to them, after whom, in 1917, city streets in the free Armenian Republic were named. Among them were lovers, Don Juans, who, however, could sacrifice meetings with Donna Annas for meetings with the Commendatore simply to question him in more detail about affairs of the other world. They raged at life, perhaps, because their ancestors had not slept calmly under portraits of tsars near icon-lamps, but moved for centuries from the Persian frontier to Cilicia and the Mesopotamian frontier, around the shores of the Black Sea, to be reborn at the mouth of the Don, and became in a hundred years the aristocracy of the city, moneyed and intellectual. This means that at the time when Yury (no patronymic), the descendant of Kara-Ul, received his lands, another great-great-great-grandfather of mine – whose name, like that of other ancestors on my father's side, has not been preserved, and who was by profession maybe a ploughman, or a barber (to judge from our surname), or perhaps even a counterfeiter – received his corner plot. After the city had been planned by uninventive city builders, this corner received the name of Sofiyskaya Street and Line 18.

In a very Russian, very church-going, very conservative family, the marriage of my mother and father was received like a shock; recovery was not rapid. My father's Armenian religion, although Christian, seemed somehow alien, and he himself was a foreigner, his southern temperament inspiring fear. This man, having come from God knows where, was nevertheless accepted by all, and he and Mother loved each other their entire lives, never separating until death divorced them.

If my mother's family reconciled itself with difficulty to her marrying a 'foreigner', my father's family found it even more complicated. To admit a 'Russian' daughter-in-law to one's family, to have a son beget 'Russian' children, was considered a betrayal of Armenia. But, of course, neither side imposed a ban. The marriage took place in January 1900, and in August of the following year, on the eighth, I was born in the house on Great Morskaya Street in St Petersburg, which was later rebuilt to make way for a yacht club whose large glass entrance I remember well to this very day.

However much I tried to persuade my grandfather to let me sit in a corner of his office when he examined his patients, he would not consent. I told him many times that I had my *own* armchair in my other grandfather's study, and that he had no secrets with the Timofeys and the Savva Kuzmiches that he kept from me, yet he firmly uttered his 'No, no,' or 'What silly fantasies!' But once I hid behind the curtains and heard Grandfather examining two patients. One was a middle-aged woman with a sickness I did not understand, the other was a boy with an ear inflammation. I emerged from behind the curtains half sick myself, with the realization that I had at least learned a lesson. Medicine dropped from the list of professions that every now and then I considered in my mind, seeking a suitable one for me. I would never like my own kidneys and future interest in my middle ear seemed total nonsense to me. I was severely punished and it was explained to me that a visit to a doctor is a secret protected by law, that I had committed a crime for which one can be put in jail. I suddenly passionately wanted to be in jail, only to break out to liberty to prove to myself as well as to others that I could be blind, one-armed, one-legged, and criminal, and yet still live, live, live!

Instead of thirty-eight horses, there were just two here. They were harnessed by the coachman, Selifan, who was the prototype if not of the Almighty, then of Santa Claus as the children of the West know him. He did not have to place pillows under his backside, because he was so fat, but nevertheless he did and from behind he looked like a globe of the world. He did not give me the reins, but ordered me to sit down in the elegant carriage, every spoke shining. I did not especially try to become friendly with the horses because they were too *fine* – reminiscent in character and even in appearance of my grandmother of Tver.

I sat next to Grandfather and we went for a ride. For the first time in my life I wanted to be clean, well dressed, and pretty. The last, as I then knew, was, of course, quite impossible, but I managed to be clean and well dressed for the duration of the ride, while Grandfather, having made his beard fluffy, leaning both hands on the walking stick with the view of Paris, and wearing a striking top hat which he had brushed before with a special velvet cloth, looked around and severely criticized the straw on the pavement on bazaar day, the barber's bright sign with the half-naked beauty, the cooper who banged too loudly in his shed.

Writers, poets, public figures, publicists, and members of the Dashnaktsutiun Party would come from the Transcaucasus to visit him. I could not understand them because I did not know their language: I could recognize only two letters of the Armenian alphabet – N and B – a marking on towels and napkins which

29

seemed to me signs of my own still mysterious world. At about five I met the Catholikos, the head of the Armenian church. All in violet – a violet cassock, a violet beard – he was solemnly brought into the house and seated in a corner of the living room. I was ordered to go to him for a blessing along with the other children, cousins, among whom the closest to me in age at the time is now a retired general in the Soviet Air Force. Seeing that none of the children moved, but only stared and shifted from one leg to the other, I decided that the Catholikos was getting bored sitting and waiting. Not sensing the significance of the moment, and, as usual, fearful of losing precious time, I went up to him first and quite casually extended my hand for a hand-shake. He did not offer me his violet hand, but placed it on my head, read a prayer containing the well-known exclamation 'Ter Bohormya!' and gave me his huge violet signet ring to kiss. After this I did not know whether to move away and give my place to another or talk to him, if allowed; and if the latter then with what subject should I entertain him? I was led away and pushed out into the yard.

This yard, completely square, then seemed the most protected place in the world. Next to the kitchen door were the rubbish bins. Selifan cleaned the harnesses or slept sitting on a bench, while dogs wandered about near him. In this yard, in 1919, a certain Magner, a tenant relocated into the house by the Red authorities, was shot. During those terrible nights of the Civil War, long, narrow shells flew above the yard and exploded with a bang near by. But those nights were still far off; nothing was known about them. The future was firmly hidden, as only the future can be from human eyes. Any other secret can be known, can be drawn from the lips of another by caresses or tortures, but the secret of the future is hidden, kept from us as if there were no future and no secret. Yes, that's the way it is. The future does not exist. It does not lie in store and does not await us. It is created by life and our very selves. It is born with each new day. It is prescribed by no one. So that cellar, which many years later became a bomb shelter where we buried the ear-rings and brooches of my late grandmother, was, at that time, only a most ordinary cellar in which sauerkraut, cucumbers, hams, and French wines were kept, along with the many goodies that Grandfather called poison.

Having graduated from Moscow University with a major in mathematics and physics, my father oscillated between continuing in his special field or entering government service. He chose the second, went to Petersburg, and entered the ministry of finance as a young aide to a bureau chief. In 1917 he had the rank of state councillor, was a civil servant for 'special missions' during the time of the last tsar's finance minister, Bark, and one of the obscure specialists in income tax, which tsarist Russia was preparing to introduce.

Differentials and integrals did not seem to suit him. Perhaps, however, I am still in the throes of an old prejudice that mathematics is a dry discipline and that a mathematician is not a man of this world. Our time of cybernetics and electronic machines has shown how close mathematics is to everything we live by, but then I understood science differently and could not grasp in what way this fiery, quick, lively man could have something in common with water flowing from taps in pools, or with Pythagorean propositions, or with the binomial theorem. I had no interest at all in those things at that time.

For me, he was never the personification of power, strength, authority, and will. So I loved him. There was certainly nothing feminine and weak, will-less and faded in him, and he seems to me now, as I write of him, the incarnation of what is masculine, the essential masculine principle. I have not often met a man of my own or his generation so wholesome in that sense. There were no attempts by him to shelter me, to defend me, to lead me, to direct me, and this made him priceless. In my childhood women exerted much more power over me, told me what to do and what not to do, and often, with the best intentions, tried to take me 'under their wing', but I feared this most of all, and with the years fled their 'wings' and warmth and care, all that is usually considered so indispensable at the beginning of every life. I see Father next to me, his hand in mine or mine in his. We are walking side by side. I take big steps or he small ones, and we speak of something, always essential and interesting to both of us, and we marvel equally at the world and the other people walking past us.

He infected me, however, with his weaknesses, his phobias, of which he had not a few. One of these was hydrophobia. He hated to live by the seashore, to look at the waves, to hear waterfalls, and in my earliest years this fear passed on to me. Sitting in a boat was unthinkable for him; a steamer was torture merely at a glance, and the splash of a river or even the smooth surface of a lake forced him to quicken his steps and not look back. The explanation of this came later. It was, of course, told to me in childhood, but I completely forgot it; and then in a dream once, when I was over thirty, I saw a surface of water, right in the centre of which rested the sun. The evening was full of flowers, warmth, charm, and peace. Everything in me rejected the fear of water, the fear of the blue sea, but I could not free myself from it and was bound to it. I understood that at that hour in my life I could not do anything with it, that it was with me, in me. But I knew all this could not be innate, it had to be overcome. Someone looking scornfully at me said that there was nothing surprising in this fear, that my father nearly drowned at seventeen by losing his balance while swimming, and that ever since he had suffered from hydrophobia. So, in a dream, my subconscious brought back to me the explanation I had heard many years before. Waking up, I understood I had shown myself the way, as has happened more than once in my life, to free myself from something that was in essence alien to me. I emerged from this phobia much later; it was one of the most important events of my inner life, one of the steps towards an equilibrium which is acquired through such an act of liberation.

Father was tall and thin, so thin that he was not taken for military service because his chest was an inch too small. Military people were, however, his second phobia. We never had them in our house, and only in 1916 when the reserves were called up do I remember seeing field jackets and shoulder straps on two of his young comrades.

I knew he loved women. I knew he loved women of a certain type, who have now, in our time, disappeared or almost disappeared. They had to be 'society' women, yet at the same time easy to conquer, beautiful, gay, and not too intelligent. They had to love love. These women occupied his thoughts and these women loved him, for in him, in full accordance with his masculinity, there was everything that pleased a woman – strength combined with tenderness, reserve and softness combined with energy. It always seemed to me that the fact that he passionately wanted a daughter and not a son was in harmony with his nature. He was genuinely pained when he saw me bring unattractive girls into our house. He loved to seek and find femininity in me and never tried to diminish or ignore its meaning, but did all he could to let it flower. I

32

understood a great deal about him when once, at about twelve, I whirled with him through a ballroom in a country hall to the strains of a Strauss waltz. No one ever danced so smoothly, with so much assurance and such complete abandon as my father.

In a warm jacket, a dark red tarboosh with a long black silk tassel, a string of amber beads in his fingers, the end of his Havana cigar swelling into a heavy blue ash (woe if it falls!), looking at me as I sat on the floor at his feet, *he spoke with his eyes*. I felt for the first time then that if I had to pick one man among a thousand, I would pick the one who *spoke with his eyes*: When thoughts pass, clear to me without words, borne here and floating there, like clouds in a sky, complete in themselves, light and transparent, I know what he wants to say, what he will presently say to me. I loved his eyes, his hands, his smell of cigar mixed with 'triple' eau-de-cologne. I loved his elegant figure (which he inherited from his father) when he returned from Paris in 1913 in a stylish coat and soft hat, which was a novelty among all the bowlers and top hats. I loved his bewilderment at my early independence, his ecstasy in February 1917, and his slow ageing, the decline of his energy after privations and pursuits, and finally his short movie career before World War Two when, on Nevsky Avenue in 1935, the director, Kozintsev, came to him and said: 'We need your type.' 'Why mine?' asked Father. 'I have neither experience nor talent.' 'But you are the right type,' was the answer. 'With that beard, that starched collar, and that walk – there are only two or three such men in all of Leningrad. We hired one of them yesterday.' This was the former chamberlain and balletomane Kovraysky, who had miraculously survived with such a beard and such a collar. So my father played his first role, a man of the 'ancien régime' who is destroyed in the end. There were others later. My father scarcely needed to use make-up.

In 1937, somewhere in a dirty, smelly street near the Boulevard Sébastopol (in Paris there are numerous streets about our shame – Boulevard Sébastopol, the Austerlitz Bridge, Malakoff Avenue, Boulevard Inkermann), I found the headquarters of a small Communist cell; it handled the showing of Soviet movies, which were not commercially exhibited in France because they were poor and coarsely propagandistic. I was told that such-and-such a film would play somewhere sometime but that they could not sell me a ticket, that I would have to join a French Communist cell and pay

33

my annual dues. Without delay I became a member of the cell of the 13th Arrondissement of Paris, paid what was demanded, and on the appointed day sat in a dark hall among other members, all in ecstatic mood. The film was a story of a counter-revolutionary bastard, director of the State Bank, a saboteur and agent of a foreign power, who upset Lenin's restoration of the Russian budget. So Lenin sent a sailor from the Baltic fleet to the State Bank who, though he could neither read nor write, restored the financial balance of Russia in three days. (The affair took place in 1918.) The director of the bank was arrested together with his cronies, and the crowd screamed wildly on the screen and in the hall, 'Beat him! Hit him in the teeth! Chop down the enemies of the working class!' At the last moment my father managed to pour ink onto the open page of a ledger, proving that he would oppose Lenin's deed to his last breath. They led him to the exit. At the gates of the State Bank, he was given a minute to pause, look at the Ekaterininsky Canal, at the Petersburg sky, growing turbid with rain, and straight at me, sitting in the Paris hall. Our eyes met. He was led away under escort. I never saw him again. But several words he uttered brought back his voice, his smile, his quick hazel-eyed glance that spoke without words. After fifteen years of separation, what a meeting! The joy of meeting after such a separation, before parting for ever, is not pre-ordained for everyone.

With a little push of the imagination, I can see him again, but he cannot see me. I see Leningrad in the winter of 1941–2 during the siege. I see Saltykov-Shchedrin (formerly Kirochnaya) Street, a huge courtyard, a thoroughfare leading to Manezhny Alley. I see my father, now very small, old, and thin, as white as the deep snow, with a little pan in his hands, walking to the Neva ice hole and slipping on the ice of Chernyshevsky Street (once Voskresensky Avenue). I see him return home and heat the iron stove, slowly, with great effort, cracking the parquet in the darkness of the dead apartment. Later, I see how both of them, my father and mother, are evacuated. She dies on the road. He survives. He is left somewhere in the provinces – at the home of strangers, in a strange place, completely alone. Where? In the Urals? Or in the Caucasus? Or in Turkestan? He lives there for several months and dies. The one place in which he still lives is my memory.

This vision of a Leningrad courtyard, or my grandfather's provincial one where the engineer Magner lay axed or shot to death, or even that courtyard where my father lived in the final months of his life and which I will never find, pass by in my mind like places whose genuine significance no one could guess. No fortune-tellers, astrologers or poets could deal in such visions. There are houses where the future is joined from the past, there are courtyards where the future is made. Chaliapin's voice growls on the first gramophone, the first telephone rings, the first electric bulb shines over a house porch, and the first automobile stands at an entrance to take us to some field near St. Petersburg to see the flight of the first biplane. The warm house (the incubator I hate) rears people only to release them to the elements, war, revolution, siege, air raid, camp, execution, atomic bomb. Mine is the first generation that is, perhaps, doomed not just to die, but to scatter into dust. The train with prisoners leaving for extermination camps in the north, the boats sinking at sea, death from hunger on a bench in a municipal square in a foreign city – everything is for everyone. Nothing is fore-ordained, all is possible.

In this connection, I remember one of my dreams about Dostoevsky. I am playing chess with someone. There are many people in the room. Dostoevsky stands near me and looks attentively at the board. And I say to him, 'Well, Fedor Mikhailovich, in chess you can foresee everything and allow for it. If we move here, then all twenty-five or thirty-five moves to the very end of the game are pre-ordained and known beforehand. If we move there, a whole chain of causalities again unfolds, a chain from which there is no escape. But in human life even you cannot foresee what will happen. You can be given a heap of facts about two people and you will still not be able to tell us today what they, together or alone, will do tomorrow. The law of cause and effect does not work when you talk about men.'

He smiles, squints with one eye, is silent for about a minute, and then says:

'Yes, very likely this is so. Twenty-five or thirty-five moves you can, of course, foresee, but only on condition the ceiling does not collapse during the game and that one of the players does not die of a stroke. If this happens, then chess becomes like life, it moves into a dimension where there are neither social nor biological laws, nor the possibility for the best mind to work out the "pattern" of the future.'

'What! No social or biological laws? Is there really such a place on earth?'

'In the meeting of two people and in man's creativity,' he answers. 'There these laws do not work.'

I see my opponent take my pawn. Suddenly I notice that Dostoevsky has small, exquisite, well-cared-for hands.

If I played with dolls sometimes, they were not ordinary ones. They were always little boys, and they were all either sick or crippled. They were called Alexandre, Alfred, Albert, Arthur, and so on. The enthusiasm was strong, but short-lived. It lasted, in all, probably a few months. Where it came from, I don't know. All these pale, dumb little boys, bandaged and covered with blankets, lay enveloped, half alive, at a time when cheeky little-girl dolls, over-dressed, in yellow wigs, saying 'Mama' and 'Papa', did not interest me in the least. But I forgot this enthusiasm very quickly and when I went to secondary school, there was not a trace of dolls. There were just slight remains of the obsession in my conviction that little boys are less happy than little girls and more defenceless, that men are brittle beings who require careful attention. This was seemingly rooted in overheard opinions of elders that there are fewer men in the world than women and that their lives are somehow shorter.

Again I return to that image, to the seam, the fusing of opposites, one of the most important themes of my inner life. In people around me, in books and in my own self, I saw how often the human personality is broken, ripped, or split in two and felt this to be one of the fatal factors in human life and one of the riddles put to man. Then came the day – suddenly, as it almost always has come in my life (therefore, perhaps, my belief in evolutionary 'jolts' rather than smooth waves) – then came the day when suddenly the fog around me lifted: I understood that what I had thought were factions in me were a union, that contradictions within myself were an organized system, my individual counterpoint. The personality supposedly divided in two was actually a personality that in itself, in its closed quintessence, connected the two in one process. This was the great day of my life, the end of my doubts about my 'dichotomy' and the beginning of calmness and moderation in my knowing and organizing myself.

Historically, as I now see it, admitting my joined nature was especially fruitful. It responded to the life of my generation, a generation that lived in two worlds, one moving towards an end, the other hardly beginning. It brought peace and fullness of existence into a shattered, distorted, and troubled world. At that junction of the old and the new, the dying of one epoch and the birth of another, a process that has lasted fifty years, *we* fuse the two. And, in a certain sense we even feel we are a *privileged class* because we breathe freely in both the old and the new, for we are *capable* of such breathing. Biologically we are 'phenomena' of this harmony. On the symbolic plane we will probably later come to *stand for something*, like the sign for a bridge or a curve. In this last sense I see that even my dreams have a functional relation to my thinking when awake, and that my subconscious answers my conscious – an eternally vigilant element in me to which a hidden, mysterious, and puzzling friend and counsellor adds his voice.

Snowy Petersburg winters and early evenings on a huge couch, that seemed a hulk to me on which you could go for a far-off trip (it later appeared in the first part of my novel *Without Sunset*), were my childhood scenery. I remember particularly the winters during my first years of secondary school (at eight I had entered a junior preparatory class), when I was living not only among grown-ups, but also among girls like myself. Some of them were already close friends, a word in which there was something holy and serious. Friendship always attracted me and attracts me even now. I have been boundlessly happy with friends all my life. My girl friends were varied and grouping them together was incredibly hard. After a while I despaired of achieving any proper order in this matter. One of them in particular, Natasha van der Fleet, the great-granddaughter of the Decembrist Ivashev, did not fit into any category. She lived in a wooden house on Vasilievsky Island which was very unlike our bourgeois apartment at No. 6 Zhukovsky Street. Three generations lived together there, including two remarkable grandmothers. One was the daughter-in-law of the Decembrist Vasily Ivashev, who had been exiled to Siberia with his wife, born Camilla Ledantu (one of the three Frenchwomen celebrated by Nekrasov in his *Russian Women*). Their daughter was born in Siberia and was a cousin of the writer Grigorovich, his mother, Sidonia Petrovna, being Camilla's sister. The paternal grandmother was the Pelageya Nikolaevna (born Pypina) about whom Nabokov wrote in *The Gift* that she had a 'faithful, firm skirt, in Euclidean pleats' which 'Chernyshevsky's son held on to'. Natasha's mother was a schoolteacher, while her father was Konstantin Petrovich van der Fleet, the very man who played such a role in the early work of Aleksey Tolstoy. The floors squeaked in the house and there was no maid in lace apron or stiff head-dress as at our place, but there were many books, small windows with views of a quiet courtyard, and the calm of the Sixth Line near Sredny Avenue. The light-haired, blue-eyed Natasha, who later lost her husband in tragic circumstances in the early 1930s, was inwardly somehow very like me. We understood each other well, spoke of the choice of professions, of the secrecy of life, of Decembrists, and both trembled with inward impatience at the thought of the future, which sped towards us with insufficient speed and strength, or so we thought, as if we were both sails ready to rush out to the sea, though there was still no wind to blow us along and whirl us away.

Another spot I remember is the huge flat in the same building as the Nikolaevsky Station. It belonged to the railways director, had windows that looked out onto the noisy carousel-like square with its recently unveiled monument to Alexander III, and a little girl who had been adopted by the railways director lived in it. He and his wife seemed very ancient to me. They were dignitaries and, like my grandmother, were from Tver (I could now recognize the species). There were reception halls in the flat, drawing rooms in a row, a ballroom, and satin chairs in the playroom in which bored-looking dolls sat in satin dresses and lace pantaloons. I loved pale, quiet Lucia, who was my age, for the mystery of her birth, and once, while we sat embracing each other in the doll-house – a real one, which you could enter and which had miniature furniture, a toy piano and even a miniature sewing machine – I leaned towards her ear and asked her if she knew who she was and where she came from. She answered into my ear that she did not know and would never know. She was later sent to a concentration camp in Vorkuta to chop timber.

We spent one summer on the shores of the Gulf of Finland instead of on the estate of my grandfather from Tver. Until then I had had only a dim notion of the Finnish Gulf. The pine forest, all dry and fragrant, that was so near our cottage (made from those very pine trees) was much more appealing to me. We wandered there, the two of us, lobster-eyed, near-sighted Yura, who wore glasses so thick that his eyes, without quite bulging, seemed huge, motionless, and very angry, and I. It never entered my head that he had some kind of feeling of love for me, endured a type of torture and joy which I caused. He told me about it in 1921, before he was sent on a construction project to Arkhangelsk from which he never returned.

I think that writing verse came completely naturally to me, owing to an *overflowing of the soul*, as with some romantics. If I was at one point a romantic, it was precisely in those first years after a profession had finally been chosen. But the beginning was quite disgraceful. Carried away by Lermontov's poem 'At an anguished moment of life', I felt I could not part with such ecstasy, and took a clean notebook in which I wrote *Poems* and accurately copied in it all twelve lines. It enraptured me with its melody, and here, at about nine, I unconsciously felt that unity of form and content which people still argue about. The content of Lermontov's poem, as I remember, was totally alien to me. I knew *prayers*, as one is supposed to know them, but they were never *miraculous* to me, and the *holy* charm of something was totally incomprehensible to me. Yet what sounds these were! Moments were hard, yet they were also marvellous, for the sadness that played in their vowel sounds was marvellous. The chords of the living words sang and sparkled in my head, and what Lermontov confessed – that something in life was incomprehensible (to me as well) – touched me to the point of tears. Instead of crying because of doubts, it seemed that you could cry after you had settled them. That 'easy-easy' feeling at the end I knew well, had felt it for a long time already. So everything that inspired beauty settled in me, and I thought I would no longer 'recite by heart' a 'prayer' but would recite Lermontov himself, with the same feeling of fullness and happiness he had when reciting a prayer by heart. A circle emerged where Lermontov and I were at one, a blessed circle! Later still others appeared.

'This is plagiarism!' said my father, when I boasted of the notebook. Presently he explained that difficult word to me. But I felt differently. I could compromise, and in the last resort confess to the fact that Lermontov and I had written the poem together.

That summer I first heard Balmont's name. Yura's older sister (who perished during the siege of Leningrad) recited to music 'The Dying Swan', which I did not understand, because it seemed obscure that a bird could 'speak with its past' and 'see the truth' (exactly like Leo Tolstoy). From Vasilievsky Island came Blok's 'Little candles and little willows', which I remained indifferent to. On the other hand, having read Pushkin's *The Captive of the Caucasus* I was elated with the 'Dedication' to it. This again was something that related to me –

> When I guiltless, cheerless – was perishing
> And heard the murmur of curses from all sides

– something that operated directly on me. Unjustly punished and standing in a corner picking at the wallpaper, I said over and over:

> And thus the storms over me weakened their ferocity.
> And I blessed the Gods in calm refuge . . .

The rest, such as 'the cold dream of love' and 'the dagger of cold betrayal', worked on me abstrusely, by their sounds only, through their sound-harmony, through the tension and charm of the pauses.

I loved my mother and I didn't love her, often falling in love with her and then out again. I began to judge her much earlier than I did my father. The reason for my vacillating love for her was my opposition to her, which arose very early. I saw her virtues as though from a distance, while my continual opposition to her authority was close at hand, automatic like a conditioned reflex. I remember my struggle, the constant 'no' to everything that came from her. In this uninterrupted duel of many years there was no room for anything else, not tenderness, understanding, forgiveness, or agreement. Everything from her brought out a wariness in me, an arming of all my forces like a porcupine bristling. Or, outwardly, I would camouflage myself in defensive colours like a chameleon, or become tense as a tiger ready to attack another tiger. She was a woman of her time: of distorted upbringing, social conventions, preconceptions, when what was considered most important in life was not to appear as you really were, and to speak in one tone to children, another to the servants, a third to guests, a fourth to a store clerk, a fifth to a man who admired you. Voices changed according to the surroundings. The women of that era, supposedly coached in the roles of wife and mother (of course, actually neither the one nor the other) repressed, hid, and masked something alive in themselves; and this liveliness was killed in the end, crushed by the severe rules of behaviour. Mother was of the same generation as Chekhov's seagull's, Dora Brilliant's, from whom so many of 'our' women emerged, having liberated themselves from the frame of artificial life, of hothouse mimosa psychology. They were born at the beginning of the 1880s, and many of them, although they did not make a genuine step towards freedom and did not liberate themselves outwardly, liberated themselves inwardly – there, somewhere, a butterfly flew out of its cocoon. The problem was not in their ordering of personal life, but in their awareness of themselves and their place in the surrounding world. Such women were noticeable during my childhood even in bourgeois society living rooms. At first small escape breaches were opened, then the doors were thrown wide open (they had been tightly closed in the time of Queen Victoria and Great-Aunt Olga Dmitrievna). It was not talent that was necessary but rather the desire to accept a new century and to become a member of it. My mother was unable and unwilling to do this, and for a long time I could not forgive her.

It seemed to me in those years that everything in her was not completely *genuine*. And where was the sincere part? Crushed by the hard rules of behaviour, the empty forms of her class. When I began to live with self-awareness (at eight or nine), that sincerity had completely disappeared. What was left was the outward form of gestures, glances, dress, walk, superstitions and taboos, forced smiles, general opinions, the trappings of a motionless and mute soul. Perhaps I, and only I, had made her so? Was it the fear that in her house something foreign, inimical, new, distant was growing? She could not help feeling how far she had moved from her mother (or rather, not moved away but been carried by life), how much from her own grandmother and great-grandmother. Perhaps she sometimes had a premonition of where we were ready to move and what we were preparing to destroy? Was it both fear and bewilderment when facing our future? Fear of the break between the two of us but also between our two generations, the division

41

within our class and explosion of our common history, the presentiment of the decline of *their* firm universe that made her so? There was a photograph of her in an old album at sixteen, light, beautiful, alive, with curls on her forehead, eyes smiling, full of mischief. It was as if all of her, like the feet of Chinese women of old, had been bound so that she would not grow, as though someone had taken her in hand once and for all and threatened that the world would collapse if she, and only she, did not hold up its foundations. Her beauty took on a dry, severe tone, her lips became thinner, her voice louder, her movements were monotonous, and her grey eyes, which looked so clever in the old photograph, became motionless, as if stopped by a constant worry: to be like everybody else. Yet, the world of Queen Victoria, Franz Josef and Alexander III collapsed all the same!

A profession had now been chosen. At the last minute the Muses helped. There were nine of them – I had read about them in a wonderful book on mythology. My choice had narrowed. I went through a sleepless night and in the morning when my temperature went up the doctor was called. Of course I knew it was not the measles! It was clearly not mumps! But I didn't say anything to anyone. And after passing a second night without sleep, I reread the next morning, for the last time, the long register I had composed the previous summer, which I always carried with me. Finally sure I had no talent whatever for drawing or tragic acting, I made my choice. I tore the register into little pieces, threw them in a gaily crackling stove and so began that *vita nuova* for which I longed.

Here was a child's crisis that meant much to me. Now I knew what I had to do, what I wanted to do. When the 'overflowing of the soul' began at night, I was sure I would have to yield to it. The beat of the metronome and the clicking of rhymes would crackle for entire days in my brain and crawl into my dreams. 'Sorrow' led to 'tomorrow', 'weep' led to 'deep', 'kiss' led to 'bliss'. Lightly stepping, trochees and iambs came to me as I sat in a corner of the hulk and looked out into the icy, bluish Petersburg night where the street began, the city, Russia, the whole universe started, where there was no longer any turning back for me.

Yes, at that time I had already understood that for me there was no retreat, that I myself was the centre of my universe, like man at the dawn of civilization. The years came and taught me to see the world as a sphere with a radius of infinity, a centre on each point of the sphere. I again and again found myself, in a sense, at its centre, like everybody else around me. For there is no limit to the number of points, while a sphere contains everything: the world of Euclid, of Einstein, and all that will replace them. On those evenings when snow fell, the windows froze, and I was overcome with expectations in that atmosphere, the initial music of genuine life, eagerness to live and know one's self, which forced me to shudder at its seriousness and grandeur as it resounded in me through those childish verses. I remember that feeling with my entire body. When I experienced them, and that is now most precious to me, the solemnity, responsibility, and uniqueness of those moments were clear to me. It seemed I heard, in jolts, my own sprouting into the future.

Together with this there was still a very childish, domestic, and scholastic existence in which life went on as with other children – pranks today, shirking one's lesson tomorrow, fibbing the day after, bragging, then breaking something and not telling, stealing sweets from the pantry and carefully covering one's traces, and all those underground feelings that are peculiar to children. A *children's underground*, special in its perverseness, was quite familiar to me. I lived like all children except, however, those exemplary ones I have never managed to meet.

The secondary school I entered was one of the progressive ones which began to appear in Petersburg after 1905. The decision to enrol was not taken without advice from Vasilievsky Island. The choice came from there and Mother yielded to it. Spartanism was her law, and like many women of the time she feared snobbishness. There could never be talk of sending me to a fashionable secondary school, one of those where my cousins studied. So I found myself at Maria S. Mikhelson's. Her father, the oldish, weak-sighted Semen, who walked around in a civil-service uniform and was the author of an arithmetic textbook, taught arithmetic. Her sister Vera, the wife of Professor K. (later liquidated for deviations), taught French, another sister German; her brother's wife sang. (I became friends with this brother in Paris. Before his death he was constantly troubled by the thought that he did not know *how Stalin's rule would end*. His last words were about this.) Another brother was a professor at the Technological Institute and our inspector. This was a family of pedagogues, and in the first years when the school had just opened and moved into two adjacent flats on Vladimirsky Avenue, the teaching had a certain family flavour. But within two or three years everything had changed. The teaching staff became excellent, and Miss Mikhelson's relatives soon disappeared from the horizon.

In the third winter (I was in the fifth grade) there was an event after which my mother took a long time to return to her senses. I proposed to a classmate that we exchange parents. I had noticed that after classes her mother came with a little brother to fetch her, and I rather liked her mother. I also liked the fact that her father wrote for newspapers. And I was especially glad she still had sisters at home. I explained to her that it would be very, very interesting to exchange parents for a time. She would live in our house and I in hers for, perhaps, a month, after which we would move to a third place. In this way, we would come to know more about life, I said. We would grow up quicker. On the other hand, if we sat at home for years with the same parents we would learn nothing and come to know nothing.

Struck dumb, she looked at me and suddenly began to whimper. I shrugged my shoulders, pulled her braid hard and walked away. This idea of 'coming to know more' had struck me during the summer when Dasha had said that a cook she knew had not had a protracted stay anywhere, had changed employers every year, and therefore was very 'experienced'. I decided to become 'experienced', too, as soon as possible.

The next day during the break I noticed that some girls looked at me with curiosity. Three girls of about fourteen from the ninth grade came and surrounded me.

'What are you, a foundling? Tell us . . .'

'No, I am not a foundling. Although . . . who knows?'

'What's the matter with you? Are you beaten at home?'

'No, I am not beaten.' There was, however, one experience – only one, it seems. I was about five and had torn a little watch from my German governess's bodice. With the watch had come a piece of the bodice ('with meat', as they say) and I had thrown it on the floor. My father, having seized me by the belt from behind, carried me into the bedroom, threw me face down on the bed, lifted my dress and with his own slipper . . . Yes, but why remember this? I shifted from one leg to the other.

'Then why exactly did you pick Tusia?'

I knew exactly why I had picked Tusia. I had always wanted to have sisters and brothers so they would distract others from me. It seemed to me that there would be more liberty, more solitude, less 'nestling' and sheltering under the domestic wing. Let them sit there, not me.

'Which means that you want to be among strange parents?'

I even licked my lips in pleasure at this idea.

'Well, wait, you'll catch it from la Marsemionna.'

The next day Miss Mikhelson, whose attention had been brought to my strange behaviour, summoned my mother. She decided to find out if I was being ill treated at home.

Mother returned before dinner in tears. I understood now what it meant 'to disgrace oneself', 'to shame one's own mother', 'to inflict shame on one's family'. This was a grim day in my life, and I even dreamt of dying. I pleaded to be allowed to stay for at least three days at home until everything was forgotten, but the following morning I was sent packing out of the house.

Girls from the upper classes came to look at me for a long time. They discussed my plan and some partly liked it. They even talked about me with each other. Some turned away from me. Lower-class girls were afraid of me. When the 'shame' had passed and there was only the memory of my impudence, I began to feel as if there were a light halo above me; and though this was a pleasant feeling I continued to be ashamed until the summer.

Once, during the Christmas holidays, I went with my father through snowdrifts and the roar of snow ploughs to a carpenter's workshop to buy a small French table of inlaid work, called 'marquetry', which for some reason we needed for the living room. We had a music cabinet there with incrustations, and I had learned only that morning that this was called 'marquetry'. I nursed the word and was overjoyed that my father was taking me with him. We set off; I was no longer led by the hand but went arm in arm with him. And we arrived at the carpenter's. He was an elderly, staid man, and Father discussed in much detail the problems of 'marquetry' and 'buhl' (about which I had not the slightest knowledge). As we went out into the yard I said to my father (I envied his relationship with the carpenter, whom he clearly found more interesting than me):

'You spoke to him about marquetry and he probably didn't even know what that meant.'

No doubt the mere pronunciation of this word gave me an inexplicable abstruse pleasure which I could not resist.

The carpenter, having taken off his hat, said in a quiet and polite voice, walking behind me:

'I knew what marquetry was, little lady, before you were born.'

It seemed to me that the earth shook under my feet and I, hoping to fall through it, slowed down my walking, but unfortunately this was an illusion. I looked at Father. He calmly looked to one side.

'That's exactly what you deserve,' he said coldly. 'Thanks, Trofimov.'

And we left. I didn't know where to look. I wanted to return and beg the carpenter's pardon.

'Well, enough foolishness,' said Father. 'You are not only uneducated and ill-mannered, but sentimental also.'

I returned home crushed. I am ashamed even now to think that this happened when my plays were already being put on at school (I don't remember at all what they were about, only that they were in verse), when the huge majority of the class (and I) lived through the Beilis affair, when Tolstoy's 'Answer to the Synod' was being read.

The morning when Beilis was acquitted (in 1913), I stood in the cloakroom and looked at my two friends Lola and Lida, covered with joyful tears, embracing one another. For a moment I felt cut off from them. They had a common joy and I was not included. Perplexed, I stood at the clothes rack, not moving, not wanting to go away and remain completely alone, yet afraid of staying, as if I were looking on from outside. Suddenly they stood back from each other, saw me and rushed at me, grabbed me, and all three of us embraced, our faces streaming with tears.

Lola Zeiliger was the daughter of a well-known Petersburg lawyer, a member of the K.-D. Party in whose house one found the pick of the Petersburg intelligentsia, political and artistic. In the huge flat on Nadezhdinskaya Street we usually played in Filipp Nikolaevich's study when he was not home. Six windows opened onto the street. The walls were covered with books, and bear hides lay on thick rugs. We made crypts out of them in which we sat for a long time and talked about our store of secrets, already quite a lot of them. Sometimes I stayed for dinner, and was shy in front of Lola's mother, a gay, active, energetic woman who was also connected with the K.-D. Party, Lola's older sister (later married to the journalist Azov), and her brother, Serezha, who shot himself in Berlin in the late 1920s. One found Miliukov of the Duma here, Khodotov of the Aleksandrinsky Theatre, violinists from the Mariinsky orchestra, eminent lawyers, actresses, and writers. But, of course, I never saw them. I only imagined with a reverent quiver that they came and walked through the rooms. I imagined how it all looked when the magnificent chandelier was lit up and the piano thundered, when a crowd of guests filled the living room, the dining room, the study, and all the other rooms where Mr Zeiliger's aides now scurried about. Lola was curly-haired, small, thin, and understood nothing about poetry nor why I wrote it, yet something united us, a curiosity about the world, an interest in one another. She was in the class above me. I very quickly lost track of her. She may still be alive now. The last I knew of her was that she lived in Kazan where she had been exiled during the Terror. Cordelia or Antigone, she gave all her life to her father after 1917. In school, however, she was not at all like the heroine of a tragedy.

There is something overly touching and artificially sweet in adults' recollections about their school classes, yet when I think of my classmates of the time I see before me not naïve mama's daughters in exquisite plissé dresses with ribbons in their hair, but completely mature beings with definite tastes, political convictions, who could judge, argue, reason, choose books to read and communicate with fellow humans like themselves. Here, the era played its role. Every year changed Russia and every year aged us. The most immature, it seems to me now, was myself, with my 'underground' feelings, my abstruse joys, my partial knowledge of the facts of life. (I had been initiated into the latter by a certain Musia R. who had stayed in each class for two years and was then five years older than the majority of us.) My sole advantage over them all was that I wrote verse, but even this quickly paled when Natasha Shklovskaya appeared in the eighth grade. She also wrote verse, and what verse! But I will speak about this later. At eleven we all more or less knew what we wanted and we all wanted something special. From the age of twelve we read forbidden literature and discussed the advantages of the Social Democrats vis-à-vis the Social Revolutionaries. We were all – there were five or six of us –

linked together, and in the evenings we finished saying on the telephone what had been left unsaid in the afternoons, asking the telephone operator to join us together in threes, which was possible then. On Sundays we would visit each other, look up foreign words together, which we did not understand, in *Granat's Encyclo-paedia*. We had opinions about everything, sometimes general and noisy, sometimes individual and secret.

Musia and I stayed after the lessons, and in the empty classroom, in half darkness, near the cold window, not only would she explain everything to me but she gave me Kuprin's *The Pit* to read to prevent me making unfounded claims. This book had a stunning impression on me. No other book has had such an effect on me. I told Aleksandr Kuprin this when once, as a guest at Prince V. V. Baryatinsky's in Paris in 1929, I was left alone with him in the living room after all the others had gone into the dining room. Kuprin was like an old Tatar in those years, in some ways reminiscent of my grandfather of Tver. With his head swaying and his hands drooping, he seemed decrepit and sleepy. He heard me out, slowly picked a cherry from a vase and asked me to take it in my mouth by the stem. The cherry hung on my chin. He moved over towards me and carefully took the cherry in his mouth, hardly touching me. When he had spat out the pit, he said:

'This is my last phase.'

I was terribly sorry for him but said nothing. He kissed my hand, shedding a tear as if the tear in his mournful eye had long awaited the moment when it could fall on my hand. We went into the dining room.

After reading *The Pit* I wanted to be blank for several weeks. I said to myself that if 'demand' gave birth to 'supply', then it was impossible to remain 'pure' and endure the prostitution of London, Hamburg, Paris, and Nevsky Avenue as inescapable evils, that something had to happen with all of us, with me, all my classmates, the girls in the whole world who were then growing up in millions of families, so that the horrors of *The Pit* could be abolished. It was not enough to ban it, not enough to tear it up, it was necessary to change something essential within our very selves. Now, after fifty years, this has happened partially in the world of 'Western' people (by 'Western' I mean those who live in modern cities conditioned by modern techniques). I did not concretely imagine this vaguely wished-for change then. I did not guess I would belong to that generation for whom the old state of things would end, to the time when women would be prevented from dividing into respectable and unrespectable, an era in which the burden carried by those considered unrespectable (so easing life for those considered respectable) would be the concern of everybody and would lose the meaning of *burden*. Modern literature, liberal legislation, new psychology, and even science helped this. The inward mutiny of modern man accomplished a great deal, economics the rest.

My first feeling of the great chain of being belongs to this time. Many years later I would come to talk about this feeling with Mark Aldanov. The idea always excited him and he returned to it in conversations. It was expressed in concrete terms by his having known Empress Eugénie in his youth in Paris, when she was already an old woman. She in turn had seen public figures of the French Revolution in her youth. When I was young I knew the daughter-in-law of the Decembrist Ivashev, and was friends with a Russified Englishman, a former uhlan of the Imperial Guard who had personally seen Nicholas I more than once. He was the son of an Englishman, a subject of George III who had come to Russia and got stuck there. Despite his having been brought to Russia at the age of three, he seemed a total foreigner to me. He could say little about England, was more interested in the harvest and family affairs (he was the neighbouring landowner of the Karaulovs), and astonished me by hanging in his study, next to a rifle and a pair of pistols and in full view of everyone, a douche for his daily enema, with a long hose and a clyster point.

Nevertheless I managed to squeeze out of him some of the names of English cities and towns; this was after a long description of a parade of the regiments who returned in 1856 from Bendery 'in the presence of the august personalities'. With him, geography came into its own for me, listening to a host of names with complex and powerful sound: the Himalayas and the Andes, Ispahan, Lisbon, and Peruvian cities overgrown with lianas. The map of the stellar universe one saw for the first time also had to be borne in mind constantly, so one could never forget – such as the fact, of course, that we not only hang, swim, and spin round but we rush headlong into the constellation of Hercules.

The feeling of 'rushing headlong' was constant: to the constellation of Hercules, to revolution, from school to home, to read, think, write poetry, and in all haste away from the Liebestraums to real awaiting storms. The more the domestic 'wing' spread out above me, the more I wanted to get further from it; the warmer and kinder all were around me, the stronger the protest grew in me against the protecting hand on my shoulder, against the attentive look and question: Are you all right? – against rules and regulations that regimented my outward life. Oh, how intolerable I was! What a cruel, reckless, wilful being, greedy for life! Why was I loved? I far from always loved myself.

Moments of ecstasy and 'overflowing of the soul' always occurred in solitude. Life bared its essence gradually to me: at first a picture, then its meaning – a landscape, as though on the run, and then its significance. It taught me to read books and see behind the entertaining story; to find a net of questions and answers behind a play, and the fabric of problems behind people's conversations. Nothing hung in mid-air without contact with what surrounded it, all was bound by threads, every part with the whole – or to use a simile, everything was like a great cobweb of the firmament, and I stood looking it over for hours, like fireworks which people ordinarily set up and then flee from.

My first contact with animals brought cruel disenchantment with the Greek Orthodox religion (in which I was christened at birth): I discovered that it never said anything about them. True, there were lions and tigers that became friends with saints, but in the first place the initiative in the friendship was the animals', and in the second all the warmth in communication came from them. A horse's muzzle, a dog's ears, a cat's chest and belly – though this list recalls 'Diana's bosom, Flora's cheeks' (Pushkin) – remained some of the sweetest impressions I had of our world. I melt with the camel's proud and sad glance, I feel a mute kinship to the bear and zebra. A hungry dog, an abandoned cat – nothing is more grievous to me than such creatures.

Once in a year of starvation I had to kill a chicken. (I like meat, rare steak; I don't understand vegetarianism, don't see any inconsistency in this: my aim is not to tie loose ends together, but to untie knots.) A huge sandy-coloured sheep dog of indescribable beauty, with eyes circled in black, brought to me in his teeth a big, red, brown-spotted chicken, half dead of fear. It was a Sunday, in occupied France in October of 1941, and Olga (later to die in Auschwitz) had said there was nothing at all to feed to the four guests who were to arrive from Paris; so she was going to the forest to look for mushrooms, to make a mushroom pie. A farmer's wife who had the evening before sold all her butter and a barrel of salted pork to German soldiers (who had paid in radiant French money printed in Frankfurt in infinite quantity) refused to sell me anything because she felt that business with Germans was a surer thing than with Russians – the Germans were then near Moscow. I stayed in the garden, beneath the pear trees planted by us two years before (and which, I have heard, after twenty years now yield a great harvest of *beurré Alexandre*), and I looked with melancholy around me, wondering how I would feed my hungry Paris friends, who would come thirty kilometres by bike. At that moment Rex appeared with the chicken. He brought it to me from a neighbouring meadow and placed it at my feet. I grabbed it by the legs, ran for the axe, swinging the bird's head downwards on the run and, on the stump where we chopped wood for the small stove, I axed the chicken through the neck. It fluttered in my hand twice and all was over. Rex stood and looked on, grave and attentive. He was proud of himself and he was right. And though for the first time in my life I had killed a living being, I was also right. He had committed a crime for my sake. I had committed a crime for the sake of Olga and our friends. He loved me, as I him, and from that day on it was as if he began to love me still more.

The Church, however, said nothing about beasts; it forgot about them. Generally speaking, the 'good news' brought to the world occasioned much blood-spilling that did not correspond to its importance (everything meaningful, essential, lofty had been said earlier). On the other hand, little has changed in twenty centuries: Christianity did not affect the social side of life. If man in our time is moving towards pity and forgiveness and refusal of ostentation, to reach a levelling in kindness, and considers lies, revenge, flattery, scorn, and envy as unworthy of him, it is because of democracy – that is, purchasing power, freedom of the press, universal suffrage, the absence of military parades and much else. All this perhaps has, for some people, lost the *aroma of novelty* and acquired a *tinge of pragmatism*, while for others it does not correspond to the principles of dialectical materialism; but for me it was and always will be precious, even without *aroma* and the support of Engels.

Life revealed its three-dimensional space to me, letting me reflect on the fourth dimension; it placed me in a landscape that had neither limit nor end. It half revealed Europe. I was twelve and just managed to grab what was in the air, the foretaste of all that many years later became my own. Of Berlin (which eight years later I discovered in all its rigid and hard essence), of Paris (which later became the capital of my life), of London (foreign even now), there remain scraps of those days and nights – hotels (the first in my life), the tempi of street life (unlike Russian ones), the old and luxurious Europe which made it a special kind of *anti-Russian* world. In these travels there were hours that seemed to anticipate the future, and there is something strangely similar in my solitary walks around Geneva in 1914 and my walks around Zurich more than twenty years later – along one lake and another, but in that same unchanging Switzerland where torpor possesses the people and one lives by the slogan 'I don't give a hang about the world around me.'

. . . Days rush by, and – the train takes us to the nocturnal Alps, to a black tunnel where wheels grumble, and the wind whistles at the train it meets. In the 1920s, returning to Paris to begin a new period of my life, I looked for but did not find that hotel where, in August 1914, we stopped (on the return trip to Russia from Vichy). On the way there, all was still as one supposed it to be; we were met at the Grand Hotel, where for some reason the lights in the rooms were on during the day, and we toured the stores; according to Mother's plan, museums and cathedrals should be seen on the trip back, after a month of Vichy life. But the trip back was wrecked by the war. The Germans approached Amiens, Belgium was occupied, Paris suddenly died, and when we arrived the taxi driver took us through empty streets in the ominous silence of a city that was dead, from the Etoile to Notre Dame, along the quays, past the Palais des Invalides. 'Benefit as much as you can! You don't know if you will come here again – look, admire, this is Paris . . .' I got there, I lived there. I spent twenty-five years there. A quarter of a century of exile.

I never again found the hotel where we stopped on the way home. Money was tight; one couldn't even think of the Grand Hotel. We stayed near the church of Saint-Roch, between the Rue de Rivoli and Marché Saint-Honoré; we were there three days in all and heard: '*Tous à Berlin!*' and '*On les aura!*' All this was new to me.

Then there was the train, and the transfer in Amiens surrounded by Germans, echelons of wounded, the rolling of cannon, and the arrival in the bursting port of Boulogne, where we boarded a ship and sailed to England. *That* time they passed through Amiens. *Before that* they had gone through Sedan. *Later* they went through Compiègne. The ninety-year-old farm woman said:

'I remember it like today, in 1870 they came along that road that leads to the Motté barn behind your beehives, and now, see, they made it the other way round past our haystacks and the Vallé buckwheat. And always such fine young men: still a gallant people, each and every one!'

There was no intonation. What could there be at ninety! She merely pointed with a crutch to the south, the north, and her single tooth moved in her mouth, as if it were ready to fall. But it held fast for another three years or so.

Vichy nights – writing verse, tennis with Russian girls, friend-ship with a French boy who recited Verlaine and his own verse by heart to me – all was behind me and already seemed far-off in England, about which I knew the little that the uhlan of Nicholas I had told me in his time, and in any case less than about Africa (Pushkin and Gumilev) or about America. For a long time I had considered Lincoln a Negro; it seemed to me that his sad, dark face looked somehow like the face of our native Moors, and I liked to think that he freed *his very own people*. Incidentally, at about eight I was certain (where the idea came from I do not know) that in America only Negroes and Indians lived and that there were no whites at all. How much absurdity feeds man's early imagination! But I now knew that even England was at war. In spite of this we stayed a week in London. I was taken to the National Gallery. This was when half the rooms were closed to the public because of the fury of the suffragettes who were busy pricking out the eyes from the Rembrandts and Raphaels.

I looked on but at that time was completely blind and deaf to art! Only at about twenty did 'aesthetic feeling', as it is called, awake in me, along with an understanding and love of art, and need for it. Yet at that time I already knew what distinguished Martov from Sukhanov and Spiridonova from Bliumkin!

'Soviet product!' a lady said to me in 1920, taking me by the chin and piercing me with her eyes.

'What do you want, Maria Ivanovna, we are eating barley kasha, we are dancing to the gramophone, and we are wearing rags.'

'Why do you call me Maria Ivanovna when I am Ariadna Leonidovna? . . .'

So, hurrying through London's National Gallery I saw nothing, like a savage brought from the jungle, and at my first concerts at the Petersburg Conservatory that winter, I could hardly sit through to the end because of boredom. I know I might astonish if I say that both music and painting are now *as close to me as poetry*, and I do not conceive of living without 'viewing' and 'listening', as I do not without reading.

As for *actual doing* in music, an honest friend once told me:

'I like to hear you from a distance. Best of all – to go off into the woods when you play the piano: there I can hardly hear at all.'

And about one of my water colours, which I had brought home from drawing class, a friend of our family asked:

'What are those, home-made biscuits?'

'That's a sow and her little ones.'

Meanwhile I was sensitive to poetry, lived in it, wrote it myself, learned about it imperceptibly, fed daily on old and new, mine and others'. The French boy in Vichy told me that you could write verse only in French, and though I knew why he was wrong, I could not explain to him. We argued for a long time: he wanted both of us to write a poem on the same theme, he in French, I in Russian, and then we would be judged as in a tournament. We decided to write verse with the title 'Give Me a Comet', probably by association with Halley's Comet of 1910. This was the idea: I do not fear dark rooms, robbers or ghosts; give me a comet in the sky, terrible and long, foretelling catastrophes, rushing about the world like a threat. Give me a comet so that finally I know what fear is. But since I had never written on an assigned theme before, I could not write verse on the comet. He did and so the argument was decided in his favour. Now, in Paris, there is a street with his name. I have often walked down this street and thought: They gave him a street. They gave me a comet that foretold catastrophes, that brought catas-trophes. And I found out what fear is.

The shelling of the train near Amiens was an omen of future Russian and European historical crumblings, and in its wake, a week later, there was that strange unforgettable night on the North

Sea, when we sailed from Edinburgh to Bergen and I walked the deck in a life belt: the sea was mined and on captain's orders we all came up in life belts, except my father, whom a belt could not have rescued. In complete darkness, to the even splash of a calm wave, I settled at the bow on the deck; very soon there were dark silhouettes around me with inflated life belts on their backs, and they also lay down, filling the whole space starboard to port. We went from darkness to darkness, all was permeated with the thought of danger, of a possible mine explosion, but I was drowsy: every now and then I closed my eyes and my consciousness was interrupted. Suddenly I awoke, because someone lay across my feet. There were two of them, a man and a woman, and they spoke Russian. All around, too, I heard soft Russian speech. In magical gloom these two embraced and kissed each other, laughed quietly, and someone on my left also embraced and kissed; another near by drank cognac and smoked. 'And who is this?' someone asked, obviously about me. 'A strange little girl. Give her some chocolates.' In a quarter of an hour I was already reading them verse.

I became witness to an uninhibited young lovers' romp. Some heads were resting on my knees, other leaned on my shoulder. I sat motionless, leaning against the railing like a witness or observer, without any idea that I might participate in such a nocturnal bacchanal. A hand in the darkness touched my face and my long braids (they were smooth and cold and in those days came to my knees), someone came close to me: 'Oh! It's not you! It's you!' was murmured in the darkness. The boat moved on and on, the sea rumbled, and I recited Anna Akhmatova, Briusov, Blok.

When I stopped, wondering if they had not fallen asleep in each others' embraces, they requested more and more. But they were not sleeping, they were celebrating their youth, whispering tender words to each other, covering themselves in twos (some in a blanket, others in a coat); occasionally a long moan would resound and a vibration seemed to spill into the air. I realized that I was invited in a strange way to an unusual celebration, like a minstrel at the court of a king, and felt myself bursting with a happiness that was not my own. The following morning, at breakfast, I did not recognize them, did not even try to recognize them. I already understood that there is joy in the fact that all passes, and there is gladness in not forcing it, but letting it pass.

We look at the gay flowery poster that presents to us and everyone the cheerful family life in nature's lap. Close-up: blades of grass and lovely daisies; foreground, children playing; a father and mother preparing breakfast on a background of lawn; four cows at pasture, and forests and mountains. A summer day. A picnic. We look again at the poster and see a huge ladybird crawling over the grass, the size of a house. Behind it, children in a mist, Papa and Mama, two dots; cows and mountains are not visible at all. We look a third time and see an artist sitting and drawing this poster: he looks like a kind old man (so the children see him), like a stranger without any security for his old age (so the parents see him), like a dash (so the cows see him). Finally, for the last time, we look and see some triangles and octagons, sparks and circles ('How do you hang this? Which is the top? Where is the bottom?') – the ladybird, all eyes, looks at God's world.

The train came into the Finland Station. Here is Russia, my homeland, the return home, war. The first days of September 1914, thick dust, a crowd of recruits. The sadness, first felt by me in the soldiers' chorus: 'They rose early in the morning – sounded the alarm.' The alarm is here, above this troop train, droning with anxiety, half the sky in flames, a peal above the Neva – 'Miss, give us a foreign charm for luck!' – I am giving him a small handbag mirror. It is strange that I have never valued my things, I can give them away, lose them, I have no 'sacred' things as Russians did in the old days (spoon, comb). A clean towel and a clean pillowcase – this is all I need. The rest is unimportant. I give him the little mirror. His overcoat is rolled up and strapped over one shoulder.

A brass band bursts out unexpectedly, drowning the chorus. On the Liteiny Bridge lanterns burn. Why do they burn? Why does the cab driver sit sideways? Why does a woman cry? Why does a child ask: 'Mister, give me a kopeck?' Why? Why does the policeman have such a fat stomach and the priest a still fatter one? Why does this boy, the son of our doorman, patter to my father: 'They promised, Nikolai Ivanovich, but they didn't give it to me. It didn't work out.' (This about a scholarship to a trade school.) Why everywhere: they didn't give it, it didn't turn out, it fell through, it fizzled out. Why? Why is it cold in September? Dark in

October? Why does Dasha have an embarrassed look and a black eye? 'Got drunk yesterday before leaving and smashed me with his fist. They dispatched them to Galicia.' What does all this mean? Why all this?

Wherever I look – at the ladybird the size of a house, children playing in the meadow, the papa and mama spreading out the white tablecloth or at those cows saying 'moo', I see only one thing: sadness, poverty, 'didn't work out', war, soldiers' boots, policemen's boots, generals' boots, cloudy sky over all this, the autumn sky of wartime Petersburg.

In a few days I return to school. The joy of meetings, a couple of new girls. Getting acquainted. 'And who is that? She speaks to no one.' – 'That's Shklovskaya, she writes verse.' I feel I am dying of curiosity mingled with desire to begin a friendship, and fear that my literary superiority has come to an end. She sits down next to me, to share the same desk. She, like me, is thirteen but her face is that of an adult: the serious look of grey eyes, the narrow nose, the slightly pursed lips, and the figure of a woman. Unintentionally I am flustered. We get on familiar terms, however. She says she has a cousin, a literary critic. I have never heard of him (I am embarrassed). I introduce her to Nadia Otsup, who has a poet brother; then I introduce her to Lucia M. (later shot), who has a publisher father. And also to Sonia R. (did away with herself in 1931), whose brother is a budding movie actor. We are all the cream of the class. She now is also the cream of the class. I allude to this, she understands me, but is silent.

In the Russian class she is called to the board. Is it true she writes verse? It is true. She is in no way embarrassed, she is calm as stone. Perhaps she will recite some to the class? Why, certainly she can! In her face no agitation at all. I worry for her. She looks at the ceiling and then through the window. Her brows, round and high, rise still higher. Assuredly, very distinctly, she speaks:

> Ah, if only I could fly
> From the earth into the sky
> And forget those chains of lead
> That my liberty impede.
> Live in freedom, sorrowless,
> Sing my song in happiness.

I inhale with difficulty. This is so beautiful I feel that all in me melts from rapture. Natasha continues to read:

> But my efforts are in vain,
> Swamps and dust and fog remain,
> I am not allowed to rise,
> I am forced to close my eyes,
> Chains are heavy, I must wait,
> But my time is late.

My heart beats wildly. I love her. I love her braid, the birthmark on her nose, her too white, adult hands, her little ring, her collar of lace. I love her face reminiscent of Cranach's madonna, and most of all I love her verse.

'Listen, Shklovskaya,' I say to her casually during a break, 'you have an ay-ay somewhere . . .'

'Yes? Where?'

'"My eyes . . ."'

'Ah! Good. I must revise it. I wrote it only yesterday. I didn't have time to check that it was all right.'

I decide to reveal to her my most secret secret, about which I have said nothing to anyone. It is my secret and I am fearful, ashamed of admitting to it, and until now I have revealed it to no one. I tell her that I do not like *Eugene Onegin*. Why should one like it? At first Tatiana falls in love, without saying two words to the man, simply because of a look (foppish, boring, sated, empty). Then she marries a fat general simply because her mother asks her to, a mother who till a ripe old age is full of Grandisonianisms. Then Tatiana tells Onegin that she doesn't love him and chases him away – what old-fashioned and irresponsible escapades . . . Natasha stands in front of me with a motionless expression: only her roundish brows are slightly raised and it's as if her lips were narrowed. She says: 'Is this really important? Does it make any difference? What's important is that "His beaver collar/Becomes silvery with frosty dust", what's important is how the enjambments run on from line to line, from stanza to stanza. And the language! The irony! And Pushkin himself!'

I run home to be alone and think all this over. I sense that new perspectives are opening for me. That literature is turning a completely new side to me, a new level of meanings and ideas.

In the next four years that fate let her live until her arrest, we became friends. We exchanged rings, we gave each other our baptismal crosses. She was arrested for her membership in the S.-R. left group after the murder of the German ambassador Mirbach in Moscow in 1918. In prison she exchanged my cross of pure gold for a pack of cigarettes. I don't remember when her cross, which I never wore, was stolen, or by whom.

When we became friends, everything receded from me. She replaced everyone, all friendships. Together we discovered Wilde and Maeterlinck, Hamsun and Ibsen, Baudelaire and Nietzsche, Annensky, Tiutchev. We shared all that was ours in the present, as well as our entire past – in essence so poor, for we had not been together in it. Together we loved Ibsen's *Brand* and Wilde's *Dorian Gray* and Akhmatova's verse and Blok's *Snow Mask*, and in the summer we wrote long letters to each other daily, we exchanged verse, books. I was more spontaneous and more alive than she, but she was brighter, she knew everything (so it seemed to me then), I understood everything, she answered all questions. In this friendship there was no 'older' and 'younger', no 'teacher' and 'pupil' – there was equality, devotion to one another, an insatiable curiosity in each other. And beneath all was poetry, hers and mine.

In the second year of our relationship, changes occurred in her family that fundamentally altered her life. Till then she had lived with her mother and father in a small stuffy flat crammed with furniture in a low-middle-class neighbourhood: in the entrance you couldn't get around the trunks and wardrobes. The old servant shuffled through the rooms in soft slippers, her toes, with long dirty nails, protruding through the holes. The flat smelled of cabbage, fish, onion – yellow, dim little lamps burned from the ceiling – and it was cold, crowded, restless. Her father slept in the study on a leather couch (a piece of bast stuck out of it), her mother somewhere on the other side of the kitchen, at the end of the dark corridor. She was a woman of about forty, heavily made up, with gypsy ear-rings hanging from her ears and curls burned by curling tongs on her forehead. I felt no sympathy towards her and only hid this with difficulty. Her father was a young-looking, ruddy, cheerful man with a light brown beard and grey wide-open eyes; he was always running somewhere, always hurrying, always doing things at speed. Then this life cracked and fell apart: Mr Shklovsky, suddenly, taking Natasha with him, moved into a beautiful flat on Staronevsky Avenue, furnished it, hired a cook and a maid and began waiting for a divorce, to marry another. Something happened to him in his career of mechanical engineer that completely changed his financial status and along with it his family affairs. Natasha lived quite painfully through this whole crisis. Her mother quickly married a man who was somehow like herself – there was something in him unpleasant, not straightforward, and not wholly clean. Mr Shklovsky took a wife who was beautiful, calm, affectionate, who dressed with taste and knew how to get along with everybody. She and Natasha had a good relationship. In all she was ten years older than we. It seems that all were happy with this new turn of affairs. And so was I.

I return to the first year of the war, which is called the 'First', 'One' 'World' and 'Great'. Here I must speak of someone who together with Natasha Shklovskaya had a tremendous influence on me in those years.

Tatiana Adamovich, to whom Gumilev dedicated his 'amorous' book, *The Quiver*, came to our school as a class monitor and a teacher of French. After the first lesson, as soon as the door closed behind her, I jumped up from my seat and cried out: 'There's a Fury!' – not fully understanding what 'Fury' meant, but this word, like 'marquetry' once, pleased me by its sound and I had the need to shout it out. She heard it from the corridor. Later, one day, she asked me: 'Why exactly did I then seem to you a Fury?' She was thinnish, dark-haired with large pale grey eyes, fine elegant hands and an unusual intonation in her speech, where *r* and *l* shaded into one another, and all *i* sounds were particularly sharp. She was from a special world: acquainted with Akhmatova and attending meetings of the Hyperboreus; in conversations with her I drank in every word. After class Natasha and I stayed in the teachers' study, that very room where once Musia R. initiated me into the facts of life near a window covered with snow. Tatiana spoke with us about verse, acmeism, French poetry, Koussevitzky's concerts, about artists from The World of Art, Meyerhold, Mandelstam, Tsarskoe Selo and Volkonsky and his ballet school. Like poor Lazarus I gathered crumbs from the table where all these divinities feasted. In 1936 she came to Paris (after the Russian Revolution she ran a ballet school in Warsaw). I saw her. 'Is that you?' she said, confused whether or not to be formal, and I remembered the lines of Gumilev about her:

> Dear one with a summer smile
> With fine, weak hands,
> And with dark hair perfumed
> Like the honey of two millennia.

Corridors, classrooms, halls – all was immersed in darkness. A lamp on the table was lit. Natasha and I sat on a leather couch, Tatiana walked from corner to corner, hands behind her back (she had this masculine habit), and spoke to us; we rhythmically turned our heads after her, to the right and left. Each word lodged in my memory like a playing card in a pack, and at night in bed, my head tucked under the blanket, I repeated her words as if laying out before me my whole motley pack. I marked the cards with my personal signs (there were not four suits, but an infinite number), and then again concealed them in my memory, as Gogol's Ikharev hid his in a suitcase. 'All has been lost – and nothing has been lost!' I want to cry out to her now, if she is still alive. 'All has perished, and nothing has perished!'

But, of course, the principal theme of her talks was Akhmatova. Of the two of us I, because of immaturity, imitated her a great deal at the time, and for me she was a special being. We read our own verse to Tatiana, and she spoke about what poetry was, of modern poetry, and the potentials of new Russian prosody beloved by the symbolists and the acmeists. Sometimes she took our verse and returned it to us in a week, saying she had read it to Akhmatova. She praised us quite rarely, but admitted that one of my poems was good. It ended:

> Today my long-awaited
> Thirteenth spring arrived.

'I will give it to my brother to read and he will say it is his. Only he will change "thirteenth" to "sixteenth".' She laughed. Her brother, later the critic Georgy Adamovich, was then probably about twenty.

Tatiana's closest friend was the first wife of the acmeist poet Georgy Ivanov, Gabrielle, an airy, charming being, French by birth. This entire group of people, thanks to my constant thoughts about them, started in time to transform themselves in my imagination into a kind of magical Olympus: at first they appeared out of the fog, out of nothingness, then they acquired a shape, and then they again began to lose the clarity of features when I gave them fantastic haloes that blinded my eyes. I lived in an astonishing, enticing world. An E in physics and an F in German sobered me for a moment, but again very quickly I sweetly and secretly plunged into another dimension, where there was neither physics nor German, but infinite bliss from poem to poem.

Yet what exactly did I like then in poetry? The possibility of doing what demi-gods were doing? Or of settling in a realm of abstract beauty? Of giving vent to Liebestraums inwardly muffled? Or did I strive to realize myself in the world? Apply myself to the sole art I thought I understood in those days? And how to grasp the beautiful? Was it feeling without thought? Primitive, animalistic – or passive, like a vegetable? I think all this was present; but especially the search for moments of anxiety, awe, and triumph.

Of the three realms – politics, ethics, and aesthetics – the first was the air of those years, the second the object of my protest, but the third remained alien. I felt that in the end it had to become bound up with my life, and that 'aesthetic truth' sooner or later would be revealed to me. I knew it would not slip away from me, that I would find it, but meanwhile I could only humbly meditate on the difference between our pots and pans in which kasha was being served and that vase in which a painted woman, with fine hands and a knot of dark hair, kept corn or olive oil two thousand years ago. That basic and eternal feeling for measure and beauty – those who have not ached because of it in youth will remain deaf to it for life!

It doesn't reveal itself in discursive speech. It is hidden somewhere in a deep hiding-place in man: this place has nothing to do with noisy horrors and weird omens, with all that is petty and ridiculous which surrounds man outside like a night's drunken bout, thirty leagues from all that is dear. It has nothing to do with the predicament of the nocturnal world all around. Eternity can reveal itself at a bus stop; putting out a cigarette butt we suddenly understand the particularity of each separate human being; in front of a post office window the brittleness of the whole world 'system' might flash at us; in a consulate reception room we find our own inescapable end bound up with a specific page of the calendar. There is that moment when an average man eats his average dinner, buys his average aspirin at the chemist – but in the following fraction of a second all that is average in him crumbles; his own particularity, the senselessness and wisdom of it all appears through his poor bald patch, in his glasses which slide down his sweaty nose – and we see a horizon without end.

I wandered all around the Karaulov house that summer; this was my farewell to it, and to the gardens where an alley of lime trees led out to the fields. Everything augured change, especially in the evenings when the whole village came to promenade through the orchards of this 'nest of noblemen'. Was this a premonition that in about two or three years these verandas and porches would gleefully burst into flames, and superintendents would circle convulsively, hung from apple trees? I do not know. But as soon as evening fell in the flower beds, near the ponds, alongside hammocks, in the arbor, shadows would flash by, a balalaika would be strummed, chords would be stretched out of the accordion. It seemed strange – and even now seems not altogether probable – that there was, so to speak, a 'cramping' of the landowners several years before the Revolution. Yet at the same time there was something natural in this. Indeed, the peasants seemed to feel, what was there to wait for? Our best years, mind you, will pass while one sits waiting for changes in his izba and one can be sent away to bloody Galicia. Why not rock in hammocks in which no one has rocked for a long time anyway? Why not breathe of the lordly gillyflower: it will not harm them!

I wandered in the cemetery where Oblomov lay, where it seemed to me my consciousness had first emerged. Apple-tree branches, which once I was unable to reach, now touched the ground. The dry well which we yelled down so we could hear the echo was still the same, with a familiar half-rotted wood smell. Having looked into it once I remembered how I dreamt I would be thrown in. 'I won't get out,' I said to myself calmly, 'I will remain there to die of thirst.' But then, let's say on the third day, I suddenly notice that a spring has burst through at my very feet. It runs along, babbling and gleaming, and I bend down to drink. So I begin to live – at the bottom of the well, with a source that feeds me and which no one knows of in the world. What's most important is to find the source. In the well? In myself? Why? To live! Why live? Is this necessary? Yes, but only if the source is found. What source? I meant to say the spring. I am a spring too, a spring needs a spring to spring up. A spring is looking for a spring! What's most important is to find it. Because the well without fail will exist.

At that moment I suddenly understood my future, as if illumined by lightning: I saw that the well would be, that it already was. And that if I did not find the secret source in it, I would perish.

(And if snakes crawl out, I would find the pipe to charm them.)

I returned home late. In the dark garden young voices were yelling: 'Vanka come! Mashka's waiting!' Waiting among the peasants there were the priest's daughters and others I had known since childhood.

I went to my room. The window opened onto the garden and a moon was rising over the old lime trees. For the first time I felt that a symbol rose, above me and my life, illuminated life and its meaning for me. Up to then all signs – even the comet I had asked for – were only signs, like the *a, b, c* in geometry that designate the angles or sides of a triangle. But now a symbol appeared full of meaning, there was the well and the source in it, about which I alone knew. And snakes. And a pipe. As if I had tasted of the tree of knowledge, the effect was no longer a pointless overflowing of the soul but great sadness.

(You could charm all the snakes with the pipe. But one old snake was stupid and deaf; it didn't hear the melody.)

This window always reminded me of that window in Otradnoe where Natasha and Sonya, who 'did not concern me', whispered at night, while Prince Bolkonsky listened to them from downstairs. So my mother and the Decembrist's granddaughter who sometimes visited us surrendered themselves to dreams, while downstairs there was already someone who stirred their imagination. And Oblomov's daughters, Olga and Alina, entrusted each other with their secrets about passing hussars, their mother about uhlans of Nicholas I's time. But where was I in all of this? What was mine? I felt myself foreign to them all, unlike them, terribly far from their dreams, their whispers and hopes. I lit a candle, took *War and Peace* and wanted to find that passage about Natasha and Sonya but instead I found the chapter where Natasha dances at her uncle's after the hunt and the uncle's mistress (a serf) looks lovingly at her. This again seemed to me a kind of camouflage: the mistress should have hated Natasha, should have been mean to her; the children and grandchildren of this mistress were now laughing in the park, trampling the flowers – this was truth I understood, which I could accept in its entirety. They awaited the moment when they would tear the brocade from the walls of the drawing room and make blankets out of it for their children. They were right, and all that Tolstoy wrote was illusion; I couldn't believe in it, life rose between me and it with my own metaphor.

I looked at the full moon that had risen over the quiet gardens, my eyes filled up with tears, and something shook within me; I felt death (Grandfather had had a stroke the evening before) in the house, a death that was not terrible, but somehow natural and timely. I felt a strange weakness and then through tears saw a second full moon: it convulsively tried to overtake the first and shuddered in the sky as something shuddered in me, perhaps a sob. Then it vanished. I felt I continued to sink into that frightful, narrow, lonely space into which I had looked, leaning over the wooden parapet. But Father, standing at my shoulder, said:

'You will see: very soon elephants will come after their ivory and tortoises after your comb.'

I smiled.

'They will come to take what by all rights belongs to them and which we took from them.'

'I didn't take anything, you didn't take either.'

'I don't know, I don't know, this is a complicated problem. But they will come.'

I knew he was right, and though he spoke to me then as with a child I did not protest.

Perhaps I should have told him I was now living in a deep well. Or asked him how and when his source had burst. But I did not ask. I feared he had no source or that his source would never help me.

(And how would I manage with that deaf, stupid old snake who could not hear my pipe?)

Night passed, and the moon like an hour hand moved along, rising and falling on the celestial dial strewn with stars that were more numerous the more I looked at them: they were stones, fire, lava, explosions, heat, steam, whirling, and silence.

Blok's third volume of verse came out in that first war year. The musical thunder he aroused in us is difficult to communicate today in a few words. He answered that side of us that denied Liebes-traums and sought beauty mingled with despair. Now, when I look back, I see that Pushkin was the Russian Renaissance, Blok Russian romanticism, Bely Russian cubism. All fell into place in historical perspective. And my generation grew alongside them: passing from the Pushkin of its childhood to the Blok of its adolescence and growing up into Bely. I now schematically indicate this line which, of course, I did not see at the time, the more so because in those years it was entangled and confused with other, intricate patterns, interrupting and muffling it.

Early in the spring of 1915, in the Army and Fleet Hall on Liteiny Avenue, a gathering called 'The Poets to the Warriors' took place. This was one of those many charity evenings which the intelligent-sia liked to attend. I don't know why it was decided to take me to it. It was a week night, and my homework, as always, probably had not been done. I studied in bursts and somehow managed to 'get by', for I was not squeamish about copying or being prompted, especially in algebra and physics, after too much time had been devoted to the reading and writing of verse till late at night. That evening after dinner my mother announced to me that we were going to 'listen to some poets'. We went on foot from Zhukovsky Street, where we were living,* up Liteiny. I was worried, for it seemed we would arrive too late, that there would be no seats left, and something would happen that would ruin everything. The brightly lit hall was overflowing. We sat quite far from the stage, I in my brown velvet Sunday dress, with long braids and buttoned shoes. In the first part Andreeva-Delmas sang, and then some sort of Meyerhold 'play' followed: the Aleksandrinsky classical reper-toire had not prepared me for such spectacles. I had no under-standing in those years of the new theatre, and the programme I crumpled in my hands agitated me so much that I could perceive

*Our windows faced those of Osip and Lila Brik's apartment (Zhukovsky Street 7, Apt. 35), where Mayakovsky then lived.

66

nothing, I thought, of what was happening. The actors had huge false noses and somersaulted on the stage, giving each other noisy slaps; partitions kept shuffling; Olga Sudeikina and Gabrielle Ivanova were barely covered by gossamer clothes. The audience hissed and applauded. Light shone, my insides trembled tensely. The first interval came, and I was rooted to my seat. After the break, Sologub walked onto the stage, and after him Blok, Akhmatova, Kuzmin.

Sologub recited in a stone-like way. He seemed to me very old, small, pale and gloomy; he wore glasses (or was it a pince-nez?), and a black frock coat. His voice was toneless. In recollections about him we often read that he did not change. Six years later, when I met him and spoke to him, he was exactly the same as the man in the Army and Fleet Hall. I believe he came into Russian poetry already old in appearance, and left it with an immobile face and wooden figure; perhaps he was never any different. Kuzmin, with a pale lock of hair on his forehead, recited for a long time and, despite a slight speech defect, beautifully. He sang heavily, but such singing was then almost obligatory for poets. About this singsong (not only of Kuzmin), Merezhkovsky told me once (in Paris, in 1928) that it came from Pushkin – or so Yakov Polonsky, whom he had known in his youth, explained it to him. Polonsky obviously had observed this tradition and read his poems in a singing tone, remembering those who had heard Pushkin and others. Tiutchev also sang, according to Polonsky. Generally only actors at that time slashed verse and read emotionally, underlining stops and intonation as in prose, so that the rhymes could not be heard and all the poem sank in the accelerated and slowed-down clusters of meaning, completely deprived of rhythm, sound patterns, and melody: only some specific words were singled out by pathetic sobbing shouts or intimate whispers, when even hands sometimes swung into motion to underline the 'realism' of the presentation, not to mention the facial expressions supporting the dramatic effects of the voice (it was better not to watch). On the basis of Polonsky's words, Merezhkovsky said that Pushkin read motionlessly, with a singing tone, heavily accenting pyrrhics and spondees, caesuræ and enjambments. Kuzmin sang, Sologub read gloomily and tonelessly in his gloomy and toneless singsong. Blok read, hardly parting his teeth, without melody, but with an astonishing realization of the rhythm. His manner was to exaggerate immobility. Khodasevich read with a perfect balance of all the nuances. Gumilev exaggerated the pathos and his reading was spoiled by the fact that he had a speech impediment – he did not pronounce certain sounds. Bely stressed his own melody (assimilated once and for all).

Blok came onto the stage erect and serious.* His face was slightly reddish, while his clear eyes and thick hair were exactly as in photographs; his hair, like a halo, shone more brightly than his face in the electric light. And yet he was different from his photographs. A kind of sadness, which I saw then in his manner, I never saw again but did not forget. Photographs neither retained nor transmitted it. There was something mournful in his face that evening and perhaps now, after reading his diaries, notebooks and letters, I can say that once it appeared it did not leave his mood. He stood in the left corner of the stage, hands in pockets:

> To the marshy, deserted meadows
> We fly. Alone.
> Around us like a pack of cards, in semi-circle,
> Lights disperse.

This soldering of the words 'marshy meadows' and the sudden cut of the line into 'We fly. Alone.' are the creative secret of this stanza. As almost always in Blok, the stanza is a whole in which either a chord or an arpeggio lives, where one is given the unexpected and at the same time a comment on it (or first the hint of a resolution, and only then the question and answer). And in these verses, a simile (lights *like* cards) is thrown in, and presently the Poet and the Child rush into it as into reality. Was the lighthouse of the second stanza found? No, it was not found, because not only those two, but the whole world, the world of night, mist, and fragrances, flew into aimlessness. And if the Child came to this poem from 'The Choirvoice', fogs and fragrances crawled into it out of 'The Stranger', where, incidentally, the hint and the question-answer are given with their most naked force – a portrait becomes a landscape (charmed shore, eyes blossom behind a veil and ostrich feathers in

*'28 March [1915]. She [Delmas] and I are taking part in a soirée, arranged by An. Chebotarevskaya (Army and Fleet Hall).' A. Blok. *Notebooks.*

the poet's own brain). This portrait-landscape makes Blok's romanticism almost surrealistic, drawing him to us at abnormally close distance.

Akhmatova wore a white dress, with a Stuart collar (which was then à la mode) – and was slender, beautiful, dark-haired, elegant. She was then near thirty; this was the heyday of her glory, the glory of her new prosody, her profile, her charm. 'You will receive no more letters from him, . . . From burned-out Poland . . .' she intoned, hands folded over her bosom, slowly and tenderly, with the musical seriousness that in her was so captivating.

And again there was an interval. But now I stood up and went towards the stage, and in the bright fog around me I suddenly saw Tatiana Adamovich, hand in hand with Akhmatova. Tatiana came up to her shoulder. She took me by the hands and introduced me to Akhmatova:

'Here, this is the girl . . . She writes verse.' ('Also' writes verse?)

Akhmatova extended her slim hand to me.

'Delighted.'

This 'delighted' seemed to me so worldly, addressed to me as to an adult. The handshake left an impression of something tight and cool in my palm; I wanted to run away – because of embarrassment, agitation, awareness of my insignificance. But Tatiana held me firmly. And all of a sudden, I don't remember exactly how, I found myself facing Blok in the artists' foyer behind the stage.

'Here, Aleksandr Aleksandrovich, here is the girl who writes verse.' ('Also' writes verse?)

And Blok said 'delighted', hardly looking at me, while his hand touched mine for a moment. In a minute a thick fog rose in clouds around me, and into this fog sank the immobile and sad face of Blok, Kuzmin's lock of hair, the glasses of Sologub. I hurriedly ran back, elbowed my way to my seat, sat down. The question 'What now?' came into my mind. Where to go? What to do with myself? Perhaps it was necessary to do something there, to say something, not keep silent, not take to one's heels. My heart beat loudly and strongly; it was good to know that no one besides me could hear it.

My agitation at the gate of Leonid Andreev's cottage was of another kind. For the Christmas holidays I went to Natasha Shklovskaya's in Finland, where her father had a cottage. It stood in deep snow among thick firs; Natasha and I harnessed the rust-coloured, long-maned mare to a small Finnish sleigh, and she took us at a leisurely pace along roads and through forests, past lakes and ponds dressed in ice, with a bell ringing beneath the shaft-bow. In those days Natasha revealed her gift of improvising verse (five-foot iambics or four-foot trochaics without rhyme), and she decidedly did not know what to do with it. I drove, she improvised, the short day fled, the sleigh runners screeched, and evenly and peacefully, we slid past the dwellings or the railway with rails that had fallen asleep and past a lighted little station window, or silent trees that offered us snow on their smooth wide branches. We ate chocolate, learned to smoke, and once in a burst of bold curiosity decided to drop in on the black-and-rose cottage of Andreev to announce to him that we had read his *Life of Man*. We rang the bell quite a long time, and then an old woman opened the gate and said, 'Leonid Nikolaevich has gone to Petersburg.' In snow that came up to our knees, we ran back to the sled, where our rust-coloured mare, covered with hoarfrost, twitched her ears.

At home we were scolded for our tobacco breath, which settled like a nimbus around our rosy faces; we were fed dinner, and were required to go to bed not later than ten. But in bed we chatted at times till late at night, first by the light of a kerosene lamp that burned between our beds on a knotty, unpainted night-table (all the furniture and walls were made of boards), and then in darkness. At that time we both felt like dramatizing the present: I complained that I could no longer live as I lived and would run away from people who 'could give me nothing save their love and care', for which I felt no need whatever, since I myself wanted to love and care for somebody though I had no one yet to devote myself to; I aspired to live among gods who, like pelicans, would feed me with their entrails (where are these gods? give them to me!) – godly food which would make me grow, grow, grow endlessly. 'I want to grow,' I repeated over and over, burying my face in the hot pillow and tucking my icy legs under me; 'I want to grow, grow, grow.' Meanwhile Natasha tried to apply to herself the ancient myth about the evil stepmother . . . But it was lies: I had no place to flee to and at home all was really not that bad, while at her home her stepmother (the divorce was not yet final, the marriage a year away) was a gay, tender young woman who tried to domesticate us, wild, intractable and so unlike her. And these nocturnal conversations –

despite the fact that from an adult's point of view they were verbose, inconsistent, chaotic, and rather too dramatic – seem to me important as I now remember them: much was touched on that even in later life evoked a response. And if our interpretation of themes was sometimes naïve and pathetic, the very themes were existential and did not die or dissolve. Even now they live in me.

Feelings of shelter and warmth in the house. We are cut off from the rushing snowstorm by double window frames, thick walls, a small porch-entrance, a staircase, three doors. A burning-hot stove blows heat on us; the two of us are raspberry-coloured from it. The birch firewood shoots out in all directions, the day nears its end, and when the storm quietens down, huge smooth Finnish stars will appear. From morning on, all over the high snowdrifts the wind rushes around the house and the thermometer registers so low that it is impossible to see the mercury. The blue snowy Finnish horizons with gingerbread cottages and firs slumbering around, silence and sky. The crimson square from the kitchen window falls across the snow. Skis scrape along, we rush home at twilight among the trees. A fine smoke rises from the chimney. We rush to this crimson square, to this blue smoke, we rush in all haste into the moonlit evening, into cold space, spraying the swirling, silver snow.

Valery Briusov came to Petersburg in 1916 for a celebration organized for him by the Armenians in Petersburg because of the publication of his *Poetry of Armenia*, a huge volume of translations of old and new Armenian poets. My father was on the committee. The day (14 May) of the celebration Briusov gave a reading of his translations in the Tenishev School. He had an unusual gaze of very sharp, somehow piercing eyes: that evening it was as though he pierced me for life with his look. I do not remember at all either his voice or his manner of reading. The main thing about him was his face; you had to look at, not listen to, him. And the important thing in this face was the eyes. I looked into his face and each time I moved my gaze away I encountered the eyes of someone who looked at me from the second row of the hall: Osya A. Did something like love begin between us? Yes, I think so. We wanted to be together and to touch one another. But this was broken off by events: not because the Revolution of February 1917 approached and there happened

not to be time for love, but because in the universal Russian collapse
all that had come before February suddenly seemed childish, worn
threadbare, used up, and it retreated for ever as everyone around us
flew head first into an abyss.

I am the kind of person whose childhood house did not become a
symbol of security, warmth, and joy in life, but whose destruction
brought me immense jubilation. I possess neither 'ancestral tombs'
nor a 'sacred birthplace' to lean on in difficult moments: I never
acknowledged blood relationship, and since nature did not give me
a buffalo's hide, or a panther's teeth, and since I did not look for a
way to build up a double skin or sharpen my teeth, I have gone on
living without support, without weapons, without training in
defence and attack, without kin and native land, not belonging to
any political party and not worshipping gods or ancestors. The
hardest thing for those like me to accept is that the elements we
struggle with are still not formulated: we struggle against enemies
that still have no firm shape, with phenomena that have not yet
arrived at the stage where discursive terminology and clear
deductions would help us grasp them in the light of new criteria.
We two-legged mammals, having lost the protection of the
'gaseous vertebrate' (in the witty phrase of Aldous Huxley) and, as
a matter of fact, having lost so much of what man of the past
centuries possessed, remain alone facing our own selves.

As I said at the beginning of this book, there is no question for me
of a meaning of life distinct from life itself. Life for me was and is
overflowing with meaning. Existence is the sole reality, nothing
lies beyond it. We do not reflect anything, we do not cut our way
through to anything, we are here and only here, and only the *present*
(the *now*) means something. To decipher the meaning of reality
(inside me and out), to find the links that bind the separate facets of
this meaning with each other and with the whole, always seemed to
me a necessity. In this way, life itself became its meaning, not
abstractly but in my personal concrete inter-relation with my time,
which was defined for me by five or six world events and five or six
great names. Every day brought me something I was able to take
with me into night, revealing outside something similar to what
was within me, sometimes explaining myself to myself but more
often laying bare the fact of myself in accordance with the fact of the
world. With the years my task became: to free myself from the

inherited chaos, to calm anarchy, clean up the intellectual mess and all the dichotomies which, if they are not alleviated, destroy man. I see life not in space in general, but at a definite geographical point, not in time, but in history. Not among 'neighbours' and not among similar or 'equal' beings, but among chosen or even elected ones. Thus adjustment to the world and to men is a joy for me, because it is a prerequisite of inward order and development. Within the established limits of birth and death (the only ones determined), I fully sense freedom of will and freedom of choice, that inward will which becomes more forceful and important *circumstantially* the more the thinking person becomes stronger than the morsel floating in the waves. I knew very early that one is not born with a mind, that 'we ourselves continually create our minds', in Chaadaev's expression. I learned, to the best of my ability, to create it, I learned and am learning yet, and still it seems to me not enough, because only while growing does man live in touch with history, in co-ordination with 'world events' and 'great names'. So I stand in front of Rembrandt's painting, 'Aristotle Contemplating the Bust of Homer', and feel the chain (like that chain on the portrait of the central figure) that eternally binds Homer, Aristotle, Rembrandt and me as I face the painting. As in a net of blood vessels, a vein carries blood from one, through another, to a third and finally into my own veins. We all stand in one line which is indestructible, if I myself do not destroy it. But I will not destroy it because a discharge of heat is released in me by this blood that runs through me, by which I live, and opens the way for me to possible judgements, to impulses of imagination; and they in their turn allow me to make the whole complicated system of symbols and myths my own which mankind has lived with since that first day it started to worship the sun. Since then we have come a long way: from fire-worshipers to Phoebus Apollo and through Christ to what we mean when we say 'civilization is warmth'.

In my mind I often say to people:

'Give me a stone. Out of it I will manage to make bread for myself. Don't worry. I am not asking for bread. Just hand me that cobblestone there, I know what to do with it.'

I now look at the years of my childhood without the slightest haze of sadness, without melancholy tears about what was lost for ever. All my past is with me at every hour of my life. For me all its charm lies in the fact that it has not died within me. So, as before, I sometimes sit at a window and look at the street, lights and roofs, or at trees and clouds, or the outline of the horizon. As before I listen to blood coursing through my body and all the beatings and rhythmical sounds in me that correspond to the rhythms of the world. I am aware that I live, that I am alive, that I have yearned all my life not for happiness, but for the intense feeling of being alive. I am aware that the roots of all late dreams are in my early years, all late passions stem from my childish insomnias. Riddles solved by me now were set up then. My life was (and is) development and growth, like the fate of any living thing. Nothing has left me, but on the contrary all is present and undergoes transfiguration along with me. All that was built by me on the foundation of the past is in perfect harmony with this foundation. My purpose, my meaning, my lesson, and my destiny lie in all this.

PART TWO

Poor Lazarus

I COME TO A COMPLICATED AND DIFFICULT JOB: with the help of Dasha the washing of my braids begins. The bath pipe drones, the stove is red–hot, the taps sing, water gurgles in the painted porcelain jug; leaning over the bath I see my hair, like heavy, dark seaweed, lying on the bottom. Dasha pours a heavy stream on my head. This goes on for a long time. Then for a second time she soaps my scalp with a huge, bulky piece of yellow soap. Twice it falls, once into the bath and once on the floor and for a long time plays hide-and-seek with Dasha, while she crawls all around me and finally pulls it out with a mop from under the bath. I stand patiently, leaning over. At last my hair begins to squeak – a sign that it is clean – and Dasha pitilessly winds it on her hand, twists it and squeezes it, like a towel or rag. She throws something shaggy and warm over me, and then everything around me begins to rumble: Dasha rinses out the pail, puts all in its place, rattles the enamel basins, letting steam out of the burning hot tap. I go to my room, she follows, and when I sit at my desk, burying my nose in a book, she places a kind of basin next to my chair on the floor, so that a puddle does not flow from me onto the floor. There is something debasing in this.

Friday, 9 March.* Confusion in the city. Tomorrow we are having an evening party; Mother fears that the bridges will be raised, that the Petrovs will not be able to come from the islands and that the ice cream will not be sent from the Ivanov bakery. This suddenly also seems to me a catastrophe, but I instantaneously pop up in a completely different dimension, and my world comes back to me: a world where there is neither Madame Petrov nor the

*Thanks to the old calendar, the 'February Revolution' took place in Russia in March (new style) and the October one in November.

Ivanov bakery, a world where Russia thunders, where people walk with red flags, and where there is a holiday.

I know this feeling increasingly: falling from our usual dimension into another. There, there are new laws; bodies have another weight and other inter-relations, and there are different values; there are new 'you mays' and 'you may nots', and I feel happy there, terror-stricken, and tempted to stay forever.

The guests came at ten; there were about thirty. I have always liked the gaiety of others. For the first time in my life I was allowed to remain till the end – that is, till 5:00 A.M., I heard a soprano of the Mariinsky opera sing *Lakmé*, and saw people dance the fashionable tango. All was so remote from me and yet so interesting as it is now when strangers dance and sing, almost as fascinating as when those close to me sing and dance. There are few of the latter. A tremendous liner crosses the ocean: about two thousand people are on it, and not one 'close one'. In a huge hotel, by the ocean shore, there are crowds of people who eat, converse, go here and there, and no one 'close' to me. This is how things have happened. Still it is good to be in a crowd and to pass by, move with a smile on my face, trying not to brush against anyone. And on this very significant Saturday, the last day of old Russia, after a gay supper in the dining room, it went without saying that I could not – because of some laws which I myself held to since time immemorial – I could not have anything in common with any of those present. I was among them but I was not of them.

Today that swiftness with which Russia collapsed and the gigantic effort with which she arose forty years later seem to me a kind of fantasy. In the upper classes people simply threw every-thing away and fled: first the tsar and his ministers, then the members of the K.-D. Party, then the socialists. The least competent and stupidest remained, till they too tumbled into the depths of nothingness. From the 'saints' (like Prince Lvov) to 'demons', whose names are well known, all were here, the whole gamut of Russian mediocrities, imbeciles, hysterics, and gangsters. And the principal culprit in this, the one who kept Russia back from a parliamentary system for endless years, the one who made it impossible for the K.-D.s and the socialists to learn the responsible craft of state power or at least the craft of opposition to state power, the one who led the country from shame to shame for twenty-three years, who, having on the day of his coronation uttered the prayer of the 'Lord's Anointed' then took symbol for reality, feeling he had actually become this 'Lord's Anointed' – he did not pay for his mistakes with any kind of so-called martyr's death: they remain with him. The idea that you can pay for life with death is a false notion which appeals to sentimental people. You can't. Death is a part of life. And although our Cambyses of the 1930s and 1940s are anathema to us, the main guilt for all Russian disasters rests with the tsar.

It is not necessary to go far to imagine, in our time, the temper of the old regime. A worthy disciple of Nicholas II is still alive and continues to reign in Ethiopia, and one does not have to be specially perceptive to understand that, if in Russia there had been no opposition to autocracy (and no Revolution), with tsars such as the Romanovs, it would now be a huge mechanized Ethiopia whose fine intelligentsia would probably have settled in another country (assuming Russia remained at all). Even in Saudi Arabia (where mullahs rule) there is planning, but the Russian tsar would hardly have reached that stage. Ten per cent literacy, as among the subjects of Haile Selassie: here is what awaited Russia in the twentieth century when the *anointed one* thought of himself not as metaphor but as reality. Nicholas II lived with the conviction that God had actually *anointed* him, and prohibited him from sharing power with anyone else.

A happy crowd, an angry crowd, a wavering crowd, a light that sparkled for an instant (especially among the intelligentsia and the workers), the bloody collapse of everything, an artificially prolonged war, a criminally and senselessly inflamed patriotism, cheap and harmful, and words, words, along with an inability to do what was necessary – all was present that spring and summer, but none of the quick, sure measures that were indispensable. There was no genius, and when October came we found ourselves (even Gorky, in his *Untimely Thoughts*) not on the Revolution's side, because we could accept neither the 'German money' paid to Lenin, nor the gradual destruction of whole classes of a population, nor the threat of destruction to two generations of intelligentsia, nor the 'all-is-permitted' Leninist ideology, nor the deliberate lowering of culture, nor the Bolsheviks' stake in world revolution.

Incidentally, about that German money. Now, when the facts about it have been revealed and the Berlin archives of the Kaiser's time have become known, it is incomprehensible why all this has, for fifty years, been concealed in the Soviet Union and why, being a defeatist, Lenin should not have used this money. And why, having used it, which was completely logical, he later denied this and all that surrounded it. Aleksandr Kerensky told me in 1959 that he knew for sure about this fact (Lenin's receipt of sums of money from Kühlmann-Ludendorff), but he could not reveal this secret and irrefutably prove the fact, for he was bound by an oath. What oath? Bound to whom? To the French and English ambassadors, Paléologue and Buchanan? Or to the French minister Albert Thomas?

But what oath, besides a Masonic one, could be more important for Kerensky than that oath of allegiance he took as the president of the Council of Ministers of the Russian Provisional Government? Ekaterina Kuskova left documents, in her archives in Paris, from which it appears that Nekrasov, Tereshchenko, and Pereverzev, ministers of Kerensky, were bound among themselves by such an oath and so could do nothing.

All or almost all was new for me, as for the majority – new and joyous because here was the destruction of everything that not only stirred up hate and scorn, but shame as well, shame for the baseness and stupidity of the old regime, at the way it rotted in front of the eyes of the whole world: Tsushima, *Potemkin*, debacle in East Prussia, Rasputin, Beilis, the hangings, the tsarina, and he himself, for whom there is not and cannot be any forgiveness so long as there remains on earth at least one Russian. He thought he was a second Tsar Alexis Mikhailovich and that Russia was that pre-Petrine country which needed anointed ones, synods, and gendarmes, when what Russia needed were quick steps through a parliamentary system and capitalism to planning, new taxes, freedom of speech and the press, and twentieth-century technology, civilization for all, universal education, self-respect for all. And those jokers who replaced him thought they had been invited to a festive occasion: if they didn't like it, they would leave, but if they did like it they would remain and celebrate – this was their day! But this was Russia's day, and they didn't allow for that. They didn't allow for the fact that their servile obedience to the 'democratic' ministers of

France and the 'liberal' ambassadors of England was not only ridiculous and undignified, but criminal, and that the mob was marching into history, sweeping everything away – starting with themselves – as they went.

Nothing is inescapable except death. The Revolution was not inevitable. The twentieth century has taught us that poverty and inequality, exploitation and unemployment are overcome in different ways. In Sweden a hundred years ago there were three kings in succession who introduced bills into Parliament that were too radical; Parliament vetoed them until Parliament became as radical as the Swedish kings themselves, and the bills were finally passed (on old-age pension, etc.). It was not the bestowal of a Constitution from above that was necessary, but working it out with the opposition, swinging the huge country in a direction where it could breathe and develop. A 'palace revolution' was not needed, but a calm and total rejection of any palaces, monuments, and fountains, so drawing the line between myth and reality. And if unfortunate wars were beyond Russia's capabilities, then it was necessary to abandon the thought of *Great* Russia once and for all. Only underdeveloped countries have revolutions – this lesson was taught to us by the twentieth century – while developed countries change *differently*. I can even agree that in the sixties of our century Russia would have been approximately at the same stage she is at now; but if this had come to be, it would have happened without forced collectivization, without a war whose army was deprived of a staff command, and no annihilation of a cultural layer that will not be restored in two hundred years. But, as for a folk hero musing at the junction of three roads, the country in 1917 faced trials in three directions: through Kornilov and Denikin, Trotsky, Stalin. This is the state of affairs the six last tsars brought Russia to.

The Ciniselli circus, where in my early childhood I had been taken to see trained dogs, became a place for meetings, and we went there: Natasha Shklovskaya had joined the left wing of S.-R.s, Nadia Otsup the Bolshevik Party (she perished as a Trotskyite), Sonia R. the right wing of S.-R.s (she committed suicide in 1931), Lucia M. the K.-D. Party (she was shot while fleeing abroad). I did not join any party, but considered myself close to Martov's group. We argued heatedly with one another, but we knew that no one could out-argue anyone else. We stuck together. The remainder of the class, with the exception of two or three blockheads, was divided almost equally between S.-R.s and S.-D.s.

Exams were cancelled, catechism eliminated. We sat at the teachers' council, where there were Martovists, Leninists, and secret anti-Bolsheviks as well. We abolished the prayer before the beginning of lessons, and hung portraits of Herzen, Plekhanov and Spiridonova on the classroom wall. Fs in physics appeared in my class register. As I was in love with the small, hirsute physics teacher, I even took some delight in being offended by him. I needed to cram, which wasn't easy. It was obviously hopeless to count on his lenience: he did not notice me at all.

In no way can I resurrect in my memory what attracted me to this yellowish, thin, dark-eyed, white-toothed man who gave me bad marks. I think he fell into the net of my imagination which sought something to hold on to. The physics teacher seemed to me mysterious, perhaps half Japanese, doomed to suffering, weird, cruel, and cynical. I think now he was not at all like that. I invented him and drifted about with my feeling for him; it fed my verse, caused me to swing from hot to cold. All this passed very quickly, however, and with effort I climbed to a D.

My relations with Victor Uskov were completely different. He became our teacher when I was about eleven and taught natural science – botany, anatomy, zoology. We left him in three years for the physics teacher, but every Sunday morning for two years I went to school in his lab, and there 'helped him in his occupations'. Did anyone know about this? Probably, yes. I could not hide at home or from my classmates that I 'worked' with Uskov, but all were quite indifferent about this. Usually I sat on a high chair near the 'preparations', not taking my eyes away from him, and he, 'preparing' something, inclining his high, bald forehead, talked in a rather muffled voice of Bakunin, Renan, Gibbon, Shakespeare, Aristophanes, Pascal . . . About two hours would pass in this way. Sometimes, having washed his hands, he would sit, towel in hand, on the chair opposite me. Then we continued looking at one another, and I would listen to him, my mouth open with awe. In my opinion then, he knew decidedly everything and I nothing. It was almost unnecessary for me to ask him questions – his speech flowed like a river and carried me along, and only when the wall clock in the laboratory struck would I realize that I had to go.

Still, I was not in love with him. True, sometimes I dreamt that he would propose to me and I would become his wife, would clean his boots, iron his jackets, cook dinner for him, entertain him, bestow something on him every day and adore him to the grave. But I very easily reconciled myself to the impossibility of such a future. I did not know whether he was married. What he found in me, why he wasted time with me I never found out. But those Sunday meetings continued for two years.

'Do you talk about botany?' my mother asked one day.

'No, we talk about Gibbon and Pascal.'

'About whom?'

'About Gibbon and Pascal.'

She did not answer. Sometimes I took Natasha Shklovskaya with me. She also loved to listen to him. Then we sat there together in front of him, like chicks on a perch, and he walked about the room. I wanted this to continue indefinitely.

It is possible that in those very years my protest against any dichotomy assumed real-life forms. It was in me even earlier, but gradually and in part I began unconsciously to seek a *chord* for my existence – I still did not know what it would be, in what key and what tonality. I demanded it not only mentally but bodily. The chord might be in some way similar to Beethoven's in the *Pathétique Sonata*, or to Wagner's in *Tristan*: I could neither create it nor invent it, I could only know it was indispensable and await the moment when it would resound for me. Physically, with my entire body, I reacted against any bisecting, halving, dualism. Co-ordination became for me a kind of constant necessity, a fixation, and the longer I lived the more strongly I felt a kind of purely physical nausea (with a brief feeling of deadly boredom), when I happened suddenly to suspect myself of being a kind of problem split in two, of losing if only for a moment the blessed sensation of the *seam*. I do not speak about this now metaphorically: the moments of nausea rising in me when I sensed bisection in any form have accompanied me throughout my life. This touchstone of physical reaction has never let me down.

The social problems that occupied me are still with me, but in the year of the Russian Revolution they were by their nature dichotomous (bi-sensed, ambiguous) and tortured me very much. I think now that all of us were then tortured by them – that is, all who had a conscience and could think. So a reading of Blok's diaries of that time will move me even now, for I see in them that very same blind ferment, where love or rather pity for what is distant, revulsion for and fear of the near, a heavy feeling of guilt, fused with the sorrow of a weakness beyond repair. It is customary to speak of the abyss between the Russian intelligentsia and the people. Not an abyss, but too close a bond existed between the two, a bonding of the two parts of one whole with a fatal feeling of the guilt of one half about the other, of the tragic alienation of these two parts, artificially soldered together. Why did one feel responsible for the other? Why did one repent before the other? It was necessary not to feel guilty and apologize, but to build railways, give smallpox vaccinations and print ABC books in great quantity for compulsory education.

I then only dimly realized this and reacted physically more than intellectually to contradictions. That is, I bristled inwardly, 'ejected' the easy answer that wanted to take root in me, denied there were two answers to the same question, that some problems have the right to remain unsolved, some fogs undispersed. For me there was no thought and feeling, good and evil, *here* and *there* and so on. I knew that thought is always thought *and* feeling, that evil is the absence of good and good the absence of evil (in man as in nature, for man is part of nature), and that no *there* whatsoever exists, but only a great myth which, though always changing, is the same in its essence, a game without which the life of man becomes dry, flat, and dull, that like symbols, laughter, tears, ecstasy, that Aristotelian shock of terror and bliss, like dreams is necessary to man.

My final year (the twelfth grade) in school was a year of great events, the year of the October Revolution, of the Brest-Litovsk peace with Germany, of Blok's *The Twelve*, and at the same time of my first love (and also, it seems, of my second and third), the time of my intensive friendship with Natasha Shklovskaya, of anxieties about the social inequality of people, about politics, and the first privations. From our still happy, spacious and clean apartment I went for the first time into an inferno of alien poverty. Of course, I had always known all people in the world did not have lamb chops, health, and starched cuffs and collars, a mother and father living in peace with each other, but I had not seen them close up, I had only read about them. I don't remember why I had to set out with thirty copybooks of schoolwork ('Turgenev's Bazarov as a Type') to the home of the teacher of Russian literature, Vasily Petrovich Sokolov, but apparently we had not handed them in on time; the Christmas holidays had arrived, and I was entrusted to do it. He lived on a side street in a part of Petersburg I had never been to before. He was himself an ageless man, in appearance reminiscent of Sologub's Peredonov, walking about in a yellow celluloid collar, his hair greasy and his whiskers red. To each word he added 'well-a'. Thus we called him Wellar. His frock coat was dirty, his nails black, his nose like a potato. Moreover, he was of enormous size; he stooped out of embarrassment, but in spite of this he was so feared that in class during his lessons a deadly silence set in, and the Kruglikov twin sisters sobbed violently when he called them to the board, though they were seventeen. My feelings towards him were of a very strange kind: he disgusted me but did not frighten me; at the same time I couldn't help noticing that he read verse *in our way*, that is, not like an actor, and when he spoke about Pushkin's *The Bronze Horseman* (linking it to his 'The Upas Tree') he would, after a reading, blow loudly into a dirty handkerchief, which made my own nose feel moist. 'Wellar seems to be wettar,' Natasha, who of course shared the same desk, whispered to me. But his words to the effect that *The Bronze Horseman* and 'The Upas Tree' were about the same thing (the power of man over man) sank deep into me; I began to think about Wellar quite often and was happy to be going to his house – I would see how he lived and perhaps speak with him about modern poets.

The building was old, narrow and tall, in a dark stinking side street; you entered from a courtyard where two pale little boys in rags were trying to slide down a black snow pile on a home-made sled. I opened the narrow door and started to climb the stairs, slippery because of wet patches; there was a stuffy and sweet odour of cats. Some doors were not quite shut and from behind them you heard sounds: shouts, curses, drunken sobs, a child's cry, the wild singing of some couplets, the squeal of a dog being beaten, the muttering of a prayer or incantations. Someone rumbled rather heavily, steam rose from linen boiling on a stove. Everything was filthy, sticky, and foul. A woman's head leaned out through a door: the face was red and seemed drunk, her hair was tousled, an unbuttoned jacket revealed a grey bosom that hung down to her waist. For a moment she jumped back, having seen me, then stuck out both hands and swiftly touched me. I jerked back because of her smell and because a shudder of squeamishness shook me. The door slammed shut. Finally I found apartment number 29; the door was insulated with dirty oilcloth. The bell jingled and became silent; it was a hoarse, brass, somehow Dostoevskian bell. Steps resounded, and Wellar opened the door. He was wearing that same celluloid collar and frock coat, but the cuffs were removed. The air in the room was heavy: it smelled of sauerkraut, last year's fried fish (from Lent), of something stewed in fat, of onions, stove smoke, a strange dampness – which combined with some kind of chemical odour, from a spray against moths or cockroaches perhaps, though more probably against bedbugs. Every minute it became harsher, killing the kitchen smells and triumphing over them in my throat and nose. Wellar led me into a room that resembled a dining room. In the middle was a table covered with dirty oilcloth, old and peeling, as if someone picked at it every evening, tracing out a pattern. To the right there was a cupboard, to the left an old screen with odd drawings on it of a Chinese man; someone's finger had poked a hole in his fat stomach. It was dusk, but Wellar did not switch on a light and did not ask me to sit down.

'Bazarov as a type,' I said. 'You asked that they be brought to you.'

'Well-a,' he said, and took the notebooks. In a minute he asked: 'And what are you reading?'

I answered, 'The *Karamazovs*.'

'And what poets?'

'Blok.'

He looked at me and said suddenly: 'That's good.'

I felt flowers beginning to bloom inside me.

'The cult of the eternal feminine. Do you know Goethe?'

I said yes.

'Look at the end of *Faust*. And have you read Vladimir Soloviev?'

'A little.'

'Read him. He has more about the eternal feminine. Do you like Blok's "But you, Marya, are treacherous"?'

'"He, on his knees in a dark recess",' I continued.

He suddenly went through the small door, obviously to fetch a book, and I remained alone. It became still darker. The window, covered with a dusty torn curtain, became grey. On the cupboard lay a piece of black bread and some nibbled horseradish, while next to the horseradish stood those two huge celluloid cuffs with the flat mother-of-pearl cuff links I knew well and which he daily 'screwed on' as we put it.

Suddenly I had an irresistible urge to see what was behind the screen. I took a step and craned my neck.

A huge fat woman staring at the ceiling lay on the bed. At first I decided she was dead, that this was his mother or wife who had died perhaps that morning. The woman did not stir and I, as if petrified, stared at her. She was covered to her chin with rags, her body rose like a mountain under these scraps, and on the summit, which was right at the top of her stomach, lay a small soiled doll, without nose or hair, in torn pantaloons. The woman's hand was above the rags and she stroked the doll, hardly moving her fat completely straight fingers. Her face expressed an idiotic beatitude.

Suddenly she moved her eyes to me and made the effort of smiling weakly at me. I jumped back. Sokolov entered the room.

'Well-a,' he said, sitting down, 'let's read this.'

So he began his class six times a week.

> You keep your eyes cast down demurely,
> Your shoulders covered with a veil –
> Mary, they think you are a saint,
> But you are false and fickle, surely.

At last I unfastened the hook of my winter coat.

'And do you love Sologub?'

Yes, I loved Sologub.

Finally I left. I went down the completely dark stairs to the courtyard, and walked along the side street. Verse sang in my head:

> Do not slip on these dark
> Wet and crooked steps,
> So ragged and uneven,
> Between cold and damp walls.
>
> An unkind eye greedily
> Follows us from behind doors,
> And a heavy steam floats out
> From every crack and suffocates us.

Why am I here together with you,
In a stinking and strange Hell?
Where cruel illnesses breathe,
Which reduced Sodom to ashes?

Is it possible that we are condemned
To slip with an unsure foot
On these millennial slops? . . .

I walked and walked and because of the verse, the thought of the dead woman behind the screens (I was now sure it only appeared to me that she smiled to me), of Sokolov's voice and his way of reading, the dark courtyard and the half-eaten piece of bread; a storm of thoughts, feelings and thought-feelings rose in me, so that I wound up wandering, and came to a quay of the Neva I did not know; the wind whistled, smoke rose from a factory chimney, and Petersburg was not like Petersburg; a factory hand led me to the tram stop, asking as he said good-bye if I would have a beer with him that evening in the corner tavern.

I never spoke alone again with Sokolov. From Bazarov there was the transition to Levin and Prince Andrey, and then to Tolstoy's play *The Fruits of Enlightenment*. On the last day before graduation in the spring of 1918, he decided to give a speech in class:

'Well-a,' he said, looking somewhere above our heads, 'I congratulate you: you are going out into life . . .'

His speech was long and boring, he scolded us for our insufficient knowledge of Russian literature, reminded us that though the letter *yat* (of the old orthography) had been abolished, you would always be able to distinguish a literate from an illiterate person. Then he went on to discuss himself and spoke of how we were leaving and how he would remain to do what he had always done and would do. That in his life there was no monotony but dedication, because every now and then when he sent out another twelfth grade – like Pushkin letting out his bird 'on a clear festive spring day' – he felt like Lermontov's cliff. Yes, sometimes – rarely, it was true – he felt like this cliff after the little cloud had left it. And when he quoted, 'and quietly it weeps in the wilderness', he had to take out that huge dirty handkerchief.

I was slightly shocked by the two literary quotations, dragged in one after the other. It seemed to me for a moment that during this he looked at me, but I paid no attention. And only after he had bowed and left the class, all turned to me and in chorus declared all this was about me, that Wellar's heart was bleeding at the separation from me. But in those days so much that was strange, new, and wonderful happened around me and with me that the theme 'Wellar, cliff-dweller' (thanks to a stupid rhyme) took on a kind of humorous tone. I never saw Sokolov again.

But this visit to him revealed a strange life to me. I began to like to visit people to see what and who, so to speak, lay behind their screens. I liked to look into strange windows, especially in the evenings, not in any way wanting to share someone's strange life, but only to see this life, to know and understand it and speculate about it. It was as if I were looking at illustrations in a thick book, and was not interested in the text. These pictures lived with me afterwards: before sleep, in bed, they suddenly arose in my memory (through a completely ungraspable association). Here a family sits at evening tea. There a young girl, like me, practises a Clementi sonatina. Here a man tries to pull a long, narrow dress off a woman, there a dog sleeps, one ear up and the other down, while between its hind legs a small cat in a red collar finds its place . . . Much later my inquisitive peering into strange windows found its way into my novel *Cape of Storm* and my story 'The Big City'.

Such was the farewell with my teacher of Russian literature; but the farewell with Uskov was completely different. There were about ten of us, and we decided to celebrate graduation together with two teachers – although Uskov did not teach in the senior classes he was popular, as was the mathematics teacher, Nathanson, who later married a classmate of mine. Uskov was young, good-looking, and talented, and in the final class both algebra and trigonometry were no longer a closed book for many of us. We took two boxes at the Aleksandrinsky Theatre for a play by Sumbatov, certainly a very bad one. But we weren't interested in it, and on Sunday at the very end of May we visited Pavlovsk for a whole day. We went to an empty house (or rather, cottage) there, in which we cooked dinner for twelve people, and then we went for a walk in the park, sat in the garden near the house on a large terrace, and returned home late to the city. Rozanov, in *Solitary Thoughts*, I think, says that one recollection from youth can sometimes keep a man from suicide, lead him away from hopelessness and despair. That day in Pavlovsk is such a memory.

Uskov took me home through the city, on a white night, and then accompanied Natasha on foot. 'We have something like a club of three,' he said in the end. 'My thanks to you.' I also wanted to say 'thank you', but owing to agitation and sadness I could hardly speak the words. No, I wasn't in love with him, but if – I thought later, in my room, at night – if he were to allow me every day to clean the dust from his books and sit silently in a corner while he read or wrote, I would immediately leave home to do it and would be so happy . . . This role of poor Lazarus pleased me terribly in those days. I somehow thought it out for myself just at the right moment.

Spring. Pavlovsk. Happiness is like a halo above our faces, and our eyes are ablaze in the feeling of life's fullness and the expectation of our fate. Around the big empty cottage, in the overgrown though still unrequisitioned garden, birds sing and lilacs bloom, and in the kitchen Esther slices herring with her beautiful large white hands – she is herself beautiful and large, with touched-up lips, smelling of sweet powder which she carries on her in an exquisite powder-case. She is a little impudent because she knows her worth, but we love her. She orders someone to cut the onion, and gentle Pauline takes up a knife while Tamara warms up the pie brought from home. I try with all my might to find something to do, for one who does not work does not eat, but Natasha fastidiously avoids touching anything, goes out to our two guests on the terrace and engages them there. 'They are talking about clever things' – so Esther characterizes their pastime. Some white wine is uncorked, I drink two glasses in one gulp and suddenly feel that I don't know where to put my own hands, that I have big feet, I have too large a mouth, a waist not slender enough and, perhaps, a nose not quite clean. But after the third glass all these doubts have passed and though I know I am no beauty, I feel myself to be in total harmony: stockings, firmly pulled on, my tight brassière, my hair precisely wound into a knot on my head, my clean nails, my high heels. Natasha reads verse, I read verse, Esther brings a guitar, Tamara sings – in a high, very high soprano, a kind of pleasant bird-like falsetto. Nathanson joins her, they sing a duet, sit opposite and look each other in the eye, while Esther, tossing the tablecloth over one shoulder, imitates a Spaniard and accompanies them, fingering and plucking the strings with her woman's long fingers.

Then in the train, the melancholy of happiness: this is a special feeling in youth, which comes when a happy day ends. You exaggerate everything: the white night is clearer than it is, the singing is sadder than it was, the man sitting opposite is younger and more handsome than he is in fact; it's as if I see only him and no one else, but he looks at Natasha, at Lucia . . . and no longer remembers me! You take a minute's revenge for all the rejected Liebestraums, the clacking of the wheels saddens you even more, the engine whistle carries away everything that was into nothingness.

But not everything. What remains, I care for. I tremble over my treasure; like a beggar at a church porch I walk around with hand extended and wait for something to fall in my palm – and when it does, I grasp it firmly. My flow of verse had stopped about this time. I became more self-critical and did not write down every tra-ra-tra-ra, not every fired-tired. I humbly gathered up the crumbs: a conversation with Wellar, Natasha's long improvisations, Dostoevsky, Nietzsche, Shestov, a word tossed out by someone (and gleaned by me) – I accumulated them, kept them, and thought and thought and thought about them. If new space opened up for me – in that year, the Gogolian areas between Dikanka and Mirgorod, and later Moscow, full of new (and cheerless) impressions for me – and if I looked into those distances it was as a pilgrim in the desert waiting to see if a drop of rain would fall on him from which he and the whole desert would take life. I awaited something from everybody. Every day I hoped to receive it. There were days that came and went in the Russian whirlwind of those months, and others, as it were, fashioned me; a third kind, like monuments, settled forever into my awareness. There were special days (in all perhaps four or five that year) that, until now, have been like bronze figures in my memory; others are themselves less memorable than what they did to me, and some are important because they illuminated me, uplifted me, added to me, raised me up.

The wedding of Aleksandr Shklovsky took place the day we graduated. That day the most diverse themes of my life came together and were tied into one knot. In the morning for the first time in my life a hairdresser came and did my hair. So I saw my new grown-up self for the first time. That afternoon there was the solemn service, and the wedding dinner was in the evening in the Shklovskys' apartment where Mr Shklovsky had taken Natasha and me for our graduation ceremonies (after his church vows). I had not seen a happier man; he shone, emanating joy, and was troubled only by one thing: how to contain himself, to avoid doing something mad out of the ecstasy that was suffocating him. In the large dining room the table was set for thirty guests, and I sat down next to – well, not Shklovsky the literary critic but his brother (who disappeared later at the Solovki camp).

'I know,' he said at the end of the dinner, 'that you will never forget this day' (he knew the graduation had been that afternoon) 'and I am happy I will be caught on the fringe of this recollection, and that I will be cosy and warm in it till the end of your days.'

We never met again. He turned out to be right.

As for the literary critic, with whom I became close friends much later and who, certainly, remembers me right now, I did not notice him at all that evening. Was he there? Was he not? I do not know. I was too caught up in the happenings of that day, the conversation with my dinner partner, my first conversation in the new style rather unfamiliar to me, to think about the literary critic. I was also, like Shklovsky, emanating happiness that overflowed from me, and was also troubled about how to control it.

That was the most wonderful day of my life, and that evening was definitely the first when, with so much coming together, I could sense and see myself grown up, free, armed with reason and outward loveliness. School was behind me; I was invited to a wedding not of an older friend, but of a grown man, of the generation of my mother and father. I sat next to a theologian who had graduated from the Divinity Academy, and who said things to me that no one had said before. The way he spoke was also new: as if the words he uttered were printed somewhere in the mind's eye, not in a standard linotype face but in hand-set cursive.

By June this wedding and the trip to Pavlovsk are in the past. I try in vain to convince myself that I am looking forward to the move to Moscow, that everything there will be thrilling, and the end of the old life, the mystery of the new one will give me the sense of passing time. It is difficult and sad at this age (I am sixteen) to tear myself away from all that is familiar: to break friendships, abandon favourite books, leave a city, the beauty and grandeur of which in those last months had begun to diminish because of broken windows, boarded-up stores, destroyed monuments, broken-down doors, and long sombre queues. I am leaving for a place the mail cannot reach, although Moscow is only a night's ride from Petersburg. I am going where I do not know a soul. Every day I bid someone farewell: to Dasha, who is leaving for her home in Pskov province; I say good-bye to friends, to Osya, with whom everything somehow cruelly and unjustly stopped all at once, I wish farewell to the old desk and that kind friend of our family who still loves Nadson and Apukhtin and wears a curled moustache.

I call Osya for the last time on the phone and see him run through the lit-up rooms at the ring: they live opposite us, their windows facing ours. We see each other and hear each other, but we don't rejoice.

I am not scared of him. I am not afraid that he will touch me, will kiss me, sit near me and find out what I smell of – soap and ink, probably, nothing else! I know that many girls are scared of boys, frightened that boys are not like us, and that there are many boys who fear us. But I also know well that Osya is not afraid of me. The thought that perhaps I will one day live together with a man, in one room, sleep in one bed, does not terrify me either. I still rarely think about this; it seems to me quite distant but not frightening. I persuade Osya that we are going to Moscow only for a short time, and it seems I convince myself of this (for how long?). Perhaps because I like Osya's smile more than anything and I fear that he will stop smiling and make sad eyes.

Girls are scared of boys and boys of girls. Girls, when they are afraid, say to themselves: 'It's nothing, we'll manage somehow' (but sometimes nothing 'is managed'). Boys, when they are scared, do not try to come near. But Osya and I belong to those who do not fear, do not turn to stone in the presence of each other, nor try to pretend that all is in order when in fact it is in great disorder and both – girl and boy – want to be at the other end of the world. We are free to look at one another, to speak what comes into our heads, to sit cheek to cheek and run our fingers over each other's hands. 'I have ugly hands,' I find it necessary to say to him. 'And I have beautiful ones,' he answers to tease me. But I know that is the truth. I kiss his lips, and brows. And he also kisses mine. It seems to us that we are the first in the world to think of these 'brow kisses'.

All friendships broke up the day we left for Moscow (my father followed the government when it moved), and I was left alone with myself, feeling how tense knots began to form within me which I did not have the ability to unravel, and problems arose when there was nobody to discuss them with. I have never felt myself so dispossessed as that summer, in the dust and stuffiness of Nikitsky Boulevard, in a strange place, deprived of all I had lived with to then. Heat and hunger, contact with communal dining halls, badly baked bread (rationed), barley kasha, a feeling – unknown to me before – of shyness: How to enter the Moscow Public Library? How to sit alone on a bench in public gardens? Can I be accepted into a college? Or must I look for work? And what will I do in this world of 'past' and 'future' people into which I suddenly have been pushed?

Some of these 'past' people were already completely transparent, with deep sunken eyes and an oppressive smell; others sold old junk at the secondhand market, and because they had started in business a spark of greed appeared in their eyes. The 'new' ones I saw only from afar. I was suddenly completely lost; I did not know where to go, whom to speak to, and since I did not know what to do with myself for whole days I began to wander the streets. I was seventeen. All three of us – Father, Mother, and I – lived in one room, which we had rented in a communal apartment. I went out in the morning and returned towards evening to eat kasha. I strolled all over Moscow. On the Sukharevka, the back of my coat was cut by a razor; on Smolensky Boulevard it cost me terrible efforts one day not to start crying. I hated the Pushkin monument; it was always there. I wandered to strange places. Once I heard some quiet choral singing, knocked on the door and entered a dirty, half-dark hall where members of the Tolstoy sect had assembled. Chertkov, a close friend of Leo Tolstoy's, spoke for a long time about the 'great Leo', then Sergeenko – another survivor – distributed some leaflets and we began to sing again. Towards the end something unexpected happened: a handsome, excited young man entered and said that he was – the resurrected Leo Tolstoy. This was Sergeenko's son, who had that day run away from an asylum . . . No, in that place I learned little.

Another time I went through a gate somewhere near Kudrin Square, walked through a dark gateway and entered a garden full of flowers and sunlight. The pond bloomed with water lilies, weeping willows bent over it and, on the benches, people sat half dead from hunger and fear, speaking to each other as if they were already in the next world. A man with a light beard sat down next to me and said that yesterday he informed on a deacon who lived in his apartment; now he felt he could not endure it and wanted to hang himself . . . He also seemed to me half dead, and when I looked around I found I was alone except for a crippled gardener, turning towards me, who carefully placed in front of me a stick whittled on all sides and with a sign attached: Do not touch the flowers!

Once I entered a large delicatessen – probably the last one open. I was very hungry, but I couldn't buy anything on the wide marble counter. I looked for a long time at the balyk, the smoked sausages, the poppyseed rolls, and especially at the cheese, which flowed fully ripe, a regular, thick, cheesy pool that slowly expanded before my eyes. Suddenly from behind the counter a voice said: 'Eat what you wish.'

I gulped and looked in the direction of the voice.

'Delighted. You are the daughter of Nikolai Ivanovich. I have seen you with him.' He nodded his head. 'Eat, don't stand on ceremony! And tell him to drop in.'

He was an Armenian, the last proprietor of the last delicatessen in Moscow – within a year he was executed. Yes, here something came my way – I am not speaking about the food, but about something for which I cannot find words: what came my way was debasement due to hunger, the humble feeling that I was a nobody, but as the daughter of Nikolai Ivanovich in some places I could still count on a sandwich. And more: the sense of falling down, out of the depths of my blessed well simply into a dirty pool from which I could not crawl out except on all fours.

'And here is the tsar-cannon, and here the tsar-bell,' someone was explaining to someone. I, like everyone, stood and looked on, and then went to Nikitsky Boulevard. I sat there for a long time, thought about nothing, and imperceptibly became acquainted with a student to whom the following day I brought some of my books (very likely my favourite ones), which he never returned. Then a distant relative (it seems she was someone's landlady) promised to introduce me to a highly intelligent man, saying: 'You will like each other a lot,' but apparently she forgot about this, or the highly intelligent man wasn't interested in me. Then, in a communal dining hall, a terrifying thin spotted dog, with purulent eyes, licked my kasha . . . On the Sukharevka someone stole my old shoes, which I had gone to sell so that with the money I could – no, not buy the works of Hegel, dear reader, but simply go to the hairdresser's who would curl my hair! (I suddenly felt a terrible urge to have my hair curled.) What had I been taught? I had not been taught to earn my daily bread, to elbow my way in the queues in a dining hall and use a wooden spoon for which you were required to pay a deposit. I had not been taught anything useful: I did not know how to sew felt boots, to comb out lice from children's heads, to bake a pie from potato peels. In bookstores, thin pale yellowed little books looked out at me – political brochures and collections of verse. They reminded me of Liudmilochka, also yellowish, continually hiccupping from hunger and wiping the accumulating saliva from her chin with a Valenciennes lace handkerchief. She was pale and thin. Her parents were also 'past'.

All this continued for a total of four months – solitude, not knowing what would be in the future, walks through the wild hot city with a constant rumbling in my stomach, so that I was even pleased no highly intelligent man was interested in me: I could not have hidden the rumbling from him. A little longer and I probably would have found my way into a college (because it was necessary, whatever came to pass, to master another year of trigonometry and Latin), to the library, or a meeting where someone would drop something into my empty palms, to the company of great people from whom I awaited so much, or of lesser people with whom I could rise out of my downfall. If I were to decide to write a book about the lost years of my life, it would begin with these four Moscow months. I had no corner where I could read a book, I had no money to buy, I had no friend to whom I had no seat to offer; I had to learn in silence how to think, how to look around and into myself freshly, but I just searched like a sparrow or a crow for a place where I could pick up crumbs or waited for something to fall into my mouth. I wanted to go to the Moscow Art Theatre to see Hamsun's *In the Grip of Life* and, with the same eagerness, to take a sauna bath, as well as to go to Petrovskoe-Razumovskoe and lie there under a tree. It was as though I had been deprived of all sense of values. It was not poverty or even Poverty, it was scarcity, however you saw it. What was within me was similar to a man not knowing what is *better*: the Victory of Samothrace or a slice of steaming meat; no one, that is literally no one around, would know, or else everyone would have forgotten or would simply not be interested in such problems. I walked all the crooked, round, and square Moscow alleys; sometimes I would gaze for a long time into the windows of strange houses. A kind of odd force grasped me, I was in emptiness. I didn't even feel like getting out of it. I was too young to understand what was happening: when I went out into life, all turned out to be *wrong*. As if we had ridden on a lift to the tenth floor but, when we got off, it became obvious there was no tenth floor, no walls, floor, or roof, that there was nothing around. And the lift left. I once wrote verse. I was once in love. I had friends who were like me, gay, clever, and swift in their speech. Now I didn't feel like remembering this. I dreamt of nothing. Nothing sparkled around or in me. I felt hungry. I was drowsy. Sometimes before dusk I felt like sitting in Manechka's room.

Manechka was a prostitute who walked Tverskoy Boulevard and lived with us in the communal apartment, one of the first in Moscow, which had belonged to Madame Koshkodavova. In her room, Manechka had a commode, chair, table, and a bed. On the table lay a pack of cards and a box of powder. She had nothing else. So I came to realize that it was possible to live possessing nothing, only a deck of soiled cards and a box of bright rose powder. Manechka sat opposite me and told my fortune. She was permanently astonished that I liked to read. I was always surprised that she liked to stroll near the Pushkin monument. She was careful with me, as if I were a crystal vase. Sometimes I had a great desire to go with her to the Square (this was still the wish to look 'behind her screen'), but she quietly and firmly told me it was out of the question and I did not insist. Madame Koshkodavova said that she 'took dope'. There was no one I could ask what this meant, and so I asked Manechka herself about it.

'Well, so what?' she answered, and looked at me in such a way that I never returned again to this issue.

When I left for the south of Russia, I gave her a gold brooch with a sapphire, a family piece, the only one I had. And much later I told Mother that someone had stolen it from me. In those years it was easy to lie, much easier than now. I see that then I was already doing what I wanted.

'When I left for the south of Russia'. Yes, there, in Nakhichevan the 'grateful Armenians' still ate white bread, and when my father was discharged in Moscow there was nothing left for us except to go on to Orsha and Kiev on our way to Rostov. I took in the news about our departure with complete indifference; never in my life was I so immobile, taciturn, sombre, and lost. In the Rostov station I came out wrapped in a blanket and barefoot: at night between Fastov and Kazatin everything had been taken from me, my suitcase ripped open with a knife. I was particularly ashamed, for some reason, to appear without a hat. Without shoes I mounted the porch of Grandfather's house. It was empty. There was no Grandfather. There was no Selifan. No horses. No dogs. Only furniture standing along the walls under dust covers, and an antique strongbox. I moved into the room with this strongbox, and, as no one could move it from its place, it stayed there; I kept the remainder of my books in it – those I had not managed to give to Manechka and the student on Nikitsky Boulevard.

I was fully aware that bits of me remained; and of Russia, there was still that small territory held by the White Armies where we lived now, without the possibility of meeting or corresponding with those who lived on the other side of the lines in the Civil War. It was said that the war in Europe was coming to an end – only years later did I find out when exactly it did end. I was told that in Paris ladies were wearing short (up to the ankle) skirts, new authors were being published, Shakespeare and Shaw were staged as before in London theatres, in Italy lemon trees were blooming. But in fact it was hard to believe all of this. White bread was reality, college was also. As well as the library, the municipal library of Nakhichevan where you could borrow a novel by Hermann Bang, and Bely's *Petersburg*, Ibsen's *Wild Duck* and Briusov's *Stephanos*. It was on the boulevard. Trees rustled there and the high-school students, pulling their caps on tight to let just a small tuft of hair show on their foreheads, walked about, bumping into girl students. But later, towards night, they all strolled to the gardens of the Municipal Club and the boulevard became deserted and quiet; on a bench under the streetlamps one could smell heliotrope. I imagined that today this was Amsterdam, tomorrow Barcelona, the day after tomorrow Tsarskoe Selo. Virginia sat next to me, reading Peter Altenberg or Max Stirner under the streetlamp and requested only that she be told beforehand where we found ourselves, so as to be sure not to confuse Scotland with the Aegean Sea.

In his diary (for 29 November 1851) Leo Tolstoy wrote:

> I have never been in love with women. [He was 23 at the time.] I have often been in love with men. I was in love with men before I had any understanding of the possibility of *homosexuality* [Tolstoy's italics]; but even when I found out about it, the thought of the possibility of copulation did not cross my mind. A strange example of this attraction, in no way explainable, was Gautier. I became terribly excited when he entered the room. – My love for Islavin spoiled for me as much as eight months of my life in Petersburg. Good looks always had much influence on my choice. However, there was the example of Dyakonov. And I will never forget that night when he and I rode out of Pirogov and when, having wrapped myself in the sleigh blanket, I wanted to kiss him and cry. There was voluptuousness in this feeling, but why it came there it is impossible to know, because, as I said, never has my imagination painted lewd pictures for me. On the contrary I have ['innately' is crossed out] a terrible aversion to that.

Tolstoy in 1851 did not know, as he did not to the very end of his life, that at least half of all people feel this way at one time or other in youth. And so it was with me, though I never 'wanted to cry' and never did love to 'spoil' my life. But I know now that Virginia sometimes wanted to cry. In this her feeling for me was different from my feeling for her.

I saw her the first time at a party; she flirted terribly all evening with a good-looking dark boy (who was later killed in a volunteer detachment fighting the Red Army) and paid no attention to me. That is, the whole evening she observed me without looking at me, while I plainly never took my eyes away from her, not understanding what exactly attracted me to her. She was small, very thin, with huge black eyes, crimson cheeks, and thick hair that hung over her forehead and ears. Later, in the 1920s in Paris, I noticed that the light did not go on in lifts under her weight – the lifts at that time were made so that the light went on automatically when someone went in and the floor gave a little beneath the weight; but she was so thin that the bulb in the lift did not light up. She later spent five years in various sanatoriums in the Pyrenees and died of tuberculosis, having converted to Greek Orthodoxy before her death and changed her name to mine. In Paris she reminded me – with that black hair and those crimson cheeks – of Proust's Albertine. Only Albertine did not have high cheekbones and dark circles under her eyes, the hollow cough, and those hot palms when Virginia's temperature would rise at sunset.

In Nakhichevan I carried her from room to room, listened to her play Medtner and Scriabin; then I would sit or lie with her on a couch and we would speak for hours, as if until our meeting, in Pushkin's words, 'My entire life has been the gauge/Of a sure tryst with you . . .' As if Russia had shattered into pieces only so that we would find one another. I stayed to spend the night, a couch was made up for me, we continued our conversation till two, three in the morning. I had never before experienced such joy simply because I was with someone, in my relations with someone else there had not been such magic, nor a ferment of thoughts which with her poured out in words. I cannot call this friendship, I must place it in the realm of love, a different dimension from the one I had till then accustomed myself to live and feel in. Two kinds of mood were especially common to Virginia: a quiet and deep sadness, and humour. She was susceptible, reflective, and you could not approach her with ordinary criteria. She had never left the little town where she was born (and spent twenty years), and she had just graduated from school (she was always ill, and missed classes for weeks at a time). In 1919 I entered the preparatory class before enrolling at university. Her place in class was next to mine, but she hardly ever came and was kept in seclusion because her weakness made it dangerous for her to be in the bustle of a tram. She played the piano, more by sight-reading than studying, repeating for hours the same piece with eyes full of tears of agitation and ecstasy. Then she would wrap herself in a shawl in a corner of the couch, lower her long lashes, and that wonderful, dazzling yet nevertheless sick and sleepy smile would appear on her face. The scent of Coty's l'Origan, then in fashion and one drop gave us such joy, came from her hair, which fell low on her thin, serious, sometimes sad face.

I sat down next to her, she put her head on my shoulder or I put mine on her knees, and no one entering the room was puzzled when they saw us sitting like that, unable to part for hours – yet I should have gone home long before to study Latin and trigonometry; it was time for her to be in bed; the doctor had ordered her to go to sleep early. Finally in the dark of night I ran past the market square, first past the Russian cathedral, then the Armenian one, then along Sofiskaya Street, and in my head there was only one thought: that we would see each other the next day, when I went to her house or she to mine, and we would be happy to be with each other.

A year later, when the south of Russia fell, we were already living together; she had moved into our house with her whole family. And that night when guns roared and shells exploded, we held each other close out of fear and a sense of the terrible future bearing down on us beyond those nights. I could not then know that in exactly twenty-five years I would again shelter someone at night from falling bombs, seeking always the main wall which, as is said, it is less dangerous to stand near – my trembling hand would again cover frightened (but this time blue) eyes, so that the one who clung to me in the violet light that illuminated terror-stricken Paris, would not see death fly, aiming at our roof.

The south of Russia fell. A detachment of the army of Budenny went past Grandfather's house: on one of the Red Army men a wide ermine stole was fastened with a diamond brooch, while others had white bath towels fastened on with safety pins which from a distance you could mistake for ermine stoles. I stood at the window and looked at them. Virginia was finishing Hamsun's *Pan* and slyly asked me:

'"What is love?"' and quoted: '"It is a breeze rustling in the roses."'

I turned towards her and said portentously that I had long ago considered that problem and it was solved for me for ever: love was *one* artichoke leaf eaten by *two* people. She heard the clatter of hoofs on the pavement, the neighing of horses, and swearing, and said:

'There will be no more artichokes. The artichoke will be forgotten. In dictionaries the entry for it will read: "obs.".'

Searches went on. Men were sent to clean the lavatories in the barracks and Father, putting on a clean starched collar, also went along. Virginia never knew her father: he had abandoned her mother when she was pregnant with her and was now in Erevan, an eminent member of the Party that shot and hanged and searched out those who still wore starched collars.

101

Until the last day, as long as it was possible, I attended Rostov University, the school of philology. I enrolled for Greek, archaeology, art history, linguistics, but in the general disintegration of that year (1920) I rarely managed to concentrate, was bored at lectures and studied little at home. Professors were tormented by fear and hunger; the majority of them, dull and old-fashioned people, came from the evacuated University of Warsaw. At home life gradually ebbed out of Mother and Father – I cannot put this in any other way – at the same time that life seethed in me, demanded expression, action. The worse the oppression became and the greater the deprivation, the more I began to gad about, in my mother's expression, to gad about anywhere with anyone, because with the passing of time I felt surer of myself, freer, and my yardstick for people changed: I no longer sought those who could speak to me about Briusov and Blok, Trotsky, or Scriabin – I accepted those whom chance was sending me and sometimes, in choosing, I sought the simplest, the most spontaneously rough dissipation, not truly picking or preferring anyone.

'The cult of oblivion,' said Virginia. We were not jealous of anyone vis-à-vis one another.

My '*Wanderjahre*', strictly speaking, still continue. With the Germans *Wanderjahre* follow *Lehrjahre*, and then, having returned to the starting point, so to speak, man begins life. With us in Russia, instead of the 'years of wanderings' the majority of people have 'years of dissoluteness' in the various senses of that phrase. To a small degree even I had them. I read no books, hardly wrote verse, I just barely remembered the well and the spring, and in secret despair reconciled myself to the fact that nothing would fall into my lap. About twice that year I nearly became someone's wife, but I thought it was better to run from every serious affair and not surrender my freedom to anyone. I secretly hoped that this matter of the moment could not always continue; I knew all that was mine would return because there was Virginia and those wonderful things we had in common. What would have become of me without her? Without saying anything to me about myself she understood all, but never stopped me when she saw me live and waste myself.

More than anything else in those years I was attracted by the discovery that all people are different and that my relations with them took shape differently, inadvertently, as if I turned varying

sides to people in changing circumstance. I remember that sometimes I had strong passionate relationships when, as Bunin once
said to me, two people waited only for the door to close and the
key to be turned before throwing themselves at each other like
beasts. There was almost love, with someone from Petersburg
with whom something arose like a peaceful common life, comfortable, as if we had already lived together for years. Caring
about the other: Aren't you ill? Aren't you sad? Let's go together,
and eat something nice, lie down, go to sleep, I will sit here for a
while and watch over you . . . There was also a short-lived wild
encounter that upset my pride: smashing everything, pinching and
twisting my arms ('Whom did you leave with yesterday?'), a
heavy fist in the face ('I will crush you! Don't you dare look at
another!'), which I did not relish but I learned something from it:
my own physical weakness and male physical strength.

Yet there were genuinely dramatic moments when S. skilfully
made me fall in love with him. He was more than thirty and
married to a young, pretty woman who treated me affably. He
lived in the second courtyard of a collapsing, yet somehow
spacious house where there were two huge, malicious black dogs
who threw themselves on me when I once went to his home. (On
the corner, where the street runs into Sobornaya, a dead horse lay,
half covered with snow.) These dogs cooled my passion and,
sombrely entering the ante-room, I felt a desire to be far away.
Knowing his wife would not return for a week, I agreed to his
entreaties and went to his place; my mind was restless and not at
all happy. I thought with not a little fear that I had to return
through that same courtyard and that the wolfhounds would tear
me to pieces if he did not accompany me. He was an extraordinary
man, a talented engraver and scholar. I sensed he was head and
shoulders above all the others I knew. A copy of da Vinci's 'Saint
John the Baptist' hung over the couch where he embraced me. (I
sat in a thick coat made from an old curtain; it was very cold, and
his lips were completely blue.) He held me, and in that second I
understood it would have been better for me to have stayed at
home. Pulling me towards him, he suddenly said in a trembling
voice:

'You are my goddess.'

I turned to stone.

'He said: "You are my goddess,"' I said to Virginia, all trembling out of insult and indignation, 'and I had thought that I loved him so much!'

She covered herself with a downy shawl, folded her legs under her as she sat on her couch, and laughed, her hair hanging down her crimson cheeks.

'O-o-o!'

'You understand: those terrifying hounds! Why didn't he tie them up? They nearly bit my calves. And the cold and the whispering: My goddess! Why! he could also have said: My angel!'

'I did not expect this from him,' she said, laughing pensively. 'Who would have thought it! What did you do?'

'I was scared to start howling. I left. You understand that for two months I thought I could not live without him.'

'And the dogs?'

'He had enough sense to accompany me to the gates. They did not pounce.'

We were already laughing, although at the same time I wanted to cry a bit.

Everybody got a job. I left university and also found work, bought rations, rejoiced with warmth when spring came, when there was fish from the Don at the market. The painter Sarian, sticking his two fingers in the gills of one fish, took it home and, before boiling, painted a *nature-morte* from it in oil, surrounding it with onions and carrots. Marietta Shaginian, the writer, in homemade slippers and a jacket that had seen better times, passed pensively beneath our windows, pressing to her chest a huge shankbone which looked as if someone had already picked at it. They both reminded me that there is another life. In the hall where Baptists had recently gathered to sing psalms, poets and artists got together: one *nothingist*, two *fuists*, one *imaginist* and three *egopupists*. Young girls, hungry and sad as I sometimes was, read verse but I did not. I only listened and nothing came to me, nothing bloomed in me, or sprouted as before. And I was not tempted to live as they did: there was already something in me that forced me to prefer a simple line to a broken one, and sometimes I was ashamed of this. Later my profession (and the life it conditioned) often placed me among drunkards, pederasts, drug addicts, neurotics, future suicides, and misfits, half geniuses who found good more boring than evil, and debauchery the indispensable accessory of the *littérateur*. But I gradually became convinced that normal people are much more interesting than these so-called abnormal ones who are never free and are often stereotypes, in conflict with their surroundings, while the normal are sophisticated, liberated, original, and responsible, always absorbing and unforeseeable. Yes, there was already something in me that was not interested in eccentrics. I was ill at ease among *nothingists*, *biocosmists*, and *presentists*, though probably some crumbs would have come my way had I come closer to them. Nothing in them or the world sparkled for me, only near Virginia I felt what was precious and indispensable to me. But she faded with every passing month; her eyes with black rings and her cheeks with the high cheekbones burned. As before she often sat at the piano, sight-reading; it was not from sheet music but manuscripts which a young composer, a tenant of one of our friends, left behind before joining the White Army. The girl said he left her a stack of compositions and asked her to keep them. We knew nothing about him. His name was Sergey Prokofiev. Virginia played the music for entire days. I listened.

From the first day of the Revolution I saw it not merely as a change, but as a fact which I would have to live with for the rest of my life. It could be a change for the bourgeoisie, for tsars, for White generals, for counter-revolutionaries (and it serves them right!), but not for me. I am seventeen, I am nobody – I accept it as that ground on which I will sprout. I know no other. The West? Where is it? The past? I don't need it. The breaking up of the old? I don't want even to remember those bits and broken pieces; let me build with everybody else something new; broken crockery is not for me. That is what I leave behind with my childhood. The future is certainly more important than the past. Someone near me says that all is lost, but I don't believe this, I never will. Bread has disappeared, lard has disappeared, candles have disappeared. The counter-revolution is lost. But we are alive. Aren't we?

At dusk we return from a walk. We both now love to walk far, on warm days, down to the Don River, and we often read books as we walk (I read Nietzsche's *Zarathustra*, promenading through the streets), bumping into passers-by. We return home. The first stars and the perfume of flowering acacia, the 'Appassionata' from an open window of a neighbouring house, birds . . . A pot simmers on the stove, soup is cooking. At that hour soup seems terribly important, more so, perhaps, than anything in the world. This in no way debases me, or offends me. It brings me closer to all those, near and far, who also need soup. I feel my daring fade, I become humble: I am terribly poor – without pretty dresses, books, verse – and I am tremendously rich with that library on the boulevard, my health, my youth, and my thoughts, which I cherish. I believe, I know, that they will be with me forever.

Now I want to do something good. And I do. Yet I am still not good. I am uneducated, unrestrained, flighty. I lie to Mother when I return home at two in the morning, taking my shoes off on the stairs and crawling up to my bed; I do not love children, I do not love old people, I am a coward; I fear I will be kicked out of the office of the Vladikavkaz Railway Administration, where I work, once it is known we live in a house that used to belong to us; and I will be without my ration of flour and herring. I don't want to get married because I don't want to be stuck in this town and because I am scared of getting bored; I don't read verse at the *nothingists'* because I consider myself better than all their bunch.

> Higher, higher, further to the North,
> To the famished plains and frozen woods,
> To the land where for two years the oats are poor,
> For two years the clover is meagre.

They could never have written such lines! Putting on airs, I appear at their soirée of readings and do not open my lips, which I have begun to paint lightly. (Virginia and I bought one lipstick and broke it in two. There were only two colours: yellow and dark crimson. 'Not an artichoke leaf, but still!' she laughed.)

When I get to the edge of the city to a huge typhus hospital to visit S., I don't quite understand why I am doing it. From awareness of my own power? A desire to experience danger? Or do I want to show him that this is what I can do, or perhaps give him some joy? But I no longer love him. All dissolved in the blinking of an eye with that 'goddess', and I don't love his love, his long explanations, monotonous confessions, and dull reproaches. Saying nothing to anyone, I buy a bottle of port (many stores are open) and caviar and take them to him.

The sick lie on beds, on the floor in wards or in corridors, in a once-white lobby, on staircases, on mattresses or without them. The windows are open. It is spring. But the air is heavy. A monotonous murmur is heard – this is delirium, they all talk in a chorus, some clean-shaven, others with thick beards, some half naked . . . I step over them, look for the orderly; in the passage one of those lying down grabs me by the foot and I almost fall on an old man with staring eyes and covered in a frightful rash.

'Where do you think you are going?' asks a dirty hospital attendant; he has a bedpan in his hands. 'Women are not allowed here.'

I shove money and a package into his hands and implore him to find S. Then I wait. Finally the attendant returns. A note in French: '*Je n'oublierai jamais* . . .' I go towards the exit.

'Shake yourself well, or you will carry lice home,' the attendant yells to me.

S. gets better and in two weeks he is home. I listen: will something not tinkle or ring within me? No, I am still. He is nobody to me. On the twelfth day I begin to shiver. No, this is not typhus. I walked a rope over an abyss, and – I did not fall!

Perhaps I did this out of secret anxiety, in search of a pure conscience? Perhaps. But in the desire to walk the tightrope, or lie under a train between the rails, or lean out of the tenth storey, there is always evidence of turmoil, inward drama, growing conflict with one's self. The note '*Je n'oublierai jamais*', however, was perhaps worth the trip? Who knows! I kept it quite a long time.

Then the day of departure arrived. Where? Home, to Petersburg, to Petersburg–Petrograd. Why? I don't know. Perhaps to study (if we are given rations); if not then to get a job. Rations had to be written with a capital R in those years, especially the one for a length of material, galoshes, fine flour. Father will work, Mother will work. And I? We shall see.

Meanwhile, however, I cannot consider myself a parasite: I am given half a freight car by the Railway Administration for the transportation of my family to Petrograd ('to be permanently resettled') and for three weeks we will be coupled to and uncoupled from freight, freight-passenger and passenger (if we are lucky) trains. In Moscow we stand for two days somewhere on the tracks of the Moscow freight line, I see again that huge, hungry, and

107

deformed city. There's the Pushkin monument. Does Manechka still walk there in the evenings? Surely not. A coffee-house has been opened on Tverskaya, and two little pies lie on a plate in the window. I look at them for a long time, but I don't dare go in and buy them. I am a weasel, I am scared that I will be arrested for this: pies are surely baked for local inhabitants. I am only passing through here and I don't have the right to register.

The last days there in the south are still in my memory. With some friends I part for ever; others I will meet again in Petersburg in the autumn. Virginia is in my arms, she is lighter than a feather. Will we see each other? There is no hope of this at all. We have no idea that in five years we will both be in Paris. She will come with her mother after the gloomy years of the first repressions, the first losses, displacements, reductions of living space, arrests. The lift beneath her will not light up. The circles around her eyes will have become deeper, blacker, the huge eyes still bigger. Something will be over-exerted in her, she will be condemned to a slow death in a sanatorium in the mountains, first on the frontier of Spain, then on the Italian frontier. I will go to see her there. She lies on a chaise longue, wrapped up in a blanket. She is very silent and in the evening tells me that a separate room has been taken for me in another wing: the doctor will not allow me to stay in the same room with her. But I lie with her in one bed, where she takes up so little room. I am frightened by the sight of her poor body, her protruding knees and elbows and her seemingly huge feet and hands. I kiss her and embrace her, I tell her she will get better, I drink from her glass, I take her phlegm to the toilet and then wash the spittoon in the basin; I warm her during the night until she begins to get feverish, and then she is all in sweat and I change her shirt. Tears flow from my eyes into the pillow when she finally falls asleep: she is already half gone, not the one she was; I share the artichoke leaf with her not out of love but out of pity. Her brittle bones are still whole, she listens and looks, but how far she is from me now! So imperceptibly she will stop living, as a shadow will move into a shadow, in the huge ward of tuberculars in Laennek Hospital. And on a damp, foggy day she is buried in the Versailles cemetery . . .

The train stopped somewhere on the tracks. It was a clear June evening and Petersburg was sunk in a mist – only the chimneys were visible in the lilac sky. Father and Mother remained with the luggage in the freight car till morning, and I went along the tracks to where I was told I would find the freight-yard building. I walked for a long time by semaphors, pump houses, railway crossings, finally passed through the freight-yard building and walked further along an unpaved road beside some long, stationary trains, hundreds of old freight cars (40 MEN. 8 HORSES. WARSAW – LODZ), empty train platforms, lifeless steam engines. In an hour I came out onto the Alexander III Memorial Square and an inexpressible emotion filled me. Everything appeared smaller than it had been in my memory. Three years had passed, exactly three, and it seemed thirty. The Northern Hotel, old and chipped, looked at me and carts in a file came from the Ligovka. Nevsky Avenue went off to the left and you could make out the Admiralty needle – a fixture of my childhood mythology.

> O my elusive city,
> Why did you rise above the abyss?

The carts now rumbled across the square. People walked along, strange people; there were probably none at all of the familiar ones left. People were beginning to live anew. There were the white nights – I had forgotten they existed. The tsar of my ancestors still sat on his fat nag, and a tram loaded with people was running to the end of Suvorovsky, past the Sands.

> My elusive city,
> Why?

I touched a projection of the station porch. Nothing in me seemed ready for this meeting, for this unspeakable bliss of homecoming.

> My city!

It had belonged to me once and was taken away, and in some unexplainable way I had reconciled myself to losing it. I didn't need its clear June evenings and its foggy squares, I could live without the Bronze Horseman, the Neva, Pushkin, Blok, without history, myth. Poor Lazarus, suffering from leprosy and covered with scabs, is thrown his first crumb by destiny after so much time! I stood transfigured on the steps of the Nikolaevsky Station, trembling at the thought that tomorrow I would touch everything again, rising to life out of my mental torpor – as if embracing again the fate of my native land, the wounds of my city, being resurrected to existence not from day to day but century to century.

My mother's sister and her daughter Zhenia (one of the first women to study at the Technological Institute, who a year later committed suicide because of an unsuccessful love affair) lived behind the Tavrichesky Garden, and from their windows you could see the Smolny and that side of the city unknown to me. The clock was three and a half hours fast: when I went to bed the sun was still promenading from room to room and when I awoke it was high in the sky; Smolny was again in the window and all around was the city, my city, returned to me, the city I belonged to once more despite the fact that in the office we went to the next day to register they did not want to believe at all that we had come for good and, apparently, they wanted to send us to Petrozavodsk to resettle there. It took two full days to fill out the questionnaires. I felt like screaming: It is I! Don't you recognize me? Look at me! Finally we received a registration-certificate, ration cards of the last category, the right to a dwelling-place . . . But the whole city was now my dwelling-place, what were nine square metres to me! The Summer Garden, and the quays, the arch on Galernaya Street, and that bend of the Moika which, like the outlines of a dear face, I recognized, overwhelmed by emotions.

I walked about, sat in gardens, I touched stones, stood on the bridges, I was in the harbour, on Krestovsky Island, at cemeteries: I recognized the intersections, learned to see what I had forgotten in a fresh way. How unlike my Moscow 'gadding about' these walks were! There was a rumbling in my stomach as before, but in Moscow I had been alien to everything, unloved, unhappy, and here I was rich because the city was mine; all my salvation – as I then understood – was in sticking to it, holding on to it: the Tavrichesky Garden which I could not escape wherever I went, Chernishev Bridge with its chains and Rastrelli Street, the quiet lines of Vasilievsky Island, where opposite the familiar house of the van der Fleets grass grew and someone's goat grazed, its udder shaking.

At midnight (when in fact it was only eight-thirty) the sun was high in the sky, but it was necessary to go to bed. We had settled in a communal apartment that had once belonged to Glinka's descendants; we occupied two rooms and during the summer I had my own room. Glinka's family also lived in two rooms, and the remaining two were occupied by some obscure people. But I was rarely home. Father and Mother went to work, and I submitted papers to the Institute of the History of Arts (called Zubovsky), on Senatsky Square. July came.

The summer of 1921. In the pearly flood of the white nights, in the quiet of sleepy streets (there were of course no cab drivers and very few trams), a few pedestrians walked by without hurrying, ragged and with emaciated faces. Houses were crumbling and at night doors and flooring were carried off by neighbours, diaphanous children waited to be given pencils to practise writing. Front doors were boarded up; in the large house where we rented rooms the passage to the Manezhny was nailed shut – you came and went via Kirochnaya. But Nevsky Avenue began to sparkle, and in the corner shop where the windows were still broken and boarded up yesterday, it suddenly became possible to buy a roll, a flower, a book – an old volume brought out of a dusty basement or a new one that had just appeared.

I found some of my old friends. The Shklovskys were in Finland, and Natasha, who had recently come out of prison, lived with her mother. Esther, beautiful and elegant, hardly looked at me – clearly she was not interested in old acquaintances. Osya was in Moscow, married and a member of the Party. The other Natasha, in the old house on Vasilievsky Island, had rushed from Isadora Duncan's dancing to painting; she sang, composed verse, did some sculpture, and was preparing to get married. Lola Zeiliger was not in the city. But I felt so new, so unlike the person I was three years before, that all this seemed completely natural to me. I accepted it calmly. And as I set off for the house on Vasilievsky Island, I dreamt only about taking books from there which had been promised to me long ago, perhaps to keep.

Her grandmothers were no longer alive. There was no father. The son was in Siberia and I didn't ask whether he had gone to join Kolchak's army or had been sent there to a camp or had himself fled there, forced to hide. I was led to the shelves: Take what you want, as many as you think you can carry. For four days I took books from Vasilievsky Island to Kirochnaya, and then placed them in the cabinet where Glinka's descendant had kept volumes of appellate court decisions. When I came to collect books for the fourth time, the granddaughter of the Decembrist Ivashev looked at me attentively:

'You know where you must go? To the poets.'

'?'

'To the Writers' House, on Basseinaya Street. It will be good for you. What are you doing always alone!'

I went to the Writers' House on Basseinaya Street, but found no poets there. Confused, I made inquiries. The Poets' Union had moved to the Muruzi house, on Liteiny Avenue. Their hours were from seven to eight.

'In the morning?' I said, astonished.

'No, in the evening,' came the answer, calmly.

But I took my time. What would I take to the poets? My childhood verse? Or 'higher, higher, further to the North'? Or the recently written, 'If tomorrow you are together'? This seemed to me forced: 'I will not say a word to you/I will only look . . .' I was jealous of someone, apparently, down there in the south. 'You will never find out.' How poor this was! Only the end had something, perhaps: 'And avidly shall I detect/The marks of your embraces/In the folds of her dress/Which you have helped her put on.' But why did he help her put on the dress? At the worst he could have helped her button it up, fasten the hooks . . .

In those years the House of Arts was on the corner of Nevsky and Moika, in the former Eliseev house. There was the main floor with a concert hall, reception rooms, library, kitchen, and there were apartments (perhaps five or six) converted to dormitories for scholars and writers, young and old. In one of the rooms that summer Prince Ukhtomsky, Uncle Serezha, lived, a first cousin of Mother's, the sculptor of clouded birth, son of Olga Dmitrievna, to whose home I had once gone on a tram with Grandfather. He was married to Evgenia Pavlovna, née Korsakova, granddaughter of a former serf; an invitation came from Evgenia Pavlovna, whom I hardly knew, to come to a reception with dancing on Sunday afternoon (10 July). I went with Mother.

That day I saw only the 'gala' rooms of the Eliseevs' house, gilded and decorated inside and out. There were about fifty guests in the halls, and the former Eliseev servants served tea and some greyish biscuits on heavy silver trays. A lot of young people came, but I do not remember anyone except Yury Sultanov, whom I danced with: he was the son of old Madame Sultanova (they lived next to the Ukhtomskys' room, in the dormitories on this very floor). Aleksandr Benois (at that time with a large beard) and his brother, Albert Nikolaevich, sat at two concert pianos at different ends of the hall, and a Strauss waltz thundered out from the raised lids. Sun sparkled on the gilding, the four-hundred-pound chandeliers rang out, and the Stroganov Palace looked in on us through the windows, a red flag over its decaying entrance.

'Come again,' said Evgenia Pavlovna, 'and without fail go to the Muruzi house. Gumilev and the whole Guild of Poets are there; they give readings. They read their poetry.'

Anna Vrubel (who also lived in the house) and the art historian Valerian Chudovsky, with a bandaged hand (he was squeamish about offering it to people), both smiled at me with sympathy, and Sultanova (who had known Turgenev well) invited me to pay a visit; Akim Volynsky, lean-faced, frightfully slim, in a hand-me-down coat (or had he grown that thin?) kissed my hand.

Gods dwelt here, and I was visiting gods. The gods played Strauss and ate biscuits. I danced among the gods, and Eliseev's cupids watched me from the ceiling.

Yet I still waited several days and only on the evening of 15 July did I go to the Poets' Union. I came early, not quite seven. It was half dark on the stairs with wide stairwells. I waited. A secretary appeared – mother of the poet Sergey Kolbasiev (whom Georgy Ivanov, in *Petersburg Winters*, without special grounds wrote about as an informer). The secretary looked like Catherine II, made up, hair in curls, fat; her little desk and chair stood on the first-floor landing, in front of the entrance to the Union premises (which consisted of two reception rooms and a hall). She heard me out and told me to bring ten poems, which would be examined by the presidium. The president Gumilev and the secretary Georgy Ivanov would have to discuss them. 'And if the verse is suitable,' said the fat woman indifferently, 'then you will be accepted into the Union.'

On the 19th I appeared with my re-copied verse and stealthily put the envelope on her desk, preparing to run down the stairs unnoticed. But she saw me, floated out onto the landing and took the envelope. Straightening her coiffure, without looking at me, she ordered me to fill out a questionnaire for entering the Union. Making blots with the scratchy post-office pen, I filled it out and looked inquisitively at Catherine II. She ordered me to come the following week to find out if 'the verse was suitable'.

Why the following week? And what would become of me if the verse was 'not suitable'?

I returned home through the Tavrichesky Garden where the nightingales sang. The sun was still high above the trees and houses. Petersburg's squalor lay quiet and immobile: the whole city then was majestic, silent and dead, like the cathedral of Chartres or the Acropolis.

On 27 July I entered the Muruzi house about ten minutes before the verse soirée began. I went straight to the reception room, where Georgy Ivanov came up to me and, having found out that my envelope must be somewhere there, led me to Gumilev. Tall, he looked down on me with his light blue, squinting eyes. His skull, stretching upwards like a cupola, made his face still longer. He was interestingly ugly, I would say somewhat terrifying in his unattractiveness: long hands, a speech defect, a haughty look in which one eye always stared blankly and to one side. He assessed me with his eye, lingered for a second over my bosom and legs, and they both went out, closing the door behind. 'They have gone to deliberate,' said Nikolai Otsup to me. He recalled that he had seen me once on a visit to his sister's. 'It was so very very long ago,' I said hurriedly to make these minutes easier for him. 'You cannot remember me. I was a schoolgirl then.'

'Nadia now works in the Cheka,' he said calmly, looking at me in a friendly way. 'She walks about in a leather jacket and carries a revolver. I ran into her not long ago in the street. She said that people like me should be shot, and that's what they're doing.'

Gumilev came back. I stood up. The verse was suitable – that is, four lines in all out of what I had brought:

> And avidly shall I detect
> The marks of your embraces
> In the folds of her dress
> Which you have helped her put on.

There were about twenty-five people in the hall where the

audience was listening. Georgy Adamovich was reading 'Marya, where are you now?' and I went to listen. Suddenly I was calm. I felt in complete harmony with myself and all that surrounded me. I had moved in a certain direction and now tranquillity covered me like a wave.

Immediately after the reading (Gumilev read, as did Ivanov, Otsup and one Neldikhen – who appeared in a velvet smock, with long hair, very decorous and with a splendid voice), Gumilev invited me for a cup of tea. We were served two glasses in holders and some pastry. ('He was a miser,' Georgy Ivanov said to me later, 'and when I saw that he treated you to some pastry I thought it was suspicious.') No one came over to us. We sat alone in a corner of the huge reception room, and I realized that to approach Gumilev when he sat with a woman he had chosen was not done. There was subordination. Gumilev unexpectedly spoke about it:

'Discipline is indispensable. I am the company commander here. Rank respects rank. In poetry it's the same thing, even stricter. Subordination, submission.'

I said nothing. I listened with curiosity, carefully looking for a smile on his face, but there was only the one fleeing eye and the other that impressively drilled through me.

'I created Akhmatova, I created Mandelstam. Now I am creating Otsup. I can, if I want, create you.'

Embarrassment grew in me. I was scared of offending him by smiling and at the same time could not believe all this was being said in earnest. Meanwhile his voice rang out dryly and, when he was silent, his face was completely immobile. Then again the speech, like dog barks, would pick up. He thought, in vain it seemed to me, that there was something military in the Poets' Guild. It was neither a squadron nor a platoon, its members rather recalled (in their relation to the Guild leader) the *petits-maîtres* and courtesans at a Louis's court.

'I am a monarchist. I cross myself when I see a church. If you do what I order, you can become a poet . . . But for this you must cease loving the symbolists.'

I suddenly burst into laughter. It seemed to me it was still a little early to give me an order about whom to love and whom not to. He looked at me angrily and in that same hard tone did not utter but somehow 'issued a command' about my face and legs.

My embarrassment began to turn into petrification. I shoved my legs under the couch, hid my hands under the table, only my face was turned to him, and probably in my eyes there was a prayer: Please turn all this into a joke. But he didn't notice it.

We sat so close that in appearance all was peaceful, but between us sparks of unfriendliness flew. Again he began to speak:

'I have classes in the House of Arts. There I teach young poets' (he said *po-ats*) 'to write verse. I will teach you to write verse. You don't know how to write verse.'

'Thank you, Nikolai Stepanovich,' I said quietly. 'I will come without fail to your classes.'

'Who is your favourite poet?' he barked out all of a sudden.

I was silent: I didn't want to lie, it wasn't he.

He took my hand and stroked it. I now felt that I wanted to go home. But he said he would like to go for a walk on the quays with me the following day. Since he had returned to Petersburg he often went to look at the Neva but he hadn't seen enough of it. He liked to caress the stones of the city. Near the urn in the Summer Garden, at three. All right? In those weeks I was also 'caressing' the city stones.

'Perhaps the day after tomorrow?'

'Tomorrow, at three.'

I stood up, gave him my hand. He led me to the doors.

My composure was not destroyed. I calmly walked out to the street and went home. Kolbasiev came to accompany me. He told me how he and Gumilev had met and become friends in the Crimea. I couldn't understand why all he said to me while we walked down the Liteiny was utterly uninteresting to me.

The following day I was at the urn at three.

At first we sat on a little bench and conversed quietly, calmly, in a very friendly way. I even compelled him to admit that Akhmatova had created herself, that he had been a hindrance in this, and that yesterday he had told me he created her only to shock me. He spoke about Paris, the war years in France, then about the Poets' Union and the Guild. All this was so nice that I didn't want to move from under the thick trees. After a while we went to the Petropolis bookstore and on the way he asked if I had Annensky's *Cypress Chest*, Kuzmin, Sologub's last book, and his own. I said I didn't have the Sologub or Annensky. While I searched the shelves he picked out five or six books and I, glancing inadvertently, saw that he had chosen *Cypress Chest* among them. A dim suspicion stirred in me, but of course I said nothing; we walked out and went along the streets to the quays, turning in the direction of the Hermitage. The day was clear, windy, cool; we walked and looked at a little steamer moving up the Neva, at the water, boys running up and down the granite stairs from the pavement to the river and back. Suddenly Gumilev stopped and said rather solemnly:

'Promise me that you will unquestioningly carry out my request.'

'Certainly not,' I answered.

He was astonished and asked if I was scared of him. I said I was a little. He was pleased by this. Then he offered me the books.

'I bought them for you.'

I recoiled from him. The thought of having Sologub and Annensky dimmed my reason for a second, but only for a second. I told him I could not accept a present from him.

'I already have all these books,' he continued insistently and with anger, 'I picked them for you.'

'I cannot,' I said, turning away. All my young principles suddenly, like fireworks, burst in the sky and illuminated me and him. I felt that not only could I not take anything from him but I didn't want to.

Then he suddenly lifted the books high and with a grand gesture threw them into the Neva. I screamed out loudly, the boys whistled. The books floated on the blue water. I saw birds sit on them and sink them. Slowly we walked on further.

I became very sad. We said good-bye somewhere and I walked home, going over this second meeting in my thoughts. The following day I was again at the Poets' Union, and on the following day, the 30th of July. When I went with him to the Universal Literature Publishing House, a membership card in the Union was made out for me. Gumilev signed it. It is still among my papers.

Then there were two days, 31 July and 1 August, when we went again to the Summer Garden, sat on a granite bench near the Neva, and spoke of Petersburg, Annensky, himself, and what would happen to all of us. He recited some verse. Towards evening, having grown hungry, we went to the Polish café near the Moika. We had to go down a few steps as the café was in a basement. We drank coffee, ate pastry, and remained silent for a long time. The closer he moved his face towards mine the harder it was for me to choose which of his eyes to look into. I remember how later, in Berlin, I was once having supper at Victor Shklovsky's with Roman Jakobson, who also looks in different directions with each eye. Everyone was having a good time and Roman, who sat opposite me at the table and had just been introduced to me, covered his left eye with one hand and yelled out, laughing: 'Look into the right one! Forget about the left one! The right one is the important one with me, it looks at you! . . .' But there was no humour in Gumilev, he took everyone in general and himself in particular very seriously; at times he seemed to me a conservative elderly gentleman who probably still wore tails and a top hat sometimes.

He then told me, in that Polish café where we ate pastry, that he had bought a black oilcloth notebook, where he would write verse to me. He had written some yesterday. He would not read it to me now, but would tomorrow. There was something there about the white dress I had worn yesterday (made out of an old curtain). I was troubled and he noticed it. Slowly and in silence we went to the Kazan Cathedral and walked a long time there, in the colonnade; then we sat on the steps, and he said I had to come now to his place in the House of Arts where he lived, but I did not go and went home instead, having promised him I would come the following day to the 'Resounding Shell' (his class) at three. This was where he taught one how to write verse (which so irritated Blok). Students had studied with him the whole of the past winter (1920–21) and now 'knew how to write'.

'And you will know how,' he added, 'if you listen to me.'

Leaning against one of the columns he put his hand on my head and ran it over my face, over my shoulders.

'No,' he said when I recoiled. 'You are terribly wise, grown up, serious, and dull. While I have remained as I was at twelve. I am a schoolboy of the seventh grade. And you don't want to play with me.'

This rang false. I answered that even when I was a child I didn't much like to play, and now I was happy not to be twelve any longer.

I left him in the colonnade angry and displeased. I myself was also displeased with that day, and decided not to meet him again. But of course I went to his class. There was another guest besides me, Nikolai Tikhonov. Gumilev valued him and accepted him into the union the same day as me.

Classes were held in the House of Arts. It was Tuesday, 2 August. Why the meeting was moved from Monday to Tuesday I do not remember, but it was an exception. There was a long table in one of the Eliseev drawing rooms and they all sat around it, reading verse 'in a circle' as was then the custom. The two Nappelbaum sisters were there, and Shura Fedorova (later Kostia V.'s wife), Vera Lurie, Olga Ziv (later a children's writer), Kostia V., Nikolai Chukovsky, and five or six more, all those who were represented in the group photograph around Gumilev: the picture was taken in the spring of 1921 by the photographer Nappelbaum, father of Ida and Frieda. Every member of the group published for the first time, and some for the last, in the collection *The Resounding Shell*, which apparently did not reach libraries in the West. It was brought out in the autumn of 1921, two months after the death of Gumilev and dedicated to his memory; it is doubtful that it ever went on sale.

Kostia, Nikolai Chukovsky, and Frieda were better than the others. She read:

> I shall open the doors and the windows,
> The wind will blow through my hair –
> I pretend that the coast has vanished
> Behind the blue line over there.

I immediately became friends with Chukovsky (Korney Chukovsky's son). He was then seventeen, fat and ashamed of it. Kostia V. was very quiet and sad (later he would remind me in some way of Zoshchenko) and wrote a strange verse, somewhat delirious:

> I enter the library, I enter,
> Words fly around in the library when I enter.

A man named Volkov read his review of Gumilev's *Fiery Pillar*, which had just then come out (and had also been drowned by him in the Neva). The review was written in rhythmic prose. Tikhonov sat glumly and left soon.

After the 'class' Gumilev suggested that the students play blind man's buff; we started to run around him with enjoyment, after blindfolding him with a handkerchief. I could not force myself to run together with all of them – the game seemed to me rather strained. I wanted more verse, conversations about verse, but I feared my refusal would seem offensive to them and I didn't know what to do. In the end I forced myself to join the players, though suddenly I became bored by the running about and I was happy when it came to an end: there was something false in it. After the game Gumilev took us to his room. Some left and about five of us remained. The room was large, along the walls stood long narrow couches – this was the Eliseev ante-room, outside the sauna; in the sauna, surrounded by tiled walls, Marietta Shaginian lived. When the others left, he stopped me, made me sit down, and showed me the black notebook. 'Tonight, I know, I will write again,' he said, 'because since yesterday I have been unbearably sad, as I haven't been for a long time.' And he read his verse, written to me on the first page of this notebook:

> I only laughed at myself,
> I only deceived myself,
> When I thought that there was in this world
> Anyone else but you.
>
> All white and all in white,
> Attired as a goddess of old,
> You alone hold the crystal sphere
> In your slender transparent hand.
>
> And all the oceans and mountains,
> Archangels, flowers, men –
> They are mirrored deep in the pools
> Of girlish transparent eyes.
>
> Strange that there is in this world
> Anyone else but you,
> That I am not only a song,
> A sleepless song about you.
>
> This light behind your shoulders,
> It is such blinding light;
> The two long flames rise slowly,
> Like a pair of golden wings.

I felt embarrassed in the ante-room next to this man to whom I did not dare say a tender or simply friendly word. I thanked him. He said: 'That's all?' Obviously he didn't at all suspect that I felt distant and ill at ease with him.

When I started to leave he came out with me. He said that these days it was painful for him to be alone, that we would again go and eat pastry in the basement café. We went, and all his sadness that evening – I don't know how – passed into me. For a long time he wouldn't let me go; finally we left and walked across Senate Square to the Bronze Horseman, where we sat for a long time, until it got dark. Later he accompanied me through the entire city. I didn't know what to do: let all this gradually melt, dissolve, keep silent, and in the coming days move away, or tell him he must think up a different form and content for our relationship? Never, it seemed, had I been in such a difficult position: up to then, between myself and a man, there had always been an understanding about what was right and wrong, what was possible and impossible. Here there was an unhearing wall: the self-assurance of a mentor, the false grandeur and complete absence of sensitivity. As happens during such occasions, I wanted at times to be thirty leagues away but I was also conscious that this was a great poet. 'I do not admit friendship with women,' he said, as if inadvertently, 'I do not seek friendship with you.'

Why am I here with him? I immediately asked myself. At the same time I blamed myself for not being able to dispel his endless gloom, as he put it, feeling that his sadness more and more spilled over into me, and I became inwardly more stubborn, sluggish, tense.

'I am now going to write verse about you,' he said to me as we parted.

I went through the house gates, knowing that he stood by and watched me. Mastering my feelings, I stopped, turned towards him and said simply and calmly: 'I thank you for everything, Nikolai Stepanovich.' At night in bed I decided never to see him again. And I never did meet him again, because at dawn on 3 August, a Wednesday, he was arrested.

'I found among the papers of Nikolai Stepanovich,' Georgy Ivanov said to me a month later, 'a black oilcloth notebook, and there is in all one poem in it. Do you know about this notebook?'

'Yes,' I answered.

'Would you like to have it?'

But as I could not accept books from Gumilev, so I could not accept his verse. I thanked Ivanov and refused.

I did not want questions or guesses. I never returned to this subject with Ivanov again: he published the verse in the last Guild volume in Berlin in 1923.

I now had to work out what had happened. I saw that my path had suddenly crossed with that of a man of the remote past, who not only did not understand his own time, but didn't even try to, as he didn't understand me. He said that he was a monarchist, that he crossed himself when looking at a church, and persuaded one that he was happy in feeling he was still twelve years old. All this was so foreign to me, so 'anti-I' that it seemed incredible when I discovered Gumilev was only thirty-five: in my naïveté I imagined him to be fifty. Incidentally, his face, as often happens with ugly people, appeared ageless.

In a few days I left home, not knowing at all where to go, but not wanting to stay. In those days I was very alone; friendship with Nikolai Chukovsky, Ida, and Lev Lunts only came at the beginning of autumn. I left, walked the streets, and thought of dropping in at the Writers' House, perhaps to learn something new there about Gumilev's fate. On the way I waited in a gateway for the rain to stop. I could in no way master myself, I was overcome by black melancholy. In my entire life there have probably been no more than fifty such days, when you don't know where to fit yourself in and you understand that no one can help you in any way: you anticipate nothing except that things will get a little better, night will come, and then you will fall asleep as if it were a toothache that it is necessary to endure until something changes deep inside you. Yet nothing moves, all is dead, frozen, turned to wood, and everything aches – but in the final account: I don't give a damn!

I walked along Basseinaya to the Writers' House. It was Sunday (and the eve of my birthday), about three o'clock. Perhaps I hoped to meet someone and learn something new about those who had been arrested the same morning as Gumilev – among others, Uncle Serezha Ukhtomsky, the publisher of *Speech* named Bak, Professor Lazarevsky, all of whom I knew personally. I went in at the front street door. It was empty and quiet. Through the glass door that opened onto the garden, the tree foliage was visible (the Writers' House, like the House of Arts, was in a former private residence). I saw an announcement in a black frame hanging among others: 'Today, the 7th of August, Aleksandr Aleksandrovich Blok passed away.' The announcement was still damp, it had just been stuck there.

I was seized by a feeling, which I never again experienced, that I was suddenly and sharply orphaned. The end is near . . . We will remain alone . . . The end is coming. We are lost . . . Tears spurted out of my eyes.

'What are you crying about, mademoiselle?' asked a thin little man with a huge hooked nose and beautiful eyes. 'Blok?'

This was Boris Khariton, whom I did not then know. Later he became an émigré, the editor of a Riga evening newspaper. The Soviets, after taking Riga, deported him in 1940 to the Soviet Union, where he died.

He went out to the street, taking out a handkerchief. I went after him.

Slowly I walked towards Liteiny, turned at Simeonovsky and the Fontanka. On the corner of Simeonovsky and the quay I stopped by a florist. Indeed, I remember my astonishment that in Petersburg there was a florist open. Eating-houses and second-hand shops had been started; there was something like a hardware shop on Vladimirsky and a hairdresser's in the second courtyard of a building on Troitsky. But the flower shop, it seemed to me, had not been here on Tuesday when I passed by with Gumilev; now it was open and there were flowers in it. I went in. I don't remember if I had ever entered a flower shop before, perhaps this was the first time. Petersburg florists were once among my childhood fairy-tale places. Paris florists . . . New York florists . . . All have their character. I had a little money. I bought four long-stemmed lilies. There was no wrapping paper in the store, and I carried the lilies to the Priazhka unwrapped. And I thought: Passers-by guess where I am going and to whom I am bringing flowers, they read the announcements stuck at street corners, they already know the news, and will follow me; in a subdued crowd we will arrive – the whole city – at Blok's house.

Somewhere on the corner of Kazanskaya I took a tram and when I got off at the very end of Ofitserskaya Street, I realized that I had never in my life been here and I did not know this neighbourhood at all. The river Priazhka, the green shores, factories, one-storey houses, grass on the streets, and for some reason not a soul. A ghostly, quiet part of Petersburg, where there is a smell of the Baltic Sea – or does it only seem so to me?

The office for the dead was set for five; I arrived about ten minutes earlier. So that had been in store for me on that lugubrious day! Grieving and not knowing what to do with myself, I could not divine that this day – day and month – would never be forgotten, that it would grow in the mind of people into a *date*, and that this date would live as long as Russian poetry. A big, old, and neglected house. The entrance under the gateway. A staircase, the door to the apartment half open. I enter the dark hallway, on the right is the door to his study. I go in. I put the flowers on the blanket and retire to a corner. There for a long time I stand and look at him.

He no longer resembles the portraits I keep in books, nor that live man who once read, on a stage:

To the marshy, deserted meadows . . .

The hair has become dark and thin, the cheeks emaciated, the eyes have sunk. The face is overgrown with a dark and thin beard, the nose has become sharper and more prominent. Nothing remains, nothing. An 'unknown corpse' lies there. The hands are bound, the feet too, the chin presses into the chest. Two or three candles burn. The furniture has been taken away. In the almost square room, near the wall to the left of the door is a book cabinet; behind the glass are books. The sun plays on the window, the green sloping shore of the Priazhka is visible. Nadezhda Pavlovich enters (a week ago she had flashed by me at the House of Arts), then Pyast comes, and someone else. I see them entering, I know only a few; only about two months later would I identify them all.

Propping herself up on her hand in the manner of a peasant woman, Pavlovich, with her head inclined, looks him straight in the face for a long time. Evgenia Knipovich comes in, eyes swollen with tears, light-haired, dark-browed; Georgy Annenkov, the painter, Blok's mother, and Liubov Dmitrievna enter. The tiny mother with a little red nose sees no one. Liubov seems to me tall, too stout. The priest arrives, puts on his robes in the hallway, and enters with a psalm-reader. This is the first office for the dead. As it takes place, I see Marietta Shaginian, then several men enter suddenly (K. Chukovsky, Zamiatin). In all there are twelve or fifteen. We all stand to the right and left of him – some between the book cabinet and the window, others between the bed and the door. Many years later Marietta Shaginian will write in her memoirs about these moments: 'A young girl brought the first flowers.' Zamiatin also remembered this. There were no other flowers, and mine probably lay alone that whole first night at his feet.

> On the blanket the first flowers
>
> . . . .
>
> Five years ago . . .

This is from my verse of 1926.

Then I left. Again Ofitserskaya, Kazanskaya, the tramway platform. Someone had come to our house, and now we were all drinking 'tea' (an infusion of grated carrots) and eating black bread. My twentieth birthday was being celebrated: the next day was a weekday and no one would be free.

The funeral was on Wednesday, the 10th. There for the first time I saw Bely. He, Pyast, Zamiatin, and others were carrying the coffin high on their shoulders, and descended to the sound of loud choir-singing (which always burst out so powerfully from Russian apartments onto the staircases during the bearing-out; the choir followed the deceased, modulating and droning on, as if rejoicing that finally the corpse had rushed out of his dwelling and was now floating in the air, feet first). Liubov led Blok's mother by the arm, the priest shook his censer, all turned onto the street at the gateway. A crowd had already begun to grow. Bigger and bigger. Dark, hatless – along the Priazhka, round the corner, to the Neva, across the Neva, across Vasilievsky Island to Smolenskoe cemetery. About five hundred people crawled along the sunny, hot streets, the coffin swayed on their shoulders, an empty hearse bobbed up and down on the cobblestone pavement, soles shuffled. Traffic stopped, a warm wind blew from the Gulf of Finland, and we walked and walked. Probably there was not a man in this crowd who did not think – if only for a moment – that not only Blok had died, but this city was dying with him, its special power over people was coming to an end, a historical period was closing, a cycle of Russian destinies was being completed, an epoch was stopping to turn and rush off to other predicaments.

Then all quieted down. For two weeks we lived in complete, as if underground, silence. We spoke in whispers. I went to the Muruzi house, to the Writers' House, to the House of Arts. Everywhere there was silence, waiting, uncertainty. The 24th of August arrived. Early in the morning when I was still in bed, Ida Nappelbaum came over to tell me that on the street corners an announcement had been posted: all have been shot – Ukhtomsky, and Gumilev, and of course Tagantsev – sixty-two people altogether. That August was not only 'like a yellow flame, like smoke' (Akhmatova), that August was a boundary line. An age had begun with the 'Ode on the Taking of Khotin' (1739), and had ended with August 1921; all that came afterwards (for still a few years) was only the continuation of this August: the departure of Bely and Remizov abroad, the departure of Gorky, the mass exile of the intelligentsia in the summer of 1922, the beginning of planned repressions, the destruction of two generations – I am speaking of a two-hundred-year period of Russian literature. I am not saying that it had all ended, but an age of it had.

Ida and I held hands as we stood in front of the displayed newspaper, on the corner of Liteiny. There, in those lines, our fate was written as well. Ida would lose her husband in the Stalin terror, I would never return. There all this was printed, but we were not able to make it out.

In the Kazan Cathedral there was a requiem for the sixty-two killed. Many people came and many tears were shed. Autumn arrived, lectures began at the Zubovsky Institute (as it was still called). The department of philology was in Galernaya Street, immediately beyond the arch. The classrooms were small; hungry and cold, we crowded around the table. The lectures began at about four and continued until about seven or eight: Tomashevsky, Eichenbaum, Bernstein, others . . . (that winter Tynianov was in Moscow). About verse, the word, the sound, about language, Pushkin, contemporary poetry, the eighteenth century, Tiutchev . . . The theory of literature. A few are still alive from those who sat next to me at the large table and saw Sergey Bernstein roll 'goat's legs' – special screws made out of a bit of newspaper and tobacco, not long, but round – and then with a hole in them so that they could be smoked better. Tomashevsky's coat is all patched, his eyes are swollen; Eichenbaum, transparent from starvation, has soles tied by a cord. Young Tolstoy, Flaubert, Stendhal . . . I go on foot from Kirochnaya to Galernaya and back on evenings that are already dark, rainy and cold. A turned wadded coat, a green cap 'à la Monomakh', boots sewn to order by the widow of some former minister out of a piece of broadloom (which once, it seems, lay in someone's 'boudoir'), with bronze buttons ripped off someone's court uniform. On Mondays now the workshop of Korney Chukovsky assembles, on Thursdays that of Mikhail Lozinsky who lectures at the House of Arts on the techniques of verse translation. I no longer have my own room; we have only one small stove and if there had been a second it would have made no difference since we wouldn't have had the wood to heat it. I move into my parents' room: their two beds, my couch, a table with the eternal kasha on it, potatoes which we eat in their skins, a badly baked ration of coarse black bread. Here the primus stove buzzes with the boiling kitchen towels and rags, which never dry out. Laundry, torn and always grey, is hanging on a line; in a corner (of the former Glinka drawing room), heaped up to the ceiling, lie the logs we have managed to get and which diminish with each day. A pipe from the stove goes through the whole room and out to a stone air-vent. Sometimes a black stinking liquid drips from it onto my open volume of Baratynsky, into the barley soup, or onto my nose.

Ida had a flat on the seventh floor on Nevsky, almost at the corner of Liteiny. It was a huge attic, and half was occupied by the photography studio of her father. Someone in the autumn of 1921 spilled some water in it, where it froze so that all winter there was a skating rink in the middle of the studio. Ida's father, sisters, and brothers, big and small, lived in the flat. It was cosy. Mama was there – a 'real mama', as Ida would say – fat, kind, always smiling, hospitable, and quiet. It was decided to give the first room on the left of the entrance to 'Mondays' (in memory of Gumilev and his Monday workshop, the Resounding Shell). Here poets and their friends were supposed to gather for readings and discussions of poetry. Two uncurtained windows looked out onto roofs of Nevsky Avenue and Troitskaya Street. In the room were a piano, couches, taborets, chairs, boxes, and a real little iron stove, and on the floor lay a rug sacrificed by someone. Right up to the spring we gathered once a week in this room. A huge enamel tea kettle boiled on the stove, 'tea' was poured into mugs and glasses, a hunk of black bread was given to everyone. Akhmatova ate that bread, as did Sologub, and all of us, after we had read verse 'in a circle'. In the spring when it got warm we drank water and went through the open windows onto the narrow balcony – that is, the narrow edge of the roof – and, trying not to look down, sat there when it was crowded in the room. Sometimes twenty or twenty-five people would gather.

'Who is coming today?' I asked, arranging the stools, while Nikolai Chukovsky tried to hammer a nail into the wall, and the Serapion Brother Lev Lunts and Ida in turn blew into the stove where damp logs hissed. Gods and demi-gods came. At first the Radlovs, Nikolai and Sergey, then Nikolai Evreinov, then Mikhail Kuzmin, Korney Chukovsky, Mikhail Lozinsky, the young members of the Serapion Brotherhood – Zoshchenko, Fedin, Kaverin, Tikhonov (who had joined up that year with the Serapions). In October, Akhmatova came, and after her Sologub. Evgeny Zamiatin and Yury Verkhovsky visited more than once, and Akim Volynsky and Vladimir Pyast (Blok's friend) were frequent guests. Of course the entire 'Shell' and the Guild (Georgy Ivanov, Georgy Adamovich, Nikolai Otsup). Valentin Krivich (Innokenty Annensky's son) attended, as did Benedikt Livshitz, Nadezhda Pavlovich, and Ada Onoshkovich (Kipling's translator), whom I sat next to at Lozinsky's seminar.

I now met Nikolai Chukovsky almost daily. After the lectures at the Zubovsky Institute I usually dropped in at the House of Arts where he waited for me. He was seventeen, I had just turned twenty. I called him by his first name, he used my first name and patronymic, sometimes tenderly adding 'dearest'. He was a talented and gentle young man, or rather boy, fat, dark-haired, lively. The popularity of his father disturbed him a little, and he wanted to think of a pseudonym for himself so he would not be mixed up with Korney Ivanovich. His early verse and the narrative poem 'The Goatling' (later printed in *Beseda*) were signed N. Radishchev. 'You see, Korney Ivanovich's real name is Nikolai Korneichuk,' he explained to me, 'so that in fact I am not Nikolai *Korneevich*, but Nikolai *Nikolaevich*. And as a matter of fact I even have no real surname of my own.'

Together we went to concerts, to the Muruzi house, to Korney Ivanovich's workshop. 'Dearest,' Nikolai Chukovsky would say to me, 'leave your institute, come to the university. Zhirmunsky is lecturing there. So we will be there together next year.' But as much as I wanted to listen to Zhirmunsky, I resisted the temptation and firmly resolved to stay at the Zubovsky.

The Serapion Brothers gathered in the House of Arts, in Mikhail Slonimsky's room. This was the second winter of the circle's existence. By that time they were no longer attending lectures in the workshop of Zamiatin and Viktor Shklovsky. Some were at the university (Kaverin, Lunts), some were already being published in magazines and even brought out books (Zoshchenko, Fedin, Vsevolod Ivanov). Gruzdev was working on a biography of Gorky. Six months previously they had published a collective volume (the first; the second came out in 1922 in Berlin, and in Russia, apparently, was never allowed to be published). One part of the brotherhood was spellbound by Remizov, another by Shklovsky. Zoshchenko, swarthy, serious, with big dark eyes, lay in the middle of the room on three chairs. It was said he had been gassed during his stint in the army during the war. Three or four girls who had written nothing, but had become friendly with Nikitin, Lunts, and Fedin, also came. The room was crowded, smoke-filled, dark. It was very noisy, but when someone read something of his own, they listened attentively and discussed intelligently. Only at the very end of the winter (in 1922) did the first signs of the future decline appear, hardly noticeable before: the disintegration of the group started when Nikolai Nikitin and Vsevolod Ivanov left. Lunts, Slonimsky, Kaverin, Fedin remained faithful to the circle to the very end. But dispersal was in the order of things: all gradually matured literarily and went their different ways during the difficult years when they had to choose a line in 'literary politics'; in this most essential decision there was of course no possible agreement among them.

Lev Lunts was my age. He was then fascinated by the methods of plot and suspense, and was little interested in poetry. He was a genial, cheerful, lively, spontaneous man. At about nineteen he had been left alone in Petersburg, his family being already abroad at that time. He lived on the lower storey of the House of Arts, in the same corridor as the acmeist poet Vsevolod Rozhdestvensky (who shared a room with Tikhonov), Pyast, and the novelist Aleksandr Grin. Lev Lunts's room was narrow, cold, and damp, full of books, with a bed squeezed in. He called it the apes' quarters. His fingers were spotted with ink, his jacket neat, the curls on his forehead gave him a boyish appearance. Without him no party could have taken place, he was the soul of the Serapions. In May of 1923, after a lengthy heart illness (still in these very apes' quarters), he finally left Petersburg to join his family in Hamburg and, having stayed in the hospital for about nine months, on 9 May 1924, died of endocarditis. It was said later that at a 'jubilee' his Serapion Brothers, according to an unpleasant Russian custom, heaved him into the air and let him fall, and his illness began from that. His letters to me in Berlin were published in *Experiments*, No. 1 (New York, 1953); my letters to him will soon be published.

Akim Lvovich Volynsky, the art historian, who slept during those winters not only in a fur coat and fur cap but in galoshes as well, found something Italian in Ida Nappelbaum and he was right: her black hair which fell in curls on her forehead, her lazy movements, her beautiful small hands, a kind of southern laziness, a sluggishness of smile. She had a heavy body, which looked pampered despite deprivation, the French 'r's' trilled through her Russian. She should have been wearing brocade and ankle bracelets, but she walked about (like all of us) in a coat made of curtains, in a dress made of her mother's housecoat, a blouse made of a tablecloth.

'Today Radlov promised to drop in,' she purred, rolling her lovely eyes, 'and next week actors from the Aleksandrinsky Theatre will come. I went to Aleksandr Benois's and invited him . . .' She was the hostess of the Mondays, and that part of her life which was free of romances (not those one reads, but those one experiences) she gave to these meetings and to verse.

I remember a soirée on Monday, 21 November. I went from the Zubovsky Institute to the House of Arts, to Korney Chukovsky's class, and there, like everyone, read verse 'in a circle'. Korney Ivanovich suddenly praised me. 'Yes,' he said, looking at me fixedly and, as it were, sizing me up inside and out, 'you write good verse.' Nikolai Chukovsky radiated pleasure in his large face, rejoicing for my sake.

Then I went with him from the Moika to Liteiny and arrived at Ida's rather early. We again arranged the taborets and ashtrays, and blew into the stove.

'I invited Anna Andreevna [Akhmatova],' said Ida (while her 'real mama' was preparing sandwiches with sausage for me and Nikolai). 'And I met Khodasevich. He also promised to come.'

This surname told me nothing, or at least very little.

Late that night when we were walking home (Chukovsky lived on Spasskaya Street, which was on my way), Chukovsky said to me, gesticulating exuberantly:

'Dearest! You received praise today! How glad I am for you! At first Papa praised you, and then Vladislav Felitsianovich! This is remarkable! What a fantastic day!' (Ida had whispered to me as I was leaving: 'Today was *your* day!')

Sitting on the floor at Ida's, I had read 'in a circle':

Decorated basins and pitchers
Under the warm tap I will rinse,
And my hair, still damp,
Near the smoky stove I will roll up.

And I will, like a gay little girl,
Walk about with a wound braid,
Carry a pail with heavy water,
Sweep up with an ugly broom.

And so on. So that Akhmatova smiled kindly (and inscribed to me a copy of *Anno Domini*), having said nothing, however, and someone, who for some reason had the most abnormal patronymic of 'Felitsianovich', announced that as regards the pail and the mop – excuse me! broom! – he was pleased.

And suppose he were not? I thought. If neither this Felitsianovich, nor Korney Chukovsky had praised me? Then what? Nothing would have changed anyway. Forget it!

Khodasevich had long, straight, black hair, and he himself read that evening 'Lida', 'Bacchus', 'Elegy'. He said of 'Elegy' that it was not yet completely finished. 'Elegy' impressed me. I got his books, *The Way of the Grain* and *The Happy Little House*. On 23 December he was again at Ida's and read 'Ballad'. Not only I was struck by these verses. Many in Petersburg were speaking about them.

But who was he? By his age he could have belonged to the Guild, to the 'Hyperboreans' (Gumilev, Akhmatova, Mandelstam), but he did not. The members of the Guild I knew personally always seemed to have something in common: their conservatism, anti-modernity, mannerisms, the exquisite parting of their hair, their sublime handkerchiefs showing in their breast pockets, their foot-shuffling, hand-kissing, and special enunciation of certain vowels: *krasivy* (beautiful) rather than *krasivai*, *chetsverg* (Thursday) instead of *chitverk*, the affected airs of society beaux (when 'society' itself had crumbled), a class consciousness that sometimes seemed comical, sometimes quite pleasant, but at all times was a pathetic anachronism with a touch of artificiality. Khodasevich was a completely different breed; even his Russian was more Russian. It was not for nothing that the wet nurse Elena Kuzina had brought up this half Pole. From the first meeting he gave the impression of a man *of our time*, in part even wounded by our time, perhaps mortally. Now, forty years later, *our time* has other overtones than it had in the years of my youth. Then it meant: the ruin of old Russia, Civil War, N.E.P., as a concession of the Revolution to the petit bourgeoisie; in literature the end of symbolism, the pressure of futurism, and through futurism the pressure of politics on art. Khodasevich appeared before me against the background of all of this as a prefiguration of 'the cold and gloom of coming days' (Blok).

In Lozinsky's workshop we studied the techniques of poetic translation. José María de Heredia's sonnet about the Magi in Bethlehem was chosen. The first line presented no difficulties (it was also the last):

'The Magi came: Gaspard, Melchior and Balthasar.' But there were difficulties later which were discussed in detail: first some words were suggested, then combinations of words, dozens of possibilities were rejected, the single perfect one was chosen, and in one hour we had managed to think over and work out no more than two or three lines.

From there to Galernaya. A line of Tiutchev analysed by Tomashevsky in a way that was then a novelty but is now considered in the Western world as the basis of all poetics. The great

Shcherba's shadow soared above us and literary wisdom poured into me. I go out to the snow-covered street. It is quiet under the arch, quiet on the square, and Petersburg is, as in the prophecies of Gogol and Dostoevsky (and Blok), like a boat cramped by lumps of ice in a blizzard. Where the sidewalk ends, and the pavement begins, is unknown. I run in soft felt boots, I fall down, I get up. The monument to the Bolshevik Volodarsky is on the corner of the boulevard. It is in plaster; last year a bomb was placed under it and its stomach was ripped out; it's no use repairing it, and to leave it as it is seems disrespectful; orders to remove it are awaited, and in the meantime it has been covered with a rag which, during the blizzards, flaps about in the wind in different directions, so the figure waves, threatens, beckons, and bows down. Past the monument from the boulevard corner diagonally across the square, to the corner of Morskaya, by the Hotel Astoria, sliding, falling through the snow. No light, no sound, the snowstorm howls and in the already nocturnal grey-white gloom, the dim figures of pedestrians float by (are they coming from the Twelve or from the Overcoat?). They disappear, then again emerge and slip by me.

'Careful! Slippery there!'

Someone yells this from the opposite corner as I approach the Hotel Astoria, and out of the storm a figure appears in a pointed sealskin hat and a long fur coat, almost down to his calves (a hand-me-down).

'I've been waiting for you here, I am frozen,' says Khodasevich. 'Let's get warmed up. Are you not frightened to run in such darkness?'

He knew that lectures at the Zubovsky ended at eight and had stood on the corner, waiting till I passed by. While we stand and look each other over, he says:

'The fur coat is Misha's and that's why it's so long; he's my brother, a Moscow lawyer. My field jacket is from a turned coat of Misha's. And I am warm! And you?'

I walk along with him. He walks easily; he is taller than me, thin and light and in spite of Misha's clothes looks rather elegant.

While we drink coffee in the Polish café he asks me: Living with Papa and Mama? Studying? And how are Papa and Mama? Are you in love with anyone? Have you written new verse? Again

133

something about a mop? – I do not answer some questions, others I answer in detail: Papa and Mama of course prevent a person from doing things when she is twenty, but in general, to tell the truth, I have brought them up so that they now move slowly from their previous positions. As they say – besides chains, one has nothing to lose.

'How do you like that! Of course, when a young lady is twenty . . .'

'I said: When a person is twenty.'

'Oh, I didn't hear right! . . .'

I firmly say 'no' when he offers to accompany me home in this blizzard, and he does not insist. We both remove our mittens and say good-bye at the entrance to the House of Arts, where he lives. His hand is thin and dry. He goes through the door and in the light of a yellow bulb, through the glass of the entrance door half covered with snow, I see him go up the stairs: hat, fur. Unhurriedly he turns and disappears, straight, with head held high. His silhouette remains in my memory.

There was an evening, clear and starlit, when the snow crackled and sparkled: both of us – Khodasevich and I – hurried past the Mikhailovsky Theatre, and in the square for some reason searchlights had been installed; in their rays our breath hung in wreaths. The beams of light criss-crossed, as if they were passing through us, suddenly illuminating our happy faces in the nocturnal frosted air – why happy? Yes, already happy. We caught a ray which very impudently stuck to our coats – perhaps someone was frolicking with us from the other end of the square? In a moment it became pitch dark and we nearly lost each other, but again the sparklings began and accompanied us to the corner of Karavannaya.

His window in the House of Arts faced the bridge, and you could see all of Nevsky through it. His semi-circular room and this window were a part of Khodasevich's life: for hours he would sit and look through it – the greater part of the verse of *The Heavy Lyre* was essentially born at this window, from this view. The difference between us at this time was that he looked *out of a window* while I looked *into* windows. But there was also a double meaning in this: starting at the Gostiny Dvor, in the middle of Nevsky, I tried to find his window, either a bright dot in the clear evening air or a dim drop of light appearing in the dark distance when I was at Kazan Cathedral. In his window, beneath the 'sixteen-candle sun', I saw him in winter behind double frames, in spring in the frame of the open window; he saw me from far off when he awaited my arrival, distinguishing me among others on the wide pavement of the avenue; he watched me when I left his place: in the evening a black dot disappearing among passers-by, late at night a melting silhouette, early in the morning signalling to him with my hand from the corner of the canal.

In spite of his thirty-five years, how young he still was that year! I mean that he did not yet know the taste of ashes in his mouth (later he would say: 'I get the taste of ashes in my mouth even from meat balls!'), or the bitter years of want and exile, or the fear that twists a man's guts into a knot. He still had, like all of us, a homeland, city, profession, a name. A feeling of hopelessness only rarely dashed him, a melody continued to resound within him, suggesting that you couldn't make everyone hard, that some could be used in other ways. If so, it seemed possible to organize – maybe not Russia, not a revolution, not the world, but above all one's own self. The importance of order within one's self and of the meaning behind facts could be recognized – not on a comforting level, or a defensive one, but on a cognitive and existential level. In the conversations we had with one another all of January and February (1922) it was not a matter of 'you' and 'I', of facts and events, recollections and hopes, but of chains of thoughts, of linking our minds with the awareness of our limits.

The change in our relationship is connected for me with the celebration of the 1922 New Year. After a three-year period of hunger, cold, cave life, suddenly new plans were swarming – of parties, 'balls', new dresses (for those who still had curtains or Mama's trunks); in the half-dead city words rang out: one bottle of wine for four, a rendezvous for dinner, invite a pianist. Vsevolod Rozhdestvensky, with whom I had become friends, asked me to go with him to the House of Writers on 31 December. I agreed. Khodasevich asked me where I was celebrating the New Year. I realized I had been expecting this question and said that Rozhdestvensky had invited me to supper. He was pained and happy at the same time and said he would also come.

Rozhdestvensky, as I have said, shared his room that year with the poet Nikolai Tikhonov. I was often at their place, and once Rozhdestvensky showed me Innokenty Annensky's *cypress chest*, a coffer of cypress wood that Valentin Innokentievich Krivich-Annensky, the son of the great poet, had brought to him for safe-keeping. In the chest lay notebooks scribbled in Annensky's hand, and once for a whole evening we read this verse, browsing in it, exhausted with ecstasy and awe.

At the dining room table of the House of Writers that evening were Zamiatin and his wife, Korney Chukovsky, Mikhail Slonimsky, Fedin and his fiancée, Khodasevich, Rozhdestvensky, and I.

> Honest is our life and free,
> Singing, drinking, marching on;
> Two glasses are enough for three,
> From which to drink all night till dawn.
>
> There is a wife, a future bride,
> And my father, hard as flint.
> Never mind! They stay outside –
> Outside our triple-passioned ring.
>
> Some girl I know will ask me shyly:
> 'Are you truly being shared?'
> . . . .
>
> But now I squint and look askance:
> I see them both at a single glance.
> My life meanders by the shore –
> Something to be thankful for!

'What does "meander" mean?' asked Khodasevich, who sat at my right at supper.

'It means not taking the main road, but wandering off the beaten track.' I was astonished he did not understand.

'That means an unimportant path? A negligible one? Is that it?'

'If you wish.'

'A path I take just for fun. If I want I take it. If I don't I stay home.'

136

'Well yes. Walking on the edge of something. By-passing the real. Not really meaningful.'

Having waited for the moment when Rozhdestvensky, sitting on my left, entered into conversation with Fedin who sat opposite him, Khodasevich said quietly:

'No, I don't want to be a whim. I want to be real.'

The clock struck twelve. All stood up, glass in hand.

To tell him, you are already real to me – I could not. I did not feel it, yet.

Then Rozhdestvensky disappeared somewhere – was it on purpose? – and we walked together along the Basseinaya to the House of Arts. Nevsky was lit up in holiday fashion, it was 1:00 A.M. At the corner of Sadovaya, over the entrance to the huge, recently opened International Café a sign fluttered:

> All free citizens
> To the International Café,
> A fashionable little place!
> Are hurrying, hurrying, hurrying.

And a drunken chorus sang to the whole surroundings:

> Mama, Mama, what will be our plight
> When will come the cold winter night?
> You have no warm shawl, no shawl,
> I have no winter coat, no coat!

This made us laugh. Laughing, slipping, clinging to one another we made our way along the ice-covered ground to the canal.

> Mama, Mama, what will be our plight . . .

they bawled from the former European Hotel to a rollicking orchestra.

> . . . cold winter night . . .

137

burst out of the basement of the house on the corner of Moika where the Polish café was. Surely this fashionable little ballad was being sung in all the cabarets of Petersburg! For three years they had waited and now they poured out their soul to an accordion, violin, piano, or orchestra.

There were about sixty people in the House of Arts, in the mirrored hall, the two living rooms and the huge wood-panelled dining room. Supper had just ended. All were here – from Akim Volynsky to Ida and from Lunts to Akhmatova. The composer Artur Lurie sat on a couch like an idol, between Akhmatova and Anna Gumileva, Nikolai Stepanovich's widow. Animated like fire, Nikolai Radlov's wife Elsa was in a red masquerade outfit ('Here lives a young beauty, Edie,/I'm madly in love with her,' wrote Otsup about her later). All were dressed up: one in a dress she had preserved from before the Revolution, one in borrowed clothes, a third in a theatrical or masquerade costume obtained through an acquaintance in a theatre store-room, a fourth in a remodelled outfit, a fifth in something contrived out of a piece of silk that had lain for about thirty years at the bottom of a trunk. In the mirrored hall Radlov with his partner and Otsup with Elsa danced the foxtrot, the one-step, the tango, in shiny shoes and pressed trousers.* The Serapions offered wine to some lovely actresses; the poetess Anna Radlova (Sergey's wife), considered a beautiful woman for some reason, sat, her face motionless, in an armchair between two windows.

'Is this a woman? Or is this some drapery that has fallen into an armchair?' asked a frightened Khodasevich. Actually, Radlova's long and wide dress of gold brocade was a perfect match for the Eliseevs' curtains that hung at her sides.

I see a dining room, living rooms, and a hall with the uninterrupted movement of familiar faces, young and old, near and far. In the dining room people are still eating and drinking, in the hall there are four couples dancing who have miraculously borrowed from somewhere all the fashionable dances of a Europe as distant as a dream. People feast their eyes on them, stand in doorways, greedily drink in the novel syncopations of the foxtrot,

*You felt a chain of romances in the air, and broken marriages, new unions – as if Schnitzler's *La Ronde* caught everyone up in its spinning motion.

and look at the figures swaying and fused together. Someone smells of l'Origan, another says something in French, someone drinks a glass of champagne – don't ask where it comes from: perhaps from the Eliseev cellar (a bottle fell in a distant corner), perhaps from the distributor of the Central Committee of the Party, or from grandmother's closet. We sit on a couch in the living room, people walk past us, do not look at us, or speak to us: they understood long ago that we were not interested in them.

At dawn he takes me home, from the Moika to Kirochnaya. We stand for several minutes at the house gates. His face is near mine, and my hand is in his. During those moments a bond arises between us, and with every hour it grows stronger.

That winter I think people only needed a pretext for a festive occasion. The 'Russian Christmas' of 7 January reminds me again of a kind of whirling in the Eliseevs' house, of music and a crowd. At about 3:00 A.M. Khodasevich and I walked through deep snow to his room, and sat till morning at his window, looking at Nevsky: the clarity of this January dawn was unusual: distant places became clearly visible, with the railway station tower behind the roofs, and Nevsky itself empty and clean; only at Sadovaya was there a glimmer, a solitary streetlamp, that did not want to die out, but then it too went. After the stars disappeared (at night it seemed that they hung very near – you could reach them with your hand) and a pale sunlight flooded the city, I left. The deep seriousness of that night had altered me. I felt I had become other than I was. Words had been uttered by me which I had never spoken to anyone, and words had been said to me which I had never heard before. That conversation had turned not on our mutual happiness, but on something completely different, in the key not of 'happiness' and 'unhappiness' but of magic, a new dual reality, his and mine.

Another (and I believe the last) soirée was at Zubov's place, on the eve of the Russian New Year. Count Valentin Zubov was still at that time the director of the Institute of the History of Art, which he had founded and which continued to bear his name. The same people gathered again in the huge, frozen halls of his palace (on St Isaac's Square). Some rooms were so cold people's breath was visible but in others the fireplaces were aflame. Again couples swirled and swayed, chandeliers burned, and some venerable servants watched us with scorn and disgust.

It was now the beginning of spring. Before this, on 2 March, Khodasevich had finished 'Not by my mother, but by a peasant woman of Tula' (the first four stanzas had lain untouched since 1917). Everything began to flow somehow at once, the sun shone, water dripped from the rooftops, there were sounds ringing in the courtyards and gardens. He went to buy galoshes at the Sennoy market and for this sold the herrings he had just received from the House of Scholars. In haste he bought galoshes one size larger than necessary, shoved the draft of his poem in them and came to my place. A year later, in Berlin, the draft was found in one of the galoshes – I have kept it till now.

That day several people gathered at my place; the second room, which had become icy cold in winter, was opened, heated, tidied up. There (it was Glinka's study) for the first time he read 'Not by my mother', recited it (the draft was already in one of the galoshes) by heart and, at the request of everyone, twice. On that occasion we did not read 'in a circle' – no one wanted to read their verse after his.

At the very beginning of February was the Serapions' 'jubilee': one year of their official existence and the production of the miscellany *Ushkuiniki*, which Nikolai Chukovsky published and in which Tikhonov, Nikolai Chukovsky himself, I, and someone else were represented. In April, still in Mikhailovsky Square on a bench, Khodasevich told me that two tasks lay before us: to be together and survive. Or perhaps: to survive and be together.

What did 'survive' then mean? Something physical? Moral? Could we at that time foresee the death of Mandelstam on a rubbish heap, the end of Babel, the suicides of Esenin and Mayakovsky, Party politics in literature aimed at destroying two if not three generations? Could we foresee twenty years of silence on Akhmatova's part? The destruction of Pasternak? The end of Gorky? Of course not. 'Anatoly Vasilievich will not allow it': this opinion about Lunacharsky was in the air at that time. But if Anatoly Vasilievich is himself poisoned? Or even if he dies a natural death? Or if he is removed? Or if he decides one day not to be a communist aesthete any more but to become a hammer, forging the Russian intelligentsia on the anvil of the Revolution? No, such possibilities dawned on no one, but doubts that it would be possible to survive swarmed in Khodasevich's thoughts for the first time during those months. That one would be seized for no reason, jailed, and annihilated then seemed unthinkable, but that one would be crushed, tortured, have his mouth shut and either be forced to die (as later happened with Sologub and Gershenson) or give up literature (as Evgeny Zamiatin, Mikhail Kuzmin and, for twenty-five years, Victor Shklovsky were forced to do) began dimly to take on more distinct shapes in one's thoughts. Only a few could follow Briusov into membership in the Communist Party; others could clutch for a short time at the triumphal chariot of the futurists. But the rest?

Afterwards this 'concept of survival' came to me many times in its most diverse aspects, bringing with it a rainbow of overtones: from the conception of a beast 'not to be devoured', to the ancient 'self-affirmation in the face of destruction'; the instinctive 'not to be caught by the enemy' to the lofty 'deliver oneself of the final Word'. Both the low and lofty often have one root in man. To grab on to a blade of grass as you hang over an abyss and to give the manuscript of your novel to a foreigner leaving Moscow for the West have the same foundation.

It was an April day in Mikhailovsky Square, the square where in the winter the searchlights' rays chased us; I decided now to set out for the Neva to look at the flow of ice, not with him but alone: the Ladoga wind these spring days was dangerous for Khodasevich. He had lost count of his illnesses and others still lay in wait for him. Once, in 1915, he feared tuberculosis of the bone and he had permanent chest trouble. From the Moscow life of 1918–20 and a three-year period of malnutrition (or rather hunger) he got furunculosis, of which he was barely cured and which still threatened him. He was thin, pale, weak, he had to take care of his teeth, he tired of carrying rations – though God knows how light they were, feather weight. His rations included herring (which he did not eat), matches, flour. He would sell the herring at the Sennoy market and buy cigarettes. And he bought cocoa on the black market.

In the winter a parcel was sent to me from Northern Ireland (yes, it turned out that there was such a country in the world!) by a cousin who in 1916 had married an Englishman. This parcel was a real event. Together with Father, I brought it on a sled from the customs house, opened it or rather ripped open the heavy package wrapped in matting. We spread out on the grand piano: a wool dress, a sweater, two pairs of shoes, a dozen pairs of stockings, a piece of lard, soap, ten bars of chocolate, sugar, coffee, and six tins of sweet condensed milk. Immediately – as I was, all bundled in my fur coat and huge shawl – I took a hammer and nail, made two holes in one of the tins and, without stopping, drank in one burst the thick sweet liquid. To the bottom of the tin. (Twenty-five years later, in Paris, having opened the first parcel I received from America after the war in 1945 – it was from Mikhail Karpovich, the Harvard professor of Russian history – which contained almost the same things, I ripped open the blue soap wrapper, took out the soap and kissed it.) To the bottom of the tin, that first time, like a beast. We later hung the empty tins on the stove-pipe to catch the liquid soot that was spoiling my books. And we fashioned a floor rag out of the matting. Nothing was wasted.

Then the Hoover A.R.A. parcels began to come. It is frightful and shameful now to read how Gorky asked Frenchmen, Americans, Englishmen, even Germans to help the hungry population of Revolutionary Russia. When a face was deathly pale, some rosy tone came to it because of lard, cocoa, and sugar. The arrival of each parcel seemed to give us hope of survival. We existed from parcel to parcel. As it was spring we no longer used the stove for heat, but used it simply for cooking. On the other hand, the poverty of our clothes suddenly became more noticeable in sunlight; in the winter all passed: Pyast's soles tied by string were not conspicuous, nor the turned jacket of Zamiatin, nor the patches on Chukovsky's trousers, nor Zoshchenko's field jacket worn to a sheen. Every week living became a little more difficult. Yes, it got warm and it was possible to settle in two rooms, remove one's boots and not count each log, open the windows and hope that in a month there would be at least something at the distributor's; but, with different people and in different ways, the sense of an imminent end began to appear – not so much a personal one but a kind of collective abstract one, which, however, did not impede one's way of staying alive; it was not a *physical* end certainly, because N.E.P. continued to play its role and a rosiness appeared in faces here and there, but perhaps a *spiritual* end. The end was in the atmosphere at first like some kind of metaphor, collective and abstract, which became clearer from day to day. It was said that soon everything would close down – that is, private publishing houses – and that 'all' would be turned over to Gosizdat. It was said that in Moscow censorship was even more severe than with us, and that in Petersburg it would soon be the same. People said in the Kremlin that, in spite of Anatoly Vasilievich Lunacharsky, a decree on 'literary politics' was being prepared which Mayakovsky was ready to transpose swiftly into verse. From Moscow someone brought the rumour that somewhere someone high up had reproached someone else and it smacked of a threat . . . The frosts and blizzards had held everything together somehow, but now everything started flowing, ran in streams, there was nothing to hold on to, everything was running somewhere. Don't delude yourself, fellow writers; not 'somewhere' but in a very definite direction where we will have no place, where most probably we will not survive.

Now, looking back at those months, I see that destruction of the intelligentsia did not come in a straight path but in a tortuous one, through a period of brief flowering; the way was not simple, and some people simultaneously flowered and perished, and made others perish, without being themselves aware of it; a little later there would be hundreds of victims and later still tens of thousands: from Trotsky through Voronsky, Pilniak, the formalists, and fellow travellers to the futurists and young workers and peasant poets who bloomed to the very end of the 1920s, serving the new regime wholeheartedly. From bearded elders, members of the Philosophical Society of the beginning of the century, to the members of the Association of Proletarian Writers, who had invented, at the right time it then seemed, the slogan about the debasement of culture but were killed like everybody else. Destruction did not come personally to each one who was being destroyed, but as a group, destruction of a whole profession, carefully planned. Poets were destroyed as a class *as planned*. In parallel fashion not things, but planned things, began to be produced. Mandelstam was destroyed *as a class*, Zamiatin was forbidden to write *as a class*. Literary politics (to the end of the 1930s) was a part of general politics – at first of Lenin-Trotsky, then of Zinoviev-

Kamenev-Stalin, and finally of Stalin-Ezhov-Zhdanov. And in the end three kinds of people were destroyed: those who were born around 1880, those who were born around 1895, and those who were born around 1910.

Thin and weak physically, Khodasevich all of a sudden began to display energy, not in keeping with his physical make-up, on preparations for our departure abroad. The distribution of travel passports had begun in Moscow since May 1922; this was one of the consequences of the general policy of N.E.P. Passports for our departure came into our hands – numbers 16 and 17. I would be curious to find out who got passport number 1. Perhaps Ehrenburg?

Khodasevich made the decision to leave Russia, but he certainly did not foresee that he was leaving forever. He made his choice; only a few years later he made a second one: not to return. I followed him. If we had not met and not taken the decision then to 'be together' and 'survive', he undoubtedly would have remained in Russia: there is no possibility, not even the slightest, that he would have gone abroad alone. He probably would have been sent at the end of 1922 to Berlin, in the group that included Berdyaev, Kuskova, Evreinov, and others banished from Russia as enemies of the people: his name, as we later learned, was on the list of those to be exiled. I would have remained of course in Petersburg. Having made his choice for himself and me, he arranged it so that we came out together and survived – that is, survived the terror of the 1930s, in which almost certainly I would have perished. My choice was *him* and my decision was to follow him. One can now say that we saved each other.

A passport was issued to me in Moscow. I went there in the middle of May at the summons of Khodasevich, who had gone there to petition for permission for us both to leave. I did not recognize Moscow: now it was the capital of the new state, the streets were black with people, all around things were growing and being created, shooting up, coming alive, being born anew, pulsating. From morning to evening we went to fill out questionnaires, hand over papers, sit in waiting rooms. Two signatures were needed for permission to leave: Yurgis Baltrushaitis, the Lithuanian ambassador in Moscow and an old friend of Khodasevich's, gave one and the other came from Anatoly Vasilievich. On the passports there was the inquiry 'reason for the trip'. The replies written were: for a health cure (on Khodasevich's passport), for completion of education (on mine). I was represented by a photograph with a round face, round eyes, round chin, and even a round nose. When this roundness had come to me, I had not noticed. Now, forty-five years later, in my slightly Indochinese face there is no roundness whatsoever.

While we were in Moscow there was a literary evening at the Union of Writers on Tverskoy Boulevard, and there Khodasevich read his new verse ('I don't believe in earthly beauty', 'She was misty and anonymous', 'Evidence', 'A stranger passes by'), verse about love; and Gershenzon and Zaitsev and others (not to mention his brother Misha and Misha's daughter, Valentina Khodasevich, the artist) looked at me with unconcealed curiosity. We dropped in on the Zaitsevs later in the evening, in an alley near the Arbat: they were also preparing to go abroad for a 'health cure'. From that day my relationship with Boris and Vera began, and it has lasted more than forty years. At their home I saw Pavel Muratov, one of the most remarkable men I ever met; our friendship had a tremendous influence on me – strange though it seems – only later, when it came to an end. We sat at the Zaitsevs' in the midst of open suitcases and trunks, books piled on tables. It looked as if we would be in Berlin at the same time.

The writers' bookstore then was (if I am not mistaken) some-where near Strastnoy Boulevard. We went there, Nikolai Berdyaev stood at the counter and 'did business', it was his day. There were books in manuscript (those it had been impossible to find a publisher for) and old editions, rare copies and newly published journals and brochures. Then we went to visit Misha. He was twenty-one years older than Khodasevich, and a famous counsellor at the Moscow Criminal Court. He came with us to the station (we were returning to Petersburg). There I went back to my parents' house, while Khodasevich stayed at the house next door, on Kirochnaya, in Georgy Annenkov's flat. Three days later we left for Riga.

On the eve of our departure he lay on my bed, I sat at his feet, and he spoke about the past, which suddenly in those last weeks had moved so far from us, supplanted by the present. It would move off still further, he said, as if looking into his future. I asked him to write something down as a remembrance: the groundwork for an autobiography, perhaps, a calendar of his childhood and youth. He sat down at my desk and began to write, and when he finished handed me a piece of cardboard, a calendar of his life, which is now in my archives.

His past was before me, his life *before* me. I read this record many times in succession then. It was for me a substitute for an album of family photographs, it illustrated a book dear to me, and as such I loved it. To this piece of cardboard he immediately added his comic 'Don Juan's Catalogue' – this list amused me for a long time.

> Evgenia
> Aleksandra
> Aleksandra
> Marina
> Vera
> Olga
> Alina
> Natalia
> N.N.
> Madeleine
> Nadezhda
> Evgenia
> Evgenia
> Tatiana
> Anna
> Ekaterina
> N.

At the station were my father and mother, bewildered, confused, sad, troubled. Our departure had been kept secret; this Khodasevich wanted. I said good-bye neither to Ida nor to Lunts, and said nothing to Nikolai Chukovsky. Petersburg receded from me – in rail entanglements, pump houses, empty cars (40 MEN. 8 HORSES. BRIANSK – MOGILEV), the Admiralty needle – part of my childhood mythology. The year receded, having begun in one June and ended in another, a year without which I would not have been I, a year bestowed on me that filled me to the brim with feelings, thoughts, a year that ploughed me afresh, taught me to approach people (and a man), inspired me, and brought my youth to an end. Poor Lazarus was now so rich that he was preparing already to begin distributing everything he had acquired – and much more – right and left.

In the freight car in which we were taken across the border at Sebezh, Khodasevich said to me that he had an unfinished poem with him. Here are those lines:

> In Moscow I was born. I never saw
> The smoke above a Polish roof.
> My father never left a grain of Polish soil,
> For me to cherish as a sacred proof.
>
> I, Russia's stepson, what am I to Poland,
> What do I know of her? – I could not understand . . .
> All I possess are eight slim volumes,
> And they contain my native land.
>
> Your fate is to accept the yoke,
> To live exiled in bitterness and woe.
> But I have packed my Russia in my bag,
> And take her with me anywhere I go.

Our knapsacks lay around us on the floor of the freight car.

Yes, there was his Pushkin, of course – all eight volumes. But I already knew that I would never be able completely to identify with Khodasevich, I wouldn't even try to: Russia was not just Pushkin for me. She always was outside literary categories: then (as now) she lay in historical groupings, if by history one understands not only the past and present, but the future as well. And we spoke – he and I – about other unfinished verse and my perhaps continuing a narrative poem begun by him, which he felt he was unable to finish:

> Here is a story, it came to me
> Entire, definitely and clearly,
> While in my hand lay
> Your obedient hand.

I took a piece of paper and pencil and while the train moved slowly from one frontier checkpoint to another I added to his four lines my four:

147

The Italics Are Mine

Thus from your warm palm
Into my palm blood overflowed
And I became alive and perceptive,
And this was your love.

PART THREE

Tobias and the Angel

FROM THE WINDOW OF MY ROOM IN THE KRAMPE boarding house in Berlin I can see the windows opposite. The boarding house is on the fourth and fifth floors of a huge building with a marble staircase, chandeliers, and a nude figure holding an electric torch. Our rooms lead to the courtyard; the Krampe rooms occupy both floors, and two sets of windows. All of it is Krampe. There are rooms that lead onto the square – Viktoria-Luise Platz, where two floors of rooms are also Krampe (Gershenzon lives there). Krampe herself is a humourless, business-like, bald spinster, though she goes to bed with an artist about twenty years younger than she. Out of the window of my room I see them drink coffee in the morning. In the evening she pores over account books, while he drinks Kantorowitz liqueur. Then they pull down the shades and put out the light.

Through another window are the inhabitants of room 38. She is fat and he is fat. They undress slowly and carefully spread out their underwear and outer clothes, on separate chairs, then go to sleep (it seems I can hear their groaning) in a double bed. They do not lower the shades. Let anyone who cares look in their windows: it makes no difference, they are cosy, have nothing to hide and their conscience is clear. Under the bed is a faïence chamber pot, next to the bed are night slippers, and over the head of the bed is Raphael's Madonna.

A bulb burns above them. The Serapion Brother Nikolai Nikitin who arrived yesterday from Petersburg (and brought me a letter from Lunts), wild as if broken loose, spent all day buying himself socks and ties in the Kadewe store, then had a couple of drinks and brought home a streetwalker from the corner of Motzstrasse. Completely naked, she simpers in an armchair, while he is on the bed; only a hairy leg thrust high is visible.

151

Andrey Bely's room is next to them. He pulled out a drawer of the night-table and cannot put it back: the knob is preventing it – he holds it length-way, not across its width. He struggles with it for a long time, but cannot put the drawer back. Putting it on the floor, he looks at it, then makes some strange movements over it, whispers something as though exorcizing it. Then he again grasps it, but this time the right way, and the drawer goes in easily as it should. Bely's face radiates happiness.

Under Bely's window is the room of a high tsarist official's widow. She is in deep mourning either for 'his majesty' or for Rasputin, whom she knew well. On the first day she looked at me with revulsion at the table d'hôte and asked: What is Prolet-cult? Did I study at the Prolet-cult? Did I graduate from the Prolet-cult? Am I about to return and take exams for entry into the Komsomol?

Having looked to my heart's content in strange windows, I put on Khodasevich's trousers, jacket, and shoes, hide my hair under his hat, take his cane, and go for a walk. I walk along the green Charlottenburg, along quiet streets where trees bend over with branches and the sky is not visible, along the quieted Wilmersdorf where in a Russian restaurant people are singing gypsy songs and cursing modern literature – all those Whites (Bely) and Blacks (Cherny), Bitters (Gorky), and Sweets (Sladky), where General X stands in livery in the doorway, and Gentleman of the Chamber Z is at your service. Now they are still rarities, unique. But soon there will be many of them – oh how many! Paris and London, New York and Shanghai will know them and get used to them.

Past and present interweave, fuse into one another, pour into one another. The widow and the general cursing the Revolution, and the poet Minsky, Nadson's younger contemporary, welcoming it: 'old émigrés', that is socialists of the tsarist epoch who have returned to their home in Europe having happily escaped from the Revolution; and the pioneer of the bicycle and of photography Vasily Nemirovich-Danchenko, with whiskers, wearing a pince-nez on a black ribbon, carrying his paunch in front of him, acquired during the reign of Alexander III, who tells me the first minute we meet that for quantity of written work he is second only to Lope de Vega (the third is Dumas père). And Nina Petrovskaya, the heroine of Briusov's novel The Fiery Angel, Briusov's Renata, wearing a large black hat like those worn circa 1912, old, lame, miserable. The authoress Lappo-Danilevskaya (it is said she wrote risqué trash and was no less well known than Verbitskaya) dances the Russian *kazachok* with a kerchief in a night club, while the Serapion Brother Nikitin circles with kicking steps. They were not introduced to each other, however.

The present day exists, too, parallel to this: Viktor Shklovsky and Mark Slonim come to see us, and a little later Pasternak, Nikolai Otsup and many others come from Russia (for a 'health cure'). It is not entirely clear if it's to the past or present that those who flash by us belong, either at the Literary Club (on Nollendorf Platz) or at the Russian restaurant on Gentinerstrasse: figures such as Sergey Makovsky, Sergey Krechetov, Semen Yushkevich; a swarm of publishers is there, publishing anything they can lay their hands on, from the memoirs of General Denikin and the verse of Igor Severianin to cook books.

They rush through Berlin and gradually begin to find their place: the generals and governors retreat into limbo, the Social Revolutionaries overgrown with Kerensky, Chernov, Zenzinov, move to one side, the Social Democrats (Sumsky, Dallin) to the other. The Muscovites – the Zaitsevs, Muratovs, Berdyaevs, Stepuns – link up together; Shklovsky, Bely, Ehrenburg, Remizov form a group around the Helicon publishing house. At Shklovsky's I meet Roman Jakobson, Elsa Triolet (Lily Brik's sister), the painter Ivan Puni. We don't see the K.-D.s and people remote to us write in their newspaper (*The Rudder*): the editor himself Iosif Gessen, Yuly Aikhenvald, Gleb Struve, the young Vladimir Nabokov. The publisher and friend of Blok, Alyansky, appears, as do the old Zinaida Vengerova, the actor Chabrov, the philosopher Lev Shestov, and Abram Lezhnev who is returning to Russia (to perish there).

On 30 June, 1922, we arrived in Berlin. Bely left for Zossen on 3 July and before his departure came to our place once but we were out. He hurried over later for just half an hour to say good-bye, telling us he would return to Berlin in September. I did not see him. When I returned home, the whole room was littered with ashes, butts were stuck in an inkwell, in a soap dish, and Khodasevich said that the minute Bely came through the door everything was transformed. He brought with him the magic of transfiguration. When he left, all again became as it was: the desk a desk and the armchair an armchair. He brought and took away something that no one else had. Until 11 September I waited for Bely. On the 11th he reappeared in Berlin.

A letter from Gorky awaited Khodasevich in Berlin. He left for Gorky's in Heringsdorf immediately and spent two days there. Days flashed by: 4 July – first meeting with Shklovsky abroad, the 5th – first meeting with Tsvetaeva, the 21st with Ehrenburg. On 18 August Aleksey Tolstoy gave a public reading of his comedy *Love – A Golden Book* (that day Khodasevich sent Marietta Shaginian a long letter). On 27 August both of us left for Gorky's for three days, on 1 September there was a literary soirée at the Café Landgraf (my first meeting with Pasternak), on the 8th again the Café Landgraf: Pasternak, Ehrenburg, Shklovsky, Zaitsev, Muratov, and others. On the 11th for Bely's return. On the 15th again the Landgraf, where Khodasevich read his verse. On the 22nd Nina Petrovskaya came to see us. On the 24th, in the evening at the Prager Diele (on Prager Platz), about fifteen people met around one large table at a café (Pasternak, Ehrenburg, Shklovsky, Tsvetaeva, Bely . . .). On the 25th, 26th, 27th Pasternak came to see us. On the 26th in the evening all of us (with Bely) went to *Pierrette's Veil*, an Arthur Schnitzler pantomime. (Chabrov played Harlequin; five years later he became a monk in a Jesuit monastery in Belgium.) On 1 October a meeting in honour of Gorky.* On the 10th the first appearance at our place of Wladimir Weidlé, thin, light-haired, young, and modest. On the 17th and 18th, again with Pasternak and Bely, in a café where the crowd included Mayakovsky. On the 27th a lecture by Shklovsky at the Café Landgraf, on the 3 November a lecture by the painter Ivan Puni. On the 4th Muratov and Bely came to see us, on the 10th I read verse at the Landgraf. On the 11th Pasternak, Muratov, and Bely were at our place (Khodasevich wrote in brackets 'like every day!'). So from day to day Khodasevich wrote short notes. There is also a separate list attached to them, 'Meetings with Bely':

1922, BERLIN.
July: 1, 3 (twice)
August: 8 (once)

*On 25 September thirty years of his literary activity had been commemorated.

154

September: 11, 12, 14, 15, 17, 18, 19, 20, 21, 22, 23, 25, 26, 28, 30 (15 times)
October: 1, 2, 6, 7, 9, 12, 13, 15, 16, 17, 18, 19, 21, 22, 24, 25, 26, 28, 29, 30 (20 times)
November: 1, 3, 4, 5, 7, 8, 10, 11, 12, 15 (10 times)

SAAROW.
November: 23, 24, 25 (3 times)
December: 6, 7, 8, 9, 13, 31 (6 times)

1923. SAAROW.
January: 1, 2, 10 (3 times)
February: 1, 13, 18, 19, 20, 21, 24, 25, 26 (9 times)
March: 1, 16, 17, 18, 19, 20, 21 (7 times)
May: 9, 15, 18, 22, 23 (5 times)

BERLIN.
July: 1, 4, 5, 6, 8, 11 (6 times)

PREROW.
August: 14–27 (4 times)

BERLIN.
August: 30, 31 (twice)
September: 3, 4, 5, 6, 7, 8 (6 times)

Andrey Bely was in the throes of a great crisis at this period of his life (1921–3). From the day he was born he was a 'mother's boy' and not a 'father's boy'; he had spent all his youth in search of a father, and before World War One he had found a father in the anthroposophist Dr. Rudolf Steiner. Returning to the West in 1921, after the years of hunger during the Civil War, he came face to face with a tragic fact: Steiner had renounced him, and Bely, shaken by this rejection and by being alone, was forced into his lifelong vulnerabilities; he could neither overcome them nor outgrow them nor reconcile himself to them. The reasons why Steiner had renounced him are clear to those who knew Bely well in those years in Germany. At the same time, after five years of life in Russia, Bely did not win back his first wife, Asya, who had stayed all those years in Switzerland and who, he thought, would *automatically* return to him. After his unsuccessful love for Liubov Blok, he saw in Asya the anchor of his salvation, which she never was. His drinking, verbosity, complaints, his senseless and fruitless ordeals made him at times irresponsible. He could have corrected all this only inwardly, within himself, as is always (isn't it always?) the case in life. He lived, however, in the hope that circumstances would change, that the one who had not returned would in some way 'understand' and return, and that the one who had renounced him would again receive him in the bosom of his anthroposophy. Bely did not see himself, did not understand himself, did not grasp the meaning of his life ('didn't manage to live his life', as he had said in a poem of 1908); he couldn't resolve his personal crisis or the whole tragic situation, and demanded 'pie in the sky' from those who surrounded him. It could not come his way, as happens with those who, however knowingly they observe outside themselves, do not know how to look into themselves. He lived as if deaf, not hearing the march of time and assuming in his madness that he would find 'darling Mama' in any woman and 'darling Papa' in Dr Steiner, his 'teacher of life' who had slipped away from him. But people around him became increasingly pitiless; this was the way of that time and not just a fashion. The 'pitiless' in people of our day had begun already in the 1880s and 1890s, when Strindberg wrote his *Confession of a Fool*. One can find some answers there to the dual dilemma of Andrey Bely. 'Have pity on me!' – but no one any longer knew how or wanted to pity. The word 'pity' was living out its last years, and it is not for nothing that this word is now used in many languages only in a derogatory sense, debasing to man – with an overtone of scorn in French, of vexation in German, of ill will in English. From a 'Pity me!' said in tears to the banging of his huge fist on the table – 'To hell with everyone!' – almost every evening he ran the entire gamut of his feelings for people, in a semi-delirium which he called an 'interruption of consciousness'. I saw him once playing Schumann's *Carnaval* on an old upright. No one listened to him; all were occupied with their own concerns, with themselves, that is with Herzen's 'most ferocious immanence'. The following day he didn't believe me when I told him he had played Schumann, and that I listened to him with pleasure – he remembered nothing. Another evening he twice told Khodasevich and me, in the most minute detail, the whole drama of his love for Liubov Blok and his quarrel with Aleksandr Blok, and when, without pausing for breath, he began to tell it a third time, I saw Khodasevich slipping from his chair onto the floor as if in a deep stupor. That night Bely banged loudly at my door wanting to 'finish telling' me something, and Khodasevich, in a cold sweat, implored me in a whisper not to open, not to answer: he feared that this wild, terrible story, having in essence neither meaning nor end, would begin again.

I knew and know it by heart. You can find a pale reflection of it in Bely's *Recollections* (in both editions: the first and basic one, and the second, re-worked for the Soviet printing). I know this story as I heard it innumerable times. And I am not alone. There were five or six people at that time in Berlin who would come upon Bely in the evening in Passauer, Augsburger, Prager, and Geissberg streets. Among those who went with him at night to the tavern was Zum Patzenhoffer, still alive today. But they will not tell all as I will not tell all. At the beginning of this book I said that I love *my secrets*. But I also preserve the secrets of others.

Bely loved Khodasevich. Perhaps in this period, from September 1922 to September 1923, there was not a man in the world he loved more. He loved me because I was Khodasevich's wife, but sometimes he tried to turn me against him; of course he didn't succeed. Khodasevich paid no attention to this, for there was a definite 'traitor' streak in Bely in matters small and large, and I think even now (as we both thought then) that in that crisis period he was like a wounded beast and all means of hurting others seemed legitimate to him when he himself had been so hurt. All blows were permitted, to alleviate the pain.

At the same time he was writing, sometimes for whole days, sometimes at night. This was the time of the *Recollections of Blok* which were being printed in Epopeya. That winter we lived in Saarow, near Berlin, where Gorky also lived with his family. Boris Nikolaevich often came to stay with us, wrote, and in the evening read to us what he had written. Yes, I heard him read these pages of his recollections of Blok; I had this supreme, unforgettable joy. He used to read to us from a rough copy till 2:00 A.M., sitting at a desk in his room; we sat on either side of him and listened. Once I remember I lay on his bed; it was the evening of 1 January, the celebration of the New Year had been at Gorky's, and I had gone to bed at 5:00 a.m.

157

The three of us had gone for a walk along the snowy paths of Saarow in the afternoon. Later I lay on his bed while he read and I fell asleep. I was ashamed to say I was not capable of fighting off sleep, or to ask him to interrupt his reading and put it off till the next day. I fell deeply asleep and at times, through sleep, heard his voice, but I could not wake up. Khodasevich's glasses gleamed and, grasping his thin knees with his hands and rocking, he listened attentively. These were chapters from *The Beginning of the Century*.

'What title do you imagine for that part?' Bely asked us uneasily several days in succession.

'"The Beginning of the Century",' I said rather impulsively, and so he called it.

Women around him that year saw the symptoms of his weakness, but didn't understand it. Many of them in that *Sturm und Drang* period of feminine initiative in everything (in our milieu) were more interested in the workings of a diesel engine than in sunsets; Bely did not recognize in them the finicky, over-refined (and today, for us, ridiculous), decadent beauties of his youth. When Klavdia Vasilieva (who later became his wife) came from Moscow, he found in her partly what he was seeking: a darling mama, the security, strength, and support for his foggy and tormented anthroposophical thought-feelings, together with an echo in her of orthodox, stone-like Steinerianism. She was not frightened by the terrible decline of emotional forces in him under the abnormal, excruciating pressure of a completely cerebral vision. Or did she misunderstand the crisis and merely see in Bely a stray sheep, a being not supported by any religious or philosophical idea, slipping into ruin and seeking a defence against the Eumenides? Was she in fact the strong person he sought? Or did she only succeed in pretending that she was strong and thus partly save him?

In the meantime he had the continual smile of a fool-madman, that fool-madman about whom he once wrote remarkable verse: '*I am sick! I have risen from the dead!*' ('They crushed him, they lashed him, they put a wet towel on his head.') This smile seemed painted on him; he never removed it, fearing that would be still worse. With this smile, in which his face was moulded, he tried (especially after drinking) to reappraise the cosmos, re-carve its meaning. In these instants, without a moment's pause, all his past whirled within him like a merry-go-round, rumbling with music or simply rattling, flashing with faces from the past or simply 'mugs', masks, grimaces. Now if only he could stop that infernal spinning in the depths of himself, if only he could begin living anew, in the present, but he couldn't: first because this was beyond his powers, and second because his reality would have been too terrifying. Sometimes the fool-madman, as if on a spring, suddenly jumped angrily out of him. I once asked him:

'Boris Nikolaevich, do you like Tsvetaeva?' This question, taking into account the whole context of our conversation, expressed my curiosity about his feeling for the verse of Marina and her personality. He opened his mouth still wider, recalling Nikolai Apollonovich Ableukhov, the hero of *Petersburg*, and word for word answered:

'I like Marina Ivanovna very much. How could I not like her? She is the daughter of Professor Tsvetaev, and I am the son of Professor Bugaev.'

I didn't believe my ears, and a year later in Prague, when he was in Moscow and his poem to her had already been published, I told Marina about this answer. She began to laugh with a certain melancholy and said that she had heard more than once from him similar *idiotic* answers to questions about people and books. (She used this answer to me in her recollections of Bely.)

Beside that was his genuine cry: 'I have risen from the dead! Look at me!' Then, as certainly before and probably later, in his intimate confessions and more often in his writing, he reached an improbable height from which he quickly 'tumbled' (one of his favourite words) into a pool – a metaphysical one, of course! From the frog in the pool to the image of Christ: you can follow these flights and falls in his prose and poetry, which were almost always incomprehensible to ordinary people, often offensive, and at times even repulsive.

Nikolai Apollonovich Ableukhov had a frog's smile. Bely in the Berlin period not only had that smile, but all his movements were frog-like. After a knock at the door he would appear, somewhere beneath the doorknob, then with a leap he was in the middle of the room, standing to his full height; it seemed that not only his feet but his hands were always ready for a new leap, huge strong hands with fingers brown from tobacco, spread wide in mid-air. His hair, almost completely grey, flew about a bronzed bald spot, the shoulders of his jacket – made of thick, ersatz, speckled German tweed – puffed out.

In *Confession of a Fool* by the great Swede, which I have already mentioned, there are pages in which you see Bely as through a secret glass. There are others of his predecessors and older contemporaries who, with him, were irreparably and incurably injured by their time (and some perhaps killed by it). This was when the twentieth century unleashed hurricanes, external and internal, onto its harsh path, which was open to all storms, and revealed in the sciences (about the universe in and outside us), new abysses and turning points which were blinding – not to those who moved and made their time, but to those who wanted to change it but did not know how to part with Kant, Saint Augustine, Euclid, Newton, and Aquinas. They pushed themselves away from the past with tremendous creative force, but in that very second trembled at the image of the future or turned to stone because of it, as before the Gorgon's face. All had a great ability to swim against the current, but no talent whatsoever for living in their own changing time.

You can imagine Blok, Gorky, even Mayakovsky in emigration. But Bely can be thought of in emigration in one way only: as the shadow of Dr Steiner in his Swiss Dornach, building a new Johannesbau (after the burning of the first, which had been built by the hands of Steiner's students, among them Bely's); the shadow of Steiner alive and dead (the Doctor died in 1925), and living as if behind a stone wall in the fortress of his Swiss *Weltanschauung* to the end. But there could be no fortress: on this very spot between Boris Nikolaevich and the Doctor a chasm opened in the years 1916–21 in which, as Bely himself would have put it, monsters swarmed. When Bely finally realized it was not on the path to Dornach that he would find 'father' or 'mother', he rushed back to Russia: the firm hand of Klavdia Vasilieva (who seemed to him that day stronger than she was) helped him find the road to Moscow.

But the greatness of his genius was such that in spite of his playing the fool painfully, his nightly drinking, his treacheries, the hysterical fuss over his past which would not subside, in spite of all those wounds opening and festering, each encounter with him was an illuminating event that enriched one's life.

He would come to our place and narrate something, more in the following style:

'I fly by tramway along the Kurfürstendamm. I see a little dog near a hydrant who has lifted his leg, musing sweetly. Suddenly some lady puts her foot on one of my galoshes. "Madame, whom do you take me for?" And she: "I have known you for a long time, I see you in my secret dreams. Our souls are cousins. You remember in Goethe? – '*Ach, du warst in längst vergangnen Zeiten/Meine Schwester oder meine Frau . . .*' When will I create a wonderful fairy tale with you?"

'I ran, hopping along, and German freaks ran towards me; I struggled in the crowd, elbowing through, seeking that little dog under the cigar ad . . . And then I reached you. My dearest, a cup of tea please, and if you find one, a little biscuit . . .'

He would come to our place, and we would go to 'sit' somewhere – this sometimes began at seven, or at nine in the evening, until well after midnight. Or he would take us, after some literary gathering, to the tavern Zum Patzenhoffer and there we would talk until it closed, that is about two or three in the morning. Or, when we moved to Saarow and he came to visit us for a few days, sometimes for a week, he would write, read to us what he had written, sometimes pare it down and rewrite, and again take us off to 'sit' with him – that is, to drink in a café, restaurant, or beerhall – or where people danced he would also dance – a much too frequent necessity for those like him, insecure and somehow immature, tortured till old age by temptations, fearing to give in to them and perhaps not knowing how, or not capable of doing so?

About our nocturnal walks through Berlin, Khodasevich wrote a remarkable poem: all three of us are in it, like the three witches in *Macbeth*, but with dogs' heads:

From the street in Berlin you can see the moon,
In the street in Berlin the shadows are long,
Houses like demons, blackness between,
Rows and rows of demons, and between – the wind.
Plans conceived in daytime, daytime souls – take flight!
All plans conceived in daytime are swallowed by the night.
Empty and defeated, we come out into the streets.
Through crossroads of darkness, like witches, in threes.

161

Not human our smell, not human our sounds,
On our stooping shoulders grow the heads of hounds.
Green dots of moonlight stare from every eye,
Lunacy possesses us, wild and dry,
Below – the asphalt glitters with dim and turbid sparks,
And overhead – the clatter of dry electric cracks.

Sometimes Klavdia Vasilieva would come with him to Saarow.
She resembled a nun ('the anthroposophical Virgin,' Bely would
sometimes call her in a fit of temper, behind her back of course, but
he called other anthroposophical ladies that as well). She wore a
long black dress and a black wool kerchief on her narrow shoulders.
To me (and all those around) she seemed ageless; she never smiled
with her fine, pursed lips; she had a little red nose and wore her hair
back in a stiff bun. She went to bed early in her allotted room next to
mine (we then lived in a hotel near the station), and not one sound
was heard from behind her wall. Bely never asked *her* to 'sit' with
him, or dance with him, or listen once again to the drama of his love
for Liubov Blok, or examine the ruins of the once-beautiful edifice
of his anthroposophical beliefs. She stood apart from all his fits of
anguish and of course could not have found herself a place among
those women whom he had then placed in a row – from the Sistine
Madonna to the streetwalker (one and the same woman being
sometimes the one and the other simultaneously). However,
Klavdia Vasilieva also had a whole series of incarnations: sometimes in his wild imagination she was his defence and shelter,
'almost like darling Mama', and sometimes he was ready to assign
her an insidious role: she had been sent by the 'Doctor' to follow
him and save him! She already had some thought of saving him,
apparently, but it was quite impossible to guess that she would
become his wife. She was, as was then said, a puzzling figure – that
is, she did not reveal her essence or her plans; perhaps neither one
nor the other actually existed.

In the summer of 1923 he would come to the seaside spot of
Prerow, where the Zaitsevs, the Berdyaevs, the Muratovs, and we
lived. It would rain. I would play chess with Muratov and have
long conversations, then light the stove, go for walks on the shores
of the Baltic in a raincoat in wind and rain, and in the evening watch
Doctor Mabuze at the movies. At the Zaitsevs', as always, it was

bright, warm, and lively. With a heavy walking stick Nikolai Berdyaev would leave on his daily walk along the dunes. His wife and mother-in-law were both sick with whooping cough.

Then we returned to Berlin, and suddenly it turned out that all were going somewhere, leaving in different directions, here and there. With this imminent separation in mind, we gathered on 8 September to be photographed on Tauentzienstrasse. Bely also came, but was obviously irritated and his smile was more than ordinarily forced. Gershenzon had told Khodasevich a month before that when he had gone to the Soviet consulate for a visa to Moscow for himself and his family (he left on 10 August) he had run into Bely, who was also petitioning for return. Bely had still not spoken to us of his intention. I remember Khodasevich's sadness about this – not so much because Bely had hidden something important about himself from him, but more because of his return to Russia. Not for a minute did Khodasevich think of dissuading Bely from going back to Moscow – Khodasevich said openly that it was not at all clear what would be better for Bely, to remain or return. He accepted as inescapable the return of both Gershenzon and the return of Shklovsky (after his letter of repentance to the Central Committee of the Communist Party), the return to Moscow of Aleksey Tolstoy and Boris Pasternak, and the lengthy vacillations of Muratov, who in the end remained. But anxiety on Bely's score was of a completely different kind: How, where, and for whom could he write best?

On 8 September the group picture was taken (in 1961 I added it to the collected verse of Khodasevich, published in Munich), and in the evening there was a crowded farewell dinner. Bely came in a state of fury I had never seen before. He greeted almost no one. Squeezing his huge hands between his knees, in a grey tweed suit with a jacket that hung down on him, he sat looking at no one, and when he rose at the end of the dinner, glass in hand, looking hatefully, with almost white eyes, at all those sitting at the table (there were more than twenty), he announced that he would make a speech. This was a toast, as it were, to one's self. The image of Christ in those moments came to life in this fool of a genius: he demanded that we drink to him because he was leaving to be crucified. For whose sake? For all of yours, sirs, sitting in this Russian restaurant on Gentienerstrasse, for Khodasevich,

Zaitsev, Remizov, Berdyaev . . . He is going to Russia
nself to be crucified for the sake of all Russian literature,
: will spill his blood.

ᴗнy not for me!' said Khodasevich quietly but distinctly at this
moment in the speech. 'I don't want you to be crucified, Boris
Nikolaevich, for me. I can in no way give you such a commission.'

Bely put his glass down in place and, looking ahead with
unseeing eyes, announced that Khodasevich always and everywhere had drowned all with the poison of his scepticism and that
he, Bely, would break relations with him. Khodasevich paled.
Everyone began to talk at once, turning the fact of the crucifixion
into a joke, a metaphor, a hyperbole, into an image of an after-
dinner speech. But Bely could no longer stop: Khodasevich was a
sceptic, destroying all that was around him while creating nothing;
Berdyaev was a secret enemy; Muratov an outsider who deceived
his own. In his wine-shattered fantasy, all those sitting around
suddenly turned into a ring of enemies who awaited his demise, did
not believe in his holiness, and greeted his doom with ironic smiles.
Every minute he became more and more foolish and arrogant.
Without taking notice of his rudeness or being insulted by it,
Zaitsev tried in vain to calm him down. Undoubtedly he saw
himself in those moments, if not as Christ, then as Saint Sebastian
pierced by arrows – the walls fell, the dragons opened their jaws and
there! he was ready to die, but *for no one!* He was led to the door. At
the last moment I wanted to grasp his hand, to betray Khodasevich
briefly, just to say to Bely that for me he was and would always be
great, one of the greats of my time, that his verse, and *Petersburg* and
The First Meeting were immortal, that meetings with him were for
me and would remain an *eternal memory*. Seeing that I was
approaching him, however, he shuddered, threw his head back and
prepared himself like a panther about to pounce – and I moved
back, or rather, sensible well-wishers pulled me back by the sleeve.
I never saw him again. He left Berlin for Moscow on 23 October,
1923. At first he was refused a visa, but then the Soviet consul
changed his mind.

Khodasevich and I were home, still in that same Krampe
boarding house, when towards evening, straight from the Zoo
Station, Vera Lurie our mutual friend arrived after seeing him off.
At the last minute he suddenly jumped from the train, muttering

'Not now, not now, not now!' This reminded me of the scene in *The Possessed* when Verkhovensky comes up to Kirillov who is repeating in a dark corner: 'Now, now, now.' The conductor pulled Bely into a car that was already in motion. He tried to yell out something, but nothing was heard. Whether Klavdia Vasilieva was with him or had returned to Moscow before, I don't remember. But if she was with him, then she certainly sat at that time near a window and calmly read some thick book.

Bely left. Berlin became empty – the Russian Berlin (I knew no other). The German Berlin was only the background for those years, sickly Germany, sickly money, the sickly trees of Tiergarten, where we sometimes strolled in the morning with Muratov. He was, as opposed to Bely, a quiet man who understood rages, and a man of inward order who understood the internal disorder of others. Styliz-ation in literature was his salvation, and he revealed the old and new Italy to the Russian symbolists. He was in his own way a symbolist, with his cult of the eternal feminine, his strong Europeanism, high standards, his own life-myth. He wore his symbolism like an atmosphere, an aura in which both he and those near him breathed easily. This was not a misty but a translucent symbolism, not decadent but eternal. He was always in love in a balanced and quiet way, and this feeling was also slightly stylized – sometimes as suffer-ing, sometimes as joy. His enchantments and disenchantments were more intellectual than sensual, but despite this he was a sensual man, not merely a clever *esprit*. He was generous and bestowed ideas on those talking to him which another in his place would have written down, retyped, and put in print, and he let them loose like birds – catch them who will. A part of them continues to live on in me. He could not, however, endure acknowledgement and gratitude, and loved only freedom in himself and in others. He was a whole and accomplished European and before World War One had already discovered Europe for himself; I discovered it through him in these years. For the first time, I heard from him the names of Gide, Proust, Valéry, Virginia Woolf, Spengler, Joyce, and many others who were quite familiar to him, feeding his mind, which was always alive and unburdened with the mannerisms or prejudices of his generation.

He was a frequent guest at our place. There was a time when he came every evening. He liked it when I sewed beneath the lamp (there is something about this in his story 'Scheherazade', dedicated to me). In Khodasevich's notes his name often appears in succession – with Boris Pasternak or Nikolai Otsup or Bely. I lived with him through my strongest theatrical experiences of the time: *Pierrette's Veil*, in which Chabrov appeared, and *Princess Turandot* (in Vakhtangov's production that visited Berlin). Chabrov was an actor and a mime of genius; I can refer to him in no other way, his magic and great, sparkling talent were exceptional. Fedorova (later to become mentally ill) played with him, and Samuil Vermel played Pierrot. I remember even now every detail of this striking spectacle – nothing has impressed me so much as this *Veil* – not Mikhail Chekhov in Strindberg, Jean-Louis Barrault in Molière, Zacconi in Shakespeare, Anna Pavlova as the Dying Swan, Ljuba Welitsch in *Salomé*. When Chabrov and Fedorova danced the polka in the second act, and the dead Pierrot appeared on the little balcony (Columbine does not see him, but Harlequin already knows that Pierrot is there), I understood for the first time (and forever) what real theatre is; and even now a shudder goes up my spine when I remember the Schnitzler pantomime performed by these three actors. Such theatre does something to the spectator, changes us, affects our later life and thought, becomes a kind of sacrament, swallowed and assimilated. The second recollection – Vakhtangov's production, is less strong: there was more of the actual show and less of the irrational shudder. We also more than once sat in the tavern Zum Patzenhoffer with Chabrov – he was a friend of Bely's (and at one time of Scriabin's).

More worldly were those Berlin cafés where a string orchestra played and couples swayed, where colourful lanterns at the entrance, surrounded by midges, floated beneath the greenery of Berlin streets. Sickly trees, sickly streetwalkers on the corner of Motzstrasse. All of us sleepless Russians wandered these streets sometimes till dawn – streets where in the daytime ailing German children went sedately to school, children born during the gas attacks on the Western front and slaughtered later near Stalingrad. Sometimes the artist Dobuzhinsky, whom I established friendly ties with that lasted thirty-five years, came to the Prager Diele. He belonged to a category of people new to me, and which I did not so easily get used to: I fall under their spell but I cannot like what they do. He was not an artist for me, he was only a man, a person to talk to, a friend. I pass over his paintings in silence.

Gershenzon did not go to the cafés. Once he went and spoke about it like this:

'Well, I was tired. And it was hot. Well, I thought, why not drop in to their café to rest. So I dropped in. They say: You must have dinner here, this is a restaurant. I explain to them that I have supper at the Krampe boarding house where I live with my family, and that I never eat in restaurants. They say: You can't. So I look around: another café. I drop in. They say: Only liqueurs here. Who needs their liqueurs? Give me a glass of water. Can't: This is a *Weinstube*. I was never in a *Weinstube* before, and I don't understand who needs them. No water. Again I look: a café. I enter, I ask: Is this or is this not a *Weinstube*? Not a *Weinstube*, they say. Is this a restaurant? No, this, they say, is a café. Oh – What luxury! Chandeliers, candelabras, rugs, servants in jackets, women – you understand, they have all that sort of thing . . . And can you drink water if you are thirsty? I ask. They are astonished. They don't ask me to sit down, but they bring me a glass of water on a tray. How much? I say. I was scared that I didn't have enough money. Nothing, they say, we will take nothing for water. Drink, they say, and go home. *Aufwiedersehen* . . . And you sit in such places every evening?'

Nina Petrovskaya came to see us, accompanied by her sister Nadia. Nadia was imbecilic and I was wary of her. Nina, her swarthy face covered with moles, had a short and squat body, coarse hands, was dressed in a long rustling décolleté dress, a large black hat with an ostrich feather and a cluster of black cherries: she seemed to me very old and outdated. The Renata of *The Fiery Angel*, Briusov's love, Bely's temptress – no, I hadn't imagined her like this. I don't think that even Khodasevich expected to see her like this. In her deep black eyes there was something comfortless, slightly sinister, and she spoke in a low voice of how she had written *him* a letter (she never called Briusov by his name) and now waited for *him* to answer her and invite her to Moscow. The cherries on her hat rocked and rustled like last year's leaves, and she used strange expressions that recalled Balmont even more than Briusov: hieratic, two-faced, he progressed like a black bird (about someone met on Passauerstrasse). When she kissed me I smelled the odour of tobacco and vodka on her. Once Khodasevich returned home in horror: he had sat three hours with

167

her and Bely while they squared some old accounts. 'It was exactly like 1911,' he said, 'only both of them were so old and frightful that I almost felt like crying.'

She regarded me with curiosity, as if she wanted to say: So there are people in the world who live to their heart's content as if nothing ever happened, not Briusov, not 1911, or shooting one another, not medieval witches, or Martell cognac in which *he* and she bathed their despair, not the whole *decadent saga*. Only cognac was then available (not Martell, but Kantorovitz), still I refused to drink with her; I didn't know how to. She came often, stayed for a long time, drank and smoked and spoke all the time of *him*. But Briusov did not answer her letter.

A few years later in Paris, after the death of her sister, she spent several days with us in our flat on Rue Lamblardie. In the morning, trying to hide it from me, she would drink wine on the corner of Place Dumesnil, and then made the rounds of the Russian doctors, imploring them to prescribe codeine for her, which had a special effect on her, partly substituting for the narcotics she had accustomed herself to. Her life was tragic from the day she abandoned Russia in 1912. How she made a living in Rome during World War One, no one asked; she probably lived to an extent on charity, if not worse. At night she couldn't sleep, she needed time and again to stir up the past. Khodasevich sat with her in what was called my room. I resigned myself to sleeping in his room on the couch. Tortured by conversations and smoking, grown numb from her drunken tears and codeine-inspired delirium, towards morning he came and lay down next to me, frozen (at night there was no central heating), tired, half sick himself. Sometimes I tried to force her to eat something (she ate almost nothing), to take a bath, wash her hair, launder her underwear and stockings, but she was already incapable of anything. One day she left and did not return. She had no money (we had none either at the time). A week later she was found dead in the garret of a Salvation Army hostel: she had turned on the gas. It was 23 February, 1928.

Meanwhile, at the Café Landgraf every Sunday in the year 1922–3 the Russian Club met: sometimes it was called the House of Arts. We read there: Ehrenburg, Muratov, Khodasevich, Otsup, Shklovsky, Pasternak, Bely, Zaitsev, I, and many others. Looking over Khodasevich's notes for the year 1922–3, I see that for whole days and especially evenings we were surrounded by people. Three publishing houses were especially active at the time: Sumsky's Epoch, Abram Vishniak's Helicon, and the house of Zinovy Grzhebin. For 27 October (1922) there is a short note to the effect that Khodasevich went to *Days*, Kerensky's paper which had then begun to appear in Berlin. The 15th of May (1923) is marked as the day of the arrival in Berlin of Mikhail Gershenzon. On 15 June Lunts was in Berlin. His father quickly took him to Hamburg, and on 6 August we were both at Gershenzon's, where I first met Lev Shestov and for ever joined his image with that of my father: they were unusually alike. From the 14th to the 28th August we lived in Prerow which I have already mentioned, and on 9 September, to be exact, the general separation began with the departure of the Zaitsevs to Florence. On 1 November Pasternak was at our place at Krampe's for the last time, and on the 4th Khodasevich and I left for Prague.

My acquaintance with Maxim Gorky was preceded by two myths, each of which bore the image of the man but not the writer. I saw him as a man, and a man he remained. His life and death were and are for me the life and death of a man I lived with for three years, under the same roof, and whom I saw in sickness and health, cheerful, angry, with all his weaknesses and strengths. He never was in my thoughts as a writer: at first I was immersed in Ibsen, Dostoevsky, Baudelaire, Blok; then (I was already living at Gorky's house) Gogol, Flaubert, Shakespeare, Goethe; and later (having parted with Gorky) I began to read and love Proust, Lawrence, Kafka, Gide, Valéry, and finally Joyce, the English and American moderns. As a writer Gorky had no place in my life. He still doesn't.

But as a man he entered my circle of thoughts through two legends. The first I heard while still a child. The Moscow Art Theatre had brought *The Lower Depths* to Petersburg. I saw a photo of a snub-nosed fellow in a Russian blouse: he was a tramp, he became a writer. He came from the poor classes, was well known, was photographed with Leo Tolstoy on a bench in a garden. Served in prison. Lived as he pleased. The whole world listened to him, and read him, and looked at him. He had walked all over Russia and now wrote books.

The second legend came to me through Khodasevich. Its background was Gorky's huge flat on Kronverksky Avenue in Petersburg. So many people came to stay overnight (actually – to drink tea and chat, but some for no reason stayed for years), so many people lived there, drank, ate, warmed themselves (hid from arrests), that the wall was broken through and two flats were made into one. In one room the Baroness Budberg lived (then still Zakrevskaya-Benckendorff), in a second an occasional guest who had dropped in, in the third Khodasevich's niece the painter and her husband, in the fourth the girlfriend of the artist Tatlin, the constructivist, in the fifth H. G. Wells stayed when he came to Russia in 1920, in the sixth, finally, Gorky lived himself. Khodasevich would stay in the ninth or tenth when he came now and then from Moscow. Gabriel Romanov, the former grand duke, was also there with his wife and dog in the former living room, not to mention Marya Andreeva, Gorky's second wife, and Ekaterina Peshkova, his first wife, who came from time to time.

The break in the wall particularly struck me. And the unpleasantness between Gorky and the Bolshevik Zinoviev, Lenin's right-hand man. Also the closing of *The New Life*, Gorky's newspaper of 1917–18. And finally his departure. Sick and angry at Zinoviev, Lenin, and himself, he had gone abroad. His flat became spacious and quiet. I was curious: Had the break in the wall been closed up?

Gorky then lived in Heringsdorf, on the shore of the Baltic Sea, and was still angry, especially at Aleksey Tolstoy and the newspaper *On the Eve*, with which he wished to have nothing in common. But Aleksey Tolstoy, then composing his novel *Aelita* on his typewriter, considered this a whim and, having met Khodasevich on Tauentzienstrasse in Berlin, told him openly, taking him by the lapel (this time not the turned jacket of Misha's, but the turned suit of the barrister N.): 'Listen, what kind of a suit are you wearing? Are you about to dress in Europe according to ideology? Go to my tailor, tell him to send the bill to *On the Eve*. I also order shirts. Ready-made shirts fit badly.'

This writer was famous for not liking poverty and knew how to live well. But Khodasevich did not go to the tailor: he was not about to collaborate with *On the Eve*.

At Aleksey Tolstoy's one already sensed the forthcoming departure of his whole family to Russia. His second wife, a poet, having grown plump, pregnant with her third son (the first, from her marriage with Wolkenstein, was here also), lived in complete harmony with her husband, and wrote verse about her 'passionate body' and 'unsatisfied embraces' – I felt awkward listening to Tolstoy was a good story-teller, although his sense of humour was coarse and primitive, like his writings. He knew how to make a trivial event alive and interesting, although listening to him narrate his visit to the dentist, or tell Jewish or Armenian jokes, or draw a picture of two 'wags' (he and Khodasevich) going to visit a third (Gorky), you could already foresee to what vulgarity he would stoop in his later novels. *Nikita's Childhood* he wrote in his former 'political mood'. An abyss lies between *Nikita* and *Aelita*. With astonishment I watched him type his novel directly on his Remington, in the presence of guests, in the corner of the living room – not rewrite it, but compose it, having sold it in advance to Gosizdat. This gave the impression that he liked more than anything not only to have money, but to count it, that he scorned those who had other interests and did not hide it. He had to pass through misfortunes, be directly involved in the all-Russian cataclysm, find a way to write the first volume of his *The Road to Calvary* – a thing made according to old literary prescriptions. When he felt secure, he began to decline. I now even doubt that he had *talent* (a combination of many elements, or part of them, or all to a small degree: discipline, uniqueness, ingenuity, measure, taste, intelligence, eye, language, the ability to think in abstractions, plus a 'spark').

We arrived at Gorky's in Heringsdorf on 27 August, 1922 (Khodasevich had been already there in early July, immediately after his arrival in Germany). It was not the split between the intelligentsia and the people, but the split between the two parts of the intelligentsia that always seemed to me fatal for Russian culture. The separation between intelligentsia and people was much less pronounced than in many other countries. It exists everywhere – in Sweden, in the U.S.A., in Kenya. One person watches television, another at the same time reads books, a third writes them, a fourth tumbles into bed early because tomorrow he must rise with the sun. X will not go to see a musical, Y will not go see a drama of Strindberg, Z will go neither to one nor the other but will stay home to write his own play. And a fourth has not heard that in the city there is even a theatre. All this is in the order of things. But when the intelligentsia is severed in two to its foundation, then the very hope disappears for something like a strong, spiritual civilization uninterrupted in its flow, and a national intellectual progress, because there are no values that would be respected by all. No matter how a Marxist Frenchman may reason, Valéry will always be great for him. No matter how abstractly Jackson Pollock painted, he will be great for most of the American bourgeoisie. Fifty years after his death, a marble plaque was nailed to the house where Oscar Wilde lived. One hand forbids, the other publishes the works of D. H. Lawrence. They try to force twelve- tone music into concert halls subsidized by the state – and who are they? English, American, German bureaucrats! So gradually those who a quarter of a century ago jarred and horrified people are accepted by the bourgeois, who at the same time support the state. This is the struggle of Western intelligentsia – via bureaucracy – with its own middle class.

With us the intelligentsia – on the very day when this term was born – was already cleft in two: some loved Blanqui, others Balmont. And if you loved Blanqui, you could neither love nor respect Balmont. You could love the verse of Béranger – or rather Béranger in his trashy Russian translation – but if you loved Vladimir Soloviev it meant that you were indifferent to hopes for the Russian Constitution, and only one path lay before you: obscurantism. At the same time both halves of the Russian intelligentsia hid elements of revolution and reaction in themselves: the politicians of the left were reactionary in art, those of the right were revolutionaries in art.

In the West people have one common holy 'shu' (a Chinese word that denotes what each one, whoever he may be and whatever he may think, admits to and respects). All counterbalance one another, and this equilibrium is one of the great factors in Western civilization and democracy. But in the Russian intelligentsia the elements of revolution and reaction never counterbalanced anything, there was no common 'shu', perhaps because Russians are not often capable of compromise – and the very word, in the Western world full of great moderating and creative significance, has the imprint in Russian of petty dishonesty.

The first evening at Gorky's I understood that this man belonged to a part of the intelligentsia different from the one I had known up to then.

Does he like Gogol? M-m-m, yes, of course . . . but he also likes Elpatievsky. He considers both realists, and so can fully compare them and even prefer one to the other. Does he like Dostoevsky? No, he hates Dostoevsky. So he told me then, the first evening we met, and repeated it many times later.

'Have you read Ogurtsov?' he asked me. 'No, I have not read Ogurtsov.' His eyes became moist: at that time he had placed great hopes in Ogurtsov. I never read the unknown Ogurtsov.

And so: the first moments in the dining room, the penetrating look of the deep blue eyes, the toneless, cough-laden voice, movements of hands – very smooth, clean, and even (someone said, like those of a soldier leaving a hospital) – the whole appearance of this tall, bent man with sunken chest and straight legs. Yes, he had a condescending, not always pleasing, smile, a face that knew how to become angry (when the neck reddened and the cheekbones moved beneath the skin); he had the habit of looking above whoever was talking to him when some pointed or unpleasant question was asked of him, of drumming his fingers on the table or, not listening, of singing. All this was part of him, but there was also something else: the natural charm of an intelligent man, not like others, who had lived a great, difficult, and remarkable life. That evening I saw, of course, only the charm, I still did not know that much of what Gorky said, as it seemed, for me – was in fact what he always said at every meeting with a new person whose favour he wished to gain, that the very tone of his conversation, even the movements with which he accompanied it, were due to his acting, and not to some spontaneous reaction to his companion. Tea was replaced by dinner, in the quiet of the dining room: Gorky, Khodasevich, the artist Ivan Rakitsky (who lived in the house), and I. ('What luck that you came,' Gorky repeated several times. 'This morning everyone left, Chaliapin and Maksim [his son] and someone else, I don't remember exactly who – so many people have been here these days.'

What was spoken about that evening? First Petersburg, because Gorky wanted news. He himself had come abroad ten months before, but up to now felt only half there. He cursed the Bolsheviks, complained that it was impossible to publish a magazine (publish it in Berlin and import it into Russia), that books were not published in sufficient quantity, that the censorship acted clumsily and coarsely, banning beautiful works. He spoke of disorders in the House of Writers, and outrages in the House of Scholars; at the mention of the group that wanted compromise with the Soviet regime he shrugged his shoulders, spoke with hostility of *On the Eve*. Several times in the conversation he mentioned Zinoviev and his insults of long ago.

But towards the end of dinner this discussion ended. The conversation turned to literature, to contemporary literature, to our 'avant-garde', to my Petersburg contemporaries, and finally to me. Like hundreds of beginners who did not know how to write anything besides verse, I had to read him my poems.

He listened attentively – he always listened attentively, whatever was read him, whatever was recounted him, and remembered it his whole life. Such was the uniqueness of his memory. In general he liked verse a lot; in any case it touched him to the point of tears, good verse and even quite bad. 'Keep trying,' he said. 'Don't rush to get into print, study . . .' He always wished one well – and me too. For him a person who had decided to dedicate himself to literature, to science, to art, was holy.

He liked verse, but he had determined once and for all on his own rules concerning the euphony and beauty of poetry, which he followed when he judged.

They also impeded him in prose, made his judgements sound hollow, but when he spoke or wrote about verse, it was more often than not unbearable. Here is what he once wrote to me. Very characteristic of him, it reflected his entire relation to poets and poetry:

> It seems to me that the definition, 'the poet is the echo of world life', is the most truthful . . . Is there really something better than literature, the art of the word? There is nothing.

It is hard to believe that this man could shed real tears at the verse of Pushkin, of Blok – not only Pushkin and Blok, however, but Ogurtsov and Babkin and many others.

The maid cleared the table and left. It became dark outside. Now Gorky was telling stories. After that evening I heard these very stories many times – about the same thing, told in the same words, to listeners as innocent as I was at the time. But when you first heard Gorky you had to marvel at his gift. It is hard to transmit this to people who have not heard him. In our time there are far fewer story-tellers; by and large, the generation born in this century, being itself rather tongue-tied, does not like to listen to orators at a tea table. In his oral tales Gorky told things unlike those he wrote, and his speaking was different from his writing: without moralizing, without underlining, simply as things were.

For him the *fact* was important, the occurrence in real life. He was an enemy of human imagination, and did not understand fairy tales.

'That's exactly the way it really was!' he would exclaim ecstatically, while reading some story or sketch.

'It was not at all like that,' he once said sombrely of Leonid Andreev's *Abyss*. 'He manufactured the end, and I quarrelled with him after this.'

But he had no consistency in all this, and in one of his letters (November 1925) you can find the following sentence: 'I do not like facts and distort them with the greatest pleasure.' What does this mean? Only that he liked the forward march of the revolutionary future even more than the facts and distorted the latter to the advantage of the revolutionary future.

The clock showed 2:00 A.M. I listened. I t seemed to me that I was walking with him through Russia forty years ago, from the Volga to the Don, from the Crimea to the Ukraine. Everything was there: old jokes from Nizhny-Novgorod, the time of political persecutions, the famous slaughter in one village when he stood up for a woman who was being beaten, the beginning of the Arts Theatre, the trip to America. His hands lay on the table, his face with its characteristically open nostrils and drooping moustache was raised, his voice, wavering, now drifted away from me. This meant that drowsiness was overcoming me. I opened my eyes wide, fearful of falling asleep. I couldn't help it! The sea air, the trip, and my youth made it difficult for me to restrain myself from putting my head on the table.

One didn't have to ask him questions. Propping himself up with one hand and waving the other in front of himself, he spoke and smoked; when he lit cigarettes he did not put out the matches but made a fire from them in the ashtray. Finally he looked at me fixedly:

'Time to go to bed,' he said, smiling. 'Take the poet away.'

The artist Rakitsky, who in the absence of a hostess fulfilled the role of one, led me upstairs. In that room, the previous evening, Chaliapin had spent the night. I had seen him twice on the stage in

Russia, and it seemed to me that his shadow soared in the air. When I was left alone I sat for a long time on the bed. I heard Gorky's cough on the other side of the wall, his steps, the turning of pages (he read before going to sleep). All judgement about what I saw and heard I put off till later.

On 25 September 1922, Gorky moved to Saarow, a one-and-a-half-hour rail trip from Berlin, in the region of Frankfurt on the Oder, and in early November he persuaded us to move there as well. We moved into two rooms in the hotel near the station.

The Kronverksky atmosphere, the transient-hotel character of Gorky's house, was renewed in Saarow, a quiet country spot, empty in the winter, on the shore of a large lake which Maksim once persuaded me to cross under sail in windy weather.

The Kronverksky atmosphere was renewed, it is true, only on Sundays: with the morning train from Berlin, people began to arrive – both close and casual friends, but primarily, of course, 'our gang', of which there were more than a few.

Through a window of the Bahnhof Hotel, I saw people walking from the station along the lifeless streets of the little German town, where the quiet was broken only by the whistles of rare trains and the cleanliness was such that after a long rainfall the streets seemed washed. A wood with deer was not far from Gorky's house. Each deer had a name and the trees had numbers.

For Marya Andreeva, his second wife, who came quite often, everything in the house was bad:

'And what do they feed you here?' she said, examining with disgust a chop served to him. 'And what's that you're wearing? Is it really not possible to find a better villa?'

In spite of her years, she was still handsome and carried her red-haired head proudly, played with her rings, and perched a tight slipper on her toe. Her son from her first marriage (a movie director), a man who appeared to be forty, sometimes came with his wife, but she regarded them, as all of us, with scornful condescension. I never saw in her face, never heard in her voice, any *charm*. But probably even without charm she had been beautiful in her time.

Marya Fedorovna did not come during the same times as Ekaterina Pavlovna, Gorky's first wife and mother of his son Maksim. She was totally different. She came straight from Moscow, from Kremlin reception rooms, equipped with all possible news.

Then from Gorky's study we heard: 'Vladimir Ilych said . . . Feliks Edmundovich replied to this . . .' She had the habi looking one in the eye, and in the old intelligentsia manner, acquired in youth, of speaking, as it were, 'from the heart'.

With Marya came Petr Kriuchkov, a confidential agent of Gorky's, something like a factotum. Later, during the great purges, Stalin 'proved' that he was an 'enemy of the people' and shot him after he had recanted. He has still not been rehabilitated. With Ekaterina came one Mikhail Nikolaev, head of the international book division of the state publishing house (he died in 1947). He spoke little and played more with the dog in the garden.

And so: the table is set for twenty, chairs are brought from all over the house. Baroness Budberg, Gorky's secretary and friend, pours out the soup. I must say a few words about her: Moura, born Countess Zakrevskaya (great-granddaughter of Pushkin's 'bronze Venus'), by her first marriage Countess Benckendorff, by her second Baroness Budberg, was born in 1892. A book was written about her in 1933 by Bruce Lockhart. He was the British Consul in Moscow during the Revolution and in 1918 replaced Ambassador Buchanan, who returned to England. A movie called *British Agent* was made from the book starring Leslie Howard and Kay Francis. Moura appeared on Kronverksky in 1919–20, after she had been arrested by the Cheka and was in prison in connection with the arrest of this very Lockhart. When Lockhart was released and sent to England, she started looking for work, came to the Universal Literature publishing house and met Korney Chukovsky, who introduced her to Gorky. She knew English well, better than Russian, and sought work as a translator. She settled on Kronverksky and lived there till her departure (illegal) for Tallin. In Estonia, where her children from her first marriage lived, she soon married Baron Nikolai Budberg. When Gorky came to Berlin in 1921 she again came to live with him and till 1933 remained close to him. Three times a year she left Gorky's household to visit her children in Tallin, and also went to London where she had friends, the closest of whom was H. G. Wells. After Gorky's final departure in 1933 to the U.S.S.R., she moved to London. Following Wells's death in 1946 she had a flat in London. In her time she translated Gorky's work into English, but unfortunately her translations are very weak: in a collection of Gorky's best stories of the years 1921–5 (including 'The Story of a Hero' and 'The Blue Silence') she left out entire paragraphs and often showed she did not understand idiomatic Russian. She continued to translate Soviet authors recommended by Gorky, during the 1920s and 1930s, and later, in the 1960s, also carelessly, the *Recollections* of Aleksandr Benois.

And so: Baroness Budberg pours out the soup. The conversation at the table is noisy, as though everyone were speaking to himself and listening to no one else. Marya says that the dumplings in the soup are inedible and asks if I believe in God. Semen Yushkevich looks all around with sad eyes and says that nothing is good for anything, that death will soon come, that it is time to think of the soul. Andrey Bely, his smile strained, looks with piercing eyes into his plate – someone forgot to give him a spoon and he waits silently till one of the household notices it. He is stunned by the noise, the laughter at the 'young' end of the table and the coffin-like silence of the host himself, who looks over everyone, raps his fingers on the table and keeps silent – this means that he is out of sorts. Khodasevich, Victor Shklovsky, Sumsky the owner of Epoch publishing house, Grzhebin, Ladyzhnikov (an old friend of Gorky's and also his publisher), the conductor and pianist Issay Dobrowen, are among the guests. Gorky thaws only gradually and towards the end of the dinner an orderly conversation starts. It is primarily Gorky who speaks, sometimes Khodasevich or Bely says a word. But Bely is not as usual; here his ceremonial politeness goes to extremes, he agrees with everyone, hardly understanding, even when Marya says the chicken is over-cooked. Now he is embarrassed to the point of tears.

But perhaps this was him at his truest – Bely's tone in his conversations with Gorky? It was impossible to argue with Gorky. You couldn't convince him of anything, because he had an astonishing ability: not to listen to what he didn't like, not to respond when a question was asked which he had no answer to. He 'turned a deaf ear', as Baroness Budberg put it – to such a degree that you had to shut up. Sometimes, however, not turning a deaf ear, he would, with an evil countenance, all red, stand up and go to his room, in the doorway finally stating:

'No, that's wrong.'

And the argument was at an end.

Once I saw Aleksey Rykov on a visit to Gorky; then president of the Soviet of People's Commissars, Rykov had come that year to Germany to undergo a cure for hard drinking. He spoke in a dull voice of the literary polemics then in progress between some high officials of the Party.

'How did it all end?' asked Khodasevich. This literary polemic really troubled him.

'We ordered it to be stopped,' Rykov answered dully.

I looked at Gorky, and suddenly it seemed to me that there was something in common between this answer of Rykov's and his own 'No, that's all wrong,' spoken in the doorway.

There were dozens of people who spent some time at Gorky's in those years – I speak of those who came from the Soviet Union. I could not enumerate all. The list of names, between 1922 and 1928, could begin with people's commissars and ambassadors, pass on through sailors of the Soviet fleet, to old and new writers, and end with Anastasia, the sister of Marina Tsvetaeva, who brought with her to Gorky's in Sorrento some poet-improviser in 1927 who displayed at the villa Il Sorrito his 'art', about which Anastasia spoke later in *Novy Mir* (in 1930).

One had to hear Gorky out and keep silent. Perhaps he did not himself consider his opinions infallible, but he did not want to, indeed probably already could not, reconsider or reappraise anything: you only touch something, and something else begins to slip away, the whole building crumbles, and then what? Let all remain as it was once built.

I enter his study before lunch. He has already finished writing (he writes from 9:00 A.M. on) and now sits reading émigré newspapers (*Days* and *The Rudder* from Berlin and *The Latest News* from Paris) wearing his colourful Tatar skull cap. He knows that I have come for books; there are shelves near the wall. The books come, a few at a time, from Russia.

I take a volume of Dostoevsky from the shelf.

'Aleksey Maksimovich, may I take . . .'

'Take what you like.'

He looks at me with kindly eyes, through glasses, but it is better not to tell him exactly what I took: in the course of my life with him I came to the conviction that though he cried over Russian verse, he did not like Russian prose.

Russian writers of the nineteenth century were for the most part his personal enemies: he hated Dostoevsky; he scorned Gogol as a man physically and morally sick; the names of Chaadaev and Vladimir Soloviev harassed him with spite and passionate jealousy; he laughed at Turgenev. Leo Tolstoy awoke a kind of disarray in him, a kind of restlessness that tortured him. Of course he considered him great, the greatest, but he liked to talk of his weaknesses, to rise to the defence of Sofia Andreevna, to approach Tolstoy from a peculiar angle. Once he said:

'Take three books: *Anna Karenina*, *Madame Bovary*, and Thomas Hardy's *Tess*. How much better European writers did *that* than ours! There *such* a woman is so much more remarkably described!'

But whom exactly did he like?

Above all, his disciples and followers; then simply those provincial self-taught devotees, beginners who sought support from him, of whom he spoke with great sentimentality and of whom nothing ever came. In addition he liked those he had met in his youth, writers who had disappeared from human memory, whose names now tell one nothing but who in their time were read by him as a revelation.

'And here is Karonin,' he said, 'he has described this remarkably.'

'Aleksey Maksimovich, I have not read Karonin.'

'You haven't? Without fail read him.'

Or:

'And here is Eleonsky . . .'

But there was an instance that remained unique. This was the day when he received from a Russian bookstore in Paris a recently published book of Bunin's latest stories. All was abandoned: work, letters, the reading of newspapers. Gorky locked himself in his study, came to lunch late and in such a state of absent-mindedness that he forgot to wear his dentures. Confused, he got up and went to his room for them and there blew his nose good and loud.

'What is Douka [so he was called in the family] sobbing about?' asked Maksim, but no one knew. And only at teatime was there an explanation:

'Remarkable . . . Outstanding . . . I am telling you . . .' He could say no more, but for a long time afterwards he did not touch Soviet current best-sellers or manuscripts sent to him by unknown geniuses.

Bunin in those years was his sore spot: he continually remembered that Bunin was alive somewhere, lived in Paris, hated the Soviet regime (and Gorky with it), probably lived in poverty, but wrote beautiful books, and also remembered his, Gorky's, existence, could not help remembering it. To the end of his life Gorky obviously remained curious about Bunin. Among the letters of Gorky to Aleksey Tolstoy in the U.S.S.R. there is one in which he writes from Sorrento what Bunin had said *the other day* in Paris. Baroness Budberg, who had just been in France, brought him this news. In the light of what happened much later, it is now clear that the link between the two writers had been provided by a member of the French Communist Party, who had been a house guest at Bunin's as a friend and admirer, which no one had any notion about before 1946.

Reading Bunin, Gorky did not ask whether these were facts or imaginings. True, snorting and sighing in his room over Bunin, he did not forget to correct misprints, if there were any, with a pencil (I never saw him without a pencil in his smooth, clean fingers); and in the margins opposite a questionable word combination – be this Demian Bedny himself! – he would put a question mark. Certain word combinations seemed to him inadmissible – it was one of the rules that had come to him, probably, from some self-appointed provincial teacher of euphony and had lodged itself in his memory. Other worldly rules were: death is an abomination, the aim of science is to prolong human life, all the physiological functions of man are shameful and repellent, every manifestation of the human spirit aids progress. Once he emerged from his study dancing, gesturing with his hands, singing, and expressing in his face such ecstasy that all were dumbfounded. It seemed he had read the recurrent news report that soon scientists would discover the cause of cancer.

He was trusting, and loved to trust. Many deceived him: from the Italian cook, who made up unbelievable bills, to Lenin who continually promised him an easing of the lot of writers, scholars, and doctors. To give Lenin pleasure he wrote *Mother*. But in response Lenin did not please him. Gorky believed that between him and Romain Rolland there was an understanding, unique in its way, a lofty friendship of two titans.

Now the correspondence of these two has been published in part.

It lasted many years, was quite frequent, and was conducted in French. Gorky wrote through a translator; I was that translator several times.

'Nina, be so kind, please translate for me what Rolland writes here.'

I take a thin sheet of paper and read an exquisite and fastidious handwriting that recalls Arabian script.

Dear Friend and Teacher. I received your fragrant letter, full of flowers and aromas, and reading it I wandered in a luxurious garden, finding delight in the wonderful shades and bright-lit spots of your thoughts.

'And what's this about? I asked him a question: I need the address of Panayit Istrati, see whether you have it there.'

. . . the spots of your thoughts that carry me away with smiles to the blue sky of meditations.

In the evening he brings a rough copy of an answer to be translated into French. He has written that the world for the past hundred years has been moving towards the light, that in this approach to the light all those worthy of bearing the name of man go hand in hand. Among them, in the front ranks is Istrati, 'about whom you wrote me, dear Friend and Teacher, and whose address I in earnest ask you to send me in your following letter'.

Sometimes – about once a year – Rolland sent Gorky his picture. For me to translate into Russian the inscriptions he made on them was harder than translating his letters. We did it all together, assembling in Maksim's room. Maksim, as always when musing, chewed his lower lip.

The first 'German' winter was replaced by the second – though it was spent in Czechoslovakia, but in its most German spot, in the dead distant, out-of-season Marienbad. We followed Gorky from Prague. All visits here – of friends and strangers – had already stopped. In complete solitude, surrounded only by family and people he considered close to him, Gorky sunk into work: at the time he was writing *The Artamonov Business*.

182

He would rise at eight and, alone while all slept, he drank his morning coffee and gulped down two eggs. We didn't see him before one.

The winter was snowy, the streets were in snowdrifts. We went out for a walk in furs and felt boots, all together, at dusk (after lunch Gorky usually wrote letters or read). We walked across the snow to the pine forest in the hills. Somewhere three kilometres away ski races were in progress, music thundered, photographers and reporters rushed there. We saw nothing of this. From November on, Christmas preparations began in the city, and we also ventured out for a tree. There were few distractions and Gorky liked them, especially when he was working strenuously and felt like interrupting his thoughts with something light and pleasant. We got a real tree, with presents,* charades, even a gramophone obtained from somewhere. But the principal distraction that winter was the cinema.

Once a week, on Saturday, at dinner, Gorky would put on a cunning expression and inquire if it was not too cold outside. This meant that today we were going to the cinema. Someone was sent immediately for the coachman; the theatre was on the other side of town. No one cared what film was playing, whether it was good, worth going to. All ran upstairs to get dressed, wrapped themselves in anything that was warm if there was a storm. The wide two-horse sledge is in front of the porch of the Hotel Maxhof and we sit – all seven: Moura Budberg and Gorky on the back seat, Khodasevich and Rakitsky on the front seat, Maksim's wife, nicknamed Timosha, and I on someone's knees, Maksim in the box next to the coachman. This is called the departure of the fire brigade.

The horses carried us through empty streets, the bells rang out, lights sparkled on the shafts, the cold wind cut our faces. The ride lasted about twenty minutes. At the theatre we were met with respect – besides us there was hardly anyone. Happily anticipating the film, we sat in a row, not caring whether *The Last Days of Pompeii*, *Two Orphans*, or Max Linder† was shown. The return trip was as gay as the trip there.

That winter (1923–4) all gradually gave way to work. *The*

*I have one of them to the present day, a cypress wood box with incrustations.
†And not Savarin, as is said in the *Short Literary Encyclopaedia* (Vol. 2, 1963).

Artamonov Business progressed, grew, occupied Gorky more and more intensely, and gradually pushed aside all else. Even his interest in his own journal (*Beseda*) dimmed – it was an attempt to combine émigré and Soviet literature, but nothing came from it. Intense personal effort did not let Gorky see that, in essence, he was beginning to be completely alone with his own self, having united with no one. He awaited a visa for Italy. It came in the spring, with specific instructions from Mussolini not to settle on Capri (where his presence could arouse some dim political passions, because of his stay there from 1907 to 1913), and Gorky moved to Sorrento – the last place of his existence abroad.* In the autumn of 1924 we followed him.

The last place of his independence and his free work on what he wanted to write. Lenin was dead. His recollections of 'Ilych' were the first step towards reconciliation with those who were now at the top in Moscow. 'He will go there very soon,' I told Khodasevich once. 'Actually it's incomprehensible why he still hasn't gone there.' But Khodasevich did not agree with me: it seemed to him that Gorky could not digest the regime, that a deep attachment to old principles of liberty and the dignity of man would hold him back. He did not believe in the success of those in Gorky's entourage who were working for his return. To me it seemed that this would occur sooner than they supposed. Sorrento turned out to be the last place where he could write sometimes out of tune with the regime and say aloud what he thought, and the last place to which he came relatively healthy. Here, at the seashore, in a villa from which you could see the Bay of Naples, with Vesuvius and Ischia, I first saw him ill. This illness aged him a lot.

The doctor was brought from Naples and diagnosed a severe cold and bronchitis. We feared pneumonia – all his life he himself and those near him feared this illness that (according to the first official version) led Gorky to the grave. The prescription was poultices of hot oats on the chest and back. Timosha and I were both inexperienced in such a cure. Moura Budberg was then away. Behind a screen, in his huge study, on a narrow high bed, Gorky lay red with fever and coughed (and as a result was still more ruddy), observing us without saying a word. We tried to act quickly and

*From here in 1928 he went to the U.S.S.R., and on 17 May 1933, moved there for good.

deftly: so that the oats would not cool off we put it with soup spoons onto an oilcloth and wrapped the thin feverish body in this cloth, bandaging him with the long, wide bandage.

'Very good. Thanks,' he snorted, though all was not at all good.

In the fireplace olive branches crackled, shadows moved quickly across the walls and ceiling. At night, by turns, we kept watch at Gorky's bedside. In the morning the doctor again came. Gorky was not finicky about his health and did not like doctors.

'Oh, leave me, leave me alone,' he grumbled. 'Tell that man to get out and go home.'

'What does the great writer deign to say?' asked the doctor respectfully.

'Translate to him that he can go to the devil. I will get better without him,' muttered Gorky.

He got better sooner than we expected.

His throat bandaged, with a lot of grey hair in his thinning crew-cut, he again organized his day, his work.

There were no Christmas trees here, no movies, but there was Italy, in which he found delight every minute of his stay. Capri recollections still lived firmly in him:

'I will show you . . . I will take you . . .' he would say, but everything changes, and those places, like everything, had changed since the time of the war: so he could not find the old street singers, the new ones sang American Broadway hits, and the tarantella on the town square was danced in front of the café by children who then made the rounds of the tourists with a platter.

In January there were days when all four of the windows of his study were wide open. He would go out on the balcony. Below in the garden voices rang out: that year Maksim, who was twenty-eight, had acquired a motor cycle and messed about with it. The Harley-Davidson with three passengers (two in the side-car, the third on the driver's seat) flew through hills – to Amalfi, Ravello, Graniano. Gorky merely brushed aside any invitation to go for a drive: he hated and feared speed.

Incidentally he also had a revulsion for any kind of drugs. He smoked a lot, sometimes liked to drink, but to force him to take analgesics or allow cocaine in the hollow of his tooth was impossible. He now and then performed on himself some torturing operations and was extremely resistant to any pain.

185

During our strolls he liked to tell stories about Chekhov, Andreev, about all that was quickly receding into the past. And the time of his magazine *Letopis* and his paper *The New Life* were also in the past. But he had never liked to speak about his old books – in this he was in no way different from the majority of writers – and didn't like it when one remembered his former work and praised it. To mention in his presence 'The Song of the Stormy Petrel' would have been completely tasteless. Even his story 'About Unrequited Love', written in 1923, receded into the past—it was the fault of *The Artamonov Business*, which he was finishing now with such eagerness.

In the evening there was card-playing, when in the early Italian spring the wind howled and rain poured. Maksim and I were busy with our magazine. I don't remember how it arose and why; we put it out once a month, a single copy, luxurious, copied out by hand and illustrated. Maksim's principal task was to get Gorky's unpublished work for the magazine: it was a magazine of humour. Gorky, embarrassed, would enter his son's room, holding a piece of paper in his hand.

'Well, I've brought a little poem here. Want it?'

'It was never printed anywhere?'

'Of course not, good God, my word! I just wrote it.'

'All right, let's have it.'

Gorky didn't know how to make jokes. In verse especially. I remember the following four lines: 'In the water without any reason/A fish splashed about/And on my shoulder two gadflies/Started copulating.' Maksim illustrated the whole text with a water colour. My first work in prose, 'A Novel in Letters', went into this magazine. The letters were written by a twelve-year-old girl, smart and weird, who lived in Gorky's house, where Turgenev and Pushkin dropped in for good company. Guests and hosts strolled and dined together, and played slapjack with Dostoevsky . . .

Often, looking at Gorky and listening to him, I tried to understand what exactly kept him in Europe, what he could not accept in Russia. He grumbled at the receipt of some letters, sometimes banged on the table, clenching his jaws, saying:

'Oh, the scoundrels, the scoundrels!'

Or:

'Oh, the cursed stupidity!'

But on the following day he was again pulled in the other direction and you felt that both petty and major differences *could* be smoothed over.

Too much was strange and inimical to him in the new (post-war) Europe; his need for keeping an integrated world view was too great, a need he acquired twenty-five years before from the Social-Democrats (not without Lenin's help) and he could not imagine existence without it. Now it was becoming clear: only *there* (in Russia) did people fundamentally like him live, only *there* could he save himself from oblivion as a writer, from loneliness, from money problems. The fear of losing readers *there* grew in him. Anxiously he listened to tales about how authors *there* were writing under the influence of Pilniak, of Mayakovsky. He feared that he would suddenly come to be necessary to no one.

He had barely finished *The Artamonov Business* when he wanted to read it to us – the first part of the novel was finished, the two following ones were only in rough draft (later he re-did them and spoiled them). It may seem strange that he decided to read the whole novel aloud: he read it three evenings in a row, till he was hoarse and lost his voice, but obviously this was necessary not only for him to see our impressions but so he could hear himself.

He sat in a corner at a desk, in gold-framed glasses that made him look like an old workman. Light fell on his hands and manuscript. At quite a distance from him, near the dying fire, Maksim and his wife slept soundly on a couch, leaning against each other – they could not endure a reading for more than an hour. Baroness Budberg, Rakitsky, Khodasevich, and I sat in armchairs. The dog lay on a rug. The uncurtained windows sparkled with blackness. The lights of Castellamare flickered on the horizon, the lighted staircase to the crater of Vesuvius sparkled in the sky. Now and then Gorky gulped water from a glass, smoked, and often towards the end took out a handkerchief and wiped his tear-moistened eyes. He was not squeamish about crying over one of his own works in our presence.

There were and are in *The Artamonov Business* – despite later corrections – powerful, remarkable pages. As a whole this novel ends an entire period of Gorky's creativity, but it was weaker than Gorky's writing in the immediately preceding years. Those years, between his arrival from Russia to Germany and *The Artamonov*

Business, are the best in Gorky's entire creative life. They represent the rise of all his creative powers and the weakening of his moralizing pressure. In Germany, in Czechoslovakia, in Italy, between 1921 and 1925, he didn't try to teach, he wrote with the maximum of liberty, equilibrium, and inspiration, and with the minimum of regard for what *use* his works would be to future communism. He wrote seven or eight long stores 'for his own self', as it were. They were dream stories, vision stories, madness stories. *The Artamonov Business* turned out to be a decline from this level toward his last period, which is now difficult to read.

Among Soviet critics not one, it seems, has understood and evaluated this period, but Gorky himself felt that he had begun to write differently: in a letter of 1926 he confessed that 'I have started to write better' (*Literary Heritage*, Vol. 70). This entire period (the 1920s) undoubtedly contains things that will live when his early and late writings have died. Why did these years turn out that way for him? There is an easy answer: because he was living in the West and was free of Russian political impressions, because he was not dictated to and was on his own. But this is not all: after the years of the Revolution, there was rest in comfort and peace, there was a private life that did not torture him but stayed happy; it was the 'moment of his destiny', without financial worries, problems, decisions for the future – the moment of destiny when the writer remained alone with himself, pen in hand and consciousness wide open.

He came to Europe, as I have already said, angry at many, among them Lenin. And angry not only at what was done in Russia in the three years 1918–21, but profoundly wrecked by what he had seen and experienced. I remember one conversation he had with Khodasevich: they recalled how both (but at different times) in 1920 went to a children's home, or perhaps reformatory for pre-teenagers. These were mostly girls, syphilitics, homeless from twelve to fifteen; nine out of ten were thieves, half were pregnant. Khodasevich, despite, it would seem, the nervousness of his nature, with a kind of pity and revulsion, remembered how these girls in rags and lice clung to him, ready to undress him there on the staircase, and lifted their torn skirts above their heads, shouting obscenities at him. With difficulty he tore himself away from them. Gorky went through a similar scene: when he began to speak about it, horror was on his face, he clenched his jaws and suddenly became silent. It was clear that this visit shook him deeply – more, perhaps, than his previous impressions of tramps, the horrors of the lower depths from which he took his early subject matter. Perhaps, now in Europe, he was healing certain wounds he himself was afraid to admit to; and at times (though not following the Dostoevsky he hated) he asked himself, and only himself: *Was it worth it?*

Lenin's death, which made him very tearful, settled matters between them. A sentimental attachment to Dzerzhinsky had long been characteristic of him. He began to write his recollections of Lenin the very first day he received the telegram about his death (from Ekaterina, his first wife). The following day (22 January, 1924) a condolence telegram was sent to Moscow. In it Gorky asked Ekaterina to place on Lenin's tomb a wreath with the inscription 'Farewell, friend!' Tears fell while he wrote his recollections. Something old-womanish suddenly appeared in him those days, then disappeared. This ability of his lachrymal glands to exude liquid for any reason (coarsely noted by Mayakovsky) was and remained for me a puzzle. In the deterministic world in which he lived, there would, it seemed, be no place for tears.

We left in April 1925. The night before I said to him that what I found most important in him was his 'divine electrical energy'. 'In Vyacheslav Ivanov' – I began to laugh – 'it came from Dionysus. And in you?'

'And in you?' he asked me in answer, not laughing.

I reminded him of his own words. It was in 1884, it seems; he was unloading a barge somewhere and, while unloading, felt 'a half-mad ecstasy of activity'. I said to him that I understood this well, but out of embarrassment again I began to laugh.

'I am laughing,' I confessed when he said nothing in reply, 'but I say this completely seriously.'

'I sense that,' he said, touched, and began to speak of something else.

The Italian coachman rode dashingly up to the porch, whipping his chestnut-coloured horse. Gorky stood at the gates, in his customary dress: flannel trousers, light-blue shirt, deep-blue tie, a grey knitted jacket with buttons. Khodasevich said to me: 'We will never see him again.' And then, when the carriage had rolled

n towards Sorrento and the figure on the porch became hidden by a turn in the road, he added with his usual finesse and without mercy:

'He will not be given the Nobel Prize, Zinoviev will be removed, and he will return to Russia.' Khodasevich now had no doubt of this.

Gorky returned to Russia in three years. At his feet were not only the main streets of large cities, not only theatres, learned institutions, factories, collective farms, but a whole city. There he also lost his son, perhaps cleverly 'removed' by Yagoda and perhaps not. He lost his own self. A legend exists that in the last months of his life he cried a great deal, kept a diary which he hid, requested permission to go to Europe. What is true in this legend, what is invention, will perhaps never be known or will come out only in a hundred years, when it will have lost interest. With time secrets lose their fascination: who hid beneath the Iron Mask has now no interest for anyone save historians. The publication of the letters of Natalia Herzen to Herwegh (in England), which fifty years ago would have alarmed the whole of the Russian intelligentsia, came almost unnoticed, and the Heeckeren archive, published in France, which would have caused great dismay, has not to the present day been translated or been taken into account in Russia. Everything has its time, and secrets die like everything else. Was Gorky killed by executioners hired by Stalin or did he die from pneumonia? – there is now no answer to this question. But more important: How did he feel when he began to perceive the planned destruction of Russian literati? The fall of all that he had loved and respected his whole life? Was there in his entourage at least one man whom he could trust and with whom he could talk about this? There was always ambiguity in him. Did it save him from anything?

It was always more important for him to be heard than to speak out. The very fact of speaking out was less necessary to him than that he be heard or read. For a writer like him there is nothing surprising in this fact, and the majority of writers of his generation would have agreed with him in this. But how much freer, stronger, and happier are those men for whom speaking out is the paramount urge, while to be heard is unimportant. A writer speaks out not to bring forth *in others* a corresponding reaction but to free himself. The poet who is in need of an audience does not feel alive without it.

He exists only in inter-relations with his audience, through the recognition of those who identify with him, and in this case he does not even sense the lack of freedom in which he lives. Alienation and despair come when there are no listeners, the pre-requisite to *production*. The main inducement should be to open one's flood-gates.

I am trying to sum up what I derived in my time from this man. Concern about social inequality always existed (and exists) in me. His 'creative mind' was uninteresting, his philosophy unoriginal, his judgements about life and people foreign to me. I only responded to the 'half-mad ecstasy of activity', against a background of Russian stagnation and conservatism in living conditions. And very likely, omitting his essence, something in his personality that made him calm, open, sometimes warm, always kindly disposed in his home life – and not only to Khodasevich and myself. I would say he was sometimes in awe of Khodasevich and he would close his eyes to his being from an alien literary camp, to his strangeness. Gorky was deeply tied to him, loved him as a poet and needed him as a friend. There were no such people in his entourage: some, dependent on him, flattered him; others, not dependent on him, passed by with profound, insulting indifference.

There was a time in the 1920s, long before he was declared the father of socialist realism and his novel *Mother* a cornerstone of Soviet literature, when his influence not his fame was shaken in the Soviet Union (and curiosity about him in the West began to wane quickly). The last symbolists, the acmeists, the militant Westerners, Mayakovsky and the constructivists, Pilniak, Ehrenburg, the new element that came (and went) in Olesha's novel *Envy*, the *Lef* period, the flowering of the formalists – all this worked against him. Young Soviet literature, representatives of which now remember with tears in the 1960s how Gorky blessed them at the beginning of their careers, then turned with great caution and small interest or strong critical feeling to his boring moralistic 'realistic' writings – there was no room in the avant-garde creative imagination for reality per se in its 'revolutionary development'. But *Lef* was closed down, the symbolists died, Mayakovsky shot himself, Pilniak was subdued, the formalists were silenced. Then, at the first Congress of Writers in 1934, after Gorky had been acclaimed from

191

the White Sea to the Black Sea, he was declared great, and his novel *Samgin* and his play *Bulychev* were hailed as models for literature of the present and future.

However strange it may seem, in life, if not in literature, he understood light-heartedness and enjoyed playful relaxation. In Italy he loved precisely the light-heartedness: whether shopkeepers danced in the square or a bricklayer sang while laying bricks, he eyed them with envy and tenderness, saying that the source of everything here was the sun. But in literature he not only did not understand jocularity, he feared it like a temptation. Because he always expected a lesson from literature. When Pavel Muratov, visiting in Sorrento, read his play *Daphnis and Chloe*, Gorky was so irritated that he became crimson and beat his fingers on the table, on books, on his knees, finally retreating into a corner and from there eying us all maliciously. Whereas in this charming play (which bore a strong imprint of the times, that is, of a post-war Europe dancing on a volcano, and which was symbolic throughout) there was so much humour and a complete absence of any didacticism; one felt that the author took nothing seriously (exercising a right given all of us): not himself, the world, the author of *Mother*, not any of us, not even his very own comedy, which he was not intending to print and which perhaps he wrote in jest (and perhaps not).

There was little humour in Russian life, and for the last thirty years there had been none at all. Now it is just beginning to reappear. And in the Russians – I am speaking only from my own experience, not on the words of others or on books I have read – there is also not much humour. It is not because there was and is little humour in Russian life, that it does not exist in the Russian people, but because there is a lack of it in the people there is little of it in life. And especially in that part of the intelligentsia to which Gorky belonged. All was taken seriously; men already took themselves too seriously: Marx was taken as seriously as the tsar took the prayer about God's anointed. Because of this, a thick shroud of didacticism too often hangs over them and their writings.

Meanwhile, sometimes (rarely, it is true) the wall of serious-ness collapsed and in the paroxysm of his liberating laughter Gorky suddenly came impetuously close to me. An awareness of guilt immediately appeared in his eyes: You can't laugh when Chinese children are hungry! When the bacillus of cancer is still undiscovered! When in the villages communists are killed! So it was when he read our 'magazine', *Pravda of Sorrento*, and after the visit of André Germain, one of the directors of the Crédit Lyonnais and Gorky's literary agent in France. This banker was resolutely enamoured of all that was Soviet, yet could not wash his own hands independently and held them out to his lackey, who was also his secretary and followed him everywhere. Here was one of the first representatives of the so-called 'salon bolshevism', a pitiful and comic figure. Maksim and I mimicked the scene of the hand-washing, which we had the chance to watch on the sly, and Gorky laughed to the point of tears. So it was when we put on parodies of classical ballet or Italian opera. But these were rare minutes of escape from the moralistic shell he had created for himself. When, however, you read his contemporaries and *fellow realists*, then you understand that he did not create that shell for himself, it was their collective defence against the other neighbouring world that by the 1860s had already become taboo for those like him.

For a long time I kept one picture – of the celebration of the 1923 New Year in Saarow. Against the background of a lit-up Christmas tree, at a table covered with hors d'oeuvres, glasses, and bottles, sat Gorky, Khodasevich, Bely, all three in the smoke of their own cigarettes: you felt the three had been drinking and were affecting detachment. To the left, her arms folded on her bosom, very severe, in a high-necked dress, was Andreeva. There were Shklovsky, toothless and bald, whose wit did not always suit this milieu; the actor Miklashevsky, who had photographed the group by flashbulb and had managed to sit under the tree himself, and as a result was half transparent; Maksim, his wife, Valentina Khodasevich, and I, painted like Indians. The negative was on glass, and when he saw the photo Gorky ordered that it be broken: the picture was 'shameful'. The only remaining picture was stolen from my archive – perhaps it is still intact somewhere.

And what is there to say about Gorky's archives, collected by him abroad in the 1920s (or, more exactly, 1921–33)? Is it possible that we will never know the truth about how and when they were brought to Moscow? In May 1933 the household in Sorrento was apparently liquidated and thousands of books were packed up, as were all the things that belonged to Gorky, his son, his daughter-in-law, and his two granddaughters, and all the things that belonged to Ivan Nikolaevich Rakitsky, who then lived in the house as a member of the family. This went to Moscow. But one must assume that not the whole archive but only a part was taken to the U.S.S.R. In the archive, besides manuscripts, notebooks, copies of letters, contracts with publishers, and much else, there was without any doubt the entire correspondence of Gorky with Soviet writers, both those living in the U.S.S.R. and those who had gone abroad in those years; the correspondence with émigré writers (Khodasevich, Slonim, Volsky, Mirsky, and others); the vast correspondence with émigré public figures who were close to Gorky before the Revolution – for example, Ekaterina Kuskova; the correspondence with foreigners who visited Russia in those years or were sympathetic to the Soviet system; and finally the letters from important Soviet officials, members of the Party and government, Bukharin, Pyatakov, some Soviet ambassadors to European capitals. Here, as one can imagine, were criticism of Stalin and criticism of the regime, and Gorky could hardly have taken these documents to Russia. If we are to believe certain rumours, he gave them for safekeeping to the person closest to him (who did not go to Russia with him), and who took this part of the archive to London. Was it brought or sent to Moscow in the 1930s, as rumour has it? Or was it conveyed there later, as is said in the *Short Literary Encylopaedia* (Vol. 2, 1963)? If the letters of Bukharin, Pyatakov, and others were already in Russia in the 1930s, then Stalin could not have failed to see them. Two months after the death of Gorky (still unexplained) the Moscow trials began. Now, beginning in 1958, these documents are being published in part, with the note: 'The original is in the Gorky Archive in Moscow.' There is still no detailed description of this archive. Were the letters of executed Bolsheviks destroyed by Stalin after he read them? Or are they still extant? And what has become of the hundreds of letters of Petr Kriuchkov, Gorky's 'guardian angel' and factotum, in which one can follow, as on a calendar, the whole of Gorky's life in Europe? Kriuchkov was tortured and shot – there is no doubt of that. But 'warm words' about him are beginning to appear here and there in memoirs.[*]

Shklovsky at that time (1923) wrote his letter of repentance to the Central Committee of the Communist Party; he was being

[*]See N. B., *Zhenshchina, Zhelcznaya* (Woman of Iron), pp. 119–34.

persecuted as a former S.-R., his wife was in prison as a hostage, he had fled the confines of Russia in February 1922 and now, in torment over his wife, requested his return. Compared to Khodasevich and Bely, Shklovsky was a man from another planet, but for me his talent, energy, and humour always clearly burned. He felt his life in Germany was senseless; he could not foresee his future, that he would be 'frozen' in the Soviet Union for thirty years (and unfrozen at the end of the 1950s). He outlived all his friends, but there was little humour left in him, judging by the writings of his last period. He never could think systematically and coherently; an academic career was not for him as it turned out to be for his contemporaries – Tynianov, Tomashevsky, Eichenbaum, and others. His was the fate of a wasted man, one of the most tragic. In the West, among Slavists, he is known and prized more highly than he is known or prized in Russia.

Shklovsky was a round–headed, smallish, witty man with clever sparkling eyes. There was always a smile on his face, and in this smile one could see the little black roots of his front teeth. He could be brilliant, he was full of humour and mockery, clever and sometimes impudent, especially when he sensed the presence of an 'important person', a 'haughty eminence', or people who irritated him by their pedantry, self-assurance, and stupidity. He was a talented inventor, full of ideas, discoveries, and formulations. Life seethed in him, and he loved it. His *Letters Not About Love* and other books written about himself in those years were a tour de force and a joke; he amused others and himself. He never spoke of the future, and probably suppressed within himself all premonitions, confident (in any event outwardly) that everything would 'turn out all right'. He would not otherwise have returned, because in the West he was one of the few who could have realized himself fully – Roman Jakobson, a man close to him, of course would have helped him. But the matter of his wife gave him no peace.

His plans sometimes came out badly: once he invited me to dinner at the house of the artist Ivan Puni and his wife, the painter Ksana Boguslavskaya. They decided to eat 'à la Soviet', write a small essay and see if something did not come out of it: herring was served first (there was no vobla to be found in Berlin), hard as wood which had at first been 'minced up'. Millet kasha was brought to the table next. A little vegetable oil was poured on it ('A small compromise,' explained Shklovsky). We chewed the herring and then, looking sadly at the pot with the kasha, felt that we could not eat it. And we had to go to a beer house on the corner, where we ordered sausages, sauerkraut, and beer. 'It didn't turn out well,' Viktor said later. 'We have fallen out of the habit. What a scoundrel man is!'

At times, in those months, Nikolai Otsup came to Saarow. He of course never thought of returning; he remained in the West and in my memory lives as an example of the swift decline of all one's abilities. His deterioration remains a riddle for me. He wrote his best verse in the 1920s, all that he wrote subsequently being touched by a strange decay, a certain sad inability to develop; his writing was too bland, too long, moralistic like an old-fashioned fable. Melody disappeared, forces of imagination vanished completely, the playfulness was suffocated by a 'moral'. In the course of twenty years my meetings with this man were always painful to me; it was as if he wanted desperately to become someone he could not be, and one felt this tension in him continually and with it the frustration, bitterness, impotence, the condemnation of this our sinful wicked world in which he once breathed so easily. Perhaps his personal life history prevented him from being what he promised to become in Petersburg when he wrote of 'darling Edie' or in Berlin when he wrote his charming narrative poem *The Meeting* (1928) where there were so many enchanting trifles (but spoiled by the ending), or the cycle of verse on love from his second book, *In Smoke*, which, once you had heard it, you could never forget:

> You will shake your head, and in the wind will sparkle
> The freed brow, and the malicious and tender mouth
> Will shift with a smile all the shadows of the face,
> And again becoming sombre will attentively stiffen.

What precision in the transmission of the picture! What freedom! But later, it seems, he grew ashamed of these lines and his motto became *Deo volente*. His best love verses did not even appear in his posthumous volume (1960); they are lost in some obscure periodicals. By whom were they rejected? By himself or by the person who was his literary executor?

I don't recall Boris Pasternak in Saarow, but I remember him well in Berlin. He belonged to that group of people whose literary interests were totally out of Gorky's range. In Berlin Pasternak came quite often to visit us, when Bely was there. I did not like his verse much then. Now I prize it much higher than his clumsy, strained, old-hat over-emotional novel, than his later verse about Christ, Magdalene, and Palm Sunday. Khodasevich and Bely listened to him with sympathy and attentiveness. He seemed to me not terribly interesting because he always gave the impression of a very talented but quite immature man. So he remained to the end of his life, but this sin one can almost always forgive if there is something else in a poet. At that time I could not get to the essence of much of his verse (which now seems to me simple, only weighted down by metaphors incompletely thought out). Once Bely complained to Khodasevich that he got to the essence with difficulty, but when he did get there the essence turned out to be uninteresting. Khodasevich agreed with him and added incidentally that 'they' (the futurists and members of the Centrifugue) often emphasize that they live in a dynamic world, in an unusually dynamic period, but, in contradiction to that, you have to lose so much time interpreting their intellectually elementary verse.

'And you wind up with nothing!' Bely screamed in the middle of Viktoria-Luise Platz (we were on our way from a literary meeting at which Pasternak had read verse, making them more obscure by his very artificial reading), so that Bely's voice bounced against the dark houses, and the echo of the Berlin square answered him resoundingly, which sent him into ecstasy.

But did Pasternak want people to get to the essence of his verse? Now I realize that the effort to decipher stanza by stanza was not at all obligatory – in his poetry the stanza, the line, the image, or the word work unconsciously. This is, in the full sense of the term, not cognitive but emotional poetry: through sound (and sight) something flutters in us in response and digging into it is quite unnecessary. There is a room – it is called a box with an orange; or there is spring – smelling like the discharge from a thousand hospitals; there is the beloved – carried around like the well-learned role of a provincial tragedian. Isn't this sufficient? Yes. And there is much of this, too much! There is genius here and we are grateful for it. Lofty tongue-tiedness is here too and we accept it.

197

In those Berlin months Pasternak was in his first period. Between the first and the third (the verse of *Doctor Zhivago*) he had a second: a characteristic mixture of Rilke and Igor Severianin, marked by a certain dose of graphomania, an easiness of response to 'spring' 'summer', 'autumn' 'winter', 'falling leaves', 'solitude', 'sea', and so on, as if he had written verse on an assigned topic – something Esenin never did and Mayakovsky raised into a literary device as a result of the 'social command' of his times, while making it sound new and strange.

Later, in Paris, I knew the person who is now mentioned in all biographies of Pasternak and about whom there are lines in *Safe Conduct*: 'the two Vysotsky sisters', the elder of whom was Pasternak's first love, when he was fourteen. He later met her in Marburg, where he lived as a student (in the summer of 1912), and proposed to her, but she then refused him. He suffered from this unrequited love and began to write verse 'day and night' (but mainly about nature).

She was already married when I knew her in Paris. The sisters were known as Bebochka and Reshka. Reshka was the elder, fine, red-haired, freckled. The second, with whom I was on friendly terms, was very good-looking, with beautiful eyes, a lovely profile, and lady-like. An abyss divided me from her – she lived in a wordly, bourgeois milieu, was a 'debutante', but for some reason, when we met, we were always happy to see each other: she had loveliness and intellectual charm. When the break between Reshka and Pasternak occurred, she was with her sister in Marburg.

'Obscurity' in his verse, because it is poetic, has not troubled me for a long time. But what can one say about his articles, letters, answers to questionnaires, his interviews? Now it seems to me that he created this 'obscurity' on purpose, to hide the real meaning even further, to cover up, camouflage it. In the article 'The Black Goblet' (1916), in the letters to Gorky (1921–8), in the questionnaire on behalf of the decree of the Communist Party in literary matters (1925), in the 'Minsk Speech' (1936), one cannot get to the heart of things, all is framed by vignettes of abstract words that have no relation to the principal theme. It is tempting to call this style 'Soviet rococo' – of course it could never have made any sense to Gorky or the common reader. And what if this is not camouflage? If Pasternak's very thoughts moved in such vignettes for years until he found himself a new way of thinking, which he used in *Doctor Zhivago*? This *Zhivago* method was not invented by him: it had flowered in Russian literature before the age of symbolism.

The third manner of his thinking is no longer rococo, and no longer the style of the 1880s. It is reflected in his correspondence with Renata Schweitzer.

Everyone who values Pasternak must read his correspondence with the niece of Dr. Albert Schweitzer, which was published in 1964 in the original German. In this small book (the story of the friendship, his letters, extracts from the letters of Renata, and the story of her visit to him in Peredelkino) Pasternak is revealed fully – and in his immutability. Even his face on the cover photo remained as before – the face of an adolescent (as was noted by foreign reporters). After a reading of the correspondence this much is certain: his poetry of youth, which he more or less renounced in old age, was nothing more than a beautiful and perhaps even brilliant accident. There is something that sobs and chokes, that comes from the second-rate German romantics and our tear-sodden Russian idealists, in the tone of the letters of the seventy-year-old Pasternak (and the sixty-year-old Renata Schweitzer, in love with him, calling him 'my Boria'); at the same time she recalls him as he was forty years before: lost, ecstatic, entangled in his own self, in the 'oh' and 'ah' of his epistolary style, confessing that he was not able to 'pause for breath' owing to his joy at receiving a letter from Renata. He writes to her of the fusing of their souls, the transmission of his feelings to her over a distance, of the weather – in connection with the expectation of her arrival – as a reflection of his own emotions. She describes him: on Easter Sunday they walk through the streets and he gives an Easter greeting (three embraces in the Russian way) to all those he meets, known or unknown. After he presented her to his wife, Zina, he took her to Olga Ivinskaya, saying: 'I won her [Zina], I conquered her . . . and now another has come. Zina is an ideal mother, hostess, laundress. But Olga suffered for me . . .' From time to time, overcome by emotion (Renata writes), they looked at each other and gulped down tears in silence.

Perhaps the gift of eternal youth did not let him mature? Still in Berlin, although he was beyond the age of thirty, he looked like a boy in his teens. He appeared on the Berlin horizon, then disappeared (several times in the years 1922 and 1923 he left Moscow for Berlin and then returned to Moscow from Berlin). In 1935 I met him again in Paris (he came twice). Up to that point he had published a lot: in the Michigan edition of his verse and prose, his bibliography takes thirty pages. In these last visits in the 1930s he separated from his first wife, the painter Zhenia Lurie, and prepared to marry (or had just married) his second one – Zinaida Nikolaevna Eremeeva-Neuhaus. Marina Tsvetaeva, who saw him quite often (he visited her in Meudon), described how he walked through Paris choosing what kind of dress to buy his new wife.

'And what kind of dress do you want?' Tsvetaeva asked him.

'Such as is worn by beauties,' he answered. Marina Ivanovna laughed as she said this. She added the question: 'And what, incidentally, is this new wife like?'

Pasternak answered: 'She is a beauty.'

If one can sigh with relief hearing that Gogol burned the second part of *Dead Souls* (it would not be as easy to bury it in oblivion as it is with the *Selected Passages*, and even this took more than a half century), then the fact that Pasternak did not manage to finish his verse trilogy *Blind Beauty* is also undoubted good fortune for modern Russian literature. What we know of it makes us feel that it would have been in no way worthy of his pen. Three generations were to have been 'portrayed' in it, and a large place was to have been given to arguments about art between a serf Agafon and – Alexander Dumas. Rape, the theft of family jewels, murder, the blinding of a serf girl – such were the themes of the first part. But fortunately even that remained un-written – if we are to believe people who visited Pasternak in the last year of his life.

When we left for Prague on 4 November, 1923, Marina Tsvetaeva had already been there for a long time. We could not stay in Berlin, where we had no way to live; we didn't go to Italy, because we had no visas or money; and we didn't go to Paris, because we feared Paris – yes, both of us feared Paris – and emigration (France had not yet recognized the Soviet Government). We were afraid of not returning, the finality of our fate, and the irrevocable decision to remain in exile. It seems that we wanted to prolong instability. So we set out for Prague. Here is the Prague calendar in Khodasevich's notes:

November 9. Roman Jakobson
November 10. Tsvetaeva
November 13. R. Jakobson
November 14. at Tsvetaeva's
November 16. Tsvetaeva
November 19. Tsvetaeva
November 20. R. Jakobson
November 23. Tsvetaeva and R. Jakobson
November 24. R. Jakobson
November 25. R. Jakobson, Tsvetaeva
November 27. R. Jakobson
November 28. Tsvetaeva
November 29. R. Jakobson, Tsvetaeva
December 1. R. Jakobson
December 5. the Jackobsons
December 6. departure for Marienbad

In the unstable world in which we lived at that time, where nothing had been decided and where for the second time in two years we lost people and an atmosphere I had begun to value highly, I could not genuinely appreciate Prague: it seemed to me nobler than Berlin and more out of the way. 'Russian Prague' did not open to us its embraces: the old Chirikov and Nemirovich-Danchenko and their wives were dominant there, and for them I was nothing more than a small insect and Khodasevich a bug of unknown and partly dangerous origin. Tsvetaeva – already weary – Slonim and Jakobson, men of the same stock and generation as Khodasevich, lived apart from the respectable crowd. Jakobson and Slonim not only survived but finally realized themselves – the one as the leading Slavist in the world, the other as a critic and scholar, perhaps because both were full of energy, or even of 'the half-mad ecstasy of activity'. In those weeks in Prague both Khodasevich and I, with great difficulty, could probably have latched on to something, placing one foot – like mountain climbers – tossing a rope, pulling oneself up, placing the other foot . . . At such moments one friendly hand can sustain a man even on Easter Island, but no one sustained us. And probably this was all to the good. Tsvetaeva and Slonim did not survive here long. Jakobson, spreading his wings, flew like a butterfly out of the cocoon.

At that time Marina Tsvetaeva was at the zenith of her poetic talent. Her life was very difficult materially and remained so till 1939, when she returned to Russia. She had already lost one daughter in Moscow, from starvation; the other was with her. Her son was born in 1925 and was killed in World War Two. She gave the impression of a woman, full of creative inventions, who had put off her problems, but who did not look into herself, did not know her vital (and feminine) possibilities, had not matured towards a consciousness of her present and future reactions. The part of a misfit, which she adopted and about which she wrote beautifully in the poem 'Roland's Horn', betrayed her immaturity: being a fish out of water is not, as was once thought, a sign of originality in a human being who stands *above* others, but is the misfortune – both psychological and ontological – of a person who has not matured to the point of uniting with the world, fusing with it and his time, that is with history and other people. Her involvement with the White Army was foolish; it was to a certain degree the outcome of her attachment to her husband, Sergey Efron, to whom she 'promised a son'. So she said to me: 'I will have a son, I have sworn to Serezha that I will give him a son.' She had faith in dreams, trusted in certain fantasies. In Marina this maladjustment was the more tragic because with the years she began to seek fusion, and her developed peculiarity gradually began to oppress her; she outlived it and nothing arose in its place. Maturing slowly, like the majority of Russian poets of our century (in contrast with the preceding one), she understood, perhaps in the last years of her life, that man cannot all his life remain an outcast, and that if he does the blame rests with him and not with his surroundings; her conflict was aggravated because, as a poet in emigration, she had no readers, there was no reaction to what she wrote, and perhaps she had no friends of her own stature. The poet carrying his gift like a hunchback his hump, the poet on an uninhabited island or descending into catacombs, in his tower (of ivory, brick, or whatever), on an iceberg in the ocean – all these are tempting images, but they hide a romantic essence that is sterile and dangerous in its deadliness. You might insert these images in immortal or simply good verse, and someone undoubtedly will react to them inwardly, but they will bear with them one of the most insidious elements of art – escapism, which, if it embellishes the poem, destroys the poet. The Prague isolation of Marina, her role as outcast in Paris, could only lead her to silence in

Moscow and tragedy in Elabuga. In her own personality, in the character of her relationships with people and the world, her end was masked: it was foretold in all those lines where she cried to us that she was not like everyone else, she was proud she was not like us, that she never wanted to be like us.

She yielded to the old decadent temptation of inventing a new self: the poet as a monster deformity, unrecognized and misunderstood; the mother of her children and the wife of her husband; the lover of a young ephebus; heroine of a glorious past; bard, singing the doom of an army; a young disciple; a partner in a passionate friendship. From these (and other) 'personality images' she made verse – great verse of our time. But she had no power over herself, did not create herself, did not even know herself (and cultivated this ignorance). She was defenceless, reckless, and unhappy, enclosed by a 'nest' and lonely: she found and lost and erred continually.

Khodasevich once said to me that in her youth Marina reminded him of Esenin (and vice versa) – in the colour of her hair, the colouring of her skin, even her gestures and voice. I once had a dream in which both, completely identical, were hanged, and swayed in their nooses. Since then I cannot help seeing the terrible parallel in their deaths – outwardly, of course, similar images of their end, with inward contradictory motivation. Esenin conceivably might not have done away with himself: he could have perished in exile in Siberia (like Kliuev), he could have settled down (like Marienhof), or 'made it' (like Kusikov), he might have died accidentally (like Poplavsky), the war could have saved him, or a change in literary policy in the U.S.S.R., or love for a woman, or finally friendship with the person who is addressed in his poem of 1922, the tenderest and most passionate of all his verse:

> My beloved, give me your hand . . .
> . . . .
> Farewell, farewell! Amidst moonlit fires
> Will I live until that blissful day?
> Among the famous and the young ones
> You were for me the best of all.
> . . . .
> Another might muffle me in you
> . . . .

But still among the fluttering and young
You were for me the best of all.

His end was unwarranted. Tsvetaeva, on the contrary, moved towards it her whole life, through her trumped-up love for her husband and children, through her poems praising the White Army, her image of the hump borne so proudly, the scorn for those who did not understand her, humiliation transmuted into a proud mask, through all the fiascos of her infatuations and the ephemeral nature of the roles she assigned herself: where roles were imagined and swords made of cardboard, yet genuine blood flowed nevertheless.

Just as inescapable was the suicide of Mayakovsky. Perhaps those few who read carefully and to the end the last volume of his collected works will agree with this – a volume that includes verbatim records of the literary discussions in January–March 1930 between the All-Union Association of Proletarian Writers and Mayakovsky, author of the poem (unfinished) 'At the Top of My Voice'. At first swearing 'at the top of his voice', then his hysterical yell resounded 'at the top of his voice' over all Russia. Then the 'top of the voice' died down. A shot rang out, and a life that, it seemed, had no end, ended. He was not used to giving in, he didn't know how and didn't want to. He had nothing to fall back on; a poet of his calibre and temperament could not have a comfortable retreat. He did not just shoot himself, he shot his whole generation.

Not in every beginning is an end concealed; the clue cannot always be discerned, sometimes it is hidden too well. Looking back, to the nineteenth century, you see that both the death of Pushkin and the death of Tolstoy, so like suicides, were concealed in their lives. Both became victims of their personal aberrations – Tolstoy of his dichotomy, and Pushkin ended his life because of a woman, not realizing what a woman was.

The idea of women's innocence lived in the world for about a hundred years. Now we know that all prolonged innocence is not only unnatural, but brings on a feeling of nausea, like that cretin who at sixteen has remained at the level of development of a two-year-old. I look on the mica-like eyes of virgins, on the too-white hands of nuns with revulsion; it is unpleasant for me to think of the state of the thyroids of old spinsters and the endocrine glands of ascetics.

★

Outside, the early November evening is black. We have been sitting since three in a room of the Hotel Beranek in Prague: Tsvetaeva, Efron, Khodasevich, and I. Beranek in Czech means lamb. Lambs are represented on the walls, doors, embroidered on pillowcases; lambs decorate the menu in the restaurant, a lamb smiles at us on the hotel bill. Khodasevich says we live in a herd of rose and sky-blue lambs. Some are be-ribboned, others with gilded horns, some with bells around their necks. A lamb stands at the hotel entrance and even moves its head, saying 'bah-ah-ah'.

We sit for long hours, drink tea which I brew on a small spirit lamp, eat ham, cheese, and rolls spread out on pieces of paper. All that Tsvetaeva says interests me, there is a mixture of wisdom and whimsy in her speech; but there is almost always something alien to me, a sick strain that startles me, exhilarating, provocative, 'clever', but somehow disturbing, without equilibrium, somehow dangerous for our further relations, as if we were now happy to fly over waves and thresholds, but the following moment we could bump into each other and get hurt. And I feel this. She obviously does not; she probably thinks that in the future she can either become friendly with me or quarrel. Suddenly the light goes out in the room – she has pulled the plug out of the socket; in the darkness she falls on me on the couch, tickles me, embraces me. I jump up, having cried out. The light goes on. This is not at all, not at all to my liking.

Roman Jakobson comes after dinner. Along the black streets, he, Khodasevich and I clump through the liquid snow and mud, sink into it, slip on the pavement – we are going to an ancient tavern. In the tavern Khodasevich and Roman will have long conversations about metaphors and metonymies. Jakobson suggests to Khodasevich that he translate into Russian a long poem of the Czech romantic Maha. Perhaps 'from Maha to Maha you could set yourself up in Praha?' he says pensively. But Khodasevich is not enchanted by Maha and returns the poem.

And then we are in Italy. At first a week in Venice, where Khodasevich is taken up with recollections of his early years and I, to begin with, am overcome and then carried away by what I see. Only partly do I share his emotions. I know he now confuses me with an old vision, and later lines such as

Pigeons rush up, frightened,
From my beloved's feet . . .

I will naturally share with his former beloved (Zhenia Muratova) of 1911. Nevertheless I have a distinct awareness of what belongs to me and what doesn't. His youth is not mine. For me even my own past is not worth the present. He is taken up with all that was here thirteen years before (which is reflected in the verse of his second volume, *The Happy Little House*) and is seeking traces of former shadows, enlists even me to seek them. And they become dear to me because they are his, but I do not completely understand him: if all that was has already been 'squeezed out' by him into verse, then why does it still trouble him, affect him? Of course I do not show him my perplexity and do not frighten away his ghosts; in my own way I begin to worship this magical city.

At that time as now I didn't like to make much of my own past. At present when I describe it, I want to be entertaining and exact, and extract more joy for myself from its verbal reincarnations than from the emotions connected with it. Properly speaking there are no emotions. I don't know how to love the past for its 'lost charm'. Every lost charm fills me with doubt: What if it is a hundred times better lost than it was alive? The dead can never be better than the living. If a living man thinks a corpse is better than those alive, it means that man is already half dead. Every living minute is better than the eternity of the dead. Who needs corpses? Only corpses.

Why drag, out of a whole life, some minutes, hours, and days? Why love their departed weight, when everything of the present, because it is alive, is better than anything past, which is dead? No, the only imperishable and imperishing charm is the 'most ferocious immanence' of the given moment which consists of past, present, and future, the here and now. All these recollections – even the most tender and the most grand – I am ready to yield up for those minutes of life, and not its reflections, when as now my pencil glides across paper, the shadow of a cloud flows across me, and all together we move through infinity – on three levels of time, space, and energy.

In Venice, Khodasevich was winged and earthbound: he was once young and alone here, the world stood whole around him, tame. Now the city cast towards him a reflection of his present state: he was not young, not alone, and no one and nothing stood up for him; there was no defence. Pigeons on the piazza cooed and flew above us, the vaporetto carried us by the stone lace of old palaces, 'which have so aged', said Khodasevich, 'that they will now crumble in a moment'. 'They just about hold firm, and we just about hold firm, but it's all right, perhaps we won't crumble,' I answered. We loved each other across that line that separated us: he with his morning premonitions of evening catastrophes, I with evening anticipations of diurnal joys.

Since then I have returned to Venice three times. I love this city more than all the cities of the world; it is for me unique. And each time I stayed in Venice the city was my present, as if I had come to it for the first time. There was no burden of recollections, no awakened melancholy for things gone, no regrets, or traces of decay. Each time I was happy there with a particular and unique fullness, and I was happiest of all when I spent eight days there (in 1965) in complete solitude – wandering through churches and museums in the mornings, through known and always, as it were, new districts, swimming at the Lido in the afternoons, and in the evenings either listening in old Renaissance courtyards to a chamber orchestra playing Vivaldi, Tartini, Scarlatti, or working on the manuscript of this book. Each day there came something fresh: the small square on the other side of the Canale Grande, where I wanted to settle if only for three days in order to see it in the mornings from the window of my room, or the island of Santa Helena, which I discovered on one of those strolls and where everything – people, children, dogs – seemed so beautiful. Or it was the roses and the gillyflowers of Torcello that surrounded my table and breathed on me when I dined there.

At night, in the railway station in Florence, Khodasevich and I suddenly decided not to leave the train, but go on to Rome, which neither of us knew. Next morning in Rome, straight from the station to the Hotel Santa Chiara, where Nikolai Otsup lived, we called on Muratov and toured Rome with him. There was money for exactly a month, and Muratov said this was not too little, if we were sensible about time and knew exactly where to go and what to see. At first I was sceptical about his suggestion to keep a 'schedule': I am able to plan myself, I don't like schedules. If I want to go, I go; if I don't, I don't. If I don't see a thing, I will see it another time.

'But, look, perhaps there won't be another time,' said Muratov. 'Or it might come a quarter of a century later. And if you don't see what's most important?' He was right, and thanks to his plan I saw all it was conceivable to see. And 'another time' came exactly thirty-six years later.

To be in Rome. To have Muratov as a guide. This now seems fantastic, like a dream, after which you walk about for three days in a trance. But this was reality, my reality, my most natural, ordinary fate in Rome. I see myself near the Moses of Michelangelo, next to me a silent short figure, and with him again in a long walk across the Trastevere, where we stop by ancient courtyards, all of which he knows as if he were born here. We stand near some anonymous bas-relief and look at it as attentively as at the frescoes of Raphael; we wander along the Appian Way, amidst tombs. In the evening we sit in a café near the Piazza Navona and dine in a restaurant near the Trevi. Finally we go out of town, to Tusculum. And all this in a mood of awe, not just in the presence of museum-like Italy but modern Italy, too. Muratov loved contemporary Italy and taught me to love it. At that time, however, he was mainly interested in the baroque. And I have never since returned to the baroque: thirty-six years later when I was there, in 1960, and then in 1965, so many antiquities had been dug up that ancient Rome over-shadowed all the rest for me, and there was no time for the baroque. I no longer went to the Vatican nor looked at Moses. The Thermae of Vespasian and Hadrian's Villa became my favourite places. There was no Muratov to go with me, examine every column, every bit of a column, but his image was still near by.

I often ask people what Renaissance *story* they like most. Muratov liked Saint Jerome, Khodasevich the Annunciation, Otsup the pensive ass in Bethlehem. But for my entire life I have borne a love for Tobias, who carries fish and walks abreast of the Angel. Much has changed in my tastes: I have fallen out of love with the late Renaissance (after 1500), out of love with the French eighteenth century, I pass by Tintoretto and Carpaccio, but Tobias in all his aspects invariably delights me. I love 'Tobias who carries fish' as painted by Piero di Cosimo, Botticini, Titian, Cima da Conegliano, and even by Guardi, in whose picture Tobias and the Angel are not yet on their way but only preparing to go and are saying good-bye. The Angel is in front, Tobias is directly behind him, and they are *arm in arm*, not *hand in hand* (this is the second picture in the series 'The Story of Tobias' in the church of Saint Raphael in Venice). In Botticini the Angel's pace is quiet and airy; in Titian, Tobias hardly keeps up. Most often he is small and serious, walks alongside the huge Angel, who is hurrying to a definite place and not just strolling leisurely, barefooted, with muscular legs and an upturned big toe. The Angel firmly holds in his 'man's' hand the child's hand of Tobias. A dog of unidentified breed follows them. But before I go on about them both in more detail, let me recall the Apocryphal tale:

Old blind Tobit (of the Naphtali tribe) was once a captive in Nineveh. He left ten silver talents at Gabael's, in Medea.

Twenty years passed. The receipt had been torn in two. Tobit kept his half.

He decided to send his son Tobias to Gabael's for the ten talents. First he had to find a travelling companion for young Tobias. The Angel Raphael was found. It was a two-day walk to Medea.

Raphael said: I am Azarias, son of Hananiel. Tobit promised to pay him one drachma a day, and board and lodging, if he took Tobias to Gabael's and brought him back. He promised a reward. The mother asked: Who is going with our son? The father answered: A kind Angel. He knows the way.

They went with a dog, in a threesome.

At night on the shores of the Tigris, Tobias wanted to wash his feet. A large fish jumped out of the water and tried to bite off his foot. He cried out loudly. The Angel said: Do not fear. He seized the fish with his hand. And on Raphael's advice Tobias slit open the fish, took out the liver and heart – these were important medicines.

He discarded the intestines.

They fried one part of the fish and salted the other. What kinds of medicines were these?

Liver and heart – for evil spirits.

Gall bladder – for blindness.

They passed through Ecbatana. Sarah lived in Raguel's house, and Raphael advised Tobias to take her as his wife.

But the Devil had already killed seven of Sarah's bridegrooms.

Raphael ordered Tobias to throw the first medicine into the fire.

The Devil vanished.

And then a joyous feast was arranged.

In Medea they received ten talents as stated in the halved receipt. Then they went back with the dog, in a threesome.

They brought the second medicine to old Tobit. Which made him see clearly, his blindness cured.

They also brought Sarah. And they all lived happily a hundred and seventeen years.

I know why I like this Renaissance story so much: I completely identify both with Tobias and the Angel. Looking at Tobias, I see myself, carefully carrying the fish, marching trustingly along the low horizon, one-two, one-two, my shoes tightly laced, a ring holding my hair so that it will not be blown about by the wind. I look at the Angel, and I also see myself: sandals neatly grasp my feet, the wide garment flows around my thighs, my face is pointed forwards like that of a figure on the prow of a ship which is going on a far-off journey – the brightest and most constant image of my personal symbolism. In my face there is assurance, fearlessness, a goal – this is the face of the Angel, I fuse with him in my imagination, I hold someone by the hand and lead him. I am not afraid to be the Angel, because at the same time I am also a tiny human led by this giant Angel along the Tuscan horizon. Clouds swirl in the sky, like my garments, and it seems to me that that march of a big one and small one is my own march through life, where I suddenly divide happily and know I can blend both parts of myself. Tobias is everything that is fearful and unsure in me, that does not dare or know, everything that errs or doubts, hopes, ails, and grieves. The Angel, twice the size of a human being, is all the rest, which includes the ecstasy of life, the sense of physical health, my equilibrium, my indestructibility, and the negation of fatigue, weakness, old age.

Money was running out: there was just enough for tickets to Paris, where we hoped to earn a living. We left Rome on a warm April day and the next morning got out of the train at the Gare de Lyon. The wind was blowing, it was raining, clouds were gathering above the huge city. All was grey: the sky, streets, people. Instead of the Castel Sant'Angelo (is the Angel taking out or sheathing his sword? – I always thought he was putting it in) against the background of the blue sky of Rome, there was the heavy tower of the Gare de Lyon with the clock. All was alien, comfortless, cold, cruel-seeming, threatening. Now I have come back, I was here once, but nothing responds to me, nothing speaks to me. The muteness of people and things is concealed in a cavernous roar. Only the trams throw out sparks from under their wheels as they cross the tracks to turn right and left.

We went straight to Zinovy Grzhebin, the well-known publisher. At that time he still lived in the hope that his publications would be allowed into Russia, that the books of Gorky, Zaitsev, Khodasevich, Bely, and others would be purchased at his warehouse, that he would be able to publish a magazine, and would republish the classics en masse. He had vast plans, continuing to buy manuscripts from authors. This experienced (so it seemed) businessman could not allow himself the thought that nothing would be bought from him, within three years he would be completely ruined; for non-payment of taxes and debts he would be photographed collarless at a French police station, full face and profile, like a criminal, his 'distinctive markings' pointed out, after which he would die of a heart attack, and his three pampered, fondled, adored daughters, his wife, his sister-in-law, the whole huge family with two very young sons, would for years struggle in complete destitution, fighting utmost poverty.

In 1924 he still lived in a large flat on the Champ-de-Mars. French and Russian teachers came to his daughters. Near the stove in the kitchen, cigarette in mouth, bustled a former Russian countess, now impoverished, hired as a cook; and in the dining room, from morning till late, the once-famous barrister Margulies ate, drank, argued, and laughed, with the Hebrew poet Chernikhovsky, the writer Semen Yushkevich, S.-R.s, S.-D.s, poets, parasites of all sorts, ballet dancers from the studio of the ballerina Preobrazhenskaya (formerly of the Mariinsky), former grand dukes, actors from former Imperial theatres, operetta singers, artists with a name, artists without a name, cabaret entertainers, unemployed journalists who had come from Odessa, unemployed impressari who had come from Kiev, all kinds of half-hungry, noisy hangers-on.

The first evening Grzhebin took us to the Bal Tabarin, to the can-can. Tickets to all the theatres lay in a heap in the dining room on a shelf – whoever wanted one took it. Khodasevich and I were settled on the seventh floor, in a so-called servant's room, beneath the roof: the room was filled not by a double bed but a triple bed.

211

The Eiffel Tower was visible through the window along with the sombre Paris sky, which was a greyish black. Below were gloomy, steamy trains (a railway still existed there). The following evening there was a ballet at the Théâtre des Champs-Elysées, then a night out in Montmartre. The third day I found a flat – or rather, a room with a tiny kitchen – on the Boulevard Raspail, diagonally across from the Café La Rotonde. We lived for four months in that room. Khodasevich lay on the bed for whole days, and I sat in the kitchen near a table, looking through the window. In the evening we both went to the Rotonde. The Rotonde was still alien – the kitchen, too, where I sometimes wrote verse – as was everything in the environment. There was no money at all. When someone came, I ran to the bakery on the corner, bought two cakes and sliced them in halves. Guests, out of politeness, did not touch them.

The mirror in the foyer of the Théâtre des Champs–Elysées, in which I saw myself during the interval on that evening of ballet, still exists. I have looked in it many times – nights of performances by Diaghilev, Anna Pavlova, Chaliapin, Habima, and the Moscow Arts Theatre touring company (in 1937). It hangs by the staircase, on the right, and you see yourself in it for a long time as you move towards it. There, in the depth of this mirror, I see myself that first evening, my dark blue dress with white lace, sleeveless in the fashion of the day, unfitted at the waist, and short, my feet in patent leather shoes, my hair tied at the back of my neck in an enormous knot, my thin hands. Khodasevich is at my side. Now the interval comes to an end. Nemchinova and Dolin will fly out onto the stage. I will see *Les Noces*, I will see *Le Sacre du Printemps*. Lean, slender, still in that turned jacket (or perhaps a rented tuxedo), Khodasevich takes me by the arm and escorts me into the hall.

We walk together through the city. Summer. It is hot. There is no place to go. We walk in the evenings or at night, when the city slowly cools down, becomes quiet, as if stretching out like a beast before placing one ear on a paw and half closing a huge fiery eye. A greedy desire to see this city in its past and present gradually possesses us. We walk through narrow and stinking streets of Montmartre, sit in cafés of Montparnasse, we go to a brothel on the Rue Blondel, to a dance at the Rue de Lappe, we spend half a night in a street near some railway tracks where Chinese men seize us by the arms and beckon us into a basement somewhere, breathing an unknown smell on us. We go to small vaudeville theatres with cardboard sets that would be ridiculous if they were not so sad, and to fairs, where we are shown a hermaphrodite; we sit in a tavern where naked greasy women wait on tables and, for five more sous, the client can get a clean towel, once he decides to go 'upstairs' with one of them. 'A pink-cheeked pimp in an opera hat' and 'a thin-haunched comet' (from Khodasevich's 'Stars') – all this he saw then on the Rue de la Gaité.

Museums, and gardens. And the quays. Together and alone we wander.

Some of our Berlin and Moscow friends here at this time already led a settled life, something we had still not dared decide to do. The Zaitsevs had set up their durable way of life, frugal but firm; the Tsetlins, who had had a flat in Paris before the war, were surrounded by peaceful family comfort. At the editorial offices of the Russian daily, *The Latest News*, it was crowded and dirty, but already one felt the soundness of this originally unstable enterprise. On the Rue Vineuse, in a small room with a portrait of 'granny of the Revolution' Breshkovskaya on the wall, the editorial offices of *Contemporary Annals* were set up. At this time the quarterly, later outstanding, printed a lot of second-rate stuff and even trash on the assumption that it would prove useful to the Russia of the future. Gradually the picture of Russian Paris became clear to us. The 'right' held on rather more firmly to the Orthodox church (where they prayed), Russian restaurants (where some worked as waiters and cloakroom girls), and the Renault plant (where some made a living as unskilled workers) – in other words, the valiant troops of the White Armies continued to carry on valiantly. They worked by the sweat of their brows, bore children, lamented the past and took part in military parades at the Tomb of the Unknown Soldier. And then there were those of the 'left', one of the centres of which was Ehrenburg, surrounded by all sorts of homeless figures, talented and confused, among whom were the poets Boris Poplavsky and Valentin Parnakh (brother of the forgotten poet Sofya Parnok, who died in Moscow in 1936) and future fashionable artists, Tereshkovich, Tchelitchew, Lanskoy, and Boris Bozhnev, one of the remarkable poets of my generation, who produced nothing in the 1930s owing to severe mental illness. All were slightly underfed, did not know fully what they would do the next day, how and where they would live, and instead sat in front of a cup of coffee on a café terrace; many had but a smattering of education, some had fought (on whose side was unknown) and now were making up for lost time as best they could in the post-war liveliness of Parisian art and literature circles.

I did not immediately feel the impact or realize all the intellectual luxury and novelty of Western (at that time, principally French) life which besieged me. For some time I still lived with the impressions of the last three years. They were too strong: Petersburg, August 1921, Bely, Gorky, Italy, changes in my personal life and separation from near ones. Our sudden poverty, Russian Paris, French Paris, the language that, though I knew it, suddenly seemed not at all like the one taught to me in childhood – exquisitely difficult, with unexpected impediments, which now and then cast me away from it – all this weighed heavily on me. The first stay in Paris, in 1924, before our return for one winter to Sorrento at Gorky's, left a feeling of homelessness in me: Khodasevich's indecision about remaining here, about planting both feet on ground that was considered firm, became even greater. Fear at making decisions tortured him. Earnings seemed ephemeral, an adequate job was not in view. I remember the last days and nights before our departure for Italy. At that time Khodasevich already knew his name was on the list of those writers and scholars who were exiled from Russia in 1922 – a couple of hundred men (when we were already in Berlin), and he understood that not only was return impossible but he would soon even find he could not be printed by Gosizdat. That he was on the list merely stressed something in his mind, eliminated the possibility of a return home and produced the first blueprint of the future. A breath of cold came from it. The first draught of fear blew over us and taught us very quickly not to expect too much. I remember one sleepless night – it was perhaps the last night before our departure for Sorrento (this journey was a delay of the inevitable). Khodasevich, exhausted by insomnia, could not find a place for himself: '*Here* I cannot, cannot, I cannot live and write, *there* I cannot, cannot live and write.' I saw how, in those moments, he was building up his own personal or private hell around himself and how he pulled me into that hell; and I trustingly followed him like Tobias with his fish. I turned to ice thinking that here finally was something stronger than both myself and all of us. Khodasevich said he could not exist without writing, that he could write only in Russia, he could not exist without Russia, but he could not live or write in Russia – and he pleaded with me to die with him.

Mark Vishniak, a member of the former S.-R. Party and one of the editors of *Contemporary Annals*, in his recollections of Khodasevich printed in the *New Review* (New York) in the 1940s, described how Khodasevich once came to his place and announced to him that he had decided to do away with himself. Already in 1921, as Khodasevich himself writes in the commentary to the poem 'From My Diary', he had been ready to do this. Such moods beset him early; one might even say they were with him from his earliest years. They ended only with his death, which he accepted like a long-awaited liberation.

We came to Paris for good in April 1925 (he remained there fourteen years and died, I remained twenty-five and left). Now he had resigned himself. He knew that return to Gorky's was impossible, all there would soon change. He knew he had no choice, that there was no place to go, which meant all problems had resolved themselves: one must live here, one must live, one must.

There is no other path but one that leads to the crowded and dirty Pretty Hotel on the Rue Amélie (since then mentioned more than once in the memoirs of foreign Bohemians – in particular in one of the books of Henry Miller). This is where we begin our life in Paris. We receive here a document given to those who are stateless, people without a homeland, who do not have the right to work for a salary, to belong to proletarians, white-collar workers or those who have a steady home and income. We can work only freelance; like people of bookish professions, we do piecework and are so labelled. We learn to divide one artichoke leaf in two, to divide every earned kopeck in half, share insult and injury, insomnia.

There were, as a matter of fact, no artichokes. Not at all because they had 'withered', as Virginia had once said, but simply because there was nothing to cook them in. Besides, Khodasevich did not eat them. In the electric kettle you could boil water for three cups of tea, and in the middle of the night, when we couldn't sleep, we drank tea, sitting on the bed together, and again could not sleep, talking endlessly, debating, but still we could never finally decide (although life every morning took it upon itself to decide for us). Sometimes he would cry, wring his hands. I was scared of the present, and I did not think about the future at all during those nights: what luxury it is to think of the future! Thus, the 'artichoke leaf' was only a metaphor.

But 'every earned kopeck' was no metaphor, if by kopeck one understands the round bronze French franc of that time. Francs came rarely and with difficulty, but as if in compensation, from very different places: to both of us from *Days* (the S.-R. daily, which then was published in Paris), or to him from *Contemporary Annals*, or to me from *The Latest News*. Or suddenly from the U.S.A. a small cheque from the Society to Aid Jobless Toilers of the Russian Intelligentsia, or suddenly from England, from some relatives (from relatives, however, as always, in the form of a loan). Once the first wife of Georgy Annenkov, who lived in the Pretty Hotel and was a dancer at La Chauve Souris (but she returned a year later to Moscow), came and put some embroidery on my knees to be finished without fail the following morning. The needlework was in cross-stitch, in long strips that were measured in metres, and within an hour I had earned sixty centimes. I remember how I sat and embroidered the whole night, and Khodasevich mused that unfortunately all this had already been described once, about one hundred years ago, either in a novel by Dickens or in one by Chernyshevsky – about poor and honest workers who sewed till they grew blind. So it was completely without interest. But I continued to do my cross-stitching for whoever needed it.

As for insult and injury, he sustained some, while I at that time had to swallow none. In a Russian publication office he would be told: 'Sorry, we can't pay you more than so-and-so, the public loves him so!' Or: 'You must wait with your article, this week we already have what's-his-name.' Miliukov, the chief editor of *The Latest News*, told him once (when for a short time he tried to work for them) that the daily *did not need him at all*. And at this very time, a pillar of Soviet literary publishing, *On Guard*, wrote about him:

> One of the typical bourgeois decadents, Vladislav Khodasevich, describes thus his impression of his own reflection in a restaurant window:

> . . . penetrating into a strange life
> Suddenly with revulsion I recognize
> That severed, lifeless
> Nocturnal head of mine.

I do not know – perhaps Khodasevich has erred personally, perhaps as a man he possesses a very attractive and even enchanting exterior, but socially he turns out to be unquestionably right. He has faithfully made out in the mirror the traits of the contemporary literature of his class. Contemporary bourgeois literature, looking into a mirror, can actually see its 'severed, lifeless nocturnal head'.

After this the critic turned to a similar criticism of Sologub, Mandelstam and Pasternak. The article closed:

For the present let us do away with the cultivation of Khodaseviches and other whiners of mysticism and restoration.

On another occasion, having done away with Ehrenburg, the critic turned to Khodasevich:

Let us leave Ehrenburg and address ourselves to his colleague on the magazine [*Krasnaya Nov*]. Listen:

'Beneath my feet it crackles and slides . . .'

[The whole poem is quoted.]
Of course 'no one will explain' why in his 'declining years' Khodasevich wants to 'turn numb' and perform other eccentricities. And similarly no one will explain in what way this verse made its way not into the pages of some émigré *Northern Lights* but into the columns of *Krasnaya Nov*.

And further on:

Manifestly bourgeois literature, beginning with émigré pogrom writers like the Gippiuses and Bunins, and ending with national Russian mystics and individualists like the Akhmatovas and Khodaseviches, sets the reader's psyche on the side of papal-feudal-bourgeois restoration . . .

In recent years (the 1950s and 1960s) it has become the custom in the U.S.S.R. to write that the émigrés 'feared' the masses, that they 'were scared' of the masses, that they trembled at the thought of the revolutionary masses. I do not think that Bunin,

Zaitsev, Tsvetaeva, Remizov, or Khodasevich feared the *masses*. But they certainly feared literary bureaucrats, and not for nothing: those servants of the regime who were at the same time literary critics, having gradually taken over *Krasnaya Nov* and established the magazine *On Guard* as a base, were instrumental in the closing of *Lef*, Mayakovsky's magazine, in the annihilation of Pilniak; they destroyed Voronsky, killed Mandelstam, Babel, and others, but finally perished themselves in Stalin's purges. One must hope that no one will rehabilitate them. Among them was that man who, one of the first, spoke of the necessity of simplifying culture for the sake of the masses – that is, of destroying the intelligentsia – and another who threatened the last symbolists and acmeists with bullets. One wants to believe that they have not left followers.

All this sounded grim because it cut off the road to Russia, while Miliukov's words rang out like a threat; one had to pay for the room in the Pretty Hotel, and not with 'freelance work' verse, my first stories, or my cross-stitching could I raise such a sum.

I strung beads. Many of us did – even Elsa Triolet (the future wife of Louis Aragon, the author) who lived during those years in a hotel on the Rue Campagne-Première, very like our Pretty Hotel. This was slightly more profitable than cross-stitching. I was an extra in films three times. I got paid with difficulty and I was not asked a fourth time. Autumn approached, and for Christmas I beautifully inscribed a thousand cards with a picture of the Star of Bethlehem. A thousand times I wrote 'Ah, mon doux Jésus!' for which I received ten francs: three meals, or one pair of shoes, or four Gallimard books.

On *Days*, while the daily existed (until the autumn of 1926), Khodasevich and Aldanov were editors of the literary section, and Khodasevich had regular work for several months. We found a flat far from the places where *everybody* lived, near the Place Dumesnil in the 12th Arrondissement. We bought two couches – that is, two box-springs on legs; one was supposed to buy mattresses for them, but we could buy the mattresses only after three years. In our understanding of the time this meant buying on 'instalment'. I had two hand-me-down dresses. We had a saucepan. In the small kitchen I laundered and spread out our four sheets. There was no change of bedclothes.

All around us post-war Paris flowered, went wild, in the roaring twenties which have entered history as the '*je m'en fous*' epoch. The post-war generation behaved stormily. The older one declined. I saw Claude Farrère, Paul Bourget, and Henri de Régnier, and it may now seem incredible that they still existed when Gide, Proust, Valéry, not to mention Breton and Tzara, burst into life with all their strength.

And at the summits of the French government it was the same: ancient Clemenceau left, but ancient Poincaré, and Barthou, and Briand came – all were people of the beginning of our century who very likely wanted to protect France from this century. But the more firmly the bearded contemporaries of Déroulède sat in their regalia and uniforms sewn in gold, the more despairingly the two generations that followed fought for the eight-hour working day, for public schools, cubism, dadaism, anti-academism, for Braque and Picasso, the ballets of Diaghilev, the surrealists, for confession rather than fiction, the new theatre and the music of Stravinsky.

Paris is not a city, it is the image, the symbol of France, its today and yesterday, the reflection of its history, its geography and its hidden essence. It has more meaning than London, Madrid, Stockholm, and Moscow – almost like Petersburg, New York, and Rome. It appears in a multitude of senses, has many aspects, sides, it speaks of the future, the past, is loaded with overtones of the present, with the heavy, rich, thick aura of today. You can't live in it as if it weren't there, can't run away from it or lock yourself out of it: it will enter your house, room, your own self all the same, it will begin to change you, force you to grow; it will age you, mutilate or uplift, perhaps kill.

It exists, constant, eternal, surrounding us who live in it, and it is in us. We love it or hate it, but we cannot escape it. It is a circle of associations in which man exists, being himself a circle of associations. Having entered it and come out of it we are not what we were before knowing it: it devoured us, we devoured it, and the problem is not did we or didn't we want it. We consumed each other. It courses in our blood.

On a small back street where in summer children play on the pavement, and at night rooms in cheap hotels (in ours as well) are rented by the hour, where at one end there is a post office and at the other Turkish baths, in a small room that is hot in summer and cold in winter, to the sound of the neighbours' radio, which thunders until late at night, we live until finally we find a flat. And out of the joy that we have a place, can lock the door, lower the blinds, and be alone, we walk about like lunatics in those first days. We find our first home on the Rue Lamblardie. Like an ant I drag into it a table, a bookshelf. There are no mattresses, but there is an iron, two chairs, a frying pan, and a broom. On Sundays an organ-grinder comes into the courtyard and I throw him a sou. We now have three forks and when Weidlé comes we have dinner for three. There is no sense of time. There will be no change. What exists will exist. No alterations are foreseen. We now live here and will to the end of time. Nothing can change – as the seal on our passports cannot be changed.

The city is all around us – symbol of the country, with its buildings, palaces, stores, factories, theatres, monuments – something huge, a thousand years old, rich with noises, odours, vitality, and thoughts. We feed on it, coalesce with it, celebrate its holidays, drag out its days, hide in it and come out into it for a struggle with life (and we will tremble later when bombs fall on it). Beneath one of its roofs we become aware of our outcast state, our impotence, despair, and (sometimes) hope.

I cannot leave Khodasevich for more than an hour: he is liable to jump out of a window, or switch on the gas. I cannot go off to study – above all, there is no money for this. I don't think I have to go to the Sorbonne, but I must become a linotypist, a typesetter, must learn to work as a typographer, but I can't leave him alone in the apartment. He gets up late if at all, sometimes around noon, sometimes around one. In the afternoon he reads, writes, sometimes goes out for a little while, sometimes to the offices of *Days*. He returns humiliated and worn out. We eat. He eats no greens, no fish, no cheese. I don't know how to cook. In the evenings we go out, return late. We sit in a café in Montparnasse, now here, now there, most often at La Rotonde. There Boris Poplavsky, Aleksandr Ginger, Antonin Ladinsky, Georgy Adamovich gather, and within a few years Vladimir Smolensky, Georgy Fedotov, more rarely Wladimir Weidlé, Boris Zaitsev, others . . . At night Khodasevich writes. I sleep, pressing his pajamas close to my bosom so they will be warm when he is ready to put them on. I wake up. There is light in his room. Sometimes I get up in the morning and he has still not gone to bed. Often at night he suddenly wakes me: Let's drink coffee, let's drink tea, let's talk. I am drowsy. After the coffee or tea he sometimes falls asleep, sometimes not. I too fall asleep.

There was no everyday humdrum. Nor could there be any: we didn't want it. But I remember two emotions that were peculiar to me in those years: a sense of liberty and feeling of constraint. The first was closely bound up with my life in the Western world and with my being young, with the books I read, the people I saw and among whom I chose friends, with all my inward maturing and what I then wrote. The feeling of constraint (or non-liberty) was bound up with my predicament of living out of Russia, with Khodasevich, with our home, the time and locales of my days and years. This feeling of constraint kept me for weeks in a kind of inexplicable intellectual stagnation, melancholy, anxiety. Beyond it there always stood, like the watchman of my every step, poverty, the concern (mixed with pain) of being together with him, awareness that both of us were tortuously dependent on one another. He did not hide this from me, nor did I hide it from him. The common criteria of *husband* and *wife*, *brother* and *sister* would not have applied to us. The fabric of life was woven from days and nights – nights depended on days – and our dreams mingled with reality, what sparkled in daylight was transformed during a sleepless night into musing. Four walls, two people. Each was revealed to the other, understood by the other (because between us there was psychic as well as physical closeness). How much that was mysterious arose in our life together when you realized how the very basis of our existence was woven – from noise into silence, out of a crowd into solitude, night into day and day into night. How much arises and is lost and disappears, leaving only a slight trace which suddenly begins to live quietly within you like a second layer. The first is always with me, but this second one I can only grasp from time to time; it slips away from me. I listen to it, but there are days when it is not audible at all.

Now, when I write about this, I know well the recurring themes of my life, its mythology: the well and the source, poor Lazarus, Tobias leading the Angel, and the Angel leading Tobias, the jutting bowsprit figure, and others. They appear from time to time, building bridges to each other, living within me between con-sciousness and unconsciousness, doing their uninterrupted work

221

rather like peristalsis, sucking in and discarding various elements of my existence. When I put my head on Khodasevich's shoulder, there was still nothing beyond that horizon. Only the thought that we clung to each other; but did we cling as strongly to this world? He hardly, for sure: through this world there was some other that was flickering for him, full of infinite meaning, created by him and his contemporaries, a mirror-world of reflections, meanings, and *realia* connected to our world. I cling to life; another world is not apparent to me beyond this one; I know that in this unique world I will find all the necessary links. But I also know that in every reality there is an element of nonsense, in every goal the absurd, and cruelty in every civilization. But Mother Nature is even more terrible, more cruel and absurd – so all things considered, let's stick to civilization!

However ominous the laws of our society, the laws of our political, social, and individual existence and of immanent experience, the laws of Mother Nature are still much more powerful and odious.

When I begin to talk about this, Khodasevich covers my eyes with his hand (the Angel's gesture towards Tobias) and within me a calm and free world is born. He falls asleep on my shoulder (that's his gesture – the gesture of Tobias towards the Angel), and I want to take on myself all the nightmares that make him scream in his sleep.

These recurring themes, the structural symbolism, is not placed on me from outside, it does not cover me but it makes my very essence: it is indivisible from me, like form and content. Without it I am only bones, muscles, skin, or water and salt, or a formula. This symbolism is my form which is my content, my content which is my form. In it I die and resurrect my whole life, clinging to it, for without it I am not I, and the senselessness and vacillation of the universe begin to show themselves to me. Only within myself can I find what I can (and must) stand on, at the same time, perhaps, grasping someone else firmly, holding him close, helping him not to slip, though not promising him eternity yet promising him a chance, the possibility of attaining the final limits of reality which he seeks. And promising him memory, the protector of the imagination, in defiance of time.

'It is impossible to destroy you, you can *only* die,' Khodasevich said to me once.

I wanted to write; I sought all possible paths of personal liberation, but I could never sacrifice a living instant of life for the sake of a line to be written, my balance for the sake of a manuscript, a storm within me for the sake of a poem. I loved life itself too much for this. I wanted to be first a person, second an educated one, third a modern educated person, fourth a modern educated person in harmony with herself and in harmony with the disharmony of the frightening world. And only fifth did I want to write – not for a friendly reader, but to purify myself, if I could just come to know myself before I *only* die.

He felt I couldn't be destroyed, and yet along with this he could not but see the moments of my weakness. At that time I was keen to know people and yet secretly scared of them – both those who liked me and those who didn't, indeed the former more than the latter. I remember the tension within because of my desire to hide this fear, and our misery, Khodasevich's illnesses, and my lack of self-confidence. I could not have spoken of myself in those years as I speak now. Much had not been overcome, not subdued. Yes, I did not know how to speak, I did not even know how to think. The most important thing was to learn to think. Of myself, him, us. And perhaps later to learn to think about others. He used to say: Learn to write. But I knew that what was most important for me was to think. Neither writing nor speaking was possible without this, for the very language of man is a reflection of his mind. I always dreamt of reaching maturity before I *only* died.

The 1920s and 1930s of our century were a fearful and terrible time. On the map of Europe were England, France, Germany, and Russia. In the first imbeciles reigned, in the second living corpses, in the third villains, and in the fourth villains and bureaucrats. England was disarming, France was not capable of putting any decisions into action, the Nazis were arming themselves, having announced beforehand to the whole world what they were up to, although nobody listened to them and nobody believed them. At home a political and cultural Thermidor had begun, which was to last, with short interruptions, a quarter of a century. One of the interruptions would be a war in which one-tenth of the population would perish.

Khodasevich and I would sit in a room that got cold at night – or rather he, as almost always when he was at home, would be lying down. I sat at his feet, wrapped up in a cotton housecoat, and we spoke of Russia, where the swift end of everything had begun – of the old, the new, whatever had sparkled for a moment. Of all that he loved. Briusov had died, nothing was heard of Bely, people with whom he had once had a close relationship – Marietta Shaginian, Abram Efros, Georgy Chulkov, Yury Verkhovsky – had gone far, far off. I told him that he, who had in himself not a drop of Russian blood, was for me the personification of Russia, that I knew no one more bound up with the Russian renaissance of the first quarter of this century: he could speak of the deaths of Chekhov and Tolstoy as events in his personal life, he had known Blok, he had shaken Scriabin's hand, he himself was a part of this renaissance, one of the stones of that structure of which there would soon remain nothing.

He coughed a lot. He had (already) prolonged pains somewhere deep inside. Dr Golovanov (who refused a fee) would take his pulse and say it was probably the liver, but he prescribed no diet, for Khodasevich could follow no diet: all his life (except during the hunger of the revolutionary years) he ate the same thing: meat and noodles. No salad, soup, fruits, not any of the food usually given to the sick.

Within a year the furunculosis started again. Golovanov gave injections, but they did not help. He prescribed pills, without effect. I had to change the sheets every other day. And so I set off once, on an autumn evening in 1926, at first to *Days*, where he was owed money, and then to my cousin (and friend) to borrow two clean sheets.

At *Days* Zenzinov (an S.-R. who in his day had let Azef escape) came out to see me and, looking fearfully around on all sides, explained there was no money and would not be, that the newspaper had gone bankrupt and was being liquidated. I stood and looked at this very honest and very stupid man and thought about his having dinner today and tomorrow and *seculum seculorum* (as for us, I still didn't know) and tried to convince myself it is more interesting to live when the future is unknown, but I couldn't. I knew that Zenzinov lived in Fondaminsky's flat (he also was an S.-R. terrorist), that they had a servant, and a samovar on the table, and a view from their window of all of Paris, and books, and that, as Fondaminsky always put it, they lived an intellectual life. But there was no money, as Zenzinov told me, and I left, went to the Rue Dareau, that spot where the subway near the Glacière station comes out above ground, and there on that narrow and dirty street, on the seventh floor, I sat for about two hours on a staircase step, awaiting the arrival of Asya, to borrow clean bed linen from her. I sat and felt on this dark staircase that we were lost, there was no place for us to go and that I was probably responsible for all that had happened both to me and to him, and thought if Khodasevich died then I of course would also die.

I returned late. Khodasevich, dressed, hardly alive, stood in the hall, ready to go to the police to report that I had disappeared. I sat down there on a chair, tired, my head spinning, my legs not supporting me. Finally I raised my eyes towards him and said:

'"A nos yeux les habitants du reste de l'Europe n'étaient que des imbéciles pitoyables."'

'Where is that from?' he asked and placed his hand on my head, himself hardly able to stand.

'Stendhal. And he was right.'

He didn't answer. Two tears fell from my eyes. I went to make his bed. He undressed, lay down, kissed my hands and laughed with joy that he didn't have to go to the morgue to identify me. All this – and his irony – were a part of our long-continued conversation which had begun in Petersburg, near the window of his round room (or at the smoking stove, or at the house gates on Kirochnaya Street).

In the luxury of European intellectual life of those years, it was not so simple to distinguish friend from foe and builder from destroyer. To put it more exactly, it was only in the 1920s that the self-knowledge of our era was born, though not in France. France either preserved monuments of the past (never smashing them, unlike the Russians) or tore them up with an inconsistency all her own, exalting all that should have been blown up and ridiculing what should have been preserved and respected. There was an unusual confusion of mind: the same man could become exhilarated by the reactionary philosophy of Alain as well as sent into ecstasy by 'dada', could feed on Freud and be a member of the Communist Party, and all this not because of his youthful irresponsibility but simply because of the over-abundance of the meaningless old theatricality that had got out of control. Men looked for the new for the mere sake of the new, madly rushing at what impeded their whims and washing it from the face of the earth without discernment. In this atmosphere Khodasevich felt himself alone (only later it became gradually clear *with whom* he had something in common among the modern European poets); he thought that time was working against him (and the opposite came to be). A captive of his youth and sometimes its slave (of the artificiality of Briusov, the hysterics of Bely, the mists of Blok), he did not notice a good deal around him; he was seized by a tremendous weariness and pessimism and a sense of the tragic destiny of the universe (the last stage before its total madness), not having any longer the strength to look in the direction where Europeans stood who thought like him (though only partially). Or perhaps he was destroyed by events in Russia. Or did he consciously hide from his European contemporaries and, not trusting them, turn away and become silent?

At that time in the entire Western world there was not *one single* writer of renown who would have been *for us*, who would have lifted up his voice against the persecution of the intelligentsia in the U.S.S.R., against repressions, Soviet censorship, arrests of writers, trials, the closing of periodicals, against the iron law of socialist realism, any violation of which led to the physical destruction of Russian writers. The older generation – Wells, Shaw, Rolland, Mann – was entirely for new Russia, for the interesting experiment that was liquidating the horrors of tsarism, for Stalin against Trotsky – as it had been for Lenin against the other leaders of Russian political parties. The older generation – with Dreiser, Sinclair Lewis, Upton Sinclair, André Gide (up to 1936) and Stefan Zweig – was in all matters on the side of the Communist Party against its opposition. In their wake came the not so young ones – for example, the Bloomsbury group with Virginia Woolf, and Valéry, and Hemingway – who did not express any enthusiasm for the Russian Communist Party but who were indifferent to what was happening in Russia in the 1930s. The idol of the young in Paris, Jean Cocteau, wrote that dictators were a boon because 'Dictators promote protest in art, and without protest art dies.' (One wanted to ask: And what about a bullet in the neck?) Their principal enemy was the reactionary, later the reactionary in Spain and the nascent National Socialism in Germany. What can one say about the young ones? The most glaring example of their behaviour was the physical beating by French surrealists of Andrey Levinson – a Russian literary and theatre critic, an émigré, author of many books – after his obituary on Mayakovsky was published in 1930. He had already been in trouble in 1928 with a letter to *Le Temps* in which he asked what Gorky thought of the repression of writers then beginning in the Soviet Union.

But here I come to an event I want to recount in more detail. It took place a year before Levinson's letter, in the summer of 1927.

That year Olga Forsh, whom I had known in Petersburg in 1922, when she was one of Khodasevich's closest friends, came from the Soviet Union. On arrival in Paris she came immediately to see us. She was happy to see Khodasevich; there was no end to their talk. In 1921–2 she had lived on the same corridor in the House of Arts, they had met daily, and now in Paris she took up the interrupted dialogue with him. Khodasevich knew her son and daughter. Forsh loved him and had held him in high esteem as a poet. For both, this meeting after a five-year separation was an event.

Forsh spent evenings with us, spoke of the changes in literature and in party politics concerning literature, sometimes carefully, sometimes openly, heatedly. Grey, fat, old (so she then seemed to me), she said that they all had one hope. They were waiting.

'Hope for what?' asked Khodasevich.

'For world revolution.'

Khodasevich was shocked.

'But there won't be one.'

Forsh was silent for a minute. Even without this, her face was heavy; it became sullen, the edges of her mouth drooped, her eyes dimmed.

'Then we have failed,' she said.

'Who has failed?'

'All of us. Our end will come.'

Two days passed and she did not reappear. So we went to her place in the evening to find out if she was all right. She was staying on the Left Bank, with her artist daughter, who had become an émigrée. It was a marvellous summer evening and in Nadia's courtyard there was greenery and a little bench, and her studio opened directly onto the yard. We went in. Forsh lay on a bed, dressed, dishevelled, flushed. She told us that yesterday morning she had gone to 'our' embassy and had been officially forbidden to meet Khodasevich. She could meet Berdyaev and Remizov from time to time, but not Khodasevich. 'You must now leave,' she said. 'You cannot stay here.'

We stood in the middle of the room, completely bewildered.

'Vladia, forgive me,' she forced out of herself with effort.

We went slowly towards the door. The courtyard was in sunshine. Forsh moved on the bed with her huge body and let out a sob. We stood silently in the gateway for a minute and then wandered on home. Now it had become indisputably clear: we were cut off maybe for thirty, forty years, forever . . . Now, in 1966, I can say: Yet not forever!

After this Khodasevich had two or three meetings with friends who had come from Moscow and turned away from him: they went back and would not permit themselves the luxury of disobedience. Later the Union of Writers stopped sending royalties to Khodasevich for his translation of Mérimée's *The Coach of the Holy Sacrament*, which was playing at the Maly Theatre. A year later my parents wrote to me not to send them letters, only postcards.

To that summer (1927) the now-forgotten anonymous letter belongs, sent from Moscow to the editorial boards of Russian émigré newspapers, entitled 'To the Writers of the World'. Evidently, judging from the title, it was sent to foreign papers as well, but I don't recall that it ever appeared in any French newspaper. It was printed on 10 June 1927, in *The Latest News*.

I quote it here in full:

TO THE WRITERS OF THE WORLD

Our words, writers of the world, are addressed to you.

How can one explain that you, so penetrating, who have dug to the depths of the human soul, to the inward depths of epochs and peoples, ignore us, Russians condemned to gnaw the chain of a fearful prison raised against the word? Why do you, also brought up on the great works of our geniuses of the word, keep silent, when in a great country the killing of a great literature, its most mature fruit as well as its buds, is going on?

Or is it that you do not know about our prison of the word – about communist censorship in the second quarter of the twentieth century, about the censorship of the 'socialist' state? We fear that this is the case. But why do the writers who have visited Russia –

Messrs. Duhamel, Durtain and others – why do they, on returning home, not tell you of it? Or perhaps they were not interested in the condition of the press in Russia? Or they looked and did not see, saw and did not understand? We are sick at the thought that the ring of official goblets filled with official champagne, with which foreign writers are greeted in Russia, has drowned out the rattling of the chains placed on our literature and the whole Russian people.

Listen and learn!

Idealism, that great current of Russian artistic literature, is considered a state crime. Our classics of this style are being withdrawn from all accessible libraries. Their fate is shared by the works of historians and philosophers who reject materialistic views. In raids by special inspectors, all pre-revolutionary children's literature and all editions of folk epics are being confiscated from public libraries and bookstores. Present-day writers who are suspected of idealism are deprived not only of the possibility but of all hope for the possibility of publishing their works. They themselves, like enemies and destroyers of the modern social structure, are pursued from all jobs and deprived of all earning-power.

This is the first wall of the prison in which the free word is interred. In its wake comes a second.

Any manuscript that goes to a publishing house must first be presented in two copies to the censor. When finally printed it goes there again, for a second reading and verification. There have been cases when single sentences, one word or even one letter in a word (the capital letter in the word 'God'), passed by the censor, the author, the printer, and the proof reader, have led on the second censoring to a ruthless confiscation of the whole edition.

All works are subject to the approval of the censor – even works in chemistry, astronomy, mathematics. Subsequent author's corrections in them can be made only with special (in every case) permission of the censor. Without this the publishing house will not dare set a single correction in galley.

Without the preliminary permission of the censor, without a special petition with special duty-stamps, without a long wait till the censor, deluged with work, gets to that piece of paper with your name and surname, you cannot under the communist system even print visiting cards. Messrs. Duhamel and Durtain could easily have noted that even theatre posters with inscriptions such as 'no smoking' and 'emergency exit' are marked at the bottom with that same sacramental sign of the censor which allows them to be printed.

There is still a third prison wall, a third line of barbed wire and wolf pits.

Special government permission is needed to establish a private or public publishing house. None, not even scientific publishing houses, receive it for a period of more than two years. Permissions are given with difficulty and rarely to non-governmental publishing houses. The activity of each of them can move only within the frame of the programme approved by the censor. The publishing houses must present to the censorship, a year in advance, a complete list of all the works prepared for publication, with detailed biographies of the authors. Without this list, in so far as it is approved by the censor, the publishing house will not dare publish anything.

Under such conditions, only that which agrees with the ideas of the communist censor is accepted for publication. Only that is printed which is not at variance with the communist *Weltanschauung* which is obligatory for all. All the rest, even what is important and full of talent, not only cannot be published, but must be carefully hidden. If found during a search, it means the threat of arrest, exile, and even death by firing squad. One of the best political scientists in Russia, Professor Lazarevsky, was shot solely for his project for a Russian Constitution, found at his home during a search.

Do you know all of this? Do you feel the whole horror of the position to which our language, our word, our literature are condemned?

If you know it, if you feel it, why are you silent? We have heard your loud protest against the conviction of Sacco and Vanzetti and other men of the word, but persecutions to the death of the best Russian people, who cannot even propagate their ideas because of the complete impossibility of such expression, evidently pass you by. In our torture chamber we, in any case, did not hear your voices of protest and of appealing to the moral sense of peoples. Why?

Writers! Ear, eye, conscience of the world – answer! It is not for you to affirm: 'There is no power if not from God.' You will not speak cruel words to us: 'Every nation is governed by the power it deserves.' You know: the nature of a nation and the nature of power in despotic regimes come to an accord only with the passing of long historical periods. In short periods of popular life they can be in tragic disagreement. Remember the years before our Revolution when our social organizations, the organs of local government, the state Duma and even certain members of the government called out, asked, implored the power to turn from the road leading to the abyss. Power remained deaf and blind. Remember: whom did you sympathize with then – the gang around Rasputin, or the people? Whom did you condemn and whom did you morally uphold? Where are you now?

We know: besides sympathy, moral support for the principles and defenders of freedom, and moral condemnation of the cruelest of despotisms, you can in no way help us or our people. However, we do not expect more. We wish you, with all our strength, to do what is possible, energetically, everywhere: for the social consciousness of the world to rip away for ever the artful hypocritical mask from that terrible face which is communist power in Russia. We ourselves are powerless to do this: our sole arm, the pen, has been yanked from our hands, the air we breathe – literature – shut off from us, while we are in prison.

Your voice is needed not only by us and Russia. Think of your own selves: with satanic energy, visible only to us, your peoples are being pushed along that same path of horrors and blood onto which, at a fateful moment in its history ten years ago, our people, torn by war and the politics of pre-revolutionary rule, were set. We know this path to the Golgotha of peoples and warn you about it.

We are personally doomed. The light of liberty had not yet shone near us. Many of us are no longer in a position to transmit to our descendants the terrible experience we have endured. Learn about it, study it, describe it – you, the free ones – so that the eyes of generations, present and future, will be opened to it. Do this – and it will be easier for us to die.

As from a dungeon we send you this letter. We write it at great risk, at risk of death it is sent to you abroad. We do not know if it will reach the pages of the free press. But if it does, if our voice from beyond the grave rings out among you, we beseech you: Listen, understand, think it over. The standard of conduct of our late great man, L. N. Tolstoy, who cried out in his day to the world, 'I cannot keep silent,' will then become your norm.

A GROUP OF RUSSIAN WRITERS.

Russia. May 1927.

Such was the outcry that came from Russia addressed to the whole world, but heard only by the émigrés. In *Pravda* on 23 August (of the same year, 1927) a refutation of the letter appeared. *Pravda* called it a forgery, fabricated by the émigrés. As proof of this the newspaper said that in Soviet Russia writers were the happiest in the world, the freest, and that you would not find among them a single one who would dare to complain of his condition and thereby play into the hands of enemies of the Soviet people.

And now, looking back, I will say that although it would be good to know the whole truth about the origin (and authorship) of this document, at present *I don't care* whether it was written by Ivanov-Razumnik, Chulkov, or Voloshin *in Russia* or by someone in the entourage of Merezhkovsky, Melgunov, Petr Struve *in Paris*. In the letter notes of despair resound related to the suicides of Esenin and Sobol, the persecutions of Voronsky, the flowering of the journal *On Guard*, the iron curtain that fell on Russia after the abolition of N.E.P. But if the letter is a forgery and *Pravda* was right, then what a prophetic forgery! What a bottle afloat in the sea when you remember what began in the U.S.S.R. in the space of two years and continued for a quarter of a century!

Not one 'writer of the world' answered this letter; not one newspaper or magazine commented on it. The left press of France, of course, stood on the side of *Pravda*; the right was not interested in the status of Russian literature at that stage. Emigré writers began to bend their efforts to make the voice from Moscow heard. But nobody listened to them, they were accepted nowhere, the answer everywhere was always the same: You have lost your plants and factories, your estates and bank accounts. We sympathize but don't want to have anything to do with you. Finally, Balmont and Bunin wrote letters addressed to the 'conscience' of French writers. For several months they tried to print them in the so-called 'popular' press, but they did not succeed. And then in January 1928 (the 12th) these appeals finally appeared in a small periodical, *L'Avenir*. No one paid any attention to them.

With one exception: Romain Rolland. He read the letters of Balmont and Bunin, which in essence commented on and recounted the anonymous Moscow letter, and he decided to teach them a lesson. He printed his rebuttal in the February issue of the monthly *L'Europe* (the letter is dated 20 January, 1928).

> Balmont, Bunin, I understand you. Your world has been destroyed, you are in unhappy exile. For you the alarm of the past that has gone resounds. O perceptive people, why do you seek allies among the horrid reactionaries of the West, among the bourgeoisie and imperialists? O recruits of disappointment! . . . I go towards the newborn, I take it in my arms . . . There was always in Russia a secret police, that horrible poison because of which the flowers of the souls of nations wither . . . As for motherhood and childhood, read the account by O. Kameneva of her activities . . . Your blood and the Russian people's are one. But at present between you and your people there is a ditch of blood . . . Great minds go to Russia and see what is being done there . . . Scientists are working feverishly in your homeland . . . there are more writers and readers there than here . . . Just recently I received a new book by Prishvin as a present . . . Censorship has also tortured me in my own country . . . Let us cauterize the wound with a hot iron! All power smells bad . . . And still mankind moves forward . . . It is moving forward today . . . Over you, over me . . .

But the matter did not end with this. It seemed but little to Rolland. He addressed himself to Gorky, in Sorrento, with the question asking if it was true that writers were oppressed in the Soviet Union. Was it true that their condition was a hard one? In the March issue of *L'Europe* (of the same year) one can find Gorky's answer to Rolland's inquiry (dated 29 January–12 February, 1928). This answer explained to Rolland once and for all the state of things and calmed him down for good.

Gorky wrote that not only was 'To the Writers of the World' a forgery, but that in the Soviet Union writers were ever so much happier than in bourgeois countries. There were hundreds of young talents, and old men-of-letters worked more strenuously and profitably than before the Revolution. So as not to make unsubstantiated statements, Gorky mentioned many names: after the known, even famous names of Aleksey Tolstoy, Tikhonov, Prishvin, Leonov, and others, he put on his list the following names:

> Leonid Borisov
> Nina Smirnova
> Babel
> Pilniak
> Yakovlev
> Klychkov
> Kazin
> Oreshin
> Zoshchenko

All these names without exception belong to people who were later in one way or another *repressed* – at different times and to varying degrees. Borisov stopped writing novels and stories and turned to biographical sketches of great men of the past (Maupassant, Jules Verne, Stevenson). Gorky wrote a preface to a book by Borisov, but evidently neither then nor later was it published. Six men mentioned by Gorky were *liquidated* in the 1930s during the purges. Zoshchenko was debarred from literature in 1946. It was perhaps for these reasons that this letter from Gorky to Rolland was never inserted in the complete editions of his works and letters.

But still this was not the end of the argument. Within a month, on 22–3 March, Gorky again wrote to Rolland: this time he characterized Balmont as an alcoholic and asked Rolland to publish his letter. This, however, Rolland did not do, evidently fearful of engaging in 'personalities', but it has now been published in the U.S.S.R. among some twelve hundred other letters by Gorky (by his own count he wrote in all twenty thousand).

At this very time *L'Avenir* made an attempt to inquire of French writers: Did there exist, in their opinion, persecutions of writers in the U.S.S.R., or had these ended long ago as Bernard Shaw had stated? But the magazine was read by no one, was badly distributed, and the whole affair was hushed up very quickly. In March 1928 the sixtieth anniversary of Gorky was celebrated by the 'whole world', as Rolland wrote in that same *L'Europe*. That was when Andrey Levinson sent his question to *Le Temps* in connection with Gorky's mourning for the head of the Cheka, Dzerzhinsky.

Exactly two years later Mayakovsky shot himself and the era of terror, which lasted twenty-three years, began in the Soviet state.

The roaring, the happy twenties. Riots in literature, rebellions in painting, in music. Revolution in the way of life – in the whole world. The bourgeoisie going out of its mind: We have been victorious, look at us! (Or: We have been defeated, look at us!) The thunder of martial music on Armistice Day, of fireworks on the day of the taking of the Bastille. The storm of speeches from tribunes, laughter from the stage – If there is among all of this a heavenly thunder no one hears it. And what do we have to do with all of this, we, the Akaky Akakieviches of the universe? As Blok put it: 'Let's be quieter than the water, lower than the grass . . .'

In the meantime, I thought, how can I endure, so as to make life bearable for myself and for at least one more person, or perhaps for two or three? How can I live through it without pushing too much? How can I arrive without kicking too hard? How can I overcome fear? How can I learn to see life *above all* as fair play, a noble sport founded on noble rules of competition in a game subject to honourable norms? Yes, at the most ghastly moments to learn what in English is called *sportsmanship*. So that in the end I might say (not announcing it in a high-falutin' speech, but muttering it to myself under my breath): They have pushed and kicked me more than I have pushed and kicked them. They have betrayed me more than I betrayed them. I have made things easier for them than they have for me. More often I was the Angel and not Tobias, and when I was Tobias I was not aware of my loveliness or my innocence (for neither, moreover, do I give a damn). In the desperate, hopeless years of my life, I knew how to be alone, keep silent and be strict with myself, at first not without a certain pedantry common to the young (later I rid myself of it).

'Generally speaking, you need no one, is that it?' said Khodase-vich once.

'I need you.'

'For so long and no longer . . . I would like to see you in a desperate situation.'

'More desperate than now with you?'

'Yes. Sometimes you are still able to turn minus–signs into plus–signs.'

'That would be a pretty vile picture.'

'As far as I am concerned, I always have a way out: I can *return my ticket.*'

'Not for anything. I want to use it up to the very end and even try to travel some miles free of charge.'

(Does he like my iron insides, I would wonder sometimes, or do they get on his nerves?)

My blessed years with him were not at all of the kind it is customary to define by the words happiness, bliss, well-being, joy, pleasure, serenity. They were something else: I felt life more intensely with him, I was more fully alive than before meeting him, I burned with life in its contrasts; in the sufferings I then knew, I had more life in myself than if I were just dividing my surroundings and those around me into 'yes' and 'no'. The intensity was such that any miracle seemed possible. I am not convinced that concepts such as *comfort* and *security* have the same meaning for modern man that lay in them a hundred years ago: if I am to judge by modern literature, they have to a great degree lost their meaning. I was not alone in seeking life itself in its strongest manifestation, beyond the concepts of comfort and security. And already then the idea came to me that I *was*, *am*, and *will be*, but perhaps will not *become*. This did not scare me. There was for me in *being* an intensity I did not feel in *becoming*.

Our dialogue, which lasted seventeen years, is not the past to me. It is as actual as the present day. It lives in me, acts upon me, grows in me as I grow in it, although today I no longer lead anyone anywhere and do not grasp on to anyone. I have fused the Angel and Tobias in myself, and they do not exist any more. For many years I used the pronoun 'we'. Now, as in my youth, I go to sleep and wake up alone.

PART FOUR

The Salt of the Earth

I REMEMBER THEIR GRAND ENTRANCE: THE TWO leaves of the door flew open, and they stepped into the room. Two chairs were brought in after them and they sat down. The man with the beard, short, looked about sixty, the reddish lady about forty-five. But I did not at once recognize them. Vasily Maklakov, then reading his recollections of Leo Tolstoy, stopped in the middle of a sentence, waited until the doors were shut, then continued. All heads turned to the new guests. Vinaver (all this took place in the Vinavers' large living room) raised himself a little, then sat down again. Some sort of hardly noticeable movement went through the whole salon. Who are they? I thought. For several minutes a kind of respectfulness hung in the air. And suddenly something struck me as I looked at him once more: before recognizing *her* I recognized *him*: I was misled because she looked so young, and yet at that time she was near sixty. These were the Merezhkovskys.

Having crossed her legs and tilted her head back, her eyelids half covering her near-sighted eyes (she became more wall-eyed with age) she played with her lorgnette and listened to Maklakov, who floridly and with confidence continued his story. She always liked the colour pink, which was not becoming to her dark red hair, but she had her own criteria and what in another woman might have appeared strange became with her a part of her very self. A half-transparent silk scarf streamed around her neck, her thick hair was arranged in a complex hairdo. Her thin small hands with unpainted fingernails were dry and impersonal, her legs (she always wore short dresses to display them) were beautiful, like the legs of a young woman of the past. Bunin jokingly said that forty pairs of pink silk panties lay in her commode and forty pink petticoats hung in her closet. She had some old jewels, chains, and pendants, and sometimes (though not that evening) she appeared with a long

239

emerald tear-drop on her forehead, suspended on a thin chain between her eyebrows. There can be no doubt she artificially worked up two features of her personality: poise and femininity. Within she was not poised. And she was not womanly.

He was aggressive and sad. This contrast was characteristic of him. He rarely laughed and indeed did not often smile; when he told funny stories (for example, about how once, in Luga, Anton Kartashev had a stomach-ache), he told them very seriously. There was something crisp and clean about him, in his physical appearance. He smelled good, and a kind of corporeal neatness and physical lightness were typical of him: one felt that all his things, from his comb to his pencil, were clean, not because he looked after them but because dust would not stick to him or them.

The Vinavers' living room was one of the 'salons' of Russian literary Paris in the years 1925–6 (Maksim Vinaver died in 1926). Their huge flat in the best part of Paris recalled the flats of old Petersburg – with rugs, chandeliers, a piano in the living room and bookshelves in the study. About thirty people – and not only the famous ones like Maklakov, Miliukov, the Merezhkovskys, Bunin – were invited to lectures. Those who 'showed promise' came too, the young of Montparnasse cafés, contributors to the weekly newspaper *The Link* which Vinaver edited and published. (At that time he also edited and published *The Jewish Tribune* and was the author of a book of recollections, *The Recent Past*.) A well-known member of the K.-D. Party and a past member of the Duma, he shared with Miliukov, as it were, the Russian democratic press (the daily newspaper): Miliukov published and edited *The Latest News*, Vinaver the literary newspaper supplement.

After the lecture the guests would move into the dining room, where supper awaited them. Zinaida Gippius had poor vision and was hard of hearing; her laugh was her defence; she played with her lorgnette and smiled, pretending sometimes to be more near-sighted and deafer than she was in fact, sometimes asking that something she had understood perfectly be repeated. A constant struggle-and-joke went on between her and the outside world. She (the real she) shielded herself from the life around and in her with irony, mannerisms, intrigues, affectations.

They lived in their pre-war flat. That is, when they left Soviet Russia in 1919 and arrived in Paris, they opened the door of the flat with their own key and found everything in place: books, kitchenware, linen. They did not have that feeling of homelessness which Bunin and others experienced so acutely. In those early years, when I did not know them, they frequented French literary circles, meeting Henri de Régnier, Paul Bourget, Anatole France, and writers of their Russian generation who were coming to nothing in France.

'And later they were fed up with us,' Merezhkovsky used to say, 'and they stopped inviting us.'

'Because you so tactlessly cursed the Bolsheviks,' she used to answer in her bizarre screeching voice, 'and they always so wanted to love them.'

'Yes, I trusted myself to them with my charges and prophecies [he pronounced the Russian r as if it were French] and they wanted something utterly different: they thought that the Russian Revolution was a most interesting experiment in an exotic country and that it had nothing to do with them. And that, as Lloyd George put it, you can trade even with cannibals.'

She sat in their living room in the evenings on the sofa, beneath a lamp, in some old but still elegant fur-trimmed housecoat, smoking fine cigarettes, or, drawing the work close to her eyes, she would sew something (she loved to sew), the thimble gleaming on her thin finger. The smell of perfume and tobacco filled the room.

'Where are my little pieces?' she would ask, digging into scraps of material.

'Where is my roll?' she asked at tea, drawing the bread-basket nearer to her.

Vladimir Zlobin, their secretary, placed a cup in front of her.

'Where is my cup?' and she looked all around with unseeing eyes at the walls of the room.

'My dear, it's in front of you,' answered Zlobin patiently in an appeasing, impressive tone. 'And here is your roll. No one took it. It's yours.'

This was a game, but a game that lasted many years (almost thirty) between the two and was necessary to both.

Then the door of the study was opened, and Merezhkovsky came into the dining room. I never heard him speak of anything that wasn't interesting. Gippius often asked, when speaking of people:

'But is he interested in what's interesting?'

Merezhkovsky was, and this was apparent from the first word he uttered. He created his own world for himself, where much was lacking but the indispensable was always present. His world was based on political irreconcilability with the October Revolution, while all else was immaterial. Problems of aesthetics, ethics, problems of religion, politics, science – all were subject to one thing: the sense of the loss of Russia, of the threat of Russia to the world, the bitter taste of exile, and the awareness that no one heard him in his denunciations, curses, and warnings. At times all this was only an undercurrent in his conversation, which at the very end of the evening would burst out:

'. . . and this is why we are here!' – Or:

'. . . and this is why they are there!'

But more often all the talk would be painted in one colour:

'Zina, what is dearer to you: Russia without freedom or freedom without Russia?'

She thought a minute:

'Freedom without Russia,' she would answer, 'and that is why I am here and not there.'

'I am also here and not there, because Russia without freedom does not exist for me. But . . .' And he became lost in thought, looking at no one. 'What good is freedom to me if there is no Russia? What can I do with this freedom without Russia?'

He was silent while she tried to find something to say, something slightly ironic so that such gravity and melancholy would not remain in the air.

From time to time she started to question me about my Petersburg childhood, and the past. I didn't like to talk, I preferred to listen.

Then she would speak. One felt there was in her a kind of muddy secret that gave her all her strangeness, all her suffering.

She loved her mother painfully. All four sisters (there were no brothers) did also. She, only, married, and the three others remained single, two in Soviet Russia. Kartashev once courted one of them and was ready to marry her, but Dmitri Sergeevich meddled, and the marriage did not take place. These two women turned up during the war (in 1942) in Pskov, then occupied by the Germans, and Zinaida Nikolaevna tried to exchange letters with them. They probably perished in the German retreat. These were

242

the Tata-Nata, about whom Bely wrote in his recollections. The third sister was the dried-up halfwit Anna Nikolaevna who spent her days at the cathedral on the Rue Daru, one of those who polish icons, mend vestments, and bow down and worship.

Anna sometimes ran over to Gippius, sat on the edge of a chair, and remained restlessly silent. I never saw Merezhkovsky's nephew (the son of his brother Konstantin) and his wife at their place. This nephew was a quite remarkable man, an inventor of all sorts of things, from a perfected naval mine to a lipstick that wouldn't soil napkins. Neither he nor his wife, evidently, was ever at the Merezhkovskys'.

I, like Blok, wanted to kiss Merezhkovsky's hand many times when I heard him speak from a podium – as a matter of fact always on the same subject, but touching on dozens of problems, particularly inquisitive, and existentially seeking answers, though of course never finding them. Of his writings during his emigration all has faded – from *The Kingdom of the Antichrist* to *Pascal* and *Luther* (which, it seems, has still not been published in book form). Only his writing from before 1920 is alive: *Leonardo, Julian the Apostate, Peter and Alexis, Alexander I and the Decembrists,* and also some literary articles if you read them in the light of the epoch when they were written (the 1890s, on the background of the writings of Mikhailovsky and Plekhanov). Not more than ten of his poems can be chosen for an anthology; yet this was a man impossible to forget. He was not interested in aesthetics and aesthetics repaid him: modern literature with its involved craftsmanship and magic turned out to be inaccessible to him.

In Gippius one also felt no desire to solve problems of form in poetry: she far from understood the role of the *word* in verbal art, but at least she had her own yardstick, taste, prized complexity and refinement in the realization of formal goals. Russian symbolism lived a short time, in all some thirty-five years, and Russian symbolists even less: Balmont was a poet for fifteen years, Briusov for twenty, Blok for eighteen. These were people of a short flowering. I see now that same inability to evolve in Gippius, to change and mature, that was noticeable in her contemporaries, the petrification, the deafness to the dynamics of her time, the uninterrupted cult of her own youth which became the zenith of life, a fact unnatural and sad that shows the deadening of an artist.

I also see now that in Gippius there was much that was in Gertrude Stein (in whom there was also undoubtedly hermaphroditism, but who managed to liberate and realize herself to a much greater degree): that same inclination to quarrel with people and then somehow make peace with them; and only *forgive* others their normal love, secretly scorning, a little, all that was normal and of course not understanding normal love at all. The same trait of closing one's eyes to the reality in a man and placing under a microscope one's fantasies about him, or overlooking the bad books of anyone well-disposed to her (and Merezhkovsky). As Stein ignored Joyce and did not invite people to her place who spoke of Joyce, so Gippius did not speak of Nabokov and did not listen when others spoke of him. The ambiguous and unjust definition of the 'lost generation' belongs to Stein (as if sanctioning this lost state). Gippius felt that we all (but not she and Merezhkovsky) had fallen into a 'crack of history', which was untrue and pernicious, and gave the weak a way of justifying their weakness, at the same time bearing testimony of her personal deafness to her age.

There was a strong wish in her to astound; at first – in her youth – with white dresses, loose hair, bare feet (which Gorky used to describe); later – in emigration – with such lines in her verse as 'Never mind!' or 'Skip it!' or stories such as 'Martynov's Memoirs'. (When she read it at the tea table on one of those Sundays, only two understood it, one of whom was I. While Khodasevich, perplexedly, only asked about the riddle at the very end: 'Is it venereal disease?') To astound, to impress, that is to a certain degree to be an exhibitionist: Look at me, how I am, unlike anyone, unique, astonishing . . . you looked at her sometimes and thought: During these years so much in the world has happened that is overwhelming, so much that is unlike anything else and so genuinely astounding that – we beg your pardon, we are sorry, excuse us – but we are not interested any more!

Everyone or nearly everyone came to their place, but I found it best with her when there was no one else, when a certain intimate atmosphere was created in which I felt that something 'came my way'. I once wrote a poem about something coming my way, the Lazarus way, and published it. Probably they both read it, but did not guess that it was about them.

In 1927 Gippius dedicated to me the poem 'Eternal Feminine' (I have in my possession a manuscript with the dedication; instead of the title there are the letters *E.F.*): she included it in her book of verse (1938), undated, without the dedication and under the title 'The Eternal Feminine'. When in 1927 we spent the summer in Le Cannet, in the south of France, where the Merezhkovskys lived, and saw each other daily, there was another poem (I quote it here for the first time, it has remained unpublished):

> Feather clouds have threaded
> Their cotton across the blueness.
> Daisies light up the meadow,
> The motley goat looks luminous.

> Grey branches hang round the olive tree
> In that summery, sun-drenched way.
> In July all things are jolly and free,
> And agitated and gay.

> But lazy and long-winded
> The gossamer in the corn violets;
> But always closed the long windows
> In the house with the name like paradise.

> Trying to keep my mind on verse
> Is simply a hopeless matter:
> I shall never glimpse her fluttering dress,
> White – with a flowered pattern.

Next year (1928) I spent three days at their place, in Thorenc, high in the Alps, and she gave me a sheet of paper with three poems written during those days. These verses astounded me; they showed her unexpected tenderness towards me and touched me. Two of them, under the title 'To her in the mountains' were also published in her book but the third has not been printed before. On my copy they are called 'To her in Thorenc':

1

I kept my purple flower on purpose,
My actions were deliberate,
I put the flower – long-stemmed and purple –
Down at her beloved feet.

But you refuse . . . You scorn my gift . . .
I try to catch your eye in vain.
No matter! Be it as you wish
Because I love you all the same.

2

I shall look for another flower in the forest,
Your responselessness is untrue, untrue.
I shall bring my flower, purple and new,
To your transparent house, with the narrow doorway.

But fear overcame me down by the brook,
The chasm emitted mist and miasma . . .
A hissing snake slid over my foot,
And I could not find the flower for my darling.

3

In the yellow sunset you shine like a candle.
Once again, silent, I stand before you.
Tenderly, smoothly, the folds of my mantle
Descend to the feet of my beloved.

Your childish happiness cannot last.
No need to explain, for you will guess
What it is that I bring instead of a flower:
And now you have guessed – and you accept.

I went to Thorenc, to the Merezhkovskys, by bus from Antibes.
Khodasevich was sick, and we then lived with Weidlé and his future
wife in a summer cottage. Thorenc is a spot in the mountains, high

up in the Maritime Alps, and there the Merezhkovskys rented one floor of an old castle. In the tower itself there was an improvised bathroom; all around the castle stood pine trees, black and straight, and behind them, on a tall mountain opposite the windows of the dining room, you could see the ruins of another castle –

'– which was built when *Don Quixote* was still unwritten,' Merezhkovsky announced to me the day of my arrival.

I was given a narrow, long room in the flat of the castle's owners, and there on the bookshelves were books from the seventeenth and eighteenth centuries, covered with a thick layer of dust.

In the afternoon we went for a stroll along the stream, which gurgled and jumped among the stones, and Merezhkovsky said, as he watched the water spiders trying with all their strength to hold themselves back, working with their little legs so as not to be carried away:

'Zina! They are against the current! They are exactly like you and me!'

The stream turned, calmed down, murmured very quietly, flowing away. Merezhkovsky again said, though no longer addressing anyone, quoting Lermontov:

'"It babbles to me a mysterious saga about a miraculous region, whence he comes."' Suddenly he stopped and began to recall how they had once lived near Luga (where Kartashev had had a stomach-ache), so that it was not difficult to work out that there could only be one 'miraculous region' for him on earth.

She said to me after his death that they had never been apart, were together for fifty-two years and, to my question about whether she had any letters from him, she answered: 'How can there be any letters if we were not apart for a single day?' I remember how, at his funeral service, she stood unsteadily on her beautiful legs because of her weakness, her hand resting on Zlobin's while he, straight and strong and completely attentive to her, motionless as a rock, stood and then led her behind the coffin. And how, about a year and a half later, with money from a French publisher, a tombstone was placed on his grave, with the inscription: THY KINGDOM COME! Every time I have been at his grave I have heard his voice uttering that incantation, into which he put his own special meaning.

Then her mental powers began to wane. In 1944 she confessed to me that she understood nothing in daily events; one felt already that there was no need to explain anything, nothing would reach her. She screamed often at night, called him, was tortured by the approach of death, dried up completely, began to see and hear even less, and fussed over her half-paralysed arm. When she lay small and wrinkled in her coffin, one of those who came to the requiem service looked her over and said:

'God forgive me, but she was a malicious old thing.'

Her coffin was lowered into the grave on top of his, and in my mind they unite, like one being in two guises, a voice singing a lengthy song to an accompaniment: now she sings and he accompanies, or (probably more often) he sings and she follows him. In a long (still probably Russian) beaver coat and beaver cap, ever smaller with each passing year, he takes her by the hand (and who holds on to whom I don't know). She wears a threadbare coat of reddish fur and a red or pink hat – how she loved those tones, from pink to brick-red, from bright red to dark and ruddy! She walks carefully on her high spike heels. They go for a walk in the Bois de Boulogne. They return. In the dark rooms here and there lamps are turned on, the oldish furniture, the bookshelves, her sewing, his papers – all in place. Evening is setting in. I arrive and sit down next to her on the sofa. She likes to ask me questions so as to embarrass me, but I am not often embarrassed. At times I feel that this is only a game, a deliberate one, to extract not the answer to a question from me but something of my very self. An interrogation. She is often astounded by me, my straightforwardness, my fearlessness, my outspokenness, the fact that I accept so much in life and that I have totally ceased to be embarrassed by her and him.

It seemed to me then that I had from them all I could get, that I saw through them. I moved away from them for several years but during the war returned when so few people remained around them in Paris. I would no longer enter the living room, however, or sit with her on the sofa. I would climb the dark staircase, enter the kitchen, and for a long time watch Zlobin washing dishes, scouring pots, wiping knives and forks. I would converse quietly with him. There, in the living room, it was very cold. Merezhkovsky would be lying on the sofa, bundled in a blanket, and she sat with him; I was afraid of disturbing them. Then I had the distinct impression that both were not living but surviving, that they were fading and gradually departing. When I received the telegram: 'Merezhkovsky deceased . . .' it seemed to me this was a smooth, timely conclusion, that it was natural – and her four years of existence without him were unnatural, unnecessary, a torture both for her and for others.

In the last months of her life she sometimes spoke (1945) about events, but always ended with:

'I understand nothing.'

This 'I understand nothing' resounded more and more for me as a refusal to live, a hopeless abyss between a human being and the world: death, not life.

'I am trying to understand, but I can't understand. Explain . . .'

In this 'I am trying' and 'explain' there was no content: a wall kept rising between her and the rest of us. In the end it isolated her forever.

Yet how she dominated others when, in the centre of the Vinavers' salon (or the Tsetlins'), her slightly scraping voice drowned the other voices, or when he spoke and she waited for the moment to attack him, or support him, or enter the conversation between him and his opponent. She dominated people, and she loved it – probably more than anything else she loved this 'power over souls'. All her joys and tortures were, I think, related precisely to this domination: over an unknown poet (Steiger, who wrote her a letter, and she joked about him) over whom she would spread her dark wings so as to pick at him more adroitly; over the editor of a periodical who had grown a tough fat hide, in whom she sought out the sensitive spots, to scratch till they bled.

Bunin was on his guard dealing with her, but of course managed rarely to beat her in an argument. The captivating, old-fashioned primitiveness of Bunin amused her and gave her the naughty desire to argue with him in her own personal key, because his key – pedestrian, elementary, two-dimensional – she found ridiculous. Merezhkovsky found it boring. He would express it so: 'Bunin bores me.' But she felt that there are, generally speaking, no boring people, that Bunin was amusing, amusing for her in any case, because if you couldn't change or alter his mind, you certainly could amaze him.

How I loved Bunin's style in conversation, reminiscent of the hero of Dostoevsky's *The Friend of the Family*, Foma Fomich Opiskin (who humbly asked people to call him simply *your excellency*), his strong handshake, conversations about 'birthmarks of nobility', the aristocratic shape of his ears and generally everything concerning 'gentle folk'. I of course hadn't heard the like even from Grandfather Karaulov! Here was something obsolete, feudal, and Bunin also always wanted to be with young people, and to be young himself. How I loved his stories about dogs (used long ago in his books) – bloodhounds, sporting dogs, hunting dogs, gun dogs, hounds, bird dogs, water dogs, setters, pointers, retrievers, and about taverns on the main street of the town of Orel – go, check them, probably half of them have been invented, but together they are a real wonder!

Of course, Orel signs and Irish and Siberian wolfhounds meant nothing to Merezhkovsky. It is not surprising that he was bored by this.

Bunin was standing downstairs, near the lift in the Tsetlins' house, when we entered. Khodasevich introduced us. Bunin did not want to get in the lift; some days earlier he had been nearly crushed: he had stepped into the empty cage when the lift was moving, and someone pulled him out. He was now afraid of lifts. We went up on foot. If on a first meeting the Merezhkovskys made the person they were talking to undergo some kind of examination – i.e., 'What do you believe?' – Bunin managed this in a completely different way: not 'What do you believe?' but what kind of impression do I make on you? Do you hate me? Or like me? Want more of the same? He drawled slightly ('as we noblemen do'? – or 'as the folks do at home'?) and as he spoke, he kept looking at me, trying to read in my face the impression he made on me.

He did this with men, women, littérateurs and non-littérateurs, but it was especially noticeable with women littérateurs. The first evening we met he told me about an event that had occurred to him in his youth. The story began like the first story in *Dark Alleys*, except that the lord was young and came to see a young peasant girl in her hut. The lord enters the hut and sees a strong big-bosomed girl. He is in ecstasy over the possibilities. He is ready to touch that big bosom and notes that she is ready for anything. Suddenly from among some bunks her grandpa's rattling voice resounds: 'Aunt Nastya, I've just had to shit.' The lord (that is Bunin) shot out of the hut, jumped on his horse, and fled in a gallop.

The telling of such stories ended very quickly: after he pronounced two or three times and with some special gusto an 'unprintable' word (printable, however, in all languages except Russian), and in the main he liked less the unprintable erotic words and more the so-called nursery ones – after he had pronounced them two or three times in my presence and I did not shudder but took them as simply as the rest of his vocabulary, and after I had told him how beautiful his 'Dreams of Chang' was, he stopped putting on airs in front of me. He understood, first, that he couldn't embarrass me in such a primitive way and, second, that I was not an enemy of his, but a friend. Not, however, a friend entirely:

'And of course you don't like my verse?'

'No . . . I like it . . . but much less than your prose.'

This was his sore spot; at that time I did not know it.

But within a year he returned in our conversations to the theme of verse and prose, the painful problem of his entire life. In Grasse, where I went to visit him, he once said to me:

'If I had wanted to, I could have written any of my stories in verse. Here, for example, is "The Sunstroke" – if I wanted to I would make it a verse-narrative.'

I felt embarrassed, but said I believed him. I was struck by these words: evidently he thought that any 'subject' could be dressed in any 'form', that you can add the form to the content, which is born independently, like a baby for whom you must choose a garment. From this it is clear he thought that *War and Peace* could conceivably have been written in hexameter and 'The Twelve' in triolets. I will speak later, however, about his relationship to Blok.

He was difficult to live with and carried domestic despotism into literature. He not only became irritated and angry, but flew into a fury when someone said he was like Tolstoy or Lermontov, or some similar stupidity. But he himself answered this with a still greater absurdity:

'I come from Gogol! No one understands anything! I have come out of Gogol!'

Those around him, frightened and uncomfortable, kept silent. Often his rage would suddenly turn into comedy. This was one of his most endearing traits:

'I'll kill you! Strangle you! Shut up! I come from Gogol!'

Conversations on modern art drove him to a similar rage, if not a greater one. For him even Rodin was too modern.

'His Balzac is shit,' he said once. 'For this reason the pigeons of the Left Bank shit all over him.' (Accompanied by a sharp glance in my direction.)

I answered that, for me, even in such a predicament, covered with shit, the Balzac was still better than the Gambetta which is near the Louvre, with flag and nymphs (whether there were nymphs in this atrocity, I was not sure).

'For you, then, Proust is better than Hugo?'

I was stunned by this unexpected remark: What kind of a comparison would that be?

'Proust, you say, is better?'

'Well, Ivan Alekseevich, well, of course. He is the greatest in our century.'

'And I?'

Galina Kuznetsova and I laughed at this. He liked laughter, he enjoyed every liberating function of the body, liked all that was near or around this. Once with me in a grocery store he was choosing a sturgeon fillet. It was wonderful to watch his eyes start glittering, and at the same time I was embarrassed in front of the shop-keeper and the customers. When, many times later, he would tell me he loved life, loved spring, that he could not reconcile himself to the thought that there would be springs without him, that he had not experienced everything in life, had not sniffed all smells, had not made love (he used another term) to every woman, that there was still on the Pacific Isles a species of woman he had never seen, I always recalled this fillet. And now, sure enough, I can say: As for women, all this was only words, he was not that concerned about them; but about sturgeon fillet or the smoothness and grooming of his own body, he was entirely serious.

Since he was an absolute and inveterate atheist (something I heard many times from him) and liked to frighten both himself and others (in particular, poor Aldanov) with the fact that worms would crawl out of their eyes and from mouth to ear when they both lay in the ground, he never gave a thought to religious questions and could not think abstractly. I am convinced that he was a totally *earthly* man, a wholesome human being capable of creating the beautiful in elementary ready-made forms which already existed near him, with an astounding sensitivity to the Russian language, limited imagination, and with a complete absence of vulgarity. What a lot of bad taste there was in the so-called Russian realists of the beginning of our century! Not only Amfiteatrov, Artsybashev, and Veresaev serve as examples, but also Aleksey Tolstoy, whose early stories are now difficult and rather disgusting to reread. Even in Gorky, the tardy Russian Victorian, you can sometimes find the vulgar, but not in Bunin. A sense of taste never betrayed him. If he had not been born thirty years late he would have been one of the greats of our great past.

I see him between Turgenev and Chekhov, born let us say in 1840. He himself spoke of this much later, in 1950, in his *Recollections*:

'I was born too late. Had I been born earlier, my recollections would have been different.'

But in the 1920s one would not have dared to allude to this. He would not allow any insinuations, either in print or personally, that he was a man of the past century. Once he complained to me that the 'young' reproached him for not writing anything about love. This was at the time of the infatuation with D. H. Lawrence. 'All that I wrote and write is always about love,' he said.

When the conversations moved to Soviet literature, he had no conception of it. All the modern French were for him 'like Proust'. I doubt, however, that he had read all twelve volumes of *Remembrance of Things Past*.

He treated me in different ways in the years. At first with tender irony ('"I was born near the Caucasus, I know how to use a dagger"' – quoting Pushkin. 'That's about you, about you!'); then with amazement and a certain distrust; still later with kindness, meekly accepting what at first seemed to be my impudence and lack of respect for him; and towards the end of his life he frankly regarded me as an enemy, because of my book on Blok. Why on Blok? Why not on him?

Blok was his sore spot during his whole life; so was symbolism, which he bypassed as something ridiculous, disgusting, idiotic, insignificant, to which he was either deaf or furiously inimical. 'Greater fools have not existed since the beginning of time,' he would say, and in his *Recollections* wrote: 'In my whole life I have had not a few dealings with cretins. Generally speaking, I have been allowed a life so unusual that I have been a contemporary of those very cretins whose names will remain forever in world history.'

These cretins were for him: Balmont, Sologub, Vyacheslav Ivanov. Gippius' verse brought a nasty sneer from him, Briusov was a communist and should be hanged for this alone, Bely was a dangerous madman. But the main abomination in all this company was Blok, sufferer from rickets and a degenerate, who died of syphilis. Once Georgy Ivanov and I, while guests at Bunin's, took down Blok's volume of verse on the Beautiful Lady: it was riddled with four-letter words in Bunin's pencil, his commentary on the first volume. Even Georgy Ivanov was embarrassed. 'Let's forget this,' I whispered to him.

'. . . and he was not even a handsome man,' Bunin once exclaimed, speaking of Blok. 'I was more handsome than he!'

Although in his *Recollections* he said that he was forced to pass his life among drunkards and idiots, his destiny often disturbed him. He felt something here was not quite right, and that perhaps he was left out of something which was more important than all his books. Some kind of beast ate him within, and his ever sharper judgements of his contemporaries, his ever more malicious outbursts towards the end of his life, oral and printed, bear witness to his not being able to forget these 'idiots and cretins', who obviously tortured him relentlessly his whole life and towards old age proved to be stronger than he; he weakened and sought defence in coarseness. In the little Salle Pleyel-Chopin in 1948 he once gave an evening of readings of his *Recollections* that later came out as a book (with Renaissance as its publisher and in old orthography, abolished since 1917!). At the moment when, pronouncing each word with gusto, he tried to prove Blok was a nonentity, I realized it was the right time to rise and leave the hall, without slamming the door. But some sort of weakness found its way into me: I suddenly began to vacillate about doing this or continuing to listen to these envious, malicious, insane pages. In several seconds the whole literary grandeur of the books written by Bunin passed before me, as well as all the personal elements that had bound me to him for the twenty-five years of our friendship, and my eventual cooling towards him (about which I will write later). At the moment while I vacillated about rising or remaining seated, someone at the other end of my row stood up, banged his seat, and, feet thumping, moved towards the exit. Then I also rose, without banging my seat or thumping my feet: and I went towards the door. Carefully opening and closing it I found myself in front of Ladinsky. We walked silently out onto the street; he went to the left, I to the right. After friendly relations for many years we now avoided talking to each other: he had taken out his Soviet passport, was a *Soviet patriot* and was ready to return to the Soviet Union, considering Stalin rather like Peter the Great.

I don't know how much and whom one can forgive. Perhaps one need not forgive anyone anything? (So it seemed in youth.) In any case I know it is impossible to forgive everyone everything, and when Bunin – after a lovely day spent at Longchêne (a place near Paris where N. and I had a country house in the years 1938–48), when after leisurely conversations, reading aloud, lounging in armchairs on the terrace, between the houses, under a blooming almond tree, after tender words – suddenly at dinner he was all set to sniff the chicken before eating it, and I calmly stopped his hand: I knew he always did that, at dinner at the Tsetlins', in the best Paris restaurant, and at home.

'No,' I said, 'Ivan Alekseevich, in my house you will not sniff the chicken.' And I forcibly drew aside his hand holding the piece of chicken on a fork.

'That's a woman!' he said gaily. 'Fears no one. "I was born near the Caucasus" and so on – that's why. But one must be cautious: a nobleman cannot eat rotten food.'

'Here,' I said, 'you will not be served rotten food.'

And the conversation moved on to other subjects.

I now think that the coarseness in his speech, his behaviour, the coarseness of his intellect were partly a cover-up, a camouflage: his fear of the world and people was no less than other men's of his generation, and all his *swagger* – and I am told it already existed to a great extent before the Revolution – was his self-defence. He was coarse with his wife, a dumb and very stupid woman (not middling stupid, but exceptionally so), he was coarse with those he knew and those he didn't, and after some rudeness he liked to say something flattering or make an old-fashioned deep bow. The last time I visited him was in 1947 or 1948, after my travels to Sweden, where I had carried out some of his commissions to the translator and publisher of his Swedish editions. I entered the anteroom. In the middle was a chamber pot, filled to the brim: Bunin was evidently exhibiting it out of malice towards someone who had not emptied it. He was sitting at a table in the kitchen with a certain Mr K., a well-to-do man, proprietor of a huge hotel near the Place de l'Etoile. Mr K. had just been let out of prison, where he had served a sentence for collaborating with the Germans. He was either writing or had already published a book about his childhood (it seems he was Siberian), and now both men were sitting and telling each other how beautifully they both wrote. It is possible that Mr K. was helping Bunin in those years of his new poverty (the Nobel Prize money had already been spent), and that Mr K. was obtaining from Bunin a preface for his book or a review of it; but when I saw the dirty kitchen, two slightly tight old people who embraced and were saying to each other tearfully, 'You are a genius,' 'You are our luminary,' 'You are the first,' 'I have to learn from you,' I could not overcome my numbness. After sitting about ten minutes, I went into the anteroom. Bunin said:

'This is K., my only friend. A great writer of the Russian land. All of you must learn from him how to write.'

I passed through the anteroom (the chamber pot was no longer there), went to the stairs and on to the Rue Offenbach, not returning.

I don't like to look at decay, to be curious about it, admire it; I don't like to laugh or complain about it, and try to escape it. For Bunin it began on the day when he was taken to the Soviet ambassador in Paris, Bogomolov, to drink to Stalin's health. The automobile waited below.

All this was arranged by Stupnitsky, evidently the 'eye of Moscow' on Miliukov's paper (no one then had any suspicion of this). He at first brainwashed Maklakov ('There will be an amnesty of the émigrés, all has changed in the Soviet Union'). Makovsky had the task of bringing Bunin and several others. The ambassador was waiting with champagne. This had no political consequences; it was just the beginning of the decay of the émigrés in general, and their individual representatives.

Pressure was exerted on Bunin from two sides. On the one was Stupnitsky, on the other the latter's closest friend, a certain P. Being a close relative of Aldanov, P. enjoyed an authority in Paris he hardly deserved. Having returned to Paris after the war he announced that those who had not died at the hands of the Germans had collaborated with the Germans. He slandered innumerable people, among them myself. In a few years both Stupnitsky and P. – neither really old –

died (of heart attacks). One of the most important events of the end of the 1940s for me was the general meeting of the Union of Writers and the elections to the board, in which both of them were rejected with a roar (they had thought they would be elected). I confess I acted energetically and bravely to prepare this blackballing beforehand.

Khodasevich and I were invited for the first time to the Bunins' for dinner in the winter of 1926–7. Bunin's books, recently published, lay on a table in the living room. He inscribed one copy (*The Rose of Jericho*) to me and Khodasevich, another to Galina Kuznetsova. I first saw her that evening (she was with her husband, who later left for South America); she had violet eyes (as described then), femininity, child's hands, and I heard her speech with its slight stammer that gave it a still greater defencelessness and charm. Bunin's inscription on the book was incomprehensible to her (he called her 'Riki-tiki-tavi') and she asked Khodasevich what this meant. Khodasevich said: 'It's from Kipling, it's a charming little animal that kills snakes.' She then seemed to be of porcelain (I, to my chagrin, considered myself made of pig iron). Within a year she was already living in Bunin's house. She was especially pretty in the summer, in light summer dresses, blue and white, on the shore at Cannes or on the terrace of their Grasse house. In 1932, when I lived alone on the sixth floor, without a lift, in a hotel on the Boulevard Latour-Maubourg, they both came to see me one evening and he said to her:

'You could not live like that. You couldn't live alone. No, you couldn't manage without me.'

And she answered meekly: 'No, I could not.'

But her eyes said something different.

When she left the Bunins' at the end of the 1930s, he missed her terribly. In his entire life he probably only loved her. His male ego was wounded, his pride humiliated. He could not believe that what had happened to him had really happened. He tried to think she had only left for a time, that she would return. But she did not.

It is difficult to communicate with people when there are too many taboo themes. With Bunin one could not speak of the symbolists, of his own verse, of Russian politics, of death, of modern art, of Nabokov's novels . . . and many other things. He ground the symbolists to dust; he was touchy about his verse and did not allow judgements on it; in Russian politics, before the visit to the Soviet ambassador's, he was of a reactionary outlook, but after he had drunk to Stalin's health he was completely reconciled to his rule; he feared death, raged that it existed; he didn't understand art and music at all; the name of Nabokov sent him into a fit. Thus very often the conversation was small talk and turned on other people and domestic interests. Only very rarely, especially after a bottle of wine, did Bunin 'let his hair down'. His handsome face would become animated with feeling and thought, his firm, strong hands rounded out his meaning and his talk poured forth – about himself, of course, not about himself as the petty, malicious, jealous and swaggering man, but about the great writer who had not found himself a genuine place in his time. Something then warmed his face; and this sometimes came through in his letters; it seemed that a kind of thread stretched between us, but on the following day there was nothing; suddenly he moved away a great distance. In his most immediate entourage there were people whose presence was painful to me, and among them (not to mention his wife, who disarmed not only me with her innocence) was a man who turned out to be a secret member of the French Communist Party. We, of course, learned of this much later. Mrs Bunina doted upon him, and he lived many years as a member of the family in the Bunins' house.

In the Vinavers' living room, in the Tsetlins' living room, the Merezhkovskys and Bunin were the principal décor. Aleksey Remizov had never been one of the guests. I loved his early novels, *The Pond* and *The Fifth Pestilence*, when I met him in Berlin. His *Russia in Vortex* is an immortal book, and if not all thirty of his volumes, then half of them will live and some time return to Russia, where his name, after thirty-five years, is now mentioned in print. One evening at Remizov's in Berlin in 1923, Bely, Zaitsev, Muratov, Khodasevich, and I were at a large tea table. Remizov's wife, Serafima Pavlovna, was doing laundry in the kitchen at the end of the corridor, and it was perilous to disturb her when she laundered – so Remizov himself told us. I sat down quietly at the table, crossed my legs and drank tea, which he himself brewed and poured, all the while mumbling something, wrapped up in a blanket; when he sat down, leaning his cheek on his fist like a woman, he became a sorcerer-dwarf.

After tea he announced to the guests that a pub was on the corner of his street – an unusual pub, that he went to every evening and where we were going to have beer. All rose and went to the ante-room; so did I. Remizov came to me and quietly but firmly said, raising and lowering his brows and wiggling the end of his nose, that young ladies were not admitted there. 'What do you mean?' Someone had already gone out onto the stairs. I looked at Khodasevich. He whispered to me not to contradict Remizov, to remain here and he himself would return in half an hour. They left. I remained alone in the dining room to look at the imps suspended on a lamp, the magic of which never had any effect on me: all *this* side of Remizov, including his Great Liberal Council of Apes, was incomprehensible and uninteresting to me, even an impediment to my contact with him.

It was quiet in the apartment. You couldn't hear or see Serafima Pavlovna; indeed, perhaps she was not even home. I knew that half of what Remizov said was made up, the aims of which were not clear to those he spoke to. Half an hour passed. An hour. I felt very bored and frustrated: I was obviously forgotten. I decided to leave alone for home; I was insulted and angry, in particular at Remizov as the host and also at Khodasevich, who had abandoned me. But when I went to the front door, it turned out to be locked from the outside – Remizov, foreseeing my departure, had locked me in his apartment. This offended me even more; I didn't know then what jokes Remizov could play on his guests. So locked up and insulted, I sat still another half hour. When they returned from the pub, I told Khodasevich I wanted to go home. After that I did not go to Remizov's for about three years, but he hardly realized that I had taken offence.

Remizov loved people who loved him, helped him, fenced him off from life caring for him, those who listened with veneration to his gibberish about imps, apes, goblins, all his fantasies (artificially sublimated but almost always sexual): among such people he lived, having gradually cut himself off from those it was necessary *to learn to know*. He had few readers, they could all sit around at the tea table, in his dining room, and among these reader-friend-guests there was nothing in common except their relationship and kind disposition towards him. As for Bunin, he felt that a writer had above all to be a good observer: to observe for example that the edges of the clouds are violet.

'But Chekhov said that we already had enough of violet clouds!'
He angrily changed the subject – and remained in a void.

The Merezhkovskys had pride: we don't need the small talk of the
petit bourgeois. 'Zina, what is everyday humdrum? You and I do
not have that kind of thing, do we?' Yes, this term indeed rings
badly when applied to them, an ordinary waking life somehow
does not square with them. It seems that no one ever goes to market
from their home, no one buys greens and meat, takes dirty linen to
the laundry, counts money, laughs at some silly thing, curses
himself . . . Remizov puts on a funny expression when he pronoun-
ces Merezhkovsky's name. He means – with his drooping mouth,
raised brows, eyes that say that in a moment he will start crying,
with his whole hunched sickly figure – How can we understand
such profound things! We are small folk, miserable, forgotten,
injured people. From childhood we have known only kicks and are
fit for a very humble place. The main thing for us is to find shelter;
perhaps some crumb will come our way. What about wisdom? It
is the business of the philosophers Shestov and Berdyaev!
   Of course he knew well both 'wisdom' and modern Western
thought, but such was his attitude – in the presence of friend-guest-
readers.
   Bunin, to overcome boredom, sometimes took to reading
French novels, but he didn't like to talk about them and perhaps was
unable to. He spoke of himself, of 'violet clouds', and of people he
met and lived with (accepting them on the domestic level). He read
more of the second-rate French authors, whom he sometimes
praised, sometimes cursed, praised for their 'observation', cursed
because the heroine did not marry the one she should have.
Sometimes Aldanov managed to make him talk about his meeting
with 'Lev Nikolaevich' or a friendly get-together with 'Anton
Pavlovich' – then he spoke well, in wonderful language, exactly as
he wrote of them. And he wrote of them as he spoke.
   Both in Merezhkovsky and Remizov one sensed a tremendous
nostalgia for Russia, which they both hid. But from time to time it
would burst painfully through in a glance, a word, or even a
moment of silence in the midst of conversation. In Bunin it was
hidden by pride: he tried to convince himself and others that it was
possible to create great things even 'after leaving the Believsky

district for ever.' He probably was quite right and indeed he did create them. Once, looking at the drawings of Remizov, his papers, his books lying on the desk, his books on shelves, I asked how he could live without Russia when Russia meant so much to him? In a muffled voice he answered, making his grimace of long-suffering:

'Russia has been a dream.'

And it seemed to me there were tears in his eyes.

Bundled in a blanket, coughing, hunched over, Remizov greeted guests, led them to his study piled high with books, with figurines, beasts and dolls hanging on lamp shades, with abstract drawings on the walls and even on the window panes. He led them down the corridor, past closed doors, complaining of poverty, of how crowded it was in the flat, of his own illnesses.

You didn't know what you should and what you shouldn't believe. Hardly breathing, he sat at the table, placing his huge hands in front of himself, and with a pained expression on his face began to tell of some misfortunes that had befallen one of his imps. Though his life was very burdensome, he made it more so with such stories; he, so to speak, 'exploited' his own poverty, embellished it, exaggerated it, revelled in it and fed on it. Unwittingly one thought that sometimes he too would run after a bus on the Avenue Mozart and jump into it as he ran, not different from the rest of us – and that all this talk was a slight mystification: 'Dichtung' and 'Wahrheit' understood in his own way. All four doors in the corridor opened into clean, spacious rooms, where books were set out in order, curtains hung, and it was warm, and where Serafima Pavlovna, like a huge doll, reigned.

When Muratov said that in poverty there must be at least some dignity – as with the Zaitsevs who, in the midst of poverty, had not only pride and cheerfulness, but even a kind of happy strength – I remembered Rozanov, who took all his misfortunes – debts, destitution, his wife's diseases – out onto the wide Russian street, pretending to be humble, insulted, and injured; or the Frenchman Léon Bloy, even closer to Remizov in his hysterics, in his poisonously meek speeches, where you hear a sickly desire to be even more trampled on by all those fine messieurs, from Zola to Huysmans. Khodasevich would talk about how, according to Georgy Chulkov, when Remizov worked on the magazine *Problems of Life* he as secretary would not attend meetings of the editorial board, but while the meeting was going on he would gather in a neighbouring room the galoshes of those who were there, put them in a circle, sit himself in the middle and play at a meeting with the galoshes. Marmeladov, Ivolgin, Lebedev, Snegirev – a whole swarm of Dostoevsky's heroes comes to mind.

But at a Stravinsky première Remizov sits in the first row. 'That's all Serafima Pavlovna,' he says, embarrassed.

Towards the end of her life she could hardly move, owing to her unhealthy corpulence and weight. It always seemed to me that his inventions and masks of personality had their origin in her, that she burdened him with her own dreams and fantasies, syndromes and complexes, and he accepted them, fed on them, built his myths on them, which sometimes infected, sometimes disaffected people. After her death in 1943, he was surrounded by compassionate women who lived near by: they cooked for him, tidied up the apartment, gave him medicines, and when he started to lose his sight, they read aloud to him. If there had not been in him these Dostoevskian absurdities, he would have been a great writer, but he lost control over his eccentricities. The reader tires of forgiving him them, of trying not to notice them, and is not caught up in his private mythology.

Yes, in the Zaitsevs' poverty there was dignity and even a kind of gaiety. Here also, as in Remizov's life, *she* not *he* reigned, *she* was the primary life force, the embodiment of a dual energy, but in contrast to Serafima Pavlovna, she was a good, intelligent, warm, live force, inexhaustible in her curiosity about people and the world, full of womanly wisdom and irony.

I asked her once why she didn't write. Laughing, she answered that she was 'fine even without that'. Books are interesting, but people are more interesting, she said. I agreed with her then, and agree now. Among people she herself was one of the most genuine and wondrous, one of the most alive.

She always told him something amusing in the mornings, even before breakfast. Many years later they both, Boris and Vera, lived at my place in Longchêne (the summer of 1947), and I heard her, as she combed her hair and dressed herself, sharing things with him that were important and unimportant, petty, wise, silly and serious, falling silent for a time to clean her teeth and rinse her mouth. Everything around aroused her curiosity, she was interested in and reacted to everything, the whole world was part of her personal life. Sometimes sadness would settle on her; she grieved for those close ones in Moscow, and the dead she was waiting to meet. 'Why grieve,' I would say, 'if you know that there will be a meeting?' 'Ah, von Koren [she called me by the name of the stern hero of Chekhov's 'The Duel'] it's all right for you to speak rashly. *Whoever is not with us is against us.* All this is not so simple.'

They loved each other all their life, tenderly, passionately, and though there was probably some infidelity (how can there not be among living people?), they survived it. Love between them flourished forever and this kept them both alive. They were jealous of each other and tortured each other, but lived unceasingly with each other. When in 1957 paralysis struck Vera (she was then about eighty), she lived, paralysed, many more years, simply because he was with her, looked after her persistently, sustained her with his love (and she sustained him with hers).

As a writer he is in many respects finer than Bunin, but his inertness, the intellectual laziness he acknowledged many times to me, impeded his whole life. It's as if, still in his childhood or early youth (in the 1880s and 1890s in the district of Kaluga) he had agreed that Russian or indeed *any* life *stands still*, and could in no way agree (understand and accept the fact) that life does not stand still one moment, but moves, changes, builds, and breaks apart. The thought of movement, effort, action, and energy was not only foreign to him, but inimical; he found it disturbing not only for himself to hurry, to make an effort, strive for something, struggle, but also to hear that others did this. A new fact – political, literary, domestic – a new thought which one had to ponder, even a new word, either left him indifferent or somehow prevented him from 'getting along'. He loved these expressions: I am getting along somehow, mind you, drinking some kind of little wine, sitting in a restaurant; I like to drop in on you, no hurry, I am not used to acting swiftly; let's mosey on home. Everyone knew that red wine was not only to his taste and gladdened him, it gave him the strength indispensable to 'act' and 'mosey along'. During the war years when there was no wine in the house, when he wanted to finish a page he sometimes went to the kitchen and drank a jigger of ordinary vinegar.

For forty years he called me 'Ninon', and I have preserved 120 letters from both of them. Almost all begin, 'Chère Ninon' and in almost every one he wonders to himself: How will he manage to write me four pages (or two)? He grins at himself ('I am still lying on my side'), stands in front of others with an admiration and awe: She goes to town every day! She drives a car! Rises at seven! She cooked the borshch on time! About Natasha (their daughter): How does she manage all this (a husband, two sons)? Both Vera and Natasha brought the world closer to him: it appeared not to stand in one place, but to flow and fly. And all this was done through love. Generally speaking, the chief element in the house (in the small apartment where they lived more than thirty years) was not things, not objects – there was no radio, no typewriter, electrical appliances, musical instruments, paintings, or rugs – the principal thing was love.

I saw all three of them first in Moscow, before our departure for Berlin in 1922. Boris was thin and weak after a bout of typhus, and Vera was packing the trunks to go abroad to care for him ('thanks to Lunacharsky'). Natasha was then about ten and she had, as anyone knows who has read Zaitsev's novels and short stories, flaxen braids: this pale little girl with braids passes through many of his books. She knew where a ration was being distributed and how much something cost, never had a pair of whole stockings, and knew no other way of life than the Soviet during the first years of communism. In Berlin we settled in rooms which they had until then occupied (before settling in Krampe's) and in Paris we followed in their tracks. We saw each other often. He sometimes even came to our cafés in Montparnasse. Despite their being closely tied to one another in the course of sixty years, they were not one person and I preferred being with each one of them separately. However close two people are, I often ignore their unity and take each by himself. During the war, when all around them in Billancourt was bombed out, we at one time lived together in a strange flat in Paris, not far from the Champ-de-Mars, and there 'trembled together', as Vera put it, under the bombs.

They were near me again, at the Gare Saint-Lazare, when I left for the U.S.A. in 1950. She was upset: 'You will forget us if things go well for you in America, you will forget us! You will get married again! Let things go well for you, only don't forget us.' He took me to one side, and we walked to the end of the platform.

'Promise me,' he said looking gravely at me, 'never to offend God.' 'Boris,' I screamed, 'look around, doesn't He offend everyone!' He shook his head sadly, in a reproachful way. He knew, as I also did, that my divergence from him began here, and could not be ended by any compromise.

However much I persuaded myself that he asked me not to offend God for the sake of God himself, I could not rid myself of the thought that he demanded this from me because he feared that I would shake someone's faith, perhaps his very own.

Then he blessed me three times, saying: 'Such is the custom with us folks from Kaluga.' And Vera also crossed me. 'Sin moderately,' she whispered into my ear, with her always sweet irony, beneath which was a layer of the grave. Ten years later I returned to Paris. Stricken by paralysis, she lay on a couch, under icons where an icon-lamp burned, looked at me with sparkling cheerful eyes and said, moving her tongue with difficulty:

'Granny . . . had become a complete fool . . . I forget . . . what's the name of that city . . .?'

'New York.'

'You live . . . and I, well . . . no legs . . . no arms . . . Boria is a saint, doesn't let me go . . . looks after me . . . holds me with love . . . You support your old woman with love, I say, Boria, do you hear? Tell her about it!'

It was not necessary to say anything, all was understood without words: he prolonged her life during illness for eight years.

I told her about my life in America, recollected all kinds of funny occurrences from our previous common life, how once Sergey Yablonovsky, a harmless fool, prayed in their place for Lenin's soul, of all things, and how Vera chased him out (they later made up); how once Boris came to visit me at 1:00 A.M. (Khodasevich was out of town) and sat till three: to be on the safe side we both hid it from her but she found out (it seems that Khodasevich blabbed) and scolded us for hiding such a thrilling fact. We remembered how during the occupation, about 1943, some eminent persons from a German Russian-language newspaper published in Paris came to Remizov, thrust money at him, and asked him to give them something for publication; and how he took the money but gave them nothing, and how Vera persuaded him to send the money back right away, which he did. With a beatific smile, in a white blouse very cleanly washed, perfumed, she did not take her eyes off me and only said from time to time:

'Well, more! Go on!'

I talked for five hours until I became hoarse; then Boris went to accompany me to the corner and said he had a hernia from pulling her about the apartment ten minutes in the morning and ten in the evening (the doctor had ordered this so that her legs would not become swollen), and that he no longer had the strength. He said he read aloud to her various old books and never, never went out in the evening any more.

But I persuaded him to come with me in the afternoon to eat pelmeni in the cafeteria of the Russian Conservatory. Three days later there we were, at a little table, eating pelmeni and drinking vodka, and sat about two hours opposite each other till we again became hungry, so that we ordered two more portions, and again sat and talked. He became lively and started to talk about himself, of Vera, about the present and past (there was no future), of her hopeless condition and of the moral joy and physical strain in being together with her. When we left, he took me by the arm, firmly, in a masculine way, and led me down the street.

'Let's go, let's go . . . Obey me. We'll turn at that corner, there is your bus.'

'Boris, what is this? How old are you? Where do you get such speed and such a *grip*?'

'Soon eighty. Whoever had a grip has it until he is a hundred . . . I have not walked arm in arm with a woman for a long time. Lovely!'

Laughing we came to the bus stop, embraced, said good-bye, and rushed off in different directions.

The last time I saw him was five years later, in 1965, when I again returned to Paris. She was no longer alive. After eight years of paralysis she had died, and he, coming down the stairs and towards me, burst into sobs. Later, sitting in his room, he said to me that he was now *depressed*, that the life of the young no longer interested him, he had become weak, was hard of hearing, and he asked if I thought he needed a hearing aid. Not only was it exhausting for him to listen to conversations in the dining room when several people spoke at once, but, he said to me, it was painful even to look at energetic lively people moving about. I said good-bye to him in

September, on a warm Paris evening, and Natasha (his daughter) accompanied me to the subway. Now she was the mother of two grown sons – her family surrounded Boris with care and love. When we spoke about him, we always called him *Papinka*.

I said: 'Last time I left Paris, five years ago, I knew I would see him again. Now, however, I have doubts.'

She answered: 'I too have doubts.'

Much has been said and written about his softness, of the 'pastel' mood of his writings and the warmth of his relationships with contemporaries. This, however, is not altogether just: his friendship with Bunin was broken by Bunin's visit to the Soviet ambassador, his friendship with Teffi showed signs of discord after some petty misunderstanding ('who seated whom where') that was not his fault but hers. Towards the end of his life he treated Remizov coldly. His attitude during the German occupation separated him from Shmelev. The end of his long-lasting (and cherished) relations with Bunin (fifty years) tormented him. In the end he decided to forget and forgive Bunin his visit to the Soviet embassy and his drinking to Stalin's health – forgive but not understand! He made a step in his direction (through Mrs Bunina) on the grounds that 'We are old people, Ivan, few of us are left –' but met with such a rude and coarse rebuff that he was flabbergasted. Boris wrote to me cursorily about this in 1948:

> Ivan was very sick (pneumonia). But pulled through. Tomorrow is his name day. I want to write to Ivan that I wish him good health . . . nothing more will be written, but my heart is still sad that the eternal separation is already not far and by the end of life we have so diverged.

'God be with him,' said Boris, but this did not mean, 'Well, we will forget him'; this meant in his language, 'Let God be with him', with his soul which, towards the end of his life, had grown so hard and venomous against a world flowering in its beauty, against healthy people far from death while he foresaw his own end; they were repulsive to him, baffling, terrible and disgusting, 'crowning' his 'unusual' life.

Yury Olesha, the author of *Envy*, understood Bunin:

> He is . . . a mean, sombre writer. He . . . bemoans his lost youth, à

propos of the fading of sensuality. His arguments about his inner life . . . seem at times simply stupid. His fear of death, his envy of the young and rich, even a kind of servility . . .

Cruel words, but very likely just. Not one of the émigrés dared to write in this way about Bunin. But many of the young thought exactly that.

When I speak of the young I mean the poets and writers of the *second generation*, those who were born at the very beginning of this century or at the end of the preceding one (there were none younger). Especially those who came into literature after 1920, that is, outside of Russia. Nabokov belongs to them, as do Ladinsky, Vadim Andreev (the son of Leonid), Knut, Smolensky, Zlobin, Poplavsky, myself, and some others. The majority are no longer alive; to refer to them as 'young' is impossible, but in the twenties and thirties they were young and did not pass unnoticed. *Stalin also did away with them* – not, however, in the concentration camps of Kolyma, but in another way.

Yes, with rare exceptions they are all dead. Poplavsky, Knut, Ladinsky, Smolensky were kicked out of Russia by the Civil War and they represent in the history of Russia a unique generation of deprived, broken, silenced, stripped, homeless, destitute, disenfranchised and therefore half-educated poets. It was a generation that grabbed whatever it could in the midst of civil war, hunger, the first repressions, exodus – deprived of the power of emotional reaction, language, native soil, an audience, the necessary books. It had no time for scholarship, leisure, human contact, friendly acceptance by its elders, no time to organize itself. It had emerged naked from the Revolution and compensated every possible way for whatever it could. But it could not make up for lost years.

Poplavsky had a destitute émigré father; the three others had no one they could have leaned on. Knut had younger sisters and brothers he had to look after, and a wife and son. A leg wound Ladinsky received in 1919 did not heal for thirty years. Smolensky evidently had an innate inclination to alcoholism.

The death of Poplavsky – which probably was not suicide – in October 1935, made him famous in a day: all the French newspapers wrote about him. The Russians in Paris heard about him for the first time. Literary people were suddenly told that a talented poet was among them. In the editorial offices of *The Latest News*, where I then worked as a typist (and Ladinsky as an errand-boy, though Smolensky did not find work there), his death was discovered, and a reporter was sent to Poplavsky's flat. The reporter returned to the office about four hours later. The chief editor and guiding spirit of the paper, Aleksandr Poliakov, nicknamed 'red Poliakov' (there were two other Poliakovs on the paper, not red), asked ironically, rocking on his chair:

'Well? Decadence? Rotting? Montparnasse cafés? Drugs? That's what you call poetry, I'll be damned!'

The reporter looked at him and said:

'Father [so his co-workers called Poliakov], if you had seen, as I just have, the underwear in which Poplavsky died, you would understand.' Silence fell upon the room.

I first saw Poplavsky's eyes in a picture in the tenth anniversary album of *The Latest News*, published in 1930: he never removed his black eyeglasses, so he had no *expression*. There was in his verse a lofty tongue-tiedness, a marvellous configuration of the seen and heard, but a kind of inexplicable pity always rose in me when I spoke to him: a man without expression, gesture, or voice. His vision of the world was misty, and diffuse of himself. In verse and later in prose he was freer than in life, though still not free. His main trait was an absence of language: he spoke Russian, when he spoke, somehow poorly and muddily, and sometimes like an illiterate. In his writings one senses this, an unsurmounted awkwardness, clumsiness, an unintended but organic paleness of syntax. He read the French writers; they were close to him, and he loved them, learning from them, and, I think, he would have settled into French literature (as Arthur Adamov did), leaving the Russian language completely – if only he had not fallen silent within a few years, as so many others did.

But he did not become a French poet or an 'ex-Russian poet': in search of kicks one evening with a friend (probably a casual, non-literary acquaintance) he sniffed something (or swallowed it), perhaps performing some anarchical experiment on himself. A few suspected suicide, but it was clear to those who knew Poplavsky this was not true. There were many more reasons for experiment: life was too dim, destitute, monotonous; moments to dream, of illumination and epiphany were too rare. Every one of us sought

269

them – in worn-out shoes, in torn shirts and patched trousers. And all around, the 1920s and 1930s thundered, rumbled.

One factor is exceptionally important for this entire generation ('young' I can no longer call it; I will call it 'mine' or 'second'): the moment of departure from Russia. Those who left at sixteen (like Poplavsky) took almost nothing with them. Those who left at twenty (like Nabokov) had time to take enough – that is, they managed to read, remember and sometimes even think through Bely and Kliuchevsky, Khlebnikov and Shklovsky, Mandelstam and Soloviev. Those who left at seventeen, eighteen, and nineteen were in various ways loaded with Russia. Everything depended on the circumstances in which they grew, on the life they lived in their last Russian years: Did they study in a high school till the last day? Did they fight in the White Army? Did they lie wounded in the midst of some turmoil? Did they hide from the Reds? Did they flee the Whites? Did they manage to print one poem in a student miscellany in Kiev, Odessa, Rostov?

Knut neither studied nor fought, but was a grocery boy in his father's store in Kishinev. Ladinsky was a White officer. Poplavsky lived with his family. Nabokov left with his parents, having published in Petersburg two collections (1916, 1918) of youthful verse. Smolensky was evacuated from the south of Russia with his entire school; Zlobin, having lived through the Revolution with the Merezhkovskys, came with them to Paris as their secretary; and I myself appeared in the world as 'Khodasevich's wife', having printed one poem in a Petersburg miscellany in February 1922 (together with Tikhonov and Nikolai Chukovsky). I don't know if any of them besides myself had ever been to Moscow; it is possible that some had. But neither Knut nor Smolensky had been to Petersburg. Had Knut looked into Lomonosov? Or Vyacheslav Ivanov? Had Ladinsky heard of the formalists? I don't think so. Smolensky had not read them and only dimly knew their names. Ladinsky took up books (and the French language) in the 1930s, when he switched from being a house-painter to being an errand-boy. Knut at the time read what he could, mostly books at random; Smolensky read almost nothing, as a protest, feeling this would harm his originality (and he had less originality than others). I remember speaking with him once about Tiutchev, but he didn't want to know him, fearing Tiutchev could destroy his 'integrity' and that he would not have the strength to struggle against him. Poplavsky, probably, read more than the others – the dadaists, Verlaine, the surrealists, Apollinaire, Gide. Zlobin, in the atmosphere of the Merezhkovskys, knew these very well.

The Union of Young Poets installed itself on the Rue Denfert-Rochereau, No. 79. In the 1920s 'we' read verse there, as well as Khodasevich and Tsvetaeva; there were readings by Remizov, Zaitsev, Shestov, and others. Knut was the initiator of the magazine, where he and I were editors, but after the first issue (1926), we already thought *New House* beyond our powers. The Merezhkovskys, whom we invited there (Bunin, of course, was also invited) immediately began to crush us by squaring their literary and political accounts with Remizov and Tsvetaeva, and the magazine very soon passed into their hands under a new title.

A close friendship tied me to Knut for seven years: much in his verse speaks of this relationship (the poems: 'Two eyes – two windows,' 'Away with your wild life', 'You are again with me and there was no separation', 'All these years were needed', 'By your guilty joyful eyes'). We were often together, sometimes formed a threesome with Khodasevich. Knut was short, with a big nose and sad but lively eyes. In the 1920s he had a small restaurant in the Latin Quarter, where his sisters and young brother were waiters. Before this he worked in a sugar plant, and later went into the business of silk prints, at that time fashionable. He once gave me a piece of orange silk for a dress, decorated with blue flowers. He gave the same silk to Sarochka, his sweet and soft-spoken wife, so that Sarochka and I were sometimes dressed alike.

He grew up in his father's grocery and, though from the first the older and younger valued and believed in him, he never genuinely believed in himself. The problem was the same as Poplavsky's: the language. At first he was impudent and Khodasevich would say to him:

'Russian is not spoken like that.'

'Where is it not spoken like that?'

'In Moscow.'

'But in Kishinev it is.'

He understood very quickly that Russian is not spoken very well in Kishinev, and melancholy set in. His verse lost its virile originality and became diffuse and monotonous; his whole person

271

took on an image of constant sadness. He then had a baby son and his personal life became more involved: he left Sarochka and settled down with his new girlfriend. I visited him once at that time; the girl did not leave us alone, so instead of reading verse to one another, we had to continue small talk which fell flat. When I left he went with me to the subway. I tried to persuade him on the stairs to go back. But he insisted, and we went into the street.

I said, 'It's better for you to go back.'

'Why?'

'Because you will have her with you a short time and me your whole life.'

He smiled but took me on to the subway and, at the stop, under the street lamp, recited his recent poems. He had lost something in the past year, a kind of freshness and strength. I felt scared: What if nothing will come of him? Actually nothing did come of him, in a certain sense: the best that he wrote was written in his earliest period. He himself felt he had to take a new turn, but he had neither the language nor the ability for prose which he tried, and he had no training for criticism. So, submitting to the ancient tradition of prophets and patriarchs, he began to accumulate a family: at first his own, then through his second wife (Ariadna Scriabina, daughter of the composer) her children by first and second marriages. After her death (she was killed by the Germans in Toulouse in 1944, having earlier converted to Judaism), he went to Israel with all the children – hers, his, and theirs. One of her daughters belonged to Irgun Tsevai and threw bombs at the English in the 1940s. In Tel Aviv, in the Noah's Ark he had built, surrounded by all these offspring and a new wife, evidently happy, he died in 1955, at fifty-five.

It took two or three years of friendship with Vladimir Smolensky for us to switch to the familiar *ty*. Khodasevich loved him as a person and for his outward appearance: there was a kind of innate finesse in him (as in Khodasevich himself), of manners and the way he walked. Svelte, tall, with fine hands, long-legged, swarthy with marvellous eyes, and a lovely smile, he always looked ten years younger than he was. He did not spare himself: he drank a lot, was a chain-smoker, did not sleep at night, wrecked his own life and the lives of others, gradually lost his health. He did not develop his small talent, probably because he was not clever enough; he was eclectic but would not admit it. He thought Russian poetry had solidified and would not in a thousand years change its prosody or common romanticism, already threadbare. He fell in love permanently, suffered, dramatized, threatened suicide, wrote verses from the dramas of his life, thought he lived exactly by the pattern of Blok and Andreev and in fact lived rather like Apollon Grigoriev, thinking a poet shouldn't even dream of living otherwise.

He was as he put it 'lucky': he got a scholarship the first year of his arrival in Paris, graduated from a business school, and worked as an accountant in a large concern. At night he, like Poplavsky and all of us at various times, sat in Montparnasse cafés, or in a night club we went to, in the Russian poetic tradition, to listen to gypsy songs, where the beautiful Marusya Dmitrievich (who died young) drove everybody out of their minds with her singing and dances. It did not dawn on us to eat there, of course, it was too expensive; but to sit half the night over a glass of cognac was sometimes possible. Hunger drove us from this paradise, and we used to go and eat a thick sandwich (a roll, with a leaf of salami) in one of the boulevard cafés open till dawn.

Perhaps, because we had begun to speak to each other in the *ty* way, we became close, talking to each other of our failures, at times meeting solely to complain of our personal misfortunes. There was an air of confidence between us. He told me every detail of his hidden personal life which, probably, he spoke about to no one else. He was the core of all his misfortunes, knew it, but was not prepared to change. I called this his 'drunken fatalism' and tried to persuade him to 'send it all to hell', and 'begin anew'.

He shook his head. If you took sufferings away from him, what would remain? What would he make his verse from?

When I returned to Paris in 1960 (after ten years' absence), he had cancer of the throat and the surgeon had cut a hole in the middle of his windpipe; from there he wheezed: he was forbidden to talk. I remembered how, for many successive years, when asked 'How are you?' 'How're you getting along?' he answered unchangingly:

'Living a slow death.'

A small slate now lay in front of him where he wrote and erased what he had written.

'Volodia?' I said, afraid of asking him a question because I knew it was difficult for him to answer.

He quickly wrote a line on the slate and held it out to me:

'Now for sure it won't be long.'

His wife came in. She looked after him day and night and understood his thoughts and desires from his facial expression.

'Tell him about yourself, Nina Nikolaevna.'

I began to speak. His face was quite strange to me: red, swollen, with immobile eyes, and his wheeze was audible all the time as he inhaled and exhaled. Yet he still looked ten years younger than his age. They lived together in this small apartment in one room, ate here, slept here; his mother-in-law lived in the next room; and the third room was a storehouse of unnecessary things, a dump for rubbish. A heavy motionless dejection was in the air. I spoke about my ten years in America, New York, Chicago, and Colorado, about libraries and waterfalls, people I met here and there; and when I was silent he wrote on his slate:

'MORE.'

The roofs of Paris could be seen from the sixth-floor window. 'Not every foreigner is born with a passionate love for Paris,' said Léon Bloy. And he was right. How Ladinsky hated this city! I walked with him once at night on the Rue Vaugirard and his face expressed, as usual, boredom and revulsion at everything around us. Suddenly he stopped and said:

'How I hate all this: their stores, monuments, women, their language, history, literature.'

I had a special tone, a special form of address, for him:

'Still for about three hundred years at the most modest estimate, the whole world has fed on this, and for better or worse we have also. We could land up in Belgrade or Toronto, in an open-air life in Karaganda, or on the island of Tristan da Cunha, where there are scorpions and earthquakes.'

'It could not be worse.'

I, in my previous tone:

'Now, now! Enough exaggerations. There is no place to go anyway.'

'Perhaps there is no place for you to go. For me there is. I have a mother and brother in the district of Vladimir.'

'Yes – but districts no longer exist.'

He never understood humour. Tall, terribly thin, with long arms, a small head and grey hair (he began to grey early), he never laughed and rarely smiled. When he did it was a crooked smile. The first time I heard his verse I was struck by its novelty, maturity, sound-patterns, the originality of the chain of images and the rhythms. Khodasevich pushed them through the magazines and dailies. Ladinsky began to be published, and his name became known after his first collection; but no one liked him personally and in his presence one always sensed a heaviness: he was an embittered, wounded man, tortured by a yearning for his homeland, dissatisfied with everything, frustrated by life, and constantly speaking of it.

'We have been squashed, crushed. I exist on a servant's job. And you are a typist. If this were Russia we would have villas in the Crimea, not from Grandad or Daddy but our own, self-acquired; we would be famous . . . And now one cad once gave me a tip.'

I firmly squeezed his arm (skin and bones) to silence him.

At the editorial offices Poliakov was astonished: 'And what's this about you, a friendship with him? He hates everyone, envies everybody.'

'No, he does not envy everybody. He writes beautiful poems. Give him some work.'

But he was not given other work. And one sensed that the dénouement of his life would be even more dramatic than his life itself.

In the 1930s I often saw him. Later, during the war, I did not stop seeing him. He reacted with horror to the Soviet–Japanese incident on Lake Hassan, in 1938, when Russians surrendered to the Japanese. He became sombre when speaking of the Soviet failures in the Finno–Soviet war. He grew unsociable and mean when in the first months of the Soviet–German war hundreds of thousands of Soviet fighters went over to the Germans without a fight. I once heard a gnashing of teeth – not in the metaphorical, but the literal sense – when he said that on one and the same day Sevastopol and Kronstadt had been surrendered (this proved to be wrong). Then, when the war ended, he took out a Soviet passport and signed up in the Union of Soviet Patriots.

The historian Melgunov once said to me:

'Whoever's head whirled the day the valiant Red Army took Berlin is off my list. No head should do that while Stalin is alive.'

Ladinsky disappeared from my life. Then we met on the street and he looked inquisitively at me. I took a step towards him.

He said he was leaving for the U.S.S.R. But he did not go. A year later he came to say good-bye to me, it was about midnight, and he stood in the doorway afraid to extend his hand in case I would not offer him mine. I felt that even now he would not go. 'Not now, not now' – I remembered Bely's cry at the station in Berlin (Kirillov's in *The Possessed*).

We sat for about an hour exchanging a few words. He said Europe was 'rotting', that all around us was doomed.

'I have been trampled here. You have too.'

I tried to argue my point that this was not because of our accidental personal failure. It was the result of a national catastrophe we shared.

'You will not be allowed to write and publish there,' I said.

'So much the better.'

We both knew we would not see each other again, and he left.

But once more he did not leave. In the end the French police expelled him as a 'Soviet patriot', in 1948. Ten or twelve men on the truck belonged to this organization. They were driven east and on the evening of the first day arrived in Strasbourg. Taken early in the morning, some were in pajamas. They were also held quite a while in Dresden. There was a rumour Ladinsky was forced to spend two years there, and that in Dresden he had done away with himself. But all this was untrue: he managed to get to the 'district of Vladimir' and lived there at his brother's till 1959 – the year of his death. His name flashed several times in the Soviet press; he translated from French. Then there was a short notice of his death.

In Paris in spring the chestnut trees bloom: the first on the Boulevard Pasteur where the subway emerges from underground and heated air rises in waves to the trees. Every autumn the leaves of the Champs-Elysées, before falling, turn a dark brown, the colour of a cigar. In summer there are several days when the sun sits in the centre of the Arc de Triomphe on the Etoile, if you look from the Place de la Concorde. The gardens of the Tuileries are the most beautiful in Paris because they are a part of the ensemble, and anyone who stands and looks at the red sun pouring onto the stone of the Arc on the Etoile also becomes part of the ensemble, as in front of 'Aristotle Contemplating the Bust of Homer' you 'contemplate' Rembrandt and feel alive. There are no winters, properly speaking, in Paris: rain falls, rustles, bangs, whispers at the window and on the roofs, one day, two, three. In January there is suddenly a day – towards the end of the month – when all shines and pours out warmly; the sky is blue, people sit on the terraces of cafés without coats, and women in light dresses transform the city. This is like a promise. It is the first hint that all will again be cheerful, beautiful, that all around will sparkle. It is only a single day, and though everyone knows two months of awful weather are still to come, they keep silent about it. This day comes every year like a movable holiday between 20 January and 5 February. It comes and goes, but what it promises remains in the air.

I stand for a long time on the Place de la Concorde, where there is as much sky as in a Russian rye field or a corn field in Kansas. I sit for a while on a bench behind Notre Dame Cathedral, where the Seine goes around the Ile Saint-Louis with its beautiful old houses. I stop at a *charcuterie* on the Boulevard Raspail and cannot tear myself away from their window, for me more splendid than all others in Paris. I am always hungry. I am always in hand-me-down dresses, old shoes, I have no perfumes, silks, furs, but I want nothing so much as that tasty stuff displayed in the window. On the other side of the window a girl, shiny with fat, turns the wheel of a ham-slicer. She has lips like pieces of ham, fingers that are pink sausages, eyes like black sparkling olives, and there she disappears amidst the hams and pork chops, so that when a buyer enters he must look for her. Then she again comes to life, and the wheel turns, a long sharp knife moves in her hand, a piece of oil-paper flies under the sausage, the needles of the scale rock and with a familiar sound – trakh-tararakh-trr – the cash register roars. Oh, if only it wouldn't roar! How easy it would be to exist!

In those years there were still stoves in the flats where we threw coals, briquettes – twelve pieces, calculated so that a bag would last for about five days. And there were often communal toilets on the landings. It was cold, and day and night one could hear the water gushing out with a roar from under the ceiling, when someone broke the chain it was replaced by a rope. Early in the morning heavy vans would pass under our windows, pulled by percherons, the dark ones of sewer-cleaners and dirty-white ones carrying ice. Saturdays and Sundays organ-grinders would come into the courtyard, bringing a child who would sing in a sharp voice of lost love, and sometimes trained dogs who would dance on a little rug, with eyes full of tears. The rolls would play a sad song I remember from 1914, to which soldiers in blue-red uniforms went to the Marne, assuming they would not return home; they were right. In those years in the streets of Paris shepherds still circulated with herds of goats. They sold goat's cheese, and the concierges would run out with a small vessel to milk the goats right there; their bleating resounded in a chorus when a ragged dog chased them from the pavement onto the street.

Dozens of books of recollections of the twenties and thirties have been written. It was good to be in Paris, to be young and poor. The young American journalist who had decided to break with his Chicago newspaper to write a novel 'that no one will ever publish', or the Swedish artist who had sworn not to cater to the tastes of the public, to write 'for himself', or the calypso musician from the Caribbean Islands who lived in a Latin Quarter attic, played on a timbrel and had cut his ties with the Caribbean because he opposed his government – our condition could not be compared with theirs: they decided to remain but could leave, they did not dream in front of a *charcuterie* and they belonged to the young artistic sub-layer of the city that had a future.

We were a strange collection of people – though by age we could not have been either bankers, or generals in the tsar's army – who for one reason or another did not accept what was being done in our homeland. The fate of Trotsky disturbed the West for a moment. The Moscow trials impressed the European intellectuals, the pact of Molotov and Ribbentrop shook them. But this happened later. In the years 1925–35, despite the suicides of Esenin and Mayakovsky, the difficulties of Ehrenburg, the disappearance of Pilniak, and the rumours about Gorky's troubles, the faith that the U.S.S.R. would renew the young post-war world and in particular the art of the left, bringing support and perspectives, was stronger in the West than all the vacillations and doubts. This was particularly so in France (and possibly in the U.S.A.), where people, when they do not want to know something, manage it with impunity. It is enough to say that even in the 1960s, after the exposure of the 'personality cult', a member of the French Communist Party and a famous writer, Louis Aragon, published his monumental *History of the U.S.S.R.* using predominantly documentation of the Stalinist period; and Jean-Paul Sartre, in his book on Genet, got away with calling

Nikolai Bukharin a traitor and enemy of the people, again making common cause with Stalin. Both authors could not have failed to hear of the changes in Russia after the Twentieth Congress, but they ignored them: that way it is simpler, they have not the time for change in ideology and a reassessment of values, and are not interested.

The facts were placed before us a hundred times, for example Rolland's letter of inquiry to Gorky and Gorky's answer, which I have already mentioned. When Gorky answered that there were no persecutions, many of the émigré writers tried to shout out to European public opinion, but they did not succeed in outshouting Gorky, and in the following years – twenty-five – the intellectuals in Europe and America did not believe in the persecution of the intelligentsia by the Communist Party. I will cite one of the letters from Khodasevich to me in 1928: he had succeeded in interesting the old translator of the Russian classics, Halperin-Kaminsky (who had known Leo Tolstoy personally), in this problem. Khodasevich wanted to answer Gorky in the French press, to tell of the poets and writers in the U.S.S.R. who had disappeared without trace, of the suicides, the politics of the party in literature, of censorship, the terrible years that were in store for men of letters in Russia. Halperin-Kaminsky evidently tried to help in this:

5 April, 1928. Versailles.
Yesterday morning, in a café, I read Halperin's letter and, going home, set off for Paris. I got a haircut, washed, and went to Halperin's. It was precisely his letter that convinced me not to print my answer to the questionnaire and delighted the old man. Now we have become friends to the tombstone (I hope, however, that it will cover him before me). And here's what we decided:
Halperin will write to Rolland to send him Gorky's letter [the second, with the personal insults to Balmont]. This letter of Gorky's H. will reprint not in *L'Avenir* which has no readers, no editor, no space, but in *Candide*. *There, next to it,* will be my detailed article, a column which I will write specially for the occasion. *Candide* is not *L'Avenir*. The article is not an answer to the questionnaire; the crushing of Gorky *on behalf of French editors* is not mere babble among other people in answer to an already obsolete questionnaire. To complete the picture I will demand an

honorarium and on the same day I will pull all this (both Gorky and myself) into *Renaissance*.

That's how clever I am. But: about Gorky's *second* letter, about my ensuing answer and about *Candide* – *the greatest secrecy*. Do not say anything to anyone.

Halperin-Kaminsky apparently undertook *L'Avenir's* questionnaire, asking writers what they thought of Gorky's letter to Rolland. Khodasevich, obviously, tried to take this problem to the large French weekly press, feeling that *L'Avenir*, to which Halperin was closely connected, was not a sufficiently weighty journal for such a serious matter.

Is it necessary to add that nothing came of this plan?

The great men of this world – that is, *our* world, not the totalitarian one – in which we lived and to which we bound ourselves, were either like André Gide, who for years had tried to prove the virtues of the great Stalin's regime until, suddenly going to the U.S.S.R., he changed his opinions or, like George Bernard Shaw who supported the U.S.S.R., went there and did *not* change. In the company of a couple of English aristocratic fools, atuned like himself sympathetically to the Kremlin Cambyses, Shaw *in 1931* went to bow to Stalin. Having returned to England he wrote (making an old buffoon of himself) a book about Russia (*The Rationalization of Russia*, reprinted as a matter of fact in 1964) where he announced *urbi et orbi* that in the Soviet Union 'all persecutions of the intelligentsia ended long ago'.

The Chicago journalist who had turned into an author of novels left (third class, of course) for Spanish shores, while the Swedish artist, living in a hotel, took a studio for his work (possibly without heat and with a toilet on the landing), eating in cheap restaurants. The Caribbean virtuoso regaled his girl with oysters, took her to the races, and bet on 'General Boulanger', who suddenly came in first. We could do none of this. We could not move anywhere. We had only one roof. In our home one saucepan stood on the fire.

Hemingway writes about poverty in his recollections of Paris in those years. He says money came to him for his early stories irregularly, that for sixty francs a day you could have lived modestly but tolerably à deux (loving each other – not loving cost much more), and even sometimes go away, to Senlis, Fontainebleau, to the Loire. In our best years, that is the years when Khodasevich worked regularly on *The Renaissance* and I on *The Latest News*, we had about forty francs a day for two, and before that there was no more than thirty. A new filling in an ailing tooth, a warm coat, two tickets to *Le Sacre du Printemps* left a gap in domestic arithmetic which it was impossible to fill in any way, save by actually walking through the city for weeks. Later, in 1939, when Khodasevich was dying, he was taken not to a private clinic but to the municipal hospital, a devil of a difference in the City of Light! And there he said, when I came to him:

'Whoever has not been lying here with me, who has not gone through what I have gone through, is to me a nobody.'

We knew, best of all, landlords who rented rooms to us, proprietors who rented apartments, coal-dealers who sold coal and wood for heating, the baker, the butcher, sales clerks at Damoy where we bought sugar, coffee, tea, and salt, the concierge who followed us with a sharp eye, our guests, our mail. Our reputation in the Préfecture de Police, credit in the shop, the receipt of a money order, the renewal of the apartment lease, depended on the concierges. We knew well the bald and moustached waiters of La Rotonde, La Coupole, Le Select, Le Napoli, where we could sit over a single cup of *café-crème* in the evenings, talking for hours of Annensky, Bagritsky, Olesha, Lawrence, Kafka, Huxley. But we did not know Valéry, who published his books in limited numbers in a luxurious edition, or the then fashionable Katherine Mansfield (the great admirer of Chekhov) who wrote about old English ladies having conversations at an exquisitely set tea table. In those years James Joyce dined at a restaurant on the Rue Jacob and talked to his wife and children in Italian, but we never met him, and only saw the then unknown Henry Miller and his wife June several times from a distance – in some ways these two were like us.

Our poverty could be divided into the organized and unorganized, or planned and unplanned. With Khodasevich and me it was an organized one, with Weidlé it was organized and planned, with Poplavsky it was probably neither the one nor the other, with Ladinsky it was planned, and with Smolensky it was sometimes the one, sometimes the other.

We were, however, together: there were eight or ten or at various times twelve people who needed each other in an anti-friendship.

This was not the 'sweet union' of the Pushkin Pleiad that 'bound' poets. This was a very critical, nervous, and uneven bond between people who, during fifteen years, travelled life's road together. At times I came close to this group, and several times moved very far away from it. Then the war began and blackout shutters appeared on the windows of our large, noisy, disorderly cafés. Then Paris was taken by German troops and overcome by the military. When all came to life again, these places turned out to be full of inhabitants of neighbouring quarters, prostitutes of Montparnasse, Allied soldiers, a new multi-lingual crowd, foreign to us; but you see, one shouldn't forget that *we* were no longer the same either. And it got 'dark on the Russian Parnassus', as Nabokov put it.

We had our own holidays, not the 'taking of the Bastille' or 'All Saints' Day', not 'Russian Christmas' or 'Russian Easter' either, when the Orthodox cathedral on the Rue Daru and the dozens of Russian churches in Paris and the suburbs filled with 'White Russians', as they were then called, the remains of the armies of Denikin and Wrangel, the dashing 'army ranks' with their devoted wives – dressmakers, embroideresses, milliners, who were once nurses in the Civil War or simply generals' daughters, fine innocent maidens and ladies of leisure. The army ranks appeared in church with their children: a son, registered at the City Hall as Gleb-Jean and a daughter, Kira-Jeannette. The blond, blue-eyed children crawled on all fours to the sacrament, babies were carried to the chalice, the choir thundered through the entire church, old widows of tsarist ministers stood on the parvis. (In the past they had been grandes-dames of Petersburg society, admirers of Rasputin; their husbands had long ago been slaughtered or shot.) Among them were beggars, with red eyes and swollen faces, dirty hat in hand:

'*S'il-vous-plaît*, give to a former member of the intelligentsia, who in '15 shed his blood on the fields of Galicia . . . At present – native of the Salvation Army.'

'Give to an unemployed victim of the labour laws of marvellous France . . .'

'Give to an invalid of the Kornilov campaign . . .'

'Give a Russian nobleman a slice of the bitter bread of exile . . .'

And so on. Our own holidays were: a banquet of *The Latest News*, the fifth or tenth anniversary of the newspaper, the thousandth number, the five thousandth; Bunin's Nobel Prize, its celebration in the Théâtre des Champs-Elysées, the reception for him at the offices of *The Latest News* on 15 November (1933); the twenty-fifth anniversary of the literary activity of Boris Zaitsev; dinners of 'The Nomad Camp' (a literary group connected with Mark Slonim's *Russia's Will*; in 1932 I was present at two of them, as in 1933); meetings of the newspaper *Days*; evenings at the Tsetlins' house; more intimate and friendly lunches with the closest collaborators on Miliukov's paper and dinners with friends (Zaitsev, Muratov, Aldanov, Osorgin, Tsetlin, Khodasevich, and I); and finally the best-attended and most solemn of all the celebrations – the banquet of *Contemporary Annals*, to which several hundred people were invited on 20 November, 1932 (the publication of the magazine's fiftieth issue).

I bought myself a white evening dress for this banquet, the first floor-length gown of my life, with a bright red cape and white silk shoes, and sat next to Vladimir Zhabotinsky, the famous Zionist to whom I had been bound by a friendly relationship for many years. When I met him I already knew his ideas, his previous literary activity, his legendary past, and his currently militant journalism. During World War One he created the Jewish Legion, became a lieutenant in the British Army, later was an organizer of Hagana and Irgun. He died in 1940 in the U.S.A., and eight years later the state whose creation he had worked for all his life came into being. Only twenty-six years later, in July 1964, his remains were transported to Israel, where tens of thousands of people in Tel Aviv went to his grave to bid him farewell. I knew by heart his translation into Russian of Edgar Allan Poe's 'The Raven', which he did when he was, it seems, in his teens and which I found in an anthology when I myself was fifteen. This translation is far better than Briusov's and better even than Balmont's, though Balmont's has its virtues. We met first at the offices of *The Latest News*, where he came once, and we later left together; when we parted after dinner he said to me in all seriousness:

'Register me among your admirers.'

'Register me among yours,' I answered laughing.

We began to see each other from time to time. He was short, with an irregular but most intelligent face, energetic and original, a face burned by a non-European sun. He had a military bearing. He was one of the most remarkable men I knew, if by remarkable one means someone who, in the course of any conversation, understands in half a word, and lives, changes, creates, changes others, and 'speaks with his eyes'. He had humour, and a kind of greedy interest in the people he spoke to; I often drank in his speech – lively, witty, clear and sparkling as his thought.

At the banquet there were many speeches, eulogies to the magazine and optimistic words about the future, which together left a rather sad impression in me of the concentrated but airless space in which we lived, the artificial union at these dinner tables of people who for the most part had not managed or did not want to change, compromise, or unite, and did not even know if this was necessary. I doubted if there was anything genuine, important and necessary behind all this façade.

But there was. It was not, however, on the political level, it was exclusively cultural and literary. The politics of the performing orators – Miliukov, Kerensky, Petr Struve, the editors of *Contemporary Annals* (members of the S.-R. Party) – died with them, leaving hardly a noticeable trace in the history of the Russian emigration. Literature is all that remained of those years, and art of course: painting, theatre, music. But painting, theatre, music (Tchelitchew, Archipenko, Kandinsky, Larionov, Lanskoy, Medtner, Stravinsky, the ballet, Russian dramatic actors who went to Hollywood or into the French theatre) lived a more 'normal' life, because they fused, in one way or another, with the European current (in painting more, in music less). Literature has remained, will remain, and – there is now no doubt – will live in the future. We need only die to be resurrected in our homeland. There's the irony of the expression: *if it dies, it bears much fruit.*

Nikolai Medtner lived near Paris in those years (1930–1), and I am happy to say I was received in his house several times, first in Antony, then in Montmorency. Antony and even Montmorency were not then a part of greater Paris but were suburbs, and once, returning at night with Georgy Otsup from Medtner's to Paris we got lost in a cabbage field and wandered for two hours, looking for the path to the station. Seven-storey houses have been there now for some time. Medtner played his 'Poems', and 'Fairy-Tales' and other piano pieces so beautifully that when I hear them I still hear his playing and no other. The musicologist Leonid Sabaneev, then in full possession of his intellectual powers, often came to his place, as well as the marvellous soprano Helen Frey, who sang Medtner's 'Romances' to his accompaniment. Mrs Medtner, Anna Mikhailovna, a veritable brood-hen, was always saddled with the most domestic tasks; she was even more a housewife than Anna Karlovna Benois, wife of Aleksandr Benois, the painter and art historian. These two Annas somehow become one in my mind, and I see before me a being, fat, small, in female dress without signs of femininity in face or coiffure or gestures, running here and there, and always calculating something in her mind that has in reality no relation at all to the 'genius' of the house, where taste, talent, intellect, and invention reign and no one pays any attention to that kind of chattering.

Aleksandr Benois came to Paris in the 1920s and at first, evidently, did not know (like many others) whether he would stay in the West or return to Leningrad, which to the end of his life he called Petersburg. He did not particularly attract anyone's attention in those first years; it was said he went daily to Versailles, and in the park from morning onwards, like one who had been starving for years, he made sketches – six, eight, ten a day. He shaved his beard, began to grow fat and shrink in height, and more and more with each passing year acquired the habit of fidgeting when he spoke to people, dancing, shuffling his feet, taking bows, making all sorts of pleasant spinning gestures with his short arms, though he was sick at heart: in Paris he was not acknowledged as an artist, but only as a theatrical designer for romantic ballets. In his recollections of childhood, which were printed in *The Latest News*, he spoke much of his childhood, of his 'sweet body', of his 'little hands and feet', of his beautiful mother and handsome father, and many laughed at him, but this approach to his own past never seemed to me either laughable or strange: it was his essence, a result of his upbringing; he could not have been otherwise; the entire past was cloudless and holy for him, especially the past of Petersburg, of the World of Art, of the Benois clan, with all their relatives, marked, it could be said, by the gods. He had a round belly, and once, when visiting me, could not get out of a deep armchair, no matter how he tried. He laughed, made all kinds of funny gestures, but his predicament – I saw this out of the corner of my eye – became increasingly difficult: it was time to leave, everyone around had already said good-bye to each other, and he still could not find points of support to help him jump out of the chair where he had sat comfortably for several hours. Laughing with him at what had happened, I went and, unnoticed, extended my little finger. Still laughing coyly, and grimacing with all his dear fat face, he seized it, and shot out of the armchair, then immediately took to shuffling a small foot to the right and left. Dobuzhinsky saw all this. He slyly smiled at me.

'A drowning man grasping at a straw,' he said.

Later I read in Rozanov that at some soirée in Petersburg Benois was present – 'a black beetle who had fallen deep into an armchair'.

When I published my biography of Tchaikovsky in instalments in *The Latest News*, Benois once said to me that he felt me to be his (as well as Tchaikovsky's) contemporary 'as if you had known everyone – Bob, Modest, Argo', and suddenly, carried away, he exclaimed:

'Do you remember at the première of *The Queen of Spades* –' And suddenly became terribly embarrassed, stopped, and began to sing an aria from the opera in a fine little voice. The première had taken place nine years before I was born.

I met Dobuzhinsky while still in Berlin. He was one of the most enchanting and attractive people I have ever known. His tall, handsome figure, his strong hands, his face with clever, grave eyes that changed with his smile (he had a great sense of humour) – everything in him was natually spiritualized and beautiful. In old age he remained very upright, trim, just a little stiff but not in the face. Even his voice – calm and musical – was in harmony with his whole appearance. He knew how to laugh, and he did love to laugh! In France he was appreciated even less than Benois. He was not even acknowledged as a stage designer, and as a portraitist or landscape artist he hardly existed. But all he touched always came to life, and what he wrote (his memoirs), what he retold was fascinating and intelligent. His witticisms, his jokes – how to the point they all were, in what splendid accord with his entire nature, with the way he lived, what he loved, revered, and took delight in!

In Berlin he began to collect a list of Russian surnames – with my help and dedicating it to me. I preserved narrow sheets of paper for a long time covered with his handwriting. The list began with classifications: *bird* names (Orlov, Soloviev, Snegirev, etc.); *beast* (Lvov, Koshkin, Ezhov); *object* (Gorshkov, Shkaff, Zavesov).*

*Orel – eagle, *solovei* – nightingale, *snegir* – bullfinch; *lev* – lion, *koshka* – cat, *ezh* – hedgehog; *gorschok* – pot, *shkaff* – closet, *zavesa* – curtain.

Then we moved to less traditional surnames – we called them 'pernicious': Krovopuskov, Koshkodavov, Tumbesov, von Deriabkin, Shchov, Tverdokrysh . . . It was forbidden to take names from literature, you had to have known the people personally, not invent them. He knew all the shop signs in Petersburg, Vilna, Pskov; it was easy for him and I helped as much as I could. Sitting somewhere on a visit we would suddenly look at each other and in the midst of general conversation blurt out: Mundirov-Treshchov, Abesguz, Likhosherstov, Vorobieux.* (The last was my discovery: a man living in Versailles; he said it *seemed* one of his ancestors was of Russian origin.)

Dobuzhinsky took out his list on the spot, wrote it down, read it to me, and we both laughed.

In Paris we often saw each other and were always full of fun and at ease with each other. He had a collection of old photographs of unknown people he had once bought at the Aleksandrovsky market in Petersburg. We would consider them. The women were all somehow like Polina Suslova, Dostoevsky's mistress, and the men were reminiscent of the composer Balakirev. Dobuzhinsky kept them as records of old dresses and hairdos. Later in Paris he collected funny ads in Russian émigré newspapers: 'At your home. Any time. Bringing ultra-violet lights with me' or 'I have a rabbit farm. Looking for a mate. The less educated, the better.' To amuse and divert me he would recite, eyes on the ceiling, hands crossed on the table, looking poised and important, the signs of Nevsky Avenue at the beginning of our century, from the Nikolaevsky railway station to Liteiny Avenue, first on the one side, then on the other. I felt I was having the great joy of walking with him down the Nevsky of my childhood, there and back, my child's mitten in his big hand, my small legs making one and a half steps while his big ones made one.

Then for many years I lost sight of him. I came to New York in November 1950, and the evening of that day he came to see me in the hotel on West Seventy-second Street where I was staying. I already knew what a terrible blow the failure of his staging of *Khovanshchina* at the Metropolitan Opera had been for him. He hated America, New York, modern painting, modern music, all

Vorobei – sparrow.

the mechanization of post-war life, but he also had some joy: he was writing his memoirs (which till now have not been published in their entirety). It seemed odd: he was sure of himself as an artist, but extremely unsure of himself as a memoirist; nevertheless he wrote remarkably, knew how to talk of the past, continually vacillating between autobiography and memoirs. He began to come to read them to me. He would call and ask permission to visit right away. I was always delighted with him. I sensed he needed to read aloud to someone what he had just written. I was frank with him when I told him of my enthusiasm, in no way exaggerating the strength of my impression, yet he still did not become confident; it suddenly began to seem to him that everything was emerging too intimately. I persuaded him not to cross anything out. 'Who needs all this?' he would suddenly ask, and I would answer that *everyone* did and that he must change nothing. 'And what about my style? Is this line well written? Are there not too many "thats" and "whiches"?' I tried to convince him not to dare even ask such a question.

I knew that between him and the ballerina Tamara Karsavina there had once been what is popularly called an affair. How carefully he circumvented this subject! I hesitated to ask him to write about it more openly; he was tightly closed off from all people, including me, in everything of his personal life. There were, however, several pages, read to me one evening, where I suddenly sensed the 'breath of mystery': he spoke of a young woman in a white dress, on the porch of a country house, of a woman or maybe a form slipping away from him, a spectre not in an abstract or metaphorical but in a very real sense. Was it a ballet vision? Perhaps I sensed something here out of the second act of *Giselle*, or was it the image of the Black Swan? Something moved around like a symbol of a drama of the repressed and tortured man: this symbol flashed by in a few lines. These, so far as I know, have never been published anywhere and – who knows! – perhaps were subsequently destroyed. They remained in my mind. Dobuzhinsky's voice, always so full and deep, at that minute suddenly gave way. He looked at me. I did not lift my eyes. I feared I would scare off this dim shadow of untold beauty and charm, and indicated that I understood him.

If all the harmony, order and concord of the Petersburg ensemble were reflected in the figure and intellect of Dobuzhinsky, then Nikolai Milioti was entirely – from head to foot – a Muscovite, was proud of it and loved to talk about it. He knew everyone, remembered everyone, especially artistic and bourgeois Moscow. Khodasevich did not like him and considered him a lady-killer, a mediocre Don Juan, and we even half-quarrelled with handsome Milioti. In one of his letters Khodasevich wrote to me (25 November, 1930):

> I ask you firmly not to make up with Milioti – i.e., of course, there is no need to quarrel. But I ask you insistently, after everything that has been said about him, after the ambiguous and stupid situation into which he put you (*and me*, as you know, *on purpose!*) – after all this that you never and nowhere be seen *alone* with him, and that he does not appear either as *our* guest or *yours*. In a neutral spot yes, but in our home I would not offer him my hand, about which I warn you . . . Let's face it: you are the master of your reputation, but I am the master of mine as well . . .

The details of this quarrel (or half quarrel) have disappeared from my memory, but of course after this letter Milioti was never again at our place.

At that time he was not old, but he was no longer as he had been known in Moscow, where in his own words he was considered 'the handsomest of all people alive in the world' – which was not that easy to believe. After emigrating he had a young son whom he did not acknowledge; there remained a wife and two children in Moscow. Till his final days he sought to live with women who adored him. He was very poor, despite the fact that he went to the United States in the 1920s, organized an exhibition, and, to hear him tell it, had a great success. In the last years of his life, grey with age, in a torn coat fastened with a safety-pin, a torn knapsack over his shoulders, toothless, he looked like a typical Paris *clochard* – a homeless tramp. I don't know what happened, after his death, to his studio on the Place de la Sorbonne. It was filled with portraits of worldly beauties.

Konstantin Somov also stayed a time in the States, but this small, inconspicuous, and quiet man did not squander his American money, but arranged a life annuity for himself. He lived alone, modestly and moderately, had a passion for the beauty of red-cheeked, curly-haired young boys with open collars and long-fingered pale hands, whom he painted in cheerful oil colours. When I visited him, he was always surrounded by them.

About twenty years ago I had a dream: I am standing in Leningrad at a railway station and am awaiting a train from Paris. It is a goods train, bringing émigré coffins to their homeland. I run along the platform; a long train stretches out slowly. On the first car is written in chalk: Miliukov, Struve, Rachmaninov, Chaliapin; on the second: Merezhkovsky, Bunin, Diaghilev, some others. I ask: Where is Khodasevich? A hand indicates to me the end of the train. A car flashes by with the inscription: Shestov, Remizov, Berdyaev. I continue to run. Finally, in the last car, with a beating heart, I see his coffin. Why am I so disturbed, as if I were prepared to see him in the flesh? With a rumble the doors fly open and a dozen railway workers roll luggage trolleys up to them. 'They are unloading them! They are unloading them!' someone shouts behind my back. Suddenly I see other coffins next to Khodasevich's coffin in the half-darkness of the goods wagon: Esenin, Tsvetaeva, Akhmatova . . . 'Why are they here? They did not die in Paris? There is some misunderstanding . . .'

Opposite the Closerie des Lilas in the early 1920s, near the Luxembourg gardens, the huge Bal Bullier stood, a wooden barracks in which Paris artists held their charity balls. Some of the Russian artists had been granted a long life – for example, Mikhail Larionov, who had lived long before World War One in Paris, together with his wife, Natalia Goncharova (he died in 1964). Soutine and Bakst died comparatively young. On the day of a ball in Bullier – in the summer – half-naked artists, made up as savages, Indians, or African Negroes, walked around Montparnasse, from La Rotonde to La Coupole, faces daubed in all colours of the rainbow, with their models, young and pretty, painted, hardly covered by bits of material. Here you could see everyone: the calm patrician Derain and Zadkine and Pevsner and Braque. Everything ended in a noisy and orgiastic fête at someone's studio; and once there was a nocturnal gathering at Kostya Tereshkovich's, then still a bachelor, to which he invited Bunin, Zaitsev, and Aldanov. Aldanov was what is called 'shocked' by everything he saw, and left quite early. Bunin was at first overwhelmed by the spectacle, but then not without relish joined the bacchanalia; Zaitsev sat and drank and looked around a little, and finally zealously joined: all this was very familiar to him from his own youth.

At dawn, everyone had a faded look, dishevelled and somewhat obscene. All went home along empty streets, where cesspool cleaners' barrels rumbled and farmers on high carts took cabbages and carrots to the central market.

Between the artist Mikhail Larionov (and Natalia Goncharova) and the young members of the World of Art group there was no difference in age, but a deep abyss divided them: until his last days, when he was well over eighty, Larionov preserved his *mischievousness*, a trait that had been a tradition of futurism. Shklovsky, Mayakovsky, the imaginists, the members of the society, 'The Donkey's Tail', the frequenters in the good old days of 'The Stall of Pegasus', all were mischievous. Those who died young died in the midst of their pranks, those who lived till old age never outlived theirs. This new feature of our time, an important trait of a whole circle of artists, poets, and musicians, was hardly noticed. The symbolists and members of the World of Art hated this mischief; the acmeists turned away from it in disgust. But everything was not that simple: there was in the futurists a deep connection between genius and immaturity and a coarse but in reality legitimate and healthy reaction against the *vin triste* of Blok, the sombre madness of Vrubel, the pathos of Scriabin, the melancholy of Chekhov. Like many of his contemporaries, Larionov remained a prankster all his long life. He was continually thinking something up, sometimes with a clever smile, sometimes transported by the anticipation of a practical joke, often only to spite someone. He did not give a damn about anyone save 'our gang', though with 'our gang' he was sentimentally tender; the principal element in him was a disrespect for the grey hairs of his enemies (even when he himself was grey) and a tireless worship of the slogans of early futurism, which taught mischievous ones like himself to cling to 'our gang', not to give in to the 'petite bourgeoisie' and to 'punch it in the face' when and wherever possible. This mingled in him with a generally innocuous attraction for Soviet communism, a certain sympathy for Germany, and hopes (during the war) for 'real changes' with which 'the old fool Europe would be smacked in the teeth'. Anything new would do! Anything unexpected! Only to smash the old and toss overboard from 'the ship of modernity' all highly esteemed and much revered rubbish and trash!

In their apartment, where Goncharova and Larionov lived from time immemorial and the floor was never swept, under the dust that had settled on books, papers, drawings collected over forty years, you could have found treasures that would be priceless now. No one, however – or almost no one – was allowed in this lair. 'Yes, I have some early drawings by Picasso. Yes, I have some sketches by Soutine and letters from Diaghilev, and all his programmes.' Sketches by Bakst, once forgotten by him here, are in a heap somewhere; Esenin's notebook is also lying around, as well as an impromptu work written in Mayakovsky's hand – there is no time, however, to discover where they are. The host is lying on his side or is running through the streets from one café to another – 'We bustle, oh yes, we certainly bustle' – or is sitting in a corner near a window and is painting in a yellowish woman with yellowish hair and a short pelvis – in the yellowish light of the Paris day.

His pranks in relation to me were always merciful and never offensive. They were, as I have said, not accidental; they belonged – one way or another – to a whole group of *modern art* people, if one uses this term in the widest sense. Mischief exists, of course, in the West, it is still alive and is gradually becoming history: the famous '*bateau lavoire*' in Montmartre became a museum, but those who once lived in it, though they stand with one foot in their graves, continue – as far as possible – to perform pranks. As an artist Larionov was no less talented than the remarkable painter Goncharova, but while she toiled and worked – even, for a living, painting some Paris restaurants – he squandered his talents, wasted his powers, deteriorated in endless conversations, arguments, dirty tricks, practical jokes, running about like the drop-out who, if he only wanted to, could graduate with honours. (All things considered: he didn't give a damn! And he was probably right.)

Some artists until the mid-1930s kept renewing their Soviet passports, meekly awaiting the day when they would be allowed to go to Moscow and occupy a place suited to them and their art of the 'left'. Right up to 1936, to the Moscow trials, they had hopes that in a country which had made the greatest Revolution in the world, 'left' art would at last be accepted officially as the principal if not the sole art. Mayakovsky's suicide shook their hopes but did not kill them. Zamiatin's arrival in Paris in 1931 again strongly agitated them. Could it really be true that it was easier for Kuprin to return to the U.S.S.R. than for Zamiatin to live there? This puzzled them greatly.

I once spent two hours with Zamiatin in the Café Danton on the corner of the Boulevard Saint-Germain two steps away from the Russian bookstore where we had met by chance. This was in July 1932. He associated with no one, did not consider himself an émigré, and lived in the hope of returning home at the first opportunity. I don't think he indeed believed that he would live to such a day, but it was for him too terrible to abandon this hope completely. I knew him in 1922, in Petersburg, spoke to him several times at literary soirées of the Serapion Brothers, and celebrated the New Year at the same table with him in 1922. He approached me in the bookstore on the Rue de l'Eperon and held out his hand.

'Do you recognize me?'

There was no one around. We left.

In the café he smoked his pipe, supported his face with both hands, and listened to me for a long time. Then he himself spoke. He always had the tone of a mentor, of a father-figure (which he had been for the Serapion Brothers), a tone slightly forced, and I sensed this. He was affectedly optimistic, said that it was imperative to wait, to keep quiet, that some insects and animals know this tactic: not to struggle, to allow things to pass. To be able later to live.

I was of another opinion. For me life could not be a marking of time.

His face became overcast. In general it was not cheerful, but now it had become more motionless and darker than ten years ago. Silence ensued, long and heavy, where I gathered he knew I was right, and he knew that I knew that he knew I was right. But neither of us wanted to return to the beginning of our conversation (about what's *here* and what's *there*). I now understood there was no reason for him to stay alive, no reason to live and no one to write for, and nothing to write about . . . That he hated *them*, and he slightly despised *us*. And I thought: If you are here, then talk about it loudly, do not hide what has happened to you, how you were tormented there, you a Russian writer, how you were brought to the point of despair and how you were asked to leave – make an *open* choice! No, I didn't have the courage to say this to

293

him: I was sorry for him. Exist, and be silent. This was now his tactic. But it could not be mine.

He was not alone. A second man who up to 1936 did not cast his lot with the émigrés was Vyacheslav Ivanov, the great symbolist poet. But he lived in Italy, where in calmer and more peaceful circumstances he could renew his Soviet passport every year, correspond with Gorky about granting him a pension, about a subsidy for the cure of his tubercular son, and not break all ties with Russia. In 1936 he began to publish in *Contemporary Annals*. The Moscow trials and the death of Gorky were of course paramount factors in this. Perhaps Zamiatin had no time to change: he died in 1937. He would hardly, however, have changed his views: he was an old Bolshevik, a member of the Party indeed since tsarist times. Stalin granted him six years.

There were about ten of us at his funeral. Georgy Annenkov, Marina Tsvetaeva, and Aleksey Remizov I remember; the rest have vanished from memory.

Yes, contributing to *Contemporary Annals* was in its way a sign of émigré distinction. Now, looking at these thick volumes published in Paris over twenty years, you see a literary monument and are not surprised that libraries of the Western world, aware that paper gradually turns into dust, are thinking of reprinting all seventy volumes of the quarterly. This publication, despite its editors' slim understanding of literature, and perhaps thanks to the pressure on the editorial board of the contributors themselves, became note-worthy precisely in its literary section. Of course it was neither avant-garde nor progressive and continued the tradition of the old fat Russian monthlies. But even in the absence of freedom for the majority of the authors, weighed down by the old-fashioned tastes and demands of the editors – the last representatives of Russian populism – this was the place where in the course of almost a quarter of a century significant things, the old and the new, could appear.

The admirers of Chernyshevsky and Mikhailovsky understood they had no successors, and learned to compromise, with difficulty it is true. Even the most able of the three editors, Mark Vishniak, learned something (not much) in those years of dealing with Gippius, Khodasevich, Nabokov, Tsvetaeva, and others. The financial position of the magazine was precarious; it was said that not more than ten or fifteen copies went to the Soviet Union. The rest were bought up in France, the Baltic countries, the Far East, in the U.S.A. – in fact, in the whole world. Probably in all about a thousand copies. Now some of the issues have become collectors' items. You certainly cannot buy a complete set for any amount of money.

One of the editors of *Contemporary Annals*, Ilya Fondaminsky, was the centre of a legend, but not the other two editors.* Those who lived with Fondaminsky were also part of the legend: his wife, and Vladimir Zenzinov, an S.-R. who had always been a member of the Fondaminsky family.

In his day Zenzinov was the man who let Azef, the famous double-agent, escape, but members of the S.-R. Party did not like to elaborate on this, and a kind of myth came into being in which Zenzinov stood as the embodiment of honesty, respectability, and asceticism. In fact his failures in his political as well as personal life inclined him towards gossip and some spinsterish obsessions, which his friends, fearful of examining, said was caused by solitude. In his own book *My Past* (1953), totally devoid of humour like himself, he told with open naïveté how he let Azef escape: he had been appointed by the S.-R. Party to guard him at night on the corner of the Boulevard Raspail, in Paris, but seeing that the windows in Azef's flat no longer showed light, he decided Azef had gone to bed and he went home. Azef was just waiting for this; he left comfortably by the back door and, as the saying goes, that's the last we saw of him. In those same recollections, and again with a naïveté that makes the reader uncomfortable, Zenzinov tells how in his youth he was in love with Mrs Fondaminskaya (before her marriage), but she loved his closest friend, Fondaminsky, and married him. They all lived together, the three of them, and Zenzinov at night would pace in distress past their bedroom. Friends ascribed this painful arrangement to his innocence and unselfishness.

The second part of the legend concerned Fondaminsky himself. His entourage felt that he had been in his youth (and now continued to be) handsome, sparkling, a man of exquisite intelligence, a star in

*The word 'legend' as applied to Fondaminsky I borrow from his close friend, G. Fedotov, who wrote his obituary in no. 18 of *The New Review*, New York, 1948.

the midst of his generation. In fact he was quite fat, dark, and hairy, not very clean, with eyes planted close to his nose and a constant sweet smile on his fleshy, badly shaved face. There was something false in his smile. He was very economical and since *Contemporary Annals*, like all émigré publications, had great financial difficulties, Fondaminsky created something like a 'Society of Friends of Contemporary Annals', to whom he gave tribute. The greater part of his time (when he was not writing his historical studies, signed 'Bunakov') he devoted to the collection of this tribute, principally among the generous and cultured Russian Jews (members of the White Army had not acquired the habit of reading books, and moreover every franc of theirs was accounted for). I confess I was struck when I learned from Mrs Tsetlina in New York in 1951 that Fondaminsky received from his wife's commercial interests no less than eight thousand francs a month (she, like the Tsetlins, had tea plantations in Ceylon). For a family of two or even three (together with Zenzinov), to live, keep a servant, and do a moderate amount of entertaining – that is, to live in a bourgeois way – would in those years cost about five or six thousand, even taking into account the fact that Mrs. Fondaminskaya was having spa treatments and went out to dance with paid dancers. Fondaminsky himself, it would seem, could have personally supported *Contemporary Annals* without outside aid. But then what would he have done with his time? Mrs. Tsetlina told me that the money was *not his*, that even before World War One, being a rich man, he had given away all his money to the S.-R. Party and had nothing all his life: he ate in cheap restaurants, had his hair cut in cheap barber shops, dressed badly, and lived on his wife's means.

The third part of the legend concerned Mrs. Fondaminskaya, an amiable and friendly woman. It was thought that she was unusually pretty, intelligent, and poetic. The poetic in her was really only that she did nothing while the wives of the other editors of the magazine worked as seamstresses, being paid by the hour. When she died, Fondaminsky published a miscellany in her memory, in which several of their acquaintances, members of the S.-R. Party and others, wrote their recollections of her. The main part of the book was written by Zenzinov.

Fondaminsky devoted a part of his life to the collection of the tribute, but this was not all. He organized meetings to which he invited poets, priests, and philosophers, published an Orthodox religious magazine, *The New City*, headed multiple gatherings where he spoke much and often. He also attended the Orthodox Church, though this side of his life is submerged in some secrecy. The legend developed further: it was said he was baptized (or was ready to be baptized), but wanted this to remain a secret so as not to vex his in-laws; it was also said after his wife's death in 1935 that he intended to go into a monastery. His end was tragic: when Paris was occupied by the Germans he at one time thought it not such a misfortune (his optimism at times gave an impression of paranoia). During emigration he assembled a large library, and once in 1940 I visited him to ask him if he did not want to take a part of his books to my place in the country. He looked at me distrustfully, however, and said that one German book lover who visited him informally had promised him his protection and asked him not to worry about anything. This German later took not only Fondaminsky's books but also the entire Turgenev Library, the priceless Russian library in Paris. Fondaminsky was arrested in June 1941 and perished in one of the Nazi camps. The legend continued: it was said that he had not died, but had gone to Russia 'to suffer for the Christian faith', and so on.

Splendid health, energy, free time, financial well-being, the adoration of those around him made it possible for him to devote his leisure time to good deeds. Indeed, he very often made other people's existence easier: Nabokov, on his trips to Paris, could stay in his apartment, a woman poet could have her teeth repaired – money was collected to save her from an inferiority complex. The series *Russian Poets* was published – a series of little volumes of verse of the 'younger' (and not only the younger) generation. Books by Smolensky, Kuznetsova, Ladinsky, and others were issued by *Contemporary Annals* with money collected by Fondaminsky, and he himself sold them left and right. From time to time he organized bridge games and teas at which elderly ladies, friends of his wife, played cards, allotting money to the aid of writers – Merezhkovsky, Remizov, Khodasevich.

In literature he tried, as befits the editor of a fat quarterly, to grasp 'what's being worn', in Khodasevich's expression. Khodasevich used to say: 'Is the fashion this year bouffes, pouffes, polka-dots and ruffles, or, on the contrary, are we headed for appliqués and décolletés?' Fondaminsky tried to find out why one couldn't print the verse of Z or X, though all was comprehensible in their poems which resounded sonorously with a wonderful tum-tum, while you had to print Tsvetaeva and Poplavsky, though it seemed that most of the lines were unintelligible and the verse did not resound in a familiar way. The other editor, the S.-R. Rudnev, a very dear man who in 1917 had been the mayor of Moscow (during the Provisional Government), did not even try to find out what was 'being worn'. Once, having received some verse from a poet of the 'younger' generation, he showed it to Khodasevich and asked him, perplexed, what metre it was in – one, in Rudnev's opinion, *not serious* and even *dance-like*. The poem was written in iambic trimetre. Khodasevich, returning home, stretched out, face to the wall, and said: 'That's the sort of people we depend on!'

I had known Rudnev for a long time, since the late 1920s, but suddenly, in June 1940, these business and in fact impersonal relations took an unexpected turn. Rudnev had a lady friend in Paris for many years, a relative of Mrs Fondaminskaya's, to whom he felt tied by their long-standing close relationship. On the eve of the general exodus from Paris, a day before the Germans' arrival, Rudnev came to see me and, overcoming his embarrassment and explaining the circumstances (which I had suspected like everybody else), asked me to visit Mrs. G. every now and then and write to him about her. He expected then to stay in the south of France till the end of the war. He got the assurance from me that if I were to see G. menaced by danger, I would write to him. I gave him my word.

Within a few months it was already clear to me that Mrs. G. would perish if Rudnev did not come for her. In 1940–1 it was easy to return to Paris and take someone away. When I visited Mrs. G., I found her in a kind of abnormally exalted state, wearing a tight corset, heavily powdered, with a rag in her hand, polishing her furniture continually. For me there was no doubt that Rudnev had to come to Paris and I wrote to him about it. But Rudnev could not come; he was already ill with cancer and died soon in Pau. On the tragic day of 16 July, 1942, Mrs. G. was taken and sent to Auschwitz. When his wife found my postcard among Rudnev's papers, she started a rumour saying I so liked living under the Germans that I summoned others into the occupied zone.

The third, and at one time principal, editor of *Contemporary Annals* was Mark Vishniak. This man knew that we were all aware that they understood nothing. His violent character and lack of restraint were well known. Khodasevich said that when he went to the editorial offices on the Rue de la Tour and spoke to Vishniak, he had the impression he had entered a lion's cage: whip in hand and attention sharp – lest the lion devour him!

Vishniak was a born diplomat: he knew whom to seat with whom, whom to invite with whom, whom to place first and at the end in an issue of the magazine, and how long one had to hold a manuscript without publishing it so that the author would not give himself airs. But in Vishniak, with all his boorishness, implacability, and puritanism, there was none of the unctuousness which both Fondaminsky and Rudnev had. He had a sense of reality and, despite a strong dose of provincialism, the ability to learn and a desire to know more. He also had a clear conception of what was going on in the Soviet Union, and abhorred any compromise with Stalin. He had no illusions about the politics of the Communist Party in literature – those illusions which at various times, owing to stupidity, old age and sclerosis of the brain, innocence, snobbishness, profit motive, self-interest, or the herd impulse, were upheld by some émigré politicians.

He outlived his co-editors by many years, but till advanced old age he continued to suffer from his unbearable personality, quarrelling with all his friends and fellow Party members. He was busy with rather irrelevant minutiae, such as whom one could sit with, to whom one could offer one's hand and to whom one couldn't. Much of his time was devoted to elucidating the past of his acquaintances: So-and-so was, it seems, forty years ago, a member of Komsomol! So-and-so went to Germany in 1938! So-and-so has still not publicly confessed to his Trotskyite sympathies! This sometimes gave the impression of a fixed idea against which he could not struggle.

Victorianism in the left section of Russian radicals (after Pisarev's time) comes in fact not so much from Queen Victoria as from her opposition: Edward VII, her son, though a Victorian, was in no way a puritan; the Fabians, on the other hand, founders of the English Labour Party, the first socialists, headed by Bernard Shaw, were undoubtedly puritans. So that priggish Soviet morals came to the U.S.S.R. not so much from the English queen as from the early socialists of Europe, from Proudhon with his everyday humdrum, petit-bourgeois conservatism, from the suffragettes, the radical circles of the nineteenth century who spread their priggishness from the Atlantic Ocean to the Urals. Indeed, in our times the only Frenchmen who do not use unprintable words in conversation (though now they are all printable) are the French communists!

I met Aleksandr Kerensky in Berlin in 1922. At first the S.-R.s put out the newspaper *Voice of Russia* (in Prague), then began *Days* (in Berlin), which was moved in a few years to Paris. In *Days* Aldanov and Khodasevich edited the literary page, the former prose, the latter verse, so that my first story, 'A Night of Flight', was printed in the paper by Aldanov. In Berlin, as later in Paris, meetings of the editorial board and the foremost contributors to *Days* were held, where men of letters were in the minority and members of the S.-R. (some very ancient) in the majority. They were not convinced that the newspaper needed articles on ballet (by Andrey Levinson) or poetry (Khodasevich). Kerensky dictated his editorials in a loud voice, heard in the far corners of the premises. Sometimes his editorials were published in verse.

He had — and this stayed with him until old age when he was almost completely blind — the habit of yelling at a man and thus frightening anyone unprepared for such treatment. I remember the following scene:

'Last name?'

'Ivanov.'

'First name?'

'Georgy.'

'Ah! What have you brought?'

'Verse.'

Khodasevich afterwards said he expected Kerensky suddenly to shout out:

'Show me your orders, private!'

During all this his near-sighted eyes looked over the person standing in front of him — whether man or woman — from head to foot; till you knew that he was too near-sighted to count the buttons and buttonholes on you, you were not quite yourself.

When I first met Rudnev, Khodasevich whispered into my ear:

'This is Rudnev. He made a bomb and a finger was ripped off. You see, a little finger is missing.'

When I met Kerensky, Khodasevich warned me:

'This is Kerensky. He screams terribly. He has one kidney.'

I looked intently at him: his face, known from portraits, was the same in 1922 as five years before. His crew-cut, indeed, for the forty years I have known him has not thinned out; it only became grey and then silver. The crew-cut and voice remained with him to the end, though his cheeks drooped, his spine bent over, his handwriting went from awful to completely illegible. I have kept more than a hundred letters from him, some of them typed, and even these typed letters, strange as it may seem, are also not completely legible.

He always appeared to me to be a man of little will power but great intentions, of negligible strength of conviction and mad stubbornness, of great self-assurance and limited intellect. I will allow that both the self-assurance and the stubbornness grew in him with the years, that he deliberately cultivated them in defence of himself. A man such as he, who was *killed*, in the full sense of the word, by 1917, had to build up his armour to continue to exist: beak, claws, tusks.

A politician almost never does away with himself. In France, for example, it will be shown that X is a thief, in England that Y is a seducer of under-age girls, in the U.S.A. that Z is a bribe-taker. And when you look ten years later, all three have floated again into the political arena, having waited for all to be forgotten. The short memory of people, their shiftings, the dynamics of time all help. A thief, a seducer, a bribe-taker resume life where they left it. But the President of a Republic, a Prime Minister, a high-ranking diplomat, who has made a *political* mistake? What happens to him? More often than not, exactly the same as with a politician who has made a moral mistake. Daladier returns to the National Assembly, Eden on some godforsaken island writes his memoirs. But some are hanged.

The most painful punishment for a politician is to be forgotten.

'Kerensky?'

'He is still alive?'

'It can't be! Only eighty-five?'

A Soviet girl of about thirteen once asked her mother in my

301

presence: 'Mama, was Kerensky before or after the emancipation of the serfs?'

Salt that has lost its savour – a man still physically alive but inwardly long dead. A man alone, despite children and grand-children in England, having buried all his acquaintances and contemporaries, who has gradually come to lean on the church, its rites, and with this has lost his dignity – human and masculine.

'Who is that, Kerensky? Let's go elsewhere.'

'Kerensky will be at your place tomorrow? I better come the day after.'

He liked to talk about how many miles he could do on foot (twelve, fifteen); he said he loved aeroplanes – he hoped to crash at one point; he confessed he had never been to the cinema; he was in mourning for Russia, for forty-seven years already. When he was invited, he looked into his little book: 'No, I can't, busy. Perhaps I will drop by for a short while.' In fact he was completely free, he had no place to go and few came to visit him.

But there was another side to his character: his unfortunate inflexibility, his coldness, his lack of comprehension of himself or others, his persistent frightening away of those well-disposed to him with an unending desire to bend them to his will, his unkind, tin-like glance that penetrated nowhere, and some nasty things that happened to him and about which he and those around him were ashamed.

All this I know now, in 1966, but in the 1930s and 1950s I did not see it. The history of our long relationship can be divided into three parts. First, its worldly and business period: Kerensky was the editor of a publication in which I published poems and stories, an orator at political meetings at which I was present, a guest in the salons of the Fondaminskys and Tsetlins where I was also a guest. Second, the pre-war years when he was married to Nell, with whom he had come to Longchêne. They sometimes stayed a week, and they left on the eve of the fall of Paris. Finally, the third and last period, after Nell's death: his return to Paris and our meeting in 1949, my arrival in New York and my first years in the U.S.A. Then our relations began to lose flesh and blood. In the 1960s we see each other only once or twice a year – that is, *I* see *him*. He no longer sees me and cannot read any of my letters.

In the half-dark rooms, the old-fashioned chambers of the

Simpsons' house where he lived, watched over by Japanese servants who had worked in the house from time immemorial, he wandered gropingly from his bedroom to the library to the dining room. The cataract operation had not been a success, and the first eye had been lost long ago.

Nell, like everyone who came there, loved Longchêne; she loved silent early hours, the kitchen garden where before an early dinner she picked fresh lettuce, dill, and onion; she sat between the two small houses (we called this place a terrace) where roses bloomed and, in the spring, almond trees, and shelled peas with her pretty fingers with their long and sharp nails. She was beautiful, calm, intelligent, and was always recounting something: about Australia where she was born and grew up, about Italy where she went after World War One, hoping to meet Russians there – she became infatuated with Russia after reading the diary of Marya Bashkirtseva. In Italy she met Nadezhin (grandson of the author of the old French–Russian dictionary), a singer and 'womanizer', and married him. The singer, despite his connections in London and the audition set up for him in Covent Garden, was rejected at the opera, apparently, hated work and deceived her with some crazy elderly Englishwomen who were rich and idle. Nell divorced him and he tied his fate to one of these creatures, the wife of a famous English writer, settled with her in her villa on Capri till they had used up all the resources of the villa and everything else they had.

Such was Nell's first meeting with Russians. A few years after she separated from Nadezhin, she met Aleksandr Kerensky.

She shelled beans and sliced tomatoes, and told fascinating stories about countries and people. Her shoulders and bosom were like Anna Karenina's, her eyes were always lively, and some disobedient locks curled around her ears. I did not then know English, and our conversations were carried on in French. There is a photograph where she and I are lying in tall grass, at the end of a garden, in similar cotton dresses, happily smiling at one another.

The night of their departure, two days before the fall of Paris in 1940, I was making their bed, my eyes clouded with tears. Sorting out some things in a suitcase, she demanded that I promise to come and join them any time 'if something happens', wherever she might be, and live with her 'under her wing' – she understood Russian and liked that expression. I remember my blue apron with which I wiped my eyes, the canvas shoes I stomped around the room in where guests normally stayed and, when the doors were open in the morning, swallows would fly in at the door and out through the window. Sometimes on warm nights our dog Rex would wander in through the open door and, curling up into a ball, would lie near the bed on a rug; the cat, quietly purring, would jump over him and settle on the bed. But Kerensky did not care for animals and the cat, sensing this, strove to settle near Nell's legs.

She loved our evenings, the silent starlit nights always on that terrace, among roses, under the almond tree, the quiet conversations, far-off nocturnal country sounds, the infrequent quick flight of a bat over our heads. She loved to go picking mushrooms and sit for hours under the nut tree on the little bench, looking at the woods – the same bench which three years later we swore we would never sit on again, and which later rotted.

Their car, heavily loaded down, set out at dawn on 12 June. I never saw Nell again: she died in April 1946 in Australia, where she had gone with Kerensky to her parents (her father had a furniture business), to her brothers and sisters who, as a matter of fact, had not read the diary of Marya Bashkirtseva and therefore lived peacefully in Australia without problems and anxieties. First, in Paris, his telegram came about her death, then a long, extremely emotional letter written at Easter in which he told me in intimate detail of her illness and death. He spoke of Longchêne and their last stay there in June 1940. He was lonely in Brisbane, and was stuck there for a long time because all the boats were occupied with returning troops, demobilized after the war. He had nothing in common with Nell's family, and his only solace now was religion. But he found no help in the Russian Orthodox Church of Brisbane, since, as he said, the 'priest here is a wild member of the Black Hundreds'. He planned to return to France but was under the impression that all of us then in Paris might soon be scattered around the world. This was based on the extremely pessimistic letters he had received from Vasily Maklakov, who wrote to Kerensky that the French government (which included communists at the time) could send the Russian émigrés to the Soviet Union. In a postscript to his letter to me (which he did not want me to publish in these pages), Kerensky exclaimed over Bunin's visit to the Soviet ambassador.

In October 1949 Kerensky arrived in Paris. Late at night, at the Gare des Invalides, I met him after nine years' separation.

This meeting was strange: he flew in alone, I met him alone, he had no one to stay with on the first evening, and I rented him a room in the Hotel Passy, where he was evidently unknown and no one was impressed at hearing his name. In Passy he had been very popular in the 1920s and 1930s; now there remained one place where he was still remembered: the Café des Tourelles on the corner where the Rue Alboni and the Boulevard Delessert meet. There the old waiters had called him 'monsieur le président' since 1919.

Again the crew-cut and the voice, but something more had grown numb in his eyes and his whole face; he gave the impression that he not only did not see, but did not even look. He spoke continually, agitated by his arrival, and came to see me on the following day to read me the 'History of the Illness and Death of Nell' which he had written. In Brisbane there had been such heat that she had had to be cremated less than twenty-four hours after her death. She was afraid of death, but before she had been scared of nothing except the marching German troops in June 1940, when once in Longchêne she burst into tears, saying over and over that Kerensky would be put in jail by the Germans 'like Schuschnigg'. She repeated 'like Schuschnigg' and cried. One day she asked me if there was a chance that he would sometime re-enter Moscow on a white horse. I said there was no such chance.

He was more interested in the political situation than in the fate of common friends. This was always his characteristic trait. He asked about the Russian press in Paris, about who remained here, who could do something, obviously interested in everything that could be of use in émigré politics. It was natural for him quickly to find his place in the chaos. But the 'conditions' he sought did not exist any more; there was no 'ambiance' either. There was nothing. And there was terrible destitution, intimidation, fatigue from what had been experienced, disassociation from men who had been on the side of the invaders, disassociation from those who had slandered the innocent, a differentiation between 'Soviet patriots' (often soiled by collaboration with the Germans) and us, the disbelief that our ill-fated 'statute for the stateless' would be left to us as before. Kerensky went to Germany to set up some sort of Russo-American or Americo-Russian committee. Only embarrassment for him came from this. He considered himself the sole and last legal head of the Russian state and was prepared to act in accordance with this principle, but he found no supporters of his views.

I never asked anything of him – neither then nor later, when I came to the U.S.A. I didn't even ask him for advice – and advice, incidentally, in the U.S.A. is more important than anywhere else. He did not like to give advice, and I knew this; he didn't like to deal with others' problems, others' hardships. It is possible he did not want the risk of responsibility, for in every bit of advice there is that risk. The expression 'take no risk' might appear, when applied to him, as irony. He himself was devoid of any sense of humour and of an understanding of comic predicaments, both his own and others'. In America I had a dozen 'soul-searching' conversations with him. They of course concerned his affairs, not mine.

I remember well one of the most important conversations. It was I who began it. Although difficult for me, I decided on it. I had come to know (in 1958) that, after her death in Switzerland, Ekaterina Kuskova's archives had been put in the Bibliothèque Nationale in Paris on her instructions, with the proviso that the papers relating to 1917 be published in 1987. I don't know if all of this is true. I learned also that in these papers there was an answer to the riddle of why the Russian Provisional Government in the summer of 1917 did not conclude a separate peace with Germany and insisted instead on continuing the war, so indirectly helping Lenin to come to power. The answer had to be sought in the fact of the visit to Petersburg in July 1917 of the French minister Albert Thomas, to whom the solemn promise was given that the Provisional Government would not abandon France. This oath bound the Russian ministers to the French minister as Masons. The members of the Provisional Government Tereshchenko and Nekrasov (the former was not even a member of the Duma, the latter was a member of the Duma's 'progressive bloc'), two associates of Kerensky's who remained with him to the end, belonged to the same lodge as he himself. Even when it became clear (in September 1917) that a separate peace could save the February Revolution, the Masonic oath was not violated. Kuskova, who herself belonged to Freemasonry (a rarity for a woman), evidently knew a lot.

The exact reasons why Kerensky, Tereshchenko, and Nekrasov

insisted on a continuation of the war had begun to interest me in the early 1930s, and still trouble me. I will name five people with whom in various years I had conversations about this. I heard nothing definite or factual from them, but something, especially when combined with what they said, half revealed the past to me – not enough to lead me to any historical conclusion, but enough to show firmly where the explanation can be found. These are the five: Vasily Maklakov, Aleksandr Konovalov, Aleksandr Khatisov, Nikolai Volsky, and Lidya Dan.

I spoke about this with Maklakov when we became friends (much later than the years of our mere social acquaintance). I had known him since 1925–6, had met him at Vinaver's and saw him, for about fifteen years, no more than three or four times a year. But at the beginning of the war and during the occupation of Paris by the Germans (that is in 1940–5) and in connection with the removal of the Turgenev Library to Germany, I began to drop in on him often, and right up to his arrest by the Germans I called on him at his flat on the Rue Péguy, where he lived with his sister and his old servant. Neither his brother nor sister ever married.

He, like some other former right-wing K.-D.s and 'progressivists', painfully relived his guilt and role in the Revolution. He said it had not only been unnecessary for Miliukov to give his famous speech 'Stupidity or Betrayal?' but that it had been unnecessary to murder Rasputin. Being himself a committed Mason, he of course never spoke of Masonry as such, but deeply (and probably unjustifiably) scorned those members of the lodge (in the main, Muscovite) who had become 'conspirators *already in 1915*'. I have reason to think that his notes about this are in his papers, in a part of his memoirs which, of course, could not be published.

The second person I spoke to about these matters was Konovalov. We became friends at the offices of *The Latest News*, where he was chairman of the board. I was never at his home, but he did come to mine and twice visited me in Longchêne. Our relations were warm and amiable. He told me more than once (with the understanding that he could not be serious) that he would like to see me married to his son (a professor at Cambridge University, Sergey Aleksandrovich, with whom I was distantly acquainted). Our conversations about 1917 began in the summer of 1936, when *The Latest News* printed the recollections of Aleksandr Guchkov, defence minister in the Provisional Government, who had died recently. Konovalov did not deny that he had been bound to Kerensky, Tereshchenko, and Nekrasov, and also Pavel Pereverzev, not only by common activities in the Provisional Government, but by something 'much more serious', 'important', and 'mysterious' *that had already begun in 1915.*

Now as I look back into that distant Paris émigré past, I think I made a mistake in not trying to talk face to face with General A. Spiridovich about the role of the Russian Freemasonry in the years of World War One. I knew him through Dr Golovanov, who at one time had treated Khodasevich. However biased his views and however negatively he regarded the State Duma, I could probably have learned from him at least a small portion of the truth. But, of course, in those years it was impossible for me to make contact with a man such as Spiridovich: he was a 'gendarme' and I could have nothing in common with 'gendarmes'. (Nevertheless I must confess that with another 'gendarme', M. Kuntsevich, I did have a talk; the conversation turned on the Beilis case. This was in 1931, and I asked this high official of the tsarist police who had been the initiator of the slander against Beilis: Did he, Kuntsevich, think that there was a grain of truth in the accusation? He answered me, face to face of course, that he knew that the whole affair was cooked up by the minister of justice, Shcheglovitov, and had known it from the very beginning.)

Khatisov was an old friend of my father's and an important figure in Armenia in 1917. During World War One he was the mayor of Tiflis, had known me since childhood, and in Paris was something like a 'head' of the Russian Armenians, as Maklakov was of the Russian 'stateless'. Khatisov was a Mason of the 33rd degree, and he once said to me that if I wanted to be accepted in the female lodge of the Russian Masons I should just tell him so. He also asked me if I knew what contemporary Masonry and in particular Russian Masonry were. I answered that I knew more than he thought, named for him both Russian lodges in Paris (the so-called 'right' and 'left') and also eighteen mutual acquaintances whom he saw every Thursday at the Grand Orient on the Rue Cadet (and on Tuesdays in the Grande Loge). He started to laugh and said that he, of course, was bound by an oath and could not answer me, but advised me to become a member of the female lodge and then write a *novel* about contemporary Russian Masonry.

'And how about non-contemporary Russian Masonry?' I asked him. 'How about 1915, 1916, 1917, the "progressive bloc", the State Duma, the "workers' groups", generals Alekseev and Krymov, Duma members Guchkov and Adzhemov, the ministers of the French government and their Russian friends?'

He changed the subject, but I saw I had hit the target.

Another person, whom I knew through my mother rather than my father, was Lidya Dan, née Tsederbaum, wife of F. Dan, the leader of the Mensheviks and sister of Yuly Martov, theoretician and leader of the Russian S.-D.s. As a girl my mother visited the Tsederbaum house (this was in the early 1890s). I talked to Lidya Dan in New York soon after the death of her friend Ekaterina Kuskova, and met her there three times in 1958. She was always warm towards me, at the beginning of the thirties, when I first met her, and in the late 1950s, not long before her death. Though they were not at all alike, she reminded me for some reason of the wife of Trotsky who also (for reasons unknown to me) regarded me with great tenderness and my writings with enthusiasm – the son of Victor Serge, the artist, had brought us together. Mrs. Dan in one of our last meetings told me of Kuskova's archives and named someone who 'knew about everything'. However strange it may seem, this was Ekaterina Peshkova, Gorky's first wife. She died in 1965, in Moscow. In the years before the Revolution she, as I now see it, must have been a member of the Masonic lodge together with Kuskova.

My relations with Volsky, at one time very friendly, were destroyed by a misunderstanding. After heart-to-heart conversations in the late 1940s about the present and past, a correspondence in the 1950s when I was already in New York (I have about eighty letters from him), he published his recollections of Blok and Bely, full of bile, insult, malice, and distortion. Fearing that I would break off relations with him, he stopped writing to me.

He, of course, not being entangled in the affairs of the Russian Masons and not bound by the oath of the secret society, was not tight-lipped with me. He had no doubt that a Masonic tie held Kerensky's government in a state of paralysis in the summer and autumn of 1917, that *already in 1915* this special mysterious tie had been established between ten or twelve members of the K.-D. Party (its right and left group) and some right socialists, as well as some generals of the high command; that approximately from that time on, a political plan (whose existence English and French members of friendly lodges were aware of) had been worked out and that the oath given was solemn and indissoluble. Kuskova, in Volsky's words, left some incontrovertible proof about this in her papers.

So I once asked Kerensky to explain this.

'I considered Ekaterina Dmitrievna my friend,' he answered, 'but she evidently . . .'

'But that's not the point. You have to answer, explain something about it.'

Silence.

'Perhaps all this is a lie?'

Silence.

'How much longer do you want to wait? Now there is no longer anyone alive, Tereshchenko just died. Isn't it time to speak out?'

He looked away somewhere, then suddenly began to sing the march from *Aïda* at the top of his voice.

I turned cold. He sang in a very loud baritone voice, so it could be heard through the whole house. In those moments he evidently wanted to exasperate me as he had others who, except for this singing, could sometimes get nothing out of him for days. When Kerensky had finished his march, our conversation was ended. Soon afterwards he left.

There were other 'soul-searching' conversations, when he announced that he no longer had any place to go, and I said it was time to think of organizing one's life; where, with whom, and how. I was seeing him age and lose his sight. But he either proclaimed that he would die very soon in an aeroplane crash, or said angrily that he would never be an invalid, would never go out of his mind, 'no matter what you think of me' – and 'I know you consider me senile!' Sometimes he was in a fighting mood:

'You think of me as a fool . . .'

Or:

'You always thought I understood nothing . . .'

Once, half jokingly, I said to him:

'On Stalin's night table, it turns out, the works of Machiavelli lay. On Churchill's also. Roosevelt's too. And on Napoleon's. On Bismarck's, and Disraeli's. But not on yours.'

He suddenly paled, got up, went to the corner of the room where his walking stick stood, took his hat from the rack, and went towards the door. I did not budge. When he stepped out on the stairs, I said:

'Aleksandr Fedorovich, I warn you, I will not run after you on the stairs begging you to return and asking your forgiveness.'

He went out, slamming the door so it shook the house. At one in the morning he called me on the telephone and apologized.

Suddenly he stopped hiding his age, which in any case was known to everyone. (I remember Maklakov: at his home I saw a pamphlet, published, I believe, before World War One; it was the directory of the State Duma. Facts were printed there about members of the Duma, their year of birth, and Maklakov, at the point where his year was printed, had made a little hole.) He stopped talking now about how many miles he had walked, stopped hinting that he led an intense intellectual and social life, he saw only people who were famous and had power. He became all at once an ordinary old man, quite helpless, alone, half blind, and very bitter. When I looked at him I remembered one of my uncles who had died in Paris in the 1940s from utter uselessness, saying before his death: 'Women I once courted (going to the races, drinking champagne, listening to gypsy songs) have long been grandmothers, and I am not of interest to their granddaughters.'

And so I started to visit Kerensky once or twice a year, and talked to him only about things that could be pleasant for him. I recalled cheerful happenings (it was not easy to find them). His last book, which he wrote in California, came out in 1965 and is now on the shelves of American libraries. It was hard for him to work, he said; he could not reread and correct what his secretary and translator wrote when he dictated. Scarcely any people remained around him and no 'ambiance' either. The principal interest of his life was no longer politics (it was hard for him to follow events), but vespers and Masses, fasts and communions. On this path I could not follow him. Such occupations are not for me.

Before me lies my calendar of the year 1932:

October 22.   Nabokov, in *Lat. News*, with him in a café.
October 23.   Nabokov. At Khodasevich's, then at Aldanov's.

311

October 25.   Nabokov. At Struve's lecture, then in the Café
   Danton.
October 30.   Nabokov. At Khodasevich's.
November 1. Nabokov.
November 15. Evening of reading by Nabokov.
November 22. Lunch with Nabokov at L'Ours (called for me).
November 24. At the Fondaminskys'. Nabokov read new things.

I had already heard of Nabokov in Berlin in 1922. Yuly
Aikhenvald, literary critic of the Russian newspaper *Rudder*, spoke
to Khodasevich about him as of a talented young poet. But his verse
at that time did not interest Khodasevich: it was a pale and at the
same time self-assured scanning of verse, as was written in Russia
by cultured amateurs, sounding nice and imitative, recalling no one
in particular and at the same time everyone. Here is one (1921) with
echoes of Blok:

> The black horse beneath its blue net,
> The splash of the snowstorm, the call of the snowstorm,
> Eyes burning through the hoarfrost
> And the moisture of her cloudy furs.

Pseudo–popular (1922):

> Before me, behind me, you are everywhere,
> ah, you stand everywhere, unforgotten,
> ....
> and your soul is an unharvested cornfield.

And later of course Pushkin (1927):

> Those knives and pots, and various jackets
> From nameless wardrobes here and there;
> Alone in strange positions were
> The crooked book stalls in the markets,
> Congealed, hiding scores and scores
> Of treatises on alchemic lore.

Five years later his 'University Poem' shone from *Contemporary*

312

Annals. There was not only lightness in it, but virtuosity as well; but there was still no personality. Then his first story 'Mashenka' came out; neither Khodasevich nor I read it then. Nabokov sometimes wrote criticism of verse in *Rudder.* In one review, incidentally, he mentioned my *liveliness* and spoke very sympathetically both of me and of Ladinsky as the 'hope of Russian literary Paris'. (Not long before, Aikhenvald had written a long article in the same periodical about one of my poems.)

Once, in the middle of a conversation in 1929, one of the editors of *Contemporary Annals* announced suddenly that in the coming issue of the magazine there would be a 'stupendous thing'. I remember how all pricked up their ears. Khodasevich was sceptical of this adjective; he did not have too much faith in Mark Vishniak's taste; the elder prose writers took the news with a certain discomfort. I was already publishing prose in *Contemporary Annals,* and suddenly felt a burning curiosity and very strong agitation: Indeed! If this were only the truth!

'Who?'

'Nabokov.'

Slight disappointment. Disbelief. No, this man will very likely not become 'the émigré Olesha'.*

I was the first to write in the Parisian Russian daily about Olesha (I am proud of this). It was the summer of 1927, when *Envy* was coming out in the Soviet monthly *Krasnaya Nov,* and I was writing a weekly chronicle of Soviet literature for the newspaper. It was thought that Khodasevich wrote it, but in fact I did, signing it 'Gulliver' (on Thursdays in *Renaissance*), and thus in great secrecy contributed to both competitive newspapers – which, of course, would have been quite impossible to do openly. I did this for Khodasevich, who said he was incapable of reading Soviet magazines and following the rise of new talents. This remained a secret for everyone right up to 1962, when a doctoral candidate at Harvard,† writing a dissertation on Khodasevich, told me he had learned from Professor Gleb Struve that Khodasevich, under the pseudonym 'Gulliver', wrote regular reports on Soviet literature in the newspaper *Renaissance.* I had to admit to him that Gulliver was

*Olesha, the author of *Envy,* and Nabokov were, by the way, born in the same year, 1899.

†The translator of this book.

I, but that Khodasevich, of course, edited my chronicle before printing it as his own, sometimes adding something.

So, in the summer of 1927 I read *Envy*, which made the strongest literary impression on me in many years. It was and remained for me a great event in Soviet literature, very likely even greater than Pasternak's *Waves*. Before me was a story by a young, original, talented writer, very much alive to his own time, a man who knew how to write and in a completely modern way as no one in Russia had before him, with a sense of measure and taste, knowing how to interweave drama and irony, pain and joy, and in whom literary techniques combined with the inner devices of his personal inversions in an oblique presentation of reality. He depicted people without embracing the rigid laws of 'realism', on his own plane, against the background of his own personal vision of the world, with all the freshness of a unique and original perception. I realized that Olesha was one of the few now in Russia who understood undercurrent in a text and its role in a prose work, who had a mastery of prose rhythm, grotesque fantasy, hyperbole, musical effects, and unexpected turns of the imagination. Olesha's consciousness of his goals, control over achieving them, and the exquisite balance of the novel were striking. Something had been built or created, linked not to Gladkov's *Cement*, to Gorky's *Mother* or even to Chernyshevsky's *What Can Be Done?* – but directly to Bely's *Petersburg*, *The Overcoat*, *Notes from the Underground*, the greatest works of our literature.

The summer of 1927, the issues of *Krasnaya Nov*, my lines in the chronicle on Olesha – all were lodged in my memory. A review of *Envy* also appeared a few months later in *The Latest News*. People asked Khodasevich: 'Is it true that it is so remarkable?' By that time he had read the novel and later, in 1931, under his own name, he wrote about Olesha. Khodasevich answered that the novel was undoubtedly extraordinary. We started awaiting further books from Olesha; none came out on this level, and in the *Great Soviet Encyclopaedia* (1954) he is not even mentioned. But now he has returned to life. *If it dies, it bears much fruit!*

The issue of *Contemporary Annals*, with the first chapters of Nabokov's *The Defence*, came out in 1929. I sat down to read these chapters, and read them twice. A tremendous, mature, sophisticated modern writer was before me; a great Russian writer, like a phoenix, was born from the fire and ashes of revolution and exile. Our existence from now on acquired a meaning. All my generation were justified. We were saved.

I never told Nabokov my thoughts about him. I knew him well in the 1930s when he began to visit Paris (from Berlin) and when finally, before the war, he settled there with his wife and son. I gradually got used to his manner (not acquired in the U.S.A., but always there) of not recognizing people, of addressing Ivan Ivanovich, after knowing him many years, as 'Ivan Petrovich', of calling Nina Nikolaevna 'Nina Aleksandrovna', the book of verse *In the West* 'In One's Ass',* of washing someone from the face of the earth who had been kind to him, of mocking in print a man well disposed to him (as in his review of Aldanov's *The Cave*), of taking something from a great author and then saying he had never read him. I know all that now; here, however, I am discussing his books not him. I stand at the 'dusty crossroads' and look at his 'royal procession'† with thanks and awareness that my generation (including of course myself) will live in him, and it did not disappear, did not dissolve itself between the Billancourt cemetery, Shanghai, New York, and Prague. All of us, with our entire weight, be we successful (if there are such) or unsuccessful (a round dozen), rest on him. *If Nabokov is alive, it means that I am as well!*‡

I hear someone inquiring derisively: Well, well! Why do you think that you are a participant in the whole story? Didn't you say (and with that finality of judgement that sometimes so irritated even the people who liked you) – didn't you say many times that everyone is his own man, that Pushkin, Gogol, Tolstoy, and others, not to mention the twentieth century, were their own men, and were not at all connected with the prodigious Russian people? What have you and your generation to do in all this? Was Nabokov preoccupied with redeeming his generation if he could not distinguish Ivan Ivanovich from Ivan Petrovich? And not only did not recognize him in the street but even in the Fondaminsky salon? Nabokov is very much alive and will live, indeed, but no one has

Na Zapade – Na Zadnitse.
†Blok to Vyacheslav Ivanov.
‡L. Tolstoy, 'Master and Man': '*Zhiv Nikita, znachit zhiv i ya!*'

yet said that in his shadow anyone else will survive – or among them you yourself.

And to that I reply: Yes, every man is his own man, a world, a hell, a universe, and I do not at all think that Nabokov will drag anyone with him into immortality. Some people do not deserve immortality, some people do not deserve it in his shadow, some (myself included) loved life too much to have any right to survive in the memory of posterity, loved life more than literature and fame, the feeling of being alive more than immortality, the 'half-mad ecstasy of activity' more than the results of this activity, and the path to the goal more than the goal itself. Nevertheless, in the perspective of the past and the future, Nabokov is the answer to all the doubts of the exiled, the persecuted, the insulted and the injured, the 'unnoticed' and the 'lost'!

Nabokov is the only Russian writer (both within Russia and in emigration) who belongs to the *entire* Western world (or the world in general), not Russia alone. The belonging to one specific nationality for such as he has no meaning and plays no role: native language – for Joyce, Kafka, Beckett, Ionesco, Jorge Luis Borges, and for Nabokov – has ceased to be what it was in the narrow nationalistic sense of eighty or a hundred years ago. Mere language effects related to native parlance and dialectisms that do not rest on other elements of a work are of no paramount interest and value, either for the author himself or for the reader, in modern literature.

In the last thirty years in Western literature – or rather, at its summit – there are no longer French, British, or American novels. Even earlier what was best written often became international, from Strindberg's *Confession* to Wilde's *Salomé* and from Conrad to Santayana. It is not only immediately translated into other languages, it is often printed simultaneously in two (or three) languages, and moreover it is not infrequently written in a language other than the one in which, as it were, it should have been written. In the final analysis it is incontestable that in the world there exists a minimum of *five* languages in which one can in our time express oneself to the entire Western world. In which of these languages it is done does not matter.

But Nabokov does not only *write* in a new manner, we learn from him to *read* in a new way as well. He (like some others)

316

creates a new reader. In modern literature (prose, poetry, drama) he has taught us to identify not with heroes as did our ancestors, but with the author himself, in whatever disguise he may hide from us, in whatever mask he may appear.

Let us, however, return to the basic myth of Nabokov the Expatriate, which he gradually transformed into a chain of symbols. I want now to follow this chain: it concerns the problem of poetic *creation* and the problem of *Russia* and leads by a different path to the image of 'pale fire', to the core that contains Nabokov's theme and where we find the catharsis of a whole life. 'But I have no right to speak more in detail' ('The Glory' of Nabokov, 1942), for I am not writing here a study of his work, but am only giving an outline for reflection on his myths, his basic theme, and the development of the chain of symbols.

Here are some quotations:

> The soul studied oblivion in vain:
> In a dream the problem was solved.
> ....
> What was I thinking about for so many years?
>   (1938)

> It is time. Still young, we are leaving
> With a list of still undreamed dreams,
> With a final, hardly visible Russia gleaming
> On the phosphorous rhymes of our last verse.
>   (1938)

> Let me go! I implore you!
> ....
> One who freely abandoned his homeland
> is free to howl about it on the summits,
> but now I have descended into the valley,
> and now do not dare to come near me.
> I am ready to hide for ever
> and live without a name. I am ready
> in order not to get together with you even in dreams
> to turn down all dreams.
> To drain my blood, to mutilate myself,

to not touch my most beloved books,
to exchange for any dialect
all that I have – my tongue.

(1939)

'Your poor books,' he said casually,
'Will hopelessly waste away in exile. Alas!
'These three-hundred pages of idle belles-lettres
'Will scatter . . .
'. . . Your poor books
'without soil, without path, without ditches, without threshold
'Will fall off into a void . . .'

(1942)

Verlaine had been also a teacher somewhere
In England. And what about Baudelaire,
Alone in his Belgian hell?

(1942)

From the nomadic, the idly straying ones
I crawl away.

(1943)

The last drop of Russia
has already dried up! Enough! Let's go!
But we are still trying to sign
with that crooked-beaked post-office pen.

(1943)

Insomnia, your stare is dull and ashen,
My love, forgive me this apostasy.

(1945)

When I saw in the fog
. . . .
That which I preserved
For so long . . .
. . . .
I imagine now the twittering

The Salt of the Earth

....
and the railway station,

....
And further on
All the details . . .

....
I feel like going home,
I am longing to go home.

....
I have had enough . . . May I go home?

(1951?)

Did the grey winters wash away
The unique outlines? Is the echo
All that remains of the voice? Or did we
    Arrive too late?
Only no one greets us! In the house
There is a grand piano, like a tomb on the North Pole. That's
Swallows for you! Can one believe that besides
    Ashes there could also be a thaw?

(1953)

There is a dream. It recurs like the languid
Knock of one immured. In this dream
with a pick I work in a huge hole
and find remains in the depths.

And with a lantern I light up in them
the trace of an inscription and the bareness of a worm.
'Read! Read!' – my blood cries to me:
R . . . O . . . S . . . I cannot see the letters.

(1953)

    The shadow of a Russian twig will sway
    On the marble of my hand.

(Undated, not later than 1961)

Beyond doubt all is about only one thing, is connected and fused,
and however much Nabokov assured us that a strawberry seed in

319

his tooth prevented him from enjoying life (as his namesake, another Vladimir Vladimirovich, Mayakovsky, assured us that a nail in his shoe was more nightmarish than a Goethe fantasy, and Dostoevsky's hero demanded that the world collapse if 'I have no tea to drink'), it dawned on us long before what precisely prevented him from enjoying life, and we needed no other confessions. In his Belgian hell, in his Ravenna, he remembers, and is tormented by, only one thing:

> Oh, swear to me to put in dreams your trust
> And to believe in fantasy alone!
> (*The Gift*, 1937)

I saw him for the last time at the beginning of 1940, when he lived in an ugly bare flat (in Passy), where I went to visit him. He had the grippe but was already getting better. There was hardly any furniture. He lay pale, thin, in bed, and we sat at first in his bedroom. Suddenly he got up and led me to the nursery, to his son who was then about six or seven. Toys lay on the floor, and a child of exceptional beauty and refinement crawled among them. Nabokov took a huge boxing glove and gave it to the boy, telling him to show me his art, and Mitya, having put on the glove, began with all his child's strength to beat Nabokov about the face. I saw it was painful to Nabokov but he smiled and endured it. This was training, his and the boy's. With a feeling of relief I went out of the room when it was over.

He left soon for the U.S.A. His first years in America were not easy, then he took one step, another, a third. *Lolita* was obviously begun in Paris (in Russian): Aldanov told me about it in 1939, how Nabokov read several chapters to a selected group and what these chapters were about. Then *Solus Rex* became *Pale Fire*, and *The Gift* was finally translated. In 1964 his commentary on *Eugene Onegin* (and his translation) came out, and it turned out there was nothing to compare them with: there was not and never had been anything like it, there were no standards that would help us to judge the whole thing. Nabokov himself invented the method and carried out the work in accordance with it: Pushkin was exalted and – undermined. *The Igor Tale* was translated, commented on, and questioned. He 'commented on', 'exalted', and 'undermined' himself – as is evident from the quotations from his verse of twenty-four years.

The burr of his Petersburg enunciation, the blond hair and bronzed, fine face, the thinness of the agile, dry body (sometimes dressed in a tuxedo Rachmaninov had given him, tailored, as Nabokov put it, 'in the period of the Prelude'): that is how he was in those years, before the war, in our final Paris years. He walked about as if drunk with himself and Paris. Once during a conversation of ours Nikolai Felzen was present, but I fear he was unable to insert a single word: we did not give him a chance. Another time Nabokov invited me to lunch in a Russian restaurant, we ate blinis and rejoiced in life and each other, or more exactly I rejoiced in him (this I know) and *perhaps* he rejoiced in me (though why invite me to L'Ours if he did not?). At Fondaminsky's, where he stayed when he came to Paris, we once sat for a long time in his room after a reading of his and he talked about the way he then wrote his novels (reflecting a long time, slowly accumulating, and then, all of a sudden, rushing to work for entire days, getting rid of everything inside himself, and afterwards again slowly reflecting, checking, polishing). This was the time when *The Gift* was being written.

He had begun to fill out and had started growing bald when I saw him again in New York at his last Russian reading, and he tried to appear near-sighted so as not to have to answer greetings and shake hands. He recognized me and bowed from a distance, but I am not convinced that he was bowing precisely to me: the more I think about this bow, the more it seems to me now that it was not addressed to me at all, but to the unknown bearded gentleman sitting behind me, or perhaps to one of the three fat ladies sitting in front.

PART FIVE

'Those Proud Figures on the Prows'

TWO SUBURBS OF PARIS IN ITS SOUTH-WESTERN corner merged into one: at first there was Billancourt and also Boulogne. Then it became Boulogne-Billancourt, department of the Seine – the same as Paris, of course. The word Boulogne rang out smartly: it recalled the Bois de Boulogne, suggesting it was near. In Boulogne there was a stadium, and there were races. In Billancourt there was the Renault automobile plant, a cemetery, a river, and dirty, poor, neglected blocks. People went from Paris to Boulogne along a wide green avenue, to Billancourt along a dusty ugly commercial street. In Boulogne streets were named at random, in Billancourt each street was dedicated to a figure of the working-class movement, from the Commune to our own times. There were expensive restaurants in Boulogne, and taverns, Russian and French bars in Billancourt. Lev Shestov and, for a while, Remizov lived in Boulogne; we and the Zaitsevs were in Billancourt. There were a number of suburbs where Russians lived: Berdyaev lived in Clamart, Tsvetaeva in Meudon. In Noisy, Old Believers lived, in Ozoire General Skoblin, who had kidnapped General Miller. In Asnières there was even a gypsy camp, where gypsies (who spoke Russian among themselves) lived in their covered wagons. When we began to settle in the suburbs, they still were suburbs; in a few years they became part of the city, joining Paris.

Now the city pushes people out. Then it did not let people in. In all those houses we passed, built two hundred, one hundred, or fifty years ago, there was no room for us. Old flats were passed on from father to son, from mother to daughter. They were crowded: a bathtub sometimes stood in the kitchen (more often than not there was one entrance of course), and under the tub a gas pipe ran with holes for flames, so that the water was heated in it as in a saucepan.

In other houses there were wide staircases and high ceilings, french windows from ceiling to floor. We never got a chance to go in there. Houses built at the end of the last and at the beginning of this century were in their own way luxurious, with stone balconies and a *lanterne* at the entrance; they were grey and somehow paunchy. To penetrate and settle in them you had to pay a lot of money. At that time, after World War One, they built houses differently: whole blocks of cages, seven storeys high, often without lifts, where the walls were studded with the ends of nails hammered in by your neighbour; if a nail fell out, you could see your neighbour's life through the opening. There was a long wait for these cages.

In Billancourt there was a street with Russian signs everywhere and in the spring, as in the south of Russia, it smelled of lilac, dust, and rubbish. At night (on Rue Traversière) there was noise, a din in the Russian cabaret. It was set up as a reflection of a Montmartre honky-tonk, where a gypsy chorus performed; or noise from some other night club, where Circassian dancers, with tight waists and a knife in their teeth, danced in sheepskin hats (which had then come into fashion with Parisian women and were called 'Shapska russe'). Sounds came also from another place, where Vertinsky's songs were performed (till he left for the Soviet Union), some romances of old were sung with tears, and glasses broken – by Frenchmen, Englishmen, and Americans, who learned to do it all by themselves having either heard (third-hand) of the behaviour of Mitya Karamazov, or having perhaps read about it.

In the cabaret on Rue Traversière there was a little of everything: an unemployed dzhigit in retirement did some wild Circassian squatting dance at two in the morning; a double-chinned singer with a splendid bosom, in a homemade spangled dress (who hemmed scarves during the day), approached the upright where an old cherub sat who had seen better times. She sang: 'I won't talk of my hidden sufferings' and about 'My little nook adorned with flowers', and 'The Star' (the text of which, incidentally, was taken from Innokenty Annensky). She also sang, as a gypsy song, Blok's poem 'She wanted as before', set to music probably by none other than the old cherub, and four lines of Poplavsky sprinkled into the famous 'Dark Eyes'.

Praskovya Gavrilovna would come out last. She was already near sixty. Her dark eyes still sparkled in the severe face. A frayed kerchief covered her shoulders, a flowery cotton skirt draped her thin knees. She once sang at the Yar, at the Strelna, in those glorious Moscow places; now her former colleagues were nearing the end of their singing days in Montmartre, in Montparnasse, having prepared a new generation of entertainers. Praskovya Gavrilovna no longer had a voice and wasn't good enough for the places where champagne was obligatory and 'your excellency' stood at the entrance with a beard combed in a semi-circle (he was the former governor of Perm or Irkutsk). She was good enough for this place only. Muttering rather than singing, she sometimes screeched in a whisper as she sat between two 'gypsies' (an Armenian and a Jew), who bent towards her with guitars. Yes, she was *here*, while Nastya Poliakova, Niura Masalskaya, Dora Stroeva were *there*, where there were magnificent Rumanian orchestras, fresh caviar and starched napkins.

On tables with filthy paper tablecloths stood cheap lamps with pink lamp shades, beside cracked plates, crooked forks, dull knives. You drank vodka, munched on cucumber and herring. Vodka was called 'our beloved native wine', herring was called 'mother herring'. There was a strong smell and thunder from the kitchen, blinis steamed and smoked, voices yelled out; the Crimean retreat was recalled, the evacuation to Gallipoli. The waitresses, one prettier than the next, slipped with bottles and plates among the tables. They were all 'Marya Petrovnas', 'Irochkas', 'Tanias', whom everyone had known almost since childhood, and yet after the fifth glass they seemed mysterious and accessible, like those who 'breathed perfume and mists' in someone's verse (or perhaps in a romance?) once upon a time – the devil knows where and when.

On the corner was the hairdresser's where I had my hair cut, and for me there was no tipping: 'We read your stories, we are very grateful to you, you do not scorn our way of life.' Beyond it was the children's Sunday school (near the Russian church installed in a former bistro). On Sundays children sang there in chorus, lifting up their hands, kneeling, pale and thin. The little boys were valued more highly than the girls: they were future soldiers of France and for them the parents were given French citizenship. Little girls could not help their parents to emerge from the predicament of stateless émigrés. Children burr when they pronounce the Russian *r*; Daddy is at Renault or a taxi-driver, or a waiter at La Maisonnette (near the Champs-Elysées); Mummy embroiders linen or makes hats; the older sister is a model at Chanel's; the brother is an errand boy in Pyshman's grocery store. In the summer the children would go to camp, and at sunrise gather at the tri-coloured Russian flag and sing the Lord's Prayer. Their teacher complains that they do not understand Griboedov's *Woe from Wit*, especially when it comes to old colloquialisms. One must explain every word. The teacher, also pale and skinny, seems to be the daughter of the priest, or rather the daughter of one of the priests: in Billancourt there were a number of Orthodox churches, one in the former bistro, another in a backyard in an abandoned garage, a third in an unused (for lack of clientele) old Catholic church.

A factory whistle sounds. Twenty-five thousand workers flow through wide iron gates onto the square. Every fourth man is a high-ranking officer of the White Army, military in bearing, his hands roughened by work. These are family people, obedient taxpayers and readers of the Russian daily newspapers, members of every conceivable Russian military organization who keep their regimental distinctions, Saint George Crosses and medals, epaulettes, and dirks at the bottom of what are still Russian trunks, together with faded photographs – chiefly group ones. About them it is known: (a) they are never strike instigators, (b) they rarely turn to the factory dispensary fund, for they enjoy iron health, evidently acquired as the result of training in two wars – World and Civil, and (c) they are exceptionally docile where the law and the police are concerned – crime among them is minimal. A throat-cutting was exceptional. Murder out of jealousy – one in ten years. According to statistics, counterfeiters or seducers of under-age girls – none.

I saw them at work: pouring steel into open-hearth furnaces, next to Arabs, half naked, deafened by the noise of the air hammers they handled, screwing bolts into a moving conveyor belt to the whistles of transmissions, when all around trembled and rocked and the high ceiling of the gigantic shop was not visible at all, so one had the illusion that everything trembled beneath the open sky, black and threatening, in the dead of night. But it is day, the sun pours into the square and sparkles at the very gates of Renault, on the metal carts of food vendors: one cart carries coffee and rolls, the other hot wine. The vendors shift from foot to foot and wait (a cold winter day). Now some Russian philosopher is carried past them to the cemetery. Three women step behind the coffin, the ends of their mourning veils flying in the wind. Among a dozen other men, a tiny, anonymous, Russian spectre moves that has long haunted me: he has a beard, but now no mandolin. I have noticed him since that evening when he came into the cellar of the café on the Place Saint-Michel where we were reading verse. Who was not there at one time or other! (Once even Diaghilev's librettist Boris Kokhno was there.) In the middle of all that tobacco smoke, coffee, beer, and cognac, the transparent little man, as if made of tissue paper, was also, it seems, reading poetry – in a thin small voice, pushing away from his forehead a greyish lock of hair. For some reason, it turned out, he had no surname. A pregnant Frenchwoman looks, as I do, at the philosopher's funeral. She is the daughter of the baker, and pushes a baby carriage in which two little Chinese infants sit. They are cold also. I continue to stand on the square long enough for dogs to run around the tree about eighty times.

In Pyshman's grocery store canned foods of the Kiev Worker and Peasant Food Trust are displayed: aubergine paste, stuffed peppers. Vodka and brandy of all sorts, too, 'Moskva' toffees, 'Filippov' pirozhki, and in the corner on a shelf, icons and painted wooden spoons. Madam Pyshman sits at the cash register. Every year she attends the Russian Press Ball, and always presents the buffet either with a cabbage pie or some jellied fish. The international state of affairs troubles her. She sighs and says:

'What is Stalin doing? He is killing, and killing, and killing. What is Hitler doing? He is studying at Stalin's university. He is learning to kill. He will soon get his diploma. Might not some new Jesus Christ come to stop all this?'

I sense that in her eyes the old Jesus Christ has somehow been compromised.

As a bargain in my purchase Madame Pyshman gives me toffee: she says she likes me because I am a member of the literary group and engage in artistic activity, and when she sells me groceries she feels that she herself is also partly privy to literary-artistic activity. Her husband comes out of the back room. He smiles and nods to me, but cannot say anything. He prefers to smile and keep silent: Petliura beat his hearing out of him in a pogrom.

There are customary figures: against the background of these streets, somewhere between the post office and the plant, they move day and night (or does it only seem so?) as if in circles, catching my eye. Here is a beggar, barrel-chested; the French children are frightened of him – because he speaks in such a deep bass, which no one has ever heard here before. He walks and sings something religious. He sleeps at the Salvation Army, has no shelter during the day. Twice a year he washes (at Christmas and Easter) and then sings in a choir in one of the Billancourt churches, and in the Credo, they say, emits such a G that the red bulb (a substitute for an icon-lamp) above the iconostasis shakes. Then Mademoiselle Fourreau comes; everyone knows her. She is the president of the Society of Former Frenchwomen. Such is the name of the strange union whose members consist of former governesses who have returned home to Paris after the Russian Revolution. In Paris they had no one; they had enthusiastically converted their savings in Russia of tsarist roubles into the Freedom Loan of the Provisional Government, and lost them, but it was mainly because they did not find the Paris they had known, and after two of them committed suicide because of nostalgia ('My life in Russia was one sweet unforgettable beautiful mirage,' Mademoiselle Fourreau once said in my presence), that they decided to form a society and support one another. Towards the end of the 1930s there remained no more than six or seven of them, but Mademoiselle Fourreau still ran around Billancourt on her short fat legs, until her life ended in a 1942 bombing.

Russian doctors did not have the right to work in Parisian hospitals, but old Dr Serov went daily to the Hôtel-Dieu and even on Sunday was on duty – among orderlies and nurses who put on their phonographs full blast and danced so that the whole hospital shook. Serov lived on his private practice (illegal), and worked at the hospital 'out of sheer passion', fearing all the while that someone would denounce him and he would be condemned. At one time he was very busy treating lepers. There were other 'illegal' Russians: a crazy character who gave copies of the Gospel to lepers, Russian and non-Russian (there were two Russian lepers at the height of the 'Russian dominance'), and commented on the Sermon on the Mount, and another (evidently a monk, because he walked about in an old patched cassock and a kamilavka that had lost shape and colour) who gave away nothing and explained nothing; he entertained the sick – the convalescent and the dying – and ran some of their errands, exasperating the administration of Hôtel-Dieu. He was arrested and fined, and then suddenly disappeared, and only much later (perhaps after serving in jail for his inability to pay the fine?) he turned up, on the eve of war, moving from hospitals to jails, between French and German authorities, until 1944 when the Gestapo finally clamped down on him.

There was crime, but it was insignificant. Nevertheless there were cases of murder (two out of jealousy, one for reasons of inheritance), one burglary, nineteen ordinary robberies, four cases of relatively large-scale swindling, four cases of bigamy, and so on. All this for thirty years in a population of seventy-five to eighty thousand. These statistics are approximate and of course only for those who were caught. I knew two Russian pimps (professional, not amateur) and several registered streetwalkers who in fact did not work on the streets: five of them were affiliated with night clubs and you could find about as many in bordellos (which were closed by law in the second half of the 1930s). About those who half prostituted themselves I do not speak, as I do not about those who dealt illegally in currency, kept stolen goods, or sold narcotics and contraceptives (then illegal).

The court building, in the very centre of the Cité, was at one time a place I knew well: the halls where petty criminals, fighting concierges, or drunken sailors who had thrown a bottle at a streetlamp were judged; and others where sophisticated civil lawsuits were tried; and finally those where jurors dealt with murderers threatened with the guillotine.

A mixture of horror and boredom is not so rare. At one moment your hair stands on end and an icy needle pierces your spinal column from the neck down, and a moment later your eyes stop at the hour-hand above the head of the judge and you see that dust lies on the scales of the bronze blind Themis. Dust and the seemingly motionless hour-hand, and the unchanging light on the other side of the windows: in winter it's the same at 10:00 A.M. as at 4:00 P.M. – always rain, always clouds rushing above the lead-coloured Seine, and the décor of red cloaks, moustaches, glasses, hands, wedding bands, ties, boots, police revolvers. All this is 'official', not personal, it is formal, eternal, exists all over the world, according to schedule, like a train in flat country, a schedule preserved in a fat sheaf also covered with dust. Boredom. Stupor of boredom.

Sudden horror: What are they doing to him (or her)? What are we all doing here? A moment of decision in human destiny, and we are present on the press benches during this unspeakable horror! We are participating in it! Lawyers fly here and there like butterflies, their faces intelligent, on the lips of each one a witty word; the women lawyers have clever eyes and such enchanting pensive smiles, they are like dragonflies above a lake. All this is a joke, a stage, until there is a verdict. The mixture of dull comedy (nothing changes, even dust is not wiped away) and cold shivering. A mixture of railway stupor and the last act of *Oedipus*.

Yes, it seems that everyone, even the criminal, is performing a play, that all this is not real, not true. Why? Perhaps because there are those rules of the game, nothing is spontaneous; perhaps because at the spectator entrance tickets are taken and those without a ticket are squeezed by rails into the gallery. Perhaps because everything is calculated ahead of time: when this one has to speak, when that one has to thunder, when a third must be unable to control himself or must cut himself short, or be stopped, or shout out – there are rules for everything. Far off, on an oak bench in an enclosure, a hysteric sits who stabbed his mistress with scissors. He studied in some cavalry school in Cossack country, his documents are in order: he is a night taxi-driver and now awaits what will come. He *cannot* do anything – think, decide, stand up, go, speak out, scream – he can only await the sentence, listening to the judge. Another day on the same oak bench a puffy woman with red spots on her cheeks and yellow hair sits and looks straight at me. She shot her lover. I know her. When she was sixteen she was still dressed up like a girl of ten. She had blue eyes. How she bored her lover! It must be that he had decided to leave her . . . Now she sits motionless and belongs entirely to the play that is being acted out before the public: she stands up when it's time for her to stand up, answers when she is questioned. In the hall around us words are acted out – clever, witty, of all kinds – as it's supposed to be in the theatre.

Again I am sitting in those places in that hall, now listening to the lies of Nadezhda Plevitskaya, wife of General Skoblin who had kidnapped the president of the All-Army Union, General Miller. She is dressed like a nun, leans her cheek on a fist and explains to the translator, in a peasant's Russian, 'Oh, it's very difficult for me, dear sir, to remember now what was said about this affair, for how can I, a peasant woman, understand those educated people?' In fact she speaks French tolerably well, but she is playing a role, and her lawyer is also playing a role in his attempt to rescue her. She is given fifteen years in prison. And where is Skoblin himself? They say he was shot in Soviet Russia as soon as he landed there. At this I feel horror and boredom, like two stones, weighing down on me. (Ten years later after the death of Plevitskaya in Roquette prison, her lawyer told me she summoned him to prison before her death and confessed *everything* to him – that is, that she was her husband's accomplice in the kidnapping of Miller.) Where can one run to from these games, jokes, and secrets, from the central figure who cannot rise and come off this canvas painting, who cannot step out under the greyish Paris sky where trams move, into the evening depth of liberation and solitude?

But theatricality is present not only in the courts: it is in all our *ceremonies*; I hate them even more than I hated the Christmas tree of my childhood. We have them at weddings, where they are thought to be so necessary, and at funerals, where they are the custom. There are somewhat fewer of them now than fifty years ago, but only a few. Till now a strait-jacket of decorum and conventionality has from time to time to be put on a man in what would seem his *personal* moments (or hours, or days). A strait-jacket of dead customs, when it is a man's nature to move in what, in a given moment, is at hand: ball gown, or a bearskin which sometimes might even cover two people . . . During the court recess I run downstairs, to the café, where voices of lawyers and journalists ring out, and which resembles a railway restaurant – it is panelled in wood in the old style, is uncomfortable, dark, people discuss rapidly the 'affair' – not general matters, but the affair that is being judged above. The reporter for the communist newspaper is assuring two young women lawyers that, in fact, no one kidnapped General Miller, that he simply escaped from his old wife with a young girlfriend. The old Russian journalist repeats for the tenth time:

'What has she become, my God! I remember her in a kokoshnik, in a sarafan, with beads . . . What a charmer! And her voice! "As I went to cut the sheaves . . ."'

A famous French lawyer, a handsome, well-built, greying man, author of books, friend of ministers and ambassadors, sits alone and with disgust on his face eats pastry with whipped cream. Suddenly he is surrounded: 'What do you think, maître? What is your opinion?'

He speaks his mind, picking up the cream from the plate with a spoon.

'". . . How I suffer when he leaves,"' The Russian journalist sings to himself. I am leaving. On the quay streetlamps are lit, and the trees, bare and black, lean towards the water; the stands of the booksellers are closing, a red flame flashes on the Eiffel Tower. It is visible from a distance. When planes fly from London to Paris, they see this flame. But they do not see, for example, me. No one knows me.

For a long time I walk, then ride, then walk again. In the dark streets beyond the city gates it is already night – empty, quiet. Before me walks that figure – short, indeed very short, a mandolin under his arm. At first I think: Is it night? Is it really so late? Is the lieutenant going to his job in the Alpine Rose? No. This is a special musician – he does not even play in the Alpine Rose, he is too mediocre. He plays in courtyards. And because he is so short, no one believes it when he says he is a former cuirassier of his majesty's. 'Heavens, he is mocking us! Did they really take his like into the cuirassiers under the tsar?' 'Well, perhaps not under the tsar, but under Kerensky he received a lieutenant's commission.' 'Excuse me, what cuirassiers were there during Kerensky? This one's a dwarf!' 'It seems he played in some vaudeville theatres . . .' Now he goes from courtyard to courtyard and catches the coppers that fly out of windows, and sings. I hurry to him and notice that he comes up to my shoulder. He carries his mandolin in a case. Now I walk ahead and he behind, the rain begins to fall so that the asphalt sparkles here and there. Suddenly I remember his surname:

'Konsky!'

Not Prince Volkonsky or Bolkonsky, but simply Konsky!

Five flights, five turns. And there is our door. Thin, all transparent, Konsky runs down from the sixth floor, pressing a balalaika to his chest. I will see him again several times – in the course of about fifteen years. Sometimes he will be swinging his guitar, walking in time. It will always be at dusk, not afternoon and not night-time. Then he will disappear, fade away, as a figure cut out of tissue paper flies up with the wind, as shavings soften in the rain . . . He blends with the Paris autumn mist, evaporates like a drop of Paris rain on the window, that smart and cheerful rain which falls only in Paris, an elegant rain, refined, fashionable, in galloons, ringing like bugles, waving like sleeves with jewelled cuff-links. The only rain in which all kinds of Konskys, spectres and princes, poets and destitute musicians, consort with each other. Some of them reach only to my shoulder.

Ten years together, next to and with a man, *he* and *I*, thinking of ourselves as *we*. An attempt to unite *him* and *me* when much that others have we do not, when some elements that constitute the *family* life of other people are lacking. I am constantly aware of the absence of these elements and inwardly I acknowledge the inapplicability of normal standards to our life. Above all, I see in it a complete absence of any competition between *her* and *him*, which exists almost everywhere and with everyone. Khodasevich and I are two people of one profession, but there is not and cannot be any rivalry between us, either when we are with others or alone; from the first day we met to his last moments, there could not have been for me any thought of equalling him. He is always the first, there is no doubt of that, no struggle for primacy. This is an indisputable fact of our life beyond any argument. I follow him, as women follow men in Japanese movies, and I am happy to be a step behind him. If I am given the right to express myself, I use it freely; I *vote* not asking him whom to choose, but consciously walk a step behind him.

So: a definite absence of the feminine assumption that he is the bread winner. I earn what I can, and he earns what he can: we have money in common. Not once do I think of him as a provider, and if he decides to leave *Renaissance*, where at times it is unbearable for him to work, it is only natural that all the burden of this move should fall on me. Around us, with other people, matters are different, but he and I are first of all two comrades, two friends beset by the same misfortune. Whether it is he or I, it makes no difference who earns a living. Sometimes it even seems to me proper that I should be the chief bread winner: I am stronger, healthier, younger, hardier, I can do much he cannot and endure a great deal he does not have the strength to endure. And I know how to do a lot more than he does. My constant dream: to learn to be a typesetter, to work as a linotypist. Here we are equals and I am maybe a half step ahead.

What's more: we never hurt each other. Not when we are together, not when we are among other people, not orally, not in print. All that he does is good, all that I do is good. He says in the future I will write much better than I write now. It seems to me that he believes this in all seriousness:

'In ten or fifteen years,' he says.

At these words I grow cold: Wait that long? But I cannot wait, I publish two stories every month in the paper – they have to be of a precise standard, but sometimes they don't turn out right. It can't be helped! I must try hard, otherwise we will perish.

He depends on me. I do not depend on him. We both know this, but do not speak about it. He falls ill, loses heart. He says he is drying up and cannot write verse any more. He needs someone to complain to, to pity himself aloud to, talk to about his dreams and fears. He is overwhelmed by them, and transfers them to me, but it does not enter my head or his that in this transfer there is something that should not be done and which is perhaps dangerous.

He moves off sometimes for an entire day (or a whole night) into his thoughts, and these departures remind me of his 'Elegy' (1921) verse about his soul –

> My chosen one moves
> Into its native ancient dwelling,
> And to its terrible brothers announces
> Its proud equality,
> And it will now not ever need,
> The one who in a slanting rain
> In the paths of Kronverksky garden
> Wanders in his smallness.
> And I cannot understand with my poor hearing,
> Nor grasp with my sluggish mind,
> What spirit it will become,
> In what paradise, in what hell . . .

– with its cello sound in the last four lines.

He returns 'to his smallness', that is to his home, to me, to us. He sees my passionate desire – with it I was born and with it I will die – to grow, change, mature, age. He does not like this craving in me, he likes my youth and does not want changes, he wants to brake me in my growth but he does not, he does nothing to bring this about – this is merely a desire of his, and he knows it is unrealizable, he knows he has no right to put barriers in front of me. Moreover, he knows I will, regardless, get through all barriers whether he likes it or not. I cannot be given a red or green light: I am perhaps myself a green light.

In one way or another we resolve all problems in our conversation that continues for years. Nothing is resolved by itself, by a tender conciliatory word or a minute of silence. All is talked out and resolved in reasoning, his and mine. We both *exist* and *become* in each other's eyes. We exist together and become together, each in his own way. But he likes to think and speak only of our *existence*. And I begin to understand that our – his and mine – *becoming* is one of his fears.

He fears the world, I do not. He fears the future, I rush towards it. He fears destitution (like Baudelaire in his letters to his mother) and insults (like Joyce in his letters to his wife). He is afraid of a storm, the crowd, a fire, an earthquake. He says he feels it when the earth quakes in Australia, and it's true: today it says in the papers that yesterday evening there was an earthquake at the other side of the world, and yesterday he spoke to me about it. It's all the same to me that there is an earthquake somewhere; for me, as a matter of fact, the earth is always quaking; fearing storms is for me the same as fearing a rain shower. A fire? Well then, we will take some books and papers (he his, I mine) under our arms and will go outdoors. As for the crowd, since I do not wear feathers, or fruits on my hat, or starched petticoats, I am not worried about being trampled. Why should I fear the crowd? I myself am a part of the crowd. And I do not want to be feared.

His fear is gradually transformed into hours of horror, and I notice this horror in its intensity is completely out of proportion to what brought it on. All sorts of trifles suddenly begin to acquire cosmic significance. Some devil-may-care jazz in the middle of the night on someone's radio, or the smell of fried fish coming in the open window from the yard, sends him into a despair that has

337

unlimited scope and no end. He drags it with him days and nights. It grows, and suffocates him.

He leaves, this time not for his 'terrible brothers', but for émigré editorial offices, or to have tea with some friends, or to play cards in a café, or to a literary gathering. He is increasingly defenceless in this 'wolf's life'. 'Man is a log to his fellow man,' said Remizov in his *de profundis*. Khodasevich would have said, probably, a log in motion: it rolls to shatter your arm or leg or most probably your skull, if you don't step aside. (But where? There is no place to go.) The log is, so to speak, very much in motion. I see that the fears and injuries are not always real, the majority of them being exaggerated. They only *might exist*. But the real and unreal are no longer kept apart, and the unreal is sometimes even more painful. He returns to the only spot that he has in the world – his desk, his papers, his books, his stove, and me. We have no planned and organized humdrum daily routine, but we have a roof, *domesticity*, and he loves it in his own way. I love domesticity, and to different degrees and at different times I have always loved it. In the concept of domesticity, when it is neither a 'nest' nor biological obligation, there is something warm, pleasant, and becoming to men, our own, freely chosen and built by us, in our planned poverty, in organized difficulty, something that can occasionally be shared with others (when these others enter your shaky world from their still unbuilt or crumbling one).

'How do you like that! They have an embroidered cock on the teapot!' exclaimed Bunin once as he entered our dining room. 'Who could have imagined it! Poets, as we all know, live in a ditch, and now it turns out they have a cock on the teapot!'

(The cock in *broderie anglaise* was sent to us in 1928 from Leningrad, embroidered by 'her own hands' from someone who was later exiled to Siberia – perhaps for this very cock? – for 'dealings abroad.')

In 1932, when I finally left our Billancourt apartment, a not too malicious wit recounted the circumstances:

'She cooked him enough borshch for three days, darned all the socks, and then left.'

This was almost the truth.

Slowly my fortress began to get rickety.

Once I returned home after a two-week absence (it was the spring of 1930, when I had gone for a visit to Nice) and suddenly noticed that my pig-iron nature was all set to crack. It was not life that was going to crack – that was still a long way – but I myself. 'If I crumble into pieces,' I thought, 'I will be necessary to no one, neither to myself, nor even more to him.' Suddenly it dawned on me that a human being (that is, I myself) is not a cauldron which is scoured with a crushed brick, but perhaps something finer, more brittle, more delicate. Once Virginia, in a moment of kind and tender irony, said to me: 'You are my Etruscan vase' – and how I answered her with an uproarious laugh.

I remembered the horse-comb with which Selifan curried Grandfather's horses and how I then wanted without fail to try to see if it was better to comb my own long braids (which I cut on my arrival in Paris) with this horse-comb rather than with a fine-tooth comb, as one was supposed to. I recalled the velvet cloth with which my grandfather brushed his top hat . . . I never thought I would also perhaps need a velvet cloth – though not a ground brick, a horse-comb, or a harrow (on which for so many years, as far back as I remember, I rode to my heart's content).

'And so I started to long for a little velvet cloth,' I said to myself, struck by this recollection.

But the crack appeared to me, and I looked with a mixed feeling of curiosity and surprise as it grew bigger and bigger.

I will quote a letter by Khodasevich, written to me in Nice:

18 February, 1930

. . . Today is Tuesday, morning. I received your little note, I am glad you are well, don't worry about me, my affairs are not going so badly either.

Sunday I sat home all day, and in the evening returned a hundred francs to K. and went to a café. Yesterday I was at *Contemporary Annals*. There I met the Bunins. Vera Nik. has turned into a kind of quiet smiling idiot. She announced she was intending to visit me. I said: 'Well, heavens, I'd be delighted, but now N.N. is in Nice.' 'That,' she said, 'is nothing, I want to come to visit you. When will you be at home?' Bunin reasoned with her: 'Just where are you going? Invite him to our place, he is living as a bachelor . . .' 'No, I want to go to his place!'

Oh good God! will she really come? What will I do with her?

Then I went to the Café Tabac. There Zina [Gippius] bantered gratingly, but not a word about you. She invited me to dinner on Friday. I will go. K. and the Vishniaks also invited me. But I refused. I will go only to the Merezhkovskys and on Saturday to Zhenia.

Yesterday after dinner (marvellous, home cooking is a great thing!) I rested, then took a bath (or the bath took me, which is more exact, descriptive, and somehow voluptuous), then wrote. I have written four pages in all since your departure, in the course of two days. This is normal, but today I will re-do all that I have written, and that's worse. In the evening I am going to the writers' dinner. But I will work all day, and then tomorrow all day, and the day after tomorrow, etc. . . . I took my column over on Saturday, and now I have till next Monday but one obligatory day-time chore – on Saturday at Zhenia's. It's even amusing.

Vishniak said Aldanov is planning to invite me over on Thursday; they are having a 'reception'.

There are complications with Kutepov, for today I read in the papers that Tardieu's cabinet fell. It fell because of a secondary financial issue, but *on the eve of the debate in Parliament about the Soviets*. Communists, socialists, radical socialists, and radicals have united as I foretold. You laughed at me. All were 'struck by this unexpected turn', but I was not. We shall see what will be. All these men have proven smarter than I thought: they overthrew the cabinet *on the eve* of the inquiry which, of course, is clever and shrewd.

I ordered not three but four bottles of medicine, received them yesterday, and began to take it.

Write to me about all small matters, I want to know how and what and where my Pet was, what she ate, and what she just sniffed at. Keep well, don't get tired. I don't yet miss you at all, my time is devilishly occupied. Work, housekeeping, and so on . . . I haven't played solitaire at all yet. In the whole time, I played just two hands yesterday evening . . . I kiss your hands and feet and run to post this letter and change 100 francs, because any moment now that laundress girl is coming. You must send postcards to . . ., and also to our concierge who is gushing with motherly tenderness for me.

How good you are! I pray to God for good weather in Nice. We are having a second day of frost, and last night there was snow, all white. I will not catch cold.

Write more often!

The following two letters are from the same year. In the autumn Khodasevich had gone to the Russian boarding-house at Arthies to work on *Derzhavin*.

Arthies, 29 Oct., 1930

. . . I arrived uneventfully and settled in P.'s former room, which, it turns out, is warmer. They are providing ample heat.

The room is spacious. Two tables (together longer than seven feet) are put alongside each other. Papers and books are laid out on them in an entrancing order. There are two chairs in front of the tables; I don't move the books, but change places myself. Very convenient. A lamp has been attached and shines, illuminating the whole field of action. On my right flank is a typewriter.

30 October

What a sleep I had! From ten to half-past eight. I dreamed that G. had built a shooting-gallery of live children and had shot one boy. I again saw the tsarevich Aleksey. In a word there were 'bloody boys before my eyes' [Pushkin]. This must be because I am a little worried about the weekly survey. Can you not send me two pages, hand written on Friday evening? I will receive them Sunday morning, retype them, add something from myself (I have a subject for a whole page), and send it in that very day. Ah, if only you could do this! Well, at least send it Saturday *morning*!

Write whom and what you saw as well as other things in general, or I will suddenly feel lonely. A kiss to you and the cat. Wash his ears.

3 Nov., Monday,
before supper.

. . . Yesterday I finished 'The Ministry' [a chapter from *Derzhavin*] and today sent it to Makovsky. It's now a clear day and I went for a walk. The air was so translucent that little houses were visible in the distance which were not visible in the summer. Then I read, copied some passages, made some cards for the future. After supper I hope to write about his move from his job to Shishkov's (end of chapter 8) and tomorrow set to work on Shishkov.

I still haven't shaved, but tomorrow some mama with some daughter is coming – and I have decided to make myself beautiful, so as not to frighten them. They are here for the first time: most probably, even without my beard they would be horrified. It is damp, monotonous, sort of dirty and somehow uncouth. S. is a barely tolerable man, though our friendship has by no means been clouded by anything. But to eat with him at one's table is tedious. Derzhavin, as it were, dined always at the empress's (and I am not even invited to the Tsetlins' any more).

341

After this I will go and have supper. Tomorrow I will write something more if there is anything. I can always, however, speak of my love for you, Nisya. This is an inexhaustible subject. God, how good you are! . . .

4th, Tuesday

Thanks for the money. I received three bundles of newspapers at the same time . . .

Something slowly, almost imperceptibly, began to deteriorate, to wear out, to get threadbare, at first in me, later in the course of almost two years around me, between him and me. What had been harmony slowly turned into mere habit, what had been comfort gradually began to take on the signs of automatism. Where there had been an easing of tension became mechanical, turned on and off according to desire. The measure of all things suddenly ceased to exist, or rather lost meaning and dissipated like steam. I was wrecked, and ruined everything around me; I began to fear that I would spoil what I shared with him, unaware that what we 'shared' was not what it had been even recently. Knots formed in me and I became apprehensive about thinking of them, feeling the time had come when I need no longer think, but had to act and move. I started fearing leisure hours and for the first time in my life it seemed to me that time was slowing down. Where could it move and why? Yet I wanted it to move faster and lead me to decisions. The whole life around me seemed utterly wrong: it was wrong in the morning when I drifted aimlessly from room to room (Khodasevich slept sometimes until eleven, sometimes till noon), and in the afternoon when I could neither read nor write, and finally in the evenings, which were always slightly melancholic and now became terribly sad. I remember walking around the city a lot, to distant neighbourhoods until then unknown to me, near Père Lachaise or beyond Buttes Chaumont. I had one stroll along the banks of the Saint-Martin canal and I remember it well, though I would like to forget it.

Sometimes I no longer felt alive, I felt fractured inside by all these years, this life, by all that had happened to me. 'Yes, I have suffered a fracture,' I thought, 'and now no one needs me, but mainly I don't need myself and, of course, he doesn't.' Trivial

342

things irritated me, nothings that weren't worth thinking about, which I hadn't noticed before. They irritated him also, I think, but he didn't show it. Perhaps I myself irritated him? Perhaps he saw all that was happening to me, but kept silent and waited. He thought it would *work itself out*. But nothing ever works itself out: that's the law, it seems. 'I am of no use to him as I am now,' I thought, 'nor to myself. It would be good to come to see him once a week and then all would be as before: I would again be unbroken, whole, not fractured. And I could be for him, as earlier, what he wanted me to be.'

Existence has taught me that even when nothing is happening, nothing stands still. It seems to one that nothing has happened, but the man is not what he was. The world is not immobile, it moves, today is not like yesterday, and to stop and *fix* something even in oneself is impossible. From dawn to dusk a man goes a long way. Mysterious processes are in operation; not for a moment does the appearance of new links in a chain cease, new mutations, trans-formations. I know now what I did not know then: that I cannot live my whole life with one man, cannot make him the centre of the world forever, that I cannot belong to one man forever without mutilating myself. I am not a *rock*, but a *river*; people deceive themselves by seeing me as a rock. Or it is I who deceive them and pretend that I am a rock when I am a river?

In my *inconstancy*, as I see it now in the light of my own life and the lives of other people, my contemporaries, I belong to the great majority of those living. Not all consider it necessary to confess to their inconstancy even to themselves: one knows he can change nothing and must reconcile himself to it; another is overcome by a sense of guilt; a third feels that till the right moment (if such ever presents itself) he will somehow survive; a fourth waits to change with the years; and finally, a fifth feels he is perfectly normal, that this is the process of life.

At first the crack was in me, then it appeared in our life together: it started widening. In those years we began to part – sometimes for three days, sometimes for a week, sometimes for two – and each separation showed more clearly to me that I would soon begin a new life. The separations were accidental but natural: he would go to Versailles to finish a chapter of *Derzhavin*, which was not coming easily; I went for three days to the Merezhkovskys in Thorenc, for

343

two days with Virginia at Pera–Cava; he spent two weeks at Arthies near Paris, tormented by difficulties at *Renaissance*; I returned to Paris from the Riviera (where I had stayed with Weidlé and his future wife) alone to prepare everything for his arrival . . . And each time I felt more strongly, when I was alone, the 'half-mad ecstasy' of being without him, of being solitary, free, strong, with unlimited time on my hands, life raging about me, new people waiting to be chosen by me.

When we again got together, there was no longer any meekness in me. In the evenings now he played innumerable hands of solitaire under the lamp, and sat down to work after midnight, when I was already in bed. My restlessness probably got in his way; I myself felt it spreading throughout the whole house. Having worked till about 6:00 A.M., he went to bed and woke at about two. Before then, having killed the better part of the morning with house chores and lunch, I used to leave for the library, for editorial offices, to wander, returning at about five; I cooked dinner, and afterwards left his solitaires and complaints and fears for Montparnasse, where in 1930, 1931, and 1932 about twenty people sometimes gathered at several tables placed together (not only 'younger' ones but 'elder' ones as well, like Fedotov and Zaitsev). Sometimes he too went out, to play bridge at the Café Murat, near the Porte Auteuil, and when I returned he was often still not home. Falling asleep I would hear the turn of his key in the lock, get up, give him tea, and sit with him till he went into his room and sat down at his desk.

Now I knew that I would leave him, and I knew I had to do it as quickly as possible, not wait too long, because I did not want to go *to anyone*, though if this life were to continue the day would come when I would go *to someone* and this would be many times more painful to him. I did not dare place this burden on him. I had to go to *no one* so as not to offend his pride. I was right when I thought all this out. His first question was:

'To whom?'

And that moment, as never before, I felt the great, light joy of pure conscience:

'To no one.'

But in a few days he asked again:

'To whom? To K.? To S.? To A.?'

This began to make me laugh, and I said:

'On what must I swear? Pushkin?'

In the last weeks of our life together he began to worry about my financial affairs: How did I hope to make ends meet? The accounting for my planned poverty was as follows: hotel room – 300 francs a month; food – 10 francs a day. The total – 600. These 600 francs a month I could earn at *The Latest News* with two regular feuilletons, an occasional literary column, film criticism, on Sundays typing work in the editorial offices. Well, what about shoe repairs? Laundry? Books? Clothes? 'One way or another, I will think of something.' Something will trickle to me from *Contemporary Annals*. He could not help me, but promised to leave me the literary column of 'Gulliver'. I was grateful to him for this.

I left everything in the flat as it was. I took two cases of books and my bookshelf, two suitcases of clothes, and a box of papers. Everything around remained as if nothing had happened: the cock on the teapot, furniture and curtains, the lamp and the couch, the engraving of old Petersburg I had bought in the Latin Quarter with money he had won at cards.* He stood at the open window and looked down at me as I left. I remembered how, when renting this flat, I had thought it dangerous for us to live on the fourth floor, that I never would be calm about him. But his attention had turned in another direction; on the afternoon of this day he said to me, peeping into the kitchen (where I was preparing him enough 'borshch for three days'):

'Why not switch on the gas?'

Now he stood in the wide-open window, clinging to the frame with both hands, in the pose of one crucified, in his striped pajamas.

It was the end of April 1932.

I found a room in the Hôtel des Ministères, on the Boulevard Latour-Maubourg, between the Seine and the Ecole Militaire, in a district I had always loved – its wide streets, lined with trees, were then still quiet and deserted. The Palais des Invalides was visible from my window, and on the other side the Eiffel Tower lights flashed at night. The room was on the sixth floor, and you had to climb a narrow, steep staircase; the window opened out of a sloping ceiling; behind the screen, where there was a wash basin stood a

---

*At present hanging on the wall in my home in Philadelphia.

spirit lamp on which I could brew myself tea, so that I needn't always dine on cold food. The first evening I arranged my books and hung my dresses in the closet, laid out my papers on a small, wobbly table, and fell into bed as soon at it got dark. Because of exhaustion I was numb, there was not a thought in my head, no strength at all in my body. I slept till 4:00 P.M. the following day, when he came to see how I had arranged things and took me to dinner. Returning home I again fell into bed and, having hardly managed to undress, I slept till the following evening. So three days passed, until on the fourth I awoke at the usual time at 9:00 A.M. and, looking at the ceiling of my mansard realized – in a single, all-embracing, radiantly shining instant – what I had done.

That day I walked through some gardens, sat under trees that were turning green, listened to the river flowing under bridges, in the same way the crowd was flowing over them. I wandered into the Louvre just before it closed and got lost there in the Egyptian section, where I had never been. Having heard the bell, I rushed to the exit, sat under the trees again and stood on the bridges. Then in one dash I ran back up to my place, all six flights, opened one book taken from the shelf, then another. All was mine, and I was no one's. This seemed such an improbable, fantastic, excessive joy. What would I do with it? Where would I keep it? How would I hide it?

During that hot summer in the empty city, with long stifling days and short stormy nights, I read. Starting in the morning, while still lying in bed, I would open a book and continue reading till night-time. I went out to the Champ-de-Mars and there continued to read, or sat in a café and with a cup of coffee continued my reading. My room beneath the roof was unbearably hot; it was impossible to sleep, so I continued reading at night. Of all that I then read the most precious were the greats of our age: Lawrence, Huxley, Virginia Woolf, Joyce (in translations, of course), Valéry, Claudel, Gide, Kafka, and Proust, whom I read that autumn. A book for me has always been a two-edged weapon: it disturbs me and organizes me, turns me over and puts me in place, builds. It superimposes on my eyes its picture and removes the mist. Since that year (1932) I have rarely returned to the literature of the past and have begun to love strongly all that was *ours*. About past literature Chateaubriand once expressed a remarkable idea – you

have only to substitute the nineteenth for his eighteenth century.
He said (in *Mémoires d'Outre-Tombe*):

> When I reread the majority of eighteenth-century writers, I am
> embarrassed both by the noise they made and my past delight in
> them. Perhaps language has moved forwards, or backwards, or we
> have moved in the direction of civilization, or have retreated from it
> into barbarism. Nevertheless it is quite clear to me that I find
> something threadbare, something faded, something dim, hardly
> alive, and cold in the authors who constituted the rapture of my
> adolescence. Even in the very greatest I find a lack of feeling, a
> poverty of thought and style.

I understood that year that all modern political, economic,
psychological, and personal relations could best be expressed in
modern literature by intellectual inversion and irony, if we
removed from inversion and irony their stale textbook meaning
and at the same time revealed the vital relations among people of
our century, so that through inversion and irony, using an oblique
approach, you could come near them and grasp them. In the world
there remains only man – all the descriptions of the natural world in
which he lives, the meanderings through his family affairs, all his
industrial relations have but secondary interest. Only he is important *in his modernity*, all the rest is a two-dimensional past in which
weak laws were ineffectual. To read great past literature (with a few
exceptions, which include the Greeks, Shakespeare, and Cervantes)
I must make a constant effort of historical imagination. Only
modern literature, like air, penetrates me. The new man, surrounded by modern techniques, is above all a new idea of man,
but a new idea does not come to life without a renewal of style; so it
is in the renewal of style that I take all my delight in new literature.
Our misfortune, our tragedy (of the 'younger' members of the
emigration) was precisely the absence of style, the impossibility of
renewing it because neither I nor my contemporaries could have
had style. Nabokov alone with his genius was able to bring in a
renewal of style. It was neither the problem of 'subject-matter'
('What can a writer write about away from his homeland?') that was
fatal for literature nor the problem of language ('Do you think in
French? Why don't you write in French?'). The problem of style

347

was fatal. The 'elder' writers openly confessed that they needed no renewal of style; there were ancient forms at hand, which they in one way or another would continue to use, trying not to notice their threadbare aspect. Those of the 'younger' writers who were talented could only modulate these forms. 'There can be no renewal of idea without a renewal of style,' said Chateaubriand. Neither in choice nor use of words did we bring anything new into literature.

Our *new* then could exist only in mutations of content. These mutations were expected of us by our small circle of readers, critics, and sympathizers. But mutations of content without a renewal of style were worth nothing and could not restore to life that which was in the process of coming to an end. The lack of air (absence of country, language, traditions and the struggle against them, both organized and individual) in which we lived was tragic not because there was 'nothing to write about' (obviously there were themes – European, Russian, personal), but because a style could not be created that would have expressed them. This tragedy of émigré literature is one more demonstration (if anyone needs one) that the 'content' of a work is its 'form' and 'form' is 'content'. Something at times in our eclecticism promised genuine creation or showed at least the direction it might come from, but in the end too little was achieved. I am judging here not only my generation but my very self as well, fully granting of course that in fifty years a different, much lighter sentence may be passed on this period of Russian literature.

There was also definite pressure on the part of those who expected from us a continuation of the Bunin-Shmelev-Kuprin tradition of *realism* (their term, not mine). Efforts to break away from it were understood and prized by no one. Tsvetaeva's prose – almost the best there was in those years – was not appreciated; Poplavsky was read after his death; no one liked Remizov. I myself heard Miliukov, the editor in chief of *The Latest News*, say: 'I graduated from a gymnasium, from a university, but I don't understand Tsvetaeva.' If a man does not understand something, doesn't it mean he is not suited to the place he occupies? But to this impudent remark, made behind his back in a whisper, the answer was always the same: 'A newspaper is above all a political (and commercial) affair, we only endure literature.'

Suddenly just before the war, voices rang out: What if only literature remains of this quarter of a century of exile? Even if it is rather bad, hardly alive, hardly independent, yet still expressing something, while all politics (of appeasement or of non-appeasement) are nothings which will dissipate like smoke and leave no trace? And what if 'rhymes' and 'tales' (the newspaper editor's demand was always the same: 'There has to be a plot.') live longer than the editorials of Mr Miliukov himself, than the historical thinking of Fondaminsky or the 'White ideology' of the right wing? What if the names of these politicians disappear without a trace? Where these voices first came from, I don't remember. Perhaps Khodasevich said it, perhaps Fedotov, perhaps one of the 'young' blurted out something, or a chance speaker said it at a literary panel discussion? Or maybe this question arose in the Tsetlins' drawing room as a paradox at which everyone smiled?

Almost no one had any aesthetic ideas, as if from the period of symbolism we had gone backwards, to the time when one considered that for the writing of verse 'certain techniques' were needed while prose 'wrote itself'. There were no aesthetic ideas at *Contemporary Annals*, for Fondaminsky, Rudnev and Vishniak had nothing in common with literature. There were none at *Numbers*, where some efforts were made but no terminology was found to express the basic problem: the editor lived by faith in miracles, which was natural since at that time he had fallen prey to religious fanaticism and compared his mistress to Jesus Christ, having lost all sense of proportion. But a miracle did not come to pass. The Russian God refused to help us.

I began to write prose in the mid-1920s. My first stories were printed in *Days* and in *New Home*. In these stories a complete inexperience with words is evident, but between the lines a vital imagination and an attempt at symbolizing can be found. Later, when I went to *The Latest News*, I began my cycle *Billancourt Fiestas*, which I continued for several years. This was a lyrico-ironical series of stories about Billancourt-Russian indigents, drunks, patresfamilias, Renault workers, courtyard singers, déclassé eccentrics. There was a story about a twelve-year-old girl who had adopted someone else's child; about a former countess who stood on Sunday on the parvis of the Orthodox cathedral; about generals who waited on tables in restaurants and barrel-chested colonels who at night were taxi drivers and by day wrote their memoirs about mistakes in Wrangel's retreat. The stories were uneven, some were written in a hurry for money, with low-level results, but at least half of them were very much to the point, although there were traces in them of Gogol, Zoshchenko, Dostoevsky, early Chekhov – and, of course, of myself seeking the local parlance, a plot with a lyrico-comic side, and human tears that were more like the drop-formations on a piece of Edam cheese than the dew on a rose petal.

These stories had a great success. *The Latest News* came out then in thirty or thirty-five thousand copies daily. Literally everyone, and not only in Paris, read it. Everyone knew me. Madame Pyshman strove to put a can of preserves in my shopping bag, the Russian shoemaker put on new soles for me free, when we arrived in Longchêne the movers (they were Russian) refused to take a tip. At public readings I was recognized, and once, in a subway train at night, all heads turned towards me: about thirty Russians were going home (to Billancourt, of course) from a Russian celebration and I heard my name pronounced in a whisper.

In *Contemporary Annals* I published stories. These were at first imitative, as was my first novel, which received quite a few favourable notices. In those years Dostoevsky overwhelmed me. I emerged from his influence only to lower myself into 'lighter' literature, as it were, 'to spite him'. My second novel, and in part my third, were a reaction to this dominance, yet by the middle of the 1930s I began to understand that the most suitable form for me was the long short story. In my book (six stories) my best pieces of the thirties and forties are collected (1948). Bunin told me that he had made lots of notes in the margins of his issue of *Contemporary Annals* about my story 'The Waiter and the Slut', and promised to show them to me sometime. Where is this copy? In what archive? In what basement of a secondhand book dealer?

Books were then issued in printings of eight to fifteen hundred copies. Bunin was published in 1,500 copies, my stories in 1,000. A play in the Russian theatre played ten or twelve times at the most (plays by Teffi and Aldanov); my comedy *Madame* in 1938 played four times. Once meant a failure, twice a small success. In their youth actors were coached in the Method. The public wanted a realistic theatre, it dreamt of seeing on the stage people drinking tea from a samovar, but Nabokov gave it *The Event* and *The Waltz*

Invention (where Waltz turned out to be not a dance but a man and one of the female roles was written in verse). When, at the end of my play, part of the cast of characters doubted the existence of the other, no one understood it and an old actress of the Moscow Arts Theatre, Germanova, even found that it had been written 'not without Leonid Andreev'. As a matter of fact, I could never forget the adaptation of *The Brothers Karamazov* where she acted Grushenka and Madame Insarova played Katya: on the stage they both looked as if they were grandmothers of Dostoevsky heroines, or as if they were *the very same* Grushenka and Katya who were young in the 1880s and now were still alive.

The old theatre critic of *The Latest News* was kind in his critique of my play. I came out onto the stage when summoned, and even received flowers. On the other hand the *Renaissance* critic (with whom I had never been on speaking terms), author of *Autumn Violins*, a hit at the Moscow Arts Theatre in its time, lectured me on my lack of *realism*.

Two intelligentsias made the Russian renaissance of the twentieth century. One was more or less ignorant in politics (in any case, did not read Lenin); these were the greater poets and prose writers, artists, composers, men of the theatre, the avant-garde. The other was active in one or another revolutionary movement. This second one imposed on the first criteria by which to judge Russian history and reality. The first did not succeed in imposing on the second its aesthetic standards. Their aims were different and the spirit was different too: the first, despite all its deviations, depended on Europe and the West, the second, despite its dependence on Marx and Engels, was closely bound up with traditional Russian characteristics. That is how I picture the first quarter of our century.

In my verse as in my prose there was then that *half form* which can be found in the verse of almost all my contemporaries of those years. So I did not bring out a collection of my verse before 1984. In Russian poetry no one among émigré poets of the 'younger' generation, even Nabokov, could do anything within the limits of the old prosody (which someday has to be destroyed or Russian poetry will have no future). Sensing this much later, after a twenty-year interruption, I switched to blank verse.

A link with Russia's past in those years meant to me less than a link with present-day Russia. Gradually its revolutionary façade changed: Trotsky was removed, then exiled. Gorky returned to the U.S.S.R., and was moved by all that he saw, deprived of the gift of foreseeing the near future, his and Russian literature's, or, as was his wont, closing his eyes to the future. He died and in thirty years the mystery of his death has only thickened: there is no mention of it anywhere, just dates of his illness and funeral! Then writers began to disappear: in Moscow and Leningrad magazines, dozens of names vanished, while on every page the name appeared of the man later the centre of the so-called 'cult of personality'. For me there always was and is now something deeply nauseating in any 'cult', in fanaticism in any form. Fanaticism seems to me the most terrible, mad, demeaning, and dangerous feature in man. It also brings out in me a physiological reaction: I feel all its perversity, it contradicts my nature, my belly rejects it, and my whole body reacts to it with *nausea*. It makes me feel ill and I know it is not only repellent but unnatural: this touchstone of physiological reaction has still never let me down.

Some returned to the U.S.S.R. in those years: the painter Ivan Bilibin, Natasha Serova, the sister of the actor, Elena Sofronit-skaya, Prokofiev, later Kuprin, still later Tsvetaeva. All of them were people who were counting on a happier life there, not materially but personally and perhaps creatively. The departure of Sergey Prokofiev happened without my noticing it. When he had visited the U.S.A. he had said more than once: 'There is no room for me here while Rachmaninov is alive, and he will live another ten or fifteen years. Europe is not enough for me and I do not wish to be second in America.' Thus he made his decision.

I saw Marina Tsvetaeva for the last time in the autumn of 1938 at the funeral of Prince Volkonsky, at the moment his coffin was being carried out of the church (on the Rue François Gérard). She stood at the entrance, her eyes full of tears, aged, almost grey, hands crossed on her bosom. This was soon after the murder of Ignace Reiss in which her husband, Efron, was implicated. She stood as if infected with plague: no one approached her. Like everyone else I walked by her. In June 1939 she left for the U.S.S.R.

In those years, in connection with the departure for the U.S.S.R. of some political émigrés, many of us, including myself, asked ourselves the question: What exactly prevents us from accepting the

Soviet regime? Men of letters were prevented above all by the politics of the Communist Party in literary affairs. Now after thirty years, when the rehabilitation of writers illegally repressed is in full swing in Russia, it is clear to everyone what was in store for those who, on returning, would have tried to *speak out aloud*. No one had ever had any illusions. But another idea dawned on some of us: What if we renounced literature and returned home to become white-collar workers in the provinces, or 'cultural workers' in Siberia, or, after being lumberjacks for several years, tried to go back to professional work? There was only one answer: Stalin. Personally I can say that in the course of twenty-five years there was not a day when I did not feel his presence in the world, did not feel hatred, revulsion, degradation, and fear in pronouncing this name. In March 1953, if not in everything at least to a great extent, my feeling for the Soviet regime changed.

A relationship is of course a two-sided phenomenon, and thus I did not have and could not have had any relationship with Soviet literature, but there was my (one-sided) knowledge of it, my constant digging into it, my interest in it, in its poetry, prose, literary polemics, its Congress of 1934, in the small figures who crawled up the stairs and the great ones who were thrown into oblivion. All that was even slightly valuable from them reached us. Nothing reached them from our side, however, if you do not take into account the samples of émigré publications brought to the Soviet state for information and buried in some archive accessible to practically no one.

Between the U.S.S.R. and the great figures of old Russia who gradually passed away, between our own miseries and the stone countenance of modern France, we lived almost two decades. I say 'we' because, despite our not having any genuine ties, any common activity, work, or ideas, I cannot tear myself away from my generation. I am not valuing myself so highly as to separate myself once and for all from everyone else and, on the other hand, I am not a Philistine who trembles behind his own four walls, having locked his door not only against robbers but against neighbours. I never felt and do not feel the urge for collective experience and public outpouring of feelings, but I also know what *esprit de corps* means. Collectivity in all its aspects is alien to me: I would sooner take up a murderous job alone than an easier one collectively, though at the same time I know I am bound by the laws of space and time to people of the same fate. Collective searches for culture (that characteristic Russian occurrence) and collective searches for answers to 'accursed' questions do not tempt me. I resolved my problems as best I could and can say that I hide my solutions from no one.

The stone countenance of post-war France that faced us was made up of dadaists, surrealists, abstractionists who were starting and cubists who were ending their careers, poets who had long written in free (and, of course, blank) verse, who looked on Moscow as the patron of modernism, greedily grabbing up French translations of Mayakovsky, of factory novels, the plays of Seyfullina and others, the films of Eisenstein, the 'permanent revolution' of Trotsky. They could not grasp, however, why Stravinsky was not *there* but *here*, why Diaghilev died in debt in Venice when he surely should have been given the post of director of Soviet theatres, why Ehrenburg did not reprint his old books. They understood the old generation of émigrés in this way: people who had lost liquid funds, an estate, a warm little nook, that's why they were here. Merezhkovsky could have been a governor (the majority of French writers had two professions), Bunin a banker, Balmont could have commanded a regiment of the guards. All this was clear. But where did these individuals come from who in the year of the Revolution were fifteen, or even ten years old? Maybe their fathers were grand dukes? In that case so much the worse for them!

The 1930s were the epoch of depression, world economic crisis, the rise of Hitler, the Ethiopian war, the Spanish war, the 'cult of personality' in the Soviet Union, disarmament of some and armament of others. A frightful time, a desperate time. Whether you yelled or not no one responded, no one answered; something had started rolling and it rolled. Not just when I now look back, but even then it was already clear that the present was not only menacing but mad, that people were not just condemned but doomed. But as I said in another part of this story: What business had the world with the universal Akaky Akakieviches? 'Quieter than the water, lower than the grass . . .' (Blok). We were bewildered, brow-beaten, at the end of our wits; we were not given citizenship, but in the war to come we were to be sent into the trenches. We felt as if we were to blame for everything that was happening and bore the responsibility for all that was going on: for the rise of Hitler, for Stalin, for the French president being killed. By whom? By a Russian, of course, a Russian émigré who had recently been released from a madhouse and wished to attract the attention of the world to his miserable condition. (We were told, what's more, that he wrote some sort of verse!) So we were now to blame for this. Who if not us? We would be kicked out of every place . . . A Russian reporter comes pale to the office of his paper: 'Father, all has collapsed, all that we have done here for ten years, all has gone to the dogs.'

On the following day a nameless cossack, '*un cosaque russe*', an émigré and valiant son of the quiet Don and of the White Army, throws himself out of a window: ashamed before the neighbours, though it was not he who killed the president.

At the funeral the widow, a Frenchwoman, sobs, the children cry, the church is full of people. This death, this funeral is a caricature, an ironic reflection of reality in the émigré psyche, deformed by fear, debasements, destitution, and rejection. The collective experience of collective guilt, so dear to the Russian heart.

'How we get on all their *nerves*,' says Ladinsky. 'Christ! how they are fed up with us! If I were in their place I would long ago have chased all the émigrés to the Sandwich Islands, with all their claims to unemployment benefits, to free education of children, to old-age pensions. You'll see: when war comes . . .'

This is now his story's refrain.

'When war comes . . .' Khodasevich also says; I now meet him about twice a week: he comes to my place, we dine and later until night-time play Russian billiards in the corner bistro. Or I go to his place and we breakfast there. Or we meet not far from the offices of *Renaissance* in the basement of the Café George V. Then I accompany him, or take a long walk through the streets. As before, he goes to bed at dawn.

I will quote excerpts from two of his letters to me at this time:

26 August, 1932
. . . I arrived here yesterday. I have a room in the country, but near the boarding house, better than the one we stayed in at Arthies. There is even a mirrored closet, and the bed has a canopy, which hangs down

355

slightly at an angle. It's clean. The park turned out to be a garden. After Arthies it looks like Deauville. There are even luxurious women in demonic pajamas – and, as a matter of fact, very nice-looking. The guests look 90% smarter than those in Arthies and 95% younger. This is comforting. No one has heard of *Renaissance*, many have heard of *The Latest News* but only the K.s subscribe to it. The rest either read nothing or read *Matin* and *Journal*. Today one woman (without pajamas) offered another (in pajamas) a book. The latter answered: 'I am not yet an old woman, why should I read books?' One female read a Russian book not long ago, about three years back. A very good little book, a Bolshevik opus, but funny –about some dozen chairs. All this I report to you because I have touched upon the 'reading masses' and share the information.

Write to me about Paris and yourself. In our last rendezvous you were kind and comforting. Write also about the cat–how did you find it and what has it become? It's very restful for me here, Good God! What joy – to write nothing and not think of the next feuilleton! . . .

Spring 1933

. . . I received your letter only now, on the 2nd, at night. Thanks for the voice of sincerity–it sounds really friendly. I will answer you with the same openness . . . What I know about you I know from you and only from you. Do you really think that I can gossip about you with fools? . . . Let's suppose that in the papers tomorrow it is printed that you do this or that. What right have I to prescribe this conduct or some other to you? Or control it? I am not dissatisfied with your *behaviour*. I said to Asya that I am grieved by your insane gullibility, your attraction to people who are worth nothing (*of both sexes, without any infatuation*) and your impetuous tossing about among people. This was always in you, I always told you that, and now, finding yourself alone, simply rising to a kind of ecstasy, now flying, now diving, you swim in the thick of people. This, in my opinion, makes you squander yourself to small purpose–God grant that I am wrong. This and only this is what I reproach you for. You must agree that this is not a matter of behaviour and does not lie in the same domain . . .

My dear one, nothing in any way can change all that is great and important that I have in my relationship with you. As it was, so it will be: you know only too well how I acted with people who dealt with you in an ugly way or tried to drive a wedge between us. So it will remain and those people who want to get along well with me must be proper and kind in their relations with you. I am not and was not reticent on this score with anyone.

356

Please, don't be angry for what I have written about your squandering yourself. I mentioned this only to explain the subject of my conversation with Asya (about your relations with people I have spoken with her a thousand times on the Rue des Quatre Cheminées, sometimes in your presence, and both of us scolded you to your face and behind your back: what reason have I to be cautious with Asya?) . . .

In a word I hope that our little tiff (or what should we call it?) will be remedied. On Saturday I will come to Les Trois Obus at 3:30. There I will tell you of my plans for the winter. Prospects are fairly good, but for the time being creditors are devouring and torturing me. Worst of all is the tax inspector (it was 2,000, I paid 1,000 – again it has become 2,000) and G., from whom I borrowed 1,000 in the autumn. He deducts 250 from my pay every two weeks. Having paid, I borrow again – and everything starts again! Well, this is nonsense. Keep well. I am going to bed – it will soon be 4 A.M. I kiss your hand.

Once in the morning Khodasevich knocked at my door. He had come to ask for the last time if I would return. If I would not, he had decided to get married, he no longer had the strength to live alone.

I rush about the room, hiding from him my happy face: he would no longer be alone, he is saved! And I am too!

I pester him, and joke, and play with him, I call him 'fiancé', but he is serious: this is an important moment in his life (and in mine!). Now I can think about my future; he will accept it calmly.

I kiss his dear, bony face, his hands. He kisses me and because of excitement cannot say a single word. 'Just wait,' I say to him, 'I will also marry, and we will start life . . . You cannot imagine how all four of us will start living!'

Finally he laughs through his tears, he guesses whom I am ready to marry and I, without asking, know whom he is marrying.

'When?'

'Today in the afternoon.'

I chase him out saying that she will run away. He leaves.

Olga Margolina came into our life in the winter of 1931–2. She lived with her sister. She was then about forty years old, but she looked much younger. She had big grey-blue eyes and marvellous smooth white teeth which made her smile unusually attractive. Later, when she lived with us in Longchêne during the war, I teased her:

'What a poor dentist our Olenka has! He gives her a set of dentures and it's at once obvious that they're porcelain! She should tell him . . .'

Olga was small in height, spoke softly and walked softly. She once told me how, as a girl of about fourteen, one evening, she dropped into some church accidentally. It was between Moika and the Ekaterinsky Canal. She was living and studying in Petersburg. In the church candles burned, a service was in progress and people were praying. In this church she experienced some special feeling of humbling and uplift for several unforgettable minutes, which changed her for ever: she became different altogether, unlike her two older sisters, her brothers, or anyone else around. She became very sweet and very gentle.

'And you see: I didn't marry in my day and, in general, everything somehow did not work out in an ordinary way.'

The ordinary way meant, as it happened, with people of her milieu, bourgeois, all of a pattern, who lead a family life.

Her family was wealthy, her father a jeweller. They lived in their own house and what always struck me was that in Petersburg they had their own cow! I had never heard of anyone in Petersburg who had his own cow. Olga was taken to the gymnasium in their own carriage and horses, beautifully harnessed in pairs. Then they lived in Switzerland, just lived, not doing anything. They played tennis and danced. But she played tennis badly and didn't like to dance.

Now she knitted caps and bonnets and earned her living that way. When I left Khodasevich she started to visit him from time to time to help him.

I remember when I was with her I had the feeling that I was an elephant who had entered a china shop and was aware that I could crush everything around, including the proprietor of the shop himself. You had to be careful because she was not at all like the majority of people around. She believed in God. She gradually came to the conviction that she had to be baptized. She said there was nothing for a woman to do in the Jewish religion, there was no room for her. The Jewish faith was a man's faith. There is, however, one God, because obviously there cannot be two Gods, or five, or ten. I remembered the elephant and kept silent: with a careless movement here I could trample something, spoil it, destroy it.

Khodasevich and Olga lived together six years, and the last year during his long illness, the year of Munich and the annexation of Czechoslovakia, they both came to Longchêne for several lengthy visits. That time he could hardly come out into the garden, remaining the entire day in an armchair on the patio. N. did everything to make them comfortable at our place. He liked Olga a lot.

Khodasevich's last letters show his mood at the end of his life. Here are two of them:

21 June, 1937

. . . In fact my utmost disenchantment with the emigration (with its 'spiritual leaders', with few exceptions) I no longer conceal. In fact, I learnt about Kuprin's impending departure [to the U.S.S.R.] about three weeks ago. From this the representatives of the élite have concluded I will also leave.* Alas, there is no real basis for this rumour. I have taken no decisive steps – I don't even know in what these consist. The main thing is that I don't even know how they would look on such steps in Moscow (though I'm secretly convinced that if they took into account many important circumstances, they would have to regard them positively). Quietly, however, like Kuprin (who has fallen into senility) I would not go, I would without fail slam doors loud and often so you would hear.

I sit at home or play cards. Literature fills me with loathing, now both the older and the younger. I conserve remains of tenderness towards Smolensky and Sirin.† There are two items of news: F., it seems, is changing direction and returning to his spiritual homeland – i.e., leaving literature for the already paved way, the stock market. A. yesterday married a rich and unattractive lady musician. They furnished their flat and the newly-weds went to the mountains. In a word, all is evolving in its natural order.

I heard about your little dog. I'm sorry I can't be introduced to him, but it would cost me 50 for the trip. If you are in Paris let me know and we will see each other.

'Paris-Shanghai'‡ published the contents of the first issue. Poor. Besides there are signs that these *Annals* will turn towards China as *Contemporaries* was turned towards Czechoslovakia . . . Probably

---

*There was a rumour that Khodasevich was preparing to return to the Soviet Union. – N. B.
†The pen name of V. Nabokov in the 1920s and 1930s. – N. B.
‡The magazine *Russian Annals*. The publisher lived in Shanghai. – N. B.

there will be articles about the jubilee of some Fun-Tiun-Tiun and the world view of Chiang Kai-shek, to Masaryk's envy! You are mistaken – Fondaminsky is still considered intelligent.

I saw Madame P.; it reminded me of youth (mine) and old age (hers). She was walking arm in arm with Misha Struve and speaking about Akhmatova, as old generals in the time of Nicholas I spoke about Catherine.

Ziuzya* married an Englishman. She will live near Birmingham, the English Hollywood. I fear she will become Hollywoodish, but for the time being she is satisfied. In the final analysis you sealed her fate, that's funny.

What horrors Bunin is writing about Tolstoy! . . .

X., in fact, does not radiate intelligence. But do not kick her too much. I assure you one must ask intelligence only from professionals, and besides that, all people are better than writers.

Good grief! I almost forgot! I enclose a letter sent to me through *Renaissance*. I opened it and had just begun to read when I saw on the envelope 'Mlle Berberoff'. Forgive me, please. Forgive me also that the subjects in this letter (that is, mine) are shuffled somehow idiotically. But today I finished an article, drove to town, read three French papers (about Léon Blum), and now it is 2:00 A.M., I am tired, it's time to sleep.

Keep well. Olga kisses you. My greetings to N. I bless the little dog. Try to teach him good behaviour in his childhood.

21 May, 1938

I send you, my dear, my article of yesterday.† Tomorrow I must set to work on the next. I will probably write about Boris Nikolaevich,‡ but I haven't yet decided. I borrowed the book from Fondaminsky, but I read a page an hour: I haven't the strength, what horrible, sad lying! So that perhaps I may not start writing: just give it up.

We ate at X.'s. It was deadly. One useful thing came of it: some driver said that you shouldn't plant horse-radish with other vegetables. You must do it separately and in a far corner. For that beast of horseradish is prolific, its roots will dig into the ground and crawl out where you don't expect it, so that soon all around will be killed, and the whole garden will become (how terrible to think of it!) a horseradish garden. This is terrifically important for you.

*Olga's niece, Melita Thorneloe, born Livshitz. – N. B.
†About my new book. – N. B.
‡About the three volumes of Andrey Bely's memoirs. – N. B.

Having just returned to the city, we realized how wonderful things are at your place. Only by staying at X.'s did we understand how good it is at home. Having gone to Montparnasse this evening we regretted not staying at X.'s. Well, judge for yourself how everything is hereabouts.

Keep well, please.

I will call you in a few days.

I will quote my notes, made in June 1939 (the 13th to the 23rd), on the illness and death of Khodasevich:

He took sick at the end of January 1939. The diagnosis was in part correct, but the treatment was cruel and coarse. At the end of February he was in Longchêne. He was all right. If I were to stay here with you, he said later, I would get better. He said the country would cure him and I began to look for a room for him for the summer somewhere near by.

Towards the end of March pains began, he became very thin, suffered terribly. He had pains in the intestine and the spine. We feared it was cancer of the intestine.

All of April he suffered cruelly and grew thin (he lost 25 lbs.). Sometimes a doctor who lived in the neighbourhood would come at night to inject morphine. After this he was delirious. There were three subjects in his delirium: Andrey Bely (meeting with him), the Bolsheviks (they were persecuting him), and I (anxiety about how I was). Once at night he screamed and cried terribly: he dreamt that I had been blinded in an automobile accident.*

I came twice a week, but his nerves remained in a terrible state of depression. There were days of continual tears (of kindness, self-pity, anxiety). The wallpaper in the room was olive, ashen, the blanket green. Poor, coarse sheets, narrow bed (really a couch). On it he lay, emaciated, long-haired, still smoking a lot. In May he had a bilious attack. His complexion became terrible, from yellow to brownish-green (which was a bad sign). Anguish, torment, horror were in his face. He did not sleep at all. He didn't know this might be cancer and didn't actually suspect that he was so seriously ill.

*That year I was learning to drive.

The doctors said it was necessary to treat him for two weeks in a hospital and make all the possible tests that would help in establishing a diagnosis. He was taken to the Brousset municipal hospital. It was horrible there: it's impossible to imagine that such a hell on earth can exist.

Visitors were allowed from 1:00 to 2:00 P.M. We all stood with little bundles (parcels, as in front of a prison) at the gates. At exactly 1:00 P.M. the gates flew open, all ran wherever they had to go, so as not to lose precious time. He lay in a glass cage, curtained off from the other neighbouring wards by sheets. A bright, hot sun shone in the cage; there was nowhere to turn. Hungry to the point of trembling, he attacked what was brought to him (the food was bad in the hospital, and he ate almost nothing there); he joked about himself, and then suddenly lay down, moaned, sometimes cried.

The bed was hard; a second pillow was obtained with great difficulty; hospital linen and a severe prison-like blanket; and outside, June days which somehow forced their way into the room. He said:

'Tonight I hated everyone. All were foreign to me. Anyone who has not lain on this bed as I have all these nights, has not slept, been tormented, or lived through these hours, is no one to me, is alien to me. Only someone who, like me, has endured this penal servitude is my brother.' Towards the end of the second week it was shown that he had neither a tumour nor stones in the gall bladder, so the idea of liver thrombosis had to be abandoned. No cancer of the pancreas came to light or was felt (as the doctors put it). It was decided to operate. Why? To become convinced and probably speed up his end.

He returned to his flat, even darker and thinner, overgrown with half-grey shaggy hair. He was happy at my coming, said that the operation was on Tuesday. He didn't think it would be death, he didn't believe in recovery – he himself didn't know what to think, only a shadow now remained of him.

For some moments he lay flat on his back and silently stared straight ahead with dark-yellow, greenish eyes. Inwardly something tormented him and he was on the point of tears. N. and Olga went out into Olga's room. I remained with him. This was on Friday, June 9th, at 2:00 P.M. I knew (and he knew) that we would not see each other again before the operation.

'To be somewhere,' he said, tears pouring, 'and to know nothing of you!'

I wanted to say something to him, to comfort him, but he continued:

'I know I am only an obstacle in your life . . . But to be somewhere, in a spot where I would never again know anything about you! . . . Only about you . . . Only about you . . . I love only you . . . All the time about you, day and night about you alone . . . You know . . . How will I be without you? . . . Where will I be? . . . It doesn't make any difference. Only you be happy and well, drive slowly. Now farewell.'

I approached him. He started crossing my face and hands, I kissed his wrinkled yellow brow, he kissed my hands, covering them with tears. I embraced him. He had such thin, pointed shoulders.

'Farewell, farewell,' he said, 'be happy. May God preserve you.'

I went out into the hall. Then I returned to his room. He was sitting on the bed, his head having fallen onto his hands.

On Sunday, June 11th, N. called on him and let him know that he would be operated on not in the Brousset municipal hospital but in a private clinic. His sister had arranged this. On Monday he was carried there, and at three on Tuesday the 13th he was operated on.

Many of his kind friends helped him financially; some sent him money through a so-called 'committee' for him, some came to him and simply gave it to him. His sister did more than anyone else for him. Unfortunately it was too late.

'If the operation is not successful,' he said on that last Friday, '*it* will nevertheless be rest.'

On Sunday he told N. he would not survive it and they blessed each other.

The operation lasted an hour and a half. The surgeon emerging after it was over, trembling and perspiring, said he had no doubt that it was cancer, but that he had not managed to reach it. He said he had no more than twenty-four hours to live and that he would suffer no more. Right there he gave Olga two stones he had extracted (which the X-rays had not shown!). N. summoned me to Paris and at 7:00 P.M. I entered the ward where he lay.

The nurse said: 'He must not suffer.' At nine we left. A sort of numbness came over me. We spent the night in a hotel.

At 7:30 A.M. we were already at the clinic (June 14th). He had died at 6:00 A.M., without regaining consciousness. Before his death he held out his right hand in some direction ('and a flower trembled in it,' as he once wrote), moaned deliriously. Suddenly Olga called out to him. He opened his eyes and smiled slightly to her. In a few minutes all was over. In the evening Olga and I cut two locks of his hair. They smelled of eau-de-cologne.

The evening of the 15th he was put into a coffin. Olga placed in his hands my baptismal icon of the Virgin of Kazan, which in his last years had hung above his bed. The morning of the 16th a van took him from the clinic basement and at 1:45 brought him to the Russian Catholic church on the Rue François-Gérard, where there were several hundred people and the funeral service was performed. At 2:45 the service ended. I took Olga by the arm. Behind the van that was taking the coffin (the priest sat in front) and was covered with flowers, the cars drifted along. At the Pont Mirabeau (it was a dazzling summer day) it seemed to me there was an element even of *relief* in this line of seven or eight cars. There was already quite a crowd at the cemetery gates. As is the custom, Olga was handed a spade with sand at the grave, then I. I felt a strange deliverance.

N. insisted that Olga spend the summer with us, and in September when the war broke out she did not return to Boulogne-Billancourt but remained in Longchêne. In 1939, in the autumn, N. became her godfather when she was converted to Russian Orthodoxy.

How gloomy and desolate the Church of Saint Sergius was that November evening on Rue Crimée! They both stood at the altar before the baptismal font, Olga completely blue from the cold, since in wartime the church was not heated. My teeth chattered, I sat in one of the chapels on a bench and waited. Then I insisted we go somewhere warm quickly and drink some grog, with rum or cognac, which we did. That evening Olga was happy, in so far as she could be at all happy after his death.

She now lived with her sister (when she was not living with us). When I was in Paris I always dropped in on her. More and more she spent time in the city, said that her sister was bored without her, that she needed her. Sometimes I insisted on taking Olga with us: I knew she loved Longchêne, and us, and the dogs, and the cat, loved to sit and knit on the little bench under the walnut tree, to go to the woods for mushrooms, but she felt she didn't have the right to live 'as in paradise', and when the German decree on the Jews came out, she went to register and began to wear a yellow star.

In July 1942, on the terrible day of the 16th, they were both arrested. I had happened to come to Paris the evening before and spent the night in an empty flat to which I had the key. Olga knew this. In the morning at eight the telephone woke me. Olga was calling from a neighbour's.

'Next to me,' she said in French, 'stands a policeman. I cannot talk long. We are being arrested. Try to find me.'

In half an hour I was at the Boulogne town hall. As I neared this huge modern building, I saw women dragging bundles and suitcases, some with children, approaching it like some centre. French policemen were supervising them. From all corners of Boulogne-Billancourt they were taken to one spot: this was the town hall basement, from which one heard troubled voices. No Germans could be seen.

The men had already been taken in the autumn. The women had not been touched before that day. Olga often said: first, they will not take women; second, they will not take old women. They took all, young and old, all who had not managed to escape, those who wore a yellow star and those who didn't.

Thrusting a packet of cigarettes into the hand of a fat policeman, I asked him to give Olga a note. She answered on a scrap of paper, asking me to buy her medicines, bring some things (she had lost her head and took almost nothing with her) and be at four o'clock at the exit of the town hall when they were to be taken to Drancy (to the north-east of Paris). I rushed to pharmacies, to her place to fetch some linen. It was summer and I could not decide whether to take her winter coat and blanket or not. In the end I did. All this I brought to the town hall. Again the cigarettes, again the policeman. Then back to the Place de l'Etoile, onto the wide quiet Avenue du Bois de Boulogne. There, in aristocratic quarters, the Gestapo had settled. A regiment of German soldiers marched in the middle of the deserted avenue, the most beautiful in the world.

An officer's command rang out. Flags with swastikas hung on the houses. S.S. guards stood at the entrances.

I cannot accurately remember how many offices I was in that day, my aim being to find out whether something could be done with evidence produced of her baptism. I went from house to house and could not stop, as if from 8:00 A.M. on, when the phone rang, I was set in motion by some force. I remember dimly that in one of the courtyards I saw two soldiers dragging a man with a yellow star, a bloody face: in fear I ran on further. I was chased from entrance to entrance, someone somewhere, it seems, gave me a glass of water, but I spilled it on myself and then walked around dishevelled, wet, unwashed since the day before, for some reason with the sleeve of my dirty summer dress torn (someone had pulled on it, pushing me against the doors, and then hit me in the face). I kept asking them the same question, telling them about the testimonial evidence of baptism, about a copy of the baptismal certificate, until finally I came to the right place. Sitting at one of the desks in one of the offices was a tall, trim military man who was ready to answer my questions. The conversation was more or less like this:

'Is she married?'

'A widow.'

'The husband was a Jew?'

'No, an *Aryan*.'

'Are there papers?'

'Yes, this is easy to prove.'

'But she is a Jewess?'

'She converted to Christianity.'

'The matter is not one of religion, but of *race*.'

'What does that mean?'

'It means she can marry a second time and return to the bosom of Judaism.'

'She is fifty.'

Here he thought a little.

'No,' he said, 'it's not possible to do anything. Of course if the husband were alive it would then be another matter.'

I looked at him. The thought that Khodasevich could still be alive that very day seemed to me so grotesque that I began to cry loudly, and two men dragged me out onto the street. Crying, I walked down the most beautiful street in the world. No one paid any attention to me.

Stopping at the Café Pressbourg on the Etoile – tied to my recollections of Pavel Muratov, with whom I had sometimes sat in the evening here and where German generals now sat with red stripes on their trousers – I went to the ladies' room, washed my hands, combed my hair, and decided to go to look for N. It was lunchtime and I knew where he might be. I found him sitting with Asya and learnt that he had already been at the Saint Sergius Church, got the copy of the certificate of Olga's baptism – and a document legally certifying that her husband, who had died three years before, was an *Aryan* and Catholic from the day of his birth. With these papers N. had managed to go to a lawyer and give him Olga's case. N. had even managed to borrow money to give a deposit to the lawyer (Maître R., who wore a yellow star). Moreover, he told me the lawyer had informed him that within several days two offices would be opened which would regulate all these 'Jewish affairs' and through which one could plead. (In fact, on the Rue de la Bienfaisance and in Montmartre some strange offices were opened, in one of which sat, among others, an old Russian journalist, Pavel Berlin, but what they did I do not know.) Olga, in any case, could be kept in Drancy and her departure to Auschwitz delayed.

Yes, she was kept in Drancy, thanks to these certificates, for exactly two months. All those arrested on 16 July were evidently sent to Auschwitz on the 17th. She remained in the camp, and all that time we even corresponded and sent her parcels. But N. could not obtain a pass to visit her and in her last card (written in the middle of September, of course in French) she bid us farewell on the eve of her being sent away, and told us she was not scared. And that they had shaved her.

The last time I saw her, at four in the afternoon the day of the arrest, 16 July, she was pushed with her bundle into an open truck, fourth in line, surrounded by police. Asya managed to run up to her when they brought her out from the town hall basement and embrace her, but I stood on the steps of the wide stairs and because of the intense trembling of my whole body could not move. Some strange woman hid me from others so that nobody would see me. It was a kind of Saint Vitus's dance: my teeth clattered loudly and my handbag fell from my hands. I could not stop, as if all this in fact were some kind of fit or a dance in which my whole body took part – from the knees, which banged against each other, to my head, which shook so that there was a buzzing in my ears. One of my arms was bare, the sleeve had been lost. The buzzing mixed with a strange whistling which had already begun in the morning, when a German hit me on the ear with his fist.

Suddenly I heard a gentle voice: 'Madame Berberova!'

An unknown woman called to me from one of the trucks. At once my shuddering stopped. I ran down from the stairs and through the chain of policemen; I ran to the truck. The woman whispered:

'You don't know me. Go [she told me the address, it was around the corner] and tell my husband that I was arrested in the street. Do you understand me?'

I looked at her stupidly. No, I could not understand what she wanted, memorize the number of the house; something had happened in my brain and nothing worked. But the name of the street remained there. In silence I held out a pencil to her, then a policeman was pulling me back. In an instant, through an effort of the will, my brain again came to life, an impression was made there and the house number jumped out. I yelled out in Russian, 'Sixteen!' The trucks began to move away.

The woman smiled at me weakly and kissed my pencil and, squeezing it in her hand, did not take it from her lips until she disappeared from view. Then a second truck left, then a third. Some sat, some stood in them. I don't remember if the children were crying or yelling, I don't at all remember the *sounds* of those moments, but children there undoubtedly were. In the fourth truck Olga stood, all seats occupied; her sister had put herself in a corner. Olga stood, looking at me and Asya with her clear eyes, and until the truck turned the corner made the sign of the cross over me, Asya, all who were standing around, the town hall, the sky, Billancourt and Boulogne . . . Then in complete silence (so it then seemed to me, because evidently I had grown deaf out of shock), new trucks were being driven up. They left, as we later learnt, one after another, full of women, till late at night.

The Zaitsevs were not in Paris in those days. Here is Vera's letter in answer to mine about Olga's arrest:

21 July [1942]

My Nina! We received two letters from you. What can we say to you? It's terrible to think what has happened! All of us bow low to you and Nikolasha for the energy you have displayed. Poor Olechka and Marianna. It's all so terrible, will they leave together or will they be separated? Of course I want Olga to remain . . . My dear! We beg you to write to us. You ask how we are. We are ashamed at how we live. All around are such misfortunes, and we have dug in and it's as if nothing happens, such silence . . . I have become frightened that only 5% of the hope remains. I write to you at your city address. I think you are in Paris all the time. When we received your first letter, I had had a heart attack that night. If we are troubled and tormented for them from afar, I can imagine how you are.

Don't worry about us. We are all right.

Explain your words, if only approximately: '. . . the second matter which I wish to discuss, is our common future lot, but this it seems can wait. In any case, I think nothing will change before September . . .' Explain. One thing scares me: that they will separate all of us. This would be terrible. What have they done with Olga's flat? Sealed it up? Can one take Vladya's manuscripts and books? You also write: 'I must tell you that I myself have not all my wits, so don't be surprised if I jump around in the letter . . .' What does this mean? Are you ill, my dear Ninusya? You wrote about everything in detail and well. I reread the letter many times. I embrace you, Nikolasha, Asya. Boria also embraces you . . .

Anxiety about papers and books was constant in those years. People abandoned their flats, their archives and libraries were carried off in unknown directions, or people were arrested and all was simply removed in a week or two. After the removal of the Turgenev Library it became known that Bunin's archives were hidden in the basement of the same building (Hôtel Colbert, Rue de la Bûcherie). Already in the summer of 1941 the city of Paris demanded that all that remained of the (Turgenev) library should be removed. Boris Zaitsev wrote to me about this from the department of Yonne where he was visiting some friends in the country:

8/24/41

Chère Ninon, I received from Paris the news that it has been suggested the premises be cleared of the remains of the Turgenev Library. Among things that remain there, the most important for

369

me are Ivan's archives. A librarian, thinking I was in Paris, asked me to help in the search for at least a shed. I am not very interested in their shelves, bookcases, or even the 300 various books. We will probably spend September here. But nine of Ivan's trunks? There are manuscripts, letters!

Vera and I considered it this way: Could these nine trunks not be put in your place? If I had any kind of suitable place in Paris, of course, I would take them. But in our place even the basement is piled high with junk – and it is, besides, damp, my few books and letters nearly rotted there.

I know that in your place there is also a great load of stuff, but still perhaps a corner can be found? (But what about the moving?) How much would that cost? All these questions are vital. You love Ivan, I know, and this is a serious matter. We could perhaps raise money for the moving in one way or another.

Or another idea: Perhaps you would indicate a *safe* place in Paris? (Till now I have not seen one.)

In a word, dear Nina, answer! Write me immediately what you think of all this, what you can advise. Of the members of the board [of the library] only Knorring is now in Paris – 123 Rue du Château, Paris 14ème. He is evidently busy mainly with this. It will, you see, be very grievous if the archives are lost. Bear in mind that if my immediate help is needed, I will return to Paris before the end of September.

We received your friendly card, thanks very much for Natasha. She is ecstatic about the stay with you, and wrote to us separately.

We live well here. Vera rests marvellously and is getting better. Strictly speaking I do not need a rest, for in Paris I live like a cat, as I have lived my whole life.

We look for mushrooms, eat plums – marvellous ones, from the garden. I read and write rather a lot.

I kiss your hand. Vera embraces you. My friendly best to N. All the best!

Your Boris Zaitsev

I answered that I would agree to take Bunin's archives to Longchêne, but for this, I thought, it would be necessary to obtain his permission. He did not at all understand the situation in Paris, judging from his card written to me in French from Grasse, in answer to my question about his papers (at that time you could correspond only in French from one zone to another):

. . . I wrote to Knorring on the 21st of September: 'If possible I would prefer that my trunks (nine in all) be taken to my Paris flat. In that case, let me know how much the move will cost so that I can reimburse you by mail for these expenses. If this is too difficult to do, keep my suitcases with yours.' I thank you from all my heart for your troubles, Nina. I wrote to you in August. I did not receive your parcel. What are you doing? I do not do anything. I only read, that's all. Swimming has ended. There is nothing new in my sad life. Your old man who, from the depths of his soul, kisses you,

I. BUNIN

Of course it was too risky to send the trunks to Bunin's Paris flat. On the other hand what did he mean when he wrote to Knorring to keep his archives 'together with yours'? Zaitsev returned from the country and after many speculations and much correspondence we decided to take Bunin's archives to the Rue Lourmel, where there was a Russian dormitory and public dining-hall. The place was insecure; within a year people there were arrested, but it seems to me that on Bunin's return to Paris after the war he got back his trunks. A part of the archives was later sent to Moscow.

I will quote two more letters (one from Boris, the other from Vera) of these years:

11/11/41

Chère Ninon, thanks for the letter . . . As for Lourmel, you are right, and in any case I prefer that the archives be with you. This will all be clear when we return to Paris (we are set to go on the 17th), but I am alone among the members of the board, I am not liked, I am not sure that things will be done my way. Unfortunately it is very difficult to contact Ivan by mail; maybe there will be an opportunity.

In any case, when I have returned to Paris I will want to see you. In the meantime, I can only thank you like a friend for your responsiveness – of which, however, I was sure.

Your BORIS ZAITSEV

22 Nov., 1942

Dear Nina! Forgive me for pestering you, but we have begun to get weak. If only you could get us some kasha . . . and dry beans. I would so much like to see you and talk about various things. Boris embraces you and Nikolasha, and I too. I was at Vladya's grave. All

371

is in order, though there is still no gravel. But all is tidy and clean. Nina! I very much want you to come . . .

Your VERA

I just came home, 7:45 P.M., the moonlight lay on the floor and suddenly something pierced me, terribly sad . . . Last Wednesday Zinaida Gippius's sister, Anna, fell dead at the market. Heart attack. Just as I sat down to write to you a siren sounded.

We no longer sat on the bench that stood beneath the walnut tree in Longchêne: we decided not to sit on it till Olga returned. By the day that Longchêne was sold (in 1948) the bench had fallen apart. But the walnut tree, I am told, has grown and gives more and more nuts every year. During the war we gathered them in old gloves – the fresh walnuts stain hands so badly that you cannot wash them clean.

Longchêne was bought by N. in the spring of 1938. The first five years of our life together I lived with him in Paris, but in 1938 we decided to leave the flat and move to the country. We had long sought a place where we would be able to live permanently, a wild house and a wild garden, generally speaking a 'wild' place where it would be worth settling. When, after long searches and many trips to the west and south-west of Paris, we finally found Longchêne, it seemed to us in the very first moment precisely a spot where one could live the rest of one's life, for there could be no better place on earth.

Longchêne was not a village, for a village pre-supposes in France a place with a school, a church, and a post office. In Longchêne there were no such things. There were four large farms and about ten houses in which old retired people lived. In the mornings five or six children would walk downhill to school in the nearest village. In the afternoons the postman would come, from that same village. The main road passed by a mile away, and only a country road led to our hamlet. There were no more than fifty people in the whole place.

I remember the first night in the house, then much more like a barn than the dwelling it became within a year. It was an old farm. We returned from the notary public, had supper, and went to bed in an upper-storey room (properly speaking, the attic) with a hole in the wall beneath the ceiling that was designed for hay-forking from carts. It later became my study. A neighbour brought us recently cut hay, there was no furniture, there were no curtains. We lay down directly on the floor, in the hay, looking through the open window, where stars flickered. Later I learned exactly, in the course of many years, in what place and when, out of which woods, Mars would emerge, where Sirius would crawl out from and when Venus would disappear after burning in the sunset. It was cool then, the month of May; lilac bloomed around the house. You couldn't close the windows because the hay had too strong a fragrance. We decided to install a kitchen, a bathroom, something that would serve as a dining room, and on the second floor a study and bedroom. We had to clear the little patio in front where a second house was built, a one-room affair. In the attic there we found an inscription in tar on one of the rafters: 1861. This second house was designed for N. – in this room he set up his painter's studio and visiting friends slept there.

Nell used to say, when we planted the fruit trees, set up the beehives, dug out the vegetable garden, that it all reminded her of a Chinese novel where life on a farm began with one peach pip. In the war years when I used to come from Paris on a bike along the field road, I could see from a distance two old tiled roofs in the greyish haze of Ile-de-France, a tiny one and a larger one sinking in the greenery of old apple and pear trees, while the young apple and pear trees were at the time no taller than myself. I thought: I have a home. So it will always be, it cannot be otherwise. The world stands still. It has stopped. In it I have stopped and am standing, motionless and unchanging. It cannot happen that I will someday pass through these places and not belong to them. But in 1960 I passed by, and I recognized neither garden nor house. All had been rebuilt, the pear and apple trees had grown enormously and were hiding the view, new gates led out somewhere to a completely unfamiliar spot, there were no beehives, the currants had been dug up. And the almond tree, which had stood like a fine, two–pronged fork near the house and had bloomed with pale pink flowers, now was indistinguishable in its greenery from an ash or birch tree.

Today I am not planting trees, not busy with bees, and not digging for strawberries. I am writing the saga of my life in which I am free to do as I want, to reveal things or keep them to myself, speak of myself, of others, not discuss something, stop at any point, close this notebook, forget about it, hide it somewhere. Or, having destroyed it, write another manuscript, another six hundred pages that would be quite different, though also about myself, but something like a second volume for a non-existent first. There have been many Russian autobiographies written, all different. Berdyaev, beginning with his childhood years, moved on to a description of the struggle of ideas in pre-revolutionary Russia and ended with an agonizing doubt about the good of the Soviet Union and the kindness of God; Stepun in his story told how, before World War One, he chose his real profession of travelling through the Russian provinces and giving lectures on the subject 'How to Live'; Bely, having begun his tale about Blok, subsequently rewrote it, proving he was a Marxist when Blok was still a lordling and Mama's pet; Nabokov told, with his innate talent, of the governesses he had in his lost paradise; Boborykin wrote how comfortable the European trains were and how fine the restaurants; the Tsarina's maid of honour about how she helped Rasputin change ministers; a socialist about how he killed these ministers. The émigrés wrote of how they had lived on a Russian estate among lime trees and portraits of ancestors in a hall with two tiers of windows, the associates of Lenin about how he squinted – in Simbirsk, in London, in Switzerland, at the Finland Station . . .

The choice is great. Whom should I choose as an example? From whom should I learn? Well, I discard all those who have written before me, I invite no one to look over my shoulder and direct my pen. I take upon myself the entire responsibility for the six hundred written pages and the six hundred unwritten, for all the confessions, all the silences. For what is said and what is not said. All that is being written here is being written in accordance with two laws to which I admit and which I obey. The first: reveal yourself completely. The second: conceal your life for yourself alone. The author of the first law is a contemporary of mine, the author of the second is Epicurus.

I had known N. a long time, since the period of *Days*, the S. R.'s newspaper. For me he was and remained one of those Russians who, like the hero of the popular fairy tale, is capable of anything and prepared for it. But for some reason it would turn out that in the end nothing remained of these abilities, water would pour through his fingers, the wind would carry away his words, and everything would collapse. No one expects anything of such people. The less you believed them, the more they lost faith in themselves, the less you expected of them, the more senselessly they wasted themselves and remained in the final analysis where they had started: with possibilities that were not realized, with personal charm that had been given to them at birth, like grace.

He could build a house, plant a garden, paint pictures, and improvise on the piano. He could laugh and amuse others, was always healthy, liked good weather, walks, trips, Longchêne, people and books (the ones I liked too). Such men are increasingly rare in our world, there is no room for them in modern life. Light-heartedness, as an outlook on the world, is dying, if it has not already died. After wars and revolutions and the calamities of our century, how could it be preserved?

He was one of the youngest delegates to the Constituent Assembly in 1917, a member of the S.-R. Party, a journalist, author of a book on Russia (London, 1919), considered himself a contributor to *Days* and *Contemporary Annals*, exhibited paintings in Paris salons in the thirties, and there was not a person on earth who would not have felt towards him immediate attraction. Hospitable, joyful, always kind and generous, and along with this extravagant, energetic, and able, he suddenly took notice of me (he had known me for about seven years), and having once done this, never let me go. We were two people with the same symbols: a garden for us both meant the same thing, and a house in his mind and mine merged existentially into one concept. Such words as 'present' and 'future', 'tree' and 'river', 'you' and 'I' carried one aura of connotations. He understood what it meant to be poor Lazarus, and he had his own well. He knew all the Himalayas and Dead Seas of my geography. And he too could not always differentiate between the Angel and Tobias.

The paths we walked and rode along – in a car, a bus, on a bike – were innumerable. Everywhere, from under the mist of the bluish air of the eternally winding sky, lined with plane trees and poplars, the paths of Pisarro, the hills of Monet, the bridges and creeks of Sisley would meet us. We reread Shakespeare and Cervantes, listened on the radio to Beethoven and Mozart. How happy we both were, right up to September 1939 when the war began, how young we were, how joyful our cares!

The sense of our meeting and rapprochement, our common life (ten years), the *happiness* experienced together, the meaning of our love for both of us is in the fact that he for me and I for him were the personification of all there was for us both – at a given stage of life – the most essential, vital and precious. What was vital and valuable for me then (and perhaps always?) was to change from dry, cool, efficient, calm, independent, and rational to warm, humid, responsive, dependent, and irrational. In him for me and in me for him one focal point gathered all that we had lacked till then. Here, as in two lines of a poetic narrative, as a poetic symbol, an intentional artistic hint, a musical phrase, it would be impossible to express in words without destroying its inward, hidden sense. Were we for each other a symbol of Russia? A symbol of youth, strength, and health? That strength, for which the whole world would serve as a fulcrum? Perhaps, but there was also much else we did not then think about and which, if singled out, would have been harmed. This sense of our meeting could have lived a long time (not only ten years) if what happened had been different: but there was a sudden duel between us, a struggle between him and me for a third person who deliberately became the centre of this struggle, determined to split us up.

We turned out to be rivals (enemies?) for this third person, and in this struggle what had been built between us – a union – perished. I emerged victorious, he emerged beaten, but it could have been the other way round. Both of us emerged from this duel prey to and losers of each other. Rivalry turned out to be fatal for us; my victory proved to be unwise, and his defeat not very humiliating. Neither inflated ego nor pity for the defeated friend–enemy has any place in love. Tobias, after having thrown his fish on the sand, leaves, the Angel climbs up to his heaven. The picture is left with an emptiness: the magic has disappeared. All of a sudden one wonders why the artist had to paint this Tuscan horizon, clouds, hills, bushes, and even the dog turned towards us, when he was thinking of Medea and Judea? Only symbolically, to walk a step behind the other and eat one artichoke leaf together is love. All the rest is merely competition between two people dealing in different goods, and even hand-to-hand fighting with many more illegal – that is, 'low' – than legal blows. But it happened that we did not cede to one another, both of us were adamant, and one took home the prize. I paid dearly for this victory, I probably would have paid less for my defeat. The prize in a few years turned into a burden I had neither the strength nor the desire to bear. I discarded it and remained alone: i.e., without him, as he remained without me.

From the years 1938 until 1944, when life in Longchêne began to fade, it seemed all those who visited us in the Paris days came to our place: the Kerenskys came often and stayed for days, as did Khodasevich and Olga; Bunin, Zaitsev, Weidlé, Zlobin. Ladinsky several times. Georgy Annenkov, Rudnev, Fondaminsky, my friends from *The Latest News* – and how they all loved it! It seemed carefree, cosy, charming, with a piece of uncleared woods at the end of the garden, meadows on either side of the enclosure, so that you could neither see nor hear the neighbours.

The day of the declaration of war we sat exhausted on the bench under the walnut tree; on the day Paris was taken we lay prone in a ditch, at the end of the garden. The morning a German parachutist fell in our woods and Marie-Louise, who used to wash floors in the house and serve dinner to our guests and us in shorts, brought him a ladle of water to drink, washed his wound, splashed the rest in his face before he was taken as a prisoner (both his legs were broken), we hid from everyone and sat all day at home. When the American unit arrived we were, like everyone else, on the square. In the middle of it stood a chestnut tree, once called, as Marie-Louise told me, the 'tree of liberty'. It had been planted here in the days of the Commune. We in the square looked at the jeeps moving by with a roar, and an old woman who was ninety said:

'*Then* they came that way, from the Monnier ricks to our oats, and *later* they came from the other side, from the sheds to the Vallé ponds. And *now*, just imagine, they are coming from a third direction: they cut from the woods to the clover, along the old road. Oh heavens, what a long life I have had!'

Then was the year 1870, *later* was June 1940, *now* was today. She took the Americans for Germans coming a third time.

How did we live during those five years? How did we survive to that day? How did we live through two searches, registration to be sent to work in Germany? Olga's end? Deprivations, nocturnal fears, bombardments, deaths, arrests, deportations . . . ? At first there was an empty Paris and a double despair: not only was there no one with whom to exchange a word, but there was no desire to see anyone, to find anyone; you wanted to hide from all, hide and keep silent. Then the return to organized deprivations: this time they went parallel and, so to speak, in a planned way with the decline of life around us. You didn't want to read new books, but you had no desire to reread old ones either. I not only could not write anything, I was afraid to sit at my desk, and averse to it; I even tried not to look at it when I passed through the room. When later I wrote my two stories for *New Review*, I wrote them not in my studio but wherever I could. I felt a strange sleepiness, which came from two sources: bad nourishment and physical work (the kitchen garden expanded, we planted potatoes). Such sleepiness that I could not overcome it: all day I would wait till seven o'clock when one got the basic news of the day on the radio, but at a quarter to seven – on a couch, an armchair, a chair – I would fall asleep and when all was finished I could not wake myself up. I begged not to be allowed to fall asleep, but N. was also sleepy. He sawed and chopped wood, we sat at a stove like the one we had had twenty years before in Petersburg. In the evenings we drank tea and at exactly eleven the planes started flying above us, from here to there, from there to here. Rex could hear their engines twenty seconds before us; with raised fur, he would crawl under the table, trembling all over, and the cat would also crawl there to lie under Rex's belly, while we, as the bombs fell, stood in the doorway where a thick wall, erected eighty years before, we were told, would allow us to survive.

One winter, then another. And a third, and a fourth. Finally the last, the fifth. We had lost count. I hadn't written anything for three years. But at the beginning of the war I had bought a thick notebook, with an oilskin binding and a red border. Sometimes I noted down in it some facts and thoughts, events and my reflections about them. In fact, did I not my whole life think that my existence consisted in living and thinking about life? And the meaning of life. But now I see that its meaning is only to be found in life itself and in me, alive, still alive. There is no other meaning. And there is no aim, thus ends do not justify means because there is no end. There is no end.

It does not suit Paris to be empty. Paris must pulsate, flash with lights, thunder, breathe. In Petersburg on Vasilievsky Island, on Sredny Avenue in 1921, a goat grazed. But here there are no goats;

there are only wide veins of streets, a solitary policeman at an intersection, closed shops, silence. I ride on my bicycle 'past buildings where we once danced, drank wine' (Akhmatova) – and read verse to each other, and spoke about verse. Felzen is under arrest, Raissa Bloch and Mikhail Gorlin have disappeared, perished; Mochulsky is ill with tuberculosis; Adamovich, Sofiev (who has lost his wife) are at the front; Knut and Otsup have gone into the Underground; Ladinsky, Raevsky are in hiding; Galina Kuznetsova is in the south, wanders in the '*zone libre*'. Bozhnev is in a hospital for the mentally ill; no one has heard about Anatol Steiger for a long time. Ginger is alive and waiting for a miracle.

Such and such lived here, so and so lived there. And here I myself lived, Rue des Quatre Cheminées, in Billancourt, now destroyed by bombs. Where are you, Denikin's warriors, Wrangel's riff-raff, the Russian Orthodox proletariat of noble descent who has come to stand over the furnaces of Monsieur Renault by contract? The Germans put some behind barbed wire on bread and water because they were Russian: who knows what tricks they intend to play now that the German army is stationed near Leningrad and Stalingrad! Others donned a German uniform and fought against the Soviets, still others remained quiet, no one saw them, perhaps they were trafficking in kvass on the black market, perhaps washing floors in German barracks? I lived here, on the Boulevard Latour-Maubourg, now a military district; two blocks away is the Pretty Hotel, where I once did cross-stitching. These streets are so bare today, like the streets of working districts, like the Rue Crimée, where it was so cold when Olga was baptized, and a tin font stood much like a child's bath. 'You will see, they will bathe you in it,' I said, scaring Olga, and her eyes were frightened. I slowly passed by Khodasevich's last flat, from where he was taken to hospital, and a few years later Olga was seized. I had been there twice after that. The concierge let me in, we climbed up on tiptoe, spoke in a whisper. I took a suitcase with his papers, his gold watch (his father's, with a little key), his cigarette holder and one of the etchings once bought by me on the quay: a view of the corner of Moika and Nevsky Avenue with the Eliseev house on it, that House of Arts where he lived with the window he looked through when he was expecting me. The first room was strewn with powder, the flowers had dried up in a vase and smelled bad, the beds were in disarray: when they had come for her and her sister, both were probably sleeping. In the kitchen three boiled potatoes covered with green moss lay on a plate. The concierge made me hurry, keeping watch at the door.

The second time I went, all had been taken away – books, furniture, dishes . . . 'They were here yesterday and said they would come this evening to seal the place up,' said the concierge. I stood in the empty room where a small pile of rubbish swept up by someone was in the very centre of the floor. And there was also a small pile of ashes. This is what you find in the pockets of Beckett's heroes. Or in an urn which has been immured in the wall of a columbarium. A handful of dust which the wind carries into the distance, which flies off to the whirlpools of mankind according to the laws of its destiny.

All around me was faded dirty wallpaper, where the bookshelf with Pushkin and Derzhavin had been.

I go to Montparnasse, where there is no one, as if I had ridden to Lyons or Dijon and walked around alone in between trains. I walk on Beethoven Street, which in Paris is called 'Rue Bétove'. I lived here with N. before the purchase of Longchêne. At one end it runs into the Seine, where the water has risen and floods are feared, and at the other side into a staircase which leads to Passy, to the Café des Tourelles, to the Trocadéro; but no one is there either, nothing, only marching soldiers and passers-by clinging to walls, unknown to me and to each other.

My black notebook now begins, and still smells of earth: at one time it was buried in our basement and bloomed with dark-green spots of mould.

PART SIX

The Black Notebook

1939

September

I was lying in the grass and not moving (at the end of the garden). It was the first day of the war. I lay an hour, two hours, I no longer remember how many hours I lay there. The grass grew through me, got entangled in my veins, the wild flowers blossomed out in my fingers and toes. A kind of bindweed began to strangle me, winding from one ear to the other.

October

The Russian renaissance at the end of the nineteenth and the beginning of the twentieth centuries is different from *common renaissances* in being aware of its own doom. This was a renaissance with a presentiment of its own ending. Resurrection and death. A beginning and an end in one and the same period of Russian cultural history. One of the original Russian phenomena.

November

I was going through old photographs and found one taken when I was about eleven at Grandfather Karaulov's estate. I am sitting on a window sill, my feet dangling in sandals; two braids; a serious facial expression. I said to Ladinsky:

'I will now show you an ugly child. It is simply unbelievable how unattractive I was.'

He looked the picture over and said:

'I don't understand why you find this little girl so ugly. Exquisite legs, braids, a dear face.'

For a second time I looked at myself through strange eyes, as it were, and suddenly it seemed to me indeed that perhaps I was not as unattractive as I was then told. And that Pleshcheev's verses (which

Mother wrote in my album), 'Poor child, she is unattractive,' were not addressed to me.

November

My sight is such that I easily read the last line on the chart at the eye doctor's. On the chart hanging on the wall. And the last line on the chart which he hands his patients.

'Why did you come?' asked Dr Leris angrily. 'Eight people are waiting in my reception room!'

'Pardon,' I said.

'You don't have to pay,' he said. But, of course, I paid.

December

Once upon a time there was the Russian writer D. Krachkovsky. Forty years ago Chekhov said that he was the hope of Russian literature. This killed him. He wrote badly, no one wanted to read him. He lived destitute in Monte Carlo and for about fourteen hours a day played roulette: five francs here, five francs there, just look, something will accumulate. So he lived. He walked about shabby, with long hair, unwashed. And continued to play.

Once he got ill, and the doctor said he needed an operation for a hernia. He wrote in *The Latest News* explaining who he was and asking for three hundred francs to be collected for him. With great difficulty and lack of enthusiasm the money was collected. No one wanted to give: he was not known, not published anywhere. He was sent three hundred francs and lost it all in one hour.

So in complete desperation he went to the director of the casino. He was not allowed to see the director, but some imposing employee came out to see him. Krachkovsky said:

'I am a Russian writer: I have lived as a beggar. I have a hernia. Money was collected for me in Paris to have an operation. I received the money and lost everything. Return to me my three hundred francs.'

And something happened which, it would seem, had not happened in all the time roulette had existed; the management returned his three hundred francs to him. And he had his hernia operation.

December

I think a lot these days about symbolism. It was necessary to

Russia. It proved (how many times now?) that Russia is a part of Europe. After symbolism, no 'slavophilism' is possible – neither old, nor renewed.

December
Cruelty and sentimentality always together. Characteristics of our century. Perhaps this combination seemed paradoxical before; now it seems natural. All this comes from a tearful awareness of our being abandoned and of the demands of an 'iron epoch'. The self-pity and defencelessness of man, and his resentment of the world.

December
'My solitude begins two steps away from you,' says one of the heroines of Giraudoux to her beloved.
One can also put it this way: 'My solitude begins in your arms.'

December
From a letter of mine to the south of France:

. . . There was among us a nasty, poor, pitiful (émigré) Russia: Russian newspapers, magazines, Russian rumours, Russians coming *from there*, sometimes alienation from Russia, but always an *opinion* about what was going on there. Nothing remained. They cut us off. There are no newspapers, no one is coming, and there is also no opinion, for it is not known, to me at least, if it is good or bad that Stalin is fortifying his position in the Baltic. We had a shabby, unhappy, provincial emigration: Russian books, Russian bordellos, Russian themes, but nothing has remained. My generation will be killed at war, the old will die off in quick order.
I view with suspicion the whole of world history. There was no justice, no good, no beauty. In any case, even less justice and good than in nature. I write nothing, I cannot, I don't want to write. For what? For whom? I always loved people, but now I am deprived of people dear to me. These 'dear ones' (themselves perhaps not 'nice people' at all) are inaccessibly distant. Some have died, some have left, some are preoccupied with daily bread. But the most terrible thing is that I don't even much want to see them.

385

Khodasevich once said there would come a day when all would disappear, and then several Russians would assemble and build a society . . . it mattered not what kind. For example: 'The Society of those who once walked in the Summer Garden', or 'The Society of those who prefer *Anna Karenina* to *War and Peace*', or simply 'The Society of those who distinguish iambs from trochees'. Such a day has now come.

Whom are we for? For our geniuses or our idiots who took portraits of Stalin and verses of Kumach with them into eastern Poland?

I thought of writing a part of what I wrote to you to Bunin. But I fear I will grieve him even more, he is so miserable. I said something to Boris Zaitsev and he at once agreed with me about everything.

December

We got stuck one night in Paris, too late to go home. We went to Bunin's to spend the night, on the Rue Offenbach. He was alone in the apartment. Mrs B. was away. He got a little drunk, N. got a little drunk, and I, it seems, also got slightly drunk. He put us in Galina Kuznetsova's room, where there were two narrow identical beds, but till quite late (about 3:00 A.M.) we wandered together through the apartment and talked. In Mrs B.'s room, on her desk, her famous diary lay. (Aldanov had once said to me: 'Beware, N.N.! She will write about you in there!') A page was open. On it in a perfect child's handwriting one read: '*Tuesday.* It showered the whole day. Jan had a stomach-ache. Mikhailov dropped in.'

This reminded me of the diary that Chekhov's father kept in Melekhovo: 'A peony blossomed in the garden. Maria Petrovna came. The peony faded. Maria Petrovna left.'

We sat at Bunin's in his study, and he told from the beginning (and to the end) about his love, which he still suffered from. Towards the end (they both continued to drink) he got terribly upset, tears flowed from his eyes, and he constantly repeated: 'I understand nothing. I am a writer, an old man, and understand nothing. Can such a thing really be? No, you tell me, can such a thing really be?'

N. embraced and kissed him, I stroked his head and face and was also upset; all three of us became terribly limp. In the end we went to bed. In the morning we left while he was still asleep.

1940

January

A meeting arranged by Fondaminsky and the 'Mladorossy' party. Why? I don't know. We left at midnight, and then suddenly such a sleet storm arose that it was impossible even to think of going to Longchêne. Fondaminsky took us to his place for the night, on the Avenue de Versailles. Unlocking the door, he says Zenzinov sleeps on the left, and to the right his wife's former nurse, now a tenant, and that we must be very quiet or they will be 'terribly angry' and will cause a 'scandal' in the middle of the night. N. goes to bed in the dining room on a couch, and I in the former room of Amalia. Neither sheets, nor blankets – all is locked up at Zenzinov's. It was very quiet behind the door: Zenzinov was sleeping there. Fondaminsky went to his room. I couldn't sleep; there was a kind of tense, heavy atmosphere in the apartment. Suddenly, at about two, Zenzinov began typing in his room. The machine was right next to my door and, of course, I couldn't sleep. He probably heard Fondaminsky returning, not alone; we made a noise in the dining room and bathroom, thought of drinking tea, but it turned out that (in Fondaminsky's words) 'Volodia locked everything up to hide it' (from whom: from the tenant? from the servants? or from Fondaminsky himself?). I lay about an hour without sleeping, went into the dining room to complain to N. about the banging on the machine, seeking his sympathy, but I couldn't rouse him. And suddenly, beyond the door from the dining room that led to the nurse's room, more typing rang out. So they both continued typing on their machines until 5.00 A.M., when all got quiet. I listened to the noise and still do not understand what sense this all made. Was this being done to spite someone? Or was this the normal way for people living in this apartment to pass time? Fondaminsky himself lived apart, at the other end of the corridor. Finally, at five-thirty, I pulled N. up from the couch and we left. He could not believe my story and for a long time assured me I had dreamt it all.

January

The destitute, stupid, stinking, despicable, unhappy, base, deprived, harassed, hungry Russian emigration (to which I belong)! Last year on a crushed mattress, with torn sheets, thin, his hair overgrown, without money for a doctor or medicine. Khodasevich was dying. This year I went to Nabokov's: he is lying in bed the same way. Next year someone else will be taken to a hospital and money collected from rich, generous, and kind Jews. (I brought Nab. a chicken and Vera immediately went to cook it.)

Billancourt is a drunken workman; the 15th arrondissement of Paris is a heaping-up of all the tears, banalities, and 'White Glory'. The 16th: a starched collar on the wrinkled neck of a worldly swindler, a fur coat, talk of illnesses, debts, gossip and cards. Meudon, Asnières, and all the suburbs with dozens upon dozens of Orthodox churches, where we are merely tolerated, where in the cemeteries there will soon be no room because of us!

February

Ladinsky told me in great secrecy that when the incident with the Japanese took place on Lake Hassan, the Russians gave themselves up to the Japanese, simply went over to them. Now in Finland this is happening before the eyes of the whole world.

March

Today, on the day of the concluding of peace between the U.S.S.R. and Finland, I said to Kerensky:

'Once, on a famous day, one of those close to him said to Napoleon: "Sire, we are today present at a turning-point of history."'

But Kerensky did not get the irony.

May

The German attack on the Maginot Line has begun.

Terrible news bulletins. I wait for them. Out of fatigue and nervousness I fall asleep half an hour before the main broadcast. There a voice says:

> 'sur terre
> sur mer
> et dans
> les aires – '

and my (barbarous) ear hears something like a rhyme.

June

In our hamlet there were French troops, the Red Cross, Algerians, Moroccans, Germans. Refugees passing through lived there; there was finally an evening when not ten men remained in the whole village. The three dogs of the café owner had been left behind and one was ashamed to look them in the eye: he had abandoned them. One of them lay in the middle of the road and cried. In three days he aged terribly, became completely grey, and now can hardly walk.

July

I rode to Paris and back on my bike.

Once it seemed that it was all right for Petersburg to be empty (this was when the goat grazed on Vasilievsky Island). Petersburg – but not Paris. It suits Paris to be an anthill or a beehive. And now it has become empty, as once Petersburg was.

In this new quiet on the Champs-Elysées a voice rings out: this is a loudspeaker at a cinema commenting in German on the *Wochenschau*. I go in. The dark hall is almost full. On the screen we are shown how the Maginot Line was broken through, how half a million prisoners were taken, how the struggle for the Loire went, how in Compiègne peace was signed and in Strasbourg and Colmar people greeted the Germans with flowers. Then Hitler comes to the Trocadéro and from there looks at the Eiffel Tower. Suddenly he makes a gesture . . . A gesture of such indescribable vulgarity, such ugliness, that you hardly believe that anyone in such circumstances could make it at all: with a fullness of satisfaction he smacks himself on his rear end and at the same time pivots on one heel.

At first I wanted to scream loudly out of shame and horror, then the matter became ridiculous, with the bells of Strasbourg cathedral and a military band playing . . . nearby pairs giggled, embraced, and kissed in the half gloom.

August

Read General de Gaulle's book (*History of the French Army*).

September

The conquering enemy walks around the village, the conquered looks at him and for his own calm seeks and finds in him all kinds of pleasant traits: he is clean, polite, pays for everything with real money (which is printed day and night at home in Frankfurt). And the talk begins: they are not guilty of anything, they do what they are ordered to.

October

For eight months (September–April) people came from the front and told of war. One said something interesting, a second something boring, a third something terrible, a fourth something ridiculous, a fifth something patriotic, a sixth something hopeless. I listened to all and did not realize that the one who was right was A., who said that 'the Germans will chase us in the end to the Pyrenées'. He said, however, that patriotism was an outmoded notion, that it was better to be a living coward than a dead hero. (He is a member of the French Communist Party.)

October

Last year when the war began, Frenchwomen asked the press and the government: 'What should we do? Our husbands and sons are at war, we are alone and have nothing to care for. We have a lot of free time, how can we use it to useful purpose?' The press, the leading figures (ministers, writers, the church, and in general all those who had authority over women) said to them:
'Knit.'
A year passed and women are again asking what they should do. Our husbands and sons are in captivity, in the flat all the taps glisten, we are tired of going to the cinema. What could we think up? How could we kill time? The favourite of them all, Colette, answers them on the pages of the *Petit Parisien*:
'*Dormez.*'
You are humiliated, there is nothing to eat, no source of heat, no one to rejoice in, and mainly 'our loved ones' are far away. There is no one to cling to. Thus *dormez* as much as you can, every hour of leisure time. All day Sunday. From 7:00 P.M. till the beginning of the working week.

November

This year, 1940, began for me with the thought of Blok. I reread his verse, then I wrote about him ('Sixty Years'). Afterwards I read three volumes of Bely's recollections, Blok's diary, his correspondence and notebooks. Endlessly I went over in my mind all that was related to him.

In 1922–3 in Berlin, Bely told me more about Liuba Blok than he wrote about her later. Here is what he said in a drunken delirium:

The night of the death of Dmitri Mendeleev (January 1907) Chulkov, in love with L. B., became her lover. At the time Bely was in Paris. She had supposedly promised Bely that she would marry him. But she asked Bely to leave Petersburg and said she would write to him daily. In the words of Bely, she 'wanted me to win her, to fight for her'. Soon the correspondence came to an end (this correspondence is now, certainly, in the Central Archives in Moscow). L. B. took up with Chulkov and Bely was forgotten. His nervous system suffered, he came down with a swelling of the lymphatic glands and was operated on, something he told everyone about for years. Chulkov wrote verses about his love for L. B. and printed them in the miscellany *White Nights* (1907), where they look revolting because of their similarity to Blok's verse of the time. Bely preserved traces of the illness till 1909. 'Three women perverted my life,' he would say, 'Nina Petrovskaya, Liuba Blok, and Asya Turgeneva.'

It seems to me that the myth of beautiful Joseph and the wife of Potiphar stood in the centre of his 'private mythology' all his life.

A. T. remained in Dornach in Switzerland when Bely left in 1916 for Russia (the reserve had been called up). Don't papers of his, notebooks, manuscripts, remain in Dornach? His departure was a final separation from A. T., but then he did not foresee, did not realize this. When in 1921 he saw her in Berlin and learnt of her relations with Kusikov, he endured her 'betrayal' very painfully.

'Beautiful Joseph', however strange this seems, was not indifferent to chambermaids. At his place in Moscow (when he lived with his mother) there were always pretty maids. He would say that 'Mamochka', after his unhappy love for L. B., was so preoccupied with his health that she 'tried to hire suitable maids'. Emil Medtner even advised him to marry a maid. 'Perhaps,' said Bely, 'this would have been a good thing.' 'Mamochka' brought him together with whomever she could.

'The First Meeting' of Bely describes his attraction to Margarita Morozova. First he corresponded with her in 1901–02. In 1905 they met. 'She was a great and genuinely human woman.' But here again he turned out to be Joseph the Beautiful and she left him. In 1912, together with A. T., Bely was a guest at the Morozovs', at their estate in Kaluga province. The daughter of M. M., Lenochka (the elder), was seventeen. 'She was charming and enticing in her femininity. I loved her sensually.' The thought, however, that (1) he was married and (2) once was in love with her mother forced him to 'overcome the passion' for the daughter.

'I will end as a suicide or as a saint,' he would say. 'As a matter of fact, I have already been a saint.'

Returning endlessly and disconnectedly to his love for L. B., Bely was saying (I am writing from old notes):

There was a night when Bely and L. B., hugging each other, entered Blok's study. 'Well, that's good,' said Blok. L. B. had said before this: 'Take me away. Sasha is a weight that has crushed me.' L. B. seemed to him in those moments united with him for ever. He felt that he could, as it were, take her for himself now. But 'so as not to humble Blok', not to take advantage of his conquest, he put off the 'carrying away' till another time. Leaving the Bloks he went out and got drunk. 'Blok tormented her with his holiness.'

One of the most unexpected confessions of Bely: the maid working at Emil Medtner's was the illegitimate daughter of Mendeleev – that is, L. B.'s step-sister.

About how Bely missed A. T. in 1917–21, there is the testimony of his letter to her, written after his move abroad, into Lithuania. It was never sent. It was given to me by Fraulein Krampe of the boarding house in Berlin where he was living when he left for Moscow; he forgot it among some other papers! Khodasevich published it in *Contemporary Annals*. In 1920, in the midst of the Civil War and the hunger, Bely somehow received a letter from A. T., in which she wrote to him that it would be better for them not to live together (in the future). In *Travel Notes* (Berlin, 1921) he calls A. T. 'Nelly' and 'wife'. For some reason she took offence at this.

Bely said his mother knew of his relations with Nina Petrovskaya and sympathized. In Berlin he once screamed: 'Down with decent women!' He drew a firm boundary between the concepts 'decent' and 'indecent'. An attack of impotency drew him away from the 'decent' ones.

He said:

'I curse you, women of my youth, intellectuals, decadents, hysterics! You are contrary to everything that is natural and normal.'

'You told me I had heavenly eyes, that I was Logos.'

'But for Andrey Bely it turned out there was no woman in the world!'

He also said:

'I am Michelangelo.'

'I am the Apostle John.'

'I am the ruler of the world.'

'I was buried alive in the foundations of the Johannesbau.'

'The destinies of Europe depend on me.'

'Steiner is looking for me.'

'Steiner is scared of me.'

Bely's first meeting with Steiner took place, it seems, in Brussels.

Steiner was giving his usual lecture. Bely and A. T. went to hear him. Next morning they wrote him a letter. They took it to him. All this is in Bely's letters to Blok. At first they met Steiner's wife, a Baltic Russian, Maria Siewers.

Bely spent seven months in Dornach.

He sometimes dreamt of having a grown son, and then tears would appear in his eyes.

He once said to me (alone), sitting on the floor near a stove, in Saarow:

'For me the other world is the same as a sturgeon filet. Most men in the other world are only guests and observers. Love me! Kiss me! You are Raphael's Madonna! I will take you where no one else will ever take you.'

(I became terribly frightened that this delirium would lead to various complications in his relations with Khodasevich.)

'When you write my biography, remember: Andrey Bely never had a single woman worthy of him. He received from all only slaps.'

Incidentally, in 1923, he said he would live another ten years or so. He died eleven years later.

Leaving Dornach in 1916, Bely kissed Steiner's hands. Their dramatic meeting after the Revolution in 1921 is described in Khodasevich's *Necropolis*.

He undoubtedly left his papers and manuscripts in Dornach. What did A. T. do with them? Did she preserve or burn them?

In 1922–3 we would meet him in the Zum Patzenhoffer tavern, on Augsburger Street. There Fräulein Mariechen (celebrated by Khodasevich) waited on tables. The place was 'Dürer-like'. Mariechen was about twenty. How often we sat there, all three! In 1937 one night I wandered over there (I happened to be in Berlin). I came to this spot. I looked in the door. A fat woman of about forty, in some way like Mariechen, sat at the register. Perhaps this was she?

November

Solomon Sumsky, once owner of Epoch which published *Beseda* (1923–5), died. He was an ordinary man and it's strange that he came to live his life quite stormily, as if his fate had been prepared for an energetic, intelligent, and remarkable man. Following his coffin was the cashier of the hotel where he lived. The cashier had taken him with her in June, when the Germans were approaching Paris. She had a house (and mother) in Brittany. Sumsky took his archives there (and those of Epoch), and recently said to me that he had left them there. They included: letters from Bely and perhaps even Blok, Gorky, and others, and also many papers, including (undoubtedly) unpublished Bely manuscripts. He left them somewhere in the attic of a farmer's house in Plugonven. The cashier was unselfish, gentle, and attached herself to Sumsky. He lived three months at her place in this Plugonven. As she followed his coffin, I noticed she limped slightly. He died in her arms. I fear that when the historian of Russian symbolism gets to Plugonven he will find nothing there except mouse droppings.

November

One evening in Saarow, in 1923, in a playful mood the three of us – Bely, Khodasevich, and I – decided to write a collective poem (which I translate here):

A POLKA

N.B.:The page is open
On days and nights.
BELY: Grin into the stupid faces

Of fat children.
N.B.:Grin into the wise faces
Of old people.

KHOD.: Yesterday night there was a ball
At the undertaker's.
N.B.: The river seems nearer
The distance shorter.
KHOD.: The merry-go-rounds around the graveyard
Went on all night after the party
Heavily, noisily.
N.B.: (And we stood there, watching.)

BELY: A prize-winner
Astride on a sheep
N.B.: Was yelling: What a garden!
Never saw it before!
BELY.: A beauty queen
Astride on a cow
N.B.: Was screaming: I like it!
It's new to me!
KHOD.: (Who do they think they are?)

N.B.: I was listening to the delirium
Of a dying man,
I was trying to unravel
The mystery of his misery.

KHOD.: He never gave up
And till his last breath
Hoarsely echoed over and over:
BELY: 'Delighted to be your obedient servant!'

November
I reread Tolstoy's 'The Devil'.
As we now come to understand him, he was unconditionally
possessed by sexual mania. Music is sex, the fat legs of a peasant
woman are sex, a beautiful dress is sex, the Venus de Milo is sex.

After his death, life itself began to suggest solutions to his 'insoluble' predicaments.

The hero of 'The Devil' is a man who rages with passionate needs and cannot live a month without a woman. Such a man should have married a passionate woman, 'cheerful and firm', but he married a pale sickly creature. If the hero had had a 'cheerful and firm' wife he would probably have looked with indifference at Stepanida's legs (and there would have been no story). Here Tolstoy's dualism plays tricks with him: Stepanida is 'for the body', the pale sickly one 'for the soul'. Lots of nuances in the desire for Stepanida and none at all in his love for his wife!

Tolstoy obviously did not understand that the marriage of Irtenyev and the marriage of Stiva Oblonsky were really not marriages at all, for the woman had no part in them. One might rather call them cases of artificial insemination than a marriage.

November

I cannot read, I can only reread. I reread *War and Peace*. It always seemed to me, and now I am convinced, that this book has no equal in *grandeur of the realized task*.

However, here are some remarks about it:

1. Humanity in the course of the novel is compared to (1) ants, (2) bees, and (3) sheep. Perhaps this is an oversight? Or the result of an unconscious scorn on Tolstoy's part for humanity?

2. 'The soldiers moved from west to east, to kill *each other*.' What does this mean?

3. The aims of any war: to move forward, hold on to territory, destroy the enemy. Of these aims *the first* was achieved by Napoleon.

4. As for Natasha's dancing at her uncle's, I again realized that the uncle's mistress (a serf) could not have admired her; I don't believe it. What we must have here is an instance of class-consciousness.

December

I remember several dates:

1926, 12 December. Celebration of anniversary of Boris Zaitsev in a hall near the Avenue Rapp: twenty-five years of his literary activity. There were a lot of people. We ate and then danced. I, incidentally, sat next to N. Otsup, on the other side of him sat

Galina Kuznetsova, and we had a good time. In his speech Bunin extolled Boris while Boris answered that many were indebted to Bunin. Both burst into tears, embraced, and kissed.

1927, 5 February. First session of 'The Green Lamp', a series of literary gatherings arranged by the Merezhkovskys. At these gatherings she appeared with an emerald hanging on her forehead, between her brows, on a chain, and he said something like this:

'We must in the end decide whom we are with, Christ or Adamovich.'

or:

'From Tolstoy to Felzen . . .'

or:

'How would Dostoevsky have answered Zlobin? We can only guess!'

1927, 3 June. At the Zaitsevs' P. Muratov read his new play *Mauritania*.

1928, 13 January. The day of the yearly charity ball of the Russian press; a farce of Teffi, especially written, was put on. Every year on the Russian New Year's Eve there was a ball at the Hôtel Lutétia, when money was collected for needy writers, poets, and journalists. The ball was elegant, well attended, and a good deal of money was collected so that the 'poor' sometimes got 250 to 400 francs apiece, depending on their service to Russian literature. A ladies' committee collected the money and arranged the ball, while a commission appointed by the Writers' Union disbursed the money.

It was necessary every year to think of something special to attract the rich (generous and kind Jews – in the main, Russian émigrés were not interested in Russian literature: they were either too poor or those with means scorned the modern Belys and Chernys, Gorkys and Sladkys* and said they had been 'brought up on Pushkin'). In 1928 Teffi wrote a hilarious farce in verse where some kingly offspring are kidnapped, then impersonated, the girl turns out to be a boy, the brother and sister are not at all brother and sister, and so on. Ladinsky and I played these impersonated and kidnapped offspring (whom everyone mixed up), and in the end he and I were carried on stage in someone's arms (he was huge and was folded in two).

*White and Black, Bitter and Sweet.

It seems the following year someone thought of getting an elegant, shiny chariot for the ball so that the writers could harness themselves to it and drive the wealthy 'patrons' around the hall. I remember how I, paired with M. Osorgin (I in a long evening gown, he in a tuxedo) stood in the shaft and rushed around the hall, while the Moscow barrister M. Goldstein (who later committed suicide) sat in the chariot, he placed Raphael with his small accordion next to him. Raphael was a fat Rumanian who had an orchestra and played in one of the Russian night clubs in Montmartre. Raphael sat and played the accordion together with Goldstein, who literally fell out of the chariot laughing. When we carried him to his place at his table, where there was champagne and some elegant ladies, he slid down, took out his wallet and, with a bow, gave me a hundred francs. In those years that was a lot. Osorgin said: 'And for the music?' He gave a hundred more. We dashed somewhere, to a member of the committee. To whom did this money go? Perhaps to Krachkovsky and his hernia? Or to B. Lazarevsky, the once popular author of the novel *Woman's Soul*? Or to F. Blagov, former editor-publisher of the tremendously influential Moscow daily *Russian Word*? Or to the unemployed journalist Buryshkin, a former Moscow millionaire?

In 1933 at the press ball, one act of Gogol's *The Marriage* was put on. I played Agafya Tikhonovna, the bride, while Podkolesin was played by the artist Vereshchagin (nephew of the famous one), who concerned himself very determinedly with this spectacle and prepared himself for it, putting on lots of make-up: in his soul he obviously was an actor. A golden wig was rented for me with curls, and a stylish dress. This was the first and last time in my life that I acted on the stage.

1929, 17 April. A Bunin evening at the Tsetlins'. This was done, of course, with a charitable aim.

1930, 4 April. Celebration of Khodasevich: twenty-five years of literary activity. He was fêted in a restaurant diagonally across from the famous Closerie des Lilas. There were about forty people, and the dinner bore a rather unofficial character. The most difficult thing was to unite the 'left' sector of the émigré press with the 'right' – that is, *Contemporary Annals* and *The Latest News* with *Renaissance*, where Khodasevich published. Somehow I achieved some equilibrium. I don't know how I managed to arrange all this, the aim of the celebration was, of course, to 'raise the prestige' of Khodasevich, and this I somehow managed to do. I remember that Professor N. Kulman (a representative of the 'right') in an embellished speech declared that the best creation of the one being fêted (the Pygmalion) was his Galatea. Galatea at that moment sat neither alive nor dead of anxiety that all this be, if not as at Zaitsev's celebration, then at least *as with decent people*.

1931, 10 March. My sole 'writers' dinner'. The group was quite close, friendly, made up of: Zaitsev, Muratov, Khodasevich, Osorgin, Aldanov, Tsetlin. I was invited to the group, but after the dinner of 10 March the group collapsed: between Khodasevich and Osorgin there was something of a split, owing to their relation to events in Russia. Osorgin renewed his Soviet passport annually, received honorariums from Moscow for his translation of Gozzi's *Princess Turandot*, repeated everywhere his casuistry that he was *not* an émigré though he published in the émigré press, and so on. On the other hand, Aldanov and Tsetlin felt that Muratov had moved into the anti-democratic camp, especially after his article 'Grandmothers and Grandfathers of the Russian Revolution', in which he declared the 'best people' of the old Russian radicalism to be beasts of prey.

December

In the autumn of 1937 N. broke his leg at the knee. When he received the insurance, we bought Longchêne, in May 1938. In the spring of 1939, when all the labours of rebuilding the house had come to an end, we left our Paris flat for good and moved to the country. This was five months before the war.

December

In a reactionary state the state says to the individual: 'Do not do *this*.' Censorship demands: 'Don't write *this*.' In a totalitarian state you are told: 'Do this. Write this in *this* way.' There is all the difference in the world in that *this*.

December

Women in France (in villages) give birth in the presence of their husbands. Yesterday Lisette had a child in the presence of two girl friends, her husband, and the doctor. She held her husband by the hand when she had her birth pains. Here is the picture: a basin is placed underneath, the husband and friends look to see if the little head has appeared. 'Hurray! It's a brunette!' one of the girl friends yells out. 'Try a little more! It's coming out now!' The following day the mother told me of her sensations as the child's shoulders passed through, as the fluids came out (the husband held the basin). The girl friend said: 'When I bore my first, as soon as the head emerged, I immediately came to my senses and then everything was easy, though I had to make every possible effort, grasping my knees this way.' (She showed how exactly.)

December

In the complicated system of his laboratory experiment, the chemist follows the flow of his chemical compounds through crucibles and flasks, through glass tubes. The most important thing is to feel that within me there is permanent flow, that I am not divided into top and bottom, that in the middle there is no 'Chinese wall' cutting me into two parts. This I always loved. This did not dawn on me out of nowhere, only when I became a woman. From head to foot and from foot to head I became 'one', I became an 'experiment'. These were my juices rushing through my system.

December

I see now that the most terrible thing that could happen to me would be that I *dry up*. My eyes would dry up, my mouth would dry up, my brain would dry up. There would be no *juices*, and I would go on living – perhaps for forty years. To live without juices is the most terrible thing for a human being who has recognized *juices* in himself and loved them (prized them). Who was alive because of his *juices*.

December

I dreamt of Khodasevich. There were a lot of people, no one recognized him. He had long hair, was thin, half transparent, a ghost or a spirit, elegant and young. Finally, we were left alone. I sat very close by, took his thin hand, light as a feather, and said:

'Well, tell me if you can, how is it there?'

He put on a funny face and I understood by it that he didn't feel bad, but hesitated, then answered, inhaling his cigarette:

400

'Well, you know, how could I put it? Well, it's not that simple . . .'

December

One room, one bed, one blanket. Who does not understand this understands nothing in marriage. And if you fear this, then you don't need marriage. During the day life sometimes sunders, cools, shakes, tears up something. At night again all is united. The body preserves the body with its warmth (if not heat).

Napoleon said: 'Give the empress a separate bedchamber. I want to preserve my freedom, at least at night. If the husband sleeps in the same room with his wife, he can hide nothing from her.' This is completely true.

December

Rich Chinese men when they build a house build 'gates to peace' either at the end of the garden or in some distant corner – i.e., put a small door through which they escape from revolutions and catastrophes. This secret exit is at every rich man's house. He carries the key with him. He saves himself through it at the last moment, taking his treasures with him.

I do not have these 'gates to peace', I have no key. I always had the desire to be where everyone else is, or in any case where many of *us* are.

December

As far back as I remember, there was something cowardly in me in childhood, slightly rotten, an ability to be petty and nasty, to compromise. Later this was gradually overcome. This was not 'because of our century', it existed before any contact with the century. (Belinsky once said: 'I am not a son of my century, I am simply a son of a bitch.') With the years this potential meanness began to decline. I can fully imagine now that at about ten or twelve I could have sacrificed a great deal merely to save my skin.

December

With me lives a man strong in spirit, healthy in body and soul, smooth, clear, kind. Industrious and tender. Whatever he undertakes turns out well in his hands. Well disposed towards all. Never bears malice, does not envy, nor casts aspersions. Prays every evening and sees childish dreams. Can repair electricity, draw a landscape, and play on the piano a passage from Schumann's *Carnaval*.

December

I have one recollection. It's as though I echo in it another 'self', then sixteen.

This is a recollection of a trip to Pavlovsk, on a happy day of my life in the spring of 1918, after graduation from school. There were nine or ten girls and two teachers. My heart was so full of a feeling of life that when I went back on the train, that May evening, together with everyone else, my thoughts flew on ahead; I thought that sometime I would remember this day, myself in it, and this recollection, if it would not save me, would perhaps protect me. I thought so *then* and do *now*. It's as though I had been preparing myself for this future recollection. Now I am flying back, towards that spring, wrapping my emotions in this recollection, and I see that it is standing watch, as it were, over my life. This was the day when we went on a picnic to Pavlovsk.

December

In 1918–20, when the events happened, I said to myself: 'This does not concern me, this concerns aristocrats, bourgeoisie, counter-revolutionaries, bankers, and tsarist governors. I am sixteen and I am nobody.' In 1940 something again befell us, and again I said to myself: 'This does not concern me, it concerns Europe. What am I? – I am a Russian émigré. Half Asian, no? In overall terms a nothing.'

'You won't get away with this!' I said to myself today in the mirror.

December

European artists are astonishingly haughty. They do not condescend to despair. They are self-confident: the Englishman because there is a great empire; the German because there is Hitler; the Frenchman because the bourgeois make-up of his thought fuses ideally with the bourgeois structure of his state. We were tortured by an awareness that there was illiteracy, there were lice. Even today repetitions of these countly and princely tortures occur.

December

I love a hard life. This came to me in youth undoubtedly from Nietzsche. It stuck. For my whole life. This means I love problems that must be solved and obstacles that must be overcome, and in general the complex 'sport' of human existence.

December

What is attained by thought remains forever with us. A considered idea never leaves us, whatever our mood might be, whereas an idea merely felt is unstable and treacherous: it depends on the strength with which our heart beats. Moreover, hearts are not given according to choice: whichever one you found in yourself you had to reconcile yourself to. But we constantly create our mind by ourselves.

— P. CHAADAEV. *Philosophical Letters*, III

1941

February

When such times come – of hunger and cold – matches gradually stop lighting. I noticed this already in 1920. First sign of great misery.

February

What became of all the clay pots, now so necessary? They disappeared. There are no more of them. Our old woman neighbour, who remembered the invasion of the Germans in 1870, gave me a pot. I kneaded dough in it. She assured me that the pot had been her grandfather's. And her grandfather went to Russia in 1812 with Napoleon. Perhaps the pot was Russian? N. looked it over and declared that the pot was undoubtedly from Vladimir (which meant it was his compatriot)!

February

Leonid Andreev, several weeks before his death (in 1919),

listened in his Finland home to air raids of enemy planes and dreamt of leaving for America. It is beginning to seem to me that there was no interruption between his nights and mine.

March

Not long ago I read at a literary soirée, on the Rue Lourmel at the Russian Centre, my short story 'The Resurrection of Mozart'. There were about a hundred people, a full house. Many wept. There were: Zaitsev, Weidlé, Ladinsky . . .

March

So, the most important things in the world are: kasha in one's pot, bread in the stove, wool, and fat.

April

All my life I loved conquerors more than the conquered, strong more than weak. Now I like neither the one nor the other.

April

It troubles me more that Isaac Babel is in prison than that a cruiser with all its equipment has been sunk.

April

A year ago we stood face to face with events: the fall of Holland and Belgium, the fall of Paris, the entry of Italy into the war. Now we again stand before great events, perhaps even greater, which will probably begin in May. Meanwhile every evening dozens of planes fly above us, to England. London is in flames on all sides.

April

In Nakhichevan, at Christmas of 1919 (or in January 1920) an armoured division stood in our courtyard, and every evening we climbed up to the attic and looked from there beyond the city to the steppe where Reds were carrying on an extensive attack on the fortress of Bataisk, attacking and losing horses and men. From Bataisk the Whites fired after them. When the Reds returned (to our place, in the yard), some were missing. And now every evening hundreds of planes fly above us to England to bomb cities and a peaceful population. I cannot sleep. All the time I think: This will end only with my life.

June

Monsieur Duplan (eighty years old, invented rayon, a millionaire) told of himself: he had remained in his castle, all his servants had fled (June 1940). Duplan lived a week completely alone, read Tolstoy in the evening, that chapter in *War and Peace* where old Bolkonsky is awaiting the French. Once he saw that a small unit of Germans were walking at the entrance of his estate. He came out on his threshold, hands in pockets, and placed on the ground a sheep recently killed by him. 'If you please. Let's dine.'

22 June. Sunday

Morning radio.

The Germans have invaded Russia.

June

Attila said: I am the axe of the world.

June

G. and his wife live next door (the daughter mixes with German soldiers). On the other side of the fence, on their land, a young tree grows, a mirabelle plum tree. It has bent completely over our land, and now its fruit (a hundred pounds at a glance) falls to us, ripe and sweet. Nothing falls on their side. I met his wife and told her to come when she wanted and collect the fruit. We collect it daily, and as jam making is impossible because of the absence of sugar, I make preserves for winter. But G.'s wife did not come and in the morning when I rose and went into the garden I saw that G. had chopped down this lovely tree and it lay on their land with all its fruit, on their side of the garden, in pieces and dead. 'Spite,' said Marie-Louise. They didn't collect the fruit and this was also done out of 'spite'. So this tree lay until the birds had eaten all the plums and the branches dried up. Every day we sat for a long time and looked at the leaves drying up, at the axed stem fine and strong, and no matter how long we reflected we could think of nothing except that this man, G., was possessed by some wild beastly malice towards me and N.

24 June

On the day of 22 June, in Paris, about one hundred and fifty Russian émigrés were arrested by Germans. In the main 'important' ones, but also 'unimportant' ones. They were arrested as 'Russians': 'right' and 'left'; among them, Fondaminsky, the lawyer Filonenko, and others. The barrister N. sobbed at his arrest and said he had never had anything against Germans, and that 'Mein Vater ist in Berlin begraben.'

25 June

It turns out that they have arrested mainly *Freemasons* – members of the Grande Loge (right) and Grand Orient (left).

June

The 28th of June at 8:00 A.M. I went to the cemetery to Khodasevich's grave. The earth had already been dug out and the pit covered with boards. Six workers arrived with ropes, lifted up the boards and began to haul up the coffin. The coffin (of oak) had darkened in three years, and was light. There was a little mould around the edges. A bureau employee said to me: 'This is dry earth and the deceased, evidently, did not decompose but dried up like a mummy (as he was obviously thin).' The coffin was carried on a cart to a new permanent place. Again ropes, pit, boards. It was lowered easily and quietly. Earth was strewn around.

And I went to the Zaitsevs', who lived around the corner.

June

On 22 June, 1812, in his main quarters in Wilkowiski, Napoleon declared war on Russia.

On 23 June, Bonaparte at night saw before him the Nieman River. (From Chateaubriand's *Mémoires d'Outre-Tombe*, v. III)

July

Lwow, Riga, Kishinev, Minsk, Smolensk.

August

Beethoven is often bound up for me with the rhythm of a moving train. The first part of the *Pathétique Sonata*, with the train that crushed Anna Karenina. In a newsreel I saw war on the Russian

406

front, where German tanks (hundreds) moved through marshes, roads, through ripe rye, virgin forests, fording the rivers – and all this to sounds of the *Ninth Symphony*.

August

Novgorod. The war goes in 'rings'. The city is surrounded, the army is destroyed, the city is taken. All is cut in big pieces. A 'ringed' war.

August

I was in the Kommandantur, in Rambouillet. Russians had been summoned to register. The Germans wanted to know if all were 'white', were there not some 'red' who should be put in camp? About fifteen people came. A tall old man, aristocratic-looking, a violinist at the Russian Conservatory, two women in large old-fashioned hats, a pale, puffy man with a snub-nosed little boy, and still other people, all badly dressed, worn out by need and fear, with large calloused hands.

A German interrogated. Turned out that all were 'white' – that is, émigrés, having 'Nansen' passports. The German was astonished. I began to explain what a 'Nansen passport' meant, that no one needed us and that their summons was a waste. The German didn't understand how you could distinguish Soviet from non-Soviet from documents. I made mistakes in my German and hurried a lot. Throughout I wanted to say: Look at them, these people are of no use at all to you, let them go, for twenty years they have . . .

. . . for twenty years they have suffered, sought out the hardest work (I said this at night, in my sleep, to this same German officer), they have been chased from everywhere, they have not been given the right to work . . . We stood with him in a sunbeam near the window, in the Kommandantur.

. . . for twenty years they have lived among 'foreign people', but you see, they were once just like you: healthy, young. Their children are also permanently frightened and therefore very quiet. Their wives are exhausted by sorrows and work. How humble they all are! They pay taxes and go to church. Crime among them is insignificant. They have 'Nansen' passports, and such sad faces . . . Pity them! These are the Russian émigrés . . .

And I awoke, crying.

August

Rereading Dostoevsky's letters: the letters of 1877 and *Diary of a Writer* have parallel themes. It was as though I understood afresh the movement of generations, that people who believe in progress consider it a straight rising line, but it seems to me more like a very slow and very uneven oscillation (with stops and starts) of a pendulum.

Kovner's letter to Dostoevsky and Dostoevsky's letter to Kovner: this is the clash of two different epochs. Dostoevsky listens attentively to what this new man, slightly cynical, slightly atheistic, slightly the swindler, slightly the internationalist, says to him. Dostoevsky shrugs his shoulders, is dumbfounded, inclines his ear. One feels that Kovner is alien to him. Then he passes by, forgets him. And in the meantime Kovner is an enormous event. This is a new man, with decidedly new outlooks on everything; on immortality, money, love.

Kovners appeared in the last quarter of the past century, and my generation knew them. They showed remains of vulgar idealism. But modern post-revolutionary men and all the thinking of our time would be incomprehensible to the Kovners, and the Kovners would appear as sentimentalists to us.

Pushkin would have gone mad had he known *us*. No, Pushkin would have gone mad after reading in Dostoevsky about the chamber pot (in *The Eternal Husband*); Dostoevsky would have gone mad because of Chekhov and Chekhov because of us. All would have held their noses and closed their eyes at our 'ugliness'.

August

Twenty years since the day of Blok's death. Who still remembers that day? I think about it every year on the very day; I think of it a lot. I would like to write a book on him.

September

As I thought, the child of L. B. who died in 1911 and whom both L. B. herself and Blok so mourned was not Blok's. Vera Zaitseva recounted for me her conversation with Blok in Moscow after the Revolution. They were walking down the street, Vera's son had just been shot. She spoke with Blok about him.

'And you, Aleksandr Aleksandrovich, never had children?'

'Never,' answered Blok.

September
   Schlüsselburg is taken.
   Kiev is taken on the 20th.

October
   Kiev is taken. Odessa is taken. Tver and Kaluga are taken.
Taganrog. (And I am reading Tarle's *Napoleon's March on Russia*.)

November
   In this life, distressing, uninspiring, melancholy, hungry, a
strange, unexplainable ray suddenly burst in and transformed
everything: a little Spanish girl (of eight) by the name of Ramona,
the daughter of a woodcutter, very poor, to whom I gave a ribbon.
I could not speak to her, she spoke only Spanish. But how she
looked at me, how she smiled at me! This was a jolt in my emotions
– a childish face, sad and beautiful. All in me began to shine and
sparkle. In the midst of our death suddenly there was beauty.
   Her father, evidently a Spanish Red, has been interned in France.
Now he cuts wood in the forest next to us. He has a sick wife and
five children. The older son was reported missing in action last
year. The entire family lives in a hut.

November
   On the 13th, Kronstadt and Sevastopol were at one and the same
time bombed and set ablaze from all sides.
   A million Germans are passing through Russia – to Tikhvin,
Maloyaroslavets, Tula, Kerch.

November
   The famous traveller Sven Hedin wrote an article against Russia
and Stalin. He said that the real name of Stalin was Ivan Ivanovich
Vissarionovich.

December
   War of the U.S.A. with Japan. Pearl Harbor and sinking of
ships.

It's very strange, but I sometimes sense, as it were, the odour of blood in the air. This odour makes me feel bad. It seems that all around there is a horrible quantity of dead bodies. Earth has already covered some, others are gradually being hidden by a blizzard, a third group is covered by the sands of the desert, fish chase a fourth in the depths of the sea.

December
Hong Kong is taken by the Japanese.

December
On 7 December at 9:00 A.M., Merezhkovsky died. In the last months he was very thin, very old. He ran in very small steps along the Rue Passy arm in arm with Gippius. When I went to see him three weeks ago, he was indifferent to everything (and to me). Zlobin was wrapping his legs in a blanket. He was always cold.

It was terrible to look at Gippius at the service in the church: white, lifeless, with bending legs. Next to her stood Zlobin, stout, strong. He supported her.

There were quite a few people at the service. The news of his death had spread quickly, though there were no Russian newspapers. Olga sent me a telegram. There were: Maklakov, the Zaitsevs, Liubimov, Ladinsky, Kartashev, Lifar, the priest Bulgakov, in all about eighty people. The Metropolitan performed the service along with four priests and two deacons. Gippius stood in front of me. The coffin seemed very small.

Merezhkovsky was the last of the living symbolists. Now there remain: Balmont (a living corpse) and Vyacheslav Ivanov (in Italy).

December
If only I could not tremble when looking at a map of Russia. But I tremble.

December
Spanish children, the children of the woodcutter in the forest hut, came to our place at Christmas: Anita – three, Juanito – six, José-María – eight, Ramona – nine. With them was Diego – sixteen. All were cleanly dressed. They were small with long, flat noses. They came with drums and a horn. It was a whole procession. We gave

410

them biscuits, candy, and apples. José-María was, obviously, a very cheerful and merry boy and sang Spanish songs. Ramona joined him. I could not listen to her without tears and went out to the dark kitchen. Ramona's hair was combed into braids wound around her head. I tied a little ribbon to them. All the pity, sadness, and beauty of the world united in her for me.

A month ago the encounter with her had led me – through exhilaration, pity, and humility – out of a state of dryness and icy hardening, one of my most taxing moods. It is part of a human being by nature (so I think) to be warm, alive, perceiving, vibrating, and in his essence more of an animal, bird or even plant than a piece of ice, desert sand, or rock.

All the beauty and drama of the world, all the tenderness, charm, and warmth of a peaceful life became suspect to me in the past year. Then, not long ago, walking in the rain through puddles along the dark village street to the farm for a bottle of milk, I saw Ramona in a dress, or rather, in rags; you could see her bare body. Her feet were encased in big shoes, obviously her mother's, with holes, falling off her feet; her hair, dark and smooth, was plaited into two fine braids that were placed around her head, and where they came together over her forehead they were tied with a red woollen thread. She walked, stumbling in the dark, to the same farm as I, and held in her hands an empty tin can.

When we entered the kitchen together where there was a vat with fresh milk which the farmer's fat wife measured out with a tin jug, I studied her. She seemed to come from the pages of Hans Christian Andersen as well as from a Goya drawing. She looked at me with curiosity through big, dark eyes for a long time, but quietly and humbly. Her fingers holding the rusty can were fine and dark. She suddenly smiled at me, silently and trustingly, not knowing who I was, looking me in the face with her meek eyes. Something within me revealed itself with force. Joy and pity penetrated me. 'Come to me,' I said, 'and I will give you a real ribbon for your braids.' In fact I wanted to give her a warm blouse. But she didn't understand French!

All of her, with her smile and tin can in hand, with her ignorance of the language of the people among whom she lived, with a wildness that suddenly flashed in her fear, appeared to awaken me, to turn over my dead layers, remove from my soul the blood and the mould.

1942

January

I overheard in a Paris café a conversation in Russian. A Russian grandmother (in an old seal coat) and her Russian granddaughter (about twelve):

The grandmother (looking the menu over):

'Look, they have sauerkraut for sixteen francs!'

The little granddaughter:

'Then you order, Granny. We have enough for one sauerkraut.'

'And what will you do without the sauerkraut?'

'I'll have it next time.'

'But are you sure their sauerkraut is tasty?'

'You order, you will see, we have enough money.'

'Can't we order two?'

'We don't have enough for two.'

'I haven't eaten sauerkraut for so long. No, I'll not order, I don't want to waste money.'

'I will count how much we have.' The little girl counts the money.

Two Frenchmen are in another corner. The first:

'I don't understand anything: there are cards, coupons, cheques, points. I lose everything, I am late everywhere, I have registered nowhere. Somewhere one had to register for something. My turn has come and gone. I go to stand in line and am told this is not my day. I understand nothing. I can't manage in any way. I'm hungry all the time.'

The second:

'You should entrust this to someone.'

'There is no one. So I walk around now, not having eaten for the entire day. I lost half my ration cards.'

January

In *Our Word* (a Russian newspaper) I read some sort of report about what is going on in Petersburg. How those who died of hunger and cold are buried, or how they are not, how they wait for the earth to thaw and corpses lie in courtyards heaped like logs. I imagined Petersburg. I visualized both of them clearly: old, transparent, half frozen, they hardly walk, they are almost skeletons falling out of weakness, old age, and malnutrition. For some reason in a dream I see a telegram: Mother died before Father. I can in no way believe this.*

January

Marie-Louise put my hand on her stomach and there I felt the man of the twenty-first century kick, turn, and jump about.

January

'Past dear graves.' I walk through Montparnasse cafés, where ten or fifteen years ago (even five) one could see people ranging from Ehrenburg and Savich to Bunin and Fedotov. Now there is not one familiar face, not one shadow. It's as if I were walking in Paris in the year 2000.

Suddenly – at the counter in a half-dark bistro – Georgy Raevsky. We rush towards each other. He fears nothing, for with him 'all is in order' (evidently false papers). He has grown terribly thin. He reads me verse.

January

I have seen talents in my time. I have known men of genius. These were unhappy, unhealthy, distressing people, with a jaded life and their victims around them. They had not known happiness, did not understand friendship. To everything they would add: 'We are not read,' 'We are not needed,' 'We are not understood,' 'There is no money,' 'There is no audience,' prison and exile threaten, the censorship oppresses. I cannot imagine anything more unfortunate, melancholy, sad.

February

From the south (Favières) came E. K. to say that all of Favières (a Russian spot) repeated my phrase about loving a hard life. They considered it a very funny paradox.

*In 1961 I found out from S. A. Rittenberg that this was the truth.

413

February

I read the trials of the 193 (1887). These people are direct ancestors of Lenin and Dzerzhinsky. Muratov in his time said that 'Granny' Breshkovskaya was a beast.

The Chief Judge then was Peters. Our time also had a Peters.

One took revenge on the other.

The sentence was ridiculous: it was so light.

February

The rumour passed through that Tsvetaeva hanged herself on 11 August in Moscow. *Our Word* (or *New Word*) carried a shockingly illiterate account about this. Not long ago while reading her prose, I read how someone once, seeing her from behind, mistook her for Esenin. Now I see them in front of me: both light-haired, they are hanged and rock in nooses. He to the left, she to the right, on identical hooks and ropes, both with short flaxen hair.

It is said that Efron has been shot in Moscow. The son is a Party man and probably in the war. How can you not hang yourself now, if your beloved Germany is bombing your beloved Moscow, old friends fear to speak to you, you are crushed in the magazines, and there is nothing to cram down your throat?

March

Gippius sits in her place, on the door is the sign: 'Key under the mat.' She hears nothing. Zlobin runs errands (for butter, sugar). She sits and writes or darns something. At night she screams and runs about the room.

March

On 3 March at 9:15 P.M. the bombing of Billancourt began. About a thousand dead, two hundred homes destroyed. The cemetery was closed for days: several bombs had fallen and many graves were destroyed, coffins flew out of them, bones and skulls flew through the air. Windows were broken at the Zaitsevs'.

That night we spent in Paris in Y.'s flat, whose key had been left for us. You could hear and see all from the balcony. Huge pink fiery balls stood above Paris and lit up the streets. The British threw luminous balls which floated through the air. The cannonading continued for two and a half hours and the earth shook.

For a week people buried in shelters were dug up. From one basement a child's voice rang out, yelling in Russian: 'I'm here! Mama, I'm here!'

March

Chancellor Müller writes down Goethe's words (3 February, 1823):

'Everything we nurture in ourselves is forever developing. This is an eternal law of nature. There exists in us an organ of evil will and dissatisfaction, as there exists one of doubt and opposition. The more we give it nourishment and exercise it, the stronger it becomes and in the end it is transformed into a pathological sore that devours and destroys everything around us, killing all *beneficial juices*. The more such things as repentance, pangs of conscience, and other inanities combine too, the more we become unjust vis-à-vis ourselves and vis-à-vis others. The joy that is obtained through *personal perfection* and perfection of those around us is lost.' [Italics mine.]

March

On the Rue Tolbiac there is a home for new mothers. There pregnant women go for six months before giving birth. Primarily prostitutes pregnant by Germans, or wives of prisoners, or fourteen-year-old girls who have nowhere to go. They live in warmth, do nothing, and are well fed. They are even given nuts. Nine out of ten of the women give their children away to orphanages, half hope that their child will 'peg out'. In the evenings the pregnant women dance with each other to the accompaniment of a gramophone.

March

Russians cry a lot. The Polish workers at the farm also, by comparison with the French, who never cry. When Ivan's brother died, he so wasted away with grief that the whole French village came to look at him: they had never seen anything like it. When Billancourt was bombed on Sunday, crowds of people went to walk there, moans of those buried in basements rang out, and in the streets people laughed, kissed, and ate sandwiches.

April

At night, on 3 March, when the British and the Americans were bombing Billancourt, several bombs fell on the cemetery. The moon was in clouds. Graves flew apart at the explosions. Bones, skulls, bodies flew through the air, as did tombstones which banged with a roar against each other. I could still see the gaping holes, the broken crosses, the cracking monuments, marble angels with broken wings. The bones were removed; they were removed the first four days the cemetery was closed.

Khodasevich's grave did not suffer, but now he is surrounded by graves of those killed during the March bombing – about thirty graves around him, whole families in circles: father and mother Robert, the five Robert children, grandmother Coiffard, children and grandchildren of Coiffard, etc. . . . In the midst of all this stands his grey cross.

June

The 21st I was in Paris. This day can remain a monument to our time – the debasement of our civilization, the wretchedness and mediocrity of our life. Everything came into focus, something you wouldn't have thought possible. I went to three incredibly provincial places and towards the end I realized something beyond retrieval had happened to us all.

It began with a funeral Mass in the Armenian church for R. After the requiem there were speeches. A man was glorified who had left nothing after him: not a poem, or work in progress, or simply an idea, but only because at the end of the last century he had personally known such-and-such Armenian public figure. He knew them when he was twenty-five, and now he was near seventy; all his life he had been a banker and had clipped coupons from his radical youth on.

Then at four, in the hall of the Russian Conservatory, there was a reading by Shmelev. There were a lot of people, almost all over sixty, and a couple of children. Of men of letters: Teffi, Zaitsev, Kartashev, Surguchev . . .

Shmelev read as they read in the provinces before the time of Chekhov: with shouts and muttering, like an actor. He read some old-fashioned stuff, churchy, silly, about religious processions and hearty Russian dishes. The audience was ecstatic and clapped.

In the evening we went to see *Don Carlos* at the Odéon. The enterprising French translator 'hid' the politics and 'stressed' love. *Give us this day our daily ersatz!*

July

Olga was seized and taken away at 8:30 on Thursday, the 16th.

July

I once asked Marie-Louise if there were some in the village who had gone to the altar without going to bed with each other. She said this happened only in marriages by arrangement, when it was understood that he does not go to bed with his fiancée because he is not in love with her, and has a mistress whom he will keep until the last day or even longer. In marriages for love, it would have been suspicious not to sleep together before the wedding.

July

I was at Olga's apartment and took two suitcases of books, papers, and some of Khodasevich's things.

All was in terrible chaos: stockings, manuscripts, scraps of fabric, balls of wool, books, food. I will go again to make some order there. I could not find many things (for example, Sologub's letters). Some documents were scattered about in the middle of the room, among them her certificate from a Petersburg high school.

July

The old man A. A. Pleshcheev (eighty-five?), almost blind, walks about with a white stick, tells people of Nekrasov and Dostoevsky, who once patted him on the head. When he has to cross the street, he addresses himself to passers-by: *'Traversez-moi!'* Once he was given alms.

August

I found in Khodasevich's papers the poem 'No, not as the Scottish Queen'. He didn't want to publish it in his lifetime. In 1935–6 the Katharine Hepburn film was playing. She looked like me (I was teased about this in *The Latest News*). I remember Khodasevich once saying to me: 'Yesterday we were at the movie *Mary Stuart* and saw your double. It was very pleasant.'

August

At the request of Vera Zaitseva, I visited the Archimandrite Cyprian. Pictures of Leo Tolstoy, Berdyaev, and Blok hung on the wall. I didn't like this. Books, icon-lamp, narrow bed.

I said to him:

'I am not lamenting my sins. I don't wish for a miracle. Dogma does not affect me. I am speaking of the one who said, "Blessed are those that weep." I am crying, but I will not be comforted. All this is a lie.'

He said:

'The Church is preserver of the full truth. What you are saying is heresy.'

I asked him why, if the Church possesses the full truth and he is a son of the Church, he is so gloomy. Why is he not rejoicing?

He answered that all his life he had been a desperate pessimist and that this was probably because he was a physically sick man.

I was not interested in talking with a sick man, and I left.

August

The German army is surrounding Stalingrad.

August

All through Paris stories circulate of people just arrived from Kiev and the Ukraine:

1) How one Georgian brought chrism to the Crimea, and how the inhabitants thought you had to spread it on bread.

2) How, near Poltava, a town fed on casein for three weeks.

3) About a little boy who came down a mountain on a dead German instead of a sled.

4) About how children think it's better to live without boots: then it's easier to run away from the militiamen.

September

And how did love begin?

Through outward phenomena. A smile that alternated with seriousness showed on a face, strange a minute before; the eyes spoke, and there were lovely discoveries in the whole person: in the hair line, the warmth of the hands, the aroma – or smell – of the body and breathing. The voice. Yes, the voice always played a large part, and the intensity of life in the face. Only later, through the strength of attraction, did I come to be acquainted with the internal life of the man. Through this love, somehow marvellously and intensively growing stronger, I accepted the intellect, already considering it a joy. I never had anything to do with his 'character' or his 'opinions'.

But this outward sensation of beginning had nothing to do with the handsomeness or even the attractiveness of a man. There was nothing cerebral in me, neither in registering first impressions, nor in my further adjustment. Yes, adjustment was always one of the biggest joys. I pity those women who do not know it. To adjust to a man is not only not debasing (who thought up that inanity?), but the indispensable condition of bliss.

November

I am reading Karamzin's *The History of the Russian State*.

After the time of Simeon the Proud (what exactly was he proud of?) if one counts seventy-five years, 'various plagues ran wild' uninterruptedly in Russia. They 'devastated entire cities'. Of these seventy-five years nothing remained, no architectural monument, manuscript, icon, idea, but only constant battles with the Mongols and with Lithuania, internecine wars of princes. Seventy-five years means two generations. Were there in these two generations intelligent, talented, adventurous people? Or were there none?

November

It's enough to read through two issues of the Berlin Russian paper *New Word* to understand all the stupidity, servility, venality, all the abjectness of the Russian character when it wants to curry favour and climb up.

November

Dry, thin, he comes in black to a fashionable restaurant on the Champs-Elysées and places on the tables of those eating a book, the Bible. He says:

'Do you want to be clever and prosper in life? Read this book.'

He goes up to the bartender at the bar:

'Do you want your business to go well? Read this book.'

No one buys. The bartender answers:

'If this concerns business, then see the boss.'

November

I said to Monsieur P.:

'There was bombing in Billancourt. Many killed. I saw women dragging burned children out of burning houses.'

He answered:

'*Je m'en fous*: I live in Montmartre!'

November

In all this there are four 'positive phenomena': books, unselfish feelings, one's own creative thoughts, and nature. The first and fourth boil down to Stendhal's *lecture* and *agriculture*. The third has died out. There is less and less of the second.

November

I am reading Léon Bloy.

He is an astonishing and sad combination of Rozanov, Merezh-kovsky, Remizov, and Khodasevich. He is the most 'Russian' of all Frenchmen!

Rozanov: the style, the incessant recurrence of his churchly and religious feelings, his reactionary temper and interest in the Jews, his hatred of radicals, the revelling in misery.

Merezhkovsky: paradox and tension, love of the slogan, ego-centrism and the fact that he moves about and around the important without being himself a great writer.

Remizov: his complaints, his poverty, his exploitation of friends, the love of publicity and advances.

Khodasevich: misfortunes nourishing themselves on him, en-slavement by work, the impossibility of writing 'for oneself'. The day of the appearance of one of Bloy's books was the day of the assassination of President Carnot: all were occupied with the killing, the book sank into oblivion, people forgot about it. This is exactly what could have happened to Khodasevich!

November

I received a summons to the Russian division of the Gestapo, somewhere near the Galliera Museum. N. received a summons to Versailles – that concerned his dispatch to work in Germany. I go alone. I enter. I go up to one of the clerks sitting at desks in a large room. I quickly look around at all those seated – not one familiar face, but I sense at once who these people are: I have acquired an eye for Russians in Paris. These are old, forgotten Russians, the real 'émigré, unnoticed generation' – cads, Black Hundreds, former bureaucrats 'of the court of his imperial majesty', of the ministry of internal affairs, ex-members of the Union of the Russian People, ex-governors, ex-members of the political section of some military organizations. This means that their day, not our day, had come. There is a fiesta on their street.

'You are a Mason?'

'No, I am not a Mason.'

'It says here that you are a Mason.'

He gives me a pamphlet by the lawyer Pechorin, 'Masons in the Russian Emigration'. Hundreds of surnames are listed there. Among them is R. I. Berberov.

'I am not R. I. Berberov.'

'And who is R. I. Berberov?'

'My father's brother.'

'Where is he?'

'He died several months ago in the south of France.'

Silence.

'You are not Jewish?'

'No, I am not Jewish.'

'How can you prove this?'

'I can't prove that I am *not* Jewish. You prove that I am Jewish.'

Silence.

'One of your relatives was deported as a Jewess.'

This is about Olga. I keep silent. He:

'I am asking you.'

'I don't understand whom you're talking about.'

Then he brings a thick folder out of some cupboard. This is my dossier. For a long time he browses in it. Two dozen denunciations are, apparently, contained there.

'Why are you not publishing in our newspapers?'

'I am not writing anything.'

'Why?'

'I have grown old. My talent has withered.'

We spoke in this vein for another five minutes or so, and with reluctance, he let me go.

At the exit I bumped into a man whose face I knew but whose

name I could not remember. He had a sharp eye, and with this he tried to drill through me in a second.

November

I feel as if we lived on a highway; there is nowhere to hide. At any moment they can enter the house, take me, throw out my books. I am dazzled from looking for a long time at the map of Europe (or from tears?). Planes fly above our roofs. They are flying to London. Or flying from London. Or flying to Hamburg. Or somewhere else.

November

I had not looked at the stars for a long time. I was not interested in them. And it was very cold. Today I looked for quite a while. They flashed and fell, flashed and fell. Then I went to the kitchen: the pan was on the fire; this was soup. At that moment it was terribly important.

December

Father and Mother gave me *only* a name. It was not *I*, but they, who thought it up. All the rest that is in me I 'made': invented, developed, bartered for, stole, gleaned, lent, took, and found.

December

The hero of our time:

I knew S. in Russia. Since the age of thirteen he had made love to servants in his parents' home. Twice he was expelled from school. At eighteen he went to the 'White partisans' in the Civil War and knifed someone. Then Berlin. He was jailed for forging a cheque. Then here's what happened: in Berlin there was a political assassination; a young Armenian killed the Turkish minister Talaat-Pasha, who was active in the Armenian massacres. The wife of the murdered man recognized S. as her husband's murderer from among thirty-two photos of 'students' shown to her. He was jailed. That evening he had taken a prostitute from the corner of Kurfürstendamm to the flat where he lived with his Papa and Mama, who at the time were at the opera. So he had an alibi, and all bore witness: Papa, Mama, the streetwalker (his entire salvation was in her), the house porter, the prostitute's lover who waited for her on the corner. S. was freed. He married a girl who was nineteen. The night of the wedding he disappeared and was missing for three days – carousing with women somewhere, while she sat alone and cried. For six years he lived on her means and after he had almost raped her sister (who was fifteen), she left him. He moved about somewhere, then signed up in the Foreign Legion and left for Africa (the French war with Ab-del-Krim was on).

In Africa he again knifed someone, returned within five years. When I encountered him in Paris and asked where his medals and crosses were and what rank he held, he said he could not become an officer because he couldn't pass the exam. Then a place turned up for him, as steward on a boat taking Jews, who were escaping Hitler, from Germany to Argentina. He smuggled things from Argentina to Germany, and made many runs, becoming a 'small Hitler' (in his words) on this ship. Then he disappeared somewhere.

S. knew how to hide his past, spoke in four languages, once spent a year or two in Cambridge at the university (from which, it seems, he was also expelled). He had worldly manners, and he was quite good looking. He knew how to behave with women, who went out of their minds on his account.

And now he wears a German uniform, is fighting on the Eastern front – or rather, is doing service as a translator for the Germans in Russia.

He had returned on leave from Smolensk. He said that all Russians had fled Smolensk and when the Germans entered there remained only a schoolteacher with his wife and daughter. Obviously he slept with the wife and forced the teacher to become something like a liaison man between the German command and the Russian population.

Coming back on leave he arranged a meeting with me, took a small package from his pocket. 'This is a present from your dear homeland,' he said. There were two objects in it: a handwritten pornographic poem, illiterate and coarse, and a bronze icon.

1943

January

One of the most beautiful museums I have ever seen was the

Mauritius Hus in The Hague. I remember standing there every day for a week, in front of a Vermeer. Later I went to Amsterdam with N. and for a long time the two of us walked beside canals and stopped at the Rembrandt house.

I have the feeling that neither Mauritius Hus nor Rembrandt simply exist *any longer*. Disappeared in thin air.

April

The sensation-causing novel of Fallada, *Wolf among Wolves*, in some way reminds me of my first novel, *The First and the Last*. The same 'documental interest', the same thesis poking out from everywhere, the same unpleasant style, pretence to modernity, the same lifeless people indispensable to the author. The same 'Dostoevsky'. Fallada, of course, is more skilful: he, so to say, built a kind of monument to the epoch of 1923–4.

April

After the bombing in Billancourt five hundred dead were counted. A general exodus. All the windows at the Zaitsevs' again flew out, and now Boris and Vera are at our place (in Zum's flat).

June

That dark shadow, Father Cyprian, said to Vera Zaitseva that Russian Orthodoxy values a good deed *less* than prayer. 'With a prayer you will go to God, and good deeds will remain here.' Even Vera was slightly shocked.

July

Landing in Sicily. Taking of Palermo. Bombing of Rome. Two hundred divisions stand on both sides of Orel.

July

The story of how Mr. Valmy-Baisse (of the Comédie Française) dedicated a monument in Bordeaux to Charles Morice, poet and friend of Verlaine. In 1903 the municipality of Bordeaux (Pelletan's administration) was too rightist and did not want to dedicate a monument to the poet. They erected a statue, but arranged no solemn dedication. In 1942 they finally decided to 'dedicate' it. They came with wreaths and palm twigs. But half an hour before this the Germans had taken away the monument – the commission on the use of bronze objects had confiscated it. They looked on: the empty pedestal remained. Thus they solemnly returned to the Hôtel de Ville and drank out of grief.

August

Madame Chaussade and her husband (obviously a former gentleman) settled in the empty house of the signalman – the railway has long not been in use. And they took in three Jewish girls, fed them and hid them from everyone. A Jewish committee was paying for the girls: their parents had long ago been taken away to Auschwitz.

Madame Chaussade sometimes brought them over to visit. Two twin girls of fifteen and Régine, eleven. They live without registration and without ration cards; Madame Chaussade started cultivating a big kitchen garden and even bought a few chickens. All would have been well, if Chaussade himself had been normal. But he burned with lust for one of the twins, sat her on his knees; Madame Chaussade feared for her, did not sleep at night, walked about the house and watched over the children. Finally it became necessary to set up a barricade, and then Chaussade strangled all the chickens, hung a lock on the kitchen garden, gave them nothing, he himself ate, and threatened that he would denounce his wife to the Gestapo for accepting Jewish children into their home.

I went to Paris, to the committee, where P. A. Berlin worked, among others, and there I was promised the children would be taken to some other place.

August

Yesterday at the Denfert-Rochereau subway station I had a fright.

I am standing at the chocolate vending machine and trying to tinker with the lever: perhaps a Meunier chocolate bar will fall out. Suddenly a voice: 'How are you, Nina Nikolaevna?'

G. M. I didn't at first recognize him, and didn't even remember if I had ever met him. Two trains passed. He held on to me and would not let go. His monologue went approximately like this:

'We have set up our new Union of Writers. The president is our dear Ilya Dmitrievich [Surguchev, with whom I had not been on speaking terms for fifteen years]. I am the secretary. The following . . . [there followed surnames] have signed up as members. Remizov has promised [this, I knew, was a lie]. When will you come? Send me a petition to be accepted as a member without delay. We will have meetings, readings, performances . . . You know, Nina Nikolaevna, it is better to sign up earlier: whoever does not sign up *we will not allow into liberated Russia*. I said just this to Boris Zaitsev yesterday. I went specifically to see him about it and explained to him: whoever is not a member will not receive permission to return. The initiators will go first. We want to publish a paper in Minsk. You live in the suburbs, is that not so? It's good I ran into you. So send your petition soon.'

I say:

'I do not live in the suburbs, but in the country, very far away, and have no means of communication. I cannot come to readings.'

'As you wish. As you wish. Think of the future.'

A second train approaches:

'Incidentally,' I say, 'last year it seems, N. addressed himself to your committee so that you would help save Khodasevich's library. You did nothing then, and all the books were carried off to some unknown place.'

He: 'We were very busy. Funeral services. We performed the services, and there was decidedly no time to busy ourselves with books.'

Yes, that's what I heard! A third train arrives, and I finally get on it.

'And against the fates there is no defence,' (from Pushkin) I say to myself.

Boris Zaitsev lets me know that it's better for me for the time being not to go to the city: L. is looking for me to invite me to write for *The Paris Herald*, another of their weeklies.

September

On the 5th, dedication of the tombstone at Merezhkovsky's grave in Sainte-Geneviève des Bois. Old men and women from the Russian House, the terribly old, brittle, completely transparent Gippius, Zaitsev, and two or three more acquaintances. The monument was erected owing to the charity of a French publisher. Milioti (in French) and Chuzeville (in very good French) spoke.

Gippius thanked the French. Zaitsev said two words in Russian. It became very sad. To myself I repeated lines from my poem, once dedicated to Merezhkovsky.

October
P. Ryss, an old journalist, friendly with me for some reason since 1925, arrives and says he must leave his wife in Asnières (a Frenchwoman, whom he married after the death of Anna Abramovna): she threatened to report that he had not registered as a Jew. He had left in what he was then wearing and settled in the Quartier Saint-Germain, in a room on the sixth floor. He fears he will not live through the winter without a winter coat. N. gives him his old coat (very warm, but worn) and he leaves. He says that for whole days he does crosswords and studies Spanish to kill time.

October
Gippius has a soirée: Loris-Melikov, Teffi, and several others. We were sitting at the tea table. I looked at the clock: a quarter to eight. Time to leave. Suddenly planes were flying, a siren roared. Zlobin and I rushed into the kitchen. There we saw, through the window looking onto the south, American bombers flying in threes, like geese, dropping bombs. The siren roars, bombs explode, the whole city begins to tremble, and we tremble, too. We return to the dining room and decide to go down into the shelter. I take Gippius by the arm. Zlobin takes Teffi's arm, and Loris follows. In the terrible thunder all around we begin to walk down the stairs (from the third floor), and suddenly I see that the marble staircase moves beneath my feet. Gippius sees and hears nothing. We go down and there, at the entrance, we stand quite a long time. When the all-clear is sounded, I leave.

Going out on the Avenue Mozart, I see that all is in smoke, and everyone is running somewhere, firemen are rushing, emergency first aid is hurrying down along the street to Billancourt, to Boulogne. My first thought: the Zaitsevs. I run and run, through all Auteuil to the Porte de Saint-Cloud, and there realize that Billancourt has been bombed and is now burning. All is cordoned off and no one is allowed there.

October

The première at the Russian Dramatic Theatre of Griboedov's *Married Bride* in Georgy Annenkov's staging. Teffi, Gippius, Insarova, Tsereteli, and others.

November

The Russian army is near Kherson, near Kiev, near Krivoy Rog, near Gomel, near Kerch.

November

The story of Maria Efimovna who is hiding in a French village: from the first day she pretended to be an Armenian. She was loved, invited. Finally people began eagerly to beg her to be the godmother of their newborn children. And she did.

December

S. came for the second time on leave from Smolensk. He looks awful: he has aged, grown thin, nervous, is always twitching. He said he found no one in Smolensk: the Germans hanged the teacher and his wife; where the daughter went is unknown.

Then he said he didn't see one literate man for a thousand kilometres, and that in the Ukraine the Germans were opening theatres and churches. In Odessa a 'Rumanian' university was opened. For whom?

I told him about Olga. He answered:

'They will never return.'

I don't believe him.

1944

February

At half-past eleven at night (I already wanted to go to bed), there is a careful knock on the door. I open: it's A. Ginger. I let him in.

He says he is living in his place, goes out once a week 'for exercise' and mainly when it gets dark. In the house – he is sure of this – no one will give him away. His wife is taken as an 'Aryan', as are their sons. He sits at home and 'waits for everything to end'. I am terribly worried about him, but he himself is very calm and repeats that he fears nothing.

'Sainte Thérèse will preserve me.'

I got terribly angry:

'Neither Sainte Thérèse nor Saint What's-Her-Name have preserved anyone from anything. If there had been a raid in the streets, you would have disappeared.'

But he is quite sure that he will survive. We embrace each other as we say good-bye.

March

A customary Sunday at Gippius's. She, true to an old custom, 'receives' from five to eight. Zlobin prepares tea. The constant visitors: Loris-Melikov (from the Russian home for the aged in Sainte-Geneviève-des-Bois), Teffi, some ladies, more rarely I. Loris, who is about eighty, nephew of a minister of Alexander II. He speaks eight languages, was till 1917 in the diplomatic corps, knows *Faust* by heart as well as a good part of *The Divine Comedy*.

N. Davidenkov, a 'Vlasovist',* arrives. He's a friend of Akhmatova, studied at Leningrad University. He speaks long about Akhmatova and reads her verse, unknown to any of us:

> My husband in a grave, my son in prison.
> Pray for me.

I could not hold back my tears and went out to the next room. In the dining room there was silence. Davidenkov was evidently waiting for me to return. When I sat in my place, he read about the willow tree:

> I loved burdocks and nettle,
> But more than anything – the silver willow tree,
> And strangely I have outlived it!

This was the voice of Anna Andreevna, which was carrying through twenty years, and what years! I felt like writing down the verse, but I was embarrassed to do so: for some reason the presence of Gippius and Teffi prevented me. I didn't do it. He read also 'I celebrate the last anniversary', and finally:

*He was later sent to a Gulag and the generals Vlasov and Krasnov were hanged.

> One goes in a straight path,
> Another goes in a circle . . .
> . . . .
> And I go, misfortune following me,
> Not in a straight and not in a crooked way,
> I go to no place and to no time,
> Like a derailed train.

Here I again got up and went to the salon, not to cry but to write down on a pad all of Gippius's eight lines; they stayed in my memory, I did not spill them out till I got the pencil. When I returned again, Davidenkov said: 'I didn't know, forgive me, that this would so upset you.' He read no more.

April

We turned up in a small hotel near the Rue Convention the night of a heavy bombing of the northern *quartiers* of Paris (Chapelle). We went down to the exit. Everything around was lilac-coloured, and it seemed that the bombs fell around the corner and all was burning. The sky at first was orange-red, then lilac, and the thunder was indescribable, deafening and uninterrupted. This was the heaviest bombing I had ever experienced. I stood and looked at the street through the glass entrance door, while M. stood next to me. Suddenly I saw her hair stand up on her head. Perhaps it only seemed so to me? But I clearly saw how above her forehead the hair stood up vertically. I covered her eyes with my hand and it gradually flattened out.

June

We went for a swim in a small river that runs for three kilometres from Longchêne beneath weeping willows. The water was up to our knees, but the day was so hot that this was refreshing. The water was transparent, the bottom rocky. N. and Marie-Louise tried to swim and I and M. nearly died of laughter looking at them. We came out, dried off, dressed, and went home. Suddenly the buzzing of planes above us: two fighters (obviously American) spotted us, swooped down, and began spraying the weeping willows with machine-gun fire. N., Marie-Louise, and M. lay on the ground in the reeds, and I dived into the water as I was, dressed.

Within a few minutes they flew away. We lay a few minutes longer (I in the water) and went home, sad, scared, and dirty.

June

Bombings at night, at which the house trembles. The nightingales pour forth their song. The heavier the bombings, the louder and more passionate the nightingales.

June

On 3 June at night the house shook terribly and there was thundering in the chimney, the shutters banged, all trembled. I, too, like everyone else around. To the nightingale it made no difference.

June

6th. Landing in Normandy.

July

I meet S.'s sister. She said she had received a notice from the headquarters of his unit: 'Killed in the battle near Chernovitsy, heroically defending his commander.' We stood a while silently, looked at each other, and parted.

August

G., who had chopped down the plum tree, announced in the village that now when the Germans were leaving and the Allies arriving, there would be communism in France. He would be mayor and would hang us as 'White' Russians. The Germans left Sunday, 20 August. Monday the 21st, drunk, he came for us with a rope and announced he would hang all the 'rich' on the 'tree of liberty' that stood in the middle of the village. Arrested besides us were some farmers. I lay, bound by a thick rope, in some shed of his for about an hour, but N. would not give himself up. It disturbed me that Marie-Louise, M., and Ramona should see me hang. This would certainly make an impression on them.

Marie-Louise, however, let the police know (though the telephones were not working), and we were all freed. The police arrested G. and sent him to Rambouillet, to prison. He had prepared revolvers (three), and he had pressed now one, now another, now a third against my left ear, the same one that was once struck with a fist.

In the shed I lay and prepared for death – an awkward but in part natural one – that is, one which we could have foreseen *if we all had not forgotten about the plum tree*. But you can't remember everything! I presume that fist destroyed my memory in July 1942. Strange, I thought, it did not destroy my hearing but my memory. But of course not for ever. This cannot be. And if I remain alive, then for sure *now* I will never forget the plum tree. I will sooner forget the shed . . .

Then G.'s wife threw herself at me with kisses. She was terribly worried that we would go to court. Some farmers insisted that N. begin proceedings against G. The police ordered us not to spend the night at home and told the farmers to be careful.

We went, all four, to Rochefort (eight kilometres). We rode on bicycles, through the woods, and behind the trees something rustled and moved. In Rochefort we took two rooms in a hotel.

On the 22nd the Americans entered,

on the 23rd the first French troops,

on the 25th Paris was liberated,

on the 27th we returned to Longchêne.

The house was looted in our absence. But there was really nothing to take.

On 24 August, in the morning, we sat and breakfasted at the hotel window in Rochefort. On the main street, hooting, a crowd ran chasing a half-naked, barefooted girl, just shaven, with swastikas painted on her bare body. She was short, chubby, her breasts shook, her face was swollen (they had probably beaten her when they shaved her). About sixty people ran after her. People stood at their windows. (This was because she had slept with a German.)

Marie-Louise wanted to run out and stop the crowd – obviously she was at her wit's end that moment! She is strong, tall, and thinks anything possible. We could hardly hold her back. She had certain 'sins' upon her, as I was once told: she gave water to a wounded German parachutist, and this had not been forgotten.

October

Meeting of poets in the Café Grillon, in the basement. We used to assemble here, but hadn't for five years. All had aged, including myself. Appearance of Raevsky and Ginger, who had survived.

Home through the Tuileries. Once, fifteen years ago, we strolled in the Tuileries: Smolensky, Knut, Khodasevich, and I. Everyone was a little in love with me, and I was a little in love with everyone.

October

Mme. Lefort said to me, gulping with joy, that in August she had lived her happiest day: she had managed to spit in the face of a captured German general, when he was being led along the Boulevard des Batignolles.

November

A show at a fair (Place des Nations). Poverty, dirt, rags, and spangles. A sign: For Adults Only. We go in. In the small 'hall' there are no seats, the audience is standing, the floor is slanted steeply so that those standing in the back can see well. On the tiny stage three girls are dancing, in red wigs, half dressed, in ragged clothes shiny with dirt. The violinist and pianist are, with effort, murdering a rollicking foxtrot.

Something seemed strange to me in the movements and facial expressions of the dancers. Gradually the girls started taking off their capes, then the transparent bodices of their dresses, and finally their brassières. *They were men.* It turned out that recently a law had been passed forbidding strip-tease and the display in music halls of naked *women.* We left with a feeling of disenchantment and revulsion.

1945

August

On the 8th was my birthday. With difficulty I obtained half a pound of sausage. In the dining room I set the table, cut twelve pieces of dark bread, and put on them twelve pieces of sausage. The guests came at eight and at first sat, as was proper, in my room. The kettle boiled, I prepared the tea, brought in the sugar, milk, and a bottle of red wine, and decided the birthday table looked proper. While I poured out the tea, the guests came into the dining room. Bunin entered first, looked over the sandwiches and, without even hurrying, ate one after another all twelve pieces of sausage. So when the others came to the table and sat down (including Sergey Makovsky, Smolensky, Asya, and others) they found only bread. These pieces of bread, spread out on two plates, looked rather strange and pitiful.

November

Once N. and I went from Paris to Zurich (about nine years ago). The train crushed a man. When I looked through the window I saw a bloody corpse lying on the embankment. The bloody leg lay apart.

December

Our brain is not the wisest part of us. In significant moments of life, when man decides on an important step, his actions are governed not so much by clear awareness of what to do as by an inward impulse which comes from the deepest foundations of his nature. Perhaps this inward impulse or instinct is an unconscious consequence of some prophetic dream, which is forgotten by us on awakening but which gives our life beauty and harmony and dramatic unity, which could not result from a vacillating awareness, where it is so easy to fall into error or let a false note ring out. Precisely thanks to these prophetic dreams man feels capable of great deeds and from his youth on goes in a necessary direction, moved by a mysterious inward feeling that this is his true path – like the bee who with such an instinct builds his honeycombs. This is the impulse Balthazar Gracián [1601–58] called *'la gran sindéresis'*, the great power of moral discernment: man instinctively feels that all his salvation is here, that without it he would have perished . . . Every man has concrete inner principles, they are in his blood, they flow in his veins as a result of his thoughts, feelings, and desires. Usually he does not suspect their abstract existence. Only when he looks in his past and sees how his life was formed, does he understand that he always followed them, as if they had given him signs which he unconsciously followed.

SCHOPENHAUER. *Aphorisms.*

1946

March

A dream: husband, wife and lover; I am a guest. The husband

dies. The wife and lover remain. I, however, enter the dining room and see: all three are again there. I am astonished: Was he not buried this morning? Turns out that all is *very simple*: they are living *backwards*, that is not in the future, but in the past, as if reversed in time, in what has been experienced (from Saturday to Friday, from Friday to Thursday). This is considered perfectly natural.

August

Two months at Le Cannet at Zlobin's. He had rented a house and invited me. We shared expenses.

Greta Gerell came from Sweden. She said my *Tchaikovsky* was being reprinted there and having great success. I am forced to write to the publisher.

If an answer comes, I will go to Sweden.

November

When, in the 1930s, the correspondence of Tchaikovsky and Madame von Meck was published, I decided to write a book about him. I then went to Rachmaninov's, Glazunov's, to the descendants of Madame von Meck, and many others who knew Tchaikovsky. Finally I got to Praskovya Vladimirovna (former Moscow beauty), widow of Anatoly Ilych Tchaikovsky. She told me I could not write all she would tell me. For example, she had a diary of Tchaikovsky's (she pointed to a locked trunk). What diary? I could hardly avoid shouting out, struck as I was. It turned out – one of the *copies* of the *Diary* printed in 1923. Did she think it was printed in one copy? Or did she feel it got to Paris in one copy? This I couldn't find out. When I said it was in libraries, she was very astonished and, I think, did not believe me.

December. Stockholm.

Anatoly Ilych was a senator and governor. Praskovya Vladimirovna, when I want to see her, lived in the Russian home for the aged near Paris. In her small room there were many family portraits. Anton Rubinstein had once been in love with her.

I told her how once Benois asked me if I had been at the première of *Queen of Spades*, and became terribly embarrassed when he realized what he had blurted out, and began to excuse himself.

She was a lively, heavily made-up old lady, with curls. She had a grandson (Venevitinov) and two granddaughters (Ungern-Stern-berg).

December. Stockholm.

In Stockholm a visit to the actress Harriet Bossé, third wife of August Strindberg. *The Confession of a Fool* (which she says she has not read, since she had given him her word not to) is a wail by Strindberg about himself. As a confession the whole book belongs to the twentieth century. Besides Rousseau, it seems, no one before Strindberg had written of himself so openly. A man socially, materially, and sexually conquered by women. And this at the time (1893) of 'The Kreutzer Sonata'!

December. Stockholm.

I bought everything, packed it, and took it to post. The package will arrive in Paris before me. I put no edibles in it, only warm things: two sweaters of indescribable beauty; six pairs of warm socks; wool gloves and a powder to clean them with; shoes and cream to polish them. A coat lighter than down and an Eskimo cap. All this so every passer-by will turn to look. This now brings me a special pleasure. Someone will lose his head out of joy and (without a head, but wearing a cap) will come to meet me at the railway station.

December. Stockholm.

In the twentieth century people have revealed themselves as they had never done before. Everything is about oneself, every book. The baring of what was secret. Strindberg was one of the first (if you forget Rousseau) to do this, in 1893. He told in *Confession of a Fool* how his first wife (this was Siri von Essen, she was born in Finland and spoke Russian) left him and why. All his deeply personal drama is reflected in this book. Then he married his second wife and she gave him her word never to read the *Confession*. She did not keep her word, read the book and, taking the two children with her, left him. When he married Harriet Bossé he again forced her to swear she would not read the book. All this Harriet Bossé told me and said she had kept her word. But after six years of living with Strindberg she also left him (taking the children). She was an actress and played the main roles in his plays, although she was very young. She showed me photographs. How charming she was in *Damask* and *Easter*! She gave me one photograph, where she was about forty-five, but no others. Now she is about seventy.

Confession of a Fool anticipates all the autobiographies of our time, including André Gide's. He was not the first, as was then said, who spoke of things previously taboo. Strindberg was the first to speak in the language of full truth about himself and show himself to the world. Perhaps this is why he has a monument in Stockholm where he is naked: near the City Hall stands a *bare* Strindberg.

We continue to a great degree to move on this path (of Strindberg and Gide) and tell about ourselves what our fathers and grandfathers kept hidden. We know ourselves (and them) better, so why hide ourselves? There remain very few riddles indeed. But there are a couple of secrets from time to time.

Not riddles, but equations. If A, B, C, D, E, F, etc . . . are known, then we can know X, Y, and Z if we have learned to think. Still, ten years ago outspokenness was bravado and a banner with which authors went into battle against silence, hypocrisy, and constraint. Now it seems natural when it is used, but also does not impede when it is not. Everything is so clear in the equation; enough is said so that there is no reason to go out into the square to a drumbeat. Secrets are another matter. They are a part of my *interior decoration*. They have their juices.

The first trait of modern autobiographies is the revelation of the self. The second: man often pretends to be not smarter, kinder, nicer, better, cleverer than he is, but worse, nastier, more stupid, and simple. Bely in his recollections sometimes took on the pose of an 'idiot' (this had begun in his childhood and continued, in fact, all his life, the other side of narcissism, which means a narcissism of particular strength). From which comes the device of writing the opposite of what is. Epicurus said: Hide your life. William Blake said: What can be understood by a fool does not interest me. From which comes the deliberate complication by authors of writings about themselves. (A third trait of modern literature.)

All this I must take into consideration when I decide at some point to write a book about myself. I know well: without having the old sense of 'female shame' I nevertheless do not feel capable of revealing *everything* about myself. If I were living and writing fifty years ago, there would be sense in this. Now I see no sense in it.

'The virus has been discovered' – why discover it again? Benefactors of mankind (at their head D.H. Lawrence) toiled in this field. Moreover, I always considered modesty (not shame!) a kind of virtue, together with daring and truth. What's more: at the moment when I decide to write about myself, all my masks will be stripped off and I will not have to pretend to be better or worse than I am. In the meantime I think, I never pretended and do not pretend now to be 'prettier': in the first place, this seemed to me utterly beyond my means, and in the second – unnecessary.

I must – when I write about myself at some point – say that I never suffered from being born a woman. I somehow compensated for this *deficiency*, which I never felt as a deficiency: not when I earned my daily bread, not when I built (or destroyed) my life with a man, not when I struck up friendships with women and men. Not when I wrote. I didn't even always remember that I was a woman, and yet still 'femininity' was my asset, this I knew. Perhaps one of my few assets. Moreover, I had a good deal of what men have (but I didn't cultivate it, perhaps out of fear of losing my femininity). There was physical and emotional endurance, there was a profession, financial independence, there was success, initiative and freedom in love and friendship, the know-how of making a choice. But there was also submission to man – with joy. I loved this submission, I sometimes artificially called it forth in myself and it gave me bliss. And there was the search for help from a man, the expectation of advice from a man and gratitude for his help, support and advice.

I will also say that I loved and love the human body, shoulders and knees, its smoothness and strength, the smell of a human being, his skin, his breathing, and all the noises within him.

1947

January

When I was in Sweden in November–December of last year, Fru Asplund invited me to come in the summer to her place on an island in the Skärgården, six hours from Stockholm, where there are no roads, no electricity, no telephones, and where she has a house in which she and Greta Gerell spend the summer. Fru Asplund is sixty-two, tall, straight, and she speaks in no other language but

Swedish (I communicate with her either through Greta, or in bad German). She once taught Swedish gymnastics, was a champion in sailing, and fenced. Quite a remarkable woman. I decided to go in June for a month. But how can I thank her?

She has everything, decidedly everything, and I have little money. She doesn't like perfume, so Guerlain is useless. And then I decided, instead of a present, to learn Swedish. At least this would certainly bring her pleasure and facilitate our getting on with each other.

I remembered that Loris-Melikov had been a tsarist consul in Norway. I wrote to him. Now he comes twice a week, we drink tea and have a snack (he has grown terribly thin in these two or three years), and I foist a sandwich on him when he leaves. He is a remnant of the past. Loris is wearing a suit that must be twenty years old. I asked N. if he did not have some old things (they are more or less the same size). He brought me a suit, perfectly all right, only moth-eaten. Loris was very happy though embarrassed, and while I tied up the bundle, recited something out of Schiller to me from memory about gratefulness.

Now I am cramming Swedish grammar.

January
  The year 1946 was happy for me: I began again to work. Then there were two trips: one to the south, to Zlobin's, the other to Sweden. And I wrote a book on Blok.

February
    Freedom? From what exactly?
    From intellectual anarchy
    From opinions subject to the caprices of mood
    From dualism (everything has been synthesized)
    From a sense of guilt (now gone)
    From anxiety
    From fear of the opinion of others
    From neurotic restlessness and disorders in the body
    From the pedantry of early years
    From formless overflowing with contradictory emotions
    From the fear of death
    From the temptation to escape

From a pretence that, very rarely, was necessary for some reason, but is now dumped as worthless

And when this composure had set in, when problems led to answers, the idea came to me that I was still able to revolt: the premonition came that *it would not end this way* (under a Paris roof). And the foretaste of some misty events. 'Energy is Eternal Delight' (W. Blake).

June. Hemmarö, Sweden.

Small misunderstanding: when I arrived at Fru Asplund's it proved that Loris had not taught me the Swedish language but Norwegian, which obviously he knew much better. Thus I cannot speak with Fru Asplund but am able to read Ibsen.

June. Hemmarö, Sweden.

Fru Asplund and Greta in the morning, before breakfast, having hardly risen from bed, go to the bathhouse and swim. In the afternoon, on a motorboat, they rush to a neighbouring island for the mail and groceries. In the evening, on a sailing boat, Fru Asplund goes out to sea and floats among the reefs for two hours, alone. Sometimes Greta takes a boat and oars and goes to some uninhabited island and there paints the clouds. All their life is on water. The archipelago is called Ruslagen, and from here, it is said, Rurik came and perhaps even the word Rus.

I do not bathe and do not go boating. I fear water. With the years this fear gets stronger and stronger in me. I even try not to look at the water from close up: I get sad and frightened.

In recent years I have felt more clearly that I should rid myself of hydrophobia, that it is really *not my* fear at all, in the first place, but an alien one fastened on me, that in old age I will be powerless against manias which bring in their wake other phobias. That this terrible weakness deprives me not only of a great number of pleasures but, what's more important, of that inner harmony which is basically the aim of life. To have done with battiness before fifty is indispensable, since afterwards these monsters – fears, doubts, mirages, prejudices – become fixed ideas, weaknesses, from which there is no salvation, from which personality begins to crumble, like the plaster of an old wall, and then the wall itself begins to fall apart, and this is an ugly, disgusting, and shameful sight. Fru Asplund said to me once in the morning:

'I look at you and don't understand: *du bist ja so harmonisch*! If you do not stop fearing water, which is an *element*, the element that is *in you*, your harmony, will be destroyed, because it's unstable. With the years hydrophobia, like every phobia, will outgrow you, and willy-nilly you will feed a dragon that will devour you and all your equilibrium. I don't understand how you, who do not fear life, fear water. You yourself are only water and salt. So what are you afraid of? Stop fearing water and all in you will fall into place. You must find time now to do it.'

'Water and salt?' I said. 'I think this is kind of old-fashioned.'

'I haven't heard that. If you deny water in yourself, you will gradually turn into a pillar of salt.'

It was the time of the white nights, and in the evenings I started taking the boat and rowing out to far-off islands. A huge pale moon floated above the pine woods, and the sun was motionless for hours above the horizon. There was a vague, fearful, and slightly ridiculous feeling in me, because I knew that from the balcony they were both watching me row clumsily, hardly making it through the gates of the boat shed, though four boats could easily have floated through. They watched me, laughed at me, but never gave advice and in fact made believe that they did not notice what I was doing at night. I went far away, tried to work the oars rhythmically; the Nordic pines were fragrant, the water moving around me clear; every now and then a fish would splash high. In this silence of the infinite evening which became, in the end, a morning, I was completely alone with the water in these reefs, I knew I could not be seen any more from the balcony; I was alone with the water as never before in my life. I subdued my horror of many years, lowered my hand into a wave and the wave answered me, as a panther rubs at the legs of its subduer. The rustle of the waves and the translucence of the air and the fragrance from the shore, all united for me in one indivisible feeling of life and freedom and strength, my own strength, my inner and outer health. Not exactly knowing which was west and which east, I floated further, ever further, in the direction of the sun, which hung in the sky, neither setting nor rising, and poured its tender fire on me and my boat and on all this divine northern silence.

The island I floated to had been uninhabited for five hundred years – there was once a plague here and all died, and no one since wanted to live here. Pines grew thick and it smelled of resin, birds twittered within, day and night, those indefatigable birds who fear nothing.

Now I run first to the bathhouse in the morning. The cold water gradually also becomes tame. Fru Asplund and Greta make believe that they don't notice this. The main thing is not to interfere. And then – look! – in two months all passes: my severe weakness of many years, a legacy from Father, this hydrophobia, and I feel within me something setting itself up that looks as if it cannot be destroyed: a feeling of wholeness, a sense that all the emotional anarchy that was still in me, the intellectual disorder that has not been outlived, the shaking of the 'trembling creature' are behind me.

In the afternoon now I hurry after the mail, across the blue water, past the plagued island, past the castle of some retired admiral who left his estate to serve as a home for mentally-ill sailors. I fly to the hamlet where there is a telephone, and a pharmacy, and even a school where children hurry on skis in the winter from neighbouring islands. I fetch newspapers and our mail, colourful Swedish weeklies, and rush back, through wind and water, to the buzzing of the motor. In the boathouse Fru Asplund awaits me, we drink coffee in the garden and then she takes me with her on the sailing boat, as if nothing had ever happened, as if from the first it had been like this. She is silent, sitting in the bow and holding the ropes in her hands. She doesn't like to converse when she is on water. She has her habits.

Very quickly I begin to notice with astonishment that other, pettier phobias leave me, and one of them is my aversion to the odour of liquid asphalt. Now, while they are repairing the city pavements, I don't even notice it. In general, suddenly nothing in the world seems unbearable to me: there are no odours that would make me sick, no food I could not accept into myself, no spectacle I would turn from. I can take in my hand any cuttlefish and examine any filth.

August

I returned from Sweden and went for a month to Longchêne, taking Boris and Vera Zaitsev with me. Starting in the morning, Vera tells Boris and me all kinds of funny and sad or simply curious stories. There is laughter in the house. They love Longchêne: we all three sit, comfortably and quietly. We stroll. We cook dinner.

Sometimes Boris goes for a walk alone. Vera then says: Papinka is thinking. Probably he will soon begin to invent something.

August

Ramona became fat-arsed, short-legged, and went to a hairdresser for a 'permanent'. She is fifteen. It's hard for her to study and she runs around with boys.

August

Bees do not attack when you fumigate them (fumigation for them as for us is an earthquake). They wait, immobile. They fold their wings, tuck up their feet and hardly crawl: they know this *will pass*. And it does.

September

The man I continue to live with (but am ceasing to do so) is:
not cheerful,
not kind,
not sweet.
Nothing turns out well in his hands. He has forgotten all he knew. He loves no one, and he will gradually stop being loved.

1948

April

The entire past is with me, it exists simultaneously with the present. As amoeba and man exist simultaneously.

April

Henry James and his contemporaries were sometimes distressed about the state of the working class, about the state of the peasants, and even lamented the nasty structure of life. But it never dawned on them that the fourteen-hour workday could become a seven-hour one and that education could become universal, free, and compulsory. Tchaikovsky, on seeing a worker demonstration in New York, did not understand: What is this? What are these people demanding and from whom?

July

Longchêne is sold. It was bought by an actress of the Comédie Française, Mony Dalmès. (I saw her when she acted in a Montherlant drama.)

She wants to 'wall up that door' and 'put a window through there'. Cut what you want and wall up all you want to your heart's content!

July

Again in Sweden (a third time).

Herr Lundstrom and his right leg: after an automobile accident his leg was amputated. He buried it in the family vault and once a year goes to the grave with flowers.

July. Stockholm.

Sweden pierces me with temptation. Yesterday E. K. asked me:

'Do you want to remain here?'

'Is this really possible?'

'Difficult, but possible.'

Suddenly I felt I had to decide on something. Nevertheless, perhaps not Sweden.

I must *fuse* with something, but I cannot with Sweden. Must I? Yes, I must. Isn't it too late? No, it isn't.

There was a holiday at Skansen. The sun set, but it didn't get darker. Fires were lit. Clean water, pure sky. A little boat headed somewhere. The shores were illuminated. Some warrior held out a bronze hand. Young graduates in white. Orchestras. People in a masquerade were dancing.

White bears and seals.

A distant view.

July. Back in Paris.

'At Nicholas II's memorial service a beautiful wreath with ribbons "From the new emigration" called attention to itself' (Russian daily).

August

Mougins. Halfway between Cannes and Grasse. The view all around is indescribable. The sea can be seen far off. We live in a

house, in front of which is an old fig tree; in the morning I pick two
dozen figs from the ground that have fallen from the tree during the
night, bursting with ripeness and juice and having become candied
during the night. Near by is an ancient chapel. It belongs to the
same man who owns the house. He let us live here free on condition
that on Sunday we open the chapel doors and let people see it. This I
do. Six days a week I go to Cannes to swim, and on Sunday I open
the heavy cast-iron doors and sit on a tabouret near them. There is
no charge. Entry is free. But you have to watch with one eye that no
one breaks or steals anything – there are five eighteenth-century
crèches, a whole collection. It attracts tourists.

November

> If I were to live, I would present in my memoirs principles, ideas,
> events, catastrophes, the entire epic of my time precisely because I
> saw how one epoch ended and another began, and personalities
> opposed to one another in this end and this beginning mix in my
> evaluation. I appeared between two centuries, as if between two
> rivers flowing together.
> CHATEAUBRIAND. *Mémoires d'Outre-Tombe.*

November

A Bunin reading. He read his memoirs in which he jeered at the
symbolists, depicted (aped) Balmont, Gippius, Blok, called Bely a
buffoon, etc. In the pro-Soviet *Russian News* Adamovich wrote an
account where he justified Bunin on the grounds that Russian
symbolism was a pretentious 'looking into abysses', which Tolstoy
had found ridiculous in his time (and Tolstoy, of course, could not
err). And because 'if Pushkin had read Blok, he also would have
understood nothing'.

December

Meeting in the big Salle Pleyel. Camus spoke. He reminded me
of Blok, in his appearance, his manner, and what he spoke about: in
a sad voice on the freedom of the poet. Sartre appeared, affirming
that you could no longer describe love and jealousy without

speaking of your attitude to Stalingrad and the Resistance. Breton babbled about Trotsky.

1949

January

In Paris in the Russian cathedral on the Rue Daru they built a monument to Nicholas II. In front of this monument of unspeakable ugliness candles burned.

Then in 1947–8, when the Metropolitan (a Soviet civil servant) Nikolai Krutitsky came from Moscow to transfer the émigré church to the Moscow jurisdiction, the 'left' were ready to agree with joy to the transfer. It did not work out only because the 'right' (those who so respected Nicholas II?) had the majority by one vote. The head of the church received Krutitsky with tears of tender emotion in his eyes.

Krutitsky then lived with Ilya Ehrenburg in the same hotel suite (in different rooms, but with a common reception room) and went with him in the same car to the Soviet embassy for breakfast.

February

I read in the Soviet press: 'Stalin invisibly casts his shadow on everything.'

March

Boris Nicolaevsky was in Paris. He was at my place a long time. The following day I met him at a café on Denfert-Rochereau. Margarete Buber-Neumann came. She had spent eleven years in a Soviet camp in Kolyma and wrote a book about it.

November

We, as distinguished from our fathers, were given the possibility of seeing things as they are in reality, and that's why the bases of life crackle beneath our feet.

– KARL JASPERS

November

Man in the Western world (who has conquered land and

established contact with people of the most diverse countries and told them of their common humanity) has developed on the strength of three principles: rationalism, awareness of his subjectivity, and understanding of the world as a tangible reality existing in time.

For the second time in the history of mankind man has moved away from nature (the first time was when he made the first axe) to do the work nature herself could never have done and which rivals the work of nature in its creative strength (the machine).

— KARL JASPERS

1950

February

Boris Zaitsev and I were invited to Brussels, to give a reading. A blend of 'The Society of Lovers of the Russian Culture', of 'The Union of Russian Intelligentsia in Belgium', and of something else. This was a great joy for Boris and I was also happy about the trip. We went. He said he had become 'restive', like a horse. We stopped in Brussels at the home of Dr Orlov. These cordial people were very kind. Before dinner Orlov's wife warned us nervously not to be astonished: her younger son was married to a blind girl. The older son was like everybody else. He worked in Antwerp. But the younger son had never known whether to become a monk or not, and suddenly married a blind girl, the daughter of a Belgian professor.

We sat down to dinner. The young man, a healthy and handsome blond, and with him the thin, tall, eyeless woman. He cut the roast on her plate for her. She ate and he looked at her and only at her. The next day we were invited to dinner by the chairman of the All-Military Union and after dinner were taken to a club. The hall (not large) was overflowing, more than a hundred people. We read, received a little money, and the next day went back. Now Boris remembers this trip as something tremendously fascinating, slightly adventurous. 'That was when Nina and I went to Belgium' he says and looks off dreamily to the side somewhere. I also try to think that there was a small holiday in my life.

February

I was certain that Yasha Zak would not come to our literary

soirée in Brussels: I had not heard from him for so many years. Perhaps he had perished during the war, perhaps he had long been in America. Still, in the interval after Boris's reading I looked around – what if? But he was not there.

In 1929–31 he had begun to write to me, at first at *The Latest News*, then to my home address. He wrote every day. I answered about twice a month. He was an unusual man and wrote well. When I went to Brussels for a reading (this was in 1934) he came. He was not alone, but with his fiancée, as he said to me. We spoke a little; she didn't understand Russian and this made us slightly uncomfortable. At the interval they both left. I was surprised: for so long he had waited for this day but left without saying good-bye. This all seemed to me a little mysterious.

Suddenly a letter came from her. She wrote in French and asked, 'Who is he to me?' and am I prepared to 'destroy her happiness?' The letter was polite but very disturbed. She wrote that she had been suffering for a long time and finally decided to write to ask me. She trusted me and hoped I would answer the 'whole truth'. I wrote a few words immediately to her that he was *nothing* to me, that I would no longer answer his letters, that I begged her to believe me and to ask him not to write to me any more.

So ended the friendship in letters.

In connection with this I remember another story: in 1926 one Boris Butkevich sent a story from Shanghai to *New House*, which I quickly published. He was talented and later everyone (even Bunin) said the author had promise. We started to correspond. Butkevich came from the Far East to Marseilles. In 1928 when I went from Cannes to Paris I wrote to him to come to the station, I wanted to help set him up at least as Marseilles correspondent of *The Latest News* (he worked at a plant as an unskilled workman). I jumped out of the train to the platform in Marseilles. A small man, humbly dressed, snub-nosed, with a stupid face and the manners of a provincial, stood before my car. I went up to him. We started to talk. I tried not to notice his appearance and got down to business at once. Suddenly the man said: 'I am not Butkevich. Excuse me, Butkevich did not come. I came instead.' 'And where is he?' I asked; my heart sank. I felt I would now get terribly angry.

'Them did not come,' said the man, 'because them does not have no new suit, and is ashamed of the old one.'

I was struck dumb. The idea that someone did not come because of a jacket with holes in it and was *embarrassed* before ME! It seemed completely absurd. The realization that some idiot had been sent to tell me this sent me into a rage. But I kept control and said:

'I am very sorry.'

I went to my car. The man with a stupid smile followed me with his eyes.

Later Butkevich excused himself to me, writing that he was sick and could not come to the train. I did not change my feelings: I wrote to him, I put two of his columns in the Russian paper, and when he died in a hospital bed I wrote his obituary.

April

Perhaps the whole pilgrimage of spirit was the only goal of spirit, the only home of truth.

— SANTAYANA

PART SEVEN

Not Waiting for Godot

IN THE SUMMER OF 1947 I WAS ON MY OWN AGAIN. Longchêne was advertised for sale and in Paris there was no place for me to live. There was neither flat nor room, and there was no money to rent anything. At that point Katya bought an apartment on one of the central streets of Paris, five minutes from the Elysée Palace. She had returned from Persia and decided to settle again in Paris. I will say a few words about Katya.

We had once been classmates, but for only a year. She had a Persian passport but was by origin Armenian, though she came not from those same 'grateful Armenians' as I, but from Persian ones, and her grandfather, in the middle of the last century, had a donkey. He decided to bring from Teheran to Russia a bag of dried fruits on this donkey, since he had heard that in Russia people did not know how to dry fruits and did not eat them. He set out on his way, got to the northern Caucasus and there sold his fruits. Returning to Teheran he bought a second donkey and again left. Within a few years he settled in Russia, married, and opened a dried-fruit store and later a factory. His son, Katya's father (and friend of my father), went from dried fruit to various other things, in particular to oil, both cooking and lubricating. Towards the time of the Revolution he was fabulously wealthy. Katya's mother died young, leaving him three daughters who were brought up by the grandmother.

Katya, the year we went to school together, came to class with a huge pearl, the size of a walnut, surrounded by diamonds, hanging on a chain beneath her chin. It turned out that her father had given his daughters (who were then fifteen, thirteen, and five) jewels out of pity for the poor orphans who had been left without a mother. The girls wore pearls, emeralds, and diamonds the way we wore collars and cuffs. After the Revolution the jewels were exchanged for food. Then Katya married, and since her husband did exactly nothing she opened a ladies' dress salon, supported him, her sister, and niece. She abandoned her husband after about six years, continued to work all her life, and when in September 1939 she had to return to Persia because of her Persian citizenship, she worked there, making clothes for the royal court, the princesses, the whole female half of the Shah's family. Now she had decided to buy a flat in Paris for fun, a large penthouse with an inside staircase and a balcony, in an old building (where, it was said, Chateaubriand had visited). But this flat had to be rebuilt, the roof re-covered, a bathroom put in, and to live in it then was impossible. Katya settled in a hotel near by, and builders worked from morning till night at her place. She proposed that I live in one of the rooms till the repairs were finished, that I somehow take shelter in those premises. She had always been kind, and also cheerful, industrious, and pretty – four basic female qualities.

Through the broken ceiling I saw stars at night. Near by, in the dining room, the roof had been removed. At 7:00 A.M. the masons came and started breaking walls around me. I lay and waited till I could rush into the bathroom, where plumbers were cutting up and soldering pipes. One night, coming home, I saw that my door had been removed and in its place was a gaping hole to the floor below. When I had to go to the kitchen I walked on boards placed along the outside wall of the house where house painters rocked on their suspension platforms, and sang loudly. Automobiles rushed below me and little men poked about here and there. In the evening there was no light, and I lay under the stars and mused. Once a beam fell across the passage and I was asked 'for the time being' not to wash. There was a layer of white powder on all my things, and my hair turned grey from dust.

Once (it was in June) a rain shower soaked my couch. The concierge said I was living completely illegally in this flat, mostly without walls, without ceiling, a floor with holes, and that if I fell through to the lower storey or fell out onto the street, no insurance company would pay me a thing. I tried not to catch her eye. The workers looked at me in silence and I tried to make myself very small, so that they wouldn't notice me.

At night I hung in the air over Paris, over its very centre, between streetlamps and clouds, in complete darkness, somewhere near the infrequent aeroplanes, which (it seemed to me) could touch me with their wings. At dawn, in the garret opposite, someone lengthily and generously watered flowers on the window sill. I didn't see him, but of course he saw me. Then the drilling of the walls began, the sanding of the floor in the future living room. And I went out, through a door, or a broken section of wall, or a window, and from there went down to the street by the kitchen stairs, six flights of them.

Then it ended. All was planed, joined, and painted, and I left the house. I now had a flat near the Trocadéro, a tiny one with running water, a lift, a small electric plate, bookshelves. I gradually began to sell my books. Fet went, Baratynsky, Sologub's *The Petty Demon* went, as well as the collected works of Leo Tolstoy, a huge Larousse of the nineteenth century, a *Petersburg 1908 Directory* once given to me by Maklakov (the property of the tsarist embassy). There were two purchasers: an old Russian admiral, a respected connoisseur of Russian books, and an ill-mannered chatterbox with the look of a crook. Both did business with U.S. universities. Now my Fet and Sologub are on American university library shelves. I have seen them, touched them. But I have not found the *Petersburg 1908 Directory* anywhere, alas! It was such interesting reading, particularly the section on Imperial theatres, where under the heading 'Ballet' there was a list of all the famous Kshesinskayas and Karsavinas, as if these were Ivanovs and Petrovs.

I sold books and wrote in *Russian Thought*. Its founders could not think up a wittier name for a weekly Russian paper in Paris. It was started in 1947 when the French government was reorganized and French communists excluded from it: while there were communist ministers in the government, permission for an émigré newspaper was not given. There was a 'literary page' in the paper and I was considered its editor. I struck up relationships with the 'new' émigrés (those who had left the U.S.S.R. during World War Two), who then lived in Germany and did not want to return to the Soviet Union. In January 1949, when the lawsuit of Viktor Kravchenko, author of the book *I Chose Freedom*, began, the paper started coming out twice a week, thanks to my reporting from the court chamber.

Again I sat on the press bench in court, as I had ten years ago, in the same row as correspondents from the *New York Times*, *Izvestia*, Canadian and French papers. The proceedings were noisy and at the time important; the character of Kravchenko himself, who had attacked the French communist paper for defamation, was quite colourful. André Gide, Mauriac, Aragon sometimes appeared in the audience. In the evenings on the pavement a crowd of curious people gathered to look at Kravchenko himself. I hurried home, knowing that after the caricature of me that appeared in *Lettres Françaises* people would watch me. I went home trying to avoid dark streets. I worked till late at night on my story. At 7:00 A.M. a messenger came for it from the editorial offices. Later the paper brought out the reports as a separate book, on newsprint; the book has long since scattered into dust.

The affair, now forgotten, came down briefly to this: one of the members of the Soviet lend-lease commission, sent from the U.S.S.R. to the U.S.A. in 1944, decided to defect and stay on in America. A French literary weekly, which can be called unofficially communist, began a campaign against him, defaming his name, insulting him, proving that the book was not written by him. But for many, including myself, the root of the whole affair lay in the fact that the Soviet system of concentration camps had finally received wide publicity. Kravchenko spoke about it in his book, as did witnesses called by him who were former inmates of the camps at Kolyma and Karaganda. The problem of camps suddenly grew in France to its full size. *Lettres Françaises*, of course, denied the existence of camps, and witnesses called by the weekly affirmed that all this was invention. To see with my own eyes how a former minister, or a world-known scientist, a Nobel Prize laureate, or a Sorbonne professor with the Legion of Honour in his lapel buttonhole, or a famous writer would take the oath and under oath affirm that there never had been and were not any concentration camps in the U.S.S.R., was one of the strongest impressions of my entire life. When in 1962 I read Solzhenitsyn's story about a Soviet camp and learnt that it had appeared in French translation, I waited for at least one man who had been sworn in and had lied to the court in 1949 to comment on this work. But it did not happen.

I loved to wander between the Trocadéro and the Etoile, to look at the window displays, still very poor. Among them was the window of a photographer on the corner of the Rue Lauriston. He was an old-fashioned photographer who took, in an old-fashioned way, first communicants, newlyweds, recruits, grandfathers and grandmothers on the day of their golden anniversary. On the left side of the window were rows of 1914 soldiers, on the right were the military of the last war. They looked at each other and I looked at them all. Those with moustaches looked at those without, goggle-eyed, and those without at those with; the soldiers dressed in khaki uniforms looked at those dressed in blue-red, long-skirted ones. The blue-red sometimes held in their hands long, clumsy rifles, while those in khaki had revolvers and seemed to be the sons of the long-skirted ones – which in fact they were, sons of faded and forgotten heroes. 'And here I see both!' I thought. 'Yes, I see one and the other. It will soon be half a century that I have been alive in this world.'

Without sound or music, a pictorial or visual counterpoint became increasingly familiar to me, even habitual in that period. It began, I think, in front of the photographer's window, and continues to intensify to the present day: I, as it were, settled down in it, 'sank', it became the element in which my mind worked. In one unit of time there can resound – that is, appear on various levels in the musical sphere – as well as exist in one's mind various pictures, one fading into the other, one emerging from the other, arranged in panoramic perspective with each other, in co-ordination not always susceptible to analysis. Ten or even more 'pictures', 'snap-shots', 'slides', 'drawings', or visions can at the same time (an instant, a second, a minute) make up a counterpoint not perceived by ear but seen by the imagination; it depends on its parts, on the previous chain of visions. The parts, the structural organization of this counterpoint of images, do not depend on the distance in time and space from the thinking moment. In other words, schematically, in 1970 the counterpoint of images at a given moment can consist of what happened in 1928, 1912, 1906, 1949. Though these components are static and nothing happens to them, they *appear* and coexist: now two huge dogs throw themselves on me from a strange courtyard; now a brightly coloured chicken with its head axed off shudders for the last time on the bloody stump; now I put my face in someone's dry warm hands and wipe my wet eyes with his fine fingers; now a lost face flashes by in a train window and I whisper to this face: Serves you right! . . . All this does not rise in my memory vertically or horizontally, does not unwind like a spool, is not scattered like a deck of cards, but comes all at once in layers, not as a musical text for a solo voice, but rather like the

457

conductor's copy of a symphonic score. Perhaps in this visual counterpoint there is a kind of transformation? But I cannot grasp that moment when the counterpoint becomes transformation.

It was good in those years to go to Sweden (three times), and the third time (in 1948) stay a whole summer on an island in the Skärgården; good to be in Provence, near Cannes, to visit Belgium for three days with Boris Zaitsev. It was good to wander about the Trocadéro in the evening, in the gardens leading down to the quays of the Seine, aware, after five years of war, that our end once begun was continuing, that it began 14 June, 1940, the day the Germans took Paris, and now in spite of the liberation was at full swing. To be aware of something is always good, and this time in my awareness a new truth was born for me: I learnt that I myself did *not belong* to those going to their end, that neither in age, inward forces or energy was I ready to move towards the end. That I was still alive. And that I would remain almost completely alone.

Slowly I walked through the whispering dark Trocadéro gardens. They led through wide empty alleys to the river. At night here it was dark and quiet, rare streetlamps illuminated a circle around themselves: a corner, a path, a wide, low-hanging plane-tree branch, from which brittle, already dry leaves fell with a slight rustle, the edge of a lawn trampled by children. That moment when I went through the illuminated circle of foggy white light, the centre of which resembled a moonstone, I suddenly forgot who I was for an instant, what was going on around me, what would happen tomorrow, what had been yesterday, whom I would remain with and how I would live in the future.

Municipal gardens and clouds above – I unravelled their meaning. They are like words. There are words that lead to something – 'Give me a plate,' 'Take a pencil,' 'I want to drink.' These are word streets. You can and must walk along them: from the station to the shop and from home to the office. But there are words that lead to nothing, the very meaning of which are in themselves: *'from a land of sombre exile you summoned me to another land'* (Pushkin); *'and you are ever the same, my country, in your tear-stained ancient beauty . . . '* (Blok). These are word gardens, they lead nowhere, they only exist and have meaning.

One already sensed autumn in the dark air, with that heartbreaking promise of spring everyone in Paris knows. Sometimes people walked next to me and I tried to get in step with them, one-two, one-two. This also led to nothing, like dark clouds in the sky, like plane trees suddenly whispering above my head and then falling silent. They exist and mean, but lead to nothing. My getting in step with passers-by also leads to nothing, but only exists and means. I live alone: without dinners and lunches, without holidays and workdays, and almost without books. I do not live as you do, who are alive, revitalized, going back, starting anew. For me there is no going back.

Trees, like huge flowers, already in three colours: green, yellow, brown. Like pansies. Suddenly the expanse of an empty street is revealed and I stop: it leads somewhere, but I don't know if I need to go somewhere. Better to remain with the trees, the clouds, better to live, in so far as I can, in aimlessness.

I walk back in the black night; terraces whiten, there is no one in the beautiful aimless garden. A section of the moon floats uncertainly above the river. In this pre-dawn hour Paris, for a short time (but very rarely), becomes slightly spectral, like that legendary capital of ours with its granite mythology. Particularly when leaves no longer rustle above my head, but the wind breaks bare boughs, and the grey rain – day and night of the same greyish shade – quietly runs down my eyes and lips. It falls a long time; it also promises spring, and spring comes; a bed of pink tulips edged with forget-me-nots sparkles with magnificence for robbers, beggars, Philistines, and artists – well, well, and even for me, of course. The nightingales sing. One is here, the other is opposite on the other side of the fountains (which gush up on holidays), a third beyond the bridge near the left back leg of the Eiffel Tower (which I noticed a quarter of a century ago).

Sometimes I went from these gardens onto the streets, to the quays. There was nothing to buy and no money in those days, but there were libraries, places I knew well from former years, and there I could go. The Turgenev Library had disappeared long ago; but like a fortress or an arsenal, the Bibliothèque Nationale stood not far from Les Halles, to which access for the 'stateless' was always complicated because to receive a card you had to present testimony from *your* embassy about your good conduct. Later this regulation was somehow changed, but then a new evil appeared: over-crowding. Before the entrance into the main reading room, from morning on, there was a queue of those who had not got in –

459

all the seats were taken – and you had to wait till one of the ninety-year-olds, growing drowsy over some volume, fell asleep and was then escorted out (it was forbidden to sleep here), and when this happened there was a seat. There were halls where the non-French were not allowed, and hours when suddenly the library closed. I still remember the time in the main reading room when there was no electric lighting (like, incidentally, in the Louvre), and old and young were chased out at three in the afternoon as it got dark, and you found scratched on the wall in the women's toilet: 'This place is a disgrace to France' (which was certainly the case).

Now the library closed at five, and if in the morning you could still find a place, it was better not to leave the room before five for any reason whatever: your place could be taken. On Sunday everything was closed. I went all my life to the Bibliothèque to read only 'strange' books which no one reads. 'Ordinary' books there had always either been taken out by someone or were lost or for some reason could not be provided on that given day. Wounded veterans of World War One in uniforms with bronze buttons, scraping their shoes and talking to each other, walked slowly around the room between the tables, looking to see if someone was not drawing something in books, ripping out pages, making marks in the margins, and from time to time an apparatus similar to a huge enema would be placed in the very centre of the room and a thick stream of disinfectant would be released beneath the ceiling to purify the air. Then a light rain fell on our heads.

The library of the Ecole des Langues Orientales was a much more comfortable spot. I didn't have to explain why I had come, excuse myself for sitting so long, show testimony of my loyalty. You found the Russian classics there, got Soviet magazines. Frenchmen sat there, students of the school, students of Professor Pascal, and very old Russian vagrants with university degrees, members of former Russian political parties, of all kinds of social organizations, who were conditioned to read books but were now unemployed and half starved. It was already late for these people to change their profession, as the 'young' (those who were now fifty or more) had gradually changed theirs, when it would turn out unexpectedly that a *poet* was working somewhere in a factory, and a *novelist* was a night taxi driver. Within a year or two these people suddenly revealed themselves as factory workers writing verse in leisure hours, and taxi drivers from time to time managing to write a story. This the old library visitors could not do; they had somehow to continue living in *their* age, which gradually moved further and further away from us all.

I remember the day when I also decided, if not to change my profession, then at least to move into the first stage, to do something else that would enable me to hold out till the end of the month. I could not live longer than from the first to the twentieth on what the Russian paper paid me. The ten final days of the month seemed, as it were, a luxury, for which no money remained, though fate was giving me this luxury and I had somehow to profit by it. It was impossible to order that the month be shortened by a third, the year by four months. I went to Katya, who now had a dress shop, and asked to be allowed to sit at a sewing machine. I have always been fond of all kinds of machines: motors, cranes, cement mixers, threshers, and linotypes. At the end of the day I received the money I had earned. Out of joy and inspiration, pride and hope, I lost it on the way home. The following day I came again and that morning inadvertently broke a bobbin. When you break something, you never know how exactly it happened. To break a Singer steel bobbin is not easy, but I broke it.

Bobbins in 1947–8 were, of course, irreplaceable. But there was no way out for me: saying nothing to anyone, during my lunch hour I went to the central office of Singer. I must confess: the idea of suicide had only for five minutes played in my head. The expression 'she died of a bobbin' suddenly seemed to me so ridiculous that I discarded this possibility (to throw myself into the Seine or to jump out of a window onto the street) almost immediately. In a state of despair, vacillating slightly (obviously from hunger), smiling (at the idea of suicide because of a bobbin), and undoubtedly with a quite abnormal expression (my predicament I now and then compared to the predicament of heroes of Greek and Shakespearian tragedies), I went to the Singer office on the Avenue de l'Opéra. A kind-looking but also obviously underfed receptionist, having watched me attentively and listened to my completely fantastic request to buy a new bobbin, asked me to sit down and went out. I began to wonder how much such a trifle might cost. How much money? Or will I be told: We want five pounds of soap: Or: Do you have real coffee? Or perhaps I will be

told: Give us the *old machine* and we will give you a *new bobbin* . . .
Suddenly a door opened and a solid, smooth, serious man came
out. He seemed to me very important; at that moment I thought
this was the director himself, the director of all of Singer machines
–in Melbourne, Zanzibar, Alaska, and Chile. That is General
Singer himself. He held in his fingers a new bobbin. He also looked
at me attentively and without saying anything put the bobbin in my
mechanically extended hand, bowed, and left. Going down the
stairs I saw to my astonishment in a mirror that my face was
completely green. I even stopped to verify if the mirror was not
green. No, the mirror was quite normal, but I myself was green.

And people? Where were they? Twenty-five years they, like
myself, have lived here; it cannot be that they have all suddenly
disappeared. Yes, they have, but all of them in a different way, and
this variety in disappearance is so curious that it is worth saying a
few words about it.

Some were involved in work with the Germans, and no one
heard anything more about them; among them were active people
who were judged and condemned, and passive ones who were
alienated and sent into oblivion. Then there were those who – like
Ladinsky, Ginger, Liubimov – took Soviet passports, acknowledg-
ing, with some reservations, that Stalin was the father of all
peoples. I had to meet them, but on a completely new footing.
Then there were those who for various reasons (sometimes out of
thoughtlessness, sometimes out of stupidity) sought a reconciliation with Stalin's regime and tried to prove to themselves and
others that, since the political role of the emigration had come to an
end, it was useless to over-emphasize one's anti-communist past,
better to look to the future where changes loomed: the evolution of
communist ideology, the dawn of freedom, amnesty granted by
the Kremlin to émigrés. To this group belonged Maklakov, Bunin,
Makovsky, Adamovich,* and many others. With each of these I
had a face-to-face conversation on the subject.

There were also those who fell gradually out of my range of
vision, and vanished by going to America and sometimes visited
Paris (Mrs Tsetlina, Aleksandr Kerensky, Boris Nicolaevsky);

*The manuscript of his book *L'Autre Patrie* (Paris, 1947) in its first edition
contained pages on Stalin that were later eliminated. The manuscript was given to
me by Adamovich to read in 1946.

some others were dispersed, like David Knut and Galina Kuznetsova, who did not return to France from Switzerland and Germany. Correspondence begun with new people from the Soviet Union and the so-called 'displaced persons', who lived at the time in German camps for refugees, gradually died down. People left Europe for Africa, Australia, North and South America. Finally, many died – some from old age (like Balmont, Korovin, Berdyaev, Pleshcheev), others from illness (like Mochulsky and Steiger), still others, deported by the Germans, perished (like Raissa Bloch and Mikhail Gorlin). Out of all these people who had left, one way or another, Remizov and Zaitsev remained, very quiet, very tired and old, undermined by war, by the burden of making a living and by solitude, and Georgy Ivanov, who in those years wrote his best verse. He made his personal morbid fate (poverty, illnesses, alcoholism) into a kind of myth of self-destruction, where, passing beyond our ordinary boundaries of good and evil, of the permitted (by whom?) and the taboo (for whom?), he moved in utter sordidness far beyond those who once were called 'poètes maudits' and all literary down-and-outers, from Apollon Grigoriev to Marmeladov (of *Crime and Punishment*) and from Tiniakov to the elder Babichev (of Olesha's *Envy*).

I had known him since 1921, from the time of Gumilev's notebook, but I had never had any personal relations with him. In the 1920s Khodasevich, he, and I wandered sometimes at night, all night, through Montmartre, which was closer to Ivanov than the literary Montparnasse. Then, on one of those nights when we were sitting somewhere at a table, quite sober, while he continually picked at his gloves (at the time he wore yellow gloves, a cane with a head, a monocle, a bowler), he confessed to me that in his *Petersburg Winters* there was *seventy-five per cent invention and twenty-five per cent truth*. In line with an old habit he blinked. I was in no way surprised by this, Khodasevich was not surprised either. Still, this book has been considered up to then as 'memoirs' and even a 'document'. Then for many years we did not see each other. After the war he was somehow unofficially and almost silently condemned for his Germanophilia. But he was not a Germanophile, only a man who had lost all moral sense, who at every corner declared he would rather be the chief of police in a Smolensk captured by Germans than edit a literary magazine in that very

Smolensk. Now in his next-to-last stage he gave the impression of a new lunatic. His last few years were in a home for the aged in Hyères, in that same Hyères where a hundred years before Herzen in one night had lost his mother, his son, and his friend . . . Now, in 1948–9, Ivanov gave the impression of near madness because, when speaking to him, one felt something was not right with him, that he needed something – a slice of bread, the inhalation of a cigarette, a glass of wine, the injection of a needle (medicinal or other), and that all he said was to no purpose, because if a man desperately needs something, he cannot hear you and answer you rationally.

He had at that time lost a living human appearance and recalled a cardboard silhouette of a man out of Blok's *The Puppet-Show*. When in 1949 he asked me to give a public reading of his verse I did it, and then met him from time to time, but a coherent conversation proved to be impossible; he would sustain some note, half 'ah', half 'eh', looking for words. In his presence many became ill at ease; bending at the waist – bowler, gloves, cane, handkerchief in a side pocket, monocle, narrow tie, slight odour of a pharmacy, shiny hair parted down to the neck – bending, but hardly touching a woman's hand with his lips, he would appear, say something in a drawl, no longer lisping naturally (he had an innate speech defect) but because of the absence of teeth.

In this way – ageless, sexless, without a third dimension (but with some kind of a fourth) – he would come to those rare literary or poetic gatherings that still took place. I remember once sitting at a long table in someone's apartment between him and Ladinsky. Ivanov, looking straight ahead and blinking, repeated the same sentence, banging a spoon:

'I can't bear Jews.'

Ladinsky whispered in my ear: 'I am now going to punch him in the jaw.' I took a pencil from my bag and scratched on a paper napkin: 'Stop, Ginger is next to you.' Ivanov took my note, gave it to Ginger, and said:

'She thinks you will get angry at me. As if you didn't know that I hate Jews. Can you really be offended with me?'

Ginger answered him something; this man always gave me the impression of a holy man, if not a fool of God. I got up, moved my chair, and sat down at the other end of the table. Ladinsky followed me.

Before my departure for the U.S.A. I had an encounter with Ivanov that I will not forget. At *Renaissance* (no longer a paper, but now a magazine) a farewell reception was arranged in my honour by the librarian, a very kind woman. I had no relations with the magazine; but I had not broken personal ties with workers in the bookstore and the library, and also with the current chief editor, Sergey Melgunov. A table was set in a large room with an apple pie baked by the librarian, four bottles of white wine, and glasses. About fifteen people came, among them Boris Zaitsev and Sergey Melgunov. As the party was coming to an end, Georgy Ivanov entered. I looked with fright at the remains of the refreshments: there was wine at the bottom of two bottles, one small triangular piece remained of the pie on the plate. While Ivanov was greeting everyone, I found a clean glass, poured the remains of the Sauternes in it and, giving Ivanov the glass, asked him to help himself to the last piece of pie. I pushed a fork and plate towards him, but he, drinking the wine in one gulp, suddenly said quietly but firmly:

'Allow me to take it home.'

I was out of sorts. I wrapped the pie in a paper napkin, he put it in an outside pocket of his jacket and, trying not to be noticed, left immediately. I want to say here that the strength of this scene is not where the soft-hearted reader will see it: the focal point is not that there is nothing for the poet to eat, and that at home someone is hungry to whom he is bringing a crust from a party. The point is I doubt that he took the pie home: this was done to produce a certain impression (which he did), and as for the pie he probably threw it into the rubbish bin at the door.

Ten days later, at about five, there was a knock at the door of my one-room apartment. That day I thought I would do some laundry, this was always complicated because of lack of space, and I had to make several dislocations in the so-called kitchen. The hot water was heating on the hot-plate, ropes were stretched over the bath (which literally took up the entire kitchen and in which for ten years – that is, since long before I moved here – there had been neither cold nor hot water). Tying on my apron, rolling up my sleeves, I had settled down to work when the knock came. I decided not to open the door. I never do this, but that day I decided I could not receive guests when the water had finally just warmed up. But someone stood at the door and would not go away. I kept quiet,

restraining the impulse to make a move and open the door.
Suddenly Ivanov's voice said behind the door:

'Nina Nikolaevna, open, I know you are home.'

'Who is it?' I asked, to gain time.

'The loan shark has come. Do you know what a loan shark is? I
want to cheat you out of ten francs.'

I asked him to wait a couple of minutes, put the kitchen in order,
removed my apron, combed my hair. When he entered, shuffling
and bowing, I said to him I had in all ten francs, and could not give
him more than five. 'Is there some wine?' he asked. Yes, I had a litre
of red. He sat at the table. Two could not move in the room, it was
too crowded, but when one sat the other could make five or six
steps here and there. I put the bottle on the table, gave him a glass.
He began to drink slowly. Drink and talk. It was a monologue – he
had to speak his piece. This monologue continued for about three
hours. Then he left. I remember, after his departure, lying for a
long time on the couch and looking through the window, at an
almost dark sky and the illuminated hill of Montmartre, with the
cathedral of the Sacré-Coeur at its summit – my window on the
eighth floor looked out to the north, onto Paris roofs, into the city
distance.

To forget or to remember? Or let it stay in me, let it grow, like
grass, not pay much attention? To regard what was said as the
drunken delirium of a man in a stage of disintegration? Or as
the passing mood of a neurotic artist? Or as a confession? Or as the
babble of a once worldly man who had decided to astound the
person he was talking to? It makes, of course, no difference of any
kind how one looks at his speech: my opinion, yours, that of all
future generations changes nothing in the speech itself. It was, to
put it in one word, a complaint, but a complaint not about
circumstances or people, not about Ivan Ivanovich, Lenin, Stalin,
Nicholas I and II, not about ruined health, poverty, loneliness, or
about himself as Mama, Papa, and women had made him . . . It
was a complaint about *no one*. He did not seek the culprit in his fate;
the culprit meant nothing to him, he would (as he himself said)
above all try to borrow ten francs from the culprit and then get
drunk with him. But in this complaint about no one the motif of
mortal fear arose; it continued to intensify in the presence of
everyone and everything, worms, spiders, machines, women,

governments, the cold wind, the policeman's whistle, civilization and savagery, and the inhuman urge to be drowned in fear and dirt. 'But I am really not scared of dirt,' he repeated several times.

We did not meet again. On the eve of my departure for New York I received a letter from him, which, as far as I remember, I did not answer. Here it is:

[Postmark: Paris, 31 October, 1950]

DEAR NINA NIKOLAEVNA,

Seeing my writing, you will surely be surprised . . . You see, I want to write to you several words now that you are leaving for America – that is, perhaps you and I will really never see each other again or, in any case, not only an ocean, but two different worlds, will divide us for a long time. To put it briefly, our whole everyday life here is ended forever or for a very long time and this is precisely why I want to say a couple of words to you, profiting from the 'freedom': neither you to me, nor I to you are in a practical sense real for some 'fragment of eternity'. I am writing confusingly. It's all the same. Decipher it somehow, along with this indecipherable hand-writing.

Thus profiting from this 'freedom' I want to tell you openly something which could not be said in a personal encounter or even the possibility of it while living in one city. I want, above all, to wish you from the bottom of my heart happiness and success. And to add that I feel that you are one of the few who deserve both success and happiness. We met, of course, long ago. And our acquaintance was in the main a chain of many misunderstandings. The fault was not yours, but mine, I know this well. Oh, long [before] Khodasevich, before all [one word illegible]. The more I value your impartiality towards my verse, because on the human level I am 'legally unpleasant' to you, to put it nicely. So, parting with you I use the occasion to say that for a very long time I have been from afar – how can I put it? – admiring you. You are bright, talented, and more – perhaps most important – in you there is an innate 'sense of responsibility', somehow masculine. At the same time you are very feminine. If you were to remain in Paris, I could not of course say this, but now I can. When at your 'reception' at *Renaissance* where I accidentally dropped in we conversed for a short moment, I valued the charm and youth of your appearance from the dress to your brown (?) hat, to the smile, to the sparkle of the eyes. Excuse the impudence of my expressions, but why pretend, everyone likes to hear that the impression he makes is charmingly young, as yours was then. I again wish you happiness and success. You have every 'right' to them. And I am speaking to you also 'by rights' – of my relationship to you which owing to 'force of circumstance' could never develop. There is no point in my explaining to you anything of course, but don't misunderstand my 'act', i.e. this letter. Why should I pretend? Though you like my verse (this is very important to me) you consider me a bastard. Like everyone in life you are both right and wrong. The fact is that in myself I am not even quite that, not at all that, as I 'appear' in my deeds. But this is out of Dostoevsky –

Good-bye. Think kindly of me. Spit on *New Russian Word* and émigré mud. Once you arrive in America then simply by your 'qualities' and firmness you will attain success there. I wish you this and am convinced that you will achieve a great deal there. I don't think, however disconnected this letter, that you will misunderstand it.

I kiss your charming hands.

YOUR GEORGY IVANOV

(To this letter was added Ivanov's poem, copied in his hand, 'A Melody Becomes a Flower', and a note:)

This is instead of flowers. I myself like this little poem. After my *Portrait* I wrote some forty pieces, in my opinion good ones.

G.I.

From New York I sent him a package. In answer he sent me the following letter which, like the first, I publish without correcting any clumsiness in style.

[Montmorency, end of December 1951]

DEAR NINA NIKOLAEVNA,

I thank you with unforgivable tardiness. If there is no excuse, there is an explanation for this: partly in the fact that your parcel arrived when I was only beginning somehow to get better – I had, as they say, a slight stroke – like a brain haemorrhage. But of course twenty times I should have and could have written to you and more than once started to – either there was no paper, or no money for stamps, or I began and could not finish because of laziness and fatigue. Forgive me, please, dear Nina Nikolaevna, all these 'disrespectful grounds' (there was, I think, an aesthete's book, by

Aksenov of the Centrifugue with such a title). In any case believe me that there was no element of ungratefulness in all this – on the contrary I was and continue to be *very* very touched. The things you sent are in themselves beautiful and arrived at a highly opportune moment, and because of my old age I have become especially sensitive to attention, warmth, smiles of friendship. This sentence has a literary ring, i.e. is not exactly what I would want to say. But in truth, believe in my sincerity. I do not deserve, probably, either attention or friendship – but because of this my need for them does not diminish but on the contrary perhaps increases. Well, I will not pad this out. Again I am very, very grateful to you.

Eternity has passed since you left. I was very sorry I did not say good-bye to you – I think I sent you then a letter and verses about Lermontov? Or only the verses? I don't remember now. Don't think the 'stroke' I had this summer destroyed my memory. It's that when you left [I] lived as in a fog and didn't remember if I had started to or only sent with the verses some words or had appended some to it. It's possible I did not write what I wanted to write. But I do remember very clearly the 'zigzags', the spot, somewhere on the bottom of my consciousness – you were leaving and probably 'for ever' in every sense, and I cannot change anything in what I would want to change or correct, so that you would think of me and my feelings for you not 'better' than they are – who needs that? – but differently; because my life has become so complicated and I so confused that everything that I in fact think and feel is buried by all kinds of things, not only unpleasant but complicated, accidental, and alien to me. Smolensky said not long ago you wrote to him that you liked my verse in *New Review*. If you write to me what you really liked in it I will be very grateful: you see (you can verify what I am saying now), I have more than once repeated that your review of my *Portrait without Likeness* was terribly valuable to me. It's not a matter of praises, but of the pleasure I experienced in it for the true satisfaction it gave to me, of the definition of meaning [crossed out] knowledge and of the place of my poetry. I have been praised many times, you know, and all of it was completely, right up to, perhaps you read it, Zinaida Gippius, 'wrong' in substance: more or less an intelligent or a stupid Mochulsky. Your review in this sense was unique, and because of my age, when [one word illegible] and the whole game becomes boring, and also criticism, and after reading for forty years exaggerations and lies – and I myself also wrote them, a sensible, responsible to – be it as it may – to a whole life of writing poetry is precious. I'm sorry only that your note is just a sketch, in forty or fifty lines. If you would only sometimes write about me more in detail. They tell me your article on Khodasevich has just been published – but I don't even know where.

But an article is a complicated matter and perhaps something you can't do at all now, but several words on the 'substance' you might perhaps write to me. What you don't like I also want to know. Please, as frank as possible. It will be interesting and *beneficial* to me. I believe you. The review of *Portrait without Likeness* and the fact that you didn't like my verse for so long and later prized it highly make your opinion and your advice important and necessary to me. Smolensky also said you wrote to him something like 'the old like it, the new do not understand'. I'd be curious to know in a concrete way, in two words, what you have heard from the 'new' ones. Only curious, because, as a rule, the 'new' make a critical fuss about nonsense, independent of whether they are praising or condemning something. In my opinion they are quite often talented, often strikingly 'full of energy', but their talent is indissolubly fused with provinciality like Latvian literature or the pre-symbolist period. They are naïve and primitively self-assured, as if they were not capable of organically mastering culture, I feel towards them, i.e. these D.-P.s, more than sympathy. I feel towards them a flesh-and-blood attraction. But I feel they are also 'victims' of Bolshevism, like us, only differently. Our spiritual culture has been shamed, spat on, and destroyed, we have been thrown into a desert where in fact in addition to coming to an end and 'tallying up', 'burying corpses', like my own poetry, nothing remains. They were raised in a proletarian ape-cage with a stuffed Pushkin instead of Pushkin as we know him, with a stuffed Russia, with an infamous imitation, a surrogate for all that was destroyed to its elements and ripped up from the root. And out of it came tremendous gifts exploding into life like a greenhouse torn asunder, in the spring through beaten glass that covers all and a filth of destruction and what in essence still remains from the rare cells, stunning everything, realizing nothing, burdocks triumphing and pouring out juices in the sunlight. Excuse the lyrical passage, it just came by association, it is not done, you cannot talk in images. But in fact I sense our 'young unknown tribe' exactly like that. I think that they and Russia itself even liberated in this sense are 'irretrievable', at least for a very long time. And possibly – forever. And why not? 'Kingdoms better than this have perished,' said not just anyone, but Pobedonostsev, about Russia. In our time this has a more

470

convincing and 'prophetic' ring than the 'accepted prophecies' of a Dostoevsky. Incidentally all my life I considered the work of Dostoevsky greater than all that had been written, more profound and penetrating than anything else. And now I confess I doubt that this is so. Perhaps I am mistaken, but in bed after my stroke I reread all Dostoevsky. Oh, there is genius, if it suits you. But – I repeat, I may have grown stupid and stale with the years – but to me it is so rottenly false both in its moments of summit and its collapses. Moreover, for all its universality, its understanding and penetration throughout – I am scared to say it – something emerges like affectation and spiritual insignificance. Ah! it's terribly possible I'm speaking nonsense. The more so as I concur with the mediocre side of mankind, like Melgunov. Although it seems to me personally that I do not concur, because I came to this through my own spiritual experience. But it's possible that

> There once was a poet known to us
> Who owing to old age became an ass.

But one ought not to abuse, I kiss your dear hands, again warmly thank you and wish you from my heart joyful holidays and in fact success and happiness. If you answer me I promise also to answer you – *sauf contre ordre* – if I do not begin again to pop off. This is possible – my life is hard and my health shaken by earlier drinking, etc. – but perhaps I will not croak. However strange, I don't want, despite my fatigue and the boredom of my existence, to kick the bucket because of (imagine!) some naïve literary considerations or rather instinct: when health and time allow I am writing, already for more than a year, a book. I am 'squaring accounts', only not in the way it would be natural to expect from me as I naturally seem from afar. In a word, not like Bely, in his brilliantly venomous death libel. I am 'squaring' with people and with myself without sparkle and without venom, without power of observation, clarity, etc. I am writing, or rather noting down 'by memory' my genuine relations to people and events, which were always 'deep down' very different than on the surface and if they were mirrored only in verse, it wasn't always so. But since my memory is weak, I found myself an approach to this very depth much easier than if I, as in Pushkin's (how is it called? I don't remember) 'I tremble and curse,' if recollections were to persecute me. I won't judge, since I don't know if I'll finish, but in my opinion I'll succeed in saying what's most important, what didn't come out in verse and thus I 'must'

471

write the book. However, it won't be much use to anyone. But writing for me is first of all a comfort and 'liberation'. Now I am expressing myself awkwardly and in a high-falutin' way because as always I am tired and beginning to get a headache. But it's better to finish and send you at any rate if not the book then this letter whatever it might be. 'The Life I Dreamed Of' – that's the proposed title.

However legibly I try to write I see that [one word illegible]. Then that terrible passion to put words in quotation marks. I do this mechanically, myself understanding that it must irritate you. I kiss your hands, I come to the end. Be dear, dispatch, if possible, the included notes, I confess openly, for reasons of economy; one fat air-mail letter costs less than a letter plus two 48-franc stamps.

I copy out in that space a recent little poem. Not that it's particularly important, but rather it shows that I did not succumb to brain dilution as did Tiutchev after the prologue of the 'British leopard'. Without fail tell me of your life, how you are getting along, what you are writing. I know nothing.

Your devoted
GEORGY IVANOV

To the letter was added the poem 'I begged, but no one helped'.

I think commentary on this letter would be superfluous. I answered him with a postcard and sent him another small package with clothes. After several months of silence, a final short letter arrived:

[no date, 1952]

DEAR NINA NIKOLAEVNA,

As you see, though I am a swine I am not the one you naturally thought I was. Your address was given to me by Smolensky, since I lost your card immediately. The office manager assured me the address was correct.

I kiss your hands and again thank you so much.

Yours forever,
G.I.

After this letter he sent me his book *Portrait without Likeness*. On it was the inscription: 'To dear Nina Nikolaevna Berberova, from *completely done-for* G.I. 1956'. The inscription (with two misspellings) was in red pencil. I still have the book.

His last stage began in Hyères, as I already said. In this home for the aged where he died, there are still people who were present at his death, if not in the same room, then next door. Ivanov's arms and legs were covered with needle marks, cockroaches were all over his blanket and pillow, the room had not been made up for weeks (not by fault of the management), and in the view of outsiders the sick man was subject to heavy attacks of either rage or depression. Depression, however, almost never left him, it was with him all those last years, not only months – his verses of this last period are testimony of this. When he was told he had to wash, that his room had to be tidied up, that the sheets had to be changed, he merely repeated that he 'wasn't scared of dirt'. Evidently he ascribed to this sentence not only a moral meaning, which I guessed, but a physical one. He had always feared death to the point of horror, of despair. It turned out to be a salvation for him which came too late.

Yes, such was one of the men I lived among towards the end of the 1940s, as I moved from the war period to my last Paris years. In the account of the bobbin, it was not the fact that I broke it that was terrifying, but that this fact seemed to me such a catastrophe. And then with people: the problem was not that there was no one around, but that in the final analysis I didn't want any of those whom I could find.

'But you survived!' a young woman shouted at me with unexpected strength, the niece of Olga who had come from London to Paris, the one remaining member of a whole huge family. 'Didn't you survive for some special reason?'

(For one tenth of a second did the thought flash into my head then to write this book? I don't know. Perhaps.)

Silently I looked at her: all these last days after her telegram I had been troubled about how I would meet her, tell her of all her deceased near ones, and now she was here, delighted to see me, showing me photographs of her son, speaking of the present, the future:

'This is all past. Now one must live. I have a son. I will, without fail, have a daughter – you will see! You arranged it so I would be saved. [In fact, before the war I had accidentally introduced her to her future father-in-law.] Now you must live as if you alone in all

473

the world had survived. There is no one, all have perished. With you as with me. But you and I are alive.'

In 1937 it turned out that, thanks to her marriage and departure for England, she did not return from Paris to Warsaw, where all her family perished in the ghetto. Now she extended a helping hand to me.

'And what's going on *there*?' I ask. 'Will anyone survive there?'

'Without fail, to tell the world of it. You will see. Perhaps Pasternak, perhaps Ehrenburg.'

This reminded me of something. I found one of the volumes of Chateaubriand's *Mémoires d'Outre-Tombe* on the bookshelf and showed her the paragraph about Nero going wild in Rome, *when Tacitus had already been born.*

'You see,' she said, hiding the photos of her son and husband in her bag, 'it was always so and so it will be in our time.'

That year (1948) my book of short stories came out. All my life I had been published by publishers, but now in the general collapse I had to publish the book with an 'organization', and one with a Sunday-school touch: the Russian division of the YMCA. This was the only place that could bring out a Russian book in those years: it had the means and the printing plant. The support of two members of the board was indispensable. Berdyaev and Zaitsev quickly helped me and the book was accepted without being read. When it came out, other members of the board (who had Sunday-school tastes) read it and with horror saw that there were some 'pornographic scenes' in it (as they were called a hundred years ago) that did not at all tally with the spirit of the 'organization'. In fact, some of the stories could not be digested by the Russian section of YMCA. They stopped the sale of the book and it is still lying in the basement of that Christian Association.

But there were six tales in the book, some not bad. 'The Resurrection of Mozart' and 'The Cloak', and 'Astashev in Paris' itself, which gave the book its title, I still consider remarkable stories. They are not inferior (and perhaps even better) than 'The Revolt' and 'The Black Pestilence', which were written by me later, in 1958 and 1959. Personally I have a weakness for 'In Memory of Schliemann', perhaps because when I wrote it I felt all the time like a bird laying an egg in a nest – which was my century.

Stravinsky speaks of creation, in one of his interviews, as a physiological process: he feels, when he composes, first like a swine looking for truffles, then like an oyster making a pearl. He confesses that sometimes he drools with saliva at the sounds and harmony he is putting on paper, and that every creation for him is the work of gland secretion, with a resultant discharge. All that is swallowed by us is digested, assimilated, eliminated, and creation is undoubtedly a physiological act. Nothing more just has ever been said! Creation in this way is a function of the body in a given biological and social situation, which we can by means of this function accept, change, or transcend.

Inside every biological and social situation I am free to make decisions. Here the comfortable horror of the existentialists taught us all a lot, yet it is less comfortable for us than for the existentialists themselves. Still, not every action of mine was carried out as a result of a conscious and free decision: my departure from Russia was not the consequence of a personal decision, although the choice of a profession (at ten) and my non-return to Russia undoubtedly were. My non-departure from Longchêne in June 1940 was the result of a conscious decision, but no conscious decision led me to live in Paris in the post-war years: this was inertia. I see during the course of my whole life moments of free choice and periods of inertia. But the alternation of passively following events and of active steps that changed the fabric of life ended for me with the most important, the most thought-out, and the most difficult conscious choice I have ever made in life: to leave for the U.S.A.

'And where is your luggage?' asked Roman Gul, meeting me at the pier in New York.

I was ashamed, not for my poverty but my light-headedness, and I pointed to two small suitcases, which the customs inspector didn't even want to examine. But before that moment when the New York porter put the suitcases on his trolley and Gul took me to the hotel on West Seventy-second Street, several rather unimportant but curious things happened.

First, my memory floating back from the port of New York to Europe, I hear a tale recounted to me somewhere not far from the Azores. And continuing on this mental return trip, I see in the American consulate in Paris a clerk requesting a certificate of health from me.

The M.D. proved to have irony:

'What did your parents die of?'

'Mother, evidently, from exhaustion, hunger and various deprivations connected with the siege of Leningrad by the Germans in 1941–2. And my father, I suppose, of anguish.'

'What illnesses were there?'

'With them? I don't remember them ever being sick.'

'Not them, you.'

'I . . . in the last twenty years, in the main, have not been sick. I am sorry, there were of course sometimes colds. Those, you know, terrible head-colds . . . '

'When were you last at the doctor's?'

'Not long ago. Five years ago. That was a serious illness: mastoiditis. The drum even had to be punctured. The day of the taking of Berlin.'

'Which ear?'

'The left. Once I was given a punch that was one of . . . '

'Can you hear with it?'

There was a sound of shyness in my voice:

'For some reason better than before.'

The doctor tapped me wherever he chose.

'What about your female organs?'

'They're in place.'

'Menstruation?'

'When I menstruated life was pleasant. I was literally reborn every month. Now that I no longer do it's also fine: fewer worries.'

'I must ask you to comment on your last statement.'

'No, Doctor, no commentary. It would take too much time.'

'And if I ask you to give a short report before a medical commission on this subject?'

'I would be glad to help the medical commission, but somehow I am not now up to speeches.'

'I will make the speech. I will use you to demonstrate.'

I look through the window, above his grey crew-cut head, and saw that it will soon rain. He's a nice fellow, let life be kind to him, he does not insist. He places me before an X-ray machine and photographs my lungs. This life-size negative will later be held in both hands by an American immigration official who will look over my large rib-cage, a cage similar to those in which people keep parrots; there in the middle a parrot, my heart, will sit with a dark aorta similar to the crown of a tropical bird. The official will in every way admire the picture, and I will stand and keep silent, all the time repeating to myself: 'Don't you recognize me? How strange! Don't you see, I am the same girl to whom you once sent the A.R.A. food packages. So I survived. You had a President who directed the whole affair, he was then called Gerbert Goover, and now – by decree of the Academy of Sciences of the U.S.S.R. – is called Kherbert Khoover . . .' The immigration official puts all my documents on his desk, stamps the seal on them. Owing to an inability to pronounce my surname he decides to use the first name alone to greet me on my arrival in the U.S.A.:

'Enjoy it, Nina!' he said, and I went through the door. Was it open, half open, or closed? – I don't remember. I went through it.

But before all this, before my encounter with customs inspectors, consuls, doctors, press attachés, petty civil servants and V.I.P.s in the immigration department, the man who administered the oath and the woman who demanded my signature on all four copies of some document, much else had happened. First of all there was the fact of the decision, of choice, in those days when I was deciding and choosing: I felt I was not simply tossing a coin in the air – heads or tails? – but was using my right to freedom to make or build my life which, in the world where I lived, my times gave me. I was using that right like air, which is mine, which I breathe, do not fight for, do not beg for, do not pay for, but just take, like something that belongs to me. I bear responsibility for myself, not relying on chance and, in full awareness, take the step on which depends not this and not that in me, but my very self. Not two, but three forces influenced me then in the green gardens of the Trocadéro in the summer of 1950, and perhaps the third was the most important one.

I have already spoken of the first two. Yes, the impossibility of making a living, the inability to change my profession, and, as they say, of making ends meet in Paris after the war, was one reason for my departure. For twenty-five years of life in Europe I had got used to nails being hammered in with silver spoons – as the saying goes. For many years I accepted this and in the end it began to seem even natural to me. Now I in no way rebelled against such a state of things, but this, which was always, to put it in a business-like way, 'unsatisfactory', became absolutely menacing. It was hardly financial hopelessness alone, however, that could lead me to decide on my fate. There was a second reason: I remained alone or almost alone in that city, where for a quarter of a century I had lived among friends, among enemies, among friend-enemies, in an atmosphere created (as I have said earlier) by one or two dozen people who were concerned with the form and content of Russian poetry – with the word, the 'note', the ideas and rhythms, which were cultivated for better or worse – in the spirit of some symphonic orchestra where, if not in all of us then in some of us (and in myself, of course) the *esprit de corps* was clearly separating us from other groups of Russian émigrés. It was like playing in an orchestra for about fifteen years. Now no one or almost no one remained, and a vacuum of life lay ahead, individual and as a group.

But besides these two reasons there was a third which, as I now see it, was the deciding factor. The majority of us, in any case the majority of the 'young', including me, took from France what they could with reverence and thanks. Different men took different things, but with the same greediness: some took Valéry and Gide, others Anatole France and Duhamel, a third group Maritain, a fourth took Mauriac and Green, a fifth group Baudelaire and Verlaine. Between the two wars we had much to choose from. Aldanov and Remizov, Berdyaev and Khodasevich, Poplavsky and Nabokov had something to 'nibble on' – and not only that, but also to feed their young ones on. Beginning in 1945 all changed: there was no longer 'intellectual nourishment' where it had been found, and its absence led me directly to spiritual hunger and stagnation of mind.

I use the words 'nourishment' and 'hunger' with the secret aim of returning to these clichés whose primordial meaning was stated by Plato and Dante. The first in his *Seventh Epistle*, 341, said that in the process of transmission of genuine knowledge from one man to another, there is something intangible:

'This knowledge cannot be expressed in words . . . but in the intercourse of both teacher and student it is suddenly born in the soul and immediately begins to *nourish* itself, like the light which shoots up after you have kindled the fire.'

Plato writes of this a second time in *Phaedrus*, 247:

'The mind of deity when it is *fed* by knowledge and pure science . . . is delighted at seeing the essence of things, up to then unknown to it. And when it . . . *has fed* on all this, it returns home.'

Dante, in *The Divine Comedy* (*Paradiso*, Canto 10), addresses himself to the reader, demanding that he *feed* on what the poet has placed before him:

'I served it to you. Now *feed* on it, *nourish* yourself.'

I am far from the idea of pronouncing some judgement on French literature of the post-war years. Sartre, Camus, Aragon, and Eluard were in its centre. The first embodied in himself the ambiguity of the French intellect of his time,* the second from the very beginning of his short life was a victim of some artistic non-incarnation: great not so much as a writer as a phenomenon, as a monument of the epoch more than as a poet. Towards the middle 1940s he had grown weak and sad. I was at a packed meeting in the big Salle Pleyel, on 13 December, 1948, when Camus spoke on a subject once so dear to Blok: the poet and the mob. That evening he resembled Blok; he was wearing a white turtle-neck sweater like the one Blok wore in 1920–21. His speech at that meeting was the speech of a loner: he emerged between Rousset, the orator, whose heart shook with eloquence, and the surrealist André Breton, who had become a Trotskyite and whose demeanour was that of a buffoon. Somewhere among them Camus spoke, in a muted voice, compressing his jowls, his hands in his pockets, looking above the audience. I wrote to Camus about this striking resemblance to Blok at his public speech in February 1921 (in the House of Writers). He answered me.†

The books of Marcel Aymé were characteristic of French literature in those years: ironic, melancholic, they proved the anti-universality, the localization of modern French literature, its 'small trajectory' and 'private horizon'. In these years also the name of Jean Genet rose like a black sun, to be elevated to the rank of saint and genius shortly after by Sartre. Two of Genet's books (one open, the

---

*Sartre still considers N. I. Bukharin not a victim of Stalin but a betrayer of the Revolution, who incurred a just punishment after his confession. In Sartre's book *Saint Genet* we read: 'Bukharin was a conspirator and traitor who humbly confessed to his betrayal of the Revolution, a rotten member of the revolutionary collective . . .' (Paris: Gallimard, 1952, pp. 544–6).

†He cites two of my books and mentions me in *Carnets* (1948).

other undisclosed autobiography) eclipsed all the rest for a whole decade, despite his preface to one of them about the occupying Germans as angels flying to the heavens while dropping bombs on France, whereas the other was dedicated to one Pilorge who killed his lover Escudéro, and the renowned Weideman who had stabbed six men and was executed in 1939. Sartre existentially defended these prefaces, its author, and the books, partly even admiring the ambiguity of his own choice: on the one hand he demanded 'engagement', the single-mindedness of all art, political responsibility of the intelligentsia, the *a priori* admission of the rightness of all the demands of the working class, and on the other, submission to the dark mysterious viciousness of his female nature; he was attracted to what seemed to him (and not him alone) the virile force of the anti-bourgeois race of the 'chosen', be it the muscular and tall Slavs carrying out a social revolution, or the blond warriors in *feldgrau*, or simply hirsute criminals condemned by law.

Yes, living in an absurd world, let's admit there is no truth, though there are *directions of truth*; if you don't take this into account, then all philosophy, even borrowed from Heidegger and Jaspers, becomes ambiguous, which means that art created on this basis will be devoid of *style* in the widest sense of the term. There lives in me eternal gratitude for all I have received from France, but my growth, my changing, my self-awareness could not stop. They have continued to be more important for me than all the 'localized' or even 'universal' philosophy of our present day.

There is a time of secrecy and silence, and there is a time of confession. And here I will in a few lines speak of still another reason for my departure from Paris (from France and Europe). It does not rank fourth in that list of which I have been speaking. It's as if it penetrates the first three reasons and gives them their existential sense – that is, lives in them, is bound up with them, and makes them more important and vital than in fact they are. In addition to the impossibility of subsisting materially, to the decline of what I had belonged to for a quarter of a century, and to the absence of intellectual food, there was my victory-defeat in my personal life I wanted to escape from. In this realm, all was lost yet it had the appearance of gain; all was acquired at a heavy price and turned out to be an unnecessary burden, was obtained by suffering, and I was ready to cede it free to whomever it suited – that is, ready to retreat, leave, float away without return. The poverty, the destruction, and the senselessness of life would have been overcome, probably, had this not happened. But this fourth reason coloured the first three in a menacing way. Beneath the trees of the Trocadéro, on the downward paths where I walked mumbling verse to myself, mine and others', where I sat thinking of my destiny (and sometimes, as it happened, not thinking it over but only listening to it, looking it over, groping for it), in these gardens the decision came to me. I used my right to free choice: to remain or to stay. And I left forever.

'Well, that's only half of the damn business,' said a man to me on the deck of the ocean liner, a man who had worked as an expert on counterfeit money in an American bank in Paris for thirty years and was now returning to the U.S., a lover of foreign languages and a real debater. At first, at breakfast, he said that in the United States there was no place better than South Carolina. This brought forth a thunder of protest from other Americans, but he remained deaf to it. Then he declared that the French painter Claude Lorrain had invented puff pastry, and since no one knew anything about this, no one said anything in answer – he felt insulted. He wanted to argue. At dinner he said you could see as many dolphins around us as you wanted; you had only to know how to look. He wanted to bet without fail against all of us, separately and together, who asserted there were no dolphins in these areas.

'Tell me some Russian idiomatic expression,' he said, sneaking up to me so that I started.

'To walk along railway tracks.'

'Explain it.'

I told him: 'No money, no ticket. You go somewhere as a bum.'

He listened, thought. Then wrote something in a little book.

'Which means that you can walk along tracks from Europe to the States?'

'No, it won't work.'

'But you can live on tracks?'

'Yes,' I answered, musing, 'you could live on tracks, and I myself have. Moreover [after a second thought] you can set out on tracks to the U.S. Let's not be pedants!'

'There's a dolphin!' he shouted.

But no one except him saw a dolphin.

Then, squinting all the time at the ocean looking for dolphins, he told me the story of the two frogs:

'Once two frogs fell into a pot of milk. "I am lost!" said the first frog, went to the bottom, and drowned. The other began to work its legs with all its strength and towards morning wound up sitting on a piece of freshly churned butter.'

'A dolphin!' I yelled out. And we had all to admit he was right.

'I am always right,' said the counterfeit-money hunter gloomily, shrugging his shoulders; he did not speak again to anyone.

Yet this too did not happen at once. I took a step forward and presently moved back. So I was moving towards America despite my decision. The tempo of my story corresponds to the tempo of my preparations.

I was not only leaving Paris, but Petersburg-Leningrad, Venice, Rome, Nice, Provence, the radiant and misty French country landscape, always dear to me, which when I close my eyes I see before I see Paris, its roads planted with rustling trees, with wheat fields and slanting meadows, tile roofs slumbering peacefully beyond a hill, and the sharp bell tower of the church now forgotten, empty, unnecessary, but still charming, erected a thousand years ago, before Montaigne, Aquinas and before Cervantes, as Merezhkovsky would say. I was leaving forever these places where I had learnt to seek intensity rather than happiness, not joys and prosperity but *more of life*, a concentrated sense of life, a strengthened feeling of existence, fullness and concentration of *pulse*, energy, growth, flowering, beyond the image of happiness or unhappiness. Here my life became increasingly not a chain of problems, but of solutions to problems, where the irrational, and dreams, inspiration, impulses had their place, co-ordinated with all the immanent and tangible things known to my five senses. I sought its force and persistence in every image, the condensed feeling of being, living, knowing, experiencing, remembering, and changing. I learnt this in Europe and now was leaving, taking with me all I had managed to gather from it – small and large, important and not very important – and above all the conviction that to know how to think and live a conscious life, to know oneself and 'make' oneself, is a necessary condition for a human being, in whom conservative, limited, stiff *instincts* take second

482

place, and the radical intellectual possibilities, unlimited and free, the very first.

This freedom of growth is tied for me to all the other freedoms that man wants. He wants to plant his own trees and chop them down himself; he wants the son not to answer for the father; he wants to shout his protest loudly; he wants to make his choice and when necessary 'not be like everyone else', something that will not only prove his own health but the health of the people from whom he emerges. But freedom of growth brings something else: freedom from confusion and from impulsive opinion; it brings an interpretation of the world and the ability to know, judge, and express oneself. I was now leaving the huge school where I had learned so much, moving to a new, different, unknown world. But I was not scared.

No, I was not scared. There was curiosity, a definite excitement about the future and a desire to arrange my departure as rationally as possible. Nevertheless, from the day-to-day point of view the whole thing looked gloomy: I didn't know English, I had on my arrival in New York just seventy-five dollars of which I immediately gave away twenty-five (for a debt), and I was not given a permanent visa. The Russian quota had been filled and I had to wait five years for an immigrant visa. I well knew I could not wait for five years. I got a temporary visa, and only four years later, with my third marriage, was my illegal status in the U.S.A. cleared up. Khodasevich was right when he said, looking at me cross-stitching in 1925 in Paris, that all this had once been described by Chernyshevsky or someone else, and thus was completely uninteresting. For this reason, for the story of how I received a permanent U.S. visa, I refer the reader to Kafka's *Trial* or Menotti's *Consul*, as well as to a whole array of similar works – in this way my story has been described by someone else, and there is no point in repeating it.

'You are abandoning all the cocks on all the teapots,' Vera Zaitseva said to me, embracing me at the Saint-Lazare station; at that very time I saw everyone around me with the clarity of Prince Myshkin before a fit: everything I was leaving and had already left, what lay ahead in three hours, in a week, in a year or two. And that actual moment – which is always the most important of all – fourteen persons dear to me were on the station platform, and they had a very long relationship with each other. I must whisper to one: 'Keep well, don't fret' (the two tips of friendship), embrace another, hang on the neck of a third, shake the hand of a fourth and a fifth, and return the tenderness and warmth of all. The ocean will carry me from one hemisphere to another, but I am no longer afraid of it. The decline of the West is within me, not in Europe, and within me at that moment are a thousand things: past, present, and future, and that clarity of seeing in which not 'everything is permitted' but 'everything is possible'.

In these minutes (or seconds) of 'Myshkin's clarity' there was the sense of the *seam* binding all my opposites: my solitude and my belonging to all those people, young and old, standing beneath the carriage window; my own country, and the one I had lived in for twenty-five years, and the third to which I was going. Destiny which bore me and my conscious choice. Finally myself face to face with this *seam*, as I had known myself, and those standing at the train window had known me, for thirty, twenty, ten years. And then – a rare occurrence and because of that dear to me – tears, which I could not stop till Le Havre itself, so that the Russian gentleman who sat in the compartment opposite me asked sympathetically (he had recognized me and Boris Zaitsev and several others who had accompanied me):

'May I offer you a glass of the most ordinary water?'

This very ordinary water had no effect on me and I stopped crying only when I saw the huge white steamer, the deep blue bay, cranes in the sky, and the majestic outlines of the gigantic port.

Then there were the dolphins, the tale of the two frogs, and a couple of giants – male and female – at my table who for the whole dinner were saying over and over again, with a quiet joy and ecstasy and shining eyes, that finally they would again see *taxis*. 'Had they really not seen taxis in Europe?' I thought. But it turned out they were talking about Texas. Here I got my first English lesson.

Then, on the sixth day at dawn, a city rose before me. It was narrow and tall like a gothic temple, surrounded by water, and in the light mist of a November morning – or better, at the end of a November night – it suddenly appeared, as if with a slight push it detached itself out of the invisible into the visible.

I had already been standing for an hour on deck, looking at hundreds of car lights moving here and there along the smooth shore, which had been at my right since 5:00 A.M. As if it were not morning but broad daylight. The shore appeared early, spotted with lights, white and red, then slowly and with an effort the day began to dawn, thick clouds moving towards us were revealed, and on the right a slightly wavy low horizon. Then the city appeared ahead. Two or three passengers, and I among them, came out on the bow of the boat. We entered the bay, and on the shore to the left lights moved, but the shore seemed higher. Ferries, tugs, motor-boats, and even islands came towards us, as well as the dark port of New York buildings; the gothic temple in front of us drew closer, shone brighter, and gradually lost its gothic shape, becoming a huge modern city with a hundred skyscrapers and some windows alight. They gradually went out as the blue-green air of the autumn morning began to brighten.

In this city, as I saw it then and would see it later for many years, there is something *deliberate*, with that unique mixture of functional and symbolic that exists in our former capital too. Here also, perhaps, someone had stood 'full of great thoughts'* deciding that precisely on this spot 'a city be founded', and bought a piece of land from the Indians. *There* were marshes and mists, *here* were black rocks on which dwellings had to be built, *there* blizzards and storms, *here* – sub-tropical temperatures sometimes for a spell of three months. This is not a hindrance. The watery spaces and the special light they give off bestow on everything *here* and *there* the same aura of transparency and temporality, or timelessness or untimeliness. Moscow, Rome, London, Paris stay in place. Lenin-grad and New York float, spreading all their sails, cutting space with their prows, and can disappear, if not in reality, then in the imagination of the poet creating a myth, a mythical tradition on the grounds of his secret experiences.

Mrs Tsetlina, my old friend (like her husband, Mikhail, who had died in 1945), had written to me a month before asking me to stay with her. She then lived in a small flat in a hotel, and she rented a room there for me. Roman Gul took me straight from the boat to her place. From the very first evening I found myself among people

The Bronze Horseman.

who had come to look at me – old acquaintances, new ones, Russian Americans, American Americans, and those like myself, people just arrived from Europe (old émigrés, new émigrés, 'displaced persons' who had moved, inhabitants of Poland, Czechoslovakia, Shanghai, the Baltic states) of Russian origin. Mrs. Tsetlina, in line with an old (Muscovite and Parisian) habit, organized evenings, that is parties, where the literary and non-literary public mixed. Here I met the pianists Vsevolod Pastukhov, Nikolai Orlov, Georgy Kochevitsky, the poets Ivan Elagin and Olga Anstey, another Elagin (Yury), author of *The Taming of the Arts*, Boris Filippov. I found old Parisians: Aleksandr Kerensky, Roman Grynberg, Galina Kuznetsova, Dobuzhinsky, Fedotov, and others. Then, the second day of my stay, the old Montparnasse misfit X came to see me:

'Why have you come?' he asked, and sat down. 'I have already been here ten years. It's horrible here. Impossible to live. Such poverty all around! And the pears have no aroma.'

I was at a loss.

'Pears? No aroma? This is indeed horrible!'

'I don't know what they do with them. They pick them, probably, when they are green, and they ripen in refrigerators. You can't live here. The strawberries have no taste, no taste at all! Do you have money for a return ticket? Look, hold on to it, don't waste it. You will need it.'

I answered I had no money and was scared he would offer to lend it to me, but he didn't.

'The poverty is terrible. Don't believe the papers. They all lie. Prosperity is only on the surface. Inside, deep down, the country is indigent. The Negro problem. Alcoholism. You'll see.'

He spoke for a long time. He told of how not long ago, while returning at night from one of his flats to the other (owing to family circumstances he had two flats), he saw a man sleeping on the sidewalk. The police had not picked him up: in the police precincts, said X, there was no room owing to the crowd of homeless people who slept there, picked up from the streets.

'Have you not once returned to Europe in those ten years?'

'I have no money, I cannot allow myself such luxury.'

'There, you know, pears also have no aroma now.'

'Bah, I don't believe it!'

'The pears have no aroma, because there aren't any. I don't know where they are, I saw pears only once in the window of some luxurious grocery store: they were lying in boxes, in tissue paper. However, it's not important.'

He spoke, delighted that there were no more rebuttals on my part. But when he went out to the stairs, I ran after him:

'Listen, then, why are there cigarette butts?'

'What butts?'

'Last night on the curb, before the entrance to our hotel, there were twenty butts and at least five whole cigarettes, and this morning they were still there and perhaps are there even now. Just look. Why does no one pick them up?'

He shrugged his shoulders. 'You always were witty,' he said as usual, through his teeth. 'That's very funny what you just said.'

I slipped on my coat and went down with him. In fact there were butts, some whole cigarettes, garbage on the curb.

'The city is dirty,' said X. 'They don't sweep here.'

A taxi drove up and he got in.

I spent ten days at Mrs Tsetlina's, and then found myself a room in a hotel, through an ad in the *New York Times*, and moved. Now I found myself in a section of a city unknown to me (it was Ninety-fourth Street, almost at the corner of West End Avenue), alone, with my two suitcases, twenty-seven dollars in my pocket (after paying for a room for a week), in a hotel where, despite my protests, I was considered French (obviously I then had a French accent in my beginner's-English speech). To my right lived a detective – or rather, a plainclothes man the bellboy told me about, perhaps hoping to warn me. To my left, a man lived who slept from eight in the evening till eight in the morning, and on Saturday and Sunday didn't wake up at all – this I could tell by his snoring. The snoring was audible even near the lift, in which many admonitions hung, and whose language I studied while rising to the eighteenth floor.

At night I was surrounded by neighbouring skyscrapers, and far below I could hear the city noise, at night as during the day, and in the day as at night. I occupied my evenings reading *New York Times* ads. I know nothing more interesting than reading want-ads in a new country, a new city. '150 positions for electrical engineers', '200 positions for biochemists', I would read, and see these people who were seeking but not finding anything. They needed 'librarians for openings in municipal libraries in 23 states' (apparently in unlimited quantity). 'A domestic service agency has opportunities for 12 cooks (with diplomas), 17 maids (who know how to serve at table), 5 sleep-in chauffeurs, 11 sleep-out, 8 gardeners (married), 38 nurses for new-born infants.' '45 doctors for 9 new hospitals.' 'Four clarinetists for an orchestra (on the road).' 'Three experienced journalists, specialists in the foreign policy of Indonesia.' 'An office-help agency is seeking 198 secretary-stenographers.'

I wanted at the same time to be a biochemist, a cook, a clarinetist – everything was terribly interesting.

Then there were columns where street-sweepers, furnacemen, seamstresses, kitchen-maids, dog-sitters and baby-sitters (who could do a little washing) were summoned. This was useful reading. Indeed, all reading was good for me. I thus immediately began with a then-fashionable novel, not understanding what was most important in it: where exactly did the hero turn on the last page, *towards the man* who lured him to a sure ruin or *away from him*, away from all temptations? But this circumstance could not stop me in those first months or even years of my life in the U.S.A.

Seven years, seven professions. Some of them were strange, others very banal, still others forced me to work at full strength, so that in the evening I was no longer fit to read ads and novels. I was asked to leave one job because of incompetence. Once I was a Russian announcer on the radio; it turned out suddenly, quite by accident, that my voice over the air was contralto, and this was what was called for. Another time I worked in the evening on an addressograph machine. There were no bobbins here and I was not at all scared. I respected and loved the machine, as I do all machines. It rolled with a rumble, metal on metal, through the envelopes that flew in its teeth, and I directed it to my great joy not by the *sweat of my brow* but while humming some melodies, which I tried to co-ordinate with its crackling, reflecting on the usefulness of machines in general and addressographs in particular. Returning home at about midnight, I slept little, walked about the city in the day, but now in a new way, not as in my youth when I looked dejectedly into Moscow and Paris windows, but devouring with my eyes all I could, without making my 'orphanhood' more intense than it was, on the contrary being aware permanently of my aim: the struggle for and future conquests of people, friends, the city, the country, the continent, which from the first hour of my arrival seemed to me a world in its immensity, its variety.

The first year – but only the first – I had days not of despondency, weakness, but rather of some depressing play of the imagination, which in general is more apt to come in childhood and is rather unusual in adult years: I confess I was sometimes tempted to become a vagrant. I tried to convince myself this was only a game (in childhood there was no such corrective, and at ten I could picture myself as a fireman or a postman for a long time, without realizing there is a corrective for every fantasy). Aware almost always that this was a game, I nevertheless gave into it quite seriously: several times I went to the spots where I could begin my new 'career'. Such places, dejecting, dirty, noisy, and sad, were well known to me in Paris: in their time the declassed heroes of my early stories lived there, but now I was wondering how I could do the same.

The first person I wanted to see and know was Alexandra Tolstoy, the youngest daughter of the writer. She then was director of an establishment that brought 'displaced persons' from Germany and other countries to the U.S.A. at American expense and set them up with work – literate and illiterate people, academics, stevedores, inventors, and dishwashers. In this organization employees sat at office desks and one of them, having written down my name, asked me to wait. Knowing how busy Miss Tolstoy was, I hinted that I could leave and return the next day, that I was in no hurry, but I waited no more than about twenty minutes when an office door opened and a very full, but somehow harmonious, muscular, smart person, with a broad face, smoothly combed, with traces of breeding and a particular fastidiousness in dress, looked severely at me through thick glasses: it was clear in a first glance that everything about her was kind, clean, even crackling, ironed out like herself, with a face sparkling from good soap, nails painted in colourless polish and tortoise-shell combs in her old-fashioned coiffure.

'Come in,' she said, like a woman doctor opening the door to her office and letting the patient in. 'Sit down,' she said, sitting at her desk and carefully looking me over from head to foot. 'Who are you? Daughter? Niece?'

I was stupefied. They garbled my surname, was my first thought. Whom does she take me for?

'Of whom?' I asked gently, thinking of ways not to put her in an awkward position.

'Of the writer?'

I was relieved.

'I am she.'

Her brows rose – she had almost no brows – her broad face slid into a still broader smile. Her arms opened into an embrace.

'You? I made you wait half an hour?'

We embraced. Forty years ago I had seen her pictures for the first time in some obscure weekly: in Astapovo she was following the coffin, there she sat on a bench in the Crimea under blooming oleanders, in a straw hat, and there she was at tea in Yasnaya Polyana, a corset propping up her bosom, a tie knotted under her chin, a little watch hanging on a chain from her belt. Now she was in front of me.

Khodasevich once told of playing cards in the Moscow Literary-Artistic Club: on his left sat Dostoevsky, on his right Tolstoy – that is, Fedor Fedorovich, a connoisseur of race-horses, and Sergey Lvovich, an amateur composer. I remembered the story in the first moments in her office. Something remained of that stout young girl in a pince-nez with a chain, laced tightly by a wide belt with a huge buckle. Later that day she took me to lunch in a Chinese restaurant, where we sat until about 4:00 P.M., and on Friday she took me out of town, for two days to her farm where she lived, and showed me photographs, some of which I recognized. Yes, in a threesome, with Sofia Andreevna, tall and dressed in black, and with him, already wearing a peasant cap, wrapped somehow against the wind in a coat; and another on a bench at the Black Sea: she looks at him and he into space; and finally one I had never seen, and which for some reason it seems to me no one had seen, so much does it contain, so much does it reveal: he in an armchair, a year or two before his death, she next to him; with both hands he grasps her broad, strong hands, squeezes them, it seems, with all his strength; his face is lifted up and he looks into her eyes – her near-sighted girl's eyes – through biting, piercing, passionate eyes, looks and cannot tear himself away, looks and cannot see enough of her, cannot unclasp her hands. She is wearing a corset, a little tie, a watch; it was time for her to marry. But he clings to her and will not allow it.

I was a guest at her place several times. In the evenings, at sunset, she took the boat and went on the lake to catch fish. I rowed and looked at her powerful, masculine figure, firm, in a raincoat with a hood, as she, standing in the bow, her back to me, cast the line, surprised I didn't know how to fish, play cards, sing second part in a song, play four hands on the piano, dance the waltz as they danced it in their Khamovniki house (until he finally forbade it). She took to teaching me all this. I was incompetent, most of all, at cards. After fishing we sat in the salon in the large house (she lived in the small one, which is where I stayed). Two old ladies who were living on the farm in retirement came out, and all four of us sat down to a game of canasta. I couldn't at all grasp what was required of me. Since the game was played with a partner, and my partner was usually Miss Tolstoy, she would get angry with me, call me 'African blockhead' and say I should put a ring through my nose (Gorky used to say this at times). But she played so well we almost always wound up on the winning end.

'There you see!' I would say to her. 'And you said I was no good!'

'African blockhead,' she answered. 'A ring in your nose. Barbarian!'

She had two dogs, male and female, beautiful black Labradors whom she loved dearly and who loved her. Once when I arrived she confessed to me that she had been so busy she had not managed that day to comb them. We stretched the dogs out on the floor, sat there too, and with a brush and comb started to comb them. This went on for a long time. But when we finished and stood up, the dogs did not want to let us go: they liked it and demanded that it continue endlessly. They nudged us, lay down at our feet, crawled with a sigh up to our knees, put their paws on our shoulders, looked us in the eye, stuck their heads in our hands, wagged their tails over our faces. Again and again we combed them, cleaned their shaggy hard stomachs with a brush, their silken tails, and their intelligent stern heads. Having missed animals, I was that evening no less delighted than they. 'How delighted *he* would have been here together with us,' she said suddenly, untangling some knot that had formed beneath one of the tails. 'This was one of his favourite occupations!'

He was with her everywhere. She was twenty-seven when he died, and for forty years had lived without him – her whole life. But he was alive in her; she was not ready to re-evaluate her feelings about him or to re-examine their mutual relations, or try, soberly aloof, to look at him – these possibilities she simply ignored. Everyone sooner or later begins to judge his father and mother – one at fifteen, another at twenty-five, a third at fifty – but it did not dawn on Miss Tolstoy, who had judged and condemned her mother (and later had again reconciled herself to her) to look at her father with new eyes, not those of her youth. I asked her once who the American was who had come to Leo Tolstoy at the beginning of our century and told him about American agrarian techniques, saying it is not necessary that *each sow his own* bread. There is a note by someone that Tolstoy was shaken by the news that in the U.S.A. ten per cent of the population easily feeds the remaining ninety. He was troubled and said it was *worth thinking about*, but then somehow forgot and never succeeded in returning to the problem he had solved once and for all. Miss Tolstoy knew nothing about this. 'You see, if he had thought this over, he would have had to re-do all his thinking!' I said. She did not answer. She didn't understand why this so troubled me. 'And his diary? Tell me what you think of this early entry (1855) when, as a twenty-seven-year-old, he said he would like to be the prophet of a new religion?' She didn't think anything. I didn't dare remind her of his 1851 entry.* I understood that I would get no answer to these questions.

The first TV set appeared in the house, and after cards I would sit with her in an armchair and we watched a movie. Sometimes not bad, sometimes stupid. She would be interrupted in the middle by the assistant manager, the manager, or be called to the phone. She rushed back with heavy steps, threw her heavy, well-cared-for body into the armchair. 'Who was the killer? Still undiscovered? Has the bad guy been exposed? Is the good-looking one not yet married?' Crossing her legs she would smoke a cigarette. When some dogs appeared on the screen, the Labradors, who were lying on the rug between us, started growling, and she would say: 'What fools! They are baring their teeth at a lapdog. I'm afraid they'll wake up all the old ladies.' And the Labradors beat their tails against our legs.

*The first notation is dated 4 March, 1855; the second (see p. 99 of this book), 29 November, 1851.

Indeed, why didn't I know how to fish? I thought, remembering how in Sweden in the Skärgården I was present, while night was becoming dawn, at the solemn ritual of Greta Gerell's and Fru Asplund's (at whose place I was staying): a fishing-line was cast into absolutely motionless silver water. The float remained still until it disappeared suddenly in a silver circle and within a second – one-hand stroke – a pike, like a bird, was flying in the air. From time to time I continued to read ads in the *New York Times*. I found one completely incomprehensible to me. Here is this mysterious text: 'Helen III. Leaves at 8. Returns at 6. Bring your lunch. Price 3.50 including tools.' Helen, even the third, and the tools confused me. Perhaps it was a sailing boat or a fishing boat or a brigantine? I went to everyone with this ad, but no one could explain what it meant. Finally the detective living next to me did. He told me (in Yiddish, but I understood) that this was one of the many fishing boats which left from East Twenty-third Street and the East River for the Atlantic Ocean. It took passengers, eager fishermen, provided them with perfectly suitable rods and reels and then distributed the fish that was caught: swordfish, flounder . . . but at this point my understanding ceased, since I was not knowledgeable about fish names in Yiddish. Spreading his hands this way and that, the detective let me know that the fish were not small, the size of a young goat, for example, and if I took such a fish to the lady who sat at the cashier's desk in our hotel, it would be credited to my account, for she was none other than the very manager of the hotel.

Perhaps I'd become a fisherman . . . ? It was a hot day, ninety-three degrees, but when we set out on the narrow old schooner for the ocean, we were submerged in a heavy cold fog, which made us damp all at once. The society on the *Helen* was completely classless: besides the captain, a handsome old man with a weather-beaten face (as captains are supposed to have), and three or four other members of the crew, there were no more than fifteen of us. There was a refined greyish man in a splendid fishing outfit and his two young daughters, all three with luxurious rods of their own. From their conversation with the other passengers, I gathered that they had also been fishing the day before (but on the *Margarita*) and would go again tomorrow. It was clear they did nothing else in life, either on holidays or weekdays. There were two Negroes, one of them old, with large yellow teeth and white curls. Then there were three old women in caps who had good luck with the flounder (which looked a little like them) and several other people – professional fishermen. They passionately condemned the qualities of *Helen III*, criticized the captain, were sceptical about the voyage we were making, sailing further and further out beyond Long Island.

The old Negro began to get seasick even before me, and we were both quickly laid out on bunks in the hold; the captain sent us a powder which put us both to sleep, and when we awoke, the captain's aide didn't want to take money from us for the trip and rewarded us for our torments with two huge fish. The boat was now returning to New York. I again saw the city outlines (gothic, cubist, constructivist) looming ahead, emerging from the icy fog into the trembling, sparkling heat of the July day. I viewed it later from above, when a small six-passenger plane flew me around New York after a flight to the Canadian border. The owner of the plane sat at the wheel, a flyer and hero of two wars and now a helicopter test pilot; he took me first to the north, then back along the Sound between Long Island and New England, and circled over the huge city, in the centre of which lay a green spot of a park, and along whose sides, like veins, ran the waters of the Hudson and the East River. I saw the city again from below when I went around it on a small boat, passed under all its bridges – railroad, auto, pedestrian, and those the subway merged with. Since then I have approached it from all six or eight sides, on roads which carry six lanes of cars in both directions.

A month had passed since my arrival. I had hardly managed to adjust when Mikhail Karpovich, a Harvard professor, invited me to Cambridge. He lived on the shores of the Charles, in a house rented to him by Harvard University, where he taught history. I had seen him in Paris, which he visited several times with his wife before the war, and once he even spent six months near Paris with Tanya and their four children. One evening from this time had stayed in my mind; Khodasevich and I had come to see them in Clamart and were sitting downstairs in the living room. Tanya asked me if I would like to see the children. I answered I would, thinking she would take me upstairs to the nursery. But she left alone and began to bring in all four in turn in her arms, and then take them away – first the two boys, of whom one was already quite big and probably heavy, then the girls. All were sound asleep and being carried down and up did

494

not awaken them. The elder girl was called Natasha; she was then four and was now twenty-four. She and her friend, a Harvard student, came to fetch me late at night and we rushed by car to Boston, where we arrived at six in the morning.

The house was old and spacious, with a broken-down piano in the living room on which Karpovich played old Viennese waltzes in the evening, humming them quietly to himself under his breath. It was said that in his youth he had been a dandy, loved to dance and court women, but now he was a bald, ruddy, elderly man with a round paunch, who at home was overwhelmed by domestic cares and at the university by administrative ones. Since the 1950s he was the sole editor of *New Review*, and he buried himself in strange manuscripts, in a pile of unanswered letters, in accounts. His little office was somewhere under the staircase, and there everything was in great disorder, principally for lack of space. He did not leave behind him a historical work, as the historian is supposed to – he had too much to do, too many problems, too many interests: in modern art, literature, people in all kinds of professions, of all ages and occupations – and there was a type of sadness within him he did not give vent to and which only from time to time was apparent in his subtle humour, his piano-playing, his humming of Strauss waltzes. It always seemed to me he not only had no time to write 'works', but none to converse calmly without looking at his watch or to go somewhere and just sit awhile with folded hands. He had to bear in mind all the time some urgent and forever confused *New Review* and Harvard affairs, answer without fail today that letter that had been lying (but where?) on the desk for three weeks, or rush to New York to see such and such before he returned to Europe, call up Professor X to reconcile him with Professor Y or else all of Harvard University would collapse, and so on. Towards the end of his life he began to grow deaf, while his wife began gradually to show signs of severe mental illness. After being ill for a long time, evidently cancer of the pancreas complicated by tuberculosis, this kind, lovable man died. He loved laughter, youth, all that was new, all that life brought, but it swept past him increasingly as in his last years, perhaps owing to deafness, he began to hum more and more, as if there was music in him that was bursting forth, but he hadn't the time nor strength nor means to communicate it. His death was a shock to the *New Review* and all who had grouped around it.

We arrived in Cambridge in the morning, drank some coffee, and Karpovich took me around the university to show me the library and the noble old buildings of Harvard. For the first time I saw an American campus. It was winter, just before Christmas, there were no lectures and the students were away. The luxury of the library, the offices, the laboratories, the lecture halls, the availability of everything, the ease, comfort, quiet, the open spaces struck me. 'For kings, not for simple mortals,' I said, remembering the line at the door of the reading room of the Bibliothèque Nationale in Paris. 'For American students,' said Karpovich. 'And do you know the conclusion I have come to about which people are the happiest on our planet?'

I did not know. 'In any case, neither Russian writers nor Chinese coolies,' I answered.

He began to laugh: 'American students. When you have learned more of American life, remember my words.'

We drank coffee in the student café, he humming as usual; it was deserted and quiet, as it always is during holidays on campuses. When we returned home, Roman Jakobson was already there. I was touched by his coming; we had not seen each other since Prague in 1923, twenty-eight years before! In that time he had come to rank first among Slavic scholars in the world; his cheeks were no longer rosy but his blue eyes were as I remembered from that supper at Shklovsky's in Berlin, when he had covered one eye and demanded I look into the other. Now this was a joyous meeting for me and we both tried not to speak of anything which could set us apart, start an argument or bring on bitter words: I knew, as everyone did who had read his book on Mayakovsky, that he violently hated Khodasevich for his article 'The Horse in a Décolleté' (on Maya-kovsky's poetry). Only in 1962 (that is eleven years later), when I met Jakobson at a dinner at Yale and sat next to him, did I ask him: 'Well, can you still not stand him as before?' And he answered me kindly: 'All this was so long ago – there is nothing left of it.' He was in his youth a 'formalist', and all formalists were by their nature incorrigible romantics, so, I noticed, his no longer clear blue, but slightly blue-grey, eyes filled with a light, momentary mist.

She was four then, now she was twenty-four . . . Natasha, seeing how I lived in New York, asked me to share an apartment with her not far from Columbus Avenue. Her weightiest argument was: it will be convenient for washing things. In fact, laundry took a rather large place in our household: every Sunday in the bathroom seven pairs of her panties hung on a cord, seven pairs of socks (for a week), and from time to time a brassière or two. On Sunday we put the same amount of money into a box on the mantel and spent it together. With what remained on Saturday we went to the movies. She cleaned up after my guests, and I after hers. That year I did some work for Alexandra Tolstoy.

There were three rooms in the apartment: 'mine', 'yours', and 'common'. I went into mine in the evenings and read, going to sleep early. Young people would sit in Natasha's: they listened to records of Bartok, smoked, talked, and sometimes woke me up, dragged me out of bed, and persuaded me to sit with them. At 1:00 A.M. all were hungry, but as the American custom is when guests are hungry, they themselves went to the kitchen, opened the refrigerator, and looked for suitable food. Then they would clean up everything, wash the dishes, and return to their hosts. 'You should have given them cheese and red wine,' I suggested to Natasha, 'or sausage.'

'They drink milk,' she answered with abandon. And in fact the young Harvardians drank milk and ate cookies, and then listened again to Schoenberg and Bartok.

We went to see one of them in the summer at the seaside, where he and his wife had taken a cottage. There was a box on a shelf too, and whoever needed money took and spent it, and once a week we, the entire household, went to buy groceries. In those places there is now one fashionable beach after another, but then it was wild and deserted, there was only sand, the ocean, fishermen, Portuguese natives, and at night you could build a fire on the beach of the loudly roaring ocean, cook hot dogs over the flame, and then sleep on the sand under the stars.

In this second year of my life in the U.S.A. I had two crises: the first in connection with a dream I had several times in a row. Someone would come and I would rise to meet him, but he (or she) would say: 'Not now.' And disappear. Or would say: 'Not now, but in ten years.' Or would say nothing, raise his hand, and leave. The second crisis lasted only five minutes: it was a fear that gripped me somewhere on Broadway, not far from Chambers Street, in an unfamiliar spot, where I was for the first time – I had gone to a

Russian printer to read some proofs. The skyscrapers were hidden, the sky, in clouds, made the streets dark grey, a strange cupola was visible over a roof that went from steel-grey to green in colour. On the corner the building was held up by white chipped columns and I saw myself standing in the middle of Sadovaya, somewhere near Gorokhovaya in the midst of Petersburg. At the moment when I was ready in full consciousness to submit to the nightmare and turn towards Ekaterininsky Canal to come out onto Kazanskaya, I realized this was not Sadovaya at all, but the corner of Rue Roquette and Boulevard Parmentier. However, both these crises were undoubtedly related to my giving blood at the time. The pint of blood taken from me both times caused my unusual hallucinations.

That year I became friends with Jessica. She called me once on the phone. Knowing I hardly spoke English, she spelled out her surname letter by letter and yelled into the phone: 'Shakespeare, remember Shakespeare! Not Ophelia, not Cordelia! Not Desdemona! From *The Merchant of Venice*! Do you remember that merchant?' She told me to come to dine at her place; her sister who lived in Philadelphia had phoned her about me; this sister had been told about me by a friend who had seen me somewhere, visiting. 'But you don't know me,' I muttered, as best I could. 'How can I come to dine?' 'You are quite alone and have only just arrived. You need practice in English.' 'I am all right, I am not lost, I even like it here,' I also shouted – I am always infected with shouting when people shout on the telephone. But Jessica insisted on my coming and indeed dining. Her last words were 'Don't forget about the merchant!'

She had a long, regular face, was flat-chested, beautiful, wore big hats from where splendid golden hair would shoot out, and her age was unclear: somewhere between thirty-five and forty-five. She spoke loudly, cursed all politicians with relish; she called Eisenhower and Truman names, and the night Stevenson was not elected president, she drank too much out of grief and broke a beautiful piece of Venetian glass she had kept on a table. 'It came to you from the merchant,' I said to her about the glass.

Her kindness and patience were astonishing. She was a worldly woman who loved the company of intelligent and even famous people, especially political ones: diplomats, members of Congress, senators and those who moved about them. She knew how to receive a dozen guests in her flat (one ate there without a table, from trays on which, besides a plate with food, were a glass for wine, a miniature salt cellar and pepper mill – like two thimbles). She invited me over often, took me to the theatre, to restaurants, and I began to speak English with her in earnest – until then I had tried to avoid this. In the evenings I now went to school where there were classes, some for beginners and others for those who, knowing the language, wanted to enlarge their vocabulary. But when after two months of group lessons 'practical exercises' began, the energetic, severe young teacher could not believe her ears when she heard my reading of the eighth chapter of *Paradise Lost*.

'Permit me! Where have you come from? How did you land here? You must go to the adjoining room, that's where the beginners are. You can't stay here – Who permitted this?'

But after the lesson I explained to her that I got a special incomparable pleasure from Milton, whom she had discussed, and asked her to leave me in peace and allow me to attend her class. She looked at me distrustfully, shrugged her shoulders, and decided apparently to forget about me.

Jessica said: 'Something always happens to you. Something always happens to Europeans.' But something happened to her which fundamentally changed her life: to do something, she wrote a story, taken, of course, from her own life. She wrote it in two evenings and sent it to one of those American magazines that are published in several million copies. The story was accepted, she was paid a large sum, the plot was sold over the phone to Hollywood for the movies, and she was invited to speak on TV on the 'Our Celebrities' hour. When I visited her she showed me several hundred readers' letters begging her to continue. But the most important one was a letter from the editor of the magazine that published the story, who demanded either a series now or a whole novel.

Jessica decided for a time to hide from New York. I tried to give her some professional advice, like Flaubert to Maupassant, but nothing came of it, since I myself didn't believe in advice. She left and quickly married.

By that time I was already going in the morning to Mrs Toom, and in the evening read books from the library: novels, criticism, history, philosophy, anthropology, psychology . . . Success in a new language, as is well known, goes in degrees: for a week there is nothing, and then suddenly a jolt, and you are pushed out of your stupidity and confusion into understanding and mastery of new forms. So it was with me.

Mrs Toom was seeking a secretary, but not at all an ordinary one. She was seeking a secretary for her personal correspondence. She corresponded in four languages and among those she wrote to were Albert Schweitzer, Gary Cooper, two senators, Furtwängler, a Nobel Prize laureate in nuclear physics, the widow of a well-known French philosopher, and a Russian inventor living in London. She asked me if I could type in French. 'I can,' I said. 'And in Russian?' 'I can also.' She was astonished and glad, because up till then she had not known anyone who could type on a Russian typewriter. A typewriter was quickly bought. 'And how about a German machine?' After thinking a little, I said I could if she would first dictate the letter. She didn't ask about English, having decided I could not avoid knowing such simple things. The first day I found, among other papers, a letter of Schweitzer's in which he thanked Mrs Toom for sending a large monetary sum for the roof in one of his dispensaries for lepers. This was a dispensary with which, as I understood it, Mrs Toom busied herself particularly. Now instead of a straw roof there was an iron one. Mrs Toom had just returned from Africa and could not accept the fact that this dispensary had been covered with straw.

The second week a photographer came, bringing her three reels of developed film, taken by her in Lambarene. I helped set up the screen, drew the curtains and sat down with her to view the film; she was worried about whether all was in order. But it turned out that the photographer had inserted a strange elephant into her roll.

'Where did you get this elephant? From a strange reel? The lions are mine, the bisons are mine, but I had no elephant. Take the elephant away. Give it to the one it belongs to. I don't need strange elephants.'

Lepers. Schweitzer. Mrs Toom and lepers. Mrs Toom and Schweitzer. I asked how she got to them. Did she go by plane?

'I flew to Africa, then took a taxi and arrived,' she said.

Her grandsons came to visit her in the third week. Snub-nosed, pale, they said: 'Hi, Grandma,' and stopped in the doorway, picking their noses.

'Ah!' she said. 'Have you had breakfast?'

'Yes, but we are hungry,' answered the grandsons.

'Once you have eaten, you are not hungry,' said Grandma. 'We will now go to see the Empire State Building.' She explained to me that she had promised a year and a half ago to take them there, but there had never been any time.

'We are hungry,' repeated the grandsons.

I lay aside the letter I was typing (to Furtwängler, affirming the promise of a scholarship for a young flutist), and asked if I could not give them each a glass of milk and a roll.

'No rolls. They are both lying. I will take them now to the Empire State Building.'

They went. When they returned and I asked the boys if they had had any pleasure (I had myself gone there three times and could not tear my eyes away from the New York skyline), they answered:

'No, we didn't, because we were hungry.'

Mrs Toom was pleased with me. I composed a letter to the Russian inventor myself, on the new Hermes machine:

MY ESTEEMED SEMEN PETROVICH!
The sum you are asking for your experiments in the desalinization of sea water is too large. I am sending you today (through my bank) exactly half. As for manganese deposits at the North Pole, you will have to secure the support of the Canadian government for such an expedition: at the end of the month I will be in Ottawa and will there try to talk with the Prime Minister about your plans . . .

'But is he not a swindler?'

'He is an old friend of mine,' she answered, indignant.

'Not the Prime Minister, but Semen Petrovich.'

'I don't think so.'

Silence followed.

'What beautiful names you have, you Russians,' she said dreamily. 'Semen Petrovich! Charming!'

Semen Petrovich wrote her letters in an elaborate handwriting, calling her 'Most honoured Mme Toom'. I once hinted that it would be good if he sent his picture – from a photograph we would probably be able to form an opinion of this man, who was beginning to trouble me.

'How self-confident you are!' said Mrs Toom. 'Do you consider yourself a physiognomist? Do you hope to grasp the character of a man on the basis of his picture?'

I began to speak more cautiously when the topic concerned Semen Petrovich. Gradually I noticed that something was bothering Mrs Toom. Finally the following conversation took place:

'Can you type in Italian?'

I thought a few seconds and decided to speak the truth: 'I can read Dante only with a dictionary.'

'Dante Alighieri, 1265–1321,' she said indifferently. 'Four times a year I send food and things to an orphans' school in Calabria. And in Swedish?'

'A little in Swedish. I asked for Swedish language but was given Norwegian.'

'Norwegian? Who needs Norwegian except Norwegians?'

I didn't know what to answer to this.

She needed Swedish because she had her candidate for the Nobel Prize, and from time to time reminded the secretary of the Royal Academy of it. 'Who?' And I began to run through some names in my head.

'Not a writer. A chemist!'

Suddenly a remarkable idea dawned on me:

'But, Mrs Toom,' I said, 'in Swedish you need a completely different machine, for there you have *a* and *o* with little circles like holes. Without them you can't type. There must be those little circles.'

'Connect me with Hermes,' she said, pointing to the telephone. 'Tomorrow they will send over a Swedish machine.'

There is something in her of universal absurdity, I thought – mind you, as in myself. Which means we are somehow alike. The fact that I am here is also absurd, which means I am a part of universal absurdity. With my own absurdity I must somehow get on with someone else's. Find room in it.

There had been times when I had to 'squeeze into an alien absurdity', 'settle in it', and fall into step with the entire universal absurdity. When? When I was given a sandwich in a Moscow grocery store? Or when on the day of the fall of Berlin I looked at Dr Serov taking, with a pair of tweezers, pieces of my *grey matter* from my left ear?

502

Sometimes Mrs Toom would not let me leave after lunch. There were days when she kept me till evening. From time to time her old-lady friends would come for cocktails, and then in her voice threatening notes appeared.

'Charming apartment! Charming cocktails! Charming secretary!' the old ladies cooed.

'I am not asking your opinion. Drink and eat. You were invited for that.'

After a month of working for her, Mrs Toom invited me to the Kabuki Theatre. At the theatre exit I thanked her, and she raised her brows in astonishment.

'What is there to say about it? It's already the past.'

In the spring she suggested a plan: abandon everything, get rid of the apartment and go with her to New Hampshire where she had an estate. There we would breed roses.

No, I would not agree to this.

'Well, not roses,' she said. 'Tulips.'

But I even refused for tulips.

She gave two sobs, but softened only for a moment. Quickly she spoke to me in the tone of a cavalry sergeant with a private:

'Then be gone.'

And I cleared out. Next morning at seven she called me and said she was in a horrible state; since the previous evening she had lost the paperback she was reading, a detective novel. She had read halfway through it and now did not know *who the murderer was*. She had forgotten the title of the book and was condemned not to know to the end of her life: *Who was the murderer?*

'I am an old fool,' she said firmly into the telephone. 'Find the book, I beg of you, find the book for the old fool.'

But of course I could not find the book and we parted on this painful note.

I became friends then with Vsevolod Pastukhov, a pianist, teacher, and in part a poet, who had lived between the two wars in Riga and had had a music school there. In the century's second decade he had lived in Petersburg, knew the poets Mikhail Kuzmin, Georgy Ivanov, and others well; like him they went to the Stray Dog. He brought into my life a forgotten Petersburg which I could not personally have known but which pierced me in 1921 just before it melted away in the air of revolutionary Petrograd. In the light of the Russian experience, all this part of the 'Petersburg period' – i.e., acmeism – seems infected today with some kind of disease; it seems anaemic, doomed from the first day of its existence. But the reason for this frailty lies not in the weakness of its theories and the thinness of its basis or its principles (incidentally, unrealized), but solely in the weakness, anaemia, vainness, and 'mimosa' quality of its representatives. The theories of course were never alien to the outstanding acmeist poets (Akhmatova, Mandelstam, and Gumilev), but when we take one step away from the centre to the periphery we come upon a kind of general enfeeblement, softening, an anti-strength, an anti-firmness, even an intolerance towards clear outlines, the exact word (and it was precisely for the exact word that arms had once been taken up), an intolerance for a strong voice – which the acmeists considered, to the end of their lives, as something indecent. So, though they loved Gumilev, the father of the movement, they did not like his verse, which for them had too much thunder – they preferred mumbling. It was not without reason that at our last encounter in Paris in 1965 Georgy Adamovich said in irritation to me, when speaking of Nabokov: 'I don't like smartness!' He had said this more than once about Tsvetaeva. 'But was there none in Pushkin?' I asked. He confessed he was jarred sometimes even by Pushkin's smartness. A loosely and clumsily written novel 'in which there is something' (his favourite expression) was always dearer to him, he said, than polished, self-assured things.

Pastukhov also hated pertness and boisterousness. He didn't like brilliant virtuosos and poets who read their verse too loudly; he liked to say that in judging them he was not out to convince anyone and was not in search of impartiality. He was a frequent guest in the New York salon of Mrs Tsetlina. If people invited by her in Paris were old friends, sometimes from Moscow days, guests in New York were gathered at random, selected – it was not always clear how they were selected. I remembered the witty statement of Khodasevich that a day would come for the émigré intelligentsia when men of letters would assemble together on the sole basis that they were still able to distinguish an iamb from a trochee. Not every guest at Mrs Tsetlina's could qualify on that criterion. To speak truthfully, they now did not mesh but differed essentially. They were divided along completely different lines than had once been the case in Paris.

There it had been above all a division of generations, then it was a political division: right and left, that is 'old regime' (with which there was no communication) and so-called socialistic (very loosely). There you could sense the Muscovite and the Petersburg-ite, or the former capital-dweller and the provincial, the man who had gone through the Civil War and the man who had been to university. These categories did not exist here. The main character-istic was: When did he leave Russia? In 1920? In 1943? When did he turn up in America? In 1925? In 1939? In 1950?

But there was another division, which was more important for me than all the rest. Notwithstanding how many years a man had lived in the Western world, some were taking everything they could from this world, but others lived behind their own Chinese wall which separated them from it. They had brought with them their own, personal (or clannish), folding, portable, stainless iron curtain, and hung it between themselves and the West. Sometimes they camouflaged it, sometimes they displayed it, but most of all they simply lived behind it, not interested in what surrounded them, on the old principle that 'things were better for us in Penza'.

In France there were a few of these, and they had made a basic compromise: it *was* better in Penza, but now willy-nilly we must change our tastes, and change ourselves, alas! France demanded submission more strongly, often changed people by force, 'fed' them whether they liked it or not – so that at times they even did not notice it. There were many reasons for this: there was the tradition of Russian Europeans who used to live in Paris; there was French literature, which had one way or another entered the consciousness of even the semi-intelligentsia in school years; émigré children growing up in France and bringing to their homes the ways of the new country; and, even in some, recollections of fathers and grandfathers who had come here and took something with them to Russia that for some reasons did not exist in Penza. In America matters were completely different: there was no tradition of coming here; the pressure that existed in France to subordinate to French culture was non-existent; the literature, art, and music were unfamiliar to those who came; émigré children not only did not bring into their homes new ways of life but, because of the nature of American schools, went ever further in their protest against their parents, clinging to those who generously gave them everything which was sometimes met with a sneer at home. The Russians in New York, both 'old' and 'new', were for the most part provincials (in Paris it was the other way round), and the preservation of the 'Penza attitude' was much stronger among them. Those who rushed to enter American life, of course, did not even glance back at this milieu. They, so to speak, hurried to jump from the 'first' generation to the second or even the third, and with this their artificial *Russianness* ended.

But too many lived behind their iron curtain or, to put it better, behind Grandma's screen (and all knew what was there and what its odour was), where light did not penetrate from the huge, strong, modern young country, striking in its generosity and energy, and which – precisely because it could grow like a legendary giant – they did not trust and even feared: it could – how terrible! – suppress their national pride. Because – and it is time to say it – the U.S.A., moving in fifteen years as it had been customary in history to move in fifty, offended the pride of other countries by its mere existence; not one country could vie with it on equal grounds. In fifteen years it went at full speed from a centre of outward immobility to a centre of inward revolution. Many goals have not been attained, but the extant consciousness of the people has become the guarantee of its vitality and the pledge of its future. The joy of stability has not yet come; the very foundations and principles of the institutions are being questioned. And the times in which this latent revolution is taking place are dangerous and fascinating, unexpected and challenging, awesome and promising. But for the petit bourgeois and the Philistine this seems both frightful and suspicious. In my first month in the U.S.A. I abandoned such people without hesitation. Their basic characteristics were for me: the impossibility of mastering the language, an inability to get along with Americans (or an absence of interest in them), a convulsive grasping at the remains of 'Russian problems' (a term that has lost all meaningful embodiment), a religion recalling the seventeenth century, and searches for their 'equals'. All this pedestrian tribal dust, brought along, was being spread within and around themselves.

In the old place in 1950 I did not have enough friends, work, books, and personal happiness. Now I began to live in a new place. And since all was changing, and I, my aims and searches were also, it turned out that these four elements also changed, and I found them, got them, but not at all as I had seen them in Paris.

We alter, and our desires do too. It would be strange to strive during an entire life for one single thing as if it were an immobile mountain peak to which an Alpinist was heading. There is a live, many-layered perspective, and mutations of the ideal when that *one thing* that was is no longer the same. It was one thing when I was twenty, and another when I was forty, and now finally has taken on completely new traits. In fact, it does not exist, it is nowhere, I do not move towards it with a cheerful step, it does not await me stone-like and motionless, somewhere above. It is in me. In the course of my life, I move and it moves also. Today it is a well I have looked into, tomorrow it is something that must fall into my palm, the day after tomorrow I am a frog churning butter in a milk bucket. So I was Tobias, then the Angel, then Galatea, then perhaps Pygmalion himself. These images have not turned to stone in front of me, forcing me to seize them, realize myself in them; they have vibrated with me, in my complex and yet modest destiny. Four elements lacking for me in post-war Europe, were regenerated here in America like myself. I never wished for their immutability, their monumentality, I wished them to be as flowing as I was when I changed – every year, or every five years, or every day – into something new and different.

And above all people. Yes, in my first years here there were not many more of them than on my last day in Paris. But in the 'mutations of the ideal', the accessibility of people around became their primordial feature for me, their openness, their willingness to accept me; this turned into something precious and indispensable at a given stage of my life. As once in Russia, the feeling returned here of contact and the possibility of contact with everyone, especially when their language became mine. I sensed, not only abstractly, but quite concretely, the opportunity of belonging to everyone and possessing everyone. Friends were found because my associations broadened limitlessly, first because of my seven different jobs, and then because of the last, the eighth, which became the main and permanent one. Which brings me to the second reason for my departure – to work, to that new job, one which I had never thought of before, which as a matter of fact was not even on my childish roster. My trade also did not prove to be unchanging as a rock. But then the unfortunate rock is unstable too, as scientists told us not long ago.

For I did not really change professions, but on the basis of one began another. After three stories, a play, and verse, written during my first years in America, I gradually switched my basic interest in a new direction, yet it was where the Russian literature I had lived with closely for forty-five years also lay. Now other sides of it became important to me: as all people know, 'artistic creation' has been on the decline in Russia for thirty-five years, but in recent years critical and analytical thought, in all its novelty and complexity, has begun to come to life. To draw something from that and give it to others seemed not only possible to me, but overwhelmingly important.

All this is bound up in the closest way with the third element I spoke about above: with the books in which the spirit of my time lives, the books I continue to live with and which teach me to think perhaps even more intensively than in my youth, because I have learned to read them better. They *feed* me in the sense given to that word by Plato and Dante; and I receive my food from the great men of *my* age – sometimes poets and novelists, but more often critics and thinkers, critic-interpreters, sociologists, historians. I came to them in a new language and found in them that *daily bread* which did not exist in any other country of the world, and which in my own country had only in recent years begun slightly to be reborn. With that, the sad blank that started to narrow and impoverish me and which I felt so sharply in the 1940s, was filled up. Now in an improbable, unthinkable abundance, treasures lie about me, only a small part of which I shall be able to use. With them nothing seems sad, nothing tedious, that joy always comes which people without it envy most of all. So here, there was also that mutation of the ideal, and the rock was moved from its place, as it should be.

But what can I say of personal happiness? This side of my life more than any other endured changes with the years, because more deeply than all others it was bound up with transformations in myself.

'Immovable' property, as everyone knows, does not exist: the lilac grows out and lies on the house roof, stifling the birches; the roof collapses; in the kitchen where pies were baked a bird's nest is forming; bats hang on Grandfather's portrait. And we ourselves are not what we were yesterday; what is born in us in the morning is different from what we fall asleep with at night. Not only our demands change but also our possibilities – when these are in harmony – and our strength. Fantasies change not only their shapes but their very subject matter. Aims go out of focus and, if there are any, passions and needs, ambitions and self-affirmations alter, and that point in the centre towards which the whole mechanism was striving continues like a constellation in a movement imperceptible to the naked eye; the important becomes less important and the essential no longer so. Everything has drifted and is no longer where it was ten or even five years ago. It would be foolish to pull this constellation to its former centre, strange and unnatural to push it from its new geometrical pattern in that old 'angle A' from which rays came to us recently, for there is no 'angle A' either, and the whole scheme changed from Tuesday to Wednesday.

These mutations of the ideal, reflecting the limitless plasticity of man, give me joy and do not scare me. My form and content are one and change together: the first helps the second when the second does not help the first. What I find now in personal life, in books, in people, in my work can no longer be what it once was: all four elements have remained, but their intersections, their movement into each other, are completely different.

My joy is as before in their intensity and their co-ordination and when I am busy with one I always sense the existence of the three others. Books are closely bound up with my work, my work with the people I meet and cultivate. Of these, five or six as it were *live on the top floor* and make my existence more intense than it would be without them. Since they are also related to the *food* I take from what surrounds me, the circle is closed: I am both alone and not alone in the world chosen by me seventeen years ago.

I have moved about this world more than a little, to know its cities and mountains, its rivers and roads, its skies and horizons.

I have already spoken of my going with Natasha Karpovich to the shores of the Atlantic in the summer of 1952, where for the first time I was struck by the immensity and emptiness of space. The distance was visible not between the backs, heads, and shoulders of other people, it lay freely before one's eyes, at times without a single living figure on the wide shore of that strip of land which extends into the sea in the form of a crab's claw between New

London and Boston. On the map it seems quite small, like a hook; in fact there are cities, pine forests grow, roads stretch out for trains and cars, airports have been built. Dunes divide inhabited spots from the shore, where sky and ocean are visible, and a funny inscription can be found on a tree stump: so many thousand miles to Portugal. Behind the high dunes the August sun set as we quietly scrambled down and found ourselves at the water, the waves thundering. Pale, puffy, at first hardly noticeable, the moon rose in the sky; it got dark; after swimming in water that was often warmer than the air, we set up a fire and I lay near it. The conversations that reached me, while I lay and looked up, were about modern painting, modern music, and new books, about politics in Asia, the local architect, a pupil of Wright, who built house after house in pine woods, on a hill, and arguments about why a balcony on piles was good and a mirror in the bathroom bad, about the tiles covering the garage at the intersection of the state and interstate highways (too bright in the dark green of the firs), and about the verse of Wallace Stevens, who worked on poetry in his leisure hours but was in fact an insurance executive. Then I would leave them, stroll beside waves that beat higher, finding not even a trace of a human print on the sand; when I returned the conversation was about government planning, and why it succeeded with some and not others.

Then it became cool, and carefully dousing the fire, covering it with sand, cleaning up all the papers and remains of food, we clambered up to the car, walking with bare feet at first in the cool sand and then in the last year's warm conifer needles, soft and dry.

As often happens in the U.S., the upkeep of the house was not complex; we all took part, the four inhabitants of the old Portuguese house. Portugal was, as had been noticed, so many thousand miles from us, but it was also here, with us, among the descendants of the seafarers who had settled here two hundred years ago. A quiet, dark girl came over to show us her newborn child, a tall old woman in a black kerchief and with glistening eyes sang songs similar to gypsies', which Praskovya Gavrilovna had once sung in that night tavern in the working quarters of Billancourt. A dark little boy on Sunday appeared to show off his costume with the darkening gold braid; a portrait of his grandfather with dark whiskers in naval uniform hung opposite the entrance door, so it was impossible not to see him on entering the house. The men were

510

all deep-sea fishermen and went to sea for five or six days at a time, not just for an hour or a night. The fishing villages alternated with country settlements on the peninsula and the islands near it. On one of the islands, very small and difficult to get to, all was small, particularly the houses with dangling roses, and only the shore, wide and long, was for giants; the ocean was endless, occupying, so it seemed when the sun rose from it, the entire surface of the earth, leaving no room for Portugal.

I saw space and emptiness in all their power when, as if on a straight line drawn with a ruler, I left Washington for Colorado, driving through the green hills of Maryland, through the wheat fields of Kansas. 'Kansas is boring,' I was warned. 'You drive straight for six hours and it's always the same.' For six and a half hours in Kansas there was a sky like nothing I had ever seen: it took up all the visible space, while the earth was just a thin crust, its weak support, a completely two-dimensional flatness without thickness. On all four corners of this huge sky giant cloud Monkey Laocoöns stood, resting their feet on the ground and hitting the centre of the heavenly cupola with their heads (and there, among them, the fat cupids of Bouchet turned a somersault); giant Titian apes stood with snakes enveloping them in a frozen marble struggle. They did not stir for six and a half hours, as if neither wind nor sun touched them, and I watched them for all the four hundred miles as if I too were standing in one place. I then remembered a conversation I witnessed. One man said to the other: 'You understand what it is to live in Oklahoma? It's a hole. It's the sticks. A living man there will die of boredom.' And the other answered: 'Once in Tulsa, you know, I saw a sunset I had never seen before anywhere.' Now in Kansas I realized you could see things you would not see in any other corner of the world.

On the border of Kansas and Colorado – where the wheat and corn fields end and sand and stone begin, and the scenery and the sky change – I met a storm from the west, or rather three storms, which came from a point straight in front of me, and dispersed in three directions, rushing at me in bolts of lightning, now receding from me. Fiery columns one after another would stick to the earth that trembled from thunder, and the car, braking amidst this roar, the torrential rain and the sudden gloom cut by the blue light of flashes, ploughed through the waters, rocking from side to side until it stopped.

The names of towns in Colorado would drive anyone to distraction: Indian, German, Spanish, English – they follow each other while I rise higher and higher into the mountains; there are modern cities and abandoned towns, and deserted towns that have suddenly become modern cities, where roads have been made, hospitals built, stores opened; and there is even a restaurant where bearded artists and their girlfriends eat and sing. The Rocky Mountains are close here, and I begin to rise to the place with no paved roads, telephone poles, lancet TV antennas, because there is no electricity, telephone, no pathway. Just trout.

Late at night the car arrives finally at a water reservoir, the sources of the Rio Grande. On the map this is a white spot. No post office, drugstore, gas station. Along the gurgling and gambolling river there are log cabins with benches in them, a table, some beds, a kerosene lamp, and a stove. For a whole month we will eat trout from the stream – morning, noon, and night – and we will light the stove in the evening. Once at dawn I will see snow (at the beginning of July).

There are pink trout, lilac, in our stream under the porch; rainbow trout are in the lake that lies in the shape of a heart even higher than we, who are at a height of ten thousand feet. At the very top of the Rocky Mountains a man lives with forty-five horses and three wives (Mexicans – small, smaller, smallest). He has never even been to Chicago, New York doesn't interest him, and neither does Peking nor Cape Town.

We arrived at night and I threw myself into bed, beneath the quilt. Already half asleep, I felt something alive under my pillow scratching next to my ear; but I didn't have the strength to light the candle and set the unknown beast at liberty. He was – I felt this with my cheek and temple – small and joyful, and because of some strange rapid clicks, I sensed it was not a mouse, in which there is always something depressingly stubborn – I will gnaw through or die! – something boring, monotonous in the very sound of his gnawing. Here a creature was playing under my pillow, trying to examine the space around my head. And I fell asleep exhausted, having decided that he could not in any case eat me up.

In the morning I awoke because someone was tenderly biting the toes of my right foot. This was the chipmunk that had played beneath my ear the evening before. Small, gay, with splendid tails, they run all over the U.S., standing up on their back paws when they see a human being and waving to us with the front ones as a sign of greeting. Mine preferred to settle in the kitchen, but later he left, looking only from time to time into the cabin, already in the company of a half dozen others.

Deer came at night when we were cooking the trout. The quiet steps sounded, as did the dry knock of horns on the doorpost. A huge eye sparkled on the chamois snout, and having turned towards me at first in profile and then full face, the head disappeared. He came and looked in, asked for nothing, and proudly went away, walking several quiet steps; only when leaving did he suddenly jump, resonantly and with force, piercing the evening silence with his clatter.

The bears were small but stocky, and kept away from people. The barefooted children of the host (they ran barefoot even in the July snow) once saw a she-bear with her little ones, but no one offended anyone else, as if by agreement. All around fishermen lived, and hunters, riders who rented horses from the man who had never been to Denver. In the heart-shaped lake golden clouds were reflected (at sunset), with blue sky and the Rocky Mountain aspens which grew here, making all the contours curly. Beneath the aspens, in a cold shadow, flowers bloomed that no one picked – they were the symbol of the state of Colorado, blue columbines.

The snow did not remain for as long as an hour. The aspens and firs only washed in it. The cold air cut my face, the lake reflected the rising sun. Every branch was visible on the mountain, which rose steeply, with a silvery strip of aspen, a dark green strip of firs, and finally a strip of grey, severe rocks, from which chipped-off stones would roll down to us sometimes in our high and quiet valley.

This whole marvellous, empty region lies north-west of New Mexico, of Santa Fe and the Indian reservations, and the colonies of artists and poets in Taos. When I arrived there I found Frieda Lawrence was no longer alive. She had lived in the mountain wilderness above Taos, next to the spot where D.H. Lawrence is buried. Now the Lawrence house has been rebuilt, but the valleys all around are as majestic and beautiful as ever; cities are not built there, nor factories set up. In the eternal quiet his ashes lie high and alone, and if there were a pose in his desire to live and die high and alone, in fact it was not accidental: every pose, like every gesture, gives the key to the whole personality. Yes, he loved to live high and alone (surrounded by disciples) and managed to find a spot where he could do it (he was less successful with his disciples). Now people – the old who knew him and the young who have heard about him – walk in the streets of Taos and read him.

These young ones produce the plays of Gertrude Stein in the local theatre, sit at easels on the corners of narrow streets and in front of the mesa where Indians live. The mesa consists of rows of clay houses with rounded corners, similar to old-fashioned hives. An Indian in a coloured poncho, standing the whole day on a corner of the central square, has for a long time repeated by heart his story about D. H. L. (so he's called here), and repeats it to all who wish to listen. Of course he remembers the names of the participants of the famous drama, Frieda is called Frieda, and Mabel Dodge Luhan is called Mabel – she was still alive the year I was in Taos but was not in evidence: she lived in her villa with her Indian husband outside the town.

No one saw her but every day everyone sees Dorothy Brett, the English aristocrat who in her day had followed Lawrence to New Mexico. She is one of the faithful and is covered with Mexican jewellery (on her forehead, neck, waist, on her hands and feet); dressed in white Mexican clothes, with a white lap dog in her arms, she walks about the town and from a distance one can hear the jingling of her bracelets, pendants, and beads. Sometimes Witter Bynner appears – another witness to the Mexican ravings of Lawrence; he also jingles silver, is in a homespun shirt too, with long greyish curls, in barefoot sandals and with a cane. Both of them, Bynner and Brett, have long ago written their books about Lawrence and in both, as I talk to them, there remains something of the 1920s: a mannerism in their walk, the decorations they wear, a sing-song in their speech.

In one of the clean clay huts, where homespun mats lie on the floor, an Indian cut me a ring at my request out of soft alloy (silver, tin, iron), hammered onto it an ornament, and put into it a huge piece of a marvellously blue-coloured glass. 'Those sapphires do not break,' he said with a bow, and put the ring on my finger with his long dark fingers. 'Rubies are not durable, and I am out of emeralds.'

Then I go to the mesa, to the village where you live vertically, not horizontally. I know that this will soon disappear. Old women were still sitting on their doorstep and weaving, old men were hammering heavy ornaments, in silver and lead, but the young were waiting on tables in restaurants or filling up tourists' gas tanks, getting scholarships and going away to study. A school was built between the two mesas. A portrait of Lincoln hung in the class; the young teacher was a native of Vermont. We sat with her on the hot stone and talked. Then we ate together. We were brought spicy Mexican dishes on huge smooth plates, Mexican bread that recalled the Caucasian *lavash*, tequila in tiny steamed glasses, and that evening I wrote to Paris that in America to that day I still had not met a single millionaire, or one gangster, or one basketball-player, or one jazz musician – and only two Hollywood actors. I knew: there would be disillusionment, especially on the part of one of my correspondents (age twelve). What interest could he have in a teacher in an Indian school? He was waiting for a letter from me about Indians themselves!

The teacher said I had to go to Vermont without fail. I already knew Vermont; Karpovich had a house there, and I had visited him several times before his life came to an end, first with the illness of his wife, then with his own unhappy operations. Vermont was too quiet in its traditions for me, its conservatism. In it, fifty years before, time had stopped and people, sitting on their balconies in wicker rocking chairs, reminded me of the king in Blok's 'Nocturnal Violet', who for one thousand years looked at the same spot on the horizon. If I must choose, I would pick Maine of the New England states, where I walk again on the shore of the Atlantic Ocean. All again is fused here: the local life, the fishermen, the festive, the touristic – boats fly at an angle of forty degrees on the dark blue water and rush by a hundred islands at great speed, without any visible goal, only so that we should admire them.

The water is cold, and you can't swim often; in August the air itself is sharp, prickly, icy; it pinches the body and makes your fingertips cold, reddens your face, burns your lips. In the port of the small town lamps are lit, someone sets a boat in the water, another is repairing a net, someone is offering for sale a whole family of huge lobsters crawling all over each other, and there is a row of fish on the pier. Everything is alive and silver in the slow twilight, in the splash of the heavy water, resounding loudly in amongst the piles.

I drive further down the map, along the shore, where, it is said, between Boston and Washington soon there will be one continuous city. For the time being it's not like that at all. Before and after New York, with its boundless industrial technology, all is green, and smells of flowers and sea. So to the very end, to Florida, where one hundred years ago there were still virgin forests (about which we read in our children's books), and half mermaids, half schoolgirls fly on water skis now after motorboats, and afterwards shaggy, barefooted, squeeze oranges into large icy glasses. Music is playing and palms sway, rustling with a special sound, metallic, similar to a human whisper.

Then I go to the black districts of Miami, the outskirts of this huge seaside city. People are poor there; they do not know how to work at a factory conveyor belt, and also do not know how to put glass in a window, repair a fence, weed a garden. Some houses are full of children, mostly naked, and in the kitchen and bedroom one senses a matriarchy – she bears, gives birth, feeds, cooks, works all day, is the provider and the master in the house; he weighs half as much as she and sits all day on the porch, smokes reefers, and, very often stunned by her shouting and slaps, goes wherever his eye can see. The older daughter grows up, a new man appears. The same story starts again, or rather continues, until the floor falls out of the house, and then the family moves to the empty dwelling next door, which has stood abandoned since last year or since time immemorial.

There are many abandoned houses in the outskirts of big and small cities and villages, and deserted stores, churches, garages, workshops, with a broken door, a cracked window, a balcony hanging over an abyss. It is cheaper to build a new one than to repair the old one. A thousand abandoned automobiles lie upside down, in a common grave one on top of the other, and the houses of signalmen are abandoned – theirs was an old system, no longer needed by anyone.

Once in a Western state, I wandered around an abandoned airport. It gave me one of the strongest impressions of changing life, of the mortal yesterday, the decomposition of a still young past. The airport was small, local, with open hangars; through the collapsed roof of one of them a sun ray climbed in and remained in a pile of excrement lying at the very entrance. Two huge trucks and a

516

large tractor were thrown on their sides, and, in the wind, some kind of metallic object squeaked and rocked over the door of what had been an office. In the middle of the airfield an oldish, bent, chipped plane stood, a twelve-passenger one, with a torn wing. I climbed into it. Four pigeons flew out in a flurry, not away from me but at me. The seat upholstery was torn.

All around there was silence. There were blue mountains on the horizon, sunny fog and larks in it like trembling spots. The rustling of reeds beneath the combing of the lazy, sultry wind. The corpse of a dog in the brambles of the early, small and hard, wild raspberries.

From this impression others flow: abandoned merry-go-rounds (the shows have gone elsewhere), the nailed-up hotels (the place went out of fashion, nobody comes here any more), a collapsed mine (Grandfather dug the earth, found silver, Father did not give a damn for silver – forks and knives? – no one there to clean them! – and left these places, and now makes forks and knives out of stainless steel; the son eats, they say, on gold). Should I look into the well of the silver mine? I can lower myself into it, if I wish, the bucket is still hanging over the black pit.

The car was bought in green, flower-smelling Indiana, and when I bought it I climbed into it and went straight home to Connecticut – a thousand miles – having forgotten to ask in my hurry how you switch on the headlights. There was no time to look and in the evening, having driven five hundred miles in a day, I began to push all the knobs; at first music started playing, then hot air began to blow on me, then cold, the ashtray opened and finally something started to drip on my feet. But it worked out well, the lights were turned on in the end – and it was about time, since while I played with the knobs it became quite dark.

Later I was going to Chicago on a highway that cut across the continent in a diagonal. One begins to sense the enormous city fifty miles ahead. Some signs wave a greeting in red and black letters, columns like the Eiffel Tower run here and there along the fields and meadows of Ohio and Illinois. Suddenly forests disappear. A kind of discomfort begins to rise on the wide highway: there, there, far beyond the horizon, beyond that turn and this one, something will appear, will interrupt the clean, clear monotony of the road. At some intersection of two or three highways you can still momentarily decide: circumvent, avoid it or dig into the very thick of it;

but the intersection flashed by and I did not use it, rushing past with no exit. Now the iron-steel, high-voltage, chemically fed space will show itself to me. I could have circumvented it from the left flank, and only from a distance feel the beating, the knocks, the trembling of the giant on the horizon. I enter, along a bisecting parabola, into the roaring mass of Chicago.

The first time I went to Chicago on a train, the second from a plane – a small screeching plane of a local line – to change into a huge jet at night at the airport, which by itself is a whole city. The third time I entered in a car, through its tunnels, across its airy bridges, straight to the shore of Lake Michigan. I wrote about Chicago in my story 'Black Pestilence'. Chicago for me – because I have not lived in it but only passed through – has remained a city of fantastic perspectives, luxury and poverty, elegance and dirt, suffocating odour and tender aroma of flowers near the lake shore. Much has been said of Chicago. One must see it, like Palermo, Naples, see the monstrous mixture of beauty and filth, but not when a sheet of snow smooths over its ugliness and grandeur, nor when a shower covers it with a veil, but when in the unbearable heat and humidity of a terrarium the trembling and ringing intense sun hangs over it for two or three weeks and the entire city quivers and rings and bangs in a temperature higher than that of the human body.

I could draw an arc, spiral, circle, triangle, or a rectangle inscribed in a circle on a map where I rushed in the early mornings in Missouri, Kentucky, Virginia, coming out of potato fields to a net of rivers, flying by lakes, passing through the tunnels of Appalachia. I would like to look for a long time at the rocks of Dakota where mythical figures have been carved (though once they walked about in trousers, a barber cut their hair, and a dentist pulled out their teeth); I would like to stand on the edge of the Grand Canyon when it is dark pink, and perhaps turn up in Oklahoma at sunset, and on the night of a full moon stand under the iron angels of the railings of New Orleans; look at South Carolina if only through one eye to find out if it is true that it is the best place in the world, as the man on the ocean liner insisted, astonished that I eventually could go to the U.S. 'along the tracks'; and finally see the Pacific. All this will happen of course because it depends entirely on me: to be or not to be. I have only *my* whims, no one else's, and I have no children, no grandchildren, no great-grandchildren – that is, no witnesses to my old age, and therefore I don't risk falling into senile garrulousness, starting to oppress my progeny with my caprices.

As for garrulousness, however, I am not sure: have I not spoken too much here about nature, about which Chekhov once said, 'enough, sirs, enough of it!' (concerning some violet clouds; but this didn't help and these lilac clouds still linger in the sky, filling out a line here and there as Russian oakum used to putty a wall). Enough about scenery with trout streams and humming-birds flying upright in the Vermont air, enough about cities, large and small, gigantic, consisting really of ten cities with many million inhabitants, and about small ones with only one street, sinking under dogwood and forsythia in spring – like the one I now live in. If I do not see it all, someone will see it with my eyes when my eyes are taken from the eye bank with tweezers and put in the eye-sockets of a blind little girl (or boy). But let both the humming-birds and the dogwood remain on this page. I have hidden enough things from the dear reader. It's as I once said: together with the six hundred pages of text there are six hundred pages of silences in this book; with seven chapters of a story about the 'present moment of the past' (T.S. Eliot) there are seven chapters of reticence, muteness, and secrecy.

Seven chapters, not six, for this last chapter too has another side. In the U.S. I have met people it is not timely to speak about, they are my present. Here I was given several lessons, but since I am not writing a manual for those arriving in this country, I will say nothing about any except one. It comes down to a simple truth: I have learned that intelligent people here do not take themselves too seriously.

I can remember only one Russian literary name from the past who did not want to take himself too seriously: this was Chekhov. Instead of 'You are my goddess' one should say 'Trum-trum-trum', and to Leo Tolstoy's praises of the 'Darling' not answer 'Yes, you are right, I turned it out well!' but say (rubbing his pince-nez): 'There are, it seems, some misprints.' Eighteenth-century people had those moments, in particular Pushkin ('with his arse leaning on the granite, he stands with Monsieur Onegin') and Derzhavin ('There is one God, and only one Derzhavin I dreamt in stupid temerity'), but then came the nineteenth century, man acquired a paunch, became important, and lost the sense of the ridiculous. Gogol burning the second volume of *Dead Souls* (one can imagine from what remained of it how bad it was!), and Herzen in the sixth volume of *My Life and Thoughts* (he does not describe events, but himself), and Dostoevsky in his speech on Pushkin: they were terribly serious about themselves. In our time there are two names that come to mind: first, a man who pretended all his life to be more stupid, ridiculous, insane, than he was in fact (Andrey Bely). Secondly, the author of a dialogue between Aleksandr Skertsevich and Aleksandr Serdtsevich in which he (O. Mandelstam) said a hundred times more than those suicides who wrote their last lines in blood. It was not irony, not the general gloomy collective irony of a whole decaying generation, but the secret humour about oneself that was lacking in Russia and Europe. I will be asked: But why cannot the men who wrote *Madame Bovary*, 'Master and Man' or the *Duino Elegies* take themselves seriously? If we take them seriously, why can they not dare to do it?

No, let others *respect* and *honour* me, but I know well about myself that because of the presence in me of even the tiniest speck of universal absurdity I cannot carry on like a monument to myself. The Greeks laughed at their holy places, while the Sephardim loved a God who knew how to joke. Let people think about me seriously, but the main thing is not their approach but how I myself am carrying on: sticking out my chest, offering two fingers instead of my whole hand, smiling on Sundays? Fearful of losing my dignity and stepping on toes of friends and enemies? Only the destruction of my own importance gives me the way to develop unexpected aspects of my personality in the quick course of life, gives a freedom to its metamorphoses and modulations.

But what will become of the tragic sense of life on which we were brought up? With the tragic period of our history? With the lot of my homeland, of my generation, and finally with my own lot? There is an answer to this, it seems to me: the tragic meaning of all this was given to me as the basis, the foundation of life: we who were born between 1895 and 1910 grew up on tragedy; in its time it had entered into us; we, so to speak, drank, devoured, and assimilated it. But now, when the *tragedy has come to its end and the epic has begun*, haven't I the right, ending my life, not to take myself too seriously? Tragedy cannot last eternally. In March 1953 the epic began, and the epic began in us too – that is, in those who survived the tragedy. 'Enter Fortinbras' – he is still entering, he is still in the doorway . . . In an epic, hasn't humour the right to exist?

We, the non-serious, make up a secret order and give each other signs. We know how to debunk ourselves in humour and we are bound by one *habit*. Let others call this a *Weltanschauung* – a resonant, buzzing, rattling term! It can push man onto a marble pedestal . . . This sight will be ridiculous and shameful . . . There have been examples.

There is an idea in Chateaubriand which it would have been tempting to put as the second epigraph to this book. But I didn't although I share his optimism. Here it is:

'The changes in literature of which the nineteenth century boasts came to it from emigration and exile.'

I share his optimism not in the sense of 'content' nor in the sense of 'form', but in the sense of the continuity of the tradition of freedom. But I didn't use this as an epigraph because I know how small we all were. Who am I? I have not published 'collected works' and did not learn the trade of typesetter; I almost died from a bobbin and knew well the last great men of Russia; I loved a moment of life more than fame and drew from this some conclusions; and now I watch the 'royal procession' (Blok) of Russian literature moving ever further away.

I love myself to a degree but was never possessed by the idea of remaking the world. 'I am what I am, here is the world, it must be remade' – this was unknown to me. 'Here is the world as it is, here I am, I must know myself and, once I do, change' – this was closer to me. Once every quarter of a century I was hatched out of an egg – at first when I was born, then in 1925, then in 1950. I don't know if this is enough or too little, but the strength of these births was so great that their quantity in comparison with their quality seems unimportant to me.

I know I can return from my third stage to the second: take a ticket and for a time sail whence I came. I have done this twice. But a return to the first stage is impossible for me: I can return to Russia only along the tracks of this book. I once had a dream, it was about my future homecoming: I am riding the Leningrad subway, for an hour, two, and suddenly I remember I have been riding for a month, a whole year or more. But there is no exit above. I get out at the stops, I look for a sign, an indication, I ask people rushing by: Where is the exit? Where are the stairs? Where is the street? People answer in a hurry and indistinctly. I don't understand them, and I run again. Then I get on the train, stations flash by – here's a transfer. I am *under* the city, I cannot be *in* the city itself, it is above me, but there's no access to it. I have no place in it.

Perhaps this is the basic image of my whole life, that 'fundamental personal symbol' which the critic seeks in a poet's work? Which appears to a man towards the end of his life like a 'drawing', a 'sketch', a 'pattern' of his life, and he sees suddenly that he is not Prometheus, not Orpheus, but – let us say – an ordinary locksmith who cannot fit the right key to his own house. Perhaps. But in the dream a kind of calm descends on me in the end, a kind of assurance that in fifty, a hundred years, someone will pull me out, by my hands and feet, out along the necessary escalator on Senate Square, or in the midst of Ligovka – perhaps names will then be different, but that in no way bothers me.

I return to the second stage, the European, and not only in dreams. Ten years passed after the day of my arrival in the U.S.A. when I returned to Europe for the first time, and five years later I made my second visit. In the metabolism of the Western world (Orwell's expression) both ten and five years mean a lot. The Russian cemetery at Sainte-Geneviève-les-Bois had become one of the sights of Paris: five buses stood single-file at its entrance, tourists clicked their cameras. They were taken to the old place where the graves were twenty and thirty years old, and to the new place where they were five and ten. There lie the unskilled workers of the Renault plant and Nobel laureates, grenadiers of 'his majesty' and beggars from the cathedral parvis on the Rue Daru (they say this cathedral has now also become a tourist attraction). Here lie Bunin and Merezhkovsky, Miliukov and Pevsner, generals of the White Armies and poets, seamstresses and ballerinas, unexposed agents of Stalin and men who fled Stalin and exposed him; people who awaited like great events the books of Olesha, Bagritsky, Tynianov, and people who placed candles before the icon of the 'tsar-martyr'. There are fresh flowers on the graves of heroes of the Resistance, along with the graves of traitors overgrown with thistle, men who had informed on others to the Gestapo. Here lies the history of Russian emigration in its glory, its misery, and madness. And here, as befits a cemetery, everything comes to an end. In a hundred years, in line with French tradition, this huge area will be ploughed over and made into a kitchen garden.

And the living? There are none. There are some half alive. In the year 2000 this will make an interesting story with political overtones. For it will suddenly turn out that both quantity and quality played their roles.

Paris is the same and no longer at all the same. In the gardens of the Trocadéro crowds of children rock in cribs, dig into sand, adults sit on benches, read newspapers; women are knitting, carriages, by fives and sixes, are set up like stars and babies yell in them, wet, suck on a bottle. In the quiet and emptiness of these gardens I walked, thought, thought of nothing, took decisions. It was then deserted. Intonations had changed since then: the human voice had in these years become different, the vocal melody had changed. The melody of speech now seems different: perhaps people have begun to bark so that they would not be suspected of sentimentality, the men of softness, the women of meekness, the children of submissiveness.

In Montparnasse not one familiar face; La Rotonde had again become small. Up to 1914 it had been small (when Lenin sometimes looked in); in those years *everyone* sat on the Boulevard Saint-Michel, in dark cafés panelled with wood – students, poets, philosophers, artists, prostitutes, parasites, artists' models, professors, political figures – so I was told. Then, in the 1920s, Saint-Michel declined, *everyone* wandered over to Montparnasse, and the Rotonde became a huge noisy café (and there were a dozen places where we gathered). After World War Two this came to an end too – *everyone* went over to Saint-Germain. Now the circle is closed: Saint-Michel again thunders with people, an international young crowd fills the cafés and pavements. But I don't see a single familiar face, not one.

I go to the old places. I walk in the streets 'past buildings, where we once danced and drank wine' (Akhmatova). I return through back streets again and again to this boulevard that leads from the Observatory to Montparnasse railway station. In one of the back streets I enter a restaurant – all in checked tablecloths and napkins. Dinner hour. I sit at a table. It smells of a mixture of rosemary and bay leaves, in which some meat is being stewed. I order food, and sit and look and listen to what is going on around. And as eyes looking into darkness sometimes begin to recognize objects, so my memory, slowly, groping, circling around a woman sitting in a corner, suddenly recognizes her. It is Simone de Beauvoir.

I saw her first in 1943–4, gay, lively, young. She walked along the street, her hips swaying, smoothly combed, eyes sparkling with energy and intelligence. Now twenty-two years had passed and I didn't recognize her at once. Her thick awkward fingers played with the broken lock of an old handbag, her lowered face seemed faded; it was as if it were eyeless – fat, sombre, with heavy cheeks and puffy eyelids. In the third volume of her memoirs she spoke of her appearance. How cruelly she had spoken of herself! The entire book is full of hospitals, operations, horror before death and old age; she writes of blood pressure (hers and Sartre's), of an impending heart attack. Sartre, like an automaton, is busy with *La Critique de la Raison Dialectique*, and in these last years so over-burdened with work that he doesn't even have the time to reread what he has written. He is growing deaf from sleeping pills. No friends remain . . . Now I see her in front of me, sitting with another woman, still not old, but irritated and tired, like herself. Both are silent. The thick fingers shake, all the while trying to click the lock, the dark high-necked dress compresses her big heavy body. I look at her for a long time; she does not lift her eyes, only her brows and cheeks are visible. Something must not be right with her kidneys and liver, and everything that is in her – as she herself wrote – is not working as it is supposed to, continues to serve her with difficulty, interruptions, pauses, and dangerous degeneration of some organs. For a moment I imagine clearly how all is set up inside her: the dilated veins, the stoppages of the heart, the inflated organs, the lazy glands . . . She wrote about this herself. I imagine her surroundings: her studio where she now spends days and nights and where she started to hate even music. There her Havana and Peking souvenirs hung – yes, she wrote about them in detail.

I always read her books, and I have just finished the third volume of her memoirs. In it she wrote about her headaches, the swelling of her legs. She complained that Sartre, who had all his life demanded 'engagement' and did not accept literature without it, had not been able to decide for a quarter of a century on which side he stood. What should be done? What should he be? From time to time he gloomily asks her: 'What shall we do? Where shall we go? Whom shall we be with?'

I looked at her and thought: As I see her now, she once saw Elsa Triolet, at a dinner at the Soviet embassy, and was surprised at her gloomy expression. Both were then engaged in discussion with the Soviet ambassador about how to preserve youth. Aragon was also troubled by this, oppressed and depressed by ensuing old age.

She now twirled a little spoon in her thick fingers. All her life she had tried to rid herself of bourgeois prejudices, but she didn't succeed: she fears death. To drown her awareness of it she avidly reads detective novels.

Sartre wanted to be a communist. Then he wanted to be an Algerian.* At one time he proclaimed: We can do nothing without the communists. Sartre and she took part in a street demonstration with the communists against De Gaulle. That day one of their communist friends confessed to them that he had never ridden in a subway, and was riding today one for the first time – all his life he had taken only taxis. They both condemned events in Hungary in 1956. Then they went to Moscow determined to meet only (as she wrote) 'the privileged class'. Now she had become indifferent to trips, confessed that sometimes she 'hates beauty'. 'It's all the same, I'll soon be in my grave.' 'Death stands between me and the world.' 'Death has already begun.' 'A whirlwind is carrying me to the grave, and I am trying not to think.' 'Perhaps do away with myself, so as not to have to wait?'

And where are the young? 'The young are taking the world away from me,' she confesses. Then she enumerates what will not be; 'nevermore' is applied to skiing, nights in the hay, lovers.

When I arrived they were finishing dinner. They were still sitting when I left. Perhaps they are waiting for Godot? The fresh wind, lights, motor-car horns, flashing neon, Rodin's Balzac hidden beneath the greenery of the trees. Where, where am I going? Isn't it all the same: once I have my own place in the world isn't it all the same what road one takes to get there – walking, flying, driving? One way or another I will get there. It is waiting for me.

Looking ahead and looking back I imagine what awaits me in two weeks: a huge table near a large window covered with papers,

*A certain Yvedon, dying for Algeria, exclaimed: 'I am an Algerian!'

shelves of books, sharp pencils, and silence. The window with a view of the four birches dancing in the middle of a lawn, bushes at the side of the road (soon they will be golden, crimson, yellow, purple, scarlet); the singing of the birds in the morning. In the evening silence . . . Suddenly steps, and a bell ringing. And dear, young, intelligent faces. Beautiful because the young and smart are always beautiful. What do I care if I am ageing? Let them only remain young, and they certainly will: *I will not see them old.* Friends. Books. Papers. Letters with postmarks of California, Australia, Sweden . . . My life awaits me there, in the small university town, a spasm of joy grasps my throat. In my suitcase there are three keys which I drag around Europe: to the house where I live, to the office in a university building where I work, to the library study where I keep books. There was once a certain story about a well and three springs. There a spring played a certain role. In this well two frogs once fell . . . I am confusing something, though. But three necessary doors await me. This is for sure.

I will be there again, in the warm little house: to work, think, live, and rejoice at the coming of guests, when a huge roast floats from the oven to the table with lighted candles; California wine (for me one of the best in the world) flows into glasses, and a record, after a quiet rustle, begins a concerto for violin, oboe, and strings, or a concerto for flute, violin, harpsichord, and strings . . .

I walk and walk. The spasm of joy does not leave me while I turn around the Luxembourg Gardens. Pavel Muratov once persuaded me here to abandon writing in Russian and to learn quickly to write in any other language because – I don't now remember his arguments; it is not hard, however, to guess what they were. And I once awaited someone eagerly here, with whom I later exchanged kisses under the dark trees. I waited eagerly. I thought eagerly. Now I was eagerly setting off for home. It's still the same eagerness that was in me thirty, forty, fifty years ago. It has not changed, not worn out. It has not wasted away. It is still whole, like myself.

And so: not one familiar face, either at the Closerie des Lilas or Les Deux Magots. Soon I will feel here as I feel in Munich or Athens. With, however, a small difference: in Paris there are friends who have come from England, Sweden, Finland to see me. I will see them in the midst of a thousand unknown faces.

His beret under his arm, in his hands a bouquet of sweet peas. This is Sergey Rittenberg, my dear, close and distant friend who has come from Stockholm, and I am walking through Paris with him, eating lunch, strolling along the quays, sitting on a bench in the Tuileries. Then he leaves. I will remember the date: 21 June, 1965. The evening before I promised him I would come to take him in a taxi to the Gare du Nord, lunch with him there and then, at 2:10, accompany him and wave to him when his train left.

I already know that on this train, but in the Paris–Moscow car, Anna Akhmatova is returning to the Soviet Union. She came from Oxford the day before and is to be taken to the station. Rittenberg knows her well, he has visited her in Komarovo. I am standing near a concrete pillar, on the platform, in front of her car, wearing dark glasses.

It is hot. I remove my gloves. I am wearing an open sleeveless dress; I shift my heavy handbag from hand to hand. Rittenberg is in front in the Paris–Stockholm car. Then the Paris–Copenhagen comes, and Paris–Warsaw. I continue to wait. And then I see her led into the train and seated in the car. She is wearing a long, dark blue raincoat, velvet sandals. She is hatless. Her motionless face is compressed. I remove my glasses and meet her with my eyes.

I go into the car. She is sitting immobile in a sleeping-compartment. I know she has had three heart attacks, two of them at railway stations. The upper bunk is already raised, Anichka Kaminskaya will sleep there. She had run to fetch some mineral water. I enter the compartment, again remove my glasses, and say quickly:

'Anna Andreevna, I am Berberova.'

Suddenly something happens in her face, from eyes to lips there is a movement and that moment I recognize her, take her hand and kiss it. She embraces me.

'Why didn't you come sooner?'

'I didn't know, could I have?'

'Was it a half century ago?'

'No, forty-three years in all,' I answer.

In my hands as I embrace her I feel the *water*, her terrible, huge body full of water not fat. She controls it with difficulty, her fingers do not bend; her legs are spread apart, she wipes her perspiring face, I help her remove her raincoat. We speak of the collection of Khodasevich which I published and sent to her. Yes, it reached her, she loves his verse, she thanks me. To my question about how she feels she answers:

'Barely alive.'

Perhaps she is leaving too soon? Could she perhaps spend several more days among us in Paris? No, this is not possible, already she has not done as she was told, she should have flown directly from London to Moscow. Before coming to her I managed to buy her some Caron perfume but gave it to Rittenberg: he would give it to her (he gave it to her two months later in Komarovo, near Leningrad). I tell her that Rittenberg will come to her car and if necessary bring her food from the dining car – there was no question of her going there.

I sense the others waiting, they are waiting for me to leave to go in.

I stand for a long time with three Petersburgites, painters, on the platform, and she stands in the window and looks at us each in turn, then at all of us together, until the train starts. She raises her hand and the weak shadow of a smile slides across her face.

The car was immediately locked – no one was allowed out, no one in. And in Cologne it was uncoupled.

So in the evening cafés, not one familiar face. However, there is a certain 'second generation', and in it several close and dear people, and a 'third generation', among which are several familiar faces too. There are none on the Acropolis; on the Piazza San Marco there are only pigeons. Perhaps not those that were there before, but the second or the tenth pigeon generation, after those about which it was said:

> Pigeons rush up, frightened,
> From my beloved's feet.

At the time these lines were written I thought I would *become*, but I had not *become*, I only *was*. In general I thought a lot. In fact during my lifetime I thought most of all. This sounds strange: 'I mostly travelled,' 'I treated people,' 'taught grammar' – this sounds rational. 'I mostly thought' sounds wild to my ear.

Nevertheless it's true. Wheels have turned, gears spun, there, beneath my cranium. I lean over a book – one of those just received by mail – it lies beneath my lamp, I lose myself in it. I read it, line by line, and note there are also as many pages of silences in it as of text. Six volumes of text and probably six volumes of silences. But this book is not like the one I am now writing.

In it an old writer I once knew well writes of himself, of people, of years, and I am writing of myself, of people, and of years. He also likes to think and like me learned to think late. But how terrible his life was! How tied to his silence he is, how free I am in mine! Exactly: free not only in what I can say, but free in what I want to keep quiet about. Yet I cannot tear myself away from his pages; for me his book means more than all the rest published in the forty years. I know the majority of his readers condemn him. But I do not. I am grateful to him. I thank him for each word.

He constructs a syllogism. Remember, as youths we were taught:

> Man is mortal,
> I am a man.

He constructs a syllogism, but does not give the third part. He gives the first two and it is up to us to awake and finally yell out the conclusion. Some condemn him because he stopped before the conclusion:

> I am mortal.

But isn't the conclusion really included in the premises? What use is all our education if we do not hear the conclusion in the premises?

The problem of the suffering of innocents is an old problem. It has never been solved, cannot be, never will be. We all agree that as long as one innocent suffers we cannot build universal happiness. But I want to speak about awareness, not suffering. The suffering of innocents can be justified only one way: if it leads to awareness.

Ehrenburg speaks of the execution of a million innocents (of whom hundreds were executed by Stalin out of personal revenge).

Most of them, dying, blessed the executioner, blessed his regime and at the last minute 'wished prosperity' to him and the regime. The destruction of these people can be justified and interpreted only if awareness is awakened. Otherwise it is a void without name.

He does not ask questions, does not draw conclusions. It remains for us to draw them, to put the third part of the syllogism in place, to wreck the silence, to emerge from suffering into consciousness. So long as the man tortured by a tyrant cries to the tyrant 'hurrah!' and the viewers all around the gallows second him, and the historian extols what has been done, there is no salvation. In the awakening of consciousness only, the answer lies to everything that was, and only one out of all – Ehrenburg – inaudibly mooing and gesturing in that direction, shows us (and future generations) the way to this consciousness. How can we dare demand more from him? Reproach him because he survived? Find between the lines of his book his 'reserved opinion'? Or dismiss him because he is giving us half truth? Our business is to arrive at the truth as a whole, to draw conclusions. To finish his syllogism. Otherwise all sacrifices are senseless.

The task is almost impossible because consciousness has long been asleep. It went to sleep forty years ago, in the first years of power of the half god who later became god, over whose dead body half the population of a country and some per cent of the world population wept. Ehrenburg himself hid the fact of suffering: he hid in 1946 what happened in 1937, in 1953 the year 1946, and now only partly reveals it. But we will not speak of suffering; enough has been said about it by others, though far from all. We will not ask ourselves: When will people stop loving the state that crushed them? We will speak of awareness. No suffering is too high a price to pay for awareness.

Millions of innocents will be resurrected if consciousness awakens: Mandelstam in rags on a rubbish pile, Mirsky who was pushed beneath the ice of the Sea of Okhotsk, Tukhachevsky whose death gave Germany the occasion to tear into Russia. Their sufferings were terrible, but it will be much more terrible if they do not lead to knowledge. The absence of awareness, not being informed, is ever more terrible than suffering. If consciousness comes, then we ourselves can handle sufferings.

'Suffer? All suffer! The dark beast suffers' (Fet) – but not everybody suffers consciously. Ehrenburg, in the nets of his silences, half confessions, withdrawals, vacillations, constructed two lines of his syllogism. There is not and will be no third – don't expect it from him. It must be in us. It will lead us along the right path: from a tale of sufferings to the moment of consciousness.

I read his book and I am embarrassed: pity for this famous man, friend of heads of state, world-renowned scholars, writers, immortal artists of our century. Pity for the old man who has aged before my eyes – from the first volume to the sixth, as I read his book. Pity and gratitude. He turned us all in the direction of the third part of the syllogism.

This is one aspect of his book, for me the most important: he makes the reader simultaneously its hero (that is, its author) and a witness of the past, splits him in two and again remakes him whole. Perhaps I could in part have done the same? Doesn't the theory of relativity concern literature too? In our world there is no longer any room for the privileged observer, as there is none for the observer of the universe – *we are all within*. The reader looks into himself reading me. God forbid that I should have proved anything on these pages. I just hinted, just directed the gaze of the onlooker.

So I write the last page of *how I did not wait for Godot*. This book, together with its title, appeared first in my thoughts either somewhere near the Azores or between Crete and Delos. I brought *it* – that is, the idea of the book – back from my first trip to Europe. All my crimes, fused with my punishments, once properties of myself alone, now belong to all those who care to deal with them, to look into these pages. I carried them to the point of realizing them in expression, utterance, writing. Recollections of a whole epoch and the people who lived in it grew into an autobiography and also my diary – as if it were a body with arms, legs, and a head. For the fourth time in my life I have been hatched from an egg. In this last birth I will live in *expectation of the unknown*, because life for me has no more unlived aspects, everything has been lived through, save ONE thing. It lies in a sphere still closed, but IT is not extrinsic to me, it is a part of myself. *It always was.* And so I will prepare for that last thing which I long ago gave my whole consent to, and which is not frightening, simply because it is unavoidable.

1960–1965

New Haven.
Colorado. Yaddo.
Taormina. Venice.
Princeton.

WHO IS WHO

This list of names was compiled by me instead of footnotes. I have tried to include some new biographical information about little-known people as well as forgotten bibliographical data about the well-known which might be interesting to readers of Russian literature of this century. Some names of organizations, periodicals, etc. have been added for the convenience of the reader.

Owing to the Russian habit of not including dates of birth or even death in obituaries, this list was more difficult to compile than originally expected. It might perhaps still contain a couple of minor errors. Discrepancies compared with other works may puzzle scholars, but I beg them to bear in mind that this is due to others' use of the Julian calendar; so a death (or birth) dated by one at the end of December of one year will be placed by me at the beginning of January of the following. Some libraries in the U.S.A. and Europe carry incorrect data, or lack facts completely. All data was checked by me, and often rechecked. The Soviet literary encyclopaedias of the 1930s and 1960s, as is well known, are incomplete. Dozens of émigré writers, not to mention politicians, actors, and painters, have not yet been 'rehabilitated' in Russia, are completely unknown to Soviet scholars and never mentioned by them. I have tried to provide information on them on the basis of my own old notes.

The transliteration of Russian names, as in the book itself, follows standard rules. When a spelling is considered traditional – i.e., does not follow these standard rules because used before the rules were established, it is left unchanged. This is, in my opinion, the simplest way of dealing with the intricate and diffuse way of writing Russian names in English. All said and done, I have tried to avoid both vain pedantry and irritating whimsicality. I could not avoid inconsistency.

N.B.

ACMEISM. Literary movement, begun in St. Petersburg *c.* 1912. The head of the school was N. Gumilev. Other members were A. A. Akhmatova, O. Mandelstam, M. Kuzmin, M. Zenkevich, N. Nedobrovo, V. Narbut, etc. In the early 1920s it was declared counter-revolutionary.

ADAMOV, ARTHUR (1908–). French playwright of Russian–Armenian descent. Career began in 1947 in Paris. His plays belong to the theatre of the absurd.

Who Is Who

ADAMOVICH, GEORGY VIKTOROVICH (1894–1972). Started publishing in 1915. An émigré since 1923. Minor poet of the acmeist movement. As a critic prefers the 'non-perfect', incomplete, dilettante product to the 'perfect' and polished; is interested in 'confession' and 'diary' writing more than in 'literature', but on the whole inconsistent. For more about him see: Marina Tsvetaeva in *Blagonamerenny*, No. 2 (1926), and V. V. Nabokov in *The Gift* (he is Christopher Mortus). In 1947 published in French *L'Autre Patrie*, about France and French culture, an acknowledgement of Stalin's grandeur as the commander-in-chief of the armies in World War Two. Collected verse: *Oblaka* (1916), *Chistilishche* (1922), *Na Zapade* (1939), *Edinstvo* (1967). This last volume (52 pages) has a subtitle: 'Poems from Different Years'. Unfortunately, there are no dates given for the poems. Some were written as much as fifty years ago.

ADAMOVICH, TATIANA VIKTOROVNA (b. 1892). Sister of the above. In 1914–17, friend of Akhmatova and Gumilev. Between the wars, ballet teacher in Warsaw. Married name, Vysotskaya. Author of memoirs written in Polish (Tacjanna Wysocka: *Wsponmienia*, 1962).

ADZHEMOV (AJEMIAN), MOYSEY SERGEEVICH (1878–*c*.1950). Armenian. Prominent lawyer, member of the K.-D. Party, and deputy of the State Duma (2nd, 3rd, and 4th) from the Don District. Emigré after 1920.

AIKHENVALD, YULY ISAEVICH (1872–1928). Impressionist critic. Emigré from 1921. Author of the popular *Siluety Russkikh Pisateley*. Died in an accident in Berlin.

AKHMATOVA, ANNA ANDREEVNA (1888–1966). Russian poet, member of the acmeist group. Lived in the U.S.S.R. for forty-seven years, before visiting Italy in 1964 and England and France in 1965. Her tragic life is reflected in her verse, which deals with the horrors of the 1930s when her husband and son (by Gumilev) were arrested during Stalin's terror. First married to Gumilev, divorced in 1918, she married Nikolai Nikolaevich Punin in the 1930s. Early in the Revolution Punin belonged to the futurist group, was a friend of Mayakovsky and a collaborator of *Iskusstvo Kommuny*, where in 1920 he wrote that futurism is the 'state art' of new Russia. In 1918 in collaboration with E. Poletaev he was the author of *Protiv Tsivilizatsii*. He was deported in 1935 and perished in Siberia.

AKSENOV, IVAN ALEKSANDROVICH (1884–1935). A theatre critic, translator (of the Elizabethans), and playwright, friend of Pasternak and member of *Tsentrifuga* (Centrifugue).

ALDANOV, MARK ALEKSANDROVICH (1886–1957). Emigré writer. In Paris after 1919. Wrote on the plight of émigré literature in *Sovremennye Zapiski*, No. 61. Compare his approach with such articles of V. Khodasevich as '*Literatura v izgnanii'*, *'Podvig'*, and *'Krovavaya pishcha'* (in the volume of articles and memoirs published in 1954 by the Chekhov Publishing House in New York).

ALEKSEEV, MIKHAIL VASILIEVICH (1857–1918). General, commander-in-chief of the Russian armies in March–May 1917. Chief of staff under Kerensky until September 1917. One of the founders of the White Army in 1918.

ALEXANDRA FEDOROVNA (1872–1918). Née princess of Hessen. Last empress of Russia.

ALEXIS MIKHAILOVICH (1629–76). Russian tsar, father of Peter. His reign is connected with the uprising of Stepan Razin and the religious schism of Avvakum.

ALKONOST. One of the last privately owned publishing houses (1918–23). The owner, Alyansky, published Blok, Bely, Vyacheslav Ivanov, A. M. Remizov, and many others. In the first three years he brought out more than thirty items (not counting reprints), and a non-periodical publication, now a collector's item, *Zapiski Mechtateley* (1919–22), six issues in all, where the first version of Bely's *Memoirs* appeared (in No.6). See: *Blokovsky Sbornik*, Tartu, 1964, p. 530.

ALL-UNION ASSOCIATION OF PROLETARIAN WRITERS. In Russian abridged as VOAPP, VAPP, and also RAPP, MAPP (in Moscow), LAPP (in Leningrad), etc.

ALYANSKY, SAMUIL MIRONOVICH (1891–1974). Friend of Blok and Bely, the owner of 'Alkonost'. His name was not mentioned for thirty-five years but reappeared in the 1960s when he wrote his memoirs. (See *Novy Mir*, 1967, No. 6, p. 198.) In these memoirs he recollects that when Blok gave one of his last readings in Moscow, a voice in the audience shouted: 'Your poems are dead, and you yourself are dead!' A. doesn't remember who this was. But Khodasevich was also present, and many times named the man: he was Sergey Bobrov.

AMFITEATROV, ALEKSANDR VALENTINOVICH (1862–1938). Minor writer. Emigré after 1920. Lived in Italy.

ANDREEV, LEONID NIKOLAEVICH (1871–1919). Russian writer, author of *The Seven Who Were Hanged, He Who Gets Slapped*, and many other stories and plays. Died in Finland after writing a violent diatribe against the October Revolution, 'S.O.S.'

ANDREEVA, MARYA FEDOROVNA (1872–1953). Second wife of Maxim Gorky, first married to Zhelyabuzhsky. Mother of the movie director Y. A. Zhelyabuzhsky. Herself a high official in the movie and theatre field (Soviet), member of the Communist Party before the Revolution, and personal friend of Lenin's. Actress in Moscow Arts Theatre from 1898 to 1906.

ANNENKOV, GEORGY (YURY) PAVLOVICH (1889–1974). Painter, writer of memoirs, painter of theatre sets, and costume designer in movies. Emigré. Known for his portraits of prominent Bolsheviks in the 1920s, writers and actors. Was present in Paris at the Gare du Nord in June 1965 when I saw Akhmatova off; she was leaving Paris and going to Moscow. He wrote in his memoirs: 'Among those who came to the station was Nina Berberova, who had come from America and whom I hadn't seen for a number of years. She told me she would like to talk to Akhmatova but was told that Akhmatova didn't want to see anyone. I told her that Akhmatova would be delighted to see her. N. B. went into the carriage and their meeting was very warm indeed.' The person who advised me (and others) not to go to the station and not to meet with Akhmatova was Adamovich. (See *Russkaya Mysl*, No. 2438, 1966.)

ANNENKOVA, ELENA (née Galpern). First wife of the above, an actress of La Chauve Souris and the theatre Krivoe Zerkalo. Went back to the U.S.S.R. in the 1920s.

ANNENSKY, INNOKENTY FEDOROVICH (1856–1909). One of the greatest poets of the twentieth century. A good selection of his verse came out in the U.S.S.R. in 1959, the first in thirty-five years. See also his critical articles in *Apollon* (1911, No. 6) and others.

ANNENSKY, VALENTIN INNOKENTIEVICH (pen name Krivich). Son of the above. Author of memoirs on his father in *Literaturnaya Mysl*, Issue 3, 1925. Himself a minor poet (see Boris Filippov: *Sovetskaya potaennaya muza*).

ANSTEY, OLGA NIKOLAEVNA (1912–1985). Russian poet. Emigré since 1943. Lived in New York.

APOLLON. A literary magazine, S. K. Makovsky editor. Was published in St. Petersburg in 1909–17. One of the most impressive publications of twentieth-century Russia: literature, art, music, criticism. Among the collaborators: Vyacheslav Ivanov, Annensky, Gumilev, and many others.

ARAGON, LOUIS (1897–1982). French writer, member of the Central Committee of the French Communist Party. Called in the U.S.S.R. a 'socialist realist' (until he wrote his novel *La Mise à Mort*, still not translated into Russian). He obviously believes that Gorky was murdered not by Stalin but by some doctors who were agents of Germany or Japan. In 1965 in the *Lugano Review* George Woodcock called Aragon 'a despicable Stalinist, intellectually dishonest, evading responsibility'. But in 1966 in the French communist daily, *L'Humanité*, he protested about the sentence at the Soviet trial of Sinyavsky and Daniel. (See *L'Humanité* of February 16–17, *Le Monde* of February 19, and *L'Express* of February 21–29).

ARTSYBASHEV, MIKHAIL PETROVICH (1878–1927). Author of *Sanin* and other 'risqué' stories and plays. Emigré from 1920 on. Died in Warsaw.

ASYA (1897–1975). My first cousin and good friend. At one time lived in Berlin, later in Paris. Once in Berlin, in 1922, I talked to her on the telephone when Andrey Bely was present. I noticed he was listening to what I was saying; he was crushed at that time by the rupture with his first wife, Anna (Asya) Turgeneva-Bugaeva. When I finally said tenderly: 'Good-bye, Asinka,' and put the receiver down, he came to me with his tense smile and asked me: 'Asinka? What Asinka? Is there more than one Asinka?' I calmed him down, telling him that this was my cousin, whom, as a matter of fact, I had recently introduced to him at a literary gathering.

AZEF, YEVNO (EVGENY) FISHELEVICH (1869–1918). Socialist-revolutionary, double agent, informer of the Okhrana (tsarist police) and at the same time (with Savinkov) active member of the terrorist group. Member of the Central Committee of the S.-R. Party after 1905. Active in killing grand dukes and tsarist ministers, and denouncing his fellow revolutionaries to the Okhrana. In 1908 was unmasked by V. L. Burtsev, judged, condemned, but allowed to escape by the S.-R.

BABEL, ISAAC EMMANUILOVICH (1894–1941). Published since 1916. Russian writer, already famous in the 1920s, went many times to Europe, was arrested in the mid-1930s and perished in a camp. After Stalin's death 'rehabilitated', finally mentioned in the *Short Literary Encyclopaedia*, Vol. 1 (1960), no place and exact date of death given, with the note: 'illegally repressed, posthumously rehabilitated'. Viktor Shklovsky very early (*Lef*, No. 4, 1923) had highly apt things to say about B.'s writings: 'His ideology is only a constructive device. His heroes are uninteresting to us, what is interesting is what he says about them.' The Soviet memoirist L. Nikulin wrote after the 'rehabilitation' of B.: 'He disappeared like so many of our comrades, but in spite of this he left an indelible trace on our literature . . . *It was not his fault that he did not sing his song to its end*' (*Moskva*, 1964, No. 7). (Italics mine.)

BAKST, LEONID SAMOILOVICH (1866–1924). Stage designer, born in Russia, died in France. Belonged to the World of Art group. Worked with the Diaghilev ballets, lived in France from 1909 on.

BAKUNIN, MIKHAIL ALEKSANDROVICH (1814–76). Famous Russian revolutionary and anarchist.

BALIEFF, NIKITA FEDOROVICH (?–1936). Director, producer, founder of the variety theatre La Chauve Souris (*Letuchaya Mysh*). Died in 1936 in New York after great success in the 1920s in Europe and the U.S.A. and a rapid decline. See: *N.Y. Times*, September 1936.

BALMONT, KONSTANTIN DMITRIEVICH (1867–1942). Russian symbolist poet, émigré from 1921 on. Lived and died in Paris in utter misery and oblivion. On him see: I. Annensky in his *First Book of Reflections*, 1906. The verse of B. gradually became completely detached from reality; his beautiful sound effects now seem vain. But at the turn of the century he was the most beloved of all symbolists in Russia, extremely popular, a legend in his time. When I speak about him in connection with the French socialist Auguste Blanqui, I seek to express the thought that the Russian intelligentsia was always against any compromise and was unable, or unwilling, or simply did not know how to correlate the term 'art for art's sake' (completely arbitrary, of course) with the radical teaching of the Marxists. In this connection it is appropriate to recall that in Spain the 'Francoists' and the Republicans have been buried in *one* grave as victims of *one* civil war; and also the respect which is paid by the Poles to the tomb of Pilsudski, the enemy of the communist regime and a patriot; or the esteem that the Czechs feel now, after many years, for the name of Tomas Masaryk. These three examples of 'Western compromise' could, probably, never occur in Russia, and symbolically the names of Balmont and Blanqui would never mesh in the mind of a literate Russian.

BARATYNSKY, EVGENY ABRAMOVICH (1800–44). Russian poet, second only to Pushkin and Tiutchev among nineteenth-century poets, understood and appreciated more in the twentieth century than in his own time. His museum in Muranovo near Moscow is not open to foreign visitors.

BARK, PETR LVOVICH (1869–1937). Last minister of finance of the tsarist government (from 1914 to 1917); replaced Count V. Kokovtsev. Bark's memoirs were published in *Renaissance* (Russian magazine in Paris) in 1955, 1959, 1965, 1966, and 1967. He died in London. See obituary in *Slavic and East European Review*, 1937, Vol. 16. He was knighted by George V of Great Britain.

BARYATINSKY, PRINCE VLADIMIR VLADIMIROVICH (1874–1941). Personal friend of the last tsar. Playwright, journalist; husband of the actress Yavorskaya. Emigré, collaborated in the Paris daily *The Latest News*.

BASHKIRTSEVA, MARYA KONSTANTINOVNA (1860–84). Minor painter of Russian descent; lived in France and left a diary, which was published in 1887 in French and in 1893 in Russian.

BEDNY, DEMYAN (1883–1945). Favourite poet of Lenin. Published since 1899. Official bard of the Communist Party of Russia, lived in the Kremlin, belonged to the Soviet establishment for twenty-seven years. The *Short Literary Encyclopaedia* (1960) tells us that he was 'elaborating on Kurochkin's traditions'.

BEILIS, MENDEL (1873–1934). Defendant in a famous trial on a charge of ritual murder (1911–13) in Kiev. Later (after acquittal) lived in Chicago. For more about him see: Maurice Samuel: *Blood Accusation* (Philadelphia, 1966).

BELINSKY, VISSARION GRIGORIEVICH (1811–48). Russian critic, utopian socialist. The first in Russia in a long line of politically minded literary critics.

BELY, ANDREY (pseudonym for Boris Nikolaevich Bugaev) (1880–1934). One of the greatest Russian poets, prose writers, literary critics and theoreticians of this century. Friend of Blok's and Vyacheslav Ivanov's, author of *St. Petersburg*. Disciple of the anthroposophist Rudolf Steiner. Spent the years 1916–21 in Russia and partially accepted the October Revolution; gave public lectures, published, participated in the literary gatherings of the House of Arts in Petersburg (where on 1 March, 1920, he read excerpts of his *Zapiski Chudaka*). In 1921 went abroad and stayed in Germany until October 1923, when he returned to Moscow. About his funeral, see *Pravda*, 11 January, 1934. Portraits of him can be found in *Literaturnoe Nasledstvo*, Nos. 27–8, in S. Makovsky's *Na Parnasse Serebrianogo Veka*, in V. Lidin's book *Autobiografii*, 1928, and in Nemirovskaya and Volpe's *Sudba Bloka*.

BENOIS, ALEKSANDR NIKOLAEVICH (1870–1960). One of the founders of the World of Art. Painter, stage decorator, art historian, author of an autobiography. Also author of a history of the World of Art: *Vozniknovenie Mira Iskusstv* (Leningrad, 1928). Emigré from the 1920s on. Lived and died in Paris.

BERBEROV, NIKOLAI IVANOVICH, father of N.B.; IVAN MINAEVICH, grand-father of N.B.; ALEKSANDR MOSESOVICH, first cousin of N.B., retired general of the Soviet Air Force; MINAS IVANOVICH, member of the Nationalist (Armenian) Party, uncle of N.B., a defendant at the Dashnaktsutiun trial (1912), minister of public education in free Armenia (in 1917).

BERBEROVA, NATALIA IVANOVNA, mother of N.B., née Karaulova.

BERBEROVA, NINA NIKOLAEVNA, author of this book. Work mentioned: *Biankurskie Prazdniki* (Billancourt Fiestas), short stories, published in *The Latest News*, 1928–38. *Poslednie i Pervye* (The First and the Last), a novel, Paris, 1930. *Tchaikovsky*, a biography, Paris, 1937, translated into six languages. *Borodin*, a biography, Paris, 1938. *Bez Zakata* (Without Sunset), a novel, Paris, 1938. *Madame*, a play, staged in Paris in 1938. *Oblegchenie Uchasti* (The Easing of Fate), a collection of short stories, Paris, 1948. *Alexandre Blok et Son Temps*, Paris, 1948. *Delo V. A. Kravchenko* (The Kravchenko Lawsuit), reportage, Paris, 1950. *Mys Bur* (The Cape of Storm), a novel, in *Novy Zhurnal*, 1951. 'Mysliashchy Trostnik' (The Revolt), a story, in *Novy Zhurnal*, 1958, No. 55. 'Pamiati Schliemana' (In Memory of Schliemann), a story in *Mosty*, 1958, No. 1 'Chernaya Bolezn' (The Black Pestilence), a story, in *Novy Zhurnal*, 1959, No. 58.

BERDYAEV, NIKOLAI ALEKSANDROVICH (1874–1948). Philosopher, historian, literary critic. See his article on Bely's *St. Petersburg* (1918) and his praise of Picasso (*Sofiya*, 1914, No. 3). In 1917 was a professor at Moscow University; twice arrested by the Bolsheviks, he was expelled from Russia in 1922. From 1924 on lived in Clamart, near Paris. Author of an autobiography, *Self-Knowledge*.

(English trans., *Dream and Reality*, 1950.) Editor of *Put*, a religious and philosophical periodical in Paris (in Russian).

BERLIN, PAVEL ABRAMOVICH (?–1962). Russian-Jewish journalist.

BERNSTEIN, SERGEY IGNATIEVICH (1892–1970). Professor, former 'formalist', known for his works on phonology, phonetics, and orphoepia. As early as 1921 he collected tapes of poets reading their poetry (Blok, Khodasevich, Mandelstam, Akhmatova, and others). Survived the purges and became active again in the 1960s.

BESEDA (sometimes referred to in English as *The Colloquy*). Russian magazine published in Berlin, 1923–5 (seven issues), to be sold in Russia. Editors: Gorky, Bely, Khodasevich. Never passed by the Soviets. Some good stories by Gorky appeared in it (one under a pseudonym), articles on Pushkin by Khodasevich, poems by Sofya Parnok, etc. See *Tartu, Publications of the State University*, 1965, for an interesting and well-documented note by Sergeev.

BILIBIN, IVAN YAKOVLEVICH (1876–1942). Russian painter and book illustrator, member of the World of Art. Emigré in the 1920s, later returned to the U.S.S.R.

BLACK HUNDRED. Founded in 1905, active from 1906 to 1911. A government-supported group, basically anti-Semitic, that initiated pogroms in Russia.

BLAGOV, FEDOR IVANOVICH (1866–?). Former Moscow millionaire, collaborator of the famous publisher Sytin, who published the popular daily *Russkoe Slovo*. Emigré, died in Paris before the war in great poverty.

BLIUMKIN, JAKOV (?–1929). Member of the S.-R. Party (left wing). Killed Mirbach, the German ambassador, in Moscow in 1918. Was pardoned and given a high post in the Cheka. Shot in 1929 after his meeting with Trotsky in Turkey (see Isaac Deutscher's *The Prophet Armed*).

BLOCH, RAISSA NOEVNA (1899–1943). Sister of Jakov Bloch, the owner of the publishing house Petropolis. Poet and scholar. Deported by the Germans, perished in a prison camp.

BLOK, ALEKSANDR ALEKSANDROVICH (1880–1921). Great Russian poet of the twentieth century. The street where he lived and died in Petersburg, Ofitserskaya, is now called Dekabristov (his address was No. 57, Apt. 23).

BLOK, ALEKSANDRA ANDREEVNA (1860–1923). Née Beketova. By her second marriage, Kublitskaya. Mother of the above.

BLOK, LIUBOV DMITRIEVNA (1881–1939). Wife of the poet. Her archives, now in TsGALI (State Archives), include her correspondence with Blok and Bely, notes and memoirs. Documents also in IRLI (*Acadamy of Sciences*). Wrote poetry, was a correspondent at the front during World War One (see *Otechestvo*, 1914, No. 4, p. 78, signed 'From letters by a nurse'). Actress in Meyerhold's theatre.

BOBORYKIN, PETR DMITRIEVICH (1835–1921). Minor Russian writer. Wrote an interesting novel, *Kitai-Gorod*, which influenced Bely's *St. Petersburg*. Author of memoirs (*Za Polveka*).

BORISOV, LEONID (1897–1972). After 1938 wrote, for young readers, biographies of Jules Verne, Stevenson, and others. Mentioned in Gorky's letter to Rolland along with Borisov: Nina Smirnova (1899–1931); Aleksandr Yakovlev (disappeared in the 1930s); Sergey Klychkov (1889–1940), now 'rehabilitated'; V. Kazin (b. 1898), not published between 1937 and 1964; and V. Oreshin (presumably 'rehabilitated' after being 'illegally repressed').

BOZHNEV, BORIS (1900–1938). Gifted émigré poet, in the group of Ginger and Knut. Died in a hospital for the mentally ill. His best book of verse: *The Struggle for Non-Being* (*Borba Za Nesushchestvovanie*, Paris, 1925). See my article in *Sovremennye Zapiski*, No. 24.

BRESHKOVSKAYA, EKATERINA KONSTANTINOVNA (1844–1934). The 'granny' of the Russian Revolution, member of the Central Committee of the S.-R. Party. Was a defendant in the 'Trial of 193', arrested four times during the tsarist period. After 1917 an émigré, lived and died in Prague.

BRIK, OSIP MAKSIMOVICH (1888–1945) and LILA YURIEVNA (1892–1978). Close friends of Mayakovsky. Brik was one of the initiators of *Opoyaz*, author of *Zvukovye Povtory*, a classic of 'formalism'. She was the heroine of Mayakovsky's early love verse and sister of the French writer (wife of Louis Aragon) Elsa Triolet.

BRILLIANT, DORA VLADIMIROVNA (c. 1880–1907). Terrorist, member of the terrorist arm of the S.-R. Party. Active in the execution of Grand Duke Sergey (1905).

BRIUSOV, VALERY YAKOVLEVICH (1873–1924). Great Russian poet, 'inventor' of Russian symbolism; after 1918 a member of the Communist Party.

BUDBERG, BARONESS MARYA IGNATIEVNA (1892–1974). Née Countess Zakrevskaya; through her first marriage became Countess Benckendorff. From 1921 to 1933 lived in the home of Gorky (Germany, Czechoslovakia, Italy). After 1933 in London. Went to Russia in 1936, when Gorky was on his deathbed (see L. Nikulin in *Moskva*, 1966, No. 2, p. 188). Returned to London after his death. In 1967 went for a visit to the Soviet Union where she was given a red-carpet reception. Her daughter Tatiana, son Pavel, and an adopted daughter, Kira (née Moulin), live in England.

BUDENNY, SEMEN MIKHAILOVICH (1883–1973). Soviet marshal, commandant of the Red cavalry during the Civil War; also active in World War Two.

BUGAEV, NIKOLAI VASILIEVICH (1837–1903). Father of Andrey Bely. Dean of Moscow University and prominent mathematician. For more about him see L. Lopatin, 'Filosofskoe Mirovozzrenie N. V. Bugaeva', in Voprosy Filosofii i Psikhologii, 1904, Part I, pp. 172–195.

BUKHARIN, NIKOLAI IVANOVICH (1887–1938). Prominent Marxist theoretician, friend of Lenin's. Condemned by Stalin at the Third Moscow Trial, after his confessions.

BULGAKOV, SERGEY NIKOLAEVICH (1871–1944). In his youth a Marxist, then a 'religious philosopher', since 1918 a priest. Exiled by the Bolsheviks in 1922. Was a member of the Second State Duma and of the Sobor of 1917, a friend of Berdyaev's and Bely's. Author of books on theology.

BUNIN, IVAN ALEKSEEVICH (1870–1953). Russian writer. Nobel Prize, 1933. A 'critical realist'. Emigré after 1920. After his death, published and praised in the Soviet Union. His verse has affinities with the verse of Yakov Polonsky, especially with the latter's poems about Georgia (1846–51) in the collection Sazandar.

BURYSHKIN, A. A. (c. 1880–c. 1954). A Moscow millionaire. In 1917 a representative of the Industrialist and Commercial Group. Author of memoirs (Chekhov Publishing House, New York). Died in Paris in great poverty.

CAMBYSES. Persian king: 529–522 B.C. Son of Cyr. Invaded Egypt in 525. Killed all his supporters, friends, and relatives. See Herodotus: The Histories, Book 3.

CENTRIFUGUE. A literary circle, an offshoot of futurism. Members: Sergey Bobrov, Nikolai Aseev, and Boris Pasternak. Started before World War One, disintegrated before 1917.

CHAADAEV, PETR YAKOVLEVICH (1794–1856). A philosopher, friend of Pushkin's and the Decembrists'. Author of the remarkable Philosophical Letters. (For more about him see the writings of M. Gershenzon.)

CHABROV, ALEKSEY ALEKSANDROVICH (c. 1888–c. 1935). Real name Podgaetsky. Actor, mime, dancer. Later a Jesuit (in a monastery in Belgium). Marina Tsvetaeva dedicated to him a cycle of her verse, The Side Streets (Pereulochki, 1922).

CHALIAPIN, FEDOR IVANOVICH (1873–1938). Famous Russian basso. Emigré.

CHEKA, later OGPU, then NKVD, MGB. Now KGB. Soviet secret police. See also DZERZHINSKY.

CHEKHOV, MIKHAIL ALEKSANDROVICH (1891–1955). Nephew of Anton Chekhov. Actor in the Moscow Arts Theatre, later in the First Studio. In the 1920s came to Europe. Acted in Latvia, later with Max Reinhardt; then went to Hollywood, where he opened a school (to teach the 'method'). Belonged to the anthroposophic sect. Author of memoirs and two books on the theatre: *To the Actor*, 1953, and *To the Director and Playwright*, 1963.

CHERNIKHOVSKY, SAUL GUTMANOVICH (1875–1943). Hebrew poet and writer, translated into Russian by Khodasevich. From 1931 lived in Palestine. One of the poets of the 'Hebrew renaissance'.

CHERNOV, VIKTOR MIKHAILOVICH (1876–1952). Leader of the S.-R. Party. Played a prominent role in 1917. Emigré after the 1920s. Author of memoirs. Died in the U.S.A.

CHERNYSHEVSKY, MIKHAIL NIKOLAEVICH (1858–1924). Son of the following.

CHERNYSHEVSKY, NIKOLAI GAVRILOVICH (1828–89). Radical journalist, revolutionary fighter against the tsarist regime, literary critic. In 1864 was banished to Siberia, came back in 1883. Lenin called him his teacher. For more about him see V. Nabokov: *The Gift*, a highly original and most amusing appraisal.

CHERTKOV, VLADIMIR GRIGORIEVICH (1854–1936). A friend and disciple of Leo Tolstoy, editor of his complete works. Another disciple mentioned is Peter A. Sergeenko (1854–1930).

CHIRIKOV, EVGENY NIKOLAEVICH (1864–1932). Minor writer of the Gorky group of *Znanie*. Emigré.

CHUKOVSKY, KORNEY IVANOVICH (1882–1967). Writer, critic, memoirist, translator, author of children's books. In 1921–2 lived with his family in Manezhny No. 6. For an interesting polemic between him and Aleksey Tolstoy see *Nakanune*, 1922, No. 6, Feb. 4, and *Novaya Russkaya Kniga*, 1922, No. 7.

CHUKOVSKY, NIKOLAI KORNEEVICH (1905–65). Minor Soviet writer, son of the above. Interesting memoirs on Mandelstam (where he mentions N. B.) in *Moskva*, 1964, No. 8, p. 152.

CHULKOV, GEORGY IVANOVICH (1878–1939). Minor symbolist poet, friend of Blok and Vyacheslav Ivanov. Author of memoirs: *Gody Stranstvy*, Moscow, 1930. The miscellany *Belye Nochi* (1907) contains an interesting series of poems by Chulkov where he embarrassingly apes the poetry of Blok; they are dedicated to Liubov Blok. See also his article '*Kistorii Balaganchika*' in *Kultura Teatra*, 1921, No. 7–8.

CONSTRUCTIVISTS. A group of poets, with Ilya Selvinsky as head, who broke with futurism in the 1920s. Ehrenburg belonged for a short time, along with E. Bagritsky and others. Around 1930 it was 'liquidated'.

CONTEMPORARY ANNALS. The most valuable and generally outstanding émigré periodical published in Paris from 1920 to 1940, seventy volumes in all. Indispensable for scholars of the Russian émigré period.

DALCROZE, EMIL JACQUES (1865–1950). A teacher, musician, and composer, the father of 'rhythmical gymnastics'. A Swiss with original pedagogical ideas, popular at the beginning of this century.

DALLIN (DALIN), DAVID YULIEVICH (1889–1962). Member of the Central Committee of the S.-D. Party (Menshevik). After 1920 an émigré. From 1940 lived in the U.S.A. Active in *Sotsialistichesky Vestnik*. A prominent political writer. Father of the Columbia University professor ALEXANDER DALLIN.

DAN, LIDYA OSIPOVNA (1878–1963). Née Tsederbaum. Wife of FEDOR DAN, the leader of the Mensheviks, and sister of the prominent S.-D. member Yuly Martov. Was exiled from Russia in 1922. A classmate of N. B.'s mother. About the Martov family, see L. Dan's memoirs, *Martov i Ego Blizkie*.

DASHNAKTSUTIUN. National Armenian party, founded in the 1890s. Prominent and active in March–November 1917. Liquidated in 1920–21.

DAVIDENKOV, NIKOLAI (*c.* 1910–?). A 'Vlasovist', defected to the Germans during the war, collaborated with General Vlasov and the Germans against the U.S.S.R. Arrested and deported to a gulag.

DAVYDOV, VLADIMIR NIKOLAEVICH (1849–1925). Famous actor in the Aleksandrinsky Theatre in St. Petersburg (1880–1924) and Moscow (1924–5).

DAYS (*Dni*). A daily newspaper; A. F. Kerensky, editor. First called *Golos Rossii* and published in Prague (1922); in 1923 transferred to Berlin and later to Paris. Closed in 1928.

DELMAS, LIUBOV ALEKSANDROVNA (ANDREEVA) (1884–1969). The 'Carmen' of Blok's third volume of verse. A singer (mezzo-soprano).

DEMIDOV, IGOR PLATONOVICH (1873–1947). Member of the Fourth State Duma, of the K.-D. Party. Emigré, deputy editor of P. N. Miliukov's émigré daily in Paris, *The Latest News*. D. was a grandson of V. I. Dal, the famous dictionary compiler.

DENIKIN, ANTON IVANOVICH (1872–1947). General, one of the prominent commanders in the White Army. Emigré. Author of memoirs.

DERZHAVIN, GAVRILA ROMANOVICH (1743–1816). Great Russian poet of the pre-Pushkin period. See V. Khodasevich's biography, *Derzhavin*.

DIAGHILEV, SERGEY PAVLOVICH (1872–1929). The great ballet impresario of this century. From 1907 on, active and famous in Paris. D. was the publisher of the magazine *World of Art* and an associate of the group.

DOBROWEN, ISSAY ALEKSANDROVICH (1894–1953). Composer, conductor, pianist. In 1919 director of the Bolshoi Theatre. After 1922 in Europe, later in America.

DOBUZHINSKY, MSTISLAV VALERIANOVICH (1875–1957). Painter, illustrator, theatre-set decorator, member of the World of Art. From 1925 on, an émigré. Lived in Lithuania, Germany, Paris, and New York. Author of memoirs, published only in part.

DONKEY'S TAIL (Ass's Tail – *Osliny Khvost*). A group of vanguard painters in Moscow; an exhibit of their work was organized in 1912 by M. Larionov.

DZERZHINSKY, FELIKS EDMUNDOVICH (1877–1926). Member of the Central Committee of the Bolshevik Party from August 1917 on. First in the line of the famous Chekists: Yagoda – Ezhov – Beria. Personal friend of Lenin's and of Gorky's first wife.

EFRON, SERGEY YAKOVLEVICH (*c.* 1892–1939). Husband of the poet Marina Tsvetaeva; involved in the late 1930s in the murder of Ignace Reiss.

EFROS, ABRAM MARKOVICH (1888–1954). An art historian and translator (of Dante, Petrarch, and others). Author of erotica.

EHRENBURG, ILYA GRIGORIEVICH (1891–1967). Lived at times in France, starting in 1908. From 1923 on, the European correspondent of *Izvestia*. Covered the Spanish Civil War. Prominent Soviet writer, author of memoirs, *People, Years, Life*. His novel *Julio Jurenito*, written in 1921, has now been republished in the U.S.S.R. after forty years (but minus Chapter 23). He concealed the horrors of Stalinism for a long time and even misled the wife of Babel for fourteen years, telling her that her husband was still alive, living under house arrest. In the last volume of his memoirs (in English) there is a shocking chapter on the writer A. Fadeev: this chapter is omitted in the Soviet edition. A controversial figure for many, without any doubt one of the main figures of Soviet cultural life of the past fifty years.

EICHENBAUM, BORIS MIKHAILOVICH (1886–1959). Outstanding 'formalist', author of classic books on Tolstoy, Gogol, Blok, and other writers. See also a forgotten 1920 article '*Mig Soznania*' in *Knizhny Ugol*, No. 7, where he proves to be far ahead of his time. This publication (1918–22), with Viktor Khovin as editor, is full of first-rate but completely forgotten material (Shklovsky's letter to Roman Jakobson, the last writings of V. Rozanov, a sensational article by Yakubinsky, an article by L. Lunts, some pages by Zhirmunsky).

EISENSTEIN, SERGEY MIKHAILOVICH (1898–1948). Movie-maker and director.

ELAGIN, IVAN VENEDIKTOVICH (1918–). Emigré since the 1940s. Poet. Son of the minor imaginist Matveev (Mart). Lives in New York.

ELAGIN, YURY BORISOVICH (1905–). Author of *The Taming of the Arts* (New York, 1952). Left Russia in the 1940s.

ELEONSKY, SERGEY NIKOLAEVICH (1861–1911). Theologian by training. Friend of Gorky's. Minor writer. Became mentally ill and committed suicide.

ELISEEV HOUSE. The House of Arts (q.v.), from 1920 to 1923, on the corner of Nevsky, Moika, and Morskaya. Belonged before the Revolution to a rich merchant and owner of delicatessens. The following writers and poets lived in these premises at various times (after 1917): Forsh, Gumilev, Khodasevich, Pavlovich, Lozinsky, Mandelstam, Grin, Slonimsky, Lunts, Letkova, Shaginian, Pyast, Tikhonov, V. Rozhdestvensky, Shklovsky, Punin, etc.

ELPATIEVSKY, SERGEY YAKOVLEVICH (1854–1933). Doctor and minor writer, friend of Gorky's. In tsarist times banished to Siberia; after the Revolution became the Kremlin physician (1922–8). Son of a priest. Author of memoirs (1929).

EPOCH. A publishing house owned by Solomon Gitmanovich Sumsky-Kaplun (1891–1940), a Menshevik; in Berlin from 1922 to 1925. Epoch published the magazine *Beseda* (1923–5).

EPOPEYA. A non-periodical magazine, with Andrey Bely as editor, published by Abram Vishniak, who owned the Berlin publishing house Helicon from 1921 to 1923. Four issues of *Epopeya* were published containing the authentic version of Bely's memoirs of Blok. Ehrenburg, Tsvetaeva, Remizov, and others contributed to *Epopeya*.

ESENIN, SERGEY ALEKSANDROVICH (1895–1925). From 1915 in St. Petersburg, later in Moscow. Russian poet of the 'peasant' group. Married to Isadora Duncan. Close to the left wing of the S.-R. Party at one time. An imaginist (with Marienhof and others). In 1922–3 went to Europe and the U.S.A. on a flamboyant trip. Committed suicide in 1925.

EVREINOV, NIKOLAI NIKOLAEVICH (1879–1953). Director, playwright, owner of the theatre Krivoe Zerkalo before the Revolution. Head of Starinny Teatr (1907–12). From the 1920s on, an émigré. Author of a history of Russian theatre (Chekhov Publishing House).

EXPERIMENTS. An irregular New York publication (1953–8). N. B.'s correspondence with Lev Lunts was published in No. 1. Nine issues in all.

EZHOV, NIKOLAI IVANOVICH (1894–1939). Head of the NKVD from 1936 to 1938. Helped Stalin to liquidate members of the Communist Party. Active in the Moscow trials with Stalin and Vyshinsky, the prosecutor. Later disappeared.

FEDIN, KONSTANTIN ALEKSANDROVICH (1892–1977). War prisoner (civilian) in Germany during World War One. Returned to Russia in 1918. Member of the Serapion Brothers. Member of the Academy of Sciences. A Soviet 'classic', or, in other words, a writer of the 'Stalinist generation'. A high official in the Union of Writers since 1932.

FEDOROVA, SOFYA (b. 1881). Ballerina of the Bolshoi Theatre, called Fedorova the Second. From 1909 on, danced in Diaghilev's group.

FEDOTOV, GEORGY PETROVICH (pen name Bogdanov, 1886–1951). In 1905 an S.-D. Emigré after 1925, in Paris and later in New York. Author of many books inspired by the Orthodox religion. A gifted publicist and polemicist with a strong pessimistic outlook in spite of his Christianity.

FELZEN, YURI (1895–1943). A minor émigré writer, deported by the Germans.

FET, AFANASY AFANASIEVICH (1820–92). A great Russian metaphysical poet.

FILIPPOV, BORIS ANDREEVICH (b.1905). Editor, critic, scholar of Russian literature. After 1950 in the U.S.A.

FILONENKO, MAKSIMILIAN MAKSIMILIANOVICH (? – c. 1950). A prominent lawyer of Russian descent in Paris; handled many sensational cases. In 1917 played a part in the 'affaire Kornilov', on the side of Savinkov. After 1946 became a 'Soviet patriot'.

FONDAMINSKY, ILYA ISIDOROVICH (1870–1943). A member of the S.-R. Party and the terrorist group from 1905 to 1917. One of the editors of Contemporary Annals (pen name Bunakov). His wife, AMALIA OSIPOVNA, née Gavronskaya, died in 1935. A book about her was published in 1937.

FORMALISM, FORMALISTS. A group formed in 1913–16. It published Opoyaz (1916–19), included the most prominent and talented literary critics of this century in Russia: Tynianov, Shklovsky, Eichenbaum, Tomashevsky, Brik, Jakobson, at one time Vinogradov (an academic linguist), and Zhirmunsky. During the 1920s struggled for survival, but was crushed around 1930. Interesting traces of this struggle can be found in Pechat i Revolyutsia (1921–7), when the formalists were looking for a compromise between questions of literary form and a Marxist approach to literature. Also in Lef, the magazine of Mayakovsky, and Novy Lef.

They even invented a 'formalist-sociological' method, but it did not help them. On this school, see Victor Erlich's *Russian Formalism* (The Hague, 1955, 1963).

FORSH, OLGA DMITRIEVNA (1873–1961). Lived in the House of Arts, 'Moika 59, apt. 30/a, room 9' – this was, with the exception of the room number, the address of Mandelstam and Khodasevich as well. Wrote a novel about the inmates of this house: first title *Simvolisty* (in *Zvezda,* 1933, Nos. 1, 5, 9, 10), second title *Voron,* Gosizdat, 1934. Final title *Sumasshedshy Korabl.* See also her interesting correspondence with Gorky in *Literaturnoe Nasledstvo,* No. 70, where she complains that 'in our country people do not understand and do not appreciate humour' (letter of 30 November, 1939, page 609).

FREEMASONS. Russian lodges were active before the Revolution in the main cities of the country. After 1918 they were closed by the Soviet government. In Paris among the émigrés Freemasonry was very popular; nearly everybody belonged (though *not* Bunin, Khodasevich, Remizov, Zaitsev, Muratov). Y. Frumkin, the well-known historian of the Jewish people, writes: 'As is well known [!] Russian political Freemasonry played a very great part in the composition of the Provisional Government (first and succeeding formations).' See also a volume published in memory of A. I. Braudo in Paris, 1937 (the footnote on p. 83). During the German occupation of France in 1941–4, many Russian Freemasons were deported to extermination camps. See N. B.'s book, *Lyudi i lozhi* (Russian Freemasons of the Twentieth Century).

FROMAN, MIKHAIL ALEKSANDROVICH (1891–1940). Minor Soviet poet, at one time the secretary of the Writers Union in Leningrad. Husband of Ida Nappelbaum. Arrested and deported to Siberia; 'illegally repressed' and now being rehabilitated. Returned from the camps and died in Leningrad.

GERMANOVA, MARYA NIKOLAEVNA (1884–1939). Actress in Stanislavsky's theatre in Moscow. Later émigré, lived in Paris.

GERSHENZON, MIKHAIL OSIPOVICH (1869–1925). A critic, essayist, historian of literature. Wrote on Pushkin, Chaadaev, Herzen, and many others. His daughter NATALIA (married name Chegodaeva) is an art historian, as is her husband.

GESSEN, IOSIF VLADIMIROVICH (1886–1943). Member of the K.-D. Party, member of the State Duma. Editor of the émigré paper *Rul* (*The Rudder,* Berlin) and the *Archives of Russian Revolution* (Prague). See *Novy Zhurnal,* No. 6.

GINGER, ALEKSANDR SAMSONOVICH (1897–1965). Minor émigré poet, lived in Paris.

GIPPIUS, ZINAIDA NIKOLAEVNA (1867–1945). Poet, critic (pen name Anton Krainy), novelist, diarist, memoirist. One of the remarkable women of this century. Wife of Merezhkovsky. Paradoxical, whimsical, often nasty, sometimes charming. Left Russia in 1919. Her sister, ANNA (d. 1942) was author of a book on a Russian saint, *Tikhon Zadonsky*. Two other sisters, TATIANA and NATALIA, were friends of Andrey Bely; see his memoirs.

GLINKA, MIKHAIL IVANOVICH (1804–57). Russian composer.

GOLDSTEIN, MOISEY L. Prominent lawyer in Russia before the Revolution. Emigré, first publisher of *The Latest News* (April 1920–March 1921). Author of a book about Russian lawyers, *Advokatskie Portrety* (1922). Committed suicide in the 1930s.

GONCHAROVA, NATALIA SERGEEVNA (1881–1962). Russian painter of the group *Bubnovy Valet*, wife of M. F. Larionov. In 1913 had a one-man show in Moscow. From 1906 on exhibited in Paris. Worked for Diaghilev.

GORKY, MAXIM, pseudonym of Aleksey Maksimovich Peshkov (1868–1936). My notes of him and his family were made in the early 1920s and Khodasevich used them for his article (see his *Nekropol*); thus there may be a certain similarity between my recollections and his. Amid the many praises of Gorky in Soviet criticism, now all old clichés without real meaning, less enthusiastic voices were heard from the beginning. See the article by Chuzhak (later disappeared), who was a member of the *Lef* group, about *The Artamonov Business* in *Zhizn Iskusstva*, 1926, No. 34; or Shklovsky's book on Gorky published in Tiflis (!) in 1926, which got him into trouble. Pilniak was one of those who disliked Gorky's style violently; Gorky hated Pilniak after a personal clash in 1920 in Petersburg, witnessed by a dozen guests in Gorky's dining room; Pilniak had made a 'faux pas' about Baroness Budberg. Though he broke all personal ties with émigré writers in the late 1920s, Gorky felt the need to answer their allegations in print from time to time. So he answered Andrey Levinson (on the question of Dzerzhinsky) in *Krasnaya Gazeta*, 5 September, 1928. Those who are interested in Gorky's relations with the U.S.A. after the Revolution should read his letter to the American people (*Literary Digest*, 18 March, 1922) about the food shortage in Soviet Russia.

GORLIN, MIKHAIL (1909–43). Poet and scholar, husband of Raissa Bloch. Deported by the Germans. See *Institut d'Etudes Slaves*, Paris, Vol. 30.

GORODETSKY, SERGEY MITROFANOVICH (1884–1967). Poet close to the acmeists, popular during World War One; he enthusiastically accepted the October Revolution, was not in evidence from 1930. Two collections of his verse, including work from his later years, were published in 1964 and 1966.

GOSIZDAT. The State Publishing House. In the years 1920–3, changed its Nevsky Avenue address four times: first No. 48, then No. 72 (the house where the Nappelbaums' 'Mondays' took place), then No. 33 (the City Duma), and finally

No. 28, in the building that had belonged before the Revolution to the Singer sewing-machine company.

GRIGORIEV, APOLLON ALEKSANDROVICH (1822–64). Poet, critic, slavophile; one of the Russian '*poètes maudits*'.

GRIGOROVICH, DMITRY VASILIEVICH (1822–99). Minor novelist. Among his friends were Turgenev, Dostoevsky, Nekrasov.

GRIN, ALEKSANDR STEPANOVICH (1880–1932). Soviet writer. Author of fantasy novels, mostly for teenagers.

GRYNBERG, ROMAN NIKOLAEVICH (1897–1969). Publisher and editor since 1960 of an irregular periodical, *Vozdushnye Puti*, New York; five issues.

GRZHEBIN, ZINOVY ISAEVICH (1869–1929). Publisher. At one time employed by the Soviet Commercial Mission. Friend of Gorky's. For more about him see a letter from Remizov in *Russkaya Kniga*, 1921, No. 9, p. 22. (Not everything published in this valuable journal can be considered reliable. Parts of it, especially articles signed by Remizov, were practical jokes at the expense of his friends.)

GUCHKOV, ALEKSANDR IVANOVICH (1862–1936). Member of the State Duma, Octobrist, chairman of the Third Duma, minister of war in the first cabinet of the Provisional Government (March–May 1917). Emigré.

GUILD OF POETS (*Tsekh Poetov*). Founded by Gumilev before World War One. In 1921–3 four issues of an irregular magazine appeared (including Ivanov, Adamovich, Otsup, etc.). Lev Lunts wrote a critique of issues 1 and 2 in *Knizhny Ugol*, 1922, No. 8.

GUL, ROMAN BORISOVICH (1896–1986). Since 1959 one of the editors of *Novy Zhurnal*. Has lived in the U.S.A. since 1950. Until 1927 the Berlin correspondent for *Pravda* and *Izvestia*, later an émigré.

GUMILEV, NIKOLAI STEPANOVICH (1886–1921). Head of the acmeist group, Russian poet, theoretician, critic, playwright, translator. First husband of A. A. Akhmatova. Executed in August 1921 as a member of a counter-revolutionary plot, 'the Tagantsev affair'.

GUMILEVA, ANNA NIKOLAEVNA (*c.* 1897–1942?). Née Engelhardt. Her mother was first married to K. D. Balmont. A. G. was the second wife of Gumilev. Apparently in the 1930s she was arrested and deported for a time, and later died with her daughter (by Gumilev, b. *c.* 1918) during the siege of Leningrad.

HABIMA. Hebrew theatre opened in 1916 in Moscow, directed by Vakhtangov. In 1926 left Russia and in 1931 settled in Palestine (later Israel). Famous staging of Ansky's *The Dybbuk*. The leading lady was the unforgettable Shoshana Avivit.

HECKEREN, BARON D'ANTHÈS. Lover of Pushkin's wife who killed the poet in a duel in 1837. His invaluable archives have finally been opened: the French writer of Russian–Armenian descent, Henri Troyat, in his biography of Pushkin published fascinating letters which prove what was long doubted: that Natalie never really loved Pushkin, and that between her and the Frenchman there was not a mere infatuation but a deep and shattering affair.

HELICON. Russian publishing house in Berlin, owned by Abram Vishniak (1920–3), published *Epopeya* of Bely and books by Tsvetaeva, Remizov, Ehrenburg and others.

HERZEN, ALEKSANDR IVANOVICH (1812–70). Great Russian publicist, polemicist, and essayist, mediocre novelist. Exiled in Europe from 1847 on.

HOUSE OF ARTS. St. Petersburg, Moika 59. Opened 19 December, 1919. Closed at the very end of 1922. Former house of the Eliseev family (see ELISEEV HOUSE). In the five apartments poets, writers, painters, and scholars lived. Conferences and concerts took place in the large hall. On 4 December, 1920, Mayakovsky, who had come from Moscow, read his *150,000,000*. Bely, until August 1921, was a frequent lecturer. Groups of young poets and writers (the Resounding Shell and Serapion Brothers) held classes there on the theory of literature, creative writing, translations, etc. The teachers were: Gumilev, Korney Chukovsky, M. Lozinsky, E. Zamiatin, V. Shklovsky. These classes started with a 'studio' (*studiya*) in the publishing house Universal Literature, headed by Gorky; on 1 March, 1919, Gumilev, Chukovsky, and Andrey Levinson started lecturing on different subjects related to modern trends. It became the '*studiya Doma Iskusstv*' in 1919–20. In the winter of 1920–1, the Serapion Brothers formed their circle. I was present on 2 February, 1922, at the first anniversary of their group. The Resounding Shell, of course, no longer officially existed after August 1921, when Gumilev was executed. The House of Arts was for a short time resurrected in Berlin, 1921–3, and the Helicon publishing house published a couple of 'bulletins' about its activities in Berlin in 1922. Interesting information about this place can be found in *Novaya Russkaya Kniga*, No. 1, 1922, p. 34. This valuable publication has a tremendous amount of information on Russian literary life in Berlin in the years 1921–2.

HOUSE OF SCHOLARS. St. Petersburg, Millionnaya Street. Organized by Gorky to help starving scholars. It was housed in the former palace of Grand Duke Vladimir.

HOUSE OF WRITERS. Basseinaya No. 11. Closed at the end of 1922. Organized conferences. An especially memorable one (I was not present) was on 11 February, 1921, when Blok delivered his speech '*O Naznachenii Poeta*'. The House of Writers published 'bulletins' (as did the House of Arts). There were, as far as I know, three issues (May, June, August, 1922).

HYPERBOREUS. A publishing imprint used by a group of acmeist writers during the early 1910s.

IGOR TALE. An epic depicting the campaign of Prince Igor in 1185. According to some, written in 1185–7. According to others, at the end of the eighteenth century. The MS. supposedly disappeared in the fire of Moscow in 1812, exactly like the MS. of *Beowulf*, which disappeared in a fire in Denmark.

ISTRATI, PANAYIT (1884–1935). Rumanian writer, wrote in French. Romain Rolland was the first to call him 'the Rumanian Gorky'. Until 1927 Istrati was hailed, translated into Russian, and published because he sympathized with the Soviet regime. After his visit to the U.S.S.R. he turned away from communism; his work has been banished in Russia, his name is not to be found in the encyclopaedias of later years. All the traces of his friendship with Gorky have been erased.

IVANOV, GEORGY VLADIMIROVICH (1894–1958). Emigré poet of the acmeist school. See Khodasevich's articles on him in *Renaissance* (1937, No. 4080 and 1938, No. 4116).

IVANOV, VSEVOLOD VYACHESLAVOVICH (1895–1963). Soviet writer, member of the Serapion Brothers. At one time had difficulties with the regime for his 'Freudianism', but later was accepted as one of the greats (although not a 'classic' like the Stalinists Sholokhov and Leonov). His letters to Gorky criticizing the meddling of the Party in literary affairs, after which Gorky hardly saw Ivanov again, are interesting (see their *Correspondence*).

IVANOV, VYACHESLAV IVANOVICH (1866–1949). One of the great Russian symbolists. Poet, historian, theoretician, critic, philosopher. Friend of Blok and Bely, to whom Blok once wrote:

> And I – sad, destitute, despondent . . .
> Look at your royal procession
> From a dusty crossroad.

Like Khodasevich, Gershenzon, Bely, and others, he accepted the October Revolution in part. Went to the University of Baku and returned to Moscow in 1924, where he was given a solemn reception by the Society of Lovers of Russian Literature, in May. Mayakovsky interrupted the laudatory speeches and started to declaim his own verse (see V. Manuilov's *Memoirs*, 1955). The same year I. left Russia and settled in Italy, but until 1936 (the death of Gorky) he was not an émigré writer – i.e., did not publish in émigré publications and had very little to do with his fellow writers from Russia. (See Gorky's *Archives*, Vol. 6, 1957, p. 210, where interesting details can be found.) In 1928 he continued to send his verse to

Moscow, to the address of G. I. Chulkov (see *Novy Mir*, No. 12, 1965, p. 249). A score of Ivanov's outstanding writings have not been republished for fifty or sixty years, and some of them have never even been found. In 1918 the publishing house Alkonost advertised his *Pesni Smutnogo Vremeni*, which were not published in book form but were printed once only in *Narodopravstvo* (1917). There is an article by him in *Zapiski Mechtateley*, No. 1, 1919 ('*Kruchi*'), and another in *Nauchnye Izvestia*, Gosizdat, Moscow, 1922 (No. 2, p. 164), whose title is 'On new discoveries in the realm of verbal art' – both forgotten and which, of course, would have to be translated and reprinted. The only time I saw Ivanov was in Rome, in 1925.

IVANOV-RAZUMNIK, RAZUMNIK VASILIEVICH (1878–1946). Literary critic, historian, prominent figure in the prerevolutionary Russian monthlies, friend of Bely and Blok, an S.-R. of the left wing and the chief editor of *Skify*, where Blok published 'The Twelve'. In 1943 was captured by the Germans in Pushkino, near Leningrad, and was sent to Germany. Died in a camp. Two books of his about the terror of the 1930s among the intelligentsia were posthumously published in the U.S.A. An extremely interesting article about what was in store for Russian literature was published by him under the pen name Ippolit Udushiev (!) in *Sovremennaya Literatura*, 1925.

IVANOVA, GABRIELLE EVODOVNA, née Ternisien (b. 1894). First wife of the poet GEORGY IVANOV. Actress and dancer in Meyerhold's theatre. (His second wife was the well-known poet Irina Odoevtseva, née Genike, herself married previously to a Petersburg lawyer, Popov-Odoevtsev, to whom her first book was dedicated [1920] and whom she divorced in 1922.)

IVASHEV, VASILY PETROVICH. Decembrist. Exiled to Siberia by Nicholas I. His wife, CAMILLA, who was the governess of his sisters, followed him to Siberia. His son PYOTR was the father of VERA, a classmate of my mother's. The well-known Soviet scholar VALENTINA VASILIEVNA IVASHEVA, as far as I could determine, is a great-granddaughter of the Decembrist. She is a specialist in modern American literature, a collaborator on *Voprosy Literatury*.

IVINSKAYA, OLGA. Friend of Pasternak's, at one time exiled to Siberia (after his death); lives in Soviet Russia.

JAKOBSON, ROMAN OSIPOVICH (1896–1982). Former 'formalist', associated with Shklovsky, Tynianov, and others. Later in Prague a member of the 'structuralist group'. Outstanding Russian linguist, brilliant scholar, theoretician, lecturer, for many years professor at Harvard and at M.I.T. See bibliography in *To Honour Roman Jakobson* (The Hague, 1967), Vol. I, pp. xi–xxxiii.

KAMENEVA, OLGA DAVYDOVNA. Wife of L. B. KAMENEV (1883–1936), old Bolshevik who perished in Stalin's purges, and sister of Trotsky, who was killed by Stalin. Executed by Stalin apparently with her husband, who had been a Party member since 1903, member of the Central Committee, chairman of the Moscow Soviet, and member of the Politburo.

KAMINSKAYA, ANICHKA. Companion, in her last years, of A. A. Akhmatova; granddaughter of N. N. Punin.

KARAMZIN, NIKOLAI MIKHAILOVICH (1766–1826). Russian historian, writer, poet.

KARAULOV, DMITRY LVOVICH (OBLOMOV). IVAN DMITRIEVICH, his son, grandfather of N. B.

KARAULOVA, VARVARA MIKHAILOVNA. Grandmother of N. B.

KARONIN, NIKOLAI ELPIDIFOROVICH (1853–92). Minor writer, son of a priest, early friend of Gorky.

KARPOVICH, MIKHAIL MIKHAILOVICH (1888–1959). Historian. Professor at Harvard, editor of *Novy Zhurnal* (for twelve years). In the U.S.A. from 1917 on. Daughter NATASHA, married name Anisimova.

KARSAVINA, TAMARA PLATONOVNA (1885–1978). Ballerina of the Mariinsky, one of the best of this century. Later with Diaghilev. Lived in London from 1917. Published an autobiography in 1931, reissued with new material in 1950.

KARTASHEV, ANTON VLADIMIROVICH (1875–1960). Minister of religious affairs in the Provisional Government in 1917. In France from 1919 on. Writer, professor of theology.

KAVERIN, VENIAMIN (1902–). Serapion Brother. Survived in the 1930s and 1940s to become a writer for children. Again active after 1956. Brother-in-law of Yury Tynianov. Author of extremely valuable recollections.

K.-D. The Constitutional-Democratic Party, founded in 1905, also known as the Party of the People's Freedom. Miliukov, founder and leader. Moderate liberal monarchist until 1917, later republican. In the First State Duma, had 37·4 per cent of the membership.

KERENSKY, ALEKSANDR FEDOROVICH (1881–1970). Member of the State Duma, lawyer, member of the *trudovik* group. Minister of justice in spring, 1917, then minister of war, then prime minister. Commander-in-chief of the army until October 1917. Emigré from 1918. From 1918 to 1939 in Paris, in mourning for Russia, he did not attend any theatre, movie, or show. His last book, published in 1965, *Russia and the Turning Point of History* is widely considered to have been written with the financial support of various U.S. foundations, but no acknowledgement is to be found in the volume.

KHARITON, BORIS OSIPOVICH (*c.* 1875– deported from Riga to Siberia in 1940). One of the managers of the House of Writers in 1920–2. In Riga, was editor of a Russian daily.

KHATISOV, ALEKSANDR IVANOVICH (*c.* 1879–194?). Member of the State Duma, Armenian. In 1917 the mayor of Tiflis. Head of the Armenian Committee for Refugees in France.

KHODASEVICH, MIKHAIL FELITSIANOVICH (MISHA) (1865–1925). A prominent Moscow lawyer, brother of the following. VALENTINA KHODASEVICH (b. 1894), his daughter, and niece of the poet, became a talented painter and stage decorator in the U.S.S.R.

KHODASEVICH, VLADISLAV FELITSIANOVICH (1886–1939). Born in Moscow. His father was descended from Polish émigrés; his mother, née Brafman, was daughter of the Jewish renegade, Jakov Brafman. First husband of N. B. Russian poet, critic, essayist, the biographer of Derzhavin, memoirist, and translator. After forty years was rehabilitated in the U.S.S.R. in 1963 (see his poems and a notice in *Moskva*, No. 1, 1963). The New York Public Library has a good collection of his verse and in 1962 (February–June) the Slavic Division organized an exhibition of his books and portraits. A couple of Soviet 'cultural delegations' came to admire it. His archives were partially destroyed by the German authorities in Paris in 1942. A part of them was rescued by me and is now in my archives in the Yale Library. Some papers are in the possession of the daughter of Prof. M. Karpovich (Mrs. N. Anisimova); some were given by me to B. Nicolaevsky and were taken by him to the Hoover Library. K.'s unfinished autobiographical sketch, *Infancy*, was reprinted in *Aerial Ways*.

KHODOTOV, NIKOLAI NIKOLAEVICH (1879–1932). Actor in the Aleksandrinsky Theatre in St. Petersburg from 1898 to 1929.

KHOLODNAYA, VERA (*c.* 1890–1918). Famous actress in silent films, one of the first 'stars' of the screen. Started with Khanzhonkov, in 1915. Became popular immediately.

KIPRIAN (CYPRIAN), Archimandrite. Professor of theology at the Theological Academy (Russian Orthodox) in Paris.

KISTIAKOVSKAYA, MARIA. Wife of the well-known Moscow lawyer IGOR KISTIAKOVSKY; a society woman.

KLIUEV, NIKOLAI ALEKSEEVICH (1887–1937). Russian poet, perished in eastern Siberia. A sectarian, a vagabond, a friend of Esenin. His verse was published in

555

the U.S.A. in 1954 by Professor G. Struve and B. Filippov (2 vols.). An interesting letter by a minor Soviet writer can be found in *Literaturnoe Nasledstvo*, No. 70, addressed to Gorky, where the loyal and Party-abiding writer (Chapygin) asks Gorky to intercede on behalf of K. (in July and August 1927). Apparently K. was the innocent victim of the terror against the intelligentsia. Gorky did not answer Chapygin.

KNIPOVICH, EVGENIA FEDOROVNA (b.1898). In 1920–1 a friend of Blok and his family. Later a Soviet critic and scholar. Has published since 1919.

KNORRING, IRINA NIKOLAEVNA (1906–43). Minor émigré poet, lived in Paris. Her father was on the board of the Turgenev Russian Library and went back to the U.S.S.R. as a 'Soviet patriot' in the late 1940s, as did her husband, Yury Sofiev, also a minor poet (b. 1899). In *Den Poezii* (Alma-Ata, 1965) there are poems of Irina Knorring, which Sofiev published, apparently, after being himself 'rehabilitated' (as a former émigré) and after she was 'rehabilitated', too. A rare case of the Soviet publication of an émigré of the 'young' generation.

KNUT, DAVID MIRONOVICH (1900–55). Russian poet, émigré. Later married the daughter of the composer Scriabin (Ariadna), who was killed by the Germans. Knut was one of the initiators of the early group *Palata Poetov* (with Bozhnev, Ginger, Poplavsky, and others) in the spring of 1922. Parnakh and Sharshun were also active in that group. See *Novaya Russkaya Kniga*, 1922, No. 2, p. 33.

KOKHNO, BORIS (KOCHNO) (b.1903). Started with Diaghilev as librettist; co-founder and artistic director of the Ballets des Champs-Elysées; with the Ballet Russe de Monte Carlo in the 1930s. In Paris since 1922.

KOKOVTSEV, COUNT VLADIMIR NIKOLAEVICH (1853–1942). Minister of finance in tsarist Russia (1904–14). Second cousin of my mother. Author of *Memoirs* (2 vols.). In my archives at the Beinecke Library in Yale an interesting unpublished letter of his can be found addressed to Natalia Berberova.

KOLBASIEV, SERGEY ALEKSANDROVICH (1898–1942). Minor Soviet writer. 'Illegally repressed, rehabilitated posthumously.'

KOLCHAK, A. V. (1874–1920). First an admiral, later 'Supreme Ruler of Russia', prominent in the Civil War in Siberia; executed by the Bolsheviks.

KOMSOMOL. Founded in 1918, the organization of Communist Youth.

KONOVALOV, ALEKSANDR IVANOVICH (1875–1948). 'Progressivist', member of the Fourth State Duma. In 1917 a K.-D., a minister of the Provisional Government, later deputy premier (September–October 1917). President of the Board of Directors of *The Latest News*, Inc. See his letter to N. B. in *Russian Freemasons of the Twentieth Century*.

KORNILOV, LAVR GEORGIEVICH (1870–1918). General. Active in First World War and in Civil War, a founder of the White Army. Until August 1917, commander-in-chief. Known as the initiator of the 'Kornilov uprising' against the government of Kerensky.

KOROVIN, KONSTANTIN ALEKSANDROVICH (1861–1939). Russian impressionist, stage decorator, prominent painter. Emigré.

KORSAKOV, P. A. Friend of Grandfather Karaulov; his son, IVAN, was a classmate of Osip Mandelstam; his daughter married N. B.'s cousin Prince Ukhtomsky, a sculptor, who was executed together with Gumilev in August 1921. In the 1870s K. married the daughter of his former serf.

KOUSSEVITZKY, SERGEY (1874–1951). Famous conductor of the Boston Symphony, from 1924 to 1949. Virtuoso on the contrabass. Left Russia after the Revolution. Conducted the memorable performances in Paris of *Khovanshchina* and *Boris Godunov* in 1921.

KOZINTSEV, GRIGORY MIKHAILOVICH (1905–1973). Soviet movie director, brother of Liubov Ehrenburg, the wife of the writer.

KRASNAYA NOV. A monthly magazine in the U.S.S.R. from 1921 to 1942. Sometimes referred to in English as *Red Virgin Soil*. In the 1920s (Voronsky, editor) published most valuable work of the fellow travellers. After Voronsky was eliminated, became the official mouthpiece of the newly formed Union of Soviet Writers.

KRAVCHENKO, VIKTOR ANDREEVICH (1905–66). A Soviet defector in 1944. Author of *I Chose Freedom*. Committed suicide in New York.

KRECHETOV, SERGEY ALEKSEEVICH (1879–1936). Editor and publisher of the periodical *Grif* (1903–14), where symbolists were published. First married to Nina Petrovskaya. Minor poet, very much in the centre of Moscow literary life. Second wife was Ryndina, the well-known star of silent films. After 1918 an émigré.

KRIUCHKOV, PETR PETROVICH (1889–1938). In many ways a fascinating figure, close to Gorky. Before 1917 a young lawyer, later an intimate friend of M. F. Andreeva, second wife of Gorky. In the years 1921–36 the secretary and factotum of Gorky, handling his correspondence, commuting between Sorrento and Moscow, and later, in the U.S.S.R., living in Gorky's home. Friendly with all of Gorky's friends, close to Maksim, Gorky's son, and the Baroness Budberg and all the numerous writers and Soviet officials who swarmed around Gorky in his last years. In the correspondence of Gorky with one of the Serapion Brothers, Gruzdev, who was his biographer, there is an interesting fact: letters by Gorky from Italy to Russia and letters by writers from Russia to Italy sent through

Kriuchkov (who was permanently taking trips) were *not delivered* to the addressee, and later, after K.'s death, were found in a special folder in the Gorky archives in Moscow – not delivered, but not destroyed. K. was arrested and executed by Stalin after the Third Moscow Trial, after confessing at the interrogation that he had helped to kill Gorky. Now he is partially 'rehabilitated' (but not officially) and in some memoirs is called 'charming' and 'wonderful', 'a guardian angel' of the writer. In the chronology of Gorky's life and work he is not mentioned *in the Index*, but, of course, could not have been taken out of the text – to my knowledge, this is a unique case in the practice of Soviet scholarship in literary matters.

KRUTITSKY, NIKOLAI. Moscow Metropolitan, high official of the Russian Orthodox Church after World War Two. Was sent by Stalin to Paris in the late 1940s to take over the émigré church. As a high official of the Soviet government, he contacted the Paris Metropolitan Evlogy and tried to convince him to join the Mother Church under Soviet guidance. In this he nearly succeeded. About Evlogy, who in the years between the two wars was the head of the émigré church in France, see Bertram Wolfe in *Three Who Made a Revolution* (1948 edn, p. 328) where he speaks about Evlogy before 1917 and after: 'The spiritual leader of this protofascist religious organization [*Russky Pravoslavny Komitet*] was the priest Evlogy. Forty years later, in September 1945, Ambassador Aleksandr Bogomolov sat in the first row in the Orthodox Church in Paris while this same Evlogy, a metropolitan now, said a solemn Mass and blessed the new ruler of the Russian State, Marshal Stalin.'

KRYMOV, A. M. (1871–1917). General. Commander of a unit during the uprising of General Kornilov. Committed suicide when the uprising was crushed.

KÜHLMANN, RICHARD VON (1873–1948). In 1917–18 German minister of foreign affairs. His part in helping Lenin to come to Russia in April 1917 from Switzerland was already known to Russian historians from Sukhanov to Melgunov before the archives of the German Foreign Office were published. Two publications in this respect are invaluable at the present time: Z. A. B. Zeman, *Germany and the Revolution in Russia: 1915–1918*, documents from the archives in the German Foreign Ministry (London, 1958), and Werner Hahlweg, *Lenins Rückkehr Nach Russland 1917*, Die Deutschen Akten (1957). The chain of people who made the connection between Germans and Lenin runs as follows: commander-in-chief, German Social-Democrats, Parvus, Ganetsky, Lenin.

KULMAN, NIKOLAI KARLOVICH (1871–1940). Professor of Russian literature. Emigré of the right wing. Married to the sister of the famous Bolshevik Boky.

KUMACH, VASILY IVANOVICH (LEBEDEV) (1898–1949). Author of 'Soviet songs for the masses', favourite poet of Stalin.

KUNTSEVICH, M. M. A member of the tsarist police in Kiev, 1910–14; was active in the Beilis affair. Died in France.

KUPRIN, ALEKSANDR IVANOVICH (1870–1938). Minor 'realist', friend of Bunin, author of *The Pit*, a semi-documentary study of Russian brothels.

KUSIKOV, ALEKSANDR BORISOVICH (1896–1970). Poet-imaginist of the Esenin group. Lived in Paris from 1924 on.

KUSKOVA, EKATERINA DMITRIEVNA (1869–1958). A journalist and liberal political writer. After 1917 a member of the *Vlast Naroda*, and of the *'gruppa kooperatorov'*. Exiled from Russia in 1922. Lived in Prague, died in Geneva.

KUTEPOV, A. P. (1882–1930). General. 'Abducted' in Paris by Soviet agents. Played a prominent part in the White Army during the Wrangel episode.

KUZMIN, MIKHAIL ALEKSEEVICH (1875–1937). Acmeist poet, author of novels and plays, composer; his poetry, partly surrealist, whimsical, slightly decadent, homosexual. Although not deported to Siberia, virtually forbidden to publish in the U.S.S.R. after 1930.

KUZNETSOVA, GALINA NIKOLAEVNA (*c.* 1898–1976). Minor émigré writer and poet. Lived in the home of Bunin from 1927 to 1938.

LADINSKY, ANTONIN PETROVICH (1896–1961). Emigré poet and writer, returned to the U.S.S.R. in 1948, but reached his family in Vladimir only in 1955. A White Army officer in the Civil War. A 'Soviet patriot' after World War Two.

LADYZHNIKOV, IVAN PAVLOVICH (1874–1945). Friend of Gorky's, his publisher; worked at one time at the Kniga (Soviet Publishing House).

LANSKOY, ANDRÉ (1902–1976). French painter of Russian origin. An abstractionist before World War Two.

LAPPO-DANILEVSKAYA, NADEZHDA ALEKSANDROVNA (1876– ?). Author of 'sexy' trash literature: *The Heart of a Russian, It Happened in Early Spring*, etc.

LARIONOV, MIKHAIL FEDOROVICH (1881–1964). Russian painter, lived in Paris, connected with Diaghilev. A 'rayonist', author of the Rayonist Manifesto in 1913. Left Russia in 1914. Husband of N. S. Goncharova.

LATEST NEWS, THE. Emigré daily, published in Paris with P. Miliukov as chief editor. Printed at one time 35,000 copies daily. Last issue dated 12 June, 1940. Of liberal-democratic-republican tendencies.

LAZAREVSKY, BORIS ALEKSANDROVICH (1871–1936). Minor writer, first published in 1894. Emigré.

LAZAREVSKY, NIKOLAI IVANOVICH (1868–1921). Professor of international law. Executed with Ukhtomsky and Gumilev in August 1921.

LEF (Left Front) and NOVY LEF (after the first was suppressed). A literary magazine of Mayakovsky and his friends, futurists and formalists. The first was published in 1923–5; the second, 1927–8, was also suppressed. One can see the increasing difficulties that Mayakovsky and others had at that time in surviving. Very few got the chance.

LENIN, VLADIMIR ILYCH (1870–1924).

LEONOV, LEONID MAKSIMOVICH (b.1899). Soviet writer, now called a 'classic'. Belongs to the 'Stalinist generation'.

LERMONTOV, MIKHAIL YURIEVICH (1814–41). Russian romantic poet, vastly overrated. Author of *The Hero of Our Time*.

LETOPIS. Magazine issued by Gorky, 1915–17.

LEVIDOV, MIKHAIL YULIEVICH (1891–1942). Now forgotten but in the years 1920–30 an extremely meaningful figure, vaguely connected with Mayakovsky's group at one time. Levidov launched the idea of the necessity of the 'organized [planned] debasement of culture'. See *Krasnaya Nov*, 1923, No. 1, for his article 'The Organized Simplification of Culture' *(Organizovannoe Uproshchenie Kultury)*. Also *Prostye Istiny*, 1927 (published by the author). He wrote: 'The masses like vulgarities in literature and we have no right to go against their taste.' On 27 October, 1921 he gave a public lecture in the House of the Press (Mayakovsky was present). The debates continued through 30 October in the Poets' Café (Moscow). Levidov was liquidated, and has now been 'posthumously rehabilitated'.

LEVINSON, ANDREY YAKOVLEVICH (1887–1933). Art historian, translator, author of many books in French (on Dostoevsky, the ballet, etc.). Emigré; wrote the obituary on Gumilev in *Sovremennye Zapiski*, No. 9. A man of great integrity and fine perception. His interests ranged from Rilke to Chaplin. On Gorky: *'Le solitaire de l'île de Capri'*, *Le Temps*, 10 April, 1928.

LEZHNEV, ABRAM (1893–1938). Member of the group Pereval, accused of Trotskyism. Now 'posthumously rehabilitated'. Not to be confused with ISAY LEZHNEV, editor of the last 'free' monthly, *Rossiya* (1923–4).

LIDIN, VLADIMIR GERMANOVICH (1894–1979). Minor Soviet writer, editor of *Autobiografii Pisateley*, 1928. Author of memoirs (1965).

LIFAR, SERGE (b.1905). Ballet dancer, choreographer. First with Diaghilev, later with the Paris Opéra.

LINK, THE *(Zveno)*. In 1923–5 a weekly of literature and criticism. In 1926–8 a monthly. Emigré publication in Paris; editor was M. Vinaver and, after 1926, M. Kantor.

LITERARY LEGACY *(Literaturnoe Nasledstvo)*. Non-periodical publication, uneven but some issues of invaluable interest. Started in 1931. To date, about 78 volumes have appeared. Dedicated to the history of (mostly) Russian literature.

LIUBIMOV, LEV DMITRIEVICH (1902–1976). Between the two wars a reporter at the *Renaissance*, daily émigré paper in Paris (right wing). After 1946 a 'Soviet patriot', went to the U.S.S.R. the same day as Ladinsky, expelled by the French police. In Moscow he wrote, first, *Na Chuzhbine*, about his life in emigration (1957), and, later, *12 Let Spustya* (1960). These were the first, extremely interesting, memoirs about the then hardly known phenomenon of Russian émigré cultural life in Paris. They were written in a rather impartial way and were, of course, a proof of the 'thaw' in Soviet policies. These two books by Liubimov were followed recently by a book of recollections by D. Meisner, who was a correspondent of *The Latest News* in Prague for twenty years *(Mirazhi i Deistvitelnost*, Moscow, 1966), where Meisner speaks of Nabokov, Ladinsky, and especially enthusiastically of N. B. (p. 218). This book had a printing of 200,000 copies.

LIVSHITZ, BENEDIKT KONSTANTINOVICH (1887–1939). Poet, futurist, author of memoirs on the Russian vanguard of the 1920s: *Polutoraglazy Strelets*, 1933. 'Illegally repressed, posthumously rehabilitated.'

LOCKHART, R. H. BRUCE. Before 1917, British Consul in Moscow. Later chargé d'affaires. Author of *The British Agent* (New York, 1933) and *The Two Revolutions* (1957).

LOMONOSOV, MIKHAIL VASILIEVICH (1711–65). Russian poet and scholar. Author of the *Ode on the Taking of Khotin* (1739).

LORIS-MELIKOV, A. (1860–*c.* 1950). Before 1917 Russian consul in Norway. The nephew of Alexander II's minister.

LOZINSKY, MIKHAIL LEONIDOVICH (1886–1955). Acmeist poet, translator. The head of the 'workshop of translators' in 1920–2.

LUNACHARSKY, ANATOLY VASILIEVICH (1875–1933). Minister of public education from 1917 to 1929. Ambassador to Spain, died before leaving for Madrid. Old Bolshevik, a playwright and critic. Active in the first years after the October Revolution; later gradually eliminated and stripped of his popularity.

LUNTS, LEV (1901–24). Serapion Brother, young Soviet writer. His manifesto, 'Why Are We Serapion Brothers?' was published in *Literaturnye Zapiski*, No. 3,

1922. Autobiography in Lidin's collection (1928). Letters to N. B. in *Opyty*, No. 1 (1953).

LURIE, ARTUR SERGEEVICH (LOURIÉ) (1892–1966). Composer, musicologist. In 1921 member of the *Volfila* in Petersburg. (See *Strelets*, No. 3, 1922, his lecture on Blok.) After October 1917, commissar of the music division of the Ministry of Public Education. From 1922 to 1941 in Paris, then in U.S.A. Converted to Catholicism.

LURIE, VERA SEMENOVNA (b. 1901–). Member of the Resounding Shell. Left Russia in 1921. A close friend of Bely in Berlin.

LURIE, ZHENIA. Painter, first wife of Pasternak.

LVOV, PRINCE GEORGY EVGENIEVICH (1861–1925). President of the Provisional Government, March–July 1917. Emigré.

MAHA, KARL HYNEK (1810–36). Czech romantic poet.

MAKLAKOV, VASILY ALEKSEEVICH (1870–1957). K.-D., Member of the Second, Third, and Fourth State Dumas. Russian ambassador in Paris during the Provisional Government in 1917. Emigré. Author of memoirs. Between the two wars the head of the Russian Committee for Refugees in France. In 1916 he took part in the assassination of Rasputin, but never talked about it: although a cheerful man and even something of a *bon vivant*, he was tortured by guilt, like some other K.-D. Party members, and deplored the role they had played in 1917.

MAKOVSKY, SERGEY KONSTANTINOVICH (1877–1962). Minor poet, editor of *Apollon*, wrote two volumes of memoirs – his best work. Son of an old 'realist' painter and a celebrated beauty of her time, he was from his early youth in the centre of St. Petersburg artistic life. Opportunistic throughout his whole life, he was in 1945 one of the initiators of the visit to the Soviet ambassador in Paris of Maklakov, Bunin, and others, which disrupted the unity of Russian émigrés in Paris.

MANDELSTAM, OSIP EMILIEVICH (1891–1938). Poet, acmeist, writer. Perished in a Stalin camp, suffered one of the most tragic destinies of all Russian poets. His early critical articles can be found in the early Hyperboreus publications (on Severianin, for example, in Nos. 1–2). For more about him see Clarence Brown's introduction to M.'s prose (Princeton, 1966); an early critique by Ehrenburg in *Novaya Russkaya Kniga*, 1922, No. 2; also Ehrenburg's memoirs, *People, Years, Life*; and Nikolai Chukovsky's recollections, published in *Moskva*, 1964, No. 8, p. 143. 'Illegally repressed, posthumously rehabilitated.'

MANDELSTAM, YURY VLADIMIROVICH (1908–43). Minor poet of the 'younger' generation. No relative of Osip. Deported by the Gestapo. First wife was the youngest daughter of Igor Stravinsky, LUDMILA, who died before the war.

MARGOLINA, OLGA BORISOVNA (1890–1942). Married Khodasevich in 1934.

MARGULIES, MANUIL SERGEEVICH. Member of K.-D. Party, prominent Moscow lawyer, émigré.

MARIENHOF, ANATOLY BORISOVICH (1897–1962). Imaginist poet, friend of Esenin, survived purges, left very interesting memoirs (*Russkaya Literatura*, 1964, No. 4), which have been published only in fragments. His early novels (*Roman Bez Vranya*, and others) are based on real facts of Moscow literary life in the first years after the Revolution.

MARTOV, YULY OSIPOVICH (1873–1923). Real name Tsederbaum. Leader of the Mensheviks. An S.-D. after 1891; a member of the Bund in 1893–5. Exiled to Siberia in 1896. With Plekhanov and Lenin, one of the founders of the S.-D. Party. Editor of *Iskra*; at the 2nd Party Congress in 1903 in London, was against Lenin, and the party was divided in two. In 1917 an 'internationalist'. In 1920 left Russia. The founder of *Sotsialistichesky Vestnik*. This publication continued for more than forty years and finally ceased in 1965; the Russian Menshevik Party had no 'second generation' – this can be said about all émigré political parties such as the K.-D., S.-R., etc. What has survived until now are the parties of the extreme right – but of course in their poorest and most amateurish aspect, more as a suppressed *Weltanschauung* of frustrated exiles than as an active political force.

MAYAKOVSKY, VLADIMIR VLADIMIROVICH (1892–1930). A gigantic statue of him stands in a Moscow square. In 1915 he was already full of 'futuristic sentimentality, self-hyperbolization, and hysterical emotionality' (V. Markov, *Russian Futurism*). With Osip Brik he edited *Iskusstvo Kommuny* (Dec. 1918–April 1919), where he laid futurism at the feet of the new state. In 1922 he went to Berlin. On 24 November he was in Paris, at a banquet in his honour (among others, Diaghilev was present). The speakers at the dinner were Waldemar George, Ilya Zdanevich, and N. Goncharova (see *Udar*, No. 4). When Esenin committed suicide, M. wrote: 'My background did not provide me with the necessary elements for slogans of healthy optimism' (*Kak Delat Stikhi*, March 1926). In 1928 M. was again in Paris; Tsvetaeva got in touch with him, told him about her tragic life in exile, then wrote him a letter and sent him her book of verse. He took the letter to Moscow, but left the book in Paris. In 1930 he committed suicide. Andrey Levinson wrote an obituary in *Les Nouvelles Littéraires* (31 May, 1930), after which he was beaten in a restaurant by Aragon and other surrealists (see *L'Humanité*, 3 June, 1930). On 14 June the French papers published a collective protest against Levinson. The death of M. was the outcome of many events: personal drama, his gloomy disposition (noted as early as 1915 by Gorky), the unsuccessful exhibition

'Twenty Years of Work' (in Moscow), à propos of which M. said publicly (verbatim record): 'They made incriminating remarks about so many things to me that sometimes I think of going somewhere to keep silent for maybe two years, just so as not to hear their abuse.' Now it seems that the failure of his play *Banya* was the coup de grâce, although after the first night and the explanations of M. on 25 March, it is not clear whether the play closed because it was a flop or because of an order of the government. At present a 'cybernetic investigation' of M.'s verse has begun in the U.S.S.R. (Markov, *Russian Futurism*).

MEDTNER, NIKOLAI KARLOVICH (1880–1951). Russian composer. Left Russia in 1921. Lived in France and England. EMIL, his elder brother, was a close friend of Bely (the dates of his birth and death are indeterminable; they can be given as approximately 1875–1935. He apparently died in Switzerland).

MELGUNOV, SERGEY PETROVICH (1879–1956). Russian historian, émigré. His ideas are now used more and more in contemporary works of Russian history such as Katkov's book on 1917, and others. Staunch enemy of the October Revolution; in 1945–7, when in Paris there was no way of publishing anything against Stalin and the U.S.S.R., he managed to publish a dozen small pamphlets, each under a separate title although they were obviously different issues of one (non-periodical) publication. This was the only 'émigré press' of those years.

MENDELEEV, DMITRI IVANOVICH (1834–1907). Russian scientist who developed the periodic system of elements, father of Liubov Blok. His wife, ANNA IVANOVNA, wrote recollections of Blok (1928).

MEREZHKOVSKY, DMITRI SERGEEVICH (1865–1941). Minor poet of the symbolist period, but a fiery polemicist, critic, thinker, with a certain gift for foreseeing events: in 1914 he spoke of 'the beginning of the end', in 1919–20 foretold that communism would not be a local affair but might some day affect other countries as well. A prominent figure among Paris émigrés, one-time candidate for the Nobel Prize; personally a controversial figure, highly educated, a European in the best sense of the word. His historical novels are bad and much of his polemics are now meaningless, but as a phenomenon, cultural, intellectual, and even political, he will certainly live.

MEREZHKOVSKY, KONSTANTIN SERGEEVICH (1854–1921). Brother of the above. Author of a strange Utopian novel (before Zamiatin and, of course, Orwell), *Earthly Paradise*, where the action is set in the twenty-seventh century. He was arrested for seducing a minor, was convicted and sent to Siberia (probably at the beginning of this century). He committed suicide in Geneva.

MESSENGER OF EUROPE (*Vestnik Evropy*). First publication was from 1802 to 1830 (founded by Karamzin); second from 1866 to 1918 (last editor, Ovsianiko-

Kulikovsky). At the time it was published it looked dreary, academic, old-fashioned, and law-abiding, but today it is fascinating reading.

MEYERHOLD, VSEVOLOD EMILIEVICH (1874–1942). The greatest theatre director in Russia of all time. Killed by Stalin (his wife was killed at the time of her arrest). Now 'posthumously rehabilitated'; his pupils, friends, and supporters are all dead. Interesting particularly in the years before the Revolution (bearing in mind the conservative Russian audiences conditioned to Stanislavsky's 'realism'). In the first years after the Revolution he played a leading part in the administration of the Soviet theatre. In the 1930s he got into trouble and was not allowed to go abroad again. Apparently he was tortured and killed in a cellar of the G.P.U.-N.K.V.D. building.

MIKHAILOVSKY, NIKOLAI KONSTANTINOVICH (1842–1904). A Narodnik – one of the last, an icon to many, an utterly uninteresting literary critic and head of the monthly *Russkoe Bogatstvo*. Out of time and place in his last ten years in Russian cultural life. Upheld some populist 'traditions' that were of no concern to the new century.

MIKLASHEVSKY, KONSTANTIN MIKHAILOVICH (*c.* 1888–1943). A talented actor, theoretician of the theatre, author of a book on the theatre of masks, and on the commedia dell' arte. In 1915 got a prize from the Academy of Sciences; a book of his written in French was dedicated to Charlie Chaplin. Went to Europe in the 1920s and stayed in France, but not as an actor or émigré writer: he was the owner of an antique shop on Rue du Faubourg Saint-Honoré in Paris and had nothing to do with politics. He died of gas poisoning during a cold winter. There were hints of suicide, but apparently it was an accident.

MILIOTI, NIKOLAI DMITRIEVICH (also MILLIOTTI) (1874–1962). Russian painter of the World of Art group. Emigré.

MILIUKOV, PAVEL NIKOLAEVICH (1859–1943). Leader of the K.-D. Member of the Third and Fourth State Duma. Minister of foreign affairs in the Provisional Government. Emigré after 1918. Historian, author of *Memoirs* (hampered by his dry and bland style). During his émigré years, the editor of *The Latest News*, a daily in Paris. In spite of his rather unpleasant memories of 1917, met Kerensky socially in Paris, avoiding political argument. There is a revealing paragraph in his memoirs (Paul Miliukov, *Political Memoirs 1905–17*, tr. by Carl Goldberg. Ann Arbor, 1967; Russian edition 1955, New York) concerning Russian Freemasonry, Tereshchenko, Nekrasov, and Konovalov. Miliukov writes (p. 424): 'Their friendship went beyond the limits of mutual policy. From the hints given here, the reader can conclude precisely what it was that linked this central group of four men [the fourth was Kerensky]. If I do not speak of the link more clearly here, that is because, observing the facts, I did not guess their origin at that time and learned of it from an accidental source only long after the Provisional Government ceased to exist.'

MILLER, EVGENY KARLOVICH. General. 'Abducted' in Paris in 1937 by Soviet agents. Prominent in émigré (right wing) military organizations.

MINSKY, NIKOLAI MAKSIMOVICH (1855–1937). Minor poet, precursor of the symbolists.

MIRBACH, COUNT WILHELM VON (1871–1918). German ambassador in Moscow, after Brest-Litovsk peace; killed by S.-R. (left wing) Bliumkin in Moscow.

MIRSKY, DMITRI PETROVICH, also known as PRINCE SVIATOPOLK-MIRSKY (1890–1939). Author of the classic *History of Russian Literature*, the gospel of every English-language student of Russian literature. Went to England after the Revolution, was a brilliant scholar, gradually became a sympathizer of the Soviet regime. In Paris in 1928 he announced at a lecture that he had become a Marxist. Soon he returned to the U.S.S.R. Some interesting details can be found now about his activities in Russia after 1930. V. Vishnevsky writes about him in his recollections and diaries (1961). Also see *Literaturnaya Gazeta*, October 1935, *Literaturny Kritik*, Nos. 1 and 7 (1933), and *God Shestnadtsaty*, No. 2 (1933). There is a letter from Gorky about Mirsky written to Koltsov (later executed) on 23 June, 1932. What can be deduced from all this is that Mirsky, accustomed to independent thinking and sometimes even brashness in expressing himself, ran into trouble very early. He became involved in literary polemics, and traces of a sharp exchange of opinions between him and his ideological enemies about the contemporary state of Soviet poetry can be found in the periodicals of 1935. He obviously struggled many years and finally was sent to eastern Siberia, where he was savagely killed. Now he has been 'posthumously rehabilitated', but his work has not yet been republished. During his stay in England he published in Russian in *Sovremennye Zapiski* (see his very interesting articles published before he left for Russia in the following issues: on the publications of the Zubov Institute, No. 24; on Pasternak and Mandelstam, No. 25; on Babel, No. 26; on Tsvetaeva, No. 27).

MLADOROSY. An émigré group of the 1920s and 1930s with fascist overtones. The *führer* of the group, Kazem-Beg, later taught Russian in an American college, but defected to the Soviet Union and is now the nearest person to the Moscow Patriarch: host to his visitors, secretary, middleman between the Orthodox Church holy fathers and the Soviet government.

MOCHULSKY, KONSTANTIN VASILIEVICH (1892–1948). Scholar of Russian literature, taught at the Sorbonne, author of many books – on the symbolists, Dostoevsky, Vladimir Soloviev.

MOROZOVA, MARGARITA KIRILLOVNA. Moscow society woman, wife of a millionaire Moscow businessman. In 1902 Bely corresponded with her and met her in 1905. (The correspondence has been preserved.) See his recollections about her in *Mezhdu Dvukh Revoliutsy* and the poem *'Pervoe Svidanie'*. She had a literary salon and everybody who was anybody gathered in her home for discussions, concerts, social events. There on 1 November, 1910, Bely read his paper about Dostoevsky, *Tragedia Tvorchestva*, published in 1911 (Blok was present). Madame Morozova had two daughters: LENOCHKA (see Bely's recollections) and MARIA, who in the 1950s taught Russian language in an American college but is now dead. There were rumours that Maria was the daughter of Scriabin, the composer, and not of MIKHAIL MOROZOV. (The husband of Margarita, Mikhail, must not be confused with his relative, another Moscow millionaire and businessman, SAVVA MOROZOV, a close friend of Gorky and an admirer of M. F. Andreeva, who gave money to the Moscow Arts Theatre and the Bolshevik Party.)

MOSCOW TRIALS. See TRIALS OF 1936–8.

MURATOV, PAVEL PAVLOVICH (1881–1950). Art historian, essayist, critic, novelist, translator, a 'Russian Walter Pater'. Went to Europe in 1922, stayed in Italy, later in France, and finally went to an estate in Ireland, where his friends invited him to live in a mansion in the middle of a huge apple orchard. There, in complete seclusion and solitude, he stayed for more than ten years, not writing, not publishing, hardly corresponding with anyone. Wrote before 1917 on literature, icons, art, Italy. Also see his later book on the famous battles of World War One.

NABOKOV, VLADIMIR VLADIMIROVICH (1899–1977). Russian writer until 1940, later an American writer; former émigré. The greatest writer in the Russian language of this century, and one of the greatest contemporary writers in any language. In some early Russian publications we can find interesting data about his writings in the 1920s and 1930s, now forgotten: as an occasional critic he mentions in his reviews in the *Rudder (Rul*, a Russian paper in Berlin) Bozhnev (23 May, 1928), Ladinsky (28 January, 1931), and N. B. (23 July, 1931). In Issue 4 of the *Letopis Doma Literatorov* (1921) there is an article by one of the managers of the House of Writers, Volkovyssky, which Nabokov answered in the *Rudder*, about the freedom of the press and the situation of literature in Russia. *Novaya Russkaya Kniga* (1921, No. 9, p. 47) announced that a book of verse by V. Sirin (N.'s pen name) was coming out (*Gorny Put*), and on p. 49 spoke about an 'American anthology', *Rodnaya Zemlya*, where N.'s poems were published. In the volume published by Zenzinov as a tribute to Amalia Fondaminsky, N. wrote a memoir. My recollections of V. V. N. are coloured by my immense admiration for him; the reader has to accept them as from one who was present at least once at a conversation between Godunov-Cherdyntsev and Koncheev (see *The Gift*).

567

NADEZHIN, N. (*c.* 1888–1958). First husband of Therese-Nell-Lidya Kerensky; later friend of Mrs Compton MacKenzie. In the early 1960s I chanced upon his papers in some archives. There is something striking in the fact that during my lifetime some intimate papers fell into my hands now and then by pure chance. The list of documents read by me seems, when I think of it, quite incredible. Most of them, of course, are still unpublished (letters, diaries, recollections connected with the most prominent persons of Russian literary life in our century), but they will be published someday, and the editors will find on their margins my corrections of misprints, and sometimes of misspellings, or even now and then a comment, made for the future in very sharp pencil, and also at the end of some papers a page attached with my initials on it, and a short 'who is who' made by me, so that hints and clues would not get lost.

NAKHICHEVAN. The old town is in the Transcaucasus. The new town, near Rostov, is now a part of Rostov. Mayakovsky once wrote about it: 'The word Nakhichevan is a magnificent word; no one until now has made any use of it in poetry' (1926).

NANSEN, FRIDTJOF (1861–1930). Member of the League of Nations who was at the head of the Refugee Committee at the time when we all were (more or less) 'citizens of the canton Uri' (Dostoevsky). '*Nansen passport*' means 'stateless'.

NAPPELBAUM, IDA MOISEEVNA (b.1900). Member of the Resounding Shell. Daughter of the famous Petersburg photographer (d. 1950). For more about him and his book (*Ot Remesla k Iskusstvu*) see *Moskva*, 1964, No. 6. Her sister FRIEDA (d. 1950) was a promising poet in her youth. Another sister, Olga Grudtsova, is now a Soviet critic. Ida was the wife of the poet Froman.

NEKRASOV, NIKOLAI VISSARIONOVICH (1879–1940?). Minister of the Provisional Government in 1917 and supporter of Kerensky until October. Before the Revolution, member of the Third State Duma and deputy president of the Fourth. Member of the K.-D. Party. In September 1917 was made governor of Finland. Stayed in the U.S.S.R., worked for the Soviet government. In 1930 was arrested for 'sabotage', disappeared in 1940(?). Staunch supporter of the war with Germany in March–October 1917.

NELDIKHEN, SERGEY EVGENIEVICH (1891–1942). Member of the Guild, minor poet. About him see Khodasevich's *Nekropol*. A comic figure.

NEMCHINOVA, VERA. World-renowned ballerina; started in Moscow, later with Diaghilev; danced until the late 1940s.

NEMIROVICH-DANCHENKO, VASILY IVANOVICH (1844–1936). Prolific writer, journalist, traveller. Brother of the Moscow Arts Theatre director, VLADIMIR (1858–1943).

NEW EMIGRATION. Name for the group of people who came out of the Soviet Union between 1942 and 1945, mostly displaced by the Germans during the invasion of Russia. Presumably, the 'old' emigration was composed of people who left after the Revolution (1918–26); for more about the New Emigration see an article by N. Ulianov in *Novy Zhurnal*, No. 28.

NEW HOUSE (*Novy Dom*). Later *Novy Korabl*. A magazine of the 'young' in Paris, in 1925–6. D. Knut, N. B., and two other writers were its editors.

NEW LIFE (*Novaya Zhizn*). Gorky's paper in Petersburg, in 1917–18.

NEW PATH (*Novy Put*). A magazine connected with the religious and philosophical group of Merezhkovsky, in St. Petersburg (1903–4).

NEW REVIEW (*Novy Zhurnal*). A quarterly in Russian, published in New York since 1942, founded by Aldanov and Tsetlin; Karpovich was its first editor, then it was edited by a group of four, and later of two. In great financial difficulties in 1959–61. It sharply declined in quality around 1964.

NEW RUSSIAN WORD. A Russian daily in New York. Started in 1917; since 1928 M. Weinbaum has been publisher and editor.

NICHEVOKI, FUISTY, PUPISTY, COSMISTY, etc. Groups of futurist and imaginist poets in the early years after the Revolution.

NICHOLAS II (1868–1918). Last Emperor of Russia (1894–1917). Executed with his family and servants in Ekaterininburg. In the *Memoirs* of Count V. N. Kokovtsev one can read the following words, which N. once wrote to Stolypin when the latter respectfully hinted he should share his responsibilities: 'I bear the terrible responsibilities to God for the whole power he has given me, and am ready to answer to him for everything at any moment' (p. 238). V. Maklakov also quotes this answer as a part of a letter from the tsar to Stolypin, saying that Nicholas 'was at that time under pressure from the Union of Russian People', an extreme rightist organization (*Vtoraya Duma* [Paris, 1946], p. 40).

NICOLAEVSKY, BORIS IVANOVICH (1887–1966). A prominent historian, member of S.-D., Menshevik, émigré. His brother was a brother-in-law of A. Rykov.

NIKITIN, NIKOLAI NIKOLAEVICH (1897–1963). A Serapion Brother.

NUMBERS (*Chisla*). A literary magazine in Paris, 1930–4, editor N. Otsup. Issues 1–10.

OLD BELIEVERS. A sect founded in the second half of the seventeenth century, after Raskol (the Schism).

OLESHA, YURY KARLOVICH (1899–1960). Author of *Envy* and other stories and plays. Suppressed in the 1930s, revived in the 1950s. For more about him see Khodasevich in *Renaissance*, No. 2854.

ON GUARD (*Na Postu*, 1923–5, and *Na Literaturnom Postu*, 1926–32). The tremendously powerful literary publication that denounced 'enemies of the Soviet people', paramount in liquidating Trotskyites, fellow travellers, symbolists, futurists, and all others; the names of Averbach, Lelevich, Rodov, all hangmen of Russian literature, will be remembered in the future as the executioners of two generations of the best writers and poets in Russia. They were themselves executed later, but some are now, unfortunately, being 'rehabilitated' – for unknown reasons.

ONOSHKOVICH, ADA. Member of the Guild of Poets (*Tsekh*), poet, translator, minor acmeist; close friend of M. L. Lozinsky.

ON THE EVE (*Nakanune*). A Russian paper in Berlin (March 1922–4?). The aim of this daily was to prepare the early émigré intelligentsia to return to the motherland. Most of the contributors, ideologists and editors went back, indeed, but later died in camps. A. N. Tolstoy, one of the editors, went back and prospered.

OSINSKY, N. (1887–1938). A prominent Bolshevik who was involved in 1922–6 in literary polemics. Interesting articles can be found in *Pravda* (1922, 1925, and 1926), where he defends A. Akhmatova against Mayakovsky and Averbach (from *Na Postu*). Later perished in the purges.

OSORGIN, MIKHAIL ANDREEVICH (1878–1943). Minor writer, polemicist, journalist, translator. For obituary see *Novy Zhurnal*, No. 4.

OTSUP, GEORGY AVDEEVICH (1897–*c*. 1962). Minor émigré poet, brother of Nikolai, published under the pen name Raevsky.

OTSUP, NIKOLAI AVDEEVICH (1894–1958). Acmeist, poet, editor of *Numbers*.

PARNAKH, VALENTIN. Futurist poet, Russian dadaist and surrealist. Brother of SOFYA PARNOK (!) (d. 1936). Published verse in Meyerhold's magazine *The Love of Three Oranges* (no. 3). Later Parnakh wrote articles about Russian poetry in *Europe* (1926) and in *La Nouvelle Revue Française* (1928).

PASTERNAK, BORIS LEONIDOVICH (1890–1960). Author of verse, *Doctor Zhivago* and other works of prose, translator. There is an interesting note by him on a party resolution of 1925 in *Versty*, No. 1. Also see an interview in *Na Postu* 1927, Nos. 5–6. The trilogy *Slepaya Krasa-vitsa* (unfinished) has not yet been published. Two parts dealing with 1840 and 1860 were ready, but the third one was hardly even sketched (the action takes place in 1880). For Renta Schweitzer see *Freundschaft mit Boris Pasternak, Ein Briefwechsel* (Vienna, 1963). An interesting critique by Ehrenburg can be found in *Novaya Russkaya Kniga*, No. 6, p. 192 (on *My Sister, Life*). There have been speculations on how P. found the name Zhivago for his hero; here is one: in 1925 P. translated the poems of a revolutionary German romantic poet, Herwegh (the lover of Herzen's wife), who lived from 1817 to 1875. The collection of Herwegh's poems was called *Gedichte eines Lebendiegen* – Poems of One Who Is Alive. Zhivago means in Russian 'of one who is alive'. It is easy to see that the name of Zhivago crossed P.'s mind for the first time in connection with the poems of Herwegh, although in an old catalogue of Russian physicians (of the 1870s) a Doctor Zhivago may be found: his name was Aleksandr Ivanovich (1850–82). The last line in the famous poem 'Hamlet' in *Doctor Zhivago* was taken by P. from a humorous verse of a minor Russian poet, Apukhtin ('To live one's life is not to cross a field'). Apukhtin was very stout and thought that for him to live his life was less complicated than to cross a field. It is interesting to note that at the time P. was nearing seventy foreign journalists found he had the face of a youth. The immaturity of Russian futurists had been noted by many quite early. Thus, Akhmatova said about P. that he was 'endowed with eternal youthfulness'; Lunacharsky wrote about Mayakovsky: 'He will be a youth until he goes to his grave' (1923); and Vasily Kamensky said about the whole crowd of his friends: 'At forty we are, all together, urchins.'

PASTERNAK, ZINAIDA NIKOLAEVNA. Second wife of Boris Pasternak, née Eremeeva; first married to Neuhaus.

PASTUKHOV, VSEVOLOD LEONIDOVICH (1896–1967). A pianist, minor poet, close friend of Kuzmin in St. Petersburg before the Revolution. Emigré; until 1940 in Riga, later in the U.S.A.

PAVLOVA, ANNA (1881–1931). World-renowned ballerina. First in the Mariinsky, after 1909 with Diaghilev; in 1910 in the U.S.A. Married to Victor Dandré (see his book about her, London, 1932).

PAVLOVICH, NADEZHDA ALEKSANDROVNA (1895–1980). Minor poet, author of children's books. Friend of Blok; in 1962 she published a book of poems about his death.

PECHORIN, DMITRI (d. *c.* 1947). French lawyer of Russian descent. Married to the sister of Maria Chaliapina, second wife of the famous singer.

PENZA. A town to the south-east of Moscow, in every way insignificant. The first time I heard the expression *'u nas v Penze luchshe'* was from a charming seventeen-year-old girl who had just arrived from Penza in Paris; her parents had sent her to live with her aunt (an opera singer) and her uncle (a prominent painter). This was the lovely Tanya Yakovleva, now Mrs. Alexander Liberman, whom I met near Paris, and who after being asked 'How do you like Paris?' (she had arrived the day before) said that she liked it better in Penza. But later she did change her mind and did not go back to her beloved Penza, not even to Moscow, although Mayakovsky very much wanted her to come.

PEREVERZEV, PAVEL NIKOLAEVICH. A lawyer, member of S.-R., minister of justice in May–July 1917. Close collaborator with Kerensky and Nekrasov. His fatal role in releasing the material concerning the German support of Lenin on 4 July, 1917, is described in Kerensky's memoirs (the information was received by the Provisional Government from the French minister Albert Thomas).

PESHKOV, MAKSIM ALEKSEEVICH (1896–1934). Son of M. Gorky, whose real name was Peshkov. NADEZHDA ALEKSEEVNA PESHKOVA (1901–), his wife. Two daughters, one an actress, live in Moscow. They were born in 1925 and 1927.

PESHKOVA, EKATERINA PAVLOVNA (1878–1965). First wife of Gorky and mother of the above. About her relations with Dzerzhinsky, see *Moskva*, 1966, No. 2, for the recollections of L. Nikulin.

PETERS, YAKOV KHRISTOFOROVICH (1886–1938). One of the high officials in the Cheka; for more about him see Louise Bryant in *Mirrors of Moscow* (1923). The other Peters was the judge in 1877–8 during 'the trial of the 193' (The People's Will Party).

PETERSBURG, now Leningrad. Streets that are mentioned have been named as follows: Ekaterininsky Canal now Griboedov. Ofitserskaya – Dekabristov. Basseinaya – Nekrasova. Konnogvardeisky Bulvar – Profsoyuzov. Troitskaya – Rubinshteina. Nadezhdinskaya – Mayakovskogo. Nikolaevskaya – Marata.

PETLIURA, SIMON (1879–1926). Ukrainian leader during the Civil War, assassinated in Paris by Schwarzbard in revenge for the pogroms of his army. In 1956 the Ukrainian Academy in the U.S.A. published a volume commemorating the thirtieth anniversary of his death.

PETROVSKAYA, NINA IVANOVNA (1884–1928). Wife of Krechetov, the Renata of Briusov's 'Fiery Angel'. Left Russia in 1912, lived in Italy, went to Paris; committed suicide.

PETRUNKEVICH, IVAN ILYCH (1844–1928). Member of the K.D., one of the founders of the party. Editor of *Speech (Rech)*.

PILNIAK, BORIS ANDREEVICH (1894–1937). Author of *The Naked Year*, one of the talented writers of the 1920s. Got into trouble early, first with Gorky, later with the communist press. Published novels abroad and was arrested. Now 'rehabilitated' – i.e., his novel *Solianoy Ambar* (unfinished), which he tried to write according to the rules of socialist realism in the 1930s, was partially published in *Moskva*, 1964, No. 5. One of the first to be 'illegally repressed.'

PISAREV, DMITRY IVANOVICH (1840–68). A critic of the school of Belinsky, who thought a cobbler much more useful than Shakespeare, because you can wear a pair of shoes.

PLEKHANOV, GEORGY VALENTINOVICH (1856–1918). Leader of the S.-D. Party, early Russian Marxist and Menshevik theoretician.

PLESCHEEV, ALEKSANDR ALEKSEEVICH (1858–194?). The son of the poet (and friend of Dostoevsky). Wrote his memoirs in Paris in 1931.

PLEVITSKAYA, NADEZHDA (c. 1885–c. 1940). Before the Revolution a popular cabaret singer; married a colonel, later general, of the White Army, who was a Soviet agent, Skoblin, who in Paris kidnapped General Miller in 1937 and apparently, seven years before that, General Kutepov. Skoblin escaped, but P. was arrested and condemned to fifteen years in prison. In the 1920s she published an autobiography, to which Remizov wrote a preface.

POETS' GUILD. See GUILD OF THE POETS.

POLIAKOV, ALEKSANDR ABRAMOVICH (1879–1966). The mainspring of *The Latest News*, a 'father figure' on the Russian daily, an old journalist from Odessa and Moscow. Later in the U.S.A.

POLONSKY, YAKOV PETROVICH (1820–98). Minor poet.

POPLAVSKY, BORIS YULIANOVICH (1903–35). One of the talented émigré poets of the younger generation. Also wrote prose. A contributor to *Numbers*.

POTEMKIN. The famous battleship where in 1905 a mutiny took place and was cruelly suppressed by the tsarist police.

PRAVDA. The Soviet daily since 1917.

PREOBRAZHENSKAYA, OLGA OSIPOVNA (1871–1962). Ballerina of the Mariinsky. Left Russia in 1921–2 and had a famous ballet school in Paris.

PRISHVIN, MIKHAIL MIKHAILOVICH (1873–1954). Soviet writer, mostly for young readers; a nature lover.

PROBLEMS OF LIFE (*Voprosy Zhizni*). Superseded *Novy Put*. Magazine (1904–5) of the Merezhkovskys, Berdyaev, and others of the religious–philosophical school.

PROKOFIEV, SERGEY SERGEEVICH (1891–1953). Russian composer.

PROLETKULT. The name stands for 'proletarian culture'. This organization was founded in September 1917. After the October Revolution it was affiliated with the Narkompross (Ministry of Public Education).

PUNI, IVAN (POUGNY) (1882–1956). Russian painter, lived in Paris, the grandson of the composer (*Little Hunchback* and other ballets). One of the successful émigré painters, became a member of the Paris school.

PYAST, VLADIMIR ALEKSEEVICH (1886–1940). Minor poet, friend of Blok's, one of the *'poètes maudits'* of the post-revolutionary period; for more about him see Khodasevich: 'Recollections of the House of Arts'. In 1929 Pyast published his memoirs, *Vstrechi*, an interesting document of an epoch. He was the person who discovered Strindberg for Blok and others; he went to Sweden in 1912 to meet the great Swede but found him dying, and spent days and nights at his door.

PYATAKOV, GEORGY LEONIDOVICH (1890–1937). Prominent Bolshevik, a high-ranking official, victim of the purges. Perished in the Second Moscow Trial.

PYPIN, ALEKSANDR NIKOLAEVICH (1833–1904). A historian and commentator on Russian literature of the academic kind, pillar of quasi-liberal thinking, editor of Belinsky's correspondence. Author of a history of Russian literature (1898–9).

RADLOV, NIKOLAI ERNESTOVICH (1889–1942). Son of the prominent professor of philosophy, painter, brother of SERGEY (1892–1958), the vanguard theatre director. Nikolai and his wife ELSA, and Sergey and his wife ANNA, the poet, were popular figures in Petersburg in the early 1920s.

RAKITSKY, IVAN NIKOLAEVICH (d. 1942). A kind of Oblomov of our time. In 1919 or 1920 he went to Gorky's in Petersburg (on Kronverksky Avenue) for a cup of tea and stayed twenty-three years, doing nothing, as a companion to Maksim, Gorky's son, and later to the granddaughters of Gorky. Handsome, lazy, charming, cultivated, hypochondriac, he was called Solovey (nightingale) for no reason whatever. His role in the last years of Gorky's life has still not been commented on and his place in the drama that took place in 1936 is a riddle.

RASPUTIN, EFIM GRIGORIEVICH (1872–1916). The last bosom friend and adviser and spiritual guide to the Emperor of Russia and his family.

REMIZOV, ALEKSEY MIKHAILOVICH (1877–1957). One of the great writers of twentieth-century Russia, completely ignored in the U.S.S.R. for thirty years, now being revived. Had a tremendous influence on many writers of the 1920s. He and his wife, SERAFIMA PAVLOVNA, née Dovgello, were members of one of the earliest groups of S.-R.s in 1897. He wrote about himself in the *Novaya Russkaya Kniga*, 1921, No. 9. About his later work see N.B.'s critique in *Novy Zhurnal*, Nos. 27 and 31. Between the two wars in Paris he often described his dreams – in a comic and whimsical way – involving friends in some utterly preposterous and sometimes degrading situations. Khodasevich once told him in public: 'Aleksey Mikhailovich, remember that I for one am never present in your dreams!' *(Ya vam ne snius.)*

RENAISSANCE (*Vozrozhdenie*). A Russian daily paper in Paris (1925–36), then a weekly (1936–40), then a bi-monthly (1949–54), from 1955 on a monthly. Right wing but, of course, *not* fascist or monarchist or Hitlerian. Most of the contributors belonged to the Grande Loge (Masonic), just as the collaborators of *The Latest News* belonged to the Grand Orient.

RESOUNDING SHELL. First known as the *Studiya*, opened in June 1919 in Liteiny, in the Muruzi house. In 1920–1 it was the group of young poets that gathered around Gumilev. Dispersed after his death in the autumn of 1921. At the end of that year a volume (anthology) was published, which apparently never reached the Western world and is not to be found in the U.S.S.R. There was a dedication to Gumilev (already a bold act, at that time) and a photograph: Gumilev among his young pupils (taken by M. Nappelbaum). That group photo included the following boys and girls, some of whom perished later in Stalin's terror: V. Miller, T. Roginsky, N. Stoliarov, P. Volkov, K. Vaginov, M. Gorfinkel, Nikolai Chukovsky, Olga Ziv, Vera Lurie, Aleksandra Fedorova, Frieda and Ida Nappelbaum, and Natasha Surina. For more about this group and their publication read O. Tizengauzen in *Abraksas*, 1922, and Gruzdev in *Kniga i Revoliutsiya*, 1922, No. 7.

REVISIONISM. From the Soviet point of view, revisionism *in literary criticism* is practised by two men: Georg Lukacs and the Chinese Hu-Fyn, about whom a Soviet critic recently wrote that 'his reactionary opinions do not interfere with his valuable and realistic work'. (Such statements, of course, are proof that times have changed in the Soviet Union and that the 'thaw' is at work indeed.)

RITTENBERG, SERGEY ALEKSANDROVICH (1899–1975). Left Russia in 1918, and between the wars lived in Finland, where he was a member of the editorial board of *Sodruzhestvo*, a literary publication. He taught French in a lycée, but in 1944 left for Sweden. In 1950–66 he was a professor of Russian literature at the University of Stockholm. Not a poet himself, he was a friend of many poets and a connoisseur of poetry.

RODICHEV, FEDOR IZMAILOVICH (1854–1933). One of the leaders of the K.-D. Party, a member of the State Dumas (all four) and a famous public orator.

ROLLAND, ROMAIN (1866–1944). French writer, highly thought of by the French left, author of an utterly uninteresting, sentimental, old-fashioned and extremely badly written series of novels. A pacifist during World War One, a 'martyr', living in Switzerland as an exile from France because of his convictions, a strong supporter of Stalin during the 1930s. Married to a Russian, he joined the strange crowd of French 'intellectual leftists' whose wives were of Russian descent: among them Picasso, Franz Hellens, Paul Eluard, Fernand Léger, and, of course, Louis Aragon. In one of his letters to Gorky, Rolland wrote in his flowery style: 'You were like a high arch which connected two worlds. I salute the arch! It overlooks the road, and those that will come after us will for a long time see it . . . ' (*Archives of Gorky*, Vol. 8, Moscow, 1960.) Isaac Deutscher wrote about him: 'The admirer of Gandhi, the humanitarian conscience of his generation, used his sweetly evangelic voice to justify the massacres in Russia and extol the master hangman' (*The Prophet Outcast*, 1963, p. 368).

ROMANOV, GRAND DUKE GABRIEL (KONSTANTINOVICH) (1887–1955). Author of the reminiscences *In the Marble Palace*. Emigré, one of the very few of the Romanovs who survived the terror (mainly because of his morganatic wife and Gorky) and who could escape. Lived and died in Paris.

ROSHCHINA-INSAROVA, EKATERINA NIKOLAEVNA (1885–1970). Leading lady in the Russian theatre before the Revolution, later an émigré.

ROZANOV, VASILY VASILIEVICH (1856–1919). Writer, critic, essayist, a controversial figure of the last days of old Russia. An innovator, created the 'intimate style', in which narration, dialogue, diary entries and private letters are blended. About him see a most interesting 1921 article by Shklovsky in his book *The Plot as a Phenomenon of Style*.

ROZHDESTVENSKY, VSEVOLOD ALEKSANDROVICH (1895–1977). A minor acmeist poet, son of a priest. Published in Moscow in 1961 his memoirs, *Stranitsy Zhizni*, where one finds pages on Voloshin, Mandelstam, the House of Arts, and the literary life of the 1920s. They are marred by the faulty memory of the author.

R.S.F.S.R. Russian Soviet Federated Socialist Republic. In January 1923 in Berlin there was an exhibition of paintings and sculptures of the last ten years sponsored by the government of the R.S.F.S.R. Hardly one of the painters and sculptors would be shown today in an official way in the Western world; few of them are honoured in the Soviet Union.

RUDDER, THE (*Rul*). Russian daily in Berlin, 1920–31.

RUDNEV, VADIM VIKTOROVICH (1879–1940). A member of the S.-R. and mayor of Moscow in 1917. Emigré, lived in Paris; one of the editors of *Contemporary Annals* (1920–40).

RURIK (d. 879). A Varangian, the head of the early Russian dynasty of princes.

RUSSKIE ZAPISKI. A periodical in Paris (1937–9), issues 1–21. Editor, P. Miliukov. In Nos. 4 and 11 there is some work by Nabokov.

RUSSKY SOVREMENNIK. One of the last 'free' monthlies in the U.S.S.R.; four issues in 1924.

RYKOV, ALEKSEY IVANOVICH (1881–1938). At one time chairman of the council of People's Commissars. Later perished in the Third Moscow Trial.

RYSS, PETR YAKOVLEVICH (*c.* 1875–*c.* 1948). Journalist, émigré. Brother of MORTIMER, the S.-R. who was one of the first (in 1906) to warn the S.-R. that its head, Azef, was a member of the tsarist Okhrana. But no one listened to him.

SABANEEV, LEONID LEONIDOVICH (1881–1968). Russian musicologist, author of books and articles on musicians and the now forgotten but valuable *Muzyka Rechi* (Moscow, 1923).

SARYAN, MARTIROS SERGEEVICH (1880–1972). Armenian painter, post-impressionist.

SAVICH, OVADY GERTSOVICH (1896–1967). Author of an interesting novel, *The Imagined Interlocutor* (Moscow, 1928). A friend of Ehrenburg and his wife in Paris and Moscow. Co-author with Ehrenburg of a book on France, *My i Oni* (*They and We*, 1931). At one time correspondent of TASS in France.

SCRIABIN, ALEKSANDR NIKOLAEVICH (1872–1915). Russian composer. First marriage to VERA IVANOVNA (had two daughters by her, one later married the pianist Sofronitsky); second marriage to TATIANA FEDOROVNA, née Schloezer, sister of the French writer of Russian descent, Boris Schloezer. There were two daughters from this second marriage. The eldest, ARIADNA, married the émigré poet David Knut; she was active in the Resistance during 1942–4 and was killed in Toulouse by a German.

S.-D. The Russian Social-Democratic Party, which divided in 1903 into two parts: Bolshevik and Menshevik. Was represented at all four State Dumas. After 1920 the Mensheviks went partly underground and partly into exile. Many perished in Siberia.

SERAPION BROTHERS. A group of ten young and talented writers and poets, founded in the 1920s (Fedin, Kaverin, Lunts, Vsevolod Ivanov, Nikitin, M. Slonimsky, I. Gruzdev, Zoshchenko, Tikhonov, and Polonskaya). In *Literaturnye Zapiski*, 1922, No. 3, their manifesto can be found. In February 1922 (one year after they formed as a group) Gosizdat decided to support them 'if they would not contribute to the reactionary press' (see *Novy Mir*, 1956, No. 12). Details on early years can also be found in *Krasnaya Nov*, 1922, No. 3, and in *Kniga i Revoliutsiya*, 1922, No. 6. First collective volume came out in 1922 (Alkonost, publ.). The second was never published in the U.S.S.R. and came out in Berlin in 1922 (Russkoe Tvorchestvo, publ.). Lunts died early; Ivanov, Nikitin, Kaverin at different times experienced difficulties owing to government pressure; Fedin and Tikhonov became high officials in the Union of Soviet Writers. Publication of Zoshchenko's work ceased in 1946, but he is now being republished.

SEROVA, NATASHA (b.1899). Daughter of the painter VALENTIN SEROV and sister of the actor YURY. Returned to Russia in the early 1930s.

SEVERIANIN, IGOR (1887–1941). A popular poet, futurist but not connected with Mayakovsky's group. Emigré in Estonia between the two wars, now republished in the U.S.S.R. because of his nostalgic and patriotic verse.

SEYFULLINA, LIDYA NIKOLAEVNA (1889–1954). Soviet writer, a fellow traveller in the 1920s.

SHAGINIAN, MARIETTA SERGEEVNA (b.1888). Soviet writer, author of novels depicting Soviet 'production' and labour procedures.

SHCHERBA, LEV VLADIMIROVICH (1880–1944). Professor, a great teacher of Slavic philology and an authority on linguistics in the 1920s.

SHESTOV, LEV ISAAKOVICH (1866–1938). Russian existentialist philosopher. Emigré, lived in Paris. Friend of Gershenzon, Berdyaev, and others. Prominent figure in the philosophical movement in Russia before 1917.

SHISHKOV, ALEKSEY SEMENOVICH (1754–1841). President of the Russian Academy, a reactionary, poet and literary figure, many times the target of Pushkin's epigrams.

SHKLOVSKY, VIKTOR BORISOVICH (1893–1984). In his youth a member of the S.-R. The founder of the group *Opoyaz* (1916–19), a 'formalist', critic, theoretician, writer. Associated with Mayakovsky and *Lef*. Left Russia in 1922, went back a year later. Tried to adapt himself in the late 1920s and early 1930s, survived, but lost his pungency and sharp wit; came back to life during the 'thaw' in the late 1950s. His brother, VLADIMIR, died in the Solovki concentration camp. His first cousin NATASHA was a classmate of mine.

SHMELEV, IVAN SERGEEVICH (1875–1950). Writer, émigré (right wing). 'Rehabilitated' in the U.S.S.R. because of his 'realism' and early connection with Gorky's group *Znanie*.

SKOBLIN, N. N. General. Husband of Plevitskaya; White Army officer and Soviet spy. Disappeared after kidnapping General Miller in Paris in 1937; apparently shot after going back to Russia.

SLONIM, MARK LVOVICH (1894–1976). A member of the S.-R. Party, later an émigré in Prague, where he was on the editorial board of the magazine *Volya Russii*. In Paris the president of the group *Kochevie* and editor of an émigré paper, *Novaya Gazeta* (1931). Later in the U.S.A.; a critic, literary historian, author of books on Russian literature and theatre, professor at Sarah Lawrence College, contributor to American literary magazines.

SLONIMSKY, MIKHAIL LEONIDOVICH (1896–1972). Serapion Brother, minor Soviet writer. Brother of the American musicologist NICHOLAS SLONIMSKY.

SMOLENSKY, VLADIMIR ALEKSEEVICH (1901–62). Emigré poet of the younger generation. Editor of *Orion*, an anthology (Paris, 1947). His last volume of verse was published in 1963.

SOBOL, ANDREY MIKHAILOVICH (1888–1926). Minor Soviet writer. Came to Sorrento to visit Gorky in the spring of 1925. About this visit see *Ogonek*, 1925, No. 26. Committed suicide.

SOFIEV, YURY BORISOVICH (b.1899). Minor poet of the younger émigré generation, husband of Irina Knorring. After World War Two went back to Russia and was active there in the 1950s.

SOFRONITSKAYA, ELENA ALEKSANDROVNA (1900–?). Daughter of Scriabin and wife of the pianist Sofronitsky. Went with him to Europe and after he went back to Moscow (his tour was unsuccessful) stayed in Paris. Returned and worked in the Scriabin Museum in Moscow after 1934.

SOLOGUB, FEDOR KUZMICH (1863–1927). Great symbolist poet and writer, author of *The Petty Demon*.

SOLOVIEV, VLADIMIR SERGEEVICH (1853–1900). Philosopher, poet, critic.

SOLZHENITSYN, ALEKSANDR ISAEVICH (1918–). Author of *One Day in the Life of Ivan Denisovich*, the first story about Stalin's concentration camps. In 1967 S. wrote a letter openly protesting about censorship in the Soviet Union. Left U.S.S.R. in 1974.

SOMOV, KONSTANTIN ANDREEVICH (1869–1939). Painter of the World of Art group.

SPIRIDONOVA, MARYA (1885–1935?). S.-R. of the 'left wing', imprisoned in tsarist Russia, imprisoned and deported to a camp after the October Revolution for 'anti-Soviet' activities.

SPIRIDOVICH, A. I. (1873–1959). General. From 1906 to 1916, head of the permanent personal bodyguard of the tsar. Author of memoirs, *The History of Terror in Russia, 1886–1917* (meaning, of course, revolutionary terror); a rather disappointing book. His archives are in the Yale Library. There is a rumour that there are personal 'dossiers' for each prominent émigré in Paris during the years 1920–40, which General Spiridovich built up as he had been accustomed to do in his pre-revolutionary job in the tsarist police.

S.-R. Social-Revolutionary Party, founded in 1898. In 1907 divided into 'right wing' and 'left wing'. There was also a group, partially close to its ideas and aspirations, the *Trudoviki* (Kerensky was a member), sometimes called 'the labour group'. S.-R.s, of course, were represented in the State Dumas. After the October Revolution the *Trudoviki* and the 'right wing' dispersed; the 'left wing' was liquidated in 1918.

STALIN, J. V. (1879–1953).

STALL OF PEGASUS. A café in Moscow where poets (imaginists and futurists) gathered after the Revolution. A noisy and lively place.

STEIGER, ANATOL (1907–44). A poet in Paris of the 'younger' generation. He first wrote to Z. N. Gippius and sent her poems. She jokingly decided to ask him (he was twenty at that time) to send her his photograph, which he did. Soon he appeared at the Merezhkovskys' Sundays. He died of tuberculosis in Switzerland. His correspondence with Marina Tsvetaeva was published in *Opyty*, New York (1957), No. 8.

STEINER, RUDOLF (1861–1925). The founder and head of the anthroposophists, a theosophic sect popular in Europe before and during World War One; later, in Russia, Berdyaev, Voloshin, and particularly Andrey Bely were interested in it; before 1916 Bely was the closest 'disciple' of S. The headquarters of this sect is in Dornach, Switzerland. After the death of S. and the German poet Morgenstern, who was also a close associate of S., the movement lost most of its lustre. S. published a dozen volumes 'for the initiated only'; he was considered a highly educated man in such varied fields as rhythmical ballet, philosophy, history of religion, theatre, education, science, meteorology, gymnastics, etc.

STEPUN, FEDOR AVGUSTOVICH (1884–1965). Before World War One, a popular lecturer, going on tour in Russia, talking on all possible subjects. Later a writer of fiction, unsuccessful and now completely forgotten. During the years between the wars a professor in a German university. Author of *Memoirs* (2 vols.) which are interesting since many prominent men of twentieth-century Russia were his friends, but extremely narcissistic and flowery in style.

STOLYPIN, PETR ARKADIEVICH (1862–1911). Prime minister in tsarist Russia (1906–11), killed by a double agent. His 'reform' was aimed against the village commune, to encourage the proprietor farmers.

STRAY DOG. A night club in St. Petersburg, closed in April 1915. Poets and actors did improvisations there. Later, on Moika No. 7, the same management opened the Hall of Comedians (*Prival Komediantov*, closed by the Bolsheviks in 1919). Painters decorated the premises; Meyerhold, Akhmatova, Mayakovsky, and others were often guests.

STRELNA. See YAR.

STRUVE, GLEB PETROVICH (1898–1984). Emigré, professor in the U.S.A. (formerly in England). Author of many books on Russian literature of the twentieth century. Among his very fine writings are two outstanding articles: on Chernyshevsky and the 'interior monologue', and on Bely and his experiments with novel techniques. (The first in *PMLA*, 1954, No. 5; the second in *Stil und Formprobleme in der Literatur*, Heidelberg, 1959). Son of the prominent K.-D. PETR STRUVE. Author of the only existing history of émigré literature, for many years out of print (in Russian, Chekhov Publishing House, 1956).

STRUVE, MIKHAIL ALEKSANDROVICH (1890–1948). Cousin of the above. A minor poet of the acmeist group.

STRUVE, PETR BERNGARDOVICH (1870–1944). Member of the K.-D. Party, after the Revolution an émigré. Head of the 'right wing' democratic part of the émigré political scene. A sociologist, historian, member of the Second State Duma. At one time in Paris edited *Renaissance*.

STUPNITSKY, A. F. Journalist and a member of the Union of Writers in Paris (émigrés); worked on *The Latest News*. Initiator of the visit to the Soviet ambassador of émigré writers and politicians after the war. Was active in the organization of the 'Soviet patriots', did not go back to Russia but helped others to go. On 22 November, 1947, the Union of the Writers announced a general meeting to elect a new board. Among about one hundred members present there were five or six who had already repudiated their 'Nansen passports' and received their Soviet papers. The meeting voted overwhelmingly to ask these members to leave the meeting and the union, since they were considered Soviet citizens already. The men walked out together with a group who protested about the decision of the assembled body, though still themselves émigrés: Adamovich, Bakhrakh, Varshavsky, Zurov, Mrs Bunina, Sofiev, Vadim Andreev, and some others.

SUDEIKINA, OLGA AFANASIEVNA (c. 1885–1945). Née Glebova. Married the painter SERGEY SUDEIKIN, then divorced him. Became a legend in her own time, involved in friendships with Akhmatova and the circle of the acmeists, later with ARTUR LOURIÉ, the composer, etc. Akhmatova speaks about her in 'A Poem Without a Hero'. S. was at one time an actress in vanguard theatres in Petersburg. Mandelstam knew her well, and G. Ivanov wrote: 'Where is Olechka Sudeikina now/ Akhmatova, Salomea?/ All those who were so glamorous in 1913/ Are only ghosts on the ice of St. Petersburg' (c. 1930). In Paris between the wars she was sometimes invited to literary evenings to recite poetry. To my generation she seemed a bit pathetic and ridiculous: she always recited Kuzmin's '*Bisernye Koshelki*', apparently remembering only one poem from hundreds she had known; she was the image of a remote and slightly decadent world. She lived in a servant's room on the seventh floor on the Avenue Mozart in Paris; her conversation was a kind of baby-talk, charming and heartbreaking. She had sixty birds in her room, and in a bombing they all perished. When she came out of the shelter, there was no longer a seventh floor.

SUKHANOV, NIKOLAI NIKOLAEVICH (1882–1931?). Menshevik, 'internationalist': A member of the Petrograd Soviet in 1917. A member of Martov's group. Stayed in Russia after October 1917, perished in the early repressions at the 'Menshevik trials'. Author of a seven-volume *History of the Russian Revolution*, a classic, published in Berlin (1922–3).

SULTANOVA, EKATERINA PAVLOVNA (1856–1937). Née Letkova. A translator and minor writer. One of the 'dowagers' of the House of Arts.

SUMBATOV, ALEKSANDR IVANOVICH (1857–1927). A minor playwright and leading actor. His plays (mostly drawing-room comedies) were presented at the Aleksandrinsky Theatre before the Revolution.

SURGUCHEV, ILYA DMITRIEVICH (1881–1956). Vaguely connected with the 'realist' group, minor writer, author of a play that was staged by Stanislavsky, a fact that gave him self-assurance for half a century. In Paris an arrogant reactionary, active during the German occupation as a sympathizer with Hitler's politics. Cast into the ash-can by events; died unnoticed.

TAGANTSEV AFFAIR. A counter-revolutionary plot, discovered in 1921. Sixty-two members of the intelligentsia were shot, among them Tagantsev, the son of the former senator.

TARLE, EVGENY VIKTOROVICH (1875–1955). Soviet historian, academician, author of many works, among them *Napoleon in Russia* (1936–8), the *Crimean War* (1941–3), *The History of Diplomacy* (1942–6).

TATLIN, VLADIMIR (1885–1953). Painter, sculptor, designer of theatre sets. A constructivist, prominent in the 1920s. The author of the project for a monument to the Third International.

TCHELITCHEW, PAVEL (CHELISHCHEV) (1898–1957). A talented émigré painter. Lived in Paris, worked with Diaghilev, and was a popular figure in Parisian vanguard society. There is a biography of him by Parker Tyler: *The Divine Comedy* (New York, 1967).

TEFFI, NADEZHDA ALEKSANDROVNA (1876–1952). Emigré writer, poet, playwright; a humourist of the old-fashioned kind.

TERESHCHENKO, MIKHAIL IVANOVICH (1888–1958). In 1914–16 the owner of the publishing house Sirin. In March–May 1917 minister of finance; May–October 1917, minister of foreign affairs. Emigré. During his stay in the Provisional Government he was a staunch supporter of continuation of the war with Germany.

On 26 September (1917) he again and again assured England and France of Russia's willingness to fight. On 1 September he was appointed 'in an emergency' one of the three members of the 'directorate of Kerensky'. Even the war minister, A. I. Verkhovsky, stated on 20 October that Russia must pull out of the war, but Tereschenko and Nekrasov, victims of their illusions (or deliberate liars), did not to the very end. Neither T. nor N. left memoirs of these last months of their activities in the Kerensky government (as far as is known). In emigration T. had no contacts whatsoever with other Russian political groups.

TERESHKOVICH, KONSTANTIN (1902–197?). French painter of Russian descent. Lived in Paris. A post-impressionist. Painted a life-size oil portrait of N.B. in 1933. It is now in the collection of another Parisian painter, Brianchon, a close friend of T.'s.

'THAW' PERIOD. The cautious and slow liberalization of the arts and literature after Stalin's death (1953) and the 20th Party Congress (1956). Began first in prose, then in poetry, around 1960 in literary criticism (see my articles in *Novy Zhurnal*, Nos. 85 and 86), and finally in every possible genre, including memoirs. Gradually recollections and documents started to appear that had been buried in archives. Among them were recollections of Blok by the actress Verigina (also of Meyerhold), memoirs of Evgeny Pavlovich Ivanov (small print in *Blokovsky Sbornik*), correspondence of Mayakovsky with Lili Brik, and many other items. The 'thaw' in literature came at the moment when cybernetics was given the green light and genetics was reconsidered.

THORNELOE, MELITA, called jokingly Ziuzya (*c.* 1915–?). Niece of Olga Margolina; she came from Warsaw, where she lived with her parents (Livshitz) in 1938. By a stroke of luck she got a job in Paris and stayed there, married an Englishman, and left in 1939 for England. Her family died during the war. At one time she worked as an announcer for the BBC.

TIKHONOV, NIKOLAI SEMENOVICH (b.1896). Soviet poet, Serapion Brother in 1921–2. Later a high official in the Union of Writers. A 'classic', a writer of the 'Stalinist generation'. His most popular verse was written in the 1920s. In his 'Ballad of the Nails' he speaks about the new men of the Russian Revolution. 'Out of such men one could make nails/ And there wouldn't be harder nails in the world.'

TINIAKOV (1886–1922). Pen name Odinoky. First published 1906. A *'poète maudit'*, a shady figure politically. Now forgotten, in his lifetime despised, a vagrant without any aura of 'nobility'. Georgy Ivanov used to quote him a lot.

TIUTCHEV, FEDOR IVANOVICH (1803–73). Great Russian poet, second only to Pushkin.

TOLSTAYA, ALEXANDRA LVOVNA (1884–1977). Daughter of the writer. She wrote memoirs about her father and mother (see *Sovremennye Zapiski*, Nos. 45–52, 56–7, 59, and 62). These early recollections (in the 1930s) are much more interesting than her later work. Head of the Tolstoy Foundation. From the 1930s lived in the U.S.A.

TOLSTOY, ALEKSEY NIKOLAEVICH (1883–1945). A Soviet 'classic', greatly over-rated. A supporter of Stalin and never 'repressed', but today on the way to oblivion.

TOLSTOY SECT. The followers of Tolstoy's teaching and preaching of the Gospels. Liquidated by the Soviets in the 1920s.

TOMASHEVSKY, BORIS VIKTOROVICH (1890–1957). A brilliant member of the 'formalist' school, author of many books on the theory and history of Russian literature.

TRIALS OF 1936–8. The three Moscow trials, when Stalin in grand manner liquidated 95 per cent of his closest associates. Although alluded to by Khrushchev as the cruel and insane acts of a madman, these trials are yet to be explained and the fate of the participants elucidated. No one yet has been 'rehabilitated' with the exception of a few minor figures, and those rather unofficially.

TRIOLET, ELSA (1896–1970). French writer of Russian descent, wife of Louis Aragon, member of the Central Committee of the French Communist Party. Sister of Lili Brik, a close friend of Mayakovsky's and wife of Osip Brik, the 'formalist'. Elsa and Aragon often went to Russia, and after one of their trips, in 1948, she got in touch with Remizov, who after the war had tried to obtain a visa to return. Her honesty forced her to dissuade him from going back, and he was immensely grateful to her. She is the translator of Mayakovsky into French. Her novels in France always had success, and during the German occupation, when she was especially popular with her readers, she nearly won the Prix Goncourt. Her home in Paris was the headquarters for Soviet writers and actors who came to France.

TROTSKY, LEV DAVYDOVICH (1879–1940). Second only to Lenin in the making of the October Revolution. Author of *My Life*, *Stalin*, and other works. Was a Menshevik before 1917, joined Lenin in the summer of 1917. Exiled by Stalin in 1928, finally landed in Mexico, where (after Stalin had killed his two sons, and two daughters had died of malnutrition and nervous exhaustion) he was killed by an agent of Stalin. His wife, NATALIA IVANOVNA, died in 1962. She had been with him for thirty-eight years (1902–40).

TSERETELI, IRAKLY GEORGIEVICH (1881–1959). Menshevik leader, member of the Second State Duma, member of the Provisional Government in 1917, émigré after 1919. Author of memoirs. First in France, later in the U.S.A. A witty, wise, and exceptionally worldly man. His *February Revolution* (2 volumes), published in 1963, is now a classic. I met him for the first time at a party in New York, in 1951.

TSETLIN, MIKHAIL OSIPOVICH (1882–1945). A minor poet and critic. Emigré. First in Moscow, later in Paris had a literary and political salon; a socialist, son of a very wealthy Moscow merchant. His wife MARYA SAMOILOVNA (1882–1972), née Tumarkina, was first married to N. D. Avksentiev, an S.-R. prominent in 1917.

TSUSHIMA. The battle between the Russian and Japanese navies in 1905, when the Russians lost 5,000 men and 27 battleships. The islands of Tsushima are between Japan and Korea.

TSVETAEVA, ANASTASIA IVANOVNA (b. 1894). Sister of the poet. Wrote interesting memoirs about Marina Tsvetaeva (see *Novy Mir*, 1966, Nos. 1 and 2), their childhood, her own trip to Sorrento to see Gorky, her stay with Marina in Paris (Meudon, 1927), etc. Pen name A. Mein (see *Novy Mir*, 1930, Nos. 8–9). Was deported to Siberia in 1938–40.

TSVETAEVA, MARINA IVANOVNA (1892–1941). Great Russian poet of the twentieth century. About her see P. Antokolsky in *Novy Mir*, 1966, No. 4, where he describes the death of her husband and the arrest of her daughter in 1938. Her daughter is still alive, her son (1925–42) died in the war. She committed suicide in Elabuga, not far from Kazan; her grave has now been found and she has been 'rehabilitated'.

TUKHACHEVSKY, MIKHAIL IVANOVICH (1893–1937). General. Soviet military official, visited Europe in 1936. Arrested by Stalin, condemned for 'plotting with Hitler' and executed. 'Rehabilitated' in 1956, along with some of his associates who had perished with him.

TURGENEV LIBRARY. The Russian library in Paris, started by Turgenev and Madame Viardot in the 1870s. Every tsarist émigré and every exile of the 1920s and 1930s knew this place; Lenin worked there, as did all Russians between the two wars. The Germans removed it in 1940 (see my article in *Novy Zhurnal*, No. 63). I was an eye-witness to the ruin of this wonderful book centre. All the cases were destroyed during a bombing in Germany, while they were on the way to some 'scholarly centre' in the eastern part of the country.

TURGENEVA, ANNA ALEKSEEVNA (1892–1966). Wife of Andrey Bely from 1912 to 1916 (Asya Bugaeva). A member of the anthroposophist sect, a close friend of Rudolf Steiner, did not return to Russia but stayed in Dornach for fifty years. Parts of her archives are now in Moscow. The 'Asya' of Bely's memoirs, and the 'Nelly' of his *Zapiski Chudaka*.

TYNIANOV, YURY NIKOLAEVICH (1895–1943). One of the brilliant theoreticians, scholars, critics, and literary historians of the 'formalist' group. Wrote historical novels and many books that are now classics in the field of literary scholarship and criticism. Barely survived the purges and terror. See V. Kaverin's memoir of him in *Novy Mir*, 1964, No. 10.

UKHTOMSKY, PRINCE SERGEY ALEKSANDROVICH (executed in 1921). A sculptor. His wife was EVGENYA PAVLOVNA, née Korsakova. He was a first cousin of my mother's.

UNIVERSAL LITERATURE. In 1918 at Nevsky 64, after August 1919 at Mokhovaya 36. A publishing house, founded by Gorky. It had two aims: to give work (i.e., ration cards) to the Petersburg intelligentsia, and to bring the universal classics to the masses. The first was fully achieved, the second only partially. Under the aegis of U.L., the literary *Studiya* was opened on 10 December, 1919; unofficially it had begun in the summer of 1919 (on Liteiny, in the Muruzi house, No. 24). From this studio, or around it, the Serapion Brothers emerged later and the Resounding Shell.

VAGINOV, KONSTANTIN KONSTANTINOVICH (1900–34). Poet, member of the Resounding Shell. Published three small volumes of verse and a novel, *The Goat's Song* (1930). Married Shura Fedorova. His books came out in editions of two hundred or three hundred copies and are now collector's items. Khodasevich once wrote a poem (unfinished) containing the following lines: 'They write me/ about Kostia Vaginov/ who writes beautiful verse,/ and about some others/ that are far away/' (*c.* 1926).

VAKHTANGOV, EVGENY BAGRATIONOVICH (1883–1922). Outstanding theatre director, worked with Habima and with the third Studio of Moscow Arts Theatre.

VAN DER FLEET, KONSTANTIN PETROVICH. Friend of A. N. Tolstoy and husband of VERA PETROVNA, the granddaughter of the Decembrist Ivashev. His mother, born Pypina, is mentioned in Nabokov's *The Gift*. His daughter, NATASHA, was my closest school friend. Their house was on Vasilievsky Ostrov, Sixth Line, No. 33.

VASILIEVA, KLAVDYA NIKOLAEVNA (1890–1970). Married Andrey Bely *c.* 1924 (Bugaeva). In 1952–3 had an attack of paralysis and was bedridden in her place in the suburbs of Moscow. Wrote unpublished memoirs about her life with Bely.

VEIL OF PIERRETTE. Pantomime by Arthur Schnitzler (1910) based on his earlier drama *The Veil of Beatrice* (1901).

VENGEROVA, ZINAIDA AFANASIEVNA (1867–1941). Translator, critic. The sister of PROF. SEMEN VENGEROV and the wife of N. M. Minsky. She was the first to write (in the 1890s) in correspondence from Paris about the new trends in 'decadent' and 'symbolist' poetry, and twenty-five years later the first to write about the new 'imagists' – T. S. Eliot, H. D., and Ezra Pound.

VERBITSKAYA, ANASTASIA ALEKSEEVNA (1861–1928). Popular author of pulp novels for women.

VERESAEV, VIKENTY VIKENTIEVICH (1867–1945). A writer of the Gorky group, an old servant of the Soviet regime; he first flourished, later barely survived. No worse than many others of the Znanie group.

VERESHCHAGIN, A. A minor painter, a 'realist', nephew of the famous painter of battle pieces.

VERKHOVSKY, YURY NIKANDROVICH (1878–1956). A friend of Blok, Khodasevich, and others. Translator, poet, scholar, author of articles and a book on the Pushkin Pleiad. Nicknamed Slon Slonovich (Elephant Elephantovich) for his clumsiness and heaviness.

VERMEL, SAMUIL. A talented theatre director, in the vanguard of the 1920s. Wrote memoirs on Meyerhold.

VERTINSKY, ALEKSANDR (d. 1957). A popular crooner. Emigré until 1943, when he returned to the U.S.S.R. and became a movie actor. In Kharbin in 1937 published a volume of verse (poems of 1916–37). Wrote his memoirs (published 1962).

VINAVER, MAKSIM MOISEEVICH (1863–1926). A member of the K.-D. and the State Duma. Prominent lawyer, émigré; in Paris edited *The Jewish Tribune* in three languages, and *Link* (*Zveno*). Wrote memoirs.

VISHNIAK, ABRAM GRIGORIEVICH (1895?–1943). The owner of the Helicon Publishing House in Berlin, in 1922–3. Friend of Ehrenburg. Deported by the Germans.

VISHNIAK, MARK VENIAMINOVICH (1883–1976). S.-R., secretary of the General Assembly (January 1918). Editor of *Contemporary Annals*. Emigré in Paris, later in the U.S.A. On the staff of *Time* magazine, although a socialist.

VOLFILA. A word meaning *Volnaya Filosofskaya Assotsiatsia* (Free Philosophical Association), a circle in Petersburg in which Andrey Bely played a prominent role. Opened 16 November, 1919, on Liteiny No. 21, when Blok read his *'Krushenie Gumanizma'*. On 2 May, 1920, Bely gave a lecture, later published in *Zapiski Mechtateley* under the pen name Alter Ego and with the title 'Utopia' (1921, Nos. 2–3). Bely also participated in the literary evening of 7 July, 1920. The circle was closed in 1924.

VOLKONSKY, PRINCE SERGEY MIKHAILOVICH (1860–1938). Grandson of the Decembrist. Director of the Imperial theatres. Emigré. Was theatre critic of *The Latest News*. Left memoirs about his childhood and youth. Friend of Diaghilev and the World of Art group. When I published my *Life of Tchaikovsky*, he was bitter and once said: 'Isn't it a pity that no one among *us* could do it, and a woman did it!'

VOLODARSKY, MOISEY MARKOVICH (1891–1918). Bolshevik. In May 1917 came to Russia from the U.S.A. and became a member of the party. Killed by the S.-R. Sergeev.

VOLOSHIN, MAKSIMILIAN ALEKSANDROVICH (1877–1932). Symbolist poet and painter, a colourful figure. Lived in the Crimea, where in the summer his friends in the years 1912–32 came as paying guests: Briusov, Bely, Khodasevich, Mandelstam, Tsvetaeva, and scores of others. His work has not been republished in the U.S.S.R. For more about him see the memoirs of Tsvetaeva and Ehrenburg. His first wife, MARGARITA, published a book of recollections (in German), *Die grüne Schlange*, with some fascinating pages on Vyacheslav Ivanov.

VOLSKY, NIKOLAI VLADISLAVOVICH (1879–1964). Also wrote under the names Yurievsky and Valentinov. Formerly a Bolshevik, later a Menshevik; around 1928 went to Europe as an official of the Soviet Planning Commission and did not return. In his old age a bitter, angry, and frustrated man, but author of valuable books and articles, and a fine scholar of Russian politics of the twentieth century. He had nothing in common with any group of the Russian S.-D. and, intransigent by nature, he lived his last fifteen years in complete solitude.

VOLYNSKY, AKIM LVOVICH (1863–1926). An essayist, art historian, critic. Scholar of the Italian Renaissance.

VORONSKY, ALEKSANDR KONSTANTINOVICH (1884–1943). For many years the editor of *Krasnaya Nov*, a sponsor of the fellow travellers. In 1928 removed, and sent to Siberia in 1937. Now 'posthumously rehabilitated', his books partially republished. Wrote about Freud and Proust in the 1920s.

VRUBEL, MIKHAIL ALEKSANDROVICH (1856–1910). Greatly over-rated Russian painter. His sister ANNA lived in the House of Arts.

VYSOTSKY sisters. Nieces of Madame Fondaminsky and friends of young Boris Pasternak. Their father was at one time the director of the Banque du Nord pour le Commerce Etranger, the first bank in Paris in the 1920s to start commercial relations with the Soviet Union.

WEIDLÉ, WLADIMIR WASILIEVICH (1895–1979). Emigré since 1924. In 1932–52 a professor of art history at the Russian Theological Seminary in Paris. Critic, art critic, essayist, and poet. Was my guest in Princeton in 1968.

WORLD OF ART. A group of painters in St. Petersburg at the end of the nineteenth century that included Benois, Dobuzhinsky, Somov, and many others, as well as Diaghilev, who sponsored their magazine, *The World of Art* (1899–1904; first a bimonthly, later, starting in 1901, a monthly). In 1904 there were two editors: Diaghilev and Benois. See N. N. Sokolova, *Mir Iskusstva* (Moscow–Leningrad, 1934), 219 pages, with 238 bibliographical entries.

YABLONOVSKY, SERGEY VASILIEVICH (1870–1953). A journalist, self-appointed speaker at literary meetings in Moscow as well as Paris. He was extremely small, and when the young ones wanted to make fun of him (he was 'bien pensant' and traditional), they shouted from the back rows: 'Yablonovsky, get up! We cannot see you!' At which he would answer: 'I am already standing!'

YAGODA, GENRIKH GRIGORIEVICH (1891–1938). Head of the GPU–NKVD after Dzerzhinsky and Menzhinsky, before Ezhov and Beria. One of the famous Stalin henchmen. He himself perished in the Third Moscow Trial, together with Rykov, Bukharin, Krestinsky, Rakovsky, Pletnev, and others (March 1938), after being implicated in the killing of Gorky.

YAR and STRELNA. Moscow restaurants before the Revolution, with gypsy orchestra and gypsy dancers. The tradition of gypsy songs and dances was very strong in Russia, and it was alive until the 1930s, when in Paris the Dmitrievich family arrived and started to perform in so-called 'Russian night clubs'. Before the war most of them left for Argentina – the old ones already over fifty and the young ones about twenty-five. The children went to school in France, and later in Argentina, and, of course, lost their gift when they became garage attendants and waitresses. Some gypsies were deported by the Germans as 'non-Aryans'. After 1950 there was hardly one left. At present there are gypsies performing in Moscow, but they have nothing at all in common with the artists of the past, who cultivated their own traditional art, lived as vagabonds, had their own moral code, food, language, and religion.

YUSHKEVICH, SEMEN SOLOMONOVICH (1868–1927). Minor writer of the Gorky group, now forgotten in the U.S.S.R. Author of stories on Jewish life, long before Babel, that depict the atmosphere of Odessa. His play *Miserere* was performed at Stanislavsky's theatre. An émigré.

ZAITSEV, BORIS KONSTANTINOVICH (1881–1972). Russian writer, born in Kaluga. Lived mostly in Moscow; since 1922 an émigré. Last member of the 'prewar generation' (meaning of World War One). Lived in Paris. His wife VERA ALEKSEEVNA, daughter of the director of the Moscow Historical Museum, died in 1965.

ZAMIATIN, EVGENY IVANOVICH (1884–1937). Author of *We* and other novels and stories. In 1931 was allowed to leave the U.S.S.R. and went to Paris. One of

589

those who still have not been 'rehabilitated'. A very interesting and, apparently, never-reprinted note by Z. about himself was published in *Novaya Russkaya Kniga*, 1922, No. 3, p. 42. His wife, LUDMILA NIKOLAEVNA, died in 1965. His papers are in the Russian Archives of Columbia University.

ZENZINOV, VLADIMIR MIKHAILOVICH (1880–1953). Member of the S.-R. Party. Member of the terrorist group, with Savinkov and others. When Nabokov's *Dar* (*The Gift*) was first published in *Contemporary Annals* in 1937–8, Z. pressured the S.-R. editorial board into omitting Chapter 4, the biography of the radical writer Chernyshevsky, an icon for Z. and other Russian socialists as well. This was done. It is a beautiful illustration of the 'power of darkness' which persisted during the emigration among editors, as well as of the old Russian tradition of suppressing literature and art for political reasons (in this case, connected with long-dead figures).

ZHABOTINSKY, VLADIMIR EVGENIEVICH (1880–1940). Writer, translator, prominent Zionist, contributor to *The Latest News*.

ZHDANOV, ANDREY ALEKSANDROVICH (1896–1948). Although not directly connected to the GPU-NKVD and not in the line of Yagoda-Ezhov-Beria, he was the most prominent *ideological* henchman of Russian literature. First he formulated *what it should be*, and gave the rules of socialist realism in his speech at the First Congress of the Union of the Writers (1934). Then he started to 'clean up' every corner of the Russian press of the 1930s. After the war, in 1945–6, he came back with renewed vigour, eliminating Akhmatova from every magazine, driving Zoshchenko to his death, forcing the cult of Stalin on every member of the Academy of Sciences, every translator, poet, novelist. All the killings of literary figures and all the banishments and horrors from 1932 to 1948 were either directly or indirectly his doing. Not a word has been said about him since the 'thaw'. He apparently died a natural and quiet death in the midst of a unique career.

'ZHENIA' (E. F. NIDERMILLER, 1875–1960). Sister of Khodasevich.

ZHIRMUNSKY, VIKTOR MAKSIMOVICH (1889–). In his early years a budding 'formalist', later professor at Leningrad University; an Academician, corresponding member of the Division of Literary History at the Academy of Science. Author of many outstanding books on Russian and world literature.

ZINOVIEV, GRIGORY EVSEEVICH (1883–1936). Bolshevik. Came with Lenin from Switzerland in April 1917 and was his right-hand man in Petersburg in the early years after the Revolution. Until 1926, chairman of the Comintern. Executed by Stalin at the First Moscow Trial. An outspoken enemy of Gorky.

ZLOBIN, VLADIMIR ANANIEVICH (1894–1968). Secretary to Merezhkovsky and Gippius from 1916 to 1945. A minor poet. In 1966 a lecturer in the U.S.A. in

Lawrence, Kansas. Later returned to France and died in a sanatorium for the mentally ill.

ZOSHCHENKO, MIKHAIL MIKHAILOVICH (1895–1958). Humourist, talented writer of short stories, in the 1920s a Serapion Brother. Author of an auto-biography, recently republished in the U.S.A. He was ordered (by Zhdanov) to terminate it in the 1940s. In it he tried to find out for himself why his life had been so gloomy. Instead of Freud, who apparently had a real impact on him, he mentions Pavlov, giving the reader the comic impression of a silly error. About the political control of the Communist Party on him and others see Harold Swayze's *Political Control, 1946–1959* (Harvard University Press, 1962), and an article about it by Gleb Struve in *The Russian Review* (1963), No. 1. Z. has been partially 'rehabilitated'.

ZUBOV, COUNT VALENTIN PLATONOVICH (1884–?). Descendant of the favourite of Catherine and the assassin of Paul. In 1912, in his palace near the Cathedral of St. Isaac and the monument of Peter in St. Petersburg, he founded the Institute of the History of Arts, which was called the Zubovsky Institute. A brochure, '*Otchet deyatelnosti (1912–1927),*' contains the history of the activities of this distinguished learned institution, as do the three issues of *Vremennik Otdela Poetiki*. Until 1930 when the Institute was closed, mainly for 'formalism', twenty-six volumes had been published (the work of prominent scholars teaching at the Zubovsky). Although in 1920 the school was completely remodelled, it could not survive the pressure of the government and the party. Count Zubov himself was put in prison for many years. At the end of the 1920s he was released, left Russia, and settled in Europe (Munich and Paris). To give a general idea of what the Institute of the History of Arts was like in the winter of 1921–2, I will enumerate the public lectures I attended:

1921	4 September	B. Eichenbaum: Melody of verse.
	25 September	V. Vinogradov: Plot and composition of Gogol's *Nose*.
	6 October	V. Zhirmunsky: The poetics of Blok.
	6 November	B. Tomashevsky: Pushkin's iambic pentameter.
	27 November	B. Eichenbaum: Fet's lyrics.
1922	15 January	M. Hofman: Introduction to the study of Pushkin.
	5 February	B. Eichenbaum: On Nekrasov.
	2 April	V. Zhirmunsky: On the melody of verse.

INDEX

593

Index

Marienhof, A. B. 203
Martov, Y. O. 53, 81, 309
Mayakovsky, V. V. 66, 140, 143, 154,
    160, 187, 189, 191, 204, 218, 227,
    235, 278, 291–2, 320, 354, 496
Medtner, N. K. 100, 284–5, 391–2
Melgunov, S. P. 232, 275, 465, 471
Mendeleev, D. I. 391–2
Merezhkovsky, D. S. 67, 232, 239–50,
    258, 260, 270–1, 297, 340, 343, 354,
    397, 410, 420, 426–7, 482, 522
Meyerhold, V. E. 60, 66
Mikhailovsky, N. K. 294
Miklashevsky, K. M. 193, 243
Milioti, N. D. 288–9
Miliukov, P. N. 47, 216, 218, 240, 256,
    283–4, 307, 348–9, 522
Miller, E. K. 325, 332–3
Miller, H. 215, 281
Minsky, N. M. 152
Mirbach, W. von 59
Mirsky, D. P. 194, 530
Mochulsky, K. V. 379, 463, 469
Morozova, M. K. 391–2
Muratov, P. P. 145, 153–4, 162–65,
    168, 191, 207–8, 258, 261, 283, 367,
    397, 399

Nabokov, V. V. 38, 153, 257–8, 268,
    270, 282, 294, 297, 311–13, 315–21,
    347, 351, 359, 374, 388, 478, 504
Nadezhin, N. 303
Nappelbaum, I. M. 119, 122, 126–8,
    130–1, 138, 146
Nekrasov, N. V. 306, 308, 417
Neldikhen, S. E. 115
Nemchinova, V. 212
Nemirovich-Danchenko, V. I. 152,
    201
Nicholas II (tsar) 11, 18, 79, 444, 446,
    466
Nicolaev, M. 177

Nicolaevsky, B. I. 446
Nidermiller see 'Zhenia'
Nikitin, N. N. 129, 151, 153

Oblomov see Karaulov, D. L.
Olesha, Y. K. 191, 267–8, 281, 313–15,
    463, 522
Onoshkovich, A. 128
Osorgin, M. A. 283, 398–9
Otsup, G. A. 57, 138, 284, 413, 433
Otsup, N. A. 114–15, 128, 153, 166,
    168, 196, 207–8, 379, 396
Otsup, Nadia 81, 114–15

Parnakh, V. 213
Pasternak, B. L. 140, 153–4, 163, 166,
    168–9, 197–200, 217, 314
Pasternak, Z. N., 199–200
Pastukhov, B. L. 486, 503
Pavlova, A. 166, 212
Pavlovich, N. A. 124, 128
Pechorin, D. 421
Pereverzev, P. N. 80, 308
Peshkov, M. A. 173, 176, 179, 182–3,
    185–7, 193
Peshkova, E. P. 170, 176–7, 189, 309
Peters, Y. K. 414
Petliura, S. 329
Petrovskaya, N. I. 154, 167–8, 391
Petrunkevich, I. I. 10
Pilniak, B. A. 143, 187, 191, 218, 234,
    278
Pisarev, D. I. 299
Plekhanov, G. V. 82, 243
Plescheev, A. A. 383, 417, 463
Plevitskaya, N. 332–3
Poliakov, A. A. 269, 275
Polonsky, Y. P. 67
Poplavsky, B. Y. 203, 213, 220, 268–
    71, 273, 281, 298, 326, 348, 478
Preobrazhenskaya, O. O. 211
Prishvin, M. M. 234

597

Index

Index

Index